DOS:
The Complete Reference

DOS:
The Complete Reference

Kris Jamsa

Osborne **McGraw-Hill**
Berkeley, California

Osborne **McGraw-Hill**
2600 Tenth Street
Berkeley, California 94710
U.S.A.

For information on translations and book distributors outside of the U.S.A.,
please write to Osborne **McGraw-Hill** at the above address.
A complete list of trademarks appears on page 1033.

DOS: The Complete Reference

0 DODO 898

ISBN 0-07-881259-3

CONTENTS

Introduction   xv

ONE   **Getting Started with DOS**   1
Understanding Hardware   2
Floppy Disks   6
Keyboard and Special-Purpose Keys   14
Microfloppy Disks   18
Understanding Software   21
What Is DOS?   22
Different DOS Versions   24
Turn On Your System   24
DOS Disk   28
Input-Processing-Output (IPO)   28

TWO   **Introducing DOS**   35
DATE (Set the System Date)   43
TIME (Set the System Time)   44
Resetting the Computer   46
Making a DOS Working Disk
    (DISKCOPY)   47
FORMAT (Readying a New Disk for Use by
    DOS)   52
Single-sided Versus Double-sided Disks   55
DOS Prompt   56
DOS Files   60
DIR (List All of the Files on a Disk)   61
DOS Wildcard Characters   64
DOS File-Naming Conventions   66
DOS File Specifications (file _ spec)   68
COPY (Create a Second Copy of a File)   68
Controlling Screen Display and Terminating
    Commands   72
Write-Protecting Disks   77

THREE   **Basic DOS Commands**   89
CLS (Clear the Screen)   90
VER (Display Current DOS Version)   91
TYPE (Display Contents of a File)   92
RENAME or REN (Rename a File)   95
DEL (Delete a File)   97
ERASE (Erase a File from Disk)   99
CHKDSK (Display Current Status of
    a Disk)   101

LABEL (Create a Volume Label)   104
VOL (Display Volume Label)   109
COMP (Compare Two Files)   110
DISKCOMP (Compare Two DOS Disks)   114
PROMPT (Set the DOS Prompt)   117

FOUR   **Using DOS Device Names**   **123**
Serial Versus Parallel Data
     Communication   124
Referencing DOS Device Names   126
MODE (Customizing Peripheral Devices)   128
NUL (The Nonexistent Device)   133

FIVE   **Exploiting the Power
of Your Printer**   **137**
PRINT   138
Echoing Terminal Output to the Printer
     (CTRL-PRTSC)   155
Printing the Screen Contents
     (SHIFT-PRTSC)   156
GRAPHICS (Print Graphics with the Print-Screen
     Function)   157

SIX   **Managing Your DOS Files
with Subdirectories**   **165**
Understanding DOS Subdirectories   167
MKDIR or MD (Make a Subdirectory)   171
CHDIR or CD (Change Current Working
     Subdirectory)   176
RMDIR or RD (Remove a Subdirectory)   183
TREE (Display Subdirectory Tree)   187
PATH (Where to Look for External
     Commands)   191
DOS Path Commands   194
Executing External Commands Contained
     in Subdirectories   198
Copying a Disk Containing Subdirectories   199
Renaming a Subdirectory   200
Working Directories   201
Other Applications   202

SEVEN   **Redirection of Input and Output**   **213**
MORE   216
FIND   219
SORT   221
DOS Pipe   223

EIGHT   **Batch Processing**   **229**

Creating Batch Files   234
REM   235
PAUSE   236
ECHO   237
GOTO   238
IF   238
FOR   240
SHIFT   244
AUTOEXEC.BAT   245

NINE   **Managing Your Disks**   **249**

Disk Structure   249
File Allocation Table (FAT)   261
How Hard Disks Differ from Floppies   266
FDISK Command   271
Exploiting DOS Subdirectories Fully   277
Improving System Performance   279
VERIFY Command   280

TEN   **Advanced DOS Commands**   **289**

APPEND (Specify a Search Path for
    Data Files)   290
ASSIGN (Assign a Drive Letter to Another
    Drive)   295
ATTRIB (Set a File's Read-only or Backup
    Attributes)   296
COMMAND (Invoke a Command
    Processor)   299
CTTY (Modify the Command Device)   304
EXE2BIN (Convert an EXE File to
    a COM File)   306
EXIT (Exit from a Secondary Command
    Processor)   308
JOIN (Join a Disk Drive to a DOS Path)   311
RECOVER (Recover a File or Disk
    Containing Bad Sectors)   316
REPLACE (Update Previous Versions
    of Files)   319
SET (Set an Environment String)   323
SHARE (Support File Sharing)   326
SUBST (Substitute a DOS Path with
    a Drive Letter)   330
SYS (Place Operating System on Disk)   332
VERIFY (Verify That Disk Output is
    Written Correctly)   334

XCOPY (Copy Files and Directories to
a New Disk)   335
DOS Editing Keys   343

ELEVEN   **Backing Up Your Disks**   **357**
BACKUP   359
Backup Policies and Procedures   364
Problems with BACKUP   370
RESTORE (Retrieving Files from Backup
Disks)   371

TWELVE   **International DOS Concerns**   **383**
Building an International Disk   392

THIRTEEN   **EDLIN—The DOS Line Editor**   **403**
Getting Started with EDLIN   410
Advanced Text Editing   418
Searching for Words and Phrases   431
Replace   435
Creating Disk Labels with EDLIN   438

FOURTEEN   **How DOS Really Works**   **453**
The Anatomy of DOS   453
Command Processor   454
DOS Kernel   462
BIOS (Basic Input/Output System)   464
Hidden Files   465
Boot Record   466
System Generation   468
DOS Interrupts   471

FIFTEEN   **Customizing DOS**   **479**
BREAK (Default: BREAK=OFF)   481
BUFFERS (Default:
IBM PC BUFFERS=2;
IBM PC AT BUFFERS=3)   482
COUNTRY   485
DEVICE   486
DRIVPARM   488
FCBS (Default: FCBS=4,0)   490
FILES (Default: FILES=8)   491
LASTDRIVE (Default:
LASTDRIVE=E)   492
SHELL   493

SIXTEEN   **Programming DOS**   **499**
LINK   499
DEBUG   521
Programming the DOS Pipe   538
ANSI Driver   542
DOS System Services   543
Spawn   614
Command Line Arguments   617
Backup Log   619

SEVENTEEN   **Microsoft Windows**   **627**
What Is Windows?   628
Time-Sharing   628
Requirements   633
What Comes with Windows?   635
Installing Windows   636
Windows Products   659
Microsoft Executive   660
System Menu   675
Selecting Programs from Icons   679
Windows Spooler   683

EIGHTEEN   **Advanced Microsoft Windows**   **691**
CLOCK   693
CALCULATOR   696
CALENDAR   702
CARDFILE   719
NOTEPAD   732
TERMINAL   739
REVERSI   747
The Clipboard   748
Running Multiple Applications
   Simultaneously   751
Microsoft WRITE and Microsoft PAINT   757
The Windows Control Panel   762
What Is a PIF?   770
Providing Initialization Values to
   Windows   772
RAM Drives and Windows   774

A   **DOS Reference Guide**   **777**
APPEND (Specify a Search Path for Data
   Files)   780
ASSIGN (Disk I/O Routing)   782

ATTRIB (Assign or Display File
     Attributes)   784
BACKUP (Back Up One or More Files to
     a New Disk)   785
BREAK (Enable/Disable CTRL-BREAK
     Processing)   788
CHDIR (Change Default Directory)   790
CHKDSK (Check a Disk's Current Status)   792
CLS (Clear the Screen)   795
COMMAND (Invoke a Secondary Command
     Processor)   795
COMP (Compare Two Files)   797
COPY (Copy One or More Files to a New
     Destination)   801
CTTY (Change the Standard Input/Output
     Device)   805
DATE (Set or Display the System Date)   806
DEL (Delete File from Disk)   809
DIR (Directory Listing of Files)   811
DISKCOMP (Compare Floppy Disks)   814
DISKCOPY (Copy Floppy Disks)   818
ECHO (Display Batch Command Names)   822
ERASE (Delete a File from Disk)   825
EXE2BIN (Convert EXE File to COM)   827
EXIT (Terminate a Secondary Command
     Processor)   829
FDISK (Fixed Disk Configuration)   829
FIND (Search a File or Piped Input for a
     String)   830
FOR (DOS Iterative Processing
     Construct)   833
FORMAT (Format Disk for Use by DOS)   835
GOTO (DOS Branching Construct)   839
GRAFTABL (Load Additional Character Set
     Data into Memory)   841
GRAPHICS (Print Graphics Display)   842
IF (DOS Conditional Processing
     Construct)   844
JOIN (Join a Disk Drive to a DOS Path)   846
KEYBxx (Load Foreign Keyboard Set)   848
LABEL (Specify a Disk Volume Label)   849
MKDIR (Create a Subdirectory)   851
MODE (Specify Device Characteristics)   853
MORE (Display Output a Screen at a
     Time)   858

PATH (Specify the Command Search
Directories)   860
PAUSE (Temporarily Suspend Batch
Processing)   862
PRINT (Send File to the DOS Print
Queue)   863
PROMPT (Set the System Prompt)   869
RECOVER (Recover Corrupted File)   872
REM (Display Comments During Batch
Processing)   874
RENAME (Rename a DOS File)   875
REPLACE (Selective Replacement of
Target Files)   877
RESTORE (Restore Files Saved by
BACKUP)   880
RMDIR (Remove a DOS Subdirectory)   882
SELECT (Select International Format)   884
SET (Place or Display Entries in
the Environment)   887
SHARE (Support DOS File Sharing)   890
SHIFT (Shift Batch Parameters Left)   891
SORT (DOS Sort Filter)   893
SUBST (Substitute a DOS Path with a
Drive Letter)   894
SYS (Transfer Operating System Files
to a Disk)   896
TIME (Set the System Time)   898
TREE (Display Directory Structure)   900
TYPE (Display the Contents of a File)   903
VER (Display DOS Version)   904
VERIFY (Verify Disk I/O)   905
VOL (Display Volume Label)   906
XCOPY (Copy Files to Include
Subdirectories)   907

B   ASCII Codes   913

C   DOS Error Messages   917

D   Upgrading Your DOS Version   1031

Index   1035

Few individuals in the computer science industry possess both technical expertise and the ability to share their vast knowledge and experience. I deeply appreciate the technical contributions of Phillip Schmauder during the development cycle of this text. His technical acumen of DOS internals and his unselfish nature allowed us to develop a synergy that produced significant insights into the inner workings of DOS.

Thank you again for your contribution.

—K.A.J.

ACKNOWLEDGMENTS

DOS is the disk operating system for the IBM PC and PC compatibles. Originally released in 1981 with the IBM PC, DOS has become the standard for microcomputer operating systems.

In general, an operating system provides the interface between the user and the computer. The operating system is responsible for managing system resources such as disks, printers, and other peripheral devices (modem, mouse, and so on). In addition, the operating system allows you to execute other programs, such as word processors or database packages, on the computer.

DOS has different faces depending upon the user. To most users, DOS simply appears as the command processor that executes the commands entered from the keyboard. DOS never appears to others; instead, a second application program takes control of the computer upon completion of the DOS startup procedures. These secondary applications are often called shells. Normally, a shell provides the user with a menu of options so that the user does not need to understand DOS commands. And to systems programmers, DOS serves as the low-level interface to disk, directory, file, and program control functions. As you will see, *DOS: The Complete Reference* covers all aspects of DOS.

Hardware Configuration

Each day more and more people are purchasing personal computers that run PC or MS-DOS. The uses of these computer systems are so diverse that it is impossible to cover all of the possible hardware configurations. Instead, this text assumes the use of an IBM PC with two floppy disk drives in the command examples. This configuration is the most widely used by PC users. If your system includes a hard disk, Chapter 9 provides a complete overview on hard disk management.

PC- Versus MS-DOS

Many DOS users are confused about PC- and MS-DOS. Essentially, PC- and MS-DOS are functionally equivalent: PC-DOS is the IBM implementation of DOS; MS-DOS is the Microsoft implementation. IBM and Microsoft make continual efforts to ensure that PC- and MS-DOS function identically, so the commands presented in this text are supported by both implementations. Very rarely is a command supported by only one of the two implementations.

Where to Look Next

While this text will well serve the needs of most users, programmers should also obtain a copy of the *DOS Technical Reference Guide*. The manual provides a complete examination of DOS and the services it provides. The DOS User's Group is one of the best sources of DOS information exchange. The group distributes a quarterly newsletter that includes the latest news on DOS, utility programs, product reviews, and answers to technical DOS questions. The group also offers diskette packages containing DOS utility programs and demos of popular third-party products. Many software manufacturers offer discounts to user-group members. Becoming a member of the DOS User's Group is one of the best investments that you will make after buying your computer. To join, write to

DOS User's Group
P.O. Box 26601
Las Vegas, Nevada 89126

A Brief Overview

This text provides a complete examination of DOS. The chapters are organized as follows:

• **Chapter 1** presents the information you need to get started with DOS. It examines hardware, software, floppy disks, and operating systems. In addition, the chapter presents the computer's power-on sequence and discusses several power configurations.

• **Chapter 2** introduces DOS and the DOS startup procedures. It also presents several commands essential to the daily use of DOS — the DATE, TIME, DISKCOPY, and FORMAT commands.

• **Chapter 3** introduces the basic DOS commands that you will normally use on a daily basis.

• **Chapter 4** examines DOS device names, their use, and their functions.

• **Chapter 5** presents the DOS PRINT command and methods that allow you to fully exploit the command and your system printer.

• **Chapter 6** discusses DOS subdirectories and directory-related commands. The information presented in this chapter is essential to successful disk organization.

• **Chapter 7** presents the DOS pipe and I/O redirection. In addition, the chapter examines the DOS SORT, MORE, and FIND commands.

• **Chapter 8** examines batch processing and the creation and execution of DOS BAT files. This chapter shows you how to invoke multiple DOS commands at one time, which allows them to proceed without user intervention. This frees you from having to monitor the computer constantly, waiting for one command to complete so that you can invoke the next. BAT files also allow you to abbreviate DOS commands.

• **Chapter 9** provides an in-depth examination of disk structures and DOS disk access methods. In addition, several techniques are presented to aid you in increasing your system performance by means of DOS subdirectories.

• **Chapter 10** examines the majority of DOS commands. Since the functions of these commands are diverse, they have, for the sake of simplicity, been grouped under the title "Advanced DOS Commands." The chapter also presents the DOS command editing keys.

• **Chapter 11** presents the DOS BACKUP and RESTORE commands. Several backup policies and procedures are also discussed. This chapter is essential for hard-disk users.

- **Chapter 12** examines the international DOS concerns. With the growing international success of the IBM PC, later versions of DOS have provided enhanced foreign-country support.

- **Chapter 13** introduces the DOS line editor EDLIN, which allows you to create, modify, or examine text files. If you don't have a word processor, EDLIN is essential. If you normally use a word processor for all of your text editing, it is important that you develop a basic understanding of EDLIN, since it is present on every computer that supports DOS.

- **Chapter 14** examines the DOS startup procedures and the command processor. Although the information presented in this chapter is technical, it provides even the novice DOS user with a critical understanding of DOS processing.

- **Chapter 15** shows you how to use the CONFIG.SYS file to customize DOS for your specific needs. The chapter also discusses the RAM disk and several optimization techniques.

- **Chapter 16** provides a programmers' overview of DOS and includes several useful utility programs and procedures. In addition, the chapter presents the DOS system services and explains how to access them from high-level languages. The chapter also examines the DOS linker, debugger, and librarian.

- **Chapter 17** introduces Microsoft Windows. It shows you how to install and start Windows and how to perform basic Windows functions.

- **Chapter 18** provides a detailed analysis of Microsoft Windows. Upon completion of this chapter you will have a thorough understanding of the Microsoft operating environment.

- **Appendix A** provides a complete reference guide to each DOS command. Syntax charts and examples are presented for each command.

- **Appendix B** provides an ASCII chart.

- **Appendix C** provides a summary of the DOS error messages and the steps required to resolve the errors.

- **Appendix D** outlines the steps to upgrade your system from one version of DOS to another.

In addition, each chapter includes review questions and answers.

Diskette Package

All of the routines provided in this text are available on diskette. The diskette package also contains several other useful utilities, including an on-line DOS facility that provides help for all of the DOS commands. This help facility is one of the most useful utilities you will ever use. The diskette package comes in a solid diskette folder that is ideal for carrying your floppy disks when you travel or go to work or school.

The complete cost of the diskette package is only $17.95 plus $2.00 shipping and handling ($5.00 for foreign orders).

Please send me the diskette package that accompanies *DOS: The Complete Reference*. My payment for $19.95 ($17.95 plus $2.00 for shipping and handling or $5.00 for foreign orders) is enclosed.

Name _____

Address _____

City _____ State _____ ZIP _____

Kris Jamsa Software, Inc.   Box 26031   Las Vegas, Nevada 89126

Getting Started
with DOS

Understanding Hardware
Floppy Disks
Keyboard and Special-Purpose Keys
Microfloppy Disks
Understanding Software
What Is DOS?
Different DOS Versions
Turn On Your System
DOS Disk
Input-Processing-Output (IPO)

This chapter presents several key concepts that are critical to your understanding of DOS, including

- hardware

- floppy disk

- keyboard

- microfloppy disk

- software

- operating systems

- starting up your computer

- input-processing-output

The first item to be discussed is hardware, or the physical components that make up your computer.

O
N
E

Understanding Hardware

Hardware is the boards, cables, and peripheral devices (printers, modems, and so on) that make up your computer (see Figure 1-1). In general, hardware is composed of things that you can see and touch.

Chassis

The *chassis* of the computer holds the *central processing unit* (CPU) and the computer's memory. The CPU controls all of the computer's processing. The CPU processor chip in the IBM PC is called the 8088. The IBM PC AT uses a faster processor called the 80286. Although there are several different chips that perform critical functions within the computer, the 8088, 80286, and the new 32-bit 80386 are the primary chips found in IBM PCs and PC-compatibles. DOS was designed to support each of these processors.

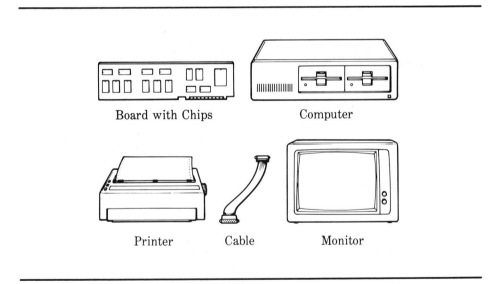

Board with Chips   Computer

Printer   Cable   Monitor

Figure 1-1.   Hardware components

In addition to the CPU, the chassis contains the computer's memory. *Memory* within the computer is defined in terms of bytes. A *byte* consists of eight binary digits or bits. Each of the hardware devices within the computer communicates with other devices based upon the presence or absence of electronic signals. A signal within the computer is either present (on) or absent (off). This on or off state can be defined by binary (base 2) digits, which are either 1 or 0 (on or off). Hence, it's a "digital" computer. Data contained in the computer is represented by a series of binary digits. To picture this sort of communication, consider what happens when the CPU adds the numbers

$$
\begin{array}{r}
7 \\
+\ 4 \\
\hline
\end{array}
$$

It manipulates the binary representations of the numbers.

$$
\begin{array}{rcr}
7 & & 0111 \\
+\ 4 & \text{or} & +\ 0100 \\
\hline
11 & & 1011 \\
\end{array}
$$

If your computer contains 256K of memory, it is capable of storing 256,000 bytes of information. Each character of the alphabet requires one byte of storage space, and 256K, therefore, is capable of storing 256,000 letters of the alphabet.

Computers have short-term (or volatile) memory. Each time you turn off the computer, it loses the entire contents of its volatile memory. Once the computer is turned off, you can never retrieve any of the information that was contained in this volatile memory. If you need to save information from one session to another, you must store your information on disks (discussed later in this chapter).

Memory in the computer is used to store programs and data. As you will see later in this chapter, computer programs (software) are nothing more than lists of instructions the computer is to perform. Before the computer can execute a program, however, the program must reside in memory. Chapter 2 will examine DOS commands. As you will see, DOS places several commands into memory each time it starts. Most programs, however, must be loaded by DOS from disk into memory before they can execute. Your computer must, therefore, have sufficient memory for these programs to reside in.

In addition to the CPU and memory, all of the chips used by the PC are contained within the chassis. If you have purchased additional hardware, such as a mouse or modem, these devices are also joined to the chassis through one of the hardware expansion slots. Lastly, the chassis provides the housing for floppy and fixed disk drives.

Most users seldom have a need to open the chassis. If you don't need to add additional hardware to your system, you should leave your chassis closed.

Monitors

A *monitor* is the screen device that DOS uses to display the result of the execution of a program. The two monitor types used with PCs are monochrome and color displays. Monochrome (green, amber, or black-and-white) displays are less expensive than color screens. They are well suited for most business applications, such as report generation and word processing. Color monitors provide programs with the ability to display information in black-and-white or in color. The number of colors supported is dependent on the monitor and the graphics board you must place in your computer. Many users find that color text is harder to read than monochrome text. The more expensive EGA monitor/card combinations actually produce good quality text in color. Although color monitors cost more than monochrome displays, you may very well find that one is worth the additional expense. Most programs support color displays, which make their output more attractive than it would be on a monochrome display.

Disk Drives

Disk drive configurations may differ for each system. Most systems today have two floppy disk drives. If you are using a standard IBM PC or PC-compatible with side-by-side disk drives, your computer will have the drive configuration shown in Figure 1-2. If your system has half-height floppy disk drives, your configuration will resemble Figure 1-3. If your system has a hard disk, your configuration will look like Figure 1-4.

Closer examination of the disk drive illustrates the disk drive types shown in Figure 1-5. Each of the disk drives contains a latch that must be open when you place the disk into the drive and closed once the drive contains the disk. Also, each drive has a small light that tells you when DOS is using the disk the drive contains. When this light is on, DOS is using the disk. Never open the latch or turn off the system while this light is on. In so doing, you risk losing all of the data the disk contains.

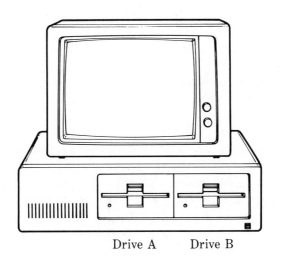

Drive A   Drive B

Figure 1-2.   Drive configuration of standard IBM PC

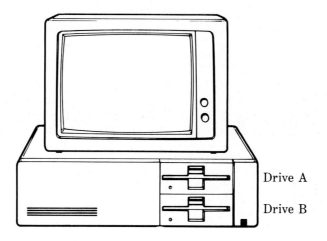

Drive A

Drive B

Figure 1-3.   Drive configuration with half-height drives

Floppy Disks

One of the most important keys to your success with DOS is a good understanding of floppy disks. After you purchase your personal computer, you will probably find that the majority of your computer-cost outlays are for floppy disks. With proper treatment, your floppy disks will last a long time, and you will greatly reduce the possibility of losing the information recorded on the disks. Always follow the rules for handling floppy disks that are shown in Figure 1-6.

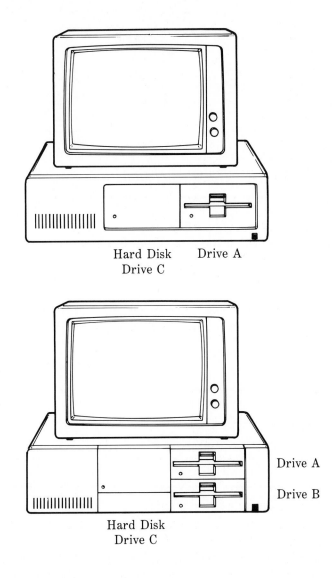

Hard Disk   Drive A
Drive C

Hard Disk
Drive C

Drive A

Drive B

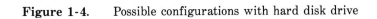

Figure 1-4.   Possible configurations with hard disk drive

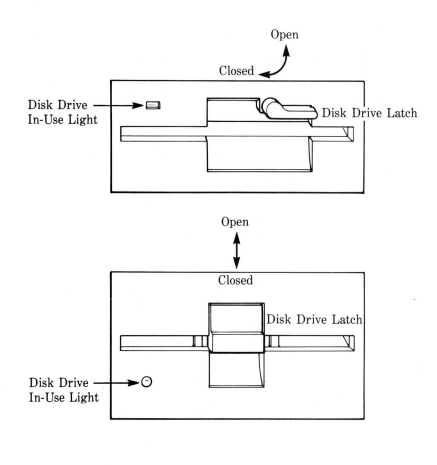

Figure 1-5.   Types of disk drives

One of the most important factors affecting the quality of your disk organization is the labels you place on each disk. You should never write on a disk label once it is placed on a disk. If your disk already contains a label and you must change it, either peel off the label or place a new label on top of it.

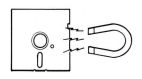

Never place the disk near
magnetic devices.

Always place disks back into a
disk envelope when you are not
using them.

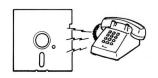

Keep the disk away from your
telephone.

Store your floppies in a safe
location.

Never touch your floppy disk
media.

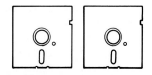

Always make a backup copy of
your floppy disk.

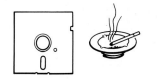

Never smoke near floppy disks.

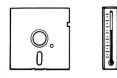

Keep room temperature in the
range 50° F to 110° F.

Never bend floppy disks.

Figure 1-6.   Rules for handling floppy disks

You may find the label format shown in Figure 1-7 helpful in organizing your disks. For PC-DOS version 3.1, you would create the labels shown in Figure 1-8. Place the label in the upper-left-hand corner of the disk, as illustrated in Figure 1-9.

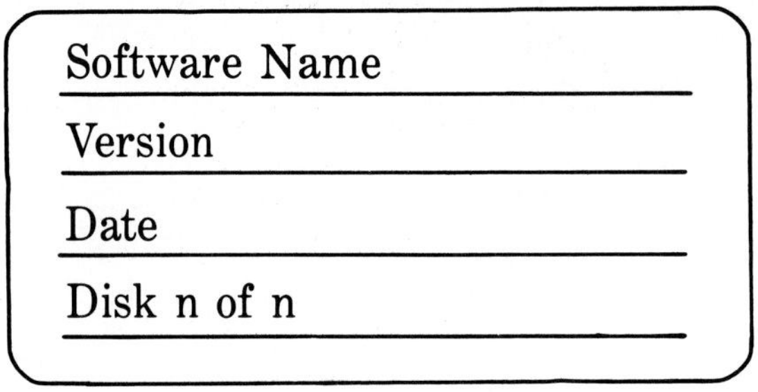

Software Name

Version

Date

Disk n of n

Figure 1-7.   Label format

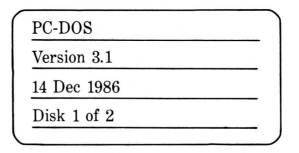

PC-DOS

Version 3.1

14 Dec 1986

Disk 1 of 2

Figure 1-8.   PC-DOS label format

Figure 1-10 provides several pieces of information about floppy disks. First, it shows the *write-protect notch*. When the notch is visible, the disk data can be modified. When you cover the notch with a write-protect tab (provided with the disk), the contents of the disk cannot be modified; this prevents accidental file deletion (although the disk can still be read and copied).

The *disk hub* is the portion of the disk that the disk drive uses to rotate the disk. The disk works in a manner similar to the way an album is played on a record player. Once in the drive, the disk spins rapidly past the computer's disk read/write head, which reads or writes information to the disk. The *jacket* surrounding the disk protects the storage media from dust, fingerprints, and scratches from other sources.

The *read/write opening* allows the read/write head inside the disk drive access to the storage media. As the disk rotates in the disk drive, the read/write head within the drive accesses the

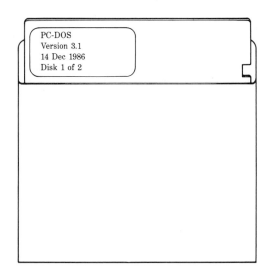

PC-DOS
Version 3.1
14 Dec 1986
Disk 1 of 2

Figure 1-9.   Placement of label on disk

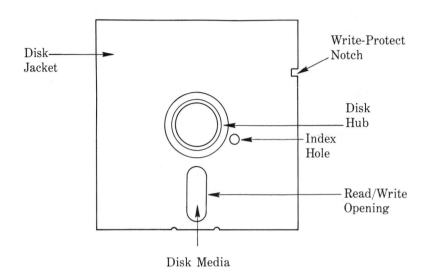

Figure 1-10.   Parts of a floppy disk

information contained on the disk via this opening. The index hole is used for timing as the disk rotates within the drive. Be careful not to touch the storage media through either of these openings.

If new personal computer users were to sacrifice one of their unused floppy disks and open it up so that they could thoroughly examine a disk, they would see something similar to Figure 1-11.

Disk Storage Capabilities

Floppy disks are categorized by density and number of sides available for recording. Common floppy disk sizes are shown in Table 1-1.

The most common disk for PC applications is the double-sided, double-density disk. DOS can store information on both sides of a *double-sided disk. Density* refers to the amount of infor-

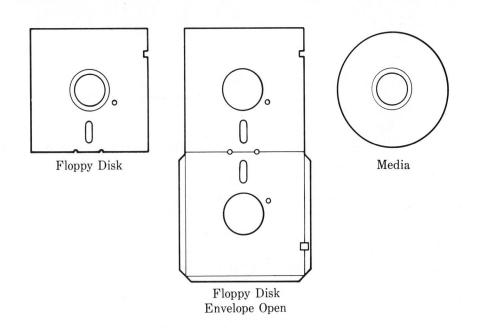

Floppy Disk

Media

Floppy Disk
Envelope Open

Figure 1-11.   Inner construction of floppy disks

Density	Number of Sides	Storage Capability
double	single	184,320 bytes
double	double	368,640 bytes
quad	double	1,228,800 bytes

Table 1-1.   Common Floppy Disk Sizes

mation DOS can place in one space on the disk. Chapter 2 examines the DOS FORMAT command and explains how you can save money and only purchase single-sided, double-density disks. As you will see, DOS allows you to treat single-sided disks as double-sided, with the same amount of storage space on the disk.

Keyboard and Special-Purpose Keys

A keyboard template for the IBM PC is shown in Figure 1-12. Several special-purpose keys will simplify your computer usage. First, the left-most collection of keys, labeled F1 through F10, are called *function keys* (see Figure 1-13). As you will see in later chapters, DOS allows you to use these keys to simplify keyboard entry. In addition, most application programs such as word processors use these keys for special purposes.

The next key of importance is the BACKSPACE key, shown in Figure 1-14. The BACKSPACE key allows you to delete the letter

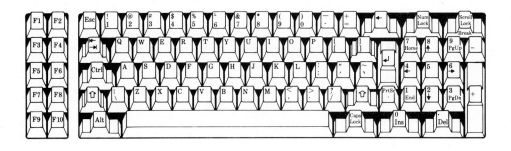

Figure 1-12.   IBM keyboard template

that precedes the cursor. For example, suppose your screen contains

```
A> DISKCOPY■
```

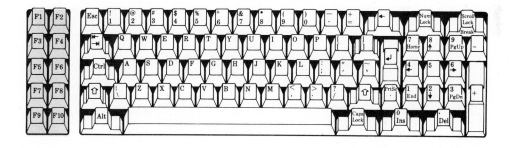

Figure 1-13.   Location of function keys

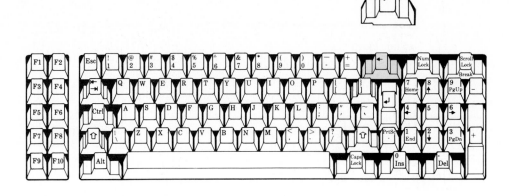

Figure 1-14. Location of BACKSPACE key

Pressing the BACKSPACE key one time will result in

```
A> DISKCOP■
```

Pressing the key again will produce

```
A> DISKCO■
```

As you will see, DOS uses the ENTER key shown in Figure 1-15 to terminate each line you type at the keyboard. For example, if you wanted to invoke the DOS DIR command presented in Chapter 2, you would simply type the letters *DIR* and then press the ENTER key.

```
A> DIR

Volume in drive A has no label
Directory of   A:\

ANSI     SYS      1651   12-30-85   12:00p
ASSIGN   COM      1536   12-30-85   12:00p
ATTRIB   EXE      8247   12-30-85   12:00p
BACKUP   COM      6234   12-30-85   12:00p
BASIC    COM     19298    2-21-86   12:00p
BASICA   COM     36396    2-21-86   12:00p
GRAFTABL COM      1169   12-30-85   12:00p
GRAPHICS COM      3220   12-30-85   12:00p
JOIN     EXE      8955   12-30-85   12:00p
SYS      COM      4620   12-30-85   12:00p
         10 File(s)      222528 bytes free
```

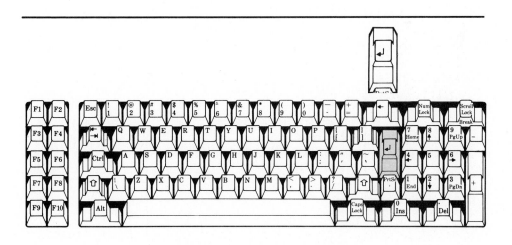

Figure 1-15.   Location of ENTER key

More and more computers are supporting 3 1/2-inch disks. These disks are called *microfloppy disks* (see Figure 1-16). Because of their unique size, microfloppy disks require special disk drives. In the future, you will notice that more and more software will appear in this disk size. Microfloppy disks are much more durable than standard 5 1/4-inch disks and are less exposed to dust, smoke, and other particles that often destroy the larger disks.

You will notice several major differences between microfloppy disks and standard floppy disks. The microfloppy disk is not flimsy like standard 5 1/4-inch disks. Each microfloppy disk is enclosed in a hard plastic case. If you look at the top of the microfloppy disk, you will notice a metal portion called a *shutter* (see Figure 1-17). Slide the shutter to the left, and you will expose

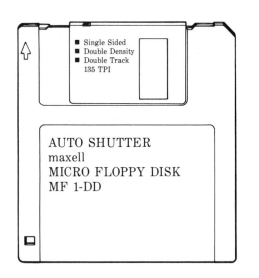

Figure 1-16.   Microfloppy disk

the actual disk media (see Figure 1-18). Each time the computer needs to read or write to the microfloppy, the disk drive will slide the shutter to the left in order to access the disk.

Turn the microfloppy disk over, as shown in Figure 1-19. The first item of importance is the *write-protect switch*. If you see light through the disk, the disk is write-protected, and its contents cannot be modified. To cover the hole, slide the switch up, as shown in Figure 1-20. When the hole is sealed, DOS can access the disk in either read or write mode.

The second element is the *disk spindle*. The disk drive uses the spindle to rotate the disk within the drive in a similar manner to the use of the disk hub on standard 5 1/4-inch floppies. Unlike floppy disks, which use the index hole for timing, the microfloppy disk uses the *sector notch*. The microfloppy disk drive must seat itself on the spindle and sector notch.

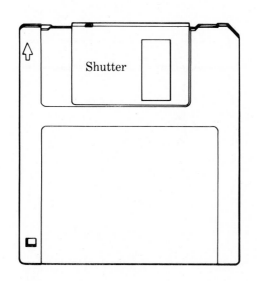

Figure 1-17.   Location of a shutter

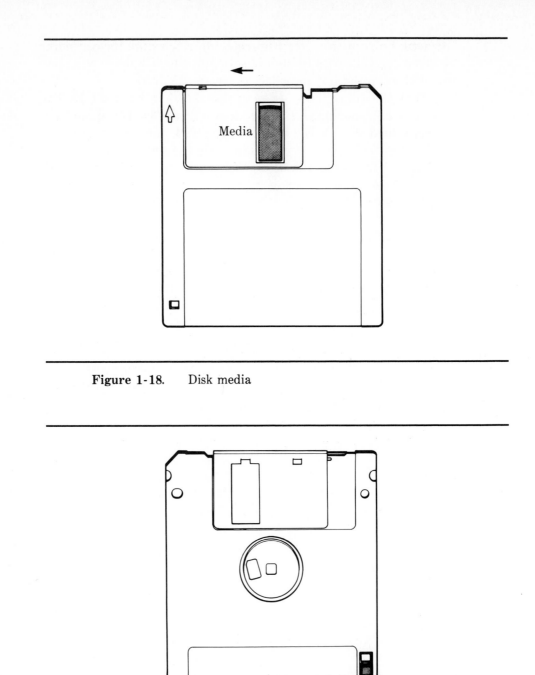

Figure 1-18.   Disk media

Figure 1-19.   Write-protect switch on microfloppy disk

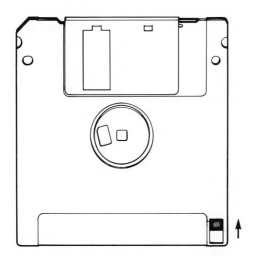

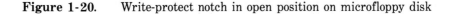

Figure 1-20.   Write-protect notch in open position on microfloppy disk

Microfloppy disks are on the verge of making a significant impact upon the computer industry. With DOS version 3.2 providing full support for microfloppy disks, you should see their uses grow at a rapid pace in the near future.

Understanding Software

Software is computer programs. A *program* is simply a list of instructions for the computer to perform. The hardware components of the computer need software to tell them what to do. Before a computer can execute a program, the program must reside in memory. This means that the program must be loaded from disk into memory. In later chapters you will see how DOS actually performs this function.

Essentially, there are two categories of software: application software and system software. *Application software* is programs written to provide a specific function such as word processing, database management, or mailing-list programs. Each day thousands of programmers develop applications for a wide range of user needs, such as billing programs, general-ledger accounting packages, and inventory management. Application software comprises the majority of software on the market today.

System software includes operating systems, such as DOS, that allow users to run application programs. In addition to operating systems, system software provides device drivers that allow programs to communicate with hardware devices (such as a mouse or plotter) and local area networks that allow several computers to communicate and share information.

System software allows application software to run on the computer. In essence, system software provides a layer between the application software and the hardware, as illustrated in Figure 1-21. It is important to note that regardless of whether the software is application or system software, it is still merely a list of instructions for the computer to perform.

What Is DOS?

DOS is an operating system for the IBM PC and PC-compatibles. An *operating system* is the overseer of the computer and the processes it performs. In general, an operating system is a collection of the programs that manage system resources and aid in the development and execution of application programs. DOS stands for *Disk Operating System*. DOS is your interface to the computer.

Many users are confused by the terms PC-DOS and MS-DOS. Essentially, the two systems are identical. PC-DOS is the IBM implementation of DOS. MS-DOS is the Microsoft version of DOS. IBM and Microsoft have gone to great lengths to ensure that the two systems are functionally identical. As you will see, all of the

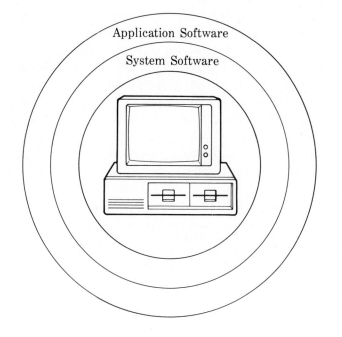

Application Software

System Software

Figure 1-21.   Relationship between application and system software

commands presented in this book are supported by both systems.

Several other operating systems exist for the IBM PC, such as XENIX, UNIX, and CP/M. DOS, however, is the standard. In the future you will see DOS incorporate many of the features of the larger operating systems. Most of these features, however, are beyond the scope of this text. The point to remember is that DOS is here to stay.

Different DOS Versions

Every operating system has a version number that allows you to keep track of whether or not the software you are running is the latest version and also of the current capabilities supported by different versions. DOS version 1.0 was originally released by IBM and Microsoft in 1981 to support the IBM PC. This version of DOS provided the basic functions required to develop and execute programs on the PC, along with the ability to perform simple file manipulations.

Each version number is broken down into two parts, a major and minor version number:

MAJOR.MINOR

In the case of DOS version 1.0, for example, 1 is the major version number, while 0 is the minor version number.

Most software developers use version numbers as follows:

• If the software package introduces significant upgrades in terms of functionality, they will increment the major version number. DOS 1.0 becomes DOS 2.0.

• If the software package fixes known bugs from the previous version or introduces only minor changes in functionality, they will increment the minor version number. DOS 1.0 will become DOS 1.1.

Table 1-2 illustrates the versions of DOS released by Microsoft since the appearance of DOS 1.0 in 1981. Table 1-3 summarizes the IBM versions of DOS.

Turn On Your System

Once you get your system put together and all of your cables are in place, it is time to turn on your computer. Chapter 2 presents the complete sequence required to begin executing DOS. For now, you will turn on the system without DOS.

DOS: The Complete Reference

Version	Date	Functionality
1.0	1981	Original disk operating system
1.25	1982	Support for double-sided disks
2.0	1983	Support for subdirectories
2.01	1983	Support for international symbols
2.11	1983	Bug fixes
2.25	1983	Extended character set support
3.0	1984	Support for 1.2M floppy disk
		Support for larger hard disk
3.1	1984	Support for PC networks
3.2	1986	Support for microfloppies

Table 1-2.   Versions of DOS

Version	Date	Functionality
1.0	1981	Original disk operating system
2.0	1983	Support for subdirectories
2.10	1983	Bug fixes
3.0	1984	Support for 1.2M floppy disk
		Support for larger hard disk
3.1	1984	Support for PC networks
3.2	1986	Support for microfloppies

Table 1-3.   IBM Versions of DOS

First, examine how your system is set up. If you have all of your plugs in one outlet via multiple-plug adapters, don't turn on the system. Instead, go to a computer or electronics store and purchase a power strip or box similar to those shown in Figure 1-22.

As you will find, there are two types of power distribution strips. The first, and least expensive, simply allows you to distribute the wires neatly. This is definitely an improvement over

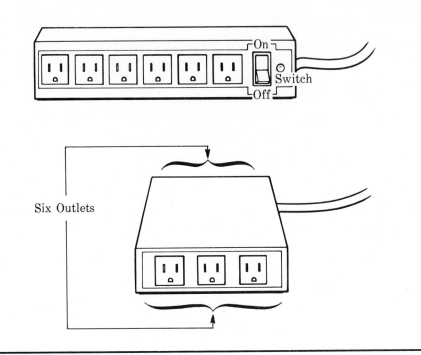

Figure 1-22. Sample power strips

multiple-plug outlets, but it provides little protection for your computer against power surges.

Many power strips also provide surge suppression. Once the power coming across the wires reaches a certain threshold, a breaker within the strip trips, and the power surge does not reach the computer. This small investment can protect the computer and software that you just spent several thousand dollars on. One such power distribution box sits under the monitor as shown in Figure 1-23. This particular box allows you to turn on and off individual components of your computer while providing surge suppression against power strikes.

Once you are satisfied with your power configuration, turn on your computer. The computer will begin its power-on diagnostics. During this time, the computer will check out most of its critical

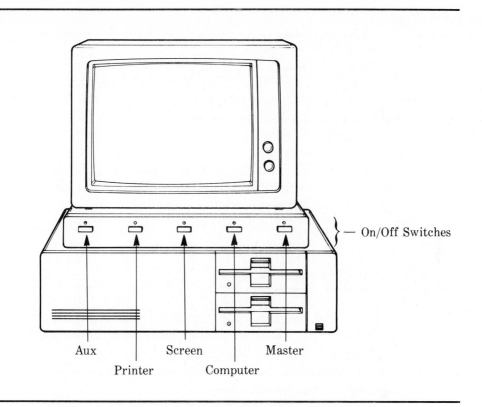

 On/Off Switches

Aux   Screen   Master
Printer   Computer

Figure 1-23.   Distribution box that sits under monitor

hardware components and display the amount of memory present in the system. If both disk drives are empty, the system will invoke a version of BASIC that is stored on a chip within the computer, and the following will be displayed:

```
The IBM Personal Computer Basic
Version C1.10 Copyright IBM Corp 1981
62940 Bytes free
Ok
1LIST 2RUN 3LOAD" 4SAVE" 5CONT 6,"LPT1 7TRON 8TROFF 9KEY 0SCREEN
```

This is a simplistic version of BASIC, but it provides you with access to the computer.

DOS Disk

Before you get started examining DOS, take out your DOS disks. You should have two disks. The first is the DOS system disk, which contains the operating system. The second is a collection of programs that the developers of DOS could not fit on the first disk. It is labeled "Supplemental Programs," since it contains a series of programs that are useful but are not necessarily required on a daily basis in your use of DOS. If differences exist between PC-DOS and MS-DOS, it is usually in the programs that you will find on the supplemental programs disk.

Input-Processing-Output (IPO)

No matter what function your computer performs, it always performs three steps: input, processing, and output. *Input* is the process of getting data into the computer from an external source. Common avenues of input include the keyboard, a modem, a mouse, and a floppy disk.

Before most programs can perform useful work, they must obtain data with which to work. Word processing programs get their input from the keyboard operator. Database and mailing-list programs obtain data from disks, and data communication programs get their data from modems.

Unless a program produces a meaningful result, it normally is of little use. The result of a program's execution is its *output*. In a word processing application, the output is the letters or reports it produces. Common output sources include a monitor, a printer, a modem, and a floppy disk.

Processing is the actual work the computer performs to produce its output.

Review

1. List several items contained within the chassis of your computer.

2. What is a byte?

3. What is a binary digit?

4. What does the term *64K of memory* mean?

5. Why do computers use the binary system?

6. List several sources of input.

7. List several sources of output.

8. What is input-processing-output?

9. What is a microfloppy?

10. How do you write-protect a disk? What does write-protecting a disk mean?

11. What are the DOS function keys?

12. What does DOS stand for?

13. How does PC-DOS differ from MS-DOS?

14. Define software.

15. Define hardware.

16. What is an operating system?

17. How does system software differ from application software?

1. *List several items contained within the chassis of your computer.*

The chassis of the computer contains the CPU and the computer's memory and houses fixed and floppy disk drives. If you have additional hardware devices, the boards for these devices are stored in the chassis within the computer's expansion slots.

2. *What is a byte?*

A byte is eight binary digits (bits). Every character in the alphabet is represented by a byte within the computer.

3. *What is a binary digit?*

A binary digit is simply a 1 or 0 in the base 2 numbering system. All digital computers are based on the binary number system. Eight binary digits combine to make a byte, which is usually the smallest unit the computer will manipulate.

4. *What does the term 64K of memory mean?*

The term *64K of memory* describes the amount of memory present in the computer. The K stands for the value 1024. This means 64K is actually 64 times 1024 or the value 65,536. When discussing computer memory, 64K means that the computer is capable of storing 64K of data or 65,536 characters of information.

5. *Why do computers use the binary system?*

Each of the hardware devices within the computer communicates with other devices based upon the presence or absence of electronic signals. A signal is either present (on) or absent (off). This on or off state can be defined by binary digits, which are either 1 or 0 (on or off). All data contained in the computer, therefore, is represented by a series of binary digits.

6. *List several sources of input.*

keyboard
disk
mouse
modem
joystick
network

7. *List several sources of output.*

screen
disk
printer
plotter
modem
network
voice synthesizer

8. *What is input-processing-output?*

No matter what your computer is doing, it always performs three steps: input, processing, and output. Input is the process of getting data into the computer from an external source. Processing is the actual computing. Output is the process of taking the computed results and writing them to an external source such as a disk, screen, or printer.

9. *What is a microfloppy?*

A microfloppy is a 3 1/2-inch disk. Microfloppy disks are much more durable than standard 5 1/4-inch disks and are exposed less to dust, smoke, and other particles that often destroy floppy disks.

10. *How do you write-protect a disk? What does write-protecting a disk mean?*

A write-protected disk cannot be written to by the computer. This prevents you from modifying or deleting files on the disk. With a standard 5 1/4-inch floppy disk, you write-protect the disk by placing a write-protect tab over the write-protect notch that is found in the upper-right-hand corner of the disk. With microfloppy disks, you must open the write-protect slide; this allows you to see through the small box in the lower corner of the disk.

11. *What are the DOS function keys?*

The keys labeled F1 through F10 are the DOS function keys. In later chapters you will see how DOS allows you to use these keys to simplify your keyboard entry.

12. *What does DOS stand for?*

DOS stands for Disk Operating System.

13. *How does PC-DOS differ from MS-DOS?*

Functionally, PC-DOS and MS-DOS are identical. PC-DOS is the IBM implementation of DOS. MS-DOS is the Microsoft version of DOS.

14. *Define software.*

Software is computer programs. Computer programs are simply lists of instructions for the computer to perform.

15. *Define hardware.*

Hardware is the boards, cables, and peripheral devices (printers, modems, and so forth) that make up your computer.

16. *What is an operating system?*

An operating system is the overseer of the computer and the processes it performs. In general, an operating system is a collection of the programs that manage system resources and aid in the development and execution of application programs.

17. *How does system software differ from application software?*

Application software is programs that provide a specific function such as word processing, database management, or mailing-list programs. System software is composed of operating systems such as DOS, which allow users to run application programs and manage system resources. System software allows application software to run on the computer. In essence, system software provides a layer between the application software and the hardware.

Introducing DOS

T
W
O

DATE (Set the System Date)
TIME (Set the System Time)
Resetting the Computer
Making a DOS Working Disk (DISKCOPY)
FORMAT (Readying a New Disk for Use by DOS)
Single-sided Versus Double-sided Disks
DOS Prompt
DOS Files
DIR (List All of the Files on a Disk)
DOS Wildcard Characters
DOS File-Naming Conventions
DOS File Specifications (file_spec)
COPY (Create a Second Copy of a File)
Controlling Screen Display and Terminating Commands
Write-Protecting Disks

Chapter 1 introduced the personal computer, differentiated between hardware and software, taught you the basics of handling floppy disks, and explained the power-on sequence for the computer. This chapter introduces you to the world of DOS. It shows you how to start DOS each time you begin working at the computer, how to copy the contents of one disk to another, and how to create new DOS disks. Finally, it introduces files. Upon completion of this chapter, you will be a bona fide DOS user.

As you will see, there are several ways to start, or boot, DOS. The remainder of this text will refer to the process of starting DOS as *booting* DOS.

The first method of booting DOS is simply to place the DOS system disk in drive A and turn on the power to your computer. Drives A and B of your computer are illustrated in Figure 2-1. After placing your DOS disk in drive A, turn on the computer.

Once started up, the computer performs its power-on hardware diagnostics. At this time, the computer examines most of its

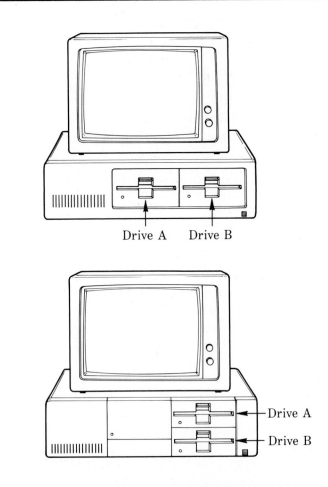

Drive A   Drive B

Drive A

Drive B

Figure 2-1.   Locations of drives A and B

critical hardware components. Next, the computer displays the amount of memory present on the system as it finds each 64K section. The disk-drive light next to drive A lights up. This tells you that the computer is accessing the disk contained in the drive; it will either read or write information to that disk. Never open the door of the disk drive or turn off the computer while this light is on; doing so may destroy all of the information contained on the disk.

The disk light is on at this time, so the computer can read DOS off the floppy disk and into memory. Before the system can execute a program, it must find that program in the computer's memory. DOS is nothing more than a large program that allows you to utilize the computer. It, too, must reside in memory. At power-up time, the computer simply knows enough to read the disk in drive A for DOS. If DOS is present, the computer will read DOS into memory. Once DOS is in memory, the system is ready for you to perform your daily tasks.

If you have placed your DOS system disk in drive A correctly, and the computer has passed all of its hardware diagnostics, DOS will gain control of the computer and display the following:

```
Current date is Thu 11-13-1986
Enter new date (mm-dd-yy):
```

This is the DOS prompt for you to enter the current date. DOS uses the date that you enter as the system date for all of the operations it will perform. Unless you have a system clock on a separate hardware board (which contains a battery to maintain the time once the system is turned off), DOS cannot retain the system time from one user session to the next. DOS expects you to enter the date in the form

mm-dd-yy

where the following is true:

mm is the two-digit number that represents the current month. It must be in the range 1-12.

dd is the two-digit number representing the current day. It must be in the range 1-31.

yy is the two-digit number that represents the current year. It must be in the range 80-99. DOS accepts the year specified as 19*xx* where *xx* is two digits in the range 80-99.

DOS allows you to use the following characters (*delimiters*) to separate the numbers of the date:

Period	9.30.87	is equivalent to	09.30.87
Slash	12/4/87	is equivalent to	12/04/87
Dash	9-3-87	is equivalent to	09-03-1987

If you enter an invalid date, DOS will respond with

```
Current date is Thu 11-13-1986
Enter new date (mm-dd-yy):14-12-86

Invalid date
Enter new date (mm-dd-yy):
```

Check for the following possible errors and reenter the date:

• Does the month precede the day? September 30, 1987, is entered as 09/30/87.

• Are you using a valid delimiter (. / or -)?

Note that the DATE command does not change the system clock on the IBM PC AT. To do so, you must use the Setup option of the diagnostic disk provided in the *AT Guide to Operations*.

If one of the characters you have entered is invalid, use the BACKSPACE key (located on the keyboard as shown in Figure 2-2) to correct the character. For example, suppose that, prior to pressing the ENTER key, you notice that you entered the date as

```
Current date is Thu 11-13-1986
Enter new date (mm-dd-yy):14-12-86▨
```

You simply press the BACKSPACE key until the cursor is at the invalid character and retype the date, as in the following:

```
Current date is Thu 11-13-1986
Enter new date (mm-dd-yy):1▨
```

Once you have successfully entered the DOS system date, DOS will prompt you to enter the current time as follows.

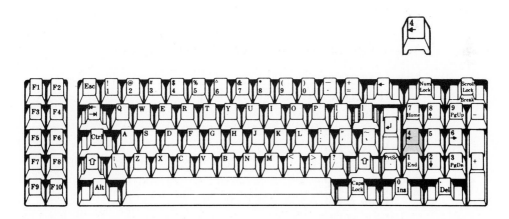

Figure 2-2. Location of BACKSPACE key

```
Current time is 13:18:15.43
Enter new time:
```

Note that the TIME command does not change the system clock on the IBM PC AT. To do so, you must use the Setup option of the diagnostic disk provided in the *AT Guide to Operations.*

DOS expects you to enter the time in the form

HH:MM:SS.hh

where the following is true:

HH is the two-digit number representing the current hour. *HH* is specified in military time as follows:

0 is 12 midnight
1 is 1 A.M.
2 is 2 A.M.
3 is 3 A.M.
4 is 4 A.M.
5 is 5 A.M.
6 is 6 A.M.
7 is 7 A.M.
8 is 8 A.M.
9 is 9 A.M.
10 is 10 A.M.
11 is 11 A.M.
12 is 12 noon
13 is 1 P.M.
14 is 2 P.M.
15 is 3 P.M.
16 is 4 P.M.
17 is 5 P.M.
18 is 6 P.M.
19 is 7 P.M.
20 is 8 P.M.
21 is 9 P.M.
22 is 10 P.M.
23 is 11 P.M.

MM is the two-digit number that represents the current minutes. It must be in the range 0-59.

SS is the two-digit number representing the current seconds. It must be in the range 0-59.

hh is the two-digit number that represents the current hundredths of seconds. It must be in the range 0-99.

DOS only requires you to specify the hours and minutes. If you enter

```
Current time is 13:18:15.43
Enter new time: 13:30
```

you have set the time to 1:30 P.M. If you enter

```
Current time is 13:18:15.43
Enter new time: 12:00:00
```

you have set the time to noon. If you enter

```
Current time is 13:18:15.43
Enter new time: 11:59:59.99
```

you have set the time to 11:59:59.99 A.M.

If you enter an invalid time, DOS will respond with

```
Current time is 13:18:15.43
Enter new time: 11:66:12

Invalid time
Enter new time:
```

Check for the following possible errors and rekey the time:

• Are you specifying the time in the form HH:MM:SS.hh within the specified ranges?

• Are you using a valid time delimiter? DOS allows the first three values (hours, minutes, seconds) to be separated by a period, a colon, or a combination of the two.

• The fourth value (hundredths of seconds) must be separated from the other values with a period.

Once you have entered the system time successfully, DOS will respond with

```
The IBM Personal Computer DOS
Version 3.00 (C)Copyright IBM Corp 1981, 1982, 1983, 1984

A>
```

Examine the following line:

```
Version 3.00 (C)Copyright IBM Corp 1981, 1982, 1983, 1984
```

It tells you the current DOS version. If you are using Microsoft's MS-DOS, as opposed to IBM's PC-DOS, the line will contain

```
Microsoft MS-DOS
Version 3.10 (C)Copyright Microsoft Corp 1981, 1985

A>
```

The A> is the DOS prompt. The prompt tells you DOS is ready for you to enter a command. Press the ENTER key three times.

```
A>
A>
A>
A>
```

DOS is still waiting for you to enter a command.

DATE (Set the System Date)

At the DOS prompt A>, type the word DATE and press the ENTER key:

```
A> DATE
```

DOS will respond with

```
Current date is Thu 11-13-1986
Enter new date (mm-dd-yy):
```

DATE is your first DOS command. Suppose you simply had pressed the ENTER key earlier when DOS prompted you to set the system date, as shown here:

```
Current date is Thu 11-13-1986
Enter new date (mm-dd-yy):

Current time is 13:31:33.33
Enter new time:
```

DOS would have used its default date of 11-13-1986. You could now reset the date via the DOS DATE command. Likewise, if you simply wanted to display today's date, you would issue the DATE command and press ENTER at the prompt for the new date. Since you did not specify a new date, the system date would remain unchanged. If you wanted to change the current system date, you would issue the DATE command and enter the date you desire.

The format of the DOS DATE command is

DATE [mm:dd:yy]

The brackets [ ] tell you that DOS allows you to provide optional command-line parameters that contain the date desired. Each time you issue a command, the entire line becomes a *command line*. If the command you want to issue is DATE, the command line is

DATE

The format of the DOS DATE command illustrates that DOS allows you to specify optional command-line parameters [mm:dd:yy]. Enter the following:

A> DATE 9/30/87

In this case, the command line not only contains the command DATE, but also the command-line parameter 9/30/87. When you press ENTER, DOS responds with

```
A> DATE 9/30/87
A>
```

Since you provided DATE with the system date you wanted, DATE did not prompt you to enter a date. Instead, DATE used the date specified by the command-line parameter to reset the system date. Suppose the date you provide is invalid, as shown here:

A> DATE 13/3/87

DATE will display an error message and prompt you for a new date, as in the following:

```
Invalid date
Enter new date (mm-dd-yy):
```

TIME (Set the System Time)

The DOS TIME command is similar to the DOS DATE command. TIME allows you to display or reset the current system time. The format of the command is

TIME [HH:MM[:SS[.hh]]]

The format of DOS TIME tells you that DOS allows you to issue the command without any parameters, as in the following:

```
A> TIME
```

In this case, TIME will display

```
Current time is 13:32:12.23
Enter new time:
```

If you simply want to display the system time, press ENTER. Since you did not specify a new system time, TIME will not reset the current time. Examine the optional command-line parameter

[HH:MM[:SS[.hh]]]

The first set of brackets tells you that the entire command-line parameter is optional. The second set tells you that if you specify a time, you need to provide the hours and minutes only. The third set of brackets states that you do not have to provide the hundredths of seconds. Consider the following examples. If you enter

```
A> TIME 12:00
```

you have set the system time to noon. If you enter

```
A> TIME 12:30:30
```

you have set the system time to 12:30:30 P.M. If you enter

```
A> TIME 11:59:59.99
```

you have set the system time to 11:59:59.99 A.M.

There are two ways to *reset* the computer. Resetting the computer is simply the process of restoring DOS to its initial state. The first method of rebooting is simply to place the DOS disk in drive A and turn on the computer. The computer will perform its power-on diagnostics and read DOS from the floppy disk into memory. The second method of rebooting DOS is to press the CTRL, ALT, and DEL keys, all at the same time. The position of these three keys is shown in Figure 2-3. Although using the CTRL-ALT-DEL sequence works to reboot DOS, turning off the computer and then turning it back on also is reliable. However, after turning off the computer, you must wait 10-30 seconds before turning on the computer.

When rebooting using the CTRL-ALT-DEL sequence, the computer will read DOS from disk into memory. Since the system was not turned off, there is no reason for the computer to perform the power-on diagnostics. Place your DOS disk into drive A and press the CTRL-ALT-DEL keys all at once. The screen will clear, and the

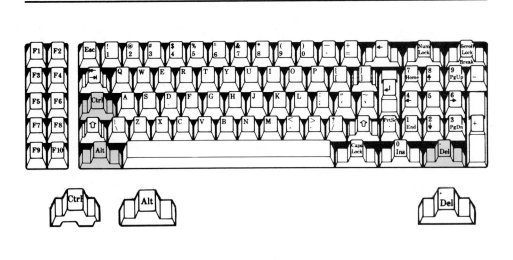

Figure 2-3. Location of CTRL, ALT, and DEL keys

disk light next to drive A will light up as the computer reads DOS from disk into memory. Once DOS is resident in memory, you must reenter the system date and time.

Making a DOS Working Disk (DISKCOPY)

If treated properly, floppy disks will last a long time. Disks will fail periodically, however, even under the best conditions, because of the everyday wear and tear of being read and written. As an immediate precaution against losing your DOS disks, make a working copy of your DOS system and supplemental disks by using the DOS DISKCOPY command.

Place your DOS system disk in drive A and a new disk in drive B. Issue the command

```
A> DISKCOPY A: B:
```

DOS will respond with

```
Insert SOURCE Diskette in Drive A :

Insert TARGET Diskette in Drive B :

Press any key when ready . . .
```

Place a new disk in drive B (if you haven't already done so). Press the ENTER key, and DOS will begin creating your working copy of DOS on the disk in drive B. This copy of DOS is called your *working copy*, since you will be using it from now on each time the system boots or when you need to issue DOS commands. As the disk copying proceeds, you should first see the disk light in drive A light up for a period of time and then see the light next to drive B light up. This is because DOS is reading the contents of drive A and then writing them to drive B.

When the copying procedure is finished, DOS will prompt you to specify whether you want to make additional copies. If so, press Y and then press ENTER; otherwise, press N. If you press Y, DISKCOPY will prompt you to

```
Insert SOURCE Diskette in Drive A :

Insert TARGET Diskette in Drive B :

Press any key when ready . . .
```

The *source* disk is the disk that you want to copy. The *target* disk is the new disk on which you want to make the copy. This procedure is illustrated in Figure 2-4.

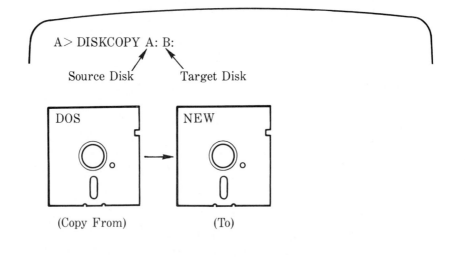

Figure 2-4.   DISKCOPY target and source disks

Use DISKCOPY to copy the DOS supplemental disk as follows:

- Place your DOS system disk in drive A.
- Issue the command

  ```
  A> DISKCOPY A: B:
  ```

- You'll see the DOS prompt

```
Insert SOURCE Diskette in Drive A :

Insert TARGET Diskette in Drive B :

Press any key when ready . . .
```

- Place your supplemental disk in drive A and a new disk in drive B. Press ENTER, and disk copying will begin.

You should now have four disks, as illustrated in Figure 2-5. Place your original disks in a safe location and use the two newly created disks as your working copies.

The format of the DOS DISKCOPY command is

[drive:][path]DISKCOPY [d1:[d2:]] [/1]

where the following is true:

drive: is the disk drive containing the file DISKCOPY.COM. DISKCOPY is an external DOS command, which means DOS must read the program from disk into memory each time the command is invoked. If you do not specify a disk drive, DISKCOPY will use the current default drive.

path: is the subdirectory path (see Chapter 6) that DOS must traverse to locate the file DISKCOPY.COM. If you do not specify a path, DOS will search the current default directory.

d1: is the disk drive (either A or B) of the disk for DISKCOPY to copy.

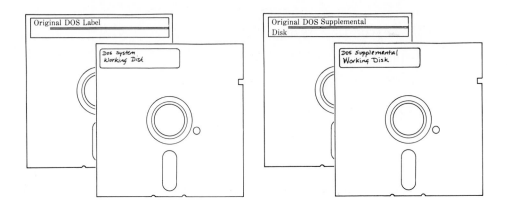

Figure 2-5.　Four disks after copying system disks

d2: is the disk drive (either A or B) of the disk DISKCOPY is to copy *d1* to.

/1 directs DISKCOPY to copy only side 1 of the floppy disk (most disks are double-sided).

If you only have a single-disk-drive system, DISKCOPY allows you to use the single drive to copy the contents of one disk to another. Place your DOS system disk in drive A and issue the command

```
A> DISKCOPY
```

Next, place the disk you want to copy into drive A and press ENTER. DISKCOPY will prompt you to place the target disk (the disk you are copying to) into the drive at the correct time as follows:

```
Insert TARGET Diskette in Drive A :

Press any key when ready . . .
```

A complete single-disk-drive copy becomes

```
A> DISKCOPY
Insert SOURCE Diskette in Drive A :

Press any key when ready

Copying 40 tracks
9 Sectors/Track, 2 Side(s)

Insert TARGET Diskette in Drive A :

Press any key when ready

Insert SOURCE Diskette in Drive A :

Press any key when ready

Insert TARGET Diskette in Drive A :

Press any key when ready

Copy another diskette (Y/N)?
```

If DISKCOPY encounters errors during disk copying, it will display the side and track (see Chapter 9) containing the error. In such cases, you should attempt the copy again with a new disk in the target (destination) drive. If the procedure still fails, see the next section, on the FORMAT command. DISKCOPY may display the message

```
Disk error while reading drive A:
Abort, Ignore, Retry?
```

You will know that the disk that you are trying to read may be copy-protected.

Note that DISKCOPY cannot copy disks that are copy-protected. To make backup copies of copy-protected disks, you need to purchase a third-party software package that breaks copy protections. It is against the law to distribute copy-protected software.

Also note that DISKCOPY does not work with fixed disk drives. If you attempt to copy to or from a fixed disk with DISK-COPY, it will display

```
Invalid drive specification.
Specified drive does not exist,
or is non-removable.
```

To place the contents of your floppy disk onto a fixed disk, you must use the COPY command presented later in this chapter.

FORMAT (Readying a New Disk for Use by DOS)

When you buy a box of floppy disks, the original manufacturer of the disks has no way of knowing on what type of computer the disks will eventually be used or what operating system the computer is using. You must, therefore, format each disk to meet your system's specific requirements.

The DOS FORMAT command prepares a disk for use by DOS. Place your DOS system disk into drive A and a new disk into drive B. Issue the command

```
A> FORMAT B:
```

DOS will respond with

```
Insert new diskette for drive B:
and strike ENTER when ready
```

If you have not yet placed a blank disk into drive B, do so now. It is important to note that FORMAT will destroy the contents of the disk in drive B. (Chapter 9 contains more information on FORMAT.) If you are ready to continue, press ENTER, and disk formatting will begin. When the procedure is finished, FORMAT will display

```
Formatting...Format complete

    362496 bytes total disk space
    362496 bytes available on disk

Format another (Y/N)?
```

The 362496 tells you the number of bytes available for use on the disk. In this case, the disk was formatted with double-sided, double-density format.

The format of the DOS FORMAT command is

[drive:][path]FORMAT [d:] [/B][/S][/V][/1][/4][/8]

where the following is true:

drive: is the disk drive containing the file FORMAT.COM.

path is the subdirectory path (see Chapter 6) that DOS must traverse to locate the file FORMAT.COM. If you do not specify a path, DOS will search the current default directory.

FORMAT is an external DOS command. Each time the command is invoked, DOS must read the program from disk into memory. If you do not specify a disk drive, *FORMAT* will use the current default drive.

d: is the disk drive (either A or B) containing the disk to be formatted.

/B requests FORMAT to allocate space on the disk for the files IBMBIO.COM (PC-DOS), IBMDOS.COM (PC-DOS), or IO.SYS (MS-DOS) and MSDOS.SYS (MS-DOS), along with COMMAND.COM. Preallocating space in this manner allows the command SYS.COM (see Chapter 10) to make the disk bootable by DOS. See the DOS reference section at the end of the book for more information on this qualifier.

/S requests FORMAT to place the files IBMBIO.CO, IBM-DOS.COM (PC-DOS), or IO.SYS and MSDOS.SYS (MS-DOS), along with COMMAND.COM, on the new disk, which makes it bootable. If you use the /S qualifier, FORMAT will display the amount of disk space consumed by the files as follows:

xxxxx bytes used by the system

The actual value for xxxxx depends on the version of DOS you are using.

/V requests FORMAT to place a volume label (see Chapter 3) on the disk drive.

/1 requests FORMAT to format the disk as a single-sided disk (most disks are double-sided).

/4 requests FORMAT to format a double-density disk in a quad-density drive. A disk formatted with the /4 qualifier may not be readable by standard double-density disk drives.

/8 requests FORMAT to format the disk with 8 sectors per track as opposed to the default values of 9 and 15 for double-density and quad-density disks. Chapter 9 provides detailed explanations on sectors and tracks.

Use of each qualifier is illustrated in the DOS reference section at the end of the text. For now, it is important only that you understand the /S qualifier. Enter the command

`A> FORMAT B:/S`

To ensure that a disk can be booted by DOS, you must format the disk with the /S qualifier. If you attempt to boot a disk that was not formatted in this manner, DOS will display

```
Non-System disk or disk error
Replace and strike any key when ready
```

If you make a complete copy of a bootable disk with the DOS DISKCOPY command, the new copy of the disk is still bootable. Simply place another bootable disk in drive A and press any key to continue. Besides readying a disk for use by DOS, the FORMAT command makes a list of damaged locations on the disk for DOS. This list prevents DOS from trying to write data to these locations. If FORMAT finds bad sectors on the disk (see Chapter 9), it will display

```
362496 bytes total disk space
  2048 bytes in bad sectors
360448 bytes available on disk
```

If there is an excessive number of bad sectors (more than 4096 on a floppy disk), you should be leery of using the disk. Some users will attempt a second FORMAT of the disk, and if this fails, they will discard it. Floppy disks have improved so much in quality over the past few years that rarely do disks have any bad sectors.

Most fixed disks will be shipped already formatted from the factory. If yours were not, see Chapter 9 for a detailed explanation on hard-disk management. FORMAT behaves in the same manner for fixed disks as it does for floppy disks.

Single-sided Versus Double-sided Disks

Most computer stores will advise you to purchase double-sided disks when you are using an IBM PC or a PC-compatible. Essentially, the only difference (other than cost) between the two disk types is that the manufacturer will only guarantee one side of a single-sided disk. FORMAT and DOS, however, are willing to treat single-sided disks as double-sided.

You can format single-sided disks as if they were double-sided (the default format). Some users may want to save the money they would spend on double-sided disks by only purchasing single-sided, double-density disks.

DOS Prompt

As previously stated, the A> is the DOS prompt. The prompt tells you that DOS is waiting for you to enter a command. Each time DOS completes the command, it displays the prompt and waits for the next command, as shown here:

```
A> DATE 12/21/87
A>
```

A DOS command is simply the function that you want DOS to perform. In the previous examples, you issued the TIME, DATE, DISKCOPY, and FORMAT commands. It is important to note that DOS categorizes commands in one of two ways: external and internal commands.

As previously stated, each time DOS boots, it stores several commands in memory. Each time you issue one of these commands, DOS simply locates it in memory and executes it. Because these commands are alway present in memory, they are called *internal DOS commands*. Figure 2-6 shows memory management within DOS.

The other category of DOS commands is external commands. Unlike internal commands, which DOS always stores in memory, *external DOS commands* reside on disk. Each time you issue an external command, DOS must read the command from disk into memory. Remember, before a program can execute, it must reside in memory.

DOS commands are simply programs that DOS runs to perform specific tasks, as shown in Figure 2-7. DATE and TIME are internal DOS commands that always reside in memory. Since internal commands are already present in memory, it doesn't matter which disks are in which drives. With external commands, however, the disks become a concern because DOS must search the disk for the command and load it into memory.

The DOS prompt A> tells you the disk drive DOS will search for the command. This drive is termed the *default drive* because, by default, DOS will look for the command on this drive unless you override it by specifying an alternate drive.

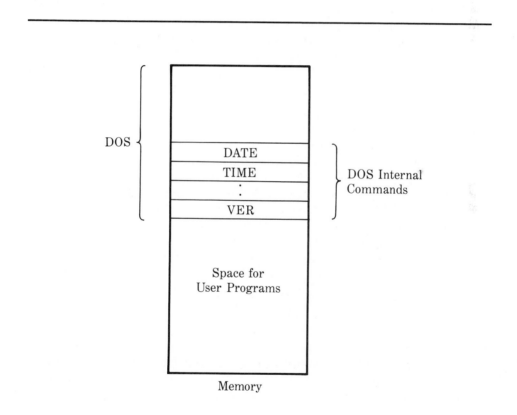

Figure 2-6.   Memory management within DOS

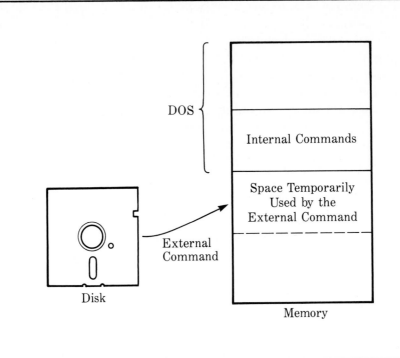

Figure 2-7. The running of programs within DOS

If your DOS system disk is in drive B instead of drive A, you can change the default drive simply by entering the desired drive as follows (be sure to include the colon):

```
A> B:
```

In this case, you are selecting drive B for the default drive. DOS acknowledges the change by modifying the system prompt, as shown here:

```
B>
```

If you have a hard disk (drive C), you can select it as the default drive by entering

```
A> C:
C>
```

To reset the system default drive to drive A, simply enter

```
C> A:
A>
```

Place your DOS disk in drive A and a newly formatted disk in drive B. Set the default drive to B by entering

```
A> B:
B>
```

Issue the command

```
B> DISKCOPY A: B:
```

DOS will respond with

```
Bad command or file name
```

This response occurs because DISKCOPY is an external command. Each time you invoke DISKCOPY, DOS must search the disk for the DISKCOPY command and load it into memory. In this case, the DISKCOPY command is located on the disk in drive A. DOS did not find the command because it was searching the default drive B, which does not contain the command.

To override the default drive, you must specify the name of the drive containing the command, as follows:

drive:command

Place your DOS system disk in drive A and a blank disk in drive B. Change the default drive to B by entering

```
A> B:
B>
```

Next, issue the command

```
B> A:DISKCOPY A: B:
```

Since you told DOS that the DISKCOPY command resides on drive A, the command overrode the default drive. In this case, press ENTER, and DOS will create a backup copy of your system disk on the disk in drive B.

DOS Files

When you store data on disk, DOS places the data into a storage facility called a *file*. You treat disk files just as you do files in your filing cabinet. You can create disk files, modify their contents, rename them, and, finally, dispose of them when they are no longer required.

Every DOS file has a name. DOS file names are made up of two parts: a file name and an extension. The file name must contain from one to eight characters. Acceptable characters are the letters of the alphabet along with the characters

~ ! @ # $ % ^ & ( ) - — { } '

The extension is optional and can contain up to three characters. A period separates the file name from the extension as follows:

filename.ext

The following are valid DOS file names:

COMMAND.COM	SEPT.SAL
OCTOBER.PAY	BOOK.RPT
BUDGET	MY_NOTES
SCIENCE.!!!	SYSTEM$1.DAT

These names are invalid file names:

TOO_MANY_CHARACTERS

.EXE	(no file name)
BOOK..EXT	(period is an illegal character)
BLANK .EXE	(the space is illegal)
NEW.DATA	(extension can be only three letters)

As you will see in Chapter 4, DOS has several reserved names for devices such as your printer. Since DOS is already using the following names, you cannot create files with the same names.

AUX	CON	LPT3
CLOCK$	LPT1	NUL
COM1	LPT2	PRN
COM2		

File names will be discussed later in this chapter.

DIR (List All of the Files on a Disk)

The DOS directory command DIR allows you to list the names and attributes of the files contained on a disk. Place your working copy of the DOS system disk in drive A and issue the command

```
A> DIR
```

DOS will respond with something like

```
Volume in drive A has no label
Directory of  A:\

COMMAND   COM     23210   3-11-86   10:00a
ASSIGN    COM      1509   3-11-86   10:00a
```

```
ATTRIB     EXE    15091    3-11-86   10:00a
FORMAT     COM     6831    5-09-86    3:52p
FDISK      COM    14448    5-13-86    9:47a
DISKCOMP   COM     3774    5-20-86    8:52a
DISKCOPY   COM     4099    5-20-86    8:52a
TREE       COM     6306    5-03-86   11:19a
EXE2BIN    EXE     2816    3-11-86   10:00a
FC         EXE    14576    3-11-86   10:00a
FIND       EXE     6403    3-11-86   10:00a
JOIN       EXE    15971    3-11-86   10:00a
LABEL      EXE     2750    3-11-86   10:00a
SHARE      EXE     8304    3-11-86   10:00a
SUBST      EXE    16611    3-11-86   10:00a
SYS        EXE     2671    3-11-86   10:00a
MORE       COM      282    3-11-86   10:00a
SORT       EXE     1664    3-11-86   10:00a
CHKDSK     COM     9435    3-11-86   10:00a
DEBUG      COM    15552    3-11-86   10:00a
EDLIN      COM     7261    3-11-86   10:00a
PRINT      COM     8291    3-11-86   10:00a
RECOVER    COM     4050    3-11-86   10:00a
MODE       COM     2868    5-21-86   11:59a
ANSI       SYS     2563    5-12-86    1:42p
SELECT     COM     6052    5-08-86    8:54a
KEYBSP     COM     2317    5-08-86    6:10p
KEYBFR     COM     2395    5-08-86    6:13p
KEYBGR     COM     2310    5-08-86    6:15p
KEYBNR     COM     2335    5-08-86    6:10p
KEYBSF     COM     2331    5-08-86    6:23p
KEYBSG     COM     2360    5-08-86    6:20p
KEYBDK     COM     2335    5-08-86    6:25p
KEYBUK     COM     1972    5-08-86    6:08p
KEYBIT     COM     2011    5-08-86    6:06p
KEYBSV     COM     2259    5-08-86    6:18p
GFTPRN     COM      292    3-18-86   10:30a
GRAFTABL   COM     2145    3-11-86   10:00a
GRAPHICS   COM     5363    4-10-86   11:37a
COMP       COM     7194    5-03-86   11:19a
SHIPZONE   EXE      779    5-12-86    9:45a
SPEED      EXE     1196    5-09-86   11:34a
      42 File(s)      54272 bytes free
```

The output of the DIR command tells you several things. First, notice the line

```
Volume in drive A has no label
Directory of A:\
```

DOS: The Complete Reference

It tells you the drive containing the disk that DIR is listing. Second, DIR tells you the name, size (in bytes), and creation date and time for each file, as illustrated here:

```
Volume in drive A has no label
Directory of   A:\

COMMAND   COM     23210   3-11-86   10:00a
```

Last, DIR tells you how many free bytes remain on the disk. The format of the DOS directory command is

DIR [file—spec][/P][/W]

where the following is true:

file—spec is the file specification (name) of the file to list. If you do not provide a file specification, DIR will list all of the files on the disk. File specifications are examined in detail later in this chapter.

/P instructs DIR to pause with each full screen of information and to display the message

```
Strike a key when ready . . .
```

Simply press a key and the directory listing will continue.

/W requests DIR only to display each file name present on the disk, suppressing the size and the creation date and time for each file, in favor of listing several file names on each line.

Consider the following examples. Enter

A> DIR /W

DIR suppresses the size, as well as the creation date and time, for each file. It displays only the file names. Enter

```
A> DIR COMMAND.COM
```

DIR only displays information on the file COMMAND.COM. If DIR cannot find the file you specify, it will display the message

```
File not found
```

Enter the DOS command

```
A> DIR FORMAT.COM
```

The result of your action is

```
Volume in drive A has no label
Directory of  A:\

FORMAT    COM     6831   5-09-86   3:52p
        1 File(s)        54272 bytes free
```

DOS Wildcard Characters

One of the best features of DOS is that it allows you to substitute the characters * and ? for other characters in a file name during file-search operations. The question mark (?) in a file name tells DOS that any character can occupy that location in the file name. Enter the following example:

```
A> DIR CHAPTER?.TXT
```

In this case, you are requesting DOS to provide a directory listing of all of the files whose names begin with the word *chapter* followed by any character and that have the extension TXT. If you perform the previous command on the disk that contains the chapters for this book, DOS will display

```
Volume in drive A has no label
Directory of  A:\

CHAPTER1 TXT     23210     3-11-86    10:00a
CHAPTER2 TXT      1509     3-11-86    10:00a
CHAPTER3 TXT      6831     5-09-86     3:52p
CHAPTER4 TXT     14448     5-13-86     9:47a
CHAPTER5 TXT      3774     5-20-86     8:52a
CHAPTER6 TXT      4099     5-20-86     8:52a
```

Perform the following directory command on your DOS system disk:

```
A> DIR DISK????.COM
```

DOS will display

```
Volume in drive A has no label
Directory of  A:\

DISKCOMP COM      3774     5-20-86     8:52a
DISKCOPY COM      4099     5-20-86     8:52a
         2 File(s)      54272 bytes free
```

The four question marks tell DOS that you don't care about the last four characters of the file name, as long as the first four are DISK and the extension is COM. The wildcard character * is more powerful than the question mark. It not only tells DOS that any character can occupy the current location, but also tells DOS which characters remain in the file name or the extension. Consider the following examples. Enter the following command, and DIR will display all files whose extension is COM, regardless of the file name:

```
A> DIR *.COM
```

Enter the following command and DIR will display all files whose names begin with DISK and have the extension COM:

```
A> DIR DISK*.COM
```

Enter the following command and DIR will display all files whose names begin with the letter D and have the extension COM.

```
A> DIR D*.COM
```

Enter the following command and DIR will display all of the files on the disk:

```
A> DIR *.*
```

Remember, the asterisk matches characters not only in the current position, but also any remaining characters in the file name or extension. The DOS wildcard characters are a feature you will use on a daily basis. Take time now to familiarize yourself with their use.

DOS File-Naming Conventions

Each DOS file stores one of two things: programs or data. Normally, you use the three-character file-name extension to differentiate between the file types. Since DOS files may contain a number of things, use extensions to help indicate what the file contains. Some commonly used examples are

```
COM     DOS  commands  or  executable  programs
EXE     DOS  executable  programs
BAT     DOS  batch  files  (Chapter  8)
SYS     Installable  device  drivers  (Chapter  15)
TXT     Word  processing  files
DAT     Data  files  for  programs
```

By examining the file-name extensions, you can categorize files, as shown in Table 2-1.

It is important that your file names be meaningful to you. For example, the files containing the chapters of this book were named as follows:

```
CHAPTER1.TXT
CHAPTER2.TXT
CHAPTER3.TXT
    .
    .
    .
CHAPTE18.TXT
APPEND1.TXT
```

Name	Function
COMMAND.COM	DOS command
ANSI.SYS	ANSI device driver
CHAPTER.TXT	Word processing document
SEPT.DAT	Data file
BUDGET.EXE	Executable program

Table 2-1.   Categories of DOS Files

DOS File Specifications
(file — spec)

The majority of the DOS commands referenced throughout the remainder of this text are designed to manipulate file specifications.

A DOS file specification differs from a DOS file name in that it provides DOS with more specific information on the location of a file. The format of a file specification is

[drive:][path][filename][.ext]

where the following is true:

drive: is the disk drive (A, B, or C) containing the disk with the file you desire. If you do not specify a drive, DOS will use the current default drive.

path is the DOS subdirectory path (see Chapter 6) that DOS must traverse to find the file. If you do not specify a path, DOS will use the current working directory.

filename is the 1- to 8-character file name. The DOS wildcard characters are valid characters.

.ext is the optional 1- to 3-character extension. The DOS wildcard characters are valid characters.

Consider the file specifications shown in Table 2-2.

COPY (Create a Second Copy
of a File)

The DOS COPY command allows you to make duplicate copies of a file. Place your DOS disk in drive A and a newly formatted disk in drive B. If you don't have a formatted disk, place a new disk in drive B and issue the FORMAT command.

```
A> FORMAT B:
```

File Specification	Drive	Path	File Name	Extension
COMMAND.COM	Default	Current Directory	COMMAND	COM
B:FORMAT.COM	B	Current Directory	FORMAT	COM
\IBM \ANSI.SYS	Default	\IBM	ANSI	SYS
B:\IBM \DATA.DAT	B:	\IBM	DATA	DAT

Table 2-2.   DOS File Specifications

When you have your DOS system disk in drive A and a formatted disk in drive B, issue the command

```
A> COPY DISKCOPY.COM B:DISKCOPY.COM
```

This command copies the contents of the file DISKCOPY.COM from drive A to drive B, as shown here:

```
A> DIR B:

 Volume in drive B has no label
 Directory of  B:\

DISKCOPY COM     4099   5-20-86   8:52a
        1 File(s)     336896 bytes free
```

A simple format of the copy command is

COPY file—spec1 file—spec2 [/V]

where the following is true:

file—spec1 is the name of the source file that you want to copy.

file_spec2 is the name of the target (destination) file of the copy.

/V is the COPY verify qualifier. When present, COPY will reread the file it copied to ensure that it read and wrote the contents of the existing file correctly to the new file. Because COPY must reread the original file, copies that use the /V qualifier will take slightly longer than copies that do not use the qualifier.

The complete format for the COPY command is provided in the DOS reference section. For now, the simple format provides all of the features you require.

Consider the following COPY commands. Enter

```
A> COPY COMMAND.COM B:NEWCMD.COM
```

COPY will copy the contents of the file COMMAND.COM on drive A to disk B with the name NEWCMD.COM. Enter

```
A> COPY *.SYS B:*.*
```

COPY will use the wildcard character * to copy all of the files on drive A with the extension SYS to drive B. The files will retain their original names. Enter

```
A> COPY *.* B:
```

COPY will copy all of the files on drive A to drive B with their original names.

Note that if a file already exists with the same name as the destination file name, COPY will overwrite the contents of the file. Enter

```
A> COPY COMMAND.COM B:COMMAND.COM
```

COPY will overwrite the contents of the file COMMAND.COM on drive B with the contents of COMMAND.COM from drive A.

COPY will not allow you to copy a file to itself, and the following display will result:

```
File cannot be copied onto itself
        0 File(s) copied
```

Likewise, if you attempt to copy a nonexistent file, COPY will display

```
A> COPY D.COM NEW.COM
D File not found
        0 File(s) copied
```

Using COPY to Append Files

Thus far, you have used COPY only to create new versions of a file. DOS, however, allows you to append one file to another with the COPY command. For example, if you have three files— PART1.TXT, PART2.TXT, and PART3.TXT—containing the information shown in Figure 2-8, you can issue the COPY command as follows to create a file called ALLPARTS.TXT,

```
A> COPY PART1.TXT+PART2.TXT+PART3.TXT ALLPARTS.TXT
```

which contains

```
I pledge allegiance to the flag
of the United States of America
and to the republic for which
it stands,
one nation, under God, indivisible,
with liberty and justice for all.
```

```
┌─────────────────────────────────────────┐
│ I pledge allegiance to the flag         │
│ of the United States of America         │
└─────────────────────────────────────────┘
              PART1.TXT

┌─────────────────────────────────────────┐
│ and to the republic for which           │
│ it stands,                              │
└─────────────────────────────────────────┘
              PART2.TXT

┌─────────────────────────────────────────┐
│ one nation, under God, indivisible,     │
│ with liberty and justice for all.       │
└─────────────────────────────────────────┘
              PART3.TXT
```

Figure 2-8.   Appending a file using COPY

Likewise, if the file for this chapter had been broken into three files, INTRO.TXT, CHAP.TXT, and REVIEW.TXT, the file CHAPTER2.TXT could have been created as follows:

```
A> COPY INTRO.TXT+CHAP.TXT+REVIEW.TXT CHAPTER2.TXT
```

Note that this is not a common use of the COPY command.

Controlling Screen Display and Terminating Commands

As DOS executes commands, it allows you to use several keyboard combinations to control the execution of the command. You have already learned the CTRL-ALT-DEL combination, which reboots DOS (see Figure 2-3). In a similar manner, the combination CTRL-S (shown in Figure 2-9) temporarily suspends the screen display.
    Consider the directory command

```
A> DIR
```

If the result of the command requires more than one screen for display, the file names will scroll off the top of the screen. You can prevent this from happening by pressing the CTRL and S keys at the same time, as shown here:

```
Volume in drive A has no label
Directory of   A:\

COMMAND  COM     23210    3-11-86    10:00a
ASSIGN   COM      1509    3-11-86    10:00a
ATTRIB   EXE     15091    3-11-86    10:00a
FORMAT   COM      6831    5-09-86     3:52p
FDISK    COM     14448    5-13-86     9:47a
DISKCOMP COM      3774    5-20-86     8:52a
DISKCOPY COM      4099    5-20-86     8:52a
TREE     COM      6306    5-03-86    11:19a
EXE2BIN  EXE      2816    3-11-86    10:00a
FC       EXE     14576    3-11-86    10:00a
FIND     EXE      6403    3-11-86    10:00a
JOIN     EXE     15971    3-11-86    10:00a
LABEL    EXE      2750    3-11-86    10:00a

CTRL-S pressed here to suspend output
```

To resume scrolling, simply press any key. Scrolling resumes, as shown here:

```
Volume in drive A has no label
Directory of   A:\

COMMAND  COM     23210    3-11-86    10:00a
ASSIGN   COM      1509    3-11-86    10:00a
ATTRIB   EXE     15091    3-11-86    10:00a
FORMAT   COM      6831    5-09-86     3:52p
FDISK    COM     14448    5-13-86     9:47a
DISKCOMP COM      3774    5-20-86     8:52a
DISKCOPY COM      4099    5-20-86     8:52a
TREE     COM      6306    5-03-86    11:19a
EXE2BIN  EXE      2816    3-11-86    10:00a
FC       EXE     14576    3-11-86    10:00a
FIND     EXE      6403    3-11-86    10:00a
JOIN     EXE     15971    3-11-86    10:00a
LABEL    EXE      2750    3-11-86    10:00a
SHARE    EXE      8304    3-11-86    10:00a
SUBST    EXE     16611    3-11-86    10:00a
```

```
SYS        EXE      2671      3-11-86     10:00a
MORE       COM       282      3-11-86     10:00a
SORT       EXE      1664      3-11-86     10:00a
CHKDSK     COM      9435      3-11-86     10:00a
DEBUG      COM     15552      3-11-86     10:00a
EDLIN      COM      7261      3-11-86     10:00a
PRINT      COM      8291      3-11-86     10:00a
RECOVER    COM      4050      3-11-86     10:00a
MODE       COM      2868      5-21-86     11:59a
ANSI       SYS      2563      5-12-86      1:42p
SELECT     COM      6052      5-08-86      8:54a
KEYBSP     COM      2317      5-08-86      6:10p
KEYBFR     COM      2395      5-08-86      6:13p
KEYBGR     COM      2310      5-08-86      6:15p
KEYBNR     COM      2335      5-08-86      6:10p
KEYBSF     COM      2331      5-08-86      6:23p
KEYBSG     COM      2360      5-08-86      6:20p
KEYBDK     COM      2335      5-08-86      6:25p
KEYBUK     COM      1972      5-08-86      6:08p
KEYBIT     COM      2011      5-08-86      6:06p
KEYBSV     COM      2259      5-08-86      6:18p
GFTPRN     COM       292      3-18-86     10:30a
GRAFTABL   COM      2145      3-11-86     10:00a
GRAPHICS   COM      5363      4-10-86     11:37a
COMP       COM      7194      5-03-86     11:19a
SHIPZONE   EXE       779      5-12-86      9:45a
SPEED      EXE      1196      5-09-86     11:34a
          42 File(s)        54272 bytes free
```

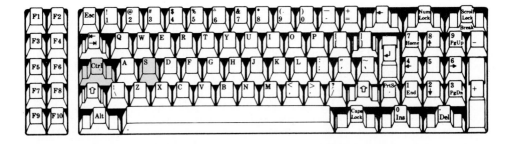

Figure 2-9.   Location of CTRL and S keys

If you have invoked a command in error or wish to terminate the current command, press the CTRL and BREAK keys at the same time (the locations of these keys are shown in Figure 2-10).

Consider the following example:

```
Volume in drive A has no label
Directory of  A:\

COMMAND   COM     23210    3-11-86    10:00a
ASSIGN    COM      1509    3-11-86    10:00a
ATTRIB    EXE     15091    3-11-86    10:00a
FORMAT    COM      6831    5-09-86     3:52p
FDISK     COM     14448    5-13-86     9:47a
DISKCOMP  COM      3774    5-20-86     8:52a
DISKCOPY  COM      4099    5-20-86     8:52a
TREE      COM      6306    5-03-86    11:19a
EXE2BIN   EXE      2816    3-11-86    10:00a
FC        EXE     14576    3-11-86    10:00a
FIND      EXE      6403    3-11-86    10:00a
JOIN      EXE     15971    3-11-86    10:00a
LABEL     EXE      2750    3-11-86    10:00a
^C
```

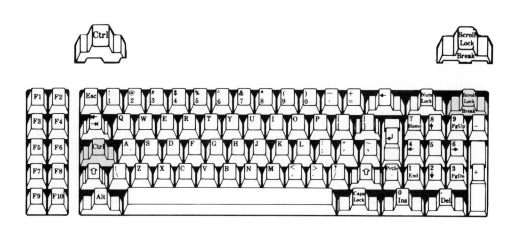

Figure 2-10.   Location of the CTRL and BREAK keys

The ^C on the screen illustrates that the CTRL-BREAK combination terminated the command. Suppose, for example, you do not want to continue a disk format.

```
A> FORMAT B:
Insert new diskette for drive B:
and strike ENTER when ready^C

A>
```

Simply press the CTRL and BREAK keys at the same time, and the command will terminate. The CTRL and C keys (shown in Figure 2-11) pressed at the same time have the same effect as the CTRL-BREAK combination.

Figure 2-11.   Location of the CTRL and C keys

Write-Protecting Disks

Chapter 1 illustrated the write-protect notch on a floppy disk, as shown in Figure 2-12. If you cover the notch with a write-protect tab, as shown in Figure 2-13, you can no longer write to the disk. This eliminates the possibility of the disk's being destroyed accidentally by FORMAT or DISKCOPY. If you attempt to write to a write-protected disk, DOS will display

```
Write protect error writing drive (n:)
```

It is a good habit to write-protect all of your disks whose contents you don't anticipate changing.

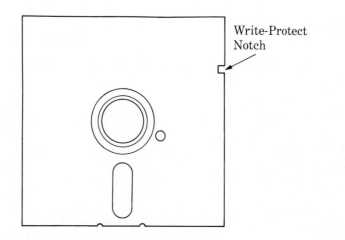

Write-Protect
Notch

Figure 2-12.   Write-protect notch on disk

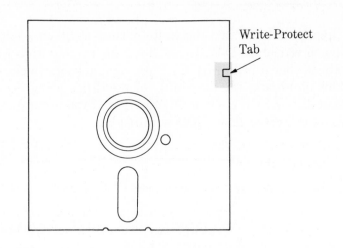

Write-Protect
Tab

Figure 2-13. Tab covering write-protect notch

Review

1. Label drives A and B for the following disk drive configurations:

2. What are the two methods of rebooting DOS?

3. What are the three delimiters (separators) that the DOS DATE command allows you to use to separate mm dd yy?

4. Do the DOS DATE and TIME commands affect the IBM PC AT system clock?

5. What do the brackets [ ] in the following DOS TIME command mean?

TIME [HH:MM[:SS[.hh]]]

6. What does the prompt DOS A> tell you? How do you change the default drive to drive B?

7. What is the function of the DOS FORMAT command?

8. Issue the command required to make a backup copy of your DOS system disk if the disk currently resides in drive A.

9. What qualifier must you add to the DOS FORMAT command to make your disk bootable by DOS?

```
Non-System disk or disk error
Replace and strike any key when ready
```

10. What does the following DOS message mean, and how do you resolve the problem?

11. What is a file?

12. What is the DOS naming convention for files? Give an example.

13. Why are the following file names illegal?

DATA..DAT
NEW.DATA
DOSFILENAME.DAT
CON.DAT
.234

14. How do you list the files contained on a disk?

15. You are given the following directory listing:

```
Volume in drive A has no label
Directory of   A:\

ATTRIB     EXE    15091    3-11-86   10:00a
EXE2BIN    EXE     2816    3-11-86   10:00a
FC         EXE    14576    3-11-86   10:00a
FIND       EXE     6403    3-11-86   10:00a
JOIN       EXE    15971    3-11-86   10:00a
LABEL      EXE     2750    3-11-86   10:00a
SHARE      EXE     8304    3-11-86   10:00a
SUBST      EXE    16611    3-11-86   10:00a
SYS        EXE     2671    3-11-86   10:00a
SORT       EXE     1664    3-11-86   10:00a
SHIPZONE   EXE      779    5-12-86    9:45a
SPEED      EXE     1196    5-09-86   11:34a
        12 File(s)       54272 bytes free
```

What files will the following DOS command display?

A> DIR S*.EXE

16. Use the DOS COPY command to make a copy of the file COMMAND.COM from drive A to drive B.

17. What does the qualifier /V on the DOS COPY command do?

18. Use the DOS COPY command to append the contents of REPORT.TXT to the file CONTENTS.TXT.

19. What are the functions of the following key combinations?

CTRL-ALT-DEL
CTRL-C
CTRL-BREAK
CTRL-S

20. What is a DOS file specification?

21. What are the DOS wildcard characters?

22. What are the common DOS file-name extensions, and what is the function of each?

23. What is the difference between internal and external DOS commands?

Answers

1. *Label drives A and B for the following disk drive configurations*:

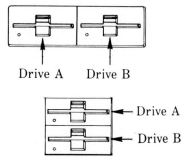

2. *What are the two methods of rebooting DOS?*

The first method of rebooting is simply to place the DOS system disk in drive A and to turn the computer off and back on. (Remember to wait a few seconds before turning the computer back on.)

The second method of rebooting DOS is to press the CTRL, ALT, and DEL keys all at the same time.

3. *What are the three delimiters (separators) that the DOS DATE command allows you to use to separate mm dd yy?*

DATE allows you to use the following characters to separate the numbers of the date:

Period 9.30.87	is equivalent to	09.30.87
Slash 12/4/87	is equivalent to	12/04/87
Dash 9-3-87	is equivalent to	09-03-1987

4. *Do the DOS DATE and TIME commands affect the IBM PC AT system clock?*

No. To set the IBM PC AT system clock, you must use the Setup option of the diagnostic disk provided in the *AT Guide to Operations*.

5. *What do the brackets [ ] in the following DOS TIME command mean?*

TIME [HH:MM[:SS[.hh]]]

The first set of brackets tells you that the entire command-line parameter is optional. The second set is shown here:

[:SS[.hh]]

It tells you that if you specify a time, you only need to provide the hours and minutes. The third set is

[.hh]

It states that you do not have to provide the hundredths of seconds.

6. *What does the prompt DOS A> tell you? How do you change the default drive to drive B?*

A> tells you the current default drive. Unless overridden by the command, DOS will search this drive for all files. To change the default drive, simply enter the drive desired as follows:

drive: (for example B: or C: or A:)

7. *What is the function of the DOS FORMAT command?*

The DOS FORMAT command provides several functions. First, the FORMAT command converts an off-the-shelf disk to a disk that DOS can use. Second, FORMAT can make a disk bootable by DOS if you use the /S qualifier in the FORMAT command. Third, FORMAT places a list of damaged disk locations on the disk so that DOS will not try to use these locations to store data. Last, FORMAT allows you to specify a volume label (see Chapter 3) for the disk.

8. *Issue the command required to make a backup copy of your DOS system disk if the disk currently resides in drive A.*

A> DISKCOPY A: B:

9. *What qualifier must you add to the DOS FORMAT command to make your disk bootable by DOS?*

The /S qualifier on the FORMAT command makes the target disk bootable by DOS.

10. *What does the following DOS message mean, and how do you resolve the problem?*

```
Non-System disk or disk error
Replace and strike any key when ready
```

Normally, this error occurs when the disk in drive A is not a bootable DOS system disk. In other words, the disk was not formatted with the /S qualifier. Place a bootable disk in drive A and press any key to boot DOS. If the disk that originally caused the error message was bootable by DOS in the past, it may have become corrupted. Try performing a directory listing of the disk after the system boots.

11. *What is a file?*

When you store data on disk, DOS places the data into a storage facility called a file. A file, therefore, is simply a storage mechanism that allows us to group related pieces of information. You can create disk files, modify their contents, rename them, and dispose of them when they are no longer required.

12. *What is the DOS naming convention for files? Give an example.*

DOS file names are of the form

    filename.ext

The file name must contain one to eight characters. The extension is optional and, if present, must contain from one to three characters. A period separates the file name from the extension. The following are valid DOS file names:

    CHAPTER.TXT   NOTES.DAT   MATH.HW
    SCIENCE.RPT   DO_TODAY   EXPENSES.$$$

13. *Why are the following file names illegal?*

DATA..DAT is illegal because of the two periods. The file name and extension are separated by a period, which makes the period an illegal character in DOS file names.

NEW.DATA is illegal because the extension DATA is more than three characters in length. The extension on DOS file names is optional and, if present, must contain from one to three characters.

DOSFILENAME.DAT is illegal because the file-name portion of a DOS file name cannot exceed eight characters.

CON.DAT is illegal because CON is a DOS device name (see Chapter 4). DOS reserves several names for the devices that are attached to your computer. The following are illegal DOS file names:

AUX	CON	LPT3
CLOCK$	LPT1	NUL
COM1	LPT2	PRN
COM2		

The .234 is illegal because it lacks a file name. Only the three-character extension in DOS file names is optional.

14. *How do you list the files contained on a disk?*

The DOS directory command DIR lists the files on a disk.

A> DIR

15. *You are given the following directory listing:*

```
Volume in drive A has no label
Directory of  A:\

ATTRIB    EXE     15091    3-11-86    10:00a
EXE2BIN   EXE      2816    3-11-86    10:00a
FC        EXE     14576    3-11-86    10:00a
FIND      EXE      6403    3-11-86    10:00a
JOIN      EXE     15971    3-11-86    10:00a
LABEL     EXE      2750    3-11-86    10:00a
SHARE     EXE      8304    3-11-86    10:00a
SUBST     EXE     16611    3-11-86    10:00a
SYS       EXE      2671    3-11-86    10:00a
SORT      EXE      1664    3-11-86    10:00a
SHIPZONE  EXE       779    5-12-86     9:45a
SPEED     EXE      1196    5-09-86    11:34a
        12 File(s)      54272 bytes free
```

What files will the following DOS command display?

A> *DIR S*.EXE*

```
Volume in drive A has no label
Directory of  A:\

SHARE    EXE    8304   3-11-86   10:00a
SUBST    EXE   16611   3-11-86   10:00a
SYS      EXE    2671   3-11-86   10:00a
SORT     EXE    1664   3-11-86   10:00a
SHIPZONE EXE     779   5-12-86    9:45a
SPEED    EXE    1196   5-09-86   11:34a
        6 File(s)     54272 bytes free
```

16. Use the DOS COPY command to make a copy of the file COMMAND.COM from drive A to drive B.

A> COPY COMMAND.COM B:

17. What does the qualifier /V on the DOS COPY command do?

The /V qualifier on the DOS COPY command requests COPY to verify that the file copy contained no errors. Including the /V qualifier on your COPY commands causes the execution of the command to take longer. Because file copies rarely contain errors, most users do not use the /V qualifier.

18. Use the DOS COPY command to append the contents of REPORT.TXT to the file CONTENTS.TXT.

A> COPY CONTENTS.TXT+REPORT.TXT NEW.TXT

19. What are the functions of the following key combinations?

CTRL-ALT-DEL
CTRL-C
CTRL-BREAK
CTRL-S

The combination CTRL-ALT-DEL reboots DOS. The CTRL-C and CTRL-BREAK combinations terminate the execution of a DOS command. CTRL-S suspends output until another CTRL-S combination is pressed.

20. *What is a DOS file specification?*

A DOS file specification differs from a DOS file name in that it provides DOS with more specific information on the location of a file. The format of a file specification is

[drive:][path][filename][.ext]

21. *What are the DOS wildcard characters?*

The DOS wildcard characters allow you to substitute the characters * and ? for other characters in a file name during file search operations. The question mark ? in a file name tells DOS that any character can occupy that location in the file name. The wildcard character * is more powerful than the question mark (?) in that it tells DOS not only that any character can occupy the current location, but also which characters remain in the file name or the extension.

22. *What are the common DOS file-name extensions and what is the function of each?*

The common DOS file-name extensions are:

COM	DOS commands or executable programs
EXE	DOS executable programs
BAT	DOS batch files (Chapter 8)
SYS	Installable device drivers (Chapter 15)
TXT	Word processing files
DAT	Data files for programs

23. *What is the difference between internal and external DOS commands?*

Internal commands are commands that DOS loads into memory each time the system boots. Since internal commands are already present in memory, DOS only needs to execute the command each time it is invoked.

External commands, however, reside on disk. Since most systems have a limited amount of memory, DOS must place many of its commands on disk and read them into memory each time they are invoked. Since DOS reads the external commands from disk, the disk that contains the command must be in the disk drive specified in the command line.

Basic DOS Commands

CLS (Clear the Screen)
VER (Display Current DOS Version)
TYPE (Display Contents of a File)
RENAME or REN (Rename a File)
DEL (Delete a File)
ERASE (Erase a File from Disk)
CHKDSK (Display Current Status of a Disk)
LABEL (Create a Volume Label)
VOL (Display Volume Label)
COMP (Compare Two Files)
DISKCOMP (Compare Two DOS Disks)
PROMPT (Set the DOS Prompt)

Chapters 1 and 2 introduced hardware and software, along with several key DOS concepts. This chapter introduces the first set of DOS commands that utilize all of the concepts presented thus far. The commands include

CLS	CHKDSK
VER	LABEL
TYPE	VOL
RENAME	COMP
DEL	DISKCOMP
ERASE	PROMPT

CLS (Clear the Screen)

The DOS command CLS erases the contents of the screen and places the cursor at the upper-left-hand corner of the screen. The format of the command is

CLS

CLS is an internal DOS command. Internal DOS commands are commands that DOS always stores in memory. External commands, however, reside on disk. DOS must read external commands from disk into memory each time the user invokes the command.

For example, suppose your screen contains the following:

```
A> DIR K*.COM

 Volume in drive A has no label
 Directory of  A:\

KEYBSP    COM    2317    5-08-86    6:10p
KEYBFR    COM    2395    5-08-86    6:13p
KEYBGR    COM    2310    5-08-86    6:15p
KEYBNR    COM    2335    5-08-86    6:10p
KEYBSF    COM    2331    5-08-86    6:23p
KEYBSG    COM    2360    5-08-86    6:20p
KEYBDK    COM    2335    5-08-86    6:25p
KEYBUK    COM    1972    5-08-86    6:08p
KEYBIT    COM    2011    5-08-86    6:06p
KEYBSV    COM    2259    5-08-86    6:18p
       10 File(s)      54272 bytes free

A>
```

You enter

A> CLS

The result will be

```
A>
```

It is important to note that CLS does not affect any of the screen attributes such as character width or reverse video.

VER (Display Current DOS Version)

The DOS VER command displays the current version of DOS. The format of the command is

VER

For DOS version 3.0, VER will display

```
IBM Personal Computer DOS Version  3.00
```

For DOS version 3.1, VER will display

```
IBM Personal Computer DOS Version  3.10
```

For version 3.2, VER will display

```
IBM Personal Computer DOS Version  3.20
```

The DOS version number is composed of two parts, the major version number and the minor version number, as shown in Table 3-1. It is important to distinguish between the major and minor version numbers. Most operating system upgrades are characterized as follows:

• If several significant enhancements are included in the new version of the operating system, the major version number will increase (DOS 4.0).

• If the new version only contains fixes to bugs, or minor enhancements, the minor version will increase (.1, .2, and so forth).

Most users find that newer versions of DOS with changes only to the minor version number are not essential.

TYPE (Display Contents of a File)

The DOS TYPE command allows you to display the contents of a file to the screen. The format of the command is

    TYPE file—spec

DOS Versions	Major Versions	Minor Versions
3.0	3	0
3.1	3	1
3.2	3	2

Table 3-1.   DOS Versions, Major Versions, and Minor Versions

where the following is true:

file—spec is the name of the file to display on the screen. TYPE does not support wildcard characters in the file-name specification.

DOS only allows TYPE to display text (ASCII) files to the screen. Files with COM, EXE, or OBJ file-name extensions contain nonprintable (nonalphanumeric) characters that prevent their displays. Suppose you try to use TYPE to display the contents of a nontext file by entering

```
A> TYPE COMMAND.COM
```

Your screen will fill up with several strange characters, and your computer bell will probably begin beeping. This is because of the unprintable characters.

Assume that the file STATES.DAT contains the following:

```
WASHINGTON
ARIZONA
COLORADO
NEVADA
UTAH
NEW YORK
```

Enter the command

```
A> TYPE STATES.DAT
```

The command will display

```
WASHINGTON
ARIZONA
COLORADO
NEVADA
UTAH
NEW YORK
```

As previously stated, TYPE does not support wildcard characters. If you attempt to use wildcard characters, TYPE will respond with

```
Invalid filename or file not found
```

If you attempt to type a nonexistent file, TYPE will display

```
File not found
```

TYPE does allow you to display files contained on a disk other than the current default disk. For example, suppose the file CITIES.DAT on disk B contains the following:

```
SEATTLE
PHOENIX
COLORADO SPRINGS
LAS VEGAS
SALT LAKE CITY
NEW YORK CITY
```

Enter the command

```
A> TYPE B:CITIES.DAT
```

The command will display

```
SEATTLE
PHOENIX
COLORADO SPRINGS
LAS VEGAS
SALT LAKE CITY
NEW YORK CITY
```

In addition, TYPE allows you to display files contained in other subdirectories (see Chapter 6).

RENAME or REN (Rename a File)

The DOS RENAME command allows you to change the name of an existing file. The format of the command is

RENAME file—spec1 file—spec2 or REN file—spec1 file—spec2

where the following is true:

file—spec1 is the name of the source (old name) file.
file—spec2 is the name of the target (new name) file.

You could create a second copy of the file ANSI.SYS and call it ANSI.SAV by entering

```
A> COPY ANSI.SYS ANSI.SAV
```

You can use RENAME later to rename the new file to ANSI.NEW as demonstrated in the following examples:

```
A> RENAME ANSI.SAV ANSI.NEW
```

or

```
A> REN ANSI.SAV ANSI.NEW
```

A directory of your disk now reveals

```
A> DIR ANSI.*

 Volume in drive A has no label
 Directory of  A:\

ANSI     SYS     1641    8-14-84    8:00a
ANSI     NEW     1641    8-14-84    8:00a
         2 File(s)      72704 bytes free
```

Unlike the COPY command, RENAME does not create a new version of the file. Instead, RENAME simply gives an existing file a new name. Enter the following examples:

```
A> RENAME DISKCOPY.COM DCOPY.COM
A> RENAME TREE.COM DTREE.COM
A> REN CONFIG.SYS CONFIG.SAV
```

Because DOS does not create a new version of the file, DOS does not allow you to rename a file contained on one disk to a different disk, as shown here:

```
A> RENAME COMMAND.COM B:COMMAND.COM
Invalid parameter
```

Likewise, DOS does not allow you to rename a file contained in one subdirectory (see Chapter 6) to a new subdirectory. The RENAME command provides full support of wildcard characters. Enter the following commands:

```
A> REN TREE.* TR.*
A> REN DISK*.COM D*.COM
```

If you try to rename a nonexistent file, RENAME will respond with

```
Duplicate file name or File not found
```

In addition, suppose you enter the following to attempt to rename a file with a name that already exists:

```
A> REN DISKCOPY.COM DISKCOMP.COM
```

RENAME will display

```
Duplicate file name or File not found
```

The rename will not occur. This command feature prevents you from accidentally overwriting a file.

DEL (Delete a File)

The DOS delete command, DEL, allows you to get rid of unwanted files on your disks. The format of the command is

DEL file—spec

where the following is true:

file—spec is the name of the file to delete.

If, for example, you want to delete the file ANSI.SAV from disk, issue the command

`A> DEL ANSI.SAV`

Be careful with the DEL command. Once you erase a file, you can no longer access it. Several software packages are on the market today that recover deleted files. These capabilities are not provided by DOS. The DOS RECOVER command (see Chapter 10) does not recover deleted files.

DEL supports the DOS wildcard characters (* and ?), as do most DOS commands. Entering the following command will delete all of the files on disk that have the SYS extension:

`A> DEL *.SYS`

Enter the command

`A> DEL *.*`

That action will delete all files from the disk. Because this command can have devastating results if you issue it in error, DEL will first prompt you with

```
Are you sure (Y/N)?
```

If you really want to delete all of the files, press Y and then
ENTER. Otherwise, press N, and the command will terminate
without deleting any files. In addition to wildcard support, DEL
allows you to delete files contained on a disk other than one on the
default drive. Enter the following command:

```
A> DEL B:PAYROLL.OLD
```

If the file PAYROLL.OLD exists on drive B, DEL will delete it.

As you will see in later chapters, it is possible to protect files
from deletion. If, for example, you attempt to delete such a file,
DEL will display

```
Access denied
```

The deletion will not occur. If you try to delete a nonexistent file,
DEL will display

```
File not found
```

DEL is a powerful DOS command. Unfortunately, a user
error involving DEL can have a catastrophic impact. Take considerable care when you issue the DEL command, especially when
you are using wildcard characters.

Advanced users will see, unless their command specifies an
alternate directory, that DEL will delete only those files contained
in the current working directory. In addition, you can only use
DEL to delete standard DOS files. Subdirectories are not affected
by the command.

ERASE (Erase a File from Disk)

The DOS command ERASE is identical to the DOS DEL command. The format of the command is

ERASE file—spec

where the following is true:

file—spec is the name of the file to erase.

Again, if you want to delete the file ANSI.SAV from disk, issue the command

```
A> ERASE ANSI.SAV
```

Be careful with the ERASE command. Once you erase a file, you can no longer access it. As stated previously, several software packages are on the market today that recover erased files. These capabilities are not provided by DOS. The DOS RECOVER command (see Chapter 10) does not recover erased files.

ERASE supports the DOS wildcard characters (* and ?). Entering the following command will erase all of the files on disk that have the BAK extension:

```
A> ERASE *.BAK
```

Suppose you enter the command

```
A> ERASE *.*
```

That action will erase all files from the disk. Because this can have devastating results if you issue the command in error, ERASE will first prompt you with

```
Are you sure (Y/N)?
```

If you really want to delete all of the files, press Y and then press ENTER. Otherwise, press N, and the command will terminate without deleting any files.

In addition to wildcard support, ERASE allows you to erase files contained on a disk other than the one in the default drive. Enter the following command:

```
A> ERASE B:BUDGET.BAK
```

If the file BUDGET.BAK exists on drive B, ERASE will erase it.

As you will see in later chapters, it is possible to protect files from deletion. If, for example, you attempt to delete such a file, ERASE will display

```
Access denied
```

The deletion will not occur. If you try to erase a nonexistent file, ERASE will display

```
File not found
```

ERASE is a powerful DOS command. Unfortunately, a user error with ERASE can have severe consequences. Take considerable care when you issue the ERASE command, especially when you use wildcard characters.

As advanced users will see, unless their command provides an alternate directory, ERASE will only erase files contained in the current working directory. In addition, you can only use

ERASE to delete standard DOS files. Subdirectories are not
affected by the command.

CHKDSK (Display Current Status of a Disk)

The DOS CHKDSK command provides several useful pieces of
information about a specific disk and about the current memory
utilization. The format of the CHKDSK command is

[drive:][path]CHKDSK [filespec] [/F] [/V]

where the following is true:

drive: is the disk drive containing the command CHKDSK.COM.
If you do not specify a disk drive, DOS will use the current
default drive.

path is the directory path to the command CHKDSK.COM. If
you do not provide a path (see Chapter 6), DOS will use the
current default directory.

filespec is the name of a file for DOS to examine for disk contiguity. The wildcard characters *.* are useful as a file specification to examine the contiguity of the disk. Chapter 9
examines disks and their structures. The CHKDSK option to
examine disk contiguity is examined in detail in that chapter.

/F directs CHKDSK to fix errors found in the file-allocation
table or in directories. The corrections are written to disk.
Periodically, DOS will lose one or more of the internal pointers it uses to track files. The /F qualifier directs CHKDSK to
repair as many damaged pointers as possible. Chapter 9 provides more information on the file allocation table.

/V directs CHKDSK to display the names and paths of all of
the files on the disk.

CHKDSK will provide you with information on the following:

Disk volume label (if present)
Total disk space (bytes)
Space consumed by hidden files (bytes)
Space consumed by directories (see Chapter 6) (bytes)
Space consumed by user files (bytes)
Space consumed by bad sectors (see Chapter 9) (bytes)
Available disk space (bytes)
Total memory present (bytes)
Total memory available (bytes)

CHKDSK assumes that the disk you want to examine is already contained in the specified disk drive. Unlike other DOS commands, CHKDSK will not prompt you to place the disk in the specified drive. Assuming you do not specify a disk drive to examine, as in

`A> CHKDSK`

CHKDSK will use the current default.

The first line displayed by CHKDSK shows the volume label of the disk. Volume labels are examined in detail later in this chapter. If the disk does not have a volume label, CHKDSK simply omits the entire line. The next six lines provide disk utilization information. The last two lines address system utilization of memory. As illustrated, 524,288 bytes of memory (512K) are present in the system. DOS allocates several thousand bytes at system startup, which leaves 485,328 bytes available.

To list all of the files contained on a disk, issue the command

`A> CHKDSK /V`

CHKDSK will respond with

```
Directory A:\
      A:\IO.SYS
      A:\MSDOS.SYS
      A:\COMMAND.COM
      A:\ASSIGN.COM
      A:\ATTRIB.EXE
```

```
A:\FORMAT.COM
A:\FDISK.COM
A:\DISKCOMP.COM
A:\DISKCOPY.COM
A:\TREE.COM
A:\EXE2BIN.EXE
A:\FC.EXE
A:\FIND.EXE
A:\JOIN.EXE
A:\LABEL.EXE
A:\SHARE.EXE
A:\SUBST.EXE
A:\SYS.EXE
A:\MORE.COM
A:\SORT.EXE
A:\CHKDSK.COM
A:\DEBUG.COM
A:\EDLIN.COM
A:\PRINT.COM
A:\RECOVER.COM
A:\MODE.COM
A:\ANSI.SYS
A:\SELECT.COM
A:\KEYBSP.COM
A:\KEYBFR.COM
A:\KEYBGR.COM
A:\KEYBNR.COM
A:\KEYBSF.COM
A:\KEYBSG.COM
A:\KEYBDK.COM
A:\KEYBUK.COM
A:\KEYBIT.COM
A:\KEYBSV.COM
A:\GFTPRN.COM
A:\GRAFTABL.COM
A:\GRAPHICS.COM
A:\COMP.COM
A:\SHIPZONE.EXE
A:\SPEED.EXE

 362496 bytes total disk space
  39936 bytes in 2 hidden files

 268288 bytes in 42 user files
  54272 bytes available on disk

 524288 bytes total memory
 274080 bytes free
```

If your disk is heavily used, direct CHKDSK to correct damaged pointers as follows:

```
A> CHKDSK /F
```

If CHKDSK finds any damaged pointers, it will respond with

```
nnnn lost clusters found in nnnn chains
Convert lost chains to files (Y/N)?
```

If you press Y, CHKDSK will begin creating files in the root directory (see Chapter 6) with the name FILE*nnnn*.CHK where *nnnn* are consecutive numbers beginning with 0000. The first file CHKDSK will create is FILE0000.CHK, the second will be FILE0001.CHK, and so on. Examine each file CHKDSK creates and erase the ones that are unusable.

A major factor affecting the speed of your disk I/O is disk contiguity. Take time to read Chapter 9 carefully. It is important that you address disk contiguity periodically. In so doing, you will find that your applications run much more efficiently.

LABEL (Create a Volume Label)

The DOS LABEL command allows you to assign a name to a volume (a fixed or floppy disk). The format of the command is

[drive:][path]LABEL [d:][volume—name]

where the following is true:

drive is the disk drive containing the external command LABEL.COM. If you do not specify a disk drive, DOS uses current default drive.

path is the subdirectory path to the command LABEL.COM. If you do not provide a path (see Chapter 6), DOS will use the current default directory.

d: is the drive containing the disk to which you will assign the label. If you do not provide a disk drive, DOS will use the current default drive.

volume—name is the name to assign to the volume. A volume name can contain 1 to 11 characters. If you do not specify a volume name, LABEL will prompt you for one.

Perform a directory listing as follows:

```
A> DIR

 Volume in drive A has no label
 Directory of  A:\

COMMAND  COM    23210   3-11-86   10:00a
ASSIGN   COM     1509   3-11-86   10:00a
ATTRIB   EXE    15091   3-11-86   10:00a
FORMAT   COM     6831   5-09-86    3:52p
FDISK    COM    14448   5-13-86    9:47a
DISKCOMP COM     3774   5-20-86    8:52a
DISKCOPY COM     4099   5-20-86    8:52a
TREE     COM     6306   5-03-86   11:19a
EXE2BIN  EXE     2816   3-11-86   10:00a
FC       EXE    14576   3-11-86   10:00a
^C
```

DOS displays the disk volume name. If the disk does not have a volume name, you can assign it one using the LABEL command as follows:

```
A> LABEL
```

LABEL will prompt you for the volume name as follows:

```
 Volume label (11 characters, Enter for none)?
```

To assign the disk in drive A the name "DOS," issue the command

```
A> LABEL DOS
```

The directory listing is

```
Volume in drive A is DOS
Directory of  A:\

COMMAND   COM    23210    3-11-86   10:00a
ASSIGN    COM     1509    3-11-86   10:00a
ATTRIB    EXE    15091    3-11-86   10:00a
FORMAT    COM     6831    5-09-86    3:52p
FDISK     COM    14448    5-13-86    9:47a
DISKCOMP  COM     3774    5-20-86    8:52a
DISKCOPY  COM     4099    5-20-86    8:52a
TREE      COM     6306    5-03-86   11:19a
EXE2BIN   EXE     2816    3-11-86   10:00a
FC        EXE    14576    3-11-86   10:00a
FIND      EXE     6403    3-11-86   10:00a
JOIN      EXE    15971    3-11-86   10:00a
LABEL     EXE     2750    3-11-86   10:00a
SHARE     EXE     8304    3-11-86   10:00a
SUBST     EXE    16611    3-11-86   10:00a
SYS       EXE     2671    3-11-86   10:00a
MORE      COM      282    3-11-86   10:00a
SORT      EXE     1664    3-11-86   10:00a
CHKDSK    COM     9435    3-11-86   10:00a
DEBUG     COM    15552    3-11-86   10:00a
EDLIN     COM     7261    3-11-86   10:00a
PRINT     COM     8291    3-11-86   10:00a
RECOVER   COM     4050    3-11-86   10:00a
MODE      COM     2868    5-21-86   11:59a
ANSI      SYS     2563    5-12-86    1:42p
SELECT    COM     6052    5-08-86    8:54a
KEYBSP    COM     2317    5-08-86    6:10p
KEYBFR    COM     2395    5-08-86    6:13p
KEYBGR    COM     2310    5-08-86    6:15p
KEYBNR    COM     2335    5-08-86    6:10p
KEYBSF    COM     2331    5-08-86    6:23p
KEYBSG    COM     2360    5-08-86    6:20p
KEYBDK    COM     2335    5-08-86    6:25p
KEYBUK    COM     1972    5-08-86    6:08p
KEYBIT    COM     2011    5-08-86    6:06p
KEYBSV    COM     2259    5-08-86    6:18p
GFTPRN    COM      292    3-18-86   10:30a
GRAFTABL  COM     2145    3-11-86   10:00a
GRAPHICS  COM     5363    4-10-86   11:37a
COMP      COM     7194    5-03-86   11:19a
```

```
SHIPZONE  EXE      779    5-12-86   9:45a
SPEED     EXE     1196    5-09-86  11:34a
      42 File(s)       54272 bytes free
```

It displays the new volume name. Many DOS users are confused
by the need to use volume names. Consider this example: A software company keeps its general ledger on a floppy disk that contains the following files:

```
ACCOUNTS  PAY      156   11-04-86  11:22a
ACCOUNTS  REC      162   11-04-86  11:23a
PAYROLL   DAT      113   11-04-86  11:23a
SALARIES  DAT       89   11-04-86  11:23a
INCOME    TAX      151   11-04-86  11:24a
LEDGER    EXE    22042    8-14-84   8:00a
```

Each fiscal year, the company creates a new disk for the accounting data. Over the past three years the company has created the
disk shown in Figure 3-1.

Figure 3-1.   Software company's general ledger system on disk

Volume labels allow the general-ledger software to determine whether or not the company is using the correct disk. As previously stated, a volume label can contain up to 11 characters. This allows the software company to use the following label names:

LEDGER85
LEDGER86
LEDGER87

A directory listing of the 1986 disk reveals

```
Volume in drive B is LEDGER86
Directory of  B:\

ACCOUNTS PAY       156  11-04-86   11:22a
ACCOUNTS REC       162  11-04-86   11:23a
PAYROLL  DAT       113  11-04-86   11:23a
SALARIES DAT        89  11-04-86   11:23a
INCOME   TAX       151  11-04-86   11:24a
LEDGER   EXE     22042   8-14-84    8:00a
       6 File(s)     334848 bytes free
```

It is now possible for the ledger software to read the disk volume before it begins processing to ensure that the company is using the disk for the current year. Chapter 16 provides a Turbo Pascal procedure that returns the name of the disk volume. A program can examine the disk volume and continue or terminate processing accordingly.

To rename a disk volume, simply enter the LABEL command

```
A> LABEL
```

The current disk label is displayed. If you press ENTER, LABEL erases the current label. If you want to rename the volume, type the new label you desire.

Note that one of the options of the FORMAT command (presented in Chapter 2) allows you to assign a volume name to a disk at this time, as follows:

```
A> FORMAT B:/V
```

VOL (Display Volume Label)

Closely related to the LABEL command is the DOS command VOL, which displays the current volume name.

The DOS VOL command displays the volume label of the disk contained in the specified drive. The format of the command is

VOL [drive:]

where

drive: is the disk drive that contains the disk to examine. If you do not specify a drive, DOS uses the current default drive.

Enter the following command:

```
A> VOL
```

VOL will display the current volume label of the disk in the default drive as follows:

```
Volume in drive A is DOS
```

Enter the command

```
A> VOL B:
```

It directs VOL to display the volume name of the disk in drive B. If the disk does not have a volume label, VOL will display

```
Volume in drive B has no label
```

COMP (Compare Two Files)

The DOS COMP command compares two files and displays the byte (or character) location of the first ten differences in the files. The format of the COMP command is

[drive:][path]COMP [file—spec] [file—spec]

where the following is true:

drive: is the disk drive containing the command COMP.COM. If you do not specify a disk drive, DOS will use the current default drive.

path is the directory path to the command COMP.COM. If you do not provide a path (see Chapter 6), DOS will use the current default directory.

file—spec is the name of a file to compare to a second file. If you do not specify file names, COMP will prompt you for the primary and secondary files to compare.

Assume that the files DAYS.DAT, WORKDAYS.DAT, WEEKDAYS.DAT, and WEEKEND.DAT contain the following:

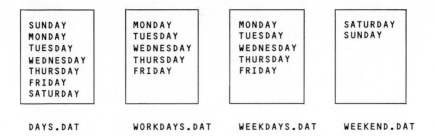

SUNDAY	MONDAY	MONDAY	SATURDAY
MONDAY	TUESDAY	TUESDAY	SUNDAY
TUESDAY	WEDNESDAY	WEDNESDAY	
WEDNESDAY	THURSDAY	THURSDAY	
THURSDAY	FRIDAY	FRIDAY	
FRIDAY			
SATURDAY			

DAYS.DAT   WORKDAYS.DAT   WEEKDAYS.DAT   WEEKEND.DAT

Enter the command

```
A> COMP DAYS.DAT WORKDAYS.DAT
```

DOS will display

```
DAYS.DAT and WORKDAYS.DAT

Compare error at OFFSET 0
File 1 = 53
File 2 = 4D

Compare error at OFFSET 1
File 1 = 55
File 2 = 4F

Compare error at OFFSET 8
File 1 = 4D
File 2 = 54

Compare error at OFFSET 9
File 1 = 4F
File 2 = 55

Compare error at OFFSET A
File 1 = 4E
File 2 = 45
```

```
Compare error at OFFSET B
File 1 = 44
File 2 = 53

Compare error at OFFSET C
File 1 = 41
File 2 = 44

Compare error at OFFSET D
File 1 = 59
File 2 = 41

Compare error at OFFSET E
File 1 = 0D
File 2 = 59

Compare error at OFFSET F
File 1 = 0A
File 2 = 0D

10 Mismatches - ending compare

Compare more files (Y/N)?
```

Since you do not want to compare additional files, simply press N
and then ENTER. Note that the first character difference occurs at
line 1, column 1. One of the difficulties of using the COMP command is that each difference is displayed as a hexadecimal byte
offset from the start of the file. You must be familiar with the
hexadecimal numbering system or have a program that converts
hexadecimal numbers to decimal. Consider the following example:

```
A> COMP

Enter primary file name
WORKDAYS.DAT

Enter 2nd file name or drive id
WEEKDAYS.DAT

WORKDAYS.DAT and WEEKDAYS.DAT

Files compare ok

Compare more files (Y/N)?
```

In this example, COMP prompted you for the names of each of the files to compare. COMP assumes that both of the files to compare reside on disks already present in the drives specified. COMP fully supports wildcard characters. Assume your directory contains the files

```
Volume in drive A has no label
Directory of  A:\

AUG      DAT      156   11-04-86   11:22a
JUL      DAT      156   11-04-86   11:22a
JUN      OLD       89   11-04-86   11:23a
JUL      OLD      156   11-04-86   11:22a
SEPT     DAT      156   11-04-86   11:22a
         5 File(s)      357376 bytes free
```

Enter the command

```
A> COMP *.DAT *.OLD
```

It will compare the files as follows:

```
B:JUN.OLD and B:JUN.DAT

B:JUN.DAT - File not found

B:JUL.OLD and B:JUL.DAT

Files compare ok

Compare more files (Y/N)?
```

Suppose you specify a drive as the second file name.

```
A> COMP CONFIG.SYS B:
```

COMP will search the drive specified for a file with the same name as the primary file and perform the comparison. If a matching file is not found, COMP will display

```
B:CONFIG.SYS - File not found

Compare more files (Y/N)?
```

One of the most useful applications of COMP is to ensure that a COPY command successfully copied a file as desired, such as when you enter

```
A> COPY COMMAND.COM B:
A> COMP COMMAND.COM B:
```

If differences between the file and copy exist, you should recopy the file. Note that COMP will not compare files of different sizes and the following display results:

```
A> COMP CHKDSK.COM COMMAND.COM

C:\DOS\CHKDSK.COM and C:COMMAND.COM

Files are different sizes

Compare more files (Y/N)?
```

DISKCOMP (Compare Two DOS Disks)

The DOS DISKCOMP command compares the contents of two DOS disks and displays the side and track numbers that differ. The format of the command is

[drive:][path]DISKCOMP [d:[d:]] [/1][/8]

where the following is true:

> *drive:* is the disk drive containing the command DISKCOMP. COM. If you do not specify a disk drive, DOS will use the current default drive.

path is the directory path to the command DISKCOMP.COM. If you do not provide a path (see Chapter 6), DOS will use the current default directory.

d is the disk drive containing one of the disks for DISKCOMP to compare. If you do not specify two disk drives, DISKCOMP will prompt you to enter the disk. If you only have a single-drive system, DISKCOMP will prompt you to place each disk into the disk drive at the correct times.

/1 directs DISKCOMP to compare only the first side of the disks (most disks are double-sided).

/8 directs DISKCOMP to use 8 sectors per track (most disks use 9 sectors per track).

DISKCOMP allows you to use the same or different disk drives for the disk comparison. If you use the same disk drive, the program will prompt you to enter the disks at the correct time:

```
A> DISKCOMP

Insert FIRST diskette in drive A

Press any key when ready . . .

Comparing 40 tracks
9 sectors per track, 2 side(s)

Insert SECOND diskette in drive A

Press any key when ready . . .
```

DISKCOMP will perform a single-drive comparison under the following conditions:

• The user omits both drive parameters.

• The system only has one floppy disk drive.

If you omit the second disk drive, DISKCOMP uses the current default drive. If the two disks DISKCOMP is comparing are identical, DISKCOMP will display

```
Compare OK

Compare another diskette (Y/N) ?
```

If DISKCOMP finds a difference between the disks, it will display the following message:

```
Compare error on
side n, track nn
```

DISKCOMP only works with floppy disks. If you use DISK-COMP to compare a fixed or virtual disk, DISKCOMP will display

```
A> DISKCOMP A: C:
Invalid drive specification
Specified drive does not exist,
or is non-removable
```

Chapter 9 provides a detailed explanation on tracks and sectors.

One of the most useful applications of DISKCOMP is to verify the completeness of a DISKCOPY command by entering

```
A> DISKCOPY A: B:
A> DISKCOMP A: B:
```

If the DISKCOPY was successful, DISKCOMP should not find any differences.

PROMPT (Set the DOS Prompt)

The DOS command PROMPT allows you to define the system prompt that DOS displays on the screen. The format of the command is

PROMPT prompt—string

where the following is true:

prompt—string is a character string containing the new system prompt. The prompt string can contain special meta-strings that are in the format $c, where c is one of the following characters:

b   results in the ¦ character
d   displays the current date
e   substitutes the string ESC
h   results in the backspace character
g   results in the > character
l   results in the < character
n   displays the current disk drive
p   displays the current directory
q   results in the = character
t   displays the current time
v   displays the DOS version number
$ results in the $ character
—   results in a carriage return line feed combination

Consider the following examples. Enter

```
A> PROMPT $D
Tue 11-04-1986
```

You will use the current date for the system prompt. Enter

```
A> PROMPT $D
A:\
```

You will use the current subdirectory (see Chapter 6). Enter

```
A> PROMPT YES$G
YES>
```

You will use the string YES> for the system prompt. Enter

```
A> PROMPT $T$G
12:00:27.04>
```

You will use the current hours, minutes, and seconds. Enter

```
A> PROMPT $T$H$H$H$H$H$H$G
12:01>
```

You will use only the current hours and minutes. Enter

```
A> PROMPT $V$_$G
IBM Personal Computer DOS Version 3.00
>
```

You will use the DOS version and the > symbol for the system prompt. If you issue the PROMPT command without any parameters, as in

```
IBM Personal Computer DOS Version 3.00
> PROMPT
```

PROMPT will restore the prompt to the current disk drive.

```
A>
```

Review

1. What DOS command clears the screen display and places the cursor in the upper-left-hand corner of the screen?

2. What is the function of the VER command? What are the major and minor version numbers for DOS 3.2?

3. Why does the following command fail?

    A> TYPE COMMAND.COM

4. Why doesn't DOS allow you to rename a file from one disk to another?

5. How do the commands DEL and ERASE differ?

6. What command displays information on current system-memory utilization?

7. What is a volume label? What command creates volume labels? What command displays the current volume label of a disk?

8. How does COMP differ from DISKCOMP?

9. Issue the command required to set the system prompt to the current date surrounded by the characters < and >.

10. Issue the command to set the system prompt back to the current disk drive.

1. *What DOS command clears the screen display and places the cursor in the upper-left-hand corner of the screen?*

CLS is the DOS clear-screen command.

2. *What is the function of the VER command? What are the major and minor version numbers for DOS 3.2?*

The VER command displays the current version number of the operating system. The major version number for DOS version 3.2 is 3. The minor version number is 2.

3. *Why does the following command fail?*

    A> TYPE COMMAND.COM

DOS only allows TYPE to display text (ASCII) files to screen. Files with COM, EXE, or OBJ extensions contain nonprintable (nonalphanumeric) characters that prevent their displays. Suppose you try to use TYPE to display a nontext file, as in

    A> TYPE COMMAND.COM

Your screen will fill up with several strange characters, and your computer bell will probably begin beeping. This is because of the unprintable characters.

4. *Why doesn't DOS allow you to rename a file from one disk to another?*

The RENAME command does not create a new version of a file. It simply allows you to rename existing files. To rename a file to a new disk, RENAME would have to create the file on that disk rather than simply rename an existing file.

5. *How do the commands DEL and ERASE differ?*

DEL and ERASE are identical in function.

6. What command displays information on current system-memory utilization?

The CHKDSK command provides memory-utilization information, as illustrated here:

```
Volume DOS            created Nov 4, 1986 11:20a

    362496 bytes total disk space
     39936 bytes in 3 hidden files
    268288 bytes in 42 user files
     54272 bytes available on disk

    524288 bytes total memory
    274080 bytes free
```

7. What is a volume label? What command creates volume labels? What command displays the current volume label of a disk?

A volume label is a name given to a disk. The DOS command LABEL creates a volume label.

    A> LABEL

The DOS command VOL displays the current volume label.

```
A> VOL B:
 Volume in drive B has no label
```

8. How does COMP differ from DISKCOMP?

The DOS COMP command compares two DOS files, whereas the DOS command DISKCOMP compares two DOS disks. Use COMP to verify the success of a file copy as follows:

```
A> COPY COMMAND.COM B:
A> COMP COMMAND.COM B:
```

Use DISKCOMP to ensure that a DISKCOPY successfully completes.

```
A> DISKCOPY A: B:
A> DISKCOMP A: B:
```

9. *Issue the command required to set the system prompt to the current date surrounded by the characters < and >.*

    <date>
    PROMPT ld$g

10. *Issue the command to set the system prompt back to the current disk drive.*

    PROMPT

If you do not specify a prompt string, PROMPT will reset the system prompt to the current disk drive.

Using DOS Device Names

Serial Versus Parallel Data Communication
Referencing DOS Device Names
MODE (Customizing Peripheral Devices)
NUL (The Nonexistent Device)

**F
O
U
R**

Chapter 1 differentiated between hardware and software. It defined peripheral devices as hardware devices attached to the computer, such as the screen, keyboard, printer, modem, and so forth. Chapter 2 stated that DOS reserves names for each of these devices. The following list provides the names reserved by DOS for device names:

AUX:	The first asynchronous communications port (used for serial communication)
COM1:	Also the first asynchronous communications port (used for serial communication)
COM2:	The second asynchronous communications port (used for serial communication)
CLOCK$	The system real-time clock
CON:	For input, CON points to the keyboard; for output, CON points to the screen
LPT1:	The first parallel printer port
LPT2:	The second parallel printer port
LPT3:	The third parallel printer port
PRN:	The first parallel printer port

Several of the devices just listed are classified as serial or parallel devices. It is important that you understand the differences between serial and parallel data communication. When the computer communicates with most peripheral devices, it does so in one of two ways: with *serial* or *parallel data communication.* The computer sends data to peripheral devices character by character. Each character the computer sends is represented by eight binary digits, or bits. The computer would send the word DOS to the printer as the string of binary digits shown in Table 4-1.

Serial devices use one wire over which data is transmitted. Each character of a word is represented by eight bits (binary digits), which are sent over the one wire one character at a time, as shown in Figure 4-1.

Serial data communication also requires additional embedded bits that ensure the coordination of the two devices. For now, however, it is important only that you understand that serial communication occurs one bit at a time over a single wire.

Parallel devices use eight wires to transmit data, which means that eight bits of a word can be sent at one time (see Figure 4-2). Additional wires provide the coordination between the communicating parallel and serial devices. Because parallel data

Character	Binary Representation
D	01000100
O	01001111
S	01010011

Table 4-1.   Binary Digits for DOS

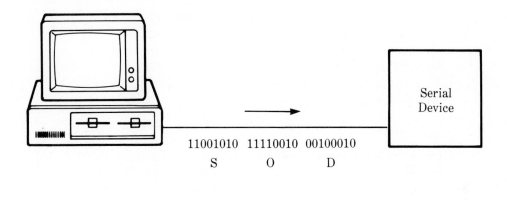

11001010 11110010 00100010
S　　　　O　　　　D

Figure 4-1. Serial data communication

communication occurs eight bits at a time, it is much faster than serial data communication. Most printers now use parallel data communication. Modems use serial data communication.

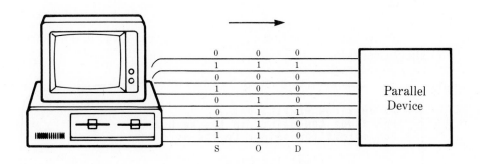

Figure 4-2. Parallel data communication

Referencing DOS Device Names

The ability to reference DOS device names is convenient in daily DOS operations. Issue the following command:

```
A> COPY CON NEWFILE.DAT
```

Your screen should now contain

```
A> COPY CON NEWFILE.DAT
▓
```

As previously stated, the device name CON points to the keyboard during input and to the screen during output, as shown in Figure 4-3. In this case, DOS will place anything that you type at the keyboard into the file NEWFILE.DAT. Type the following:

```
For input CON points to the keyboard.
For output CON points to the screen.
```

Once you have entered the sentences, your screen should contain

```
A> COPY CON NEWFILE.DAT
For input CON points to the keyboard.
For output CON points to the screen.
▓
```

Press the F6 function key and then press ENTER. The screen should contain

```
A> COPY CON NEWFILE.DAT
For input CON points to the keyboard.
For output CON points to the screen.
^Z
          1 File(s) copied
```

DOS uses the ^Z (CTRL-Z) to mark the end of a text-only file. The F6 key allows you to insert the ^Z at the end of a file you are creating from the keyboard.

Input Operations
COPY CON NEWFILE.DAT CON References

Keyboard

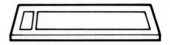

Screen

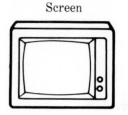

Output Operations
COPY NEWFILE.DAT CON CON References

Figure 4-3.   References of CON

Issue the command

```
A> TYPE NEWFILE.DAT
```

DOS will respond with

```
For input CON points to the keyboard.
For output CON points to the screen.
```

Turn on your printer and issue the command

```
A> COPY NEWFILE.DAT LPT1:
```

In this case, DOS will copy the contents of the NEWFILE.DAT file to the printer. Issue the command

```
A> COPY CON LPT1:
```

Using DOS Device Names   **127**

Type the following:

```
For input CON points to the keyboard.
LPT1: is the first printer port.
```

Press the F6 and ENTER keys. Your screen should now contain

```
A> COPY CON LPT1:
For input CON points to the keyboard.
LPT1: is the first printer port.
^Z
        1 File(s) copied
```

The sentences that you just entered should begin printing. The device LPT1: points to the first parallel port on the system. Normally, this port is connected to the system printer. The device name PRN: also references the system printer. Issue the command

```
A> COPY NEWFILE.DAT PRN:
```

This action will also print the contents of NEWFILE.DAT. Note that using PRN: is often safer than using LPT1: since PRN: refers to the first *connected* printer port (which may be LPT2:). The DOS PRINT command presented in Chapter 5 will increase the usefulness of your printer.

MODE (Customizing Peripheral Devices)

The MODE command allows you to set the characteristics of the asynchronous communications adapters, the color/graphics adapter, and the system printer. For video display, MODE allows you to alternate between the 40- and 80-column screen displays, enable or disable color, or modify character alignment on the screen. Note that the video MODE commands only work on the color graphics or extended graphics adapter systems.

The MODE command also allows you to modify the default character sizes on the system printer and handle printer time-

'outs in a consistent manner. In addition, MODE provides you with the ability to define the data communication parameters for each of your serial ports (such as the baud rate and the number of data bits).

The formats of the MODE command follow.

Video Display

[drive:][path]MODE N

or

[drive:][path]MODE [N],SHIFT—DIR[,T]

where the following is true:

drive: is the disk drive containing the file MODE.COM. MODE is an external DOS command; therefore, DOS must read the command from disk into memory each time the command is invoked. If you do not specify a disk drive, DOS will use the current default drive.

path is the set of subdirectories (see Chapter 6) DOS must traverse to find the file MODE.COM. If you do not specify a path, DOS will use the current working directory.

N is the video display mode. It must be one of the following values:

40	Sets the display to 40 columns per line
80	Sets the display to 80 columns per line
BW40	Sets the display to 40 columns per line with color disabled
BW80	Sets the display to 80 columns per line with color disabled
CO40	Sets the display to 40 columns per line with color enabled
CO80	Sets the display to 80 columns per line with color enabled
MONO	Sets the screen to monochrome

SHIFT_DIR specifies direction on the screen to shift all of the characters (R for right and L for left) one position.

T, if present, requests MODE to display a test pattern across the top of the screen to aid in character alignment.

Printer

[drive:][path]MODE LPT#[:] [cpl][,[lpi][,P]]

where the following is true:

LPT# is the printer port (LPT1, LPT2, or LPT3) whose characteristics are to be set.

cpl is the number of characters per line, either 80 or 132. The 80-characters-per-line setting is the DOS default.

lpi is the number of vertical lines per inch, either 6 or 8. The 6-lines-per-inch setting is the DOS default.

P specifies that MODE is using the COM port for a serial printer and will continue to retry if time-out errors occur.

Asynchronous Ports

[drive:][path]MODE COM#[:] BAUD[,PARITY[,DATABITS [,STOPBITS][,P]]]

where the following is true:

COM# is the asynchronous communications port (COM1 or COM2) whose characteristics are to be set.

BAUD is the baud rate of the port (110, 150, 300, 600, 1200, 4800, or 9600). Only the first two digits are required by MODE.

PARITY is the parity of the port: N (none), E (even), or O (odd). Even parity is the DOS default.

DATABITS is the number of data bits in a transmission, either seven or eight. The seven data bits setting is the DOS default.

STOPBITS is the number of stop bits in a transmission, either one or two. For 110 baud, two is the DOS default; otherwise, the default is one.

P specifies that MODE is using the COM port for a serial printer and will continue to retry if time-out errors occur.

Parallel Redirection to an Asynchronous Port

[drive:][path]MODE LPT#[:]=COM#

where the following is true:

LPT# is the printer port number (LPT1, LPT2, or LPT3) to reassign to a serial port.

COM# is the asynchronous communications port COM1 or COM2 to which the parallel port is assigned.

If you are using a device that does not use the DOS default data communication parameters, the installation instructions that accompanied the device should provide you with the complete setup instructions. Consider the following device customizations. Enter

```
A> MODE 40
```

DOS will set the screen to 40-column mode, as in the following:

```
A>
```

Enter

```
A> MODE 80
```

DOS will reset the screen display to 80 columns per line, as in the following:

```
A>
```

If, for some reason, you cannot see all of the characters on the screen when DOS displays information, use the MODE ,R,T or MODE ,L,T command to shift the characters to the right or to the left as required. Enter

```
A> MODE ,R,T
```

DOS will shift the characters one location to the right.

To set the printer width to 132 columns per line, issue the command that follows. (This command is not required to use the 132-column mode. Most programmers will bypass the command.)

```
A> MODE LPT1: 132
```

To set the printer to a vertical spacing of eight lines per inch, as opposed to the DOS default value of six, issue the command

```
A> MODE LPT1: ,8
```

The following command sets the first asynchronous communications port (COM1) to 4800 baud:

```
A> MODE COM1 48
```

If you are receiving nonsense characters from your asynchronous port, it is likely that you have a baud-rate problem. Issue the MODE command with the various baud rates until the characters make sense or until you have exhausted the possible baud rates. You may also check to see that you are using the correct cables for your system or that you have connected the printer to the proper port. Most devices will use seven data bits and one stop bit. If a device uses parity, it will normally use even parity. The baud rate is generally the only value you will have to modify via the MODE command. Refer to your printer manual if you continue to get "garbage" while trying to print.

If your system has only a serial printer, you can direct the printer output, which is normally destined for a parallel device (LPT#), to one of your asynchronous ports as follows:

```
A> MODE LPT1:=COM1
```

DOS assigns the parallel port LPT1 to the first communications port, COM1. DOS will now send all of the output that normally would have gone to LPT1 to COM1.

If you invoke MODE without any parameters, MODE will display

```
A> MODE

Invalid parameters
```

If one of the parameters is invalid, MODE will display an error message and return to DOS, as in the following:

```
A> MODE COM1 44

Invalid baud rate specified
```

You can access all of the DOS devices from programming languages by referencing their names in open statements and then treating them like files. Chapter 16 provides a C program that utilizes this ability.

NUL (The Nonexistent Device)

In addition to the previous device names, DOS supports a device name that points to a nonexistent device—NUL. Most DOS users will never need to reference the NUL device. Users who perform a great deal of I/O redirection or piping (see Chapter 7) may find NUL a good destination for unwanted output. DOS will ignore any information written to the NUL device.

1. List the reserved DOS device names and their functions.

2. How does serial communication differ from parallel data communication?

3. Copy the following sentences from the keyboard into the file DATA.DAT:

   The device CON has two sources: the keyboard and screen. LPT1 and PRN point to your printer.

4. Copy the contents of DATA.DAT (created in question 3) to the system printer.

5. Use the COPY command instead of the TYPE command to display the contents of DATA.DAT (created in question 3) to the screen.

6. What is the function of the F6 key when you copy a file from the keyboard?

7. Use the DOS MODE command to set your display to 40-column mode.

8. Use the DOS MODE command to shift the characters on your screen display to the left one location.

9. Use the DOS MODE command to select 132-column mode on your system printer.

10. How do you use the DOS MODE command to assign the parallel port associated with LPT2 to the serial port COM2?

1. *List the reserved DOS device names and their functions.*

AUX: The first asynchronous communications port (used for serial communication)

COM1:   Also the first asynchronous communications port (used for serial communication)

COM2:   The second asynchronous communications port (used for serial communication)

CLOCK$ The system real-time clock

CON: For input CON points to the keyboard; for output CON points to the screen

LPT1:   The first parallel printer port

LPT2:   The second parallel printer port

LPT3:   The third parallel printer port

PRN: The first parallel printer port

2. *How does serial communication differ from parallel data communication?*

With serial communication, data is sent one bit at a time over a single wire. Most modems use serial data communication.

With parallel data communication, eight (or more) bits of data are sent at once, which results in faster communication. Most printers use parallel data communication.

3. *Copy the following sentences from the keyboard into the file DATA.DAT.*

A> COPY CON DATA.DAT
The device CON has two sources: the keyboard and screen.
LPT1 and PRN point to your printer.
^Z

4. *Copy the contents of DATA.DAT (created in question 3) to the system printer.*

A> COPY DATA.DAT PRN:

5. *Use the COPY command instead of the TYPE command to display the contents of DATA.DAT (created in question 3) to the screen.*

> A> COPY DATA.DAT CON

6. *What is the function of the F6 key when you copy a file from the keyboard?*

DOS uses the ^Z (CTRL-Z) to mark the end of a text-only file. The F6 key allows you to insert the ^Z at the end of a file you are creating from the keyboard.

7. *Use the DOS MODE command to set your display to 40-column mode.*

> A> MODE 40

8. *Use the DOS MODE command to shift the characters on your screen display to the left one location.*

> A> MODE ,L,T

9. *Use the DOS MODE command to select 132-column mode on your system printer.*

> A> MODE LPT1: 132

10. *How do you use the DOS MODE command to assign the parallel port associated with LPT2 to the serial port COM2?*

> A> MODE LPT2:=COM2

Exploiting the Power of Your Printer

PRINT
**Echoing Terminal Output to the Printer
(CTRL-PRTSC)**
Printing the Screen Contents (SHIFT-PRTSC)
**GRAPHICS (Print Graphics with the Print-
Screen Function)**

Chapter 4 illustrated that you can copy files to your printer by referencing the device name LPT# or PRN as follows:

```
A> COPY FILENAME.EXT LPT1:
```

or

```
A> COPY FILENAME.EXT PRN:
```

Although the COPY command allows you to get data to the printer, it does not allow you to utilize the printer or your computer to their full potential. For example, consider the following scenario.

It's late Friday afternoon, and you are rushing to get all of your work completed before closing time. Your boss brings in a floppy disk with 20 files that she wants you to print before you leave. As illustrated in Chapter 4, you can sit at the computer and issue 20 COPY commands to the printer as follows:

```
A> COPY FILE1.EXT PRN:
A> COPY FILE2.EXT PRN:
A> COPY FILE3.EXT PRN:
        :
        :
A> COPY FILE20.EXE PRN:
```

When each file copy is complete, you can adjust the printer to the start of the next page and issue the next COPY command. By the end of the day you will have completed your boss's print request, but you will not have been able to do the rest of your work. As a result, you have to stay late at work on a Friday night.

PRINT

You use the DOS PRINT command to solve the problem of the computer's being unable to perform other functions while it is printing. The PRINT command is a background command. *Background commands* work behind the scenes to perform functions such as printing while you complete other tasks with the computer. As you will see, background commands actually share the computer (and its peripherals) with you, which makes the computer appear to be performing several functions at once.

Create the following files:

```
The DOS PRINT command is a
background command that makes
the computer appear to be performing
multiple tasks at the same time.
```

PRINTER.TXT

```
The DOS PRINT command uses
print queues.  A queue is
a waiting line.  Files waiting
to be printed are queued.
```

QUEUE.TXT

```
A> COPY CON PRINTER.TXT
The DOS PRINT command is a
background command that makes
the computer appear to be performing
multiple tasks at the same time.
^Z
        1 File(s) copied
A>
A> COPY CON QUEUE.TXT
The DOS PRINT command uses
print queues.  A queue is
a waiting line.  Files waiting
to be printed are queued.
^Z
        1 File(s) copied
A>
```

Once you have created the files, issue the following command:

```
A> PRINT PRINTER.TXT,QUEUE.TXT
```

DOS will respond with

```
Name of list device [PRN]:
```

DOS is asking you to specify the device to which the PRINT command is to print the files. By default, PRINT uses PRN. If your printer configuration is different from the one shown here, simply specify the port name that your printer is connected to (LPT2, LPT3). Otherwise, press ENTER. DOS will display the message

```
Resident part of PRINT installed
        A:\PRINTER.TXT is currently being printed
        A:\QUEUE.TXT is in queue
```

The files should begin printing. As soon printing begins, DOS returns to the A> prompt.

As previously stated, PRINT allows you to work on other things as it prints files. Before you continue examining PRINT, there are several key concepts to address. First, the DOS PRINT command uses a *queue* to store the names of files it is to print. Simply stated, a queue is a waiting line. DOS sets aside an area of memory in which to store the names of the files PRINT is to print, as shown in Figure 5-1. Each time you request PRINT to print files, it stores the file names in this area, as shown in Figure 5-2.

File names in the queue are simply the names of the files that PRINT will print in the background as you work on other tasks. A queue can have the following states:

• The queue can be empty, as shown in Figure 5-3.

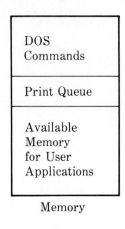

Memory

Figure 5-1.   Queue in DOS memory

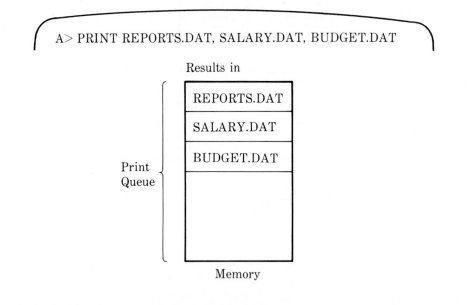

A> PRINT REPORTS.DAT, SALARY.DAT, BUDGET.DAT

Results in

Print
Queue

| REPORTS.DAT |
| SALARY.DAT |
| BUDGET.DAT |

Memory

Figure 5-2.   Storage of files in the queue

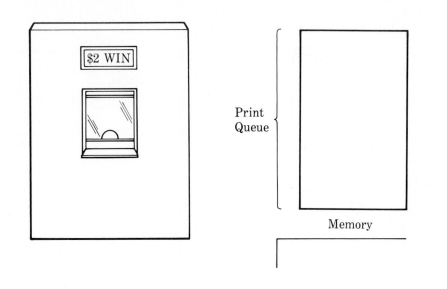

Figure 5-3.   Empty queue

• An entry can enter the queue and receive immediate service, as shown in Figure 5-4.

• If service is not available, the entry must wait, as seen in Figure 5-5.

• Additional entries can be queued, as illustrated in Figure 5-6.

• Once service is available, an entry leaves the queue, as in Figure 5-7.

• The queue can fill up and entries are denied, as shown in Figure 5-8.

• An entry can leave the queue before it is serviced, as illustrated in Figure 5-9.

By default, the DOS print queue is restricted to ten entries. As you will see, it is possible to increase this value to 32.

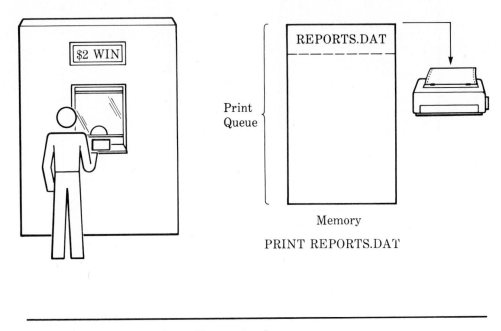

Figure 5-4. Immediate action from queue

The second important concept is a *timeslice.* As previously stated, PRINT is a background command that allows you to continue working as it prints files. PRINT can do this because DOS allows you and PRINT to share the CPU. If, for example, you have several files printing (via PRINT), and you instruct your word processor to create additional files, PRINT can continue to print files by sharing the CPU with your word processing application.

The CPU on the IBM PC and PC-compatibles is capable of working much faster than you or a mechanical device such as a printer. This means that the majority of the time you are issuing DOS commands or typing memos with a word processor, the CPU is sitting idle waiting for you to tell it to do something else. Background commands take advantage of this fact by utilizing unused CPU time.

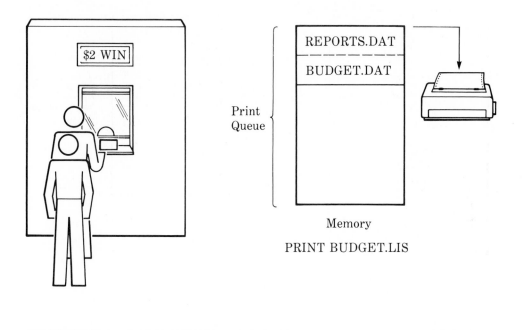

Figure 5-5. Waiting in the queue

DOS divides CPU time into timeslices. DOS then distributes these timeslices to everyone using the system. If you are not running background commands or MS Windows (see Chapter 17), you will have all of the available timeslices, and the CPU will probably be idle a considerable amount of the time. If, however, you are printing jobs in the background with PRINT, DOS will distribute some of the timeslices to print as shown in Figure 5-10. DOS will first give the CPU to your word processing application (1). After a small period of time (timeslice), DOS will give PRINT the CPU (2). When PRINT has used up its timeslice, your word processing application regains control (3). This process continues as long as background commands are present in the system.

The timeslices are so small that you normally don't notice that DOS has taken them from you. This is why it appears that the

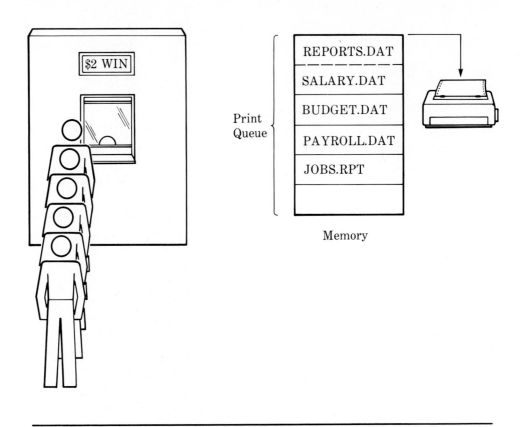

Figure 5-6.   Additional entries queued

computer is performing two tasks at once. Actually, it is just switching from one task to the other very rapidly. (*Note:* The IBM PC and PC-compatibles are capable of performing only one task at a time. Background commands give the illusion that the computer is performing multiple tasks at the same time.)

The last item to discuss before examining the DOS PRINT command is print-buffer size. As PRINT prints your files, it must read the contents of the file from disk into memory and then send it from memory to the printer, as illustrated in Figure 5-11.

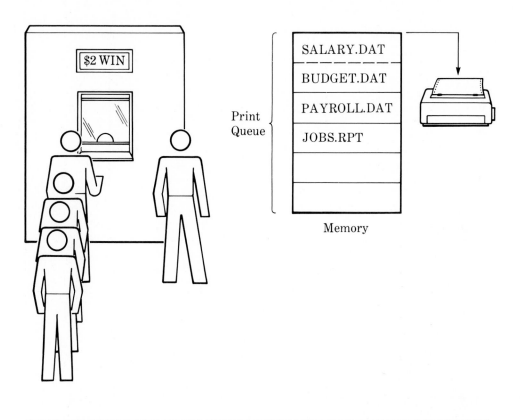

Figure 5-7. Entry leaving queue

By virtue of their mechanical nature, disk drives are slow devices when compared to the electronic CPU and memory. It is to your advantage, therefore, for PRINT to read as much of the file into memory as possible each time it reads a file from disk. By default, DOS establishes a print-buffer size (in memory) of 512 bytes. If your files are large, increasing your print-buffer size will improve your system performance. If you have sufficient memory, and you print a considerable number of files, try increasing the size of your print buffer (as illustrated later in this chapter) in

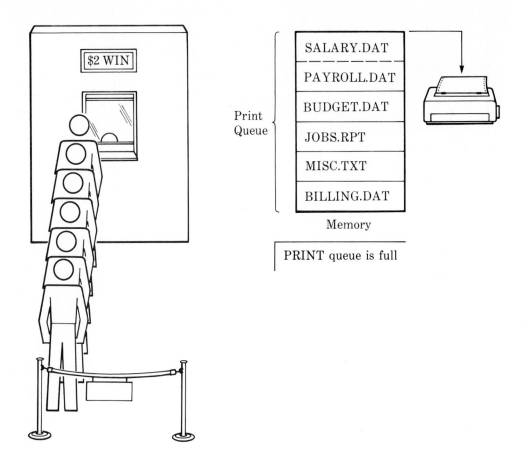

Print
Queue

SALARY.DAT

PAYROLL.DAT

BUDGET.DAT

JOBS.RPT

MISC.TXT

BILLING.DAT

Memory

PRINT queue is full

Figure 5-8. Entries denied access to queue

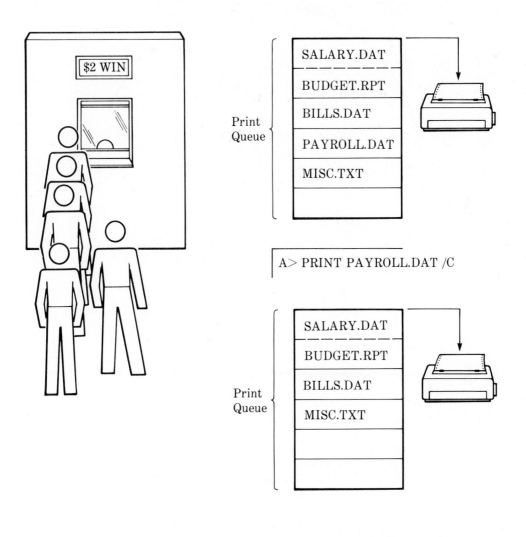

Figure 5-9. Entry leaving queue before being serviced

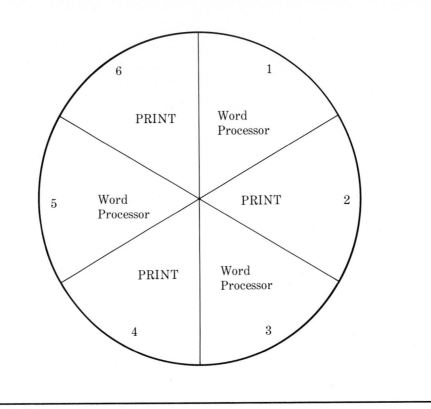

Figure 5-10. Distribution of timeslices in DOS

multiples of 512 bytes (1024, 2048, and 4096) until you are satisfied with the PRINT and system performance.

The complete format of the DOS PRINT command is

```
[drive:][path]PRINT
    [/B:buffer_size]
    [/C]
    [/D:device_name]
    [/M:max_ticks]
    [/P]
    [/Q:queue_size]
```

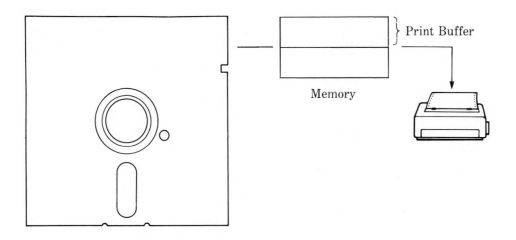

Figure 5-11. PRINT reading file contents from disk into memory and then to printer

[/S:time—slice]
[/T]
[/U:busy—ticks]

file—spec [file—spec...]

where the following is true:

drive: is the disk drive containing the file PRINT.COM. PRINT is an external DOS command; this means that DOS must read the contents of PRINT.COM from disk into memory each time you invoke the command. If you do not specify a disk drive, DOS will use the current default.

path is the subdirectory path (see Chapter 6) DOS must traverse to locate the file PRINT.COM. If you do not specify a path, DOS will use the current working directory.

/B:buffer_size specifies the size in bytes of the print-buffer size in memory. The default size is 512 bytes. Increasing this size decreases the number of disk reads PRINT must perform to print a file. Increasing this value, however, also allocates memory, making that memory unavailable to other programs. Specify this qualifier only the first time you invoke PRINT.

/C directs PRINT to cancel printing of the file name that precedes, and all file names following, the /C qualifier in the command line. Each file specified is removed from the queue.

/D:device_name specifies the device to which PRINT is to print the files. PRN is the default print device. Specify this qualifier only the first time you invoke PRINT.

/M:max_ticks specifies the maximum number of CPU clock ticks that PRINT can use to print characters before it must return control to DOS. The value you specify must be in the range 1-255. The default value is 2. Specify this qualifier only the first time you invoke PRINT.

/P tells PRINT to print the file preceding, and all files following, the /P qualifier in the command line. This qualifier is normally used in conjunction with /C.

/Q:queue_size specifies the maximum number of entries that you can place into the print queue. The value must be in the range 1-32. The default value is 10. Increasing this value allows you to queue more files. It also increases the amount of memory allocated by print, however. Specify this qualifier only the first time you invoke PRINT.

/S:time_slice specifies the number of timeslices PRINT must wait before it gains control of the CPU. The value must be in the range 1-255. The default value is 8. Specify this value only the first time you invoke PRINT.

/T requests PRINT to stop printing the current file and to emove all of the remaining files from the print queue.

/U:busy—ticks specifies the number of CPU clock ticks that PRINT will wait to print characters if the printer is currently unavailable because it is printing. The value must be in the range 1-255. The default value is 1. Specify this qualifier only the first time you invoke PRINT.

file—spec is the name of the file for PRINT to print. The [*file—spec*...] tells you that you can specify multiple files on the command line. The three periods (...) represent repetition of the preceding item. In this case, the periods tell you that PRINT allows you to repeat multiple file specifications on the command line.

As illustrated, PRINT allows you to specify several of the qualifiers only the first time that you invoke PRINT. This is because these qualifiers specify the attributes of the print queue that DOS must create. Once DOS creates the queue, you must reboot to change any of its characteristics.

Note how each of the following commands affects the print queue created by DOS. Enter

```
A> PRINT/D:LPT2:
```

PRINT will now print each file you specify to the device connected to LPT2. Enter

```
A> PRINT/B:2048
```

PRINT will allocate additional memory for its print buffer, thereby reducing the number of disk reads PRINT must perform each time it prints a file. Before PRINT can send data to the printer, the data must reside in memory. The print buffer is simply an intermediate stop for the data. The larger the print buffer, the fewer disk reads PRINT must perform to get the data into memory. Since disk reads are slow, it is to your benefit to minimize them. Increasing the buffer size too much, however, will result in wasted memory.

Enter

```
A> PRINT/Q:32
```

PRINT will allocate additional space to increase the queue size from the default size of 10 to 32. This allows you to queue more files for printing, but it also increases the amount of memory allocated by PRINT. Each queue entry requires 64 bytes of memory (see Figure 5-12).

Enter

```
A> PRINT/U:64
```

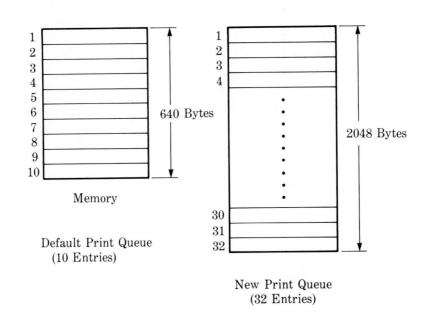

Figure 5-12. Default print queue and new print queue

If PRINT finds the printer busy, it will wait up to 64 additional clock ticks for the printer to become available. If you have a slower printer, increasing this parameter may improve your performance. If you make the value too large (255), your overall system performance will suffer, because the computer will be doing nothing other than waiting for the printer to become available.

Normally, these are the only parameters that you will want to modify when you install your print queue. Most users find the default settings for /M:max_ticks or /S:time_slice to be adequate.

As previously stated, several things can happen to a file once it is in the print queue. First, the file can print successfully. Second, if your printer runs out of paper or is taken off-line, the files will remain queued indefinitely. Third, you can terminate a specific file, removing it from the print queue. Last, you can remove all of the files from the print queue.

The /T PRINT qualifier stops printing the file currently being printed and then removes all of the files remaining in the print queue.

```
A> PRINT/T
```

The printer alarm will sound and PRINT will display the message "All files canceled by operator" at the bottom of the print page. The print queue will now be empty.

The /C PRINT qualifier is more specific than /T. The /C qualifier allows you to delete specific files from the queue. When you use /C, PRINT will cancel the file name that preceded the qualifier and any file names that follow. Consider the following examples. Enter

```
A> PRINT FILE1 /C FILE2 FILE3
```

PRINT will remove FILE1, FILE2, and FILE3 from the print queue. Enter

```
A> PRINT FILE1 /C
```

PRINT will remove FILE1 from the print queue. Enter

```
A> PRINT FILE1 /C FILE2
```

PRINT will remove FILE1 and FILE2 from the print queue. If the file you remove with the /C qualifier is the file PRINT is currently printing, the printer alarm will sound, and PRINT will terminate the printing of the file by displaying the message "File canceled by operator" at the bottom of the print page.

Some DOS users will perform multiple operations in a single PRINT command line by combining the /C and /P PRINT qualifiers. The /P qualifier tells PRINT to print the file name preceding and any file names following the qualifier. Consider the following examples: Enter

```
A> PRINT MAIL.LST /C /P NEWMAIL.LST
```

PRINT will remove the file MAIL.LST from the print queue and add the file NEWMAIL.LST. Enter

```
A> PRINT BUDGET.LST /C SALARY.LST NEWSALES.LST /P BUDGET.NEW
```

PRINT will remove the files BUDGET.LST and SALARY.LST from the print queue and add the files NEWSALES.LST and BUDGET.NEW. Experiment with combining the /C and /P qualifiers on the command line; their uses should become more apparent.

If PRINT cannot locate the file you specify, it will display the following message:

```
A> PRINT NOFILE.LST
A:\NOFILE.LST File not found
PRINT queue is empty
```

PRINT supports the DOS wildcard characters in file names. Enter

```
A> PRINT *.LST
```

PRINT will queue all of the files with the extension LST. The DOS reference section at the end of this text provides detailed explanations on all of the messages generated by PRINT.

It is often convenient to add files directly to a print queue from within an application. Chapter 16 will examine a Turbo Pascal procedure that allows you to do this.

Echoing Terminal Output to the Printer (CTRL-PRTSC)

Many DOS users find it convenient to print all of the information DOS writes to the screen. Press the CTRL and PRTSC keys simultaneously. The location of these keys is shown in Figure 5-13.

Turn on your printer and issue the following directory command:

```
A> DIR
```

As DOS displays the directory listing to your screen, it also writes the same information to your printer. To turn off character echo, simply press the CTRL and PRTSC keys again at the same time. Issue the directory command

```
A> DIR
```

DOS displays only the result of the command to the screen.

It may prove useful to place the printer into screen-echo mode when performing compiles and links. This gives an immediate hard copy of any syntax errors or undefined externals.

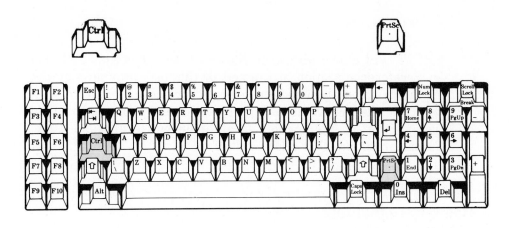

Figure 5-13. Location of CTRL and PRTSC keys

Printing the Screen
Contents (SHIFT-PRTSC)

Issue the following commands:

```
A> CLS
A> DIR
```

Turn on your printer and press the SHIFT and PRTSC keys at the same time (see Figure 5-14). DOS will print the contents of your screen display.

By default, the print-screen function only works with text data. If you need to print graphics with the print-screen function, you must first issue the DOS GRAPHICS command. Chapter 16 will examine a Turbo Pascal procedure that provides the print-screen service from within an applications program.

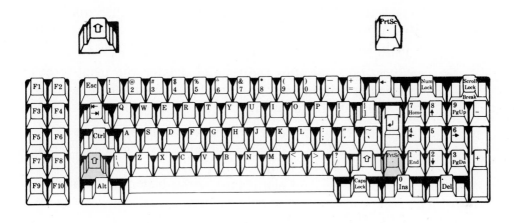

Figure 5-14. Location of SHIFT and PRTSC keys

GRAPHICS (Print Graphics with the Print-Screen Function)

The DOS GRAPHICS command allows graphics to be printed on an IBM or PC-compatible printer with the DOS print-screen function. The format of the GRAPHICS command is

[drive:][path]GRAPHICS [printer_type][/B][/R]

where the following is true:

> *drive:* is the disk drive containing the file GRAPHICS.COM. GRAPHICS is an external DOS command; this means that DOS must read the contents of GRAPHICS.COM from disk

into memory each time you invoke the command. If you do not specify a disk drive, DOS will use the current default.

path is the subdirectory path (see Chapter 6) DOS must traverse to locate the file GRAPHICS.COM. If you do not specify a path, DOS will use the current working directory.

printer_type specifies the type of printer the print-screen function is printing the graphics to. A printer type is specified as one of the following:

COLOR1	Color printer with a black ribbon
COLOR4	Color printer with a red, green, and blue ribbon
COLOR8	Color printer with a black, cyan, magenta, and yellow ribbon
COMPACT	An IBM PC Compact printer
GRAPHICS (the default)	A graphics printer

/B directs the print-screen function to print background colors. The default is no background color.

/R directs the print-screen function to reverse the screen image (in other words, to print black images as black and white images as white). The default is to print black images as white and white images as black.

If your screen is in text mode, the print-screen function will finish in less than 30 seconds; the exact amount of time it takes depends on what type of printer you have. In graphics modes (modes 4, 5, 6), however, printing the screen contents may require up to 3 minutes.

Screen modes affect your printouts as shown in Figure 5-15. Consider the following commands. Enter

```
A> GRAPHICS
```

The DOS print-screen function will support graphics output with the GRAPHICS printer as the default. There will be no printing

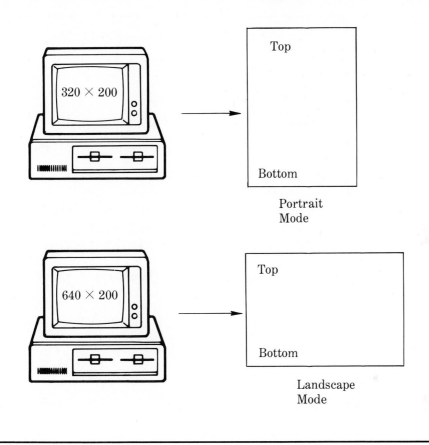

Figure 5-15.   Effect of screen modes on printouts

of background colors; black images are displayed as white and white images displayed as black. Enter

```
A> GRAPHICS COLOR8 /B
```

The DOS print-screen function will support a color printer with a four-color ribbon, and the background color will be printed.

1. What is a queue?

2. What is a print buffer?

3. What is a background command?

4. What is the function of each of the print qualifiers?

5. What is the result of each of the following print commands?

```
A> PRINT/Q:32 MYFILE.DAT
A> PRINT/T
A> PRINT/C MYFILE.DAT
A> PRINT MYFILE.DAT /C YOURFILE.DAT
A> PRINT MYFILE.DAT /C YOURFILE.DAT /P
```

6. What are the functions of the keyboard combinations CTRL-PRTSC and SHIFT-PRTSC?

7. What is the function of the DOS GRAPHICS command?

1. *What is a queue?*

A queue is a waiting line. DOS uses queues to manage the files to be sent to the printer by the PRINT command. Each time you request PRINT to print a file, the name of the file is placed into a list, contained in memory, of the other files PRINT is to print.

2. *What is a print buffer?*

When PRINT prints your files, it must read the contents of the file from disk into memory and then send that information from memory to the printer. The print buffer is the area in memory to which the file contents are read prior to being sent to the printer. Disk drives are slow when compared to the electronic CPU and memory. It is to your advantage, therefore, for PRINT to read as much of the file into memory as possible each time it reads a file from disk. By default, DOS establishes a print-buffer size in memory of 512 bytes. If your files are large, increasing your print-buffer size will improve your system's performance. If you have sufficient memory, and you print a considerable number of files, try increasing the size of your print buffer in multiples of 512 bytes (1024, 2048, and 4096) until you are satisfied with the PRINT and system performance.

3. *What is a background command?*

Background commands work behind the scenes to perform functions such as printing while you complete other tasks with the computer. Background commands actually share the computer (and its peripherals) with you, which makes the computer appear to be performing several functions at once. The DOS PRINT command is a background command.

4. *What is the function of each of the print qualifiers?*

/B:buffer—size specifies the size in bytes of the print-buffer size in memory. The default size is 512 bytes. Increasing this size decreases the number of disk reads PRINT must perform to print a file. Increasing this value, however, also allocates memory, making that memory unavailable to other programs. Specify this qualifier only the first time you invoke PRINT.

/C directs PRINT to cancel printing of the file name that precedes and all file names following the /C qualifier in the command line. Each file specified is removed from the queue.

/D:device—name specifies the device to which PRINT is to print the files. PRN is the default print device. Specify this qualifier only the first time you invoke PRINT.

/M:max—ticks specifies the maximum number of CPU clock ticks that PRINT can use to print characters before it must return control to DOS. The value you specify must be in the range 1-255. The default value is 2. Specify this qualifier only the first time you invoke PRINT.

/P tells PRINT to print the file preceding, and all files following, the /P qualifier in the command line. This qualifier normally is used in conjunction with the /C.

/Q:queue—size specifies the maximum number of entries that can be placed into the print queue. The value must be in the range 1-32. The default value is 10. Increasing this value allows you to queue more files. It also increases the amount of memory allocated by PRINT, however. Specify this qualifier only the first time you invoke PRINT.

/S:time—slice specifies the number of timeslices PRINT must wait before it gains control of the CPU. The value must be in the range 1-255. The default value is 8. Specify this value only the first time you invoke PRINT.

/T requests PRINT to stop printing the current file and to remove all of the remaining files from the print queue.

/U:busy—ticks specifies the number of CPU clock ticks that PRINT will wait to print characters if the printer is currently unavailable because it is printing. The value must be in the range 1-255. The default value is 1. Specify this qualifier only the first time you invoke PRINT.

file—spec is the name of the file for PRINT to print. The (file—spec...) tells you that you can specify multiple files on the command line. The three periods (...) represent repetition of the preceding item. In this case, the periods tell you that PRINT allows you to repeat multiple file specifications on the command line.

5. *What is the result of each of the following print commands?*

    A> *PRINT/Q:32 MYFILE.DAT*

PRINT will allocate enough memory to support a queue large enough for 32 files. In addition, PRINT will print the contents of the file MYFILE.DAT.

    A> *PRINT/T*

PRINT will stop the current file from printing and remove all of the remaining files from the print queue.

    A> *PRINT/C MYFILE.DAT*

PRINT will remove the file MYFILE.DAT from the print queue.

    A> *PRINT MYFILE.DAT /C YOURFILE.DAT*

PRINT will remove MYFILE.DAT and YOURFILE.DAT from the print queue.

    A> *PRINT MYFILE.DAT /C YOURFILE.DAT /P*

PRINT will remove the file MYFILE.DAT from the print queue while adding the file YOURFILE.DAT.

6. What are the functions of the keyboard combinations CTRL-PRTSC and SHIFT-PRTSC?

CTRL-PRTSC toggles on and off to the printer the echoing of each character DOS displays on the screen.

SHIFT-PRTSC causes DOS to print the current screen contents.

7. What is the function of the DOS GRAPHICS command?

The DOS GRAPHICS command allows graphics to be printed on an IBM or PC-compatible printer via the DOS print-screen function.

Managing Your DOS Files
with Subdirectories

Understanding DOS Subdirectories
MKDIR or MD (Make a Subdirectory)
CHDIR or CD (Change Current Working Subdirectory)
RMDIR or RD (Remove a Subdirectory)
TREE (Display Subdirectory Tree)
PATH (Where to Look for External Commands)
DOS Path Commands
Executing External Commands Contained in Subdirectories
Copying a Disk Containing Subdirectories
Renaming a Subdirectory
Working Directories
Other Applications

Most DOS users find that their everyday use of DOS quickly produces a large number of files on either their fixed or floppy disks. Unfortunately, having a large number of files often leads to confusion and a cluttered directory listing. To improve the quality of your disk organization DOS provides subdirectories. Consider the following example.

A stockbroker is tracking the stock prices of the following four computer companies:

Apple
DEC (Digital Equipment Corporation)
IBM (International Business Machines)
Intel

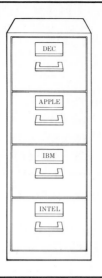

Figure 6-1.   Filing cabinet for organization of stock prices

Every day he receives several reports on each company, and every day several of the reports get lost in the shuffle of papers on his desk. To improve his office organization, the broker purchases a four-drawer filing cabinet, with each drawer labeled for the appropriate company, as shown in Figure 6-1. Each day the broker adds company reports to the correct drawer, and, in turn, the level of his office organization has increased dramatically.

DOS subdirectories allow you to perform the same type of organization on your disk. Imagine a DOS subdirectory as being equivalent to one of the drawers in the stockbroker's filing cabinet. If you create the subdirectories APPLE, DEC, IBM, and INTEL on a DOS disk, you can organize your files as illustrated in Figure 6-2.

Placing each company's files in its respective subdirectory allows you to see only the files in a specific group each time you perform a directory listing. This in turn improves your disk organization. In addition, keeping files separate in subdirectories decreases the possibility of accidental file deletion. As you will

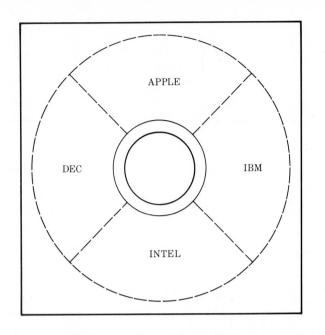

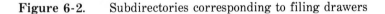

Figure 6-2. Subdirectories corresponding to filing drawers

see, most DOS commands do not affect files contained in other subdirectories, unless you explicitly reference a file by name.

Understanding DOS Subdirectories

By default, each DOS disk has a root or upper-level directory. The root directory provides the base (or root) from which all other directories grow. If you consider the stockbroker example, you can visualize the directory structure of the disk (see Figure 6-3).

The purpose of subdirectories is to improve disk organization. If, for example, the stockbroker wants to track the stock prices by

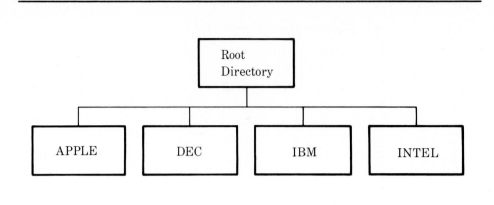

Figure 6-3.   Directory structure of stockbroker's files

each quarter of the fiscal year, he can create the subdirectories shown in Figure 6-4. He may further separate the files by company within each of the four subdirectories, as in Figure 6-5. The broker's use of subdirectories makes his disk files much easier for him to locate and maintain.

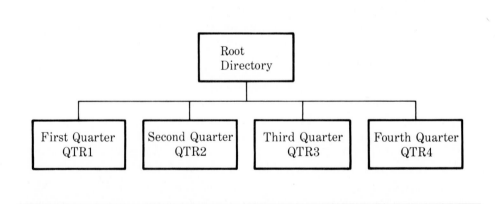

Figure 6-4.   Subdirectories for quarterly stock prices

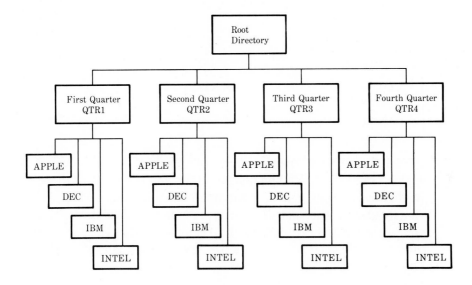

Figure 6-5.   Company distinctions in subdirectories

DOS provides the following five commands specifically for directory manipulation:

MKDIR
CHDIR
RMDIR
TREE
PATH

Before examining the DOS subdirectory commands, it is

important that you understand how DOS represents the root directory and subdirectory names.

Format a disk and place it in drive A. Issue the directory command, and DOS responds with

```
A> DIR

Volume in drive A has no label
Directory of   A:\

File not found
```

DOS tells you that the directory listing is of A:\. Obviously, the current drive is A. The backslash \tells you the current directory. In this case, \tells you that you are in the root directory. As previously stated, the root directory provides DOS with the starting point from which all other subdirectories grow. If your disk has the structure shown in Figure 6-5, you reference each of the subdirectories as

    \APPLE
    \DEC
    \IBM
    \INTEL

If, for example, you examine the name \IBM, the backslash \tells DOS to start in the root directory. IBM is the name of a subdirectory contained in the root directory.

Consider the disk directory structure shown in Figure 6-5. To reference files contained in the first quarter, you start in the root directory and move one level down, as in

    \QTR1

To reference the IBM subdirectory within \QTR1, you specify the pathname

    \QTR1\IBM

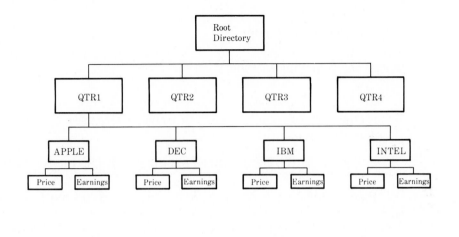

Figure 6-6. Directory structure with prices and earnings

A *pathname* is simply the series of subdirectory names DOS must combine to get to the file you desire. DOS restricts the length of a pathname to 63 characters. If you are given the directory structure shown in Figure 6-6, the following are valid pathnames:

\ specifies the root directory

\QTR1 references the first quarter subdirectory

\QTR3 \IBM \EARNINGS requests the subdirectory containing the earnings for IBM in the third quarter (not shown in Figure 6-6).

MKDIR or MD (Make a Subdirectory)

The DOS command MKDIR allows you to create subdirectories on a DOS disk. The format of the command is

MKDIR [drive:]pathname

or

MD [drive:]pathname

where the following is true:

drive: specifies the disk drive on which to create the subdirectory. If you don't specify a drive, DOS uses the current default drive.

pathname is the name of the subdirectory DOS is to create.

Place a formatted blank disk in drive A. Type the following command:

```
A> MKDIR \IBM
```

DOS will create the subdirectory illustrated in Figure 6-7. A directory listing of drive A now reveals

```
A> DIR

 Volume in drive A has no label
 Directory of  A:\

IBM            <DIR>      10-28-86    9:52a
        1 File(s)     361472 bytes free
```

The characters <DIR> tell you that IBM is a subdirectory and not a standard DOS file. Note this command:

```
A> MKDIR \IBM
```

The slash tells DOS to begin in the root directory. You must specify a pathname before the directory name

```
A> MKDIR DEC
```

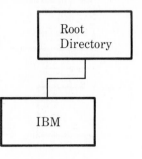

Figure 6-7. Directory structure with IBM subdirectory

If you do not, DOS will create the subdirectory in the current directory. In this case, the root is the current or working directory. Unless you specifically state otherwise, most DOS commands only affect files contained in the working directory. The DOS command CHDIR, discussed later in this chapter, allows you to

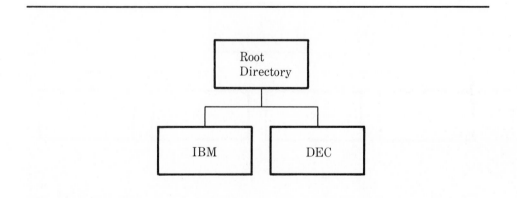

Figure 6-8. Directory structure with IBM and DEC subdirectories

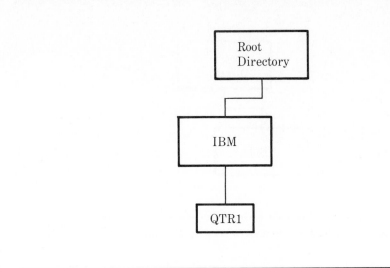

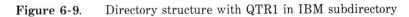

Figure 6-9. Directory structure with QTR1 in IBM subdirectory

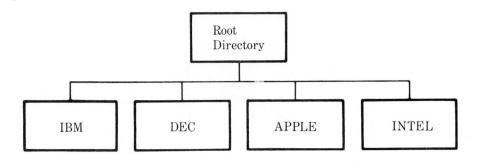

Figure 6-10. Directory structure with IBM, DEC, APPLE, and INTEL subdirectories

move from one directory to another. Your directory structure now looks like Figure 6-8. Suppose the current directory were \IBM, and you entered the command

```
A> MKDIR QTR1
```

Your action would result in the structure shown in Figure 6-9.
Create subdirectories for Apple and Intel by entering

```
A> MKDIR \APPLE
A> MKDIR \INTEL
```

Your directory structure now resembles Figure 6-10.
Perform a directory listing of drive A and DOS will now display

```
A> DIR
 Volume in drive A has no label
 Directory of   A:\

IBM           <DIR>      10-28-86     9:52a
DEC           <DIR>      10-28-86     9:56a
INTEL         <DIR>      10-28-86     9:56a
APPLE         <DIR>      10-28-86     9:56a
        4 File(s)    358400 bytes free
```

Attempt to create a second directory with the name IBM by entering

```
A> MKDIR \IBM
```

DOS will respond with

```
Unable to create directory
```

The following rules provide guidelines for creating DOS subdirectories:

- Directory names must conform to DOS file-name standards. Each name can consist of one to eight characters with a three-character extension. The following are valid directory names: IBM, IBM.ERN, IBM.PRC.

- If you do not start at the root directory by starting the pathname with a backslash (\ ), DOS will create the subdirectory in the current working directory.

- The drive specifier allows you to create directories on disk drives other than the current default drive (for example, MKDIR B:IBM).

- Do not create a subdirectory with the same name as a DOS file that is to reside in the new directory.

- Do not create a subdirectory called \DEV. DOS uses a hidden internal directory called DEV to perform I/O to devices. For example, to copy the file NEWS.DAT to the printer, you can issue the command

```
A> COPY NEWS.DAT \DEV\PRN
```

- DOS allows you to create an unlimited number of subdirectories in each directory other than the root. The number of subdirectories that the root will support is shown in Table 6-1.

- DOS pathnames cannot exceed 63 characters.

If you need to create a subdirectory for the first quarter for IBM (QTR1), you can specify the complete pathname as follows:

```
A> MKDIR \IBM\QTR1
```

CHDIR or CD (Change Current Working Subdirectory)

The DOS command CHDIR allows you to select your working subdirectory. The format of the command is

CHDIR [drive:]pathname

Disk Space	Maximum Number of Subdirectories in the Root Directory
160K	64
180K	
320K	112
360K	
1.2M	224
Fixed Disk	Based upon partition size

Table 6-1.   Subdirectories Supported by Root Directory

or you can use

CD [drive:]pathname

Use the directory structure shown here:

```
A> DIR
 Volume in drive A has no label
 Directory of  A:\

IBM          <DIR>      10-28-86   9:52a
DEC          <DIR>      10-28-86   9:56a
INTEL        <DIR>      10-28-86   9:56a
APPLE        <DIR>      10-28-86   9:56a
        4 File(s)    358400 bytes free
```

You can select IBM as your default directory as follows:

```
A> CD \IBM
```

Perform a directory listing and DOS displays the name of the current default subdirectory (\IBM).

```
A> DIR

 Volume  in  drive  A  has  no  label
 Directory  of   A:\IBM

 .               <DIR>       10-28-86      9:52a
 ..              <DIR>       10-28-86      9:52a
        2 File(s)       358400 bytes free
```

In this case, the subdirectory IBM does not contain any files. DOS does, however, list two subdirectories:

```
 .               <DIR>       10-28-86      9:52a
 ..              <DIR>       10-28-86      9:52a
```

DOS uses the period (.) as the abbreviation for the current subdirectory. Issue the command

```
A> DIR .
```

DOS will respond with

```
 Volume  in  drive  A  has  no  label
 Directory  of   A:\IBM

 .               <DIR>       10-28-86      9:52a
 ..              <DIR>       10-28-86      9:52a
        2 File(s)       358400 bytes free
```

DOS uses the double periods (..) to represent the directory one level above the current subdirectory. Assuming your current directory is \IBM, . points to the subdirectory \IBM and .. points to the root directory. Issue the command

```
A> DIR ..
```

DOS will display

```
Volume in drive A has no label
Directory of  A:\

IBM          <DIR>      10-28-86   9:52a
DEC          <DIR>      10-28-86   9:56a
INTEL        <DIR>      10-28-86   9:56a
APPLE        <DIR>      10-28-86   9:56a
        4 File(s)    358400 bytes free
```

Place your disk containing DOS in drive B. Issue the command

```
A> COPY B:*.SYS *.*
```

DOS will copy the files into the subdirectory IBM. You can now see your directory structure as shown in Figure 6-11.

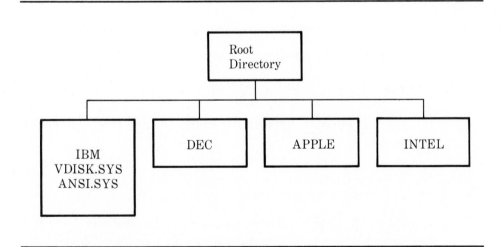

Figure 6-11. Current directory structure of IBM subdirectory

If you need to place files into the \DEC subdirectory, simply issue the command

```
A> COPY B:*.SYS \DEC\*.SYS
```

You also could have copied the files by first moving back to the root directory and then moving into the DEC subdirectory by entering one of the following:

```
A> CD \DEC
A> COPY B:*.SYS
```

or

```
A> CD ..
A> CD DEC
A> COPY B:*.SYS *.*
```

If you issue CD without specifying a subdirectory, DOS will display the name of the current directory.

```
A> CD
A:\IBM
```

Consider the following examples. Enter the command

```
A> CD \
```

It sets the current default directory to the root. Enter the command

```
A> CD B:
B:\
```

It displays the name of the current default directory on drive B. If you have the directory structure shown in Figure 6-12, you could enter the command

```
A> CD \IBM\QTR1
```

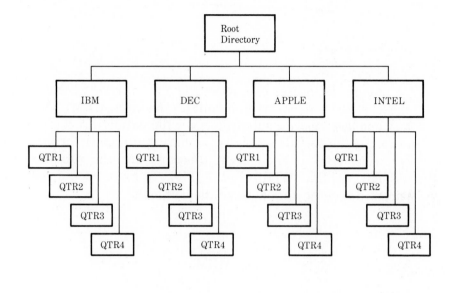

Figure 6-12. Directory structure with QTR1 as subdirectory of IBM

That action would place you into the subdirectory containing first-quarter information for IBM, as shown here:

```
A> CD
A:\IBM\QTR1
```

As previously stated, DOS uses the period (.) to represent the current directory. Issue the command

```
A> CD .
```

The current directory remains

```
A> CD
A:\IBM\QTR1
```

Again, DOS uses two periods (..) to represent the directory one level above the current default (in this case, \IBM). The directory one level above a subdirectory is the parent directory. In this example, the root directory is the parent directory for all subdirectories. IBM is the parent directory for the subdirectories \QTR1, \QTR2, \QTR3, and \QTR4. To move back up into the parent directory, simply issue the command

```
A> CD ..
```

The current default is now \IBM.

```
A> CD
A:\IBM
```

Issue the command

```
A> CD ..
```

The current default becomes the root directory.

```
A> CD
A:\
```

The following command assumes that the subdirectory \IBM \QTR1\EARNINGS exists:

```
A> CD \IBM\QTR1\EARNINGS
```

If you specify a pathname containing a nonexistent subdirectory, DOS will display

```
Invalid directory
```

It is important to note that DOS allows you to issue either of the commands CD or CHDIR.

RMDIR or RD (Remove a Subdirectory)

You may find it convenient to build and access temporary directories. When you are done using a temporary directory, you can use the DOS command RMDIR to delete it. The format of the command is

RMDIR [drive:]pathname

or

RD [drive:]pathname

where the following is true:

drive: is the disk drive containing the subdirectory to delete. If you do not specify a drive, DOS uses the current default drive.

pathname is the name of the subdirectory to remove.

Assume that you have the directory structure shown in Figure 6-11. Enter the DOS command

```
A> RMDIR DEC
```

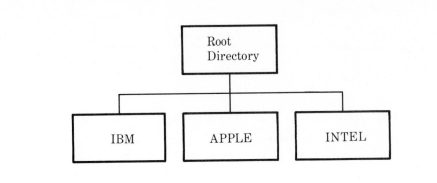

Figure 6-13.   Current directory structure after removing DEC subdirectory

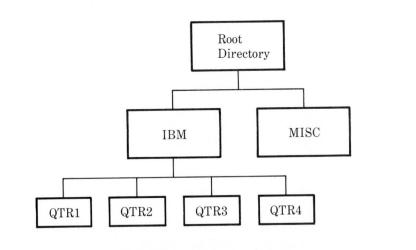

Figure 6-14.   Directory structure with quarters in IBM directory

Your action results in the directory structure in Figure 6-13.

Again, if you do not specify a complete pathname starting at the root, RMDIR will search the current working directory for the subdirectory to remove. Assume your current directory is IBM, and you have the directory structure shown in Figure 6-14. Enter the command

```
A> RMDIR \IBM\QTR1
```

This removes the subdirectory \IBM \QTR1.

Suppose you issue the command

```
A> RMDIR \QTR1
```

DOS will respond with

```
Invalid path, not directory,
or directory not empty
```

In this case, the current directory is \IBM, which contains the subdirectory QTR1. The pathname \QTR1, however, tells DOS to search the root directory \for the subdirectory QTR1, which does not exist. The correct pathname in this case is either QTR1 or \IBM\QTR1.

Before DOS allows you to remove a subdirectory, you must delete all of the files it contains. If you attempt to remove a directory that contains files, DOS will display

```
Invalid path, not directory,
or directory not empty
```

In this case, you must simply delete the files contained in the subdirectory and then remove the subdirectory.

DOS allows you to abbreviate the command RMDIR as RD. Therefore, these commands are equivalent: RMDIR \DEC and RD \DEC.

Assuming that you are given the directory structure shown in Figure 6-14, consider the following commands. Enter the command

```
A> RMDIR \IBM\QTR1
```

This removes the subdirectory containing first-quarter information for IBM, resulting in the directory structure in Figure 6-15. Enter the command

```
A> RMDIR MISC
```

The result will be the directory structure shown in Figure 6-16
Since the subdirectory IBM contains files (the subdirectories QTR2 through QTR4), this command fails:

```
A> RMDIR IBM
```

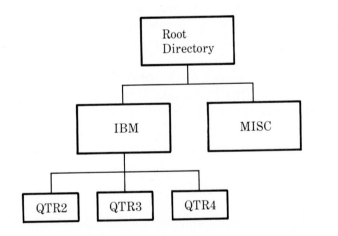

Figure 6-15.   Directory structure after removing QTR1

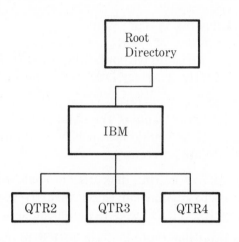

Figure 6-16. Directory structure after removing MISC

DOS will display

```
Invalid path, not directory,
or directory not empty
```

As you can see, if you create several levels of subdirectories, it is essential that you maintain a visual picture of the directory structure.

TREE (Display Subdirectory Tree)

The DOS TREE command allows you to display the directory structure of a disk. The command lists all of the subdirectories (and, optionally, their files) to the screen. The command format is [drive:][pathname]TREE [source—drive:][/F]

where the following is true:

drive: is the disk drive containing the file TREE.COM. If you do not specify a drive, DOS uses the current default disk drive.

pathname is the name of the subdirectory containing the file TREE.COM. If you do not specify a pathname, DOS uses the current default directory.

source—drive: is the disk drive containing the directory structure to display on the screen. If you do not specify a source drive, TREE uses the current default disk drive.

/F is a qualifier that requests TREE to display the names of each file contained in the subdirectories. If you do not specify /F, TREE will only display the subdirectory names.

Enter the following command:

```
A> TREE
```

TREE will display all of the subdirectories contained on the current default drive. Place your DOS disk in drive A and a disk with the subdirectories \APPLE, \DEC, \IBM, and \INTEL in drive B. Issue the command

```
A> TREE B:
```

TREE will respond by displaying

```
DIRECTORY PATH LISTING

Path: \IBM

Sub-directories:   QTR1


Path: \IBM\QTR1

Sub-directories:   None


Path: \DEC

Sub-directories:   None


Path: \INTEL

Sub-directories:   None


Path: \APPLE

Sub-directories:   None
```

Enter the command

```
A> TREE B:/F
```

This will display the names of the files contained in each of the
subdirectories on drive B.

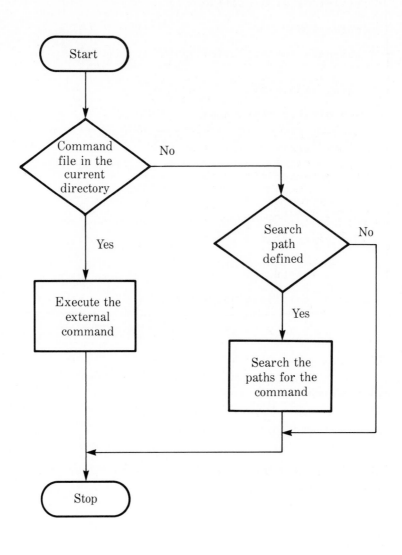

Figure 6-17.   Flowchart showing execution of PATH

PATH (Where to Look for External Commands)

The DOS PATH command provides you with a convenient method of telling DOS where to look for external commands. Each time you execute an external command (that is, a DOS file with an EXE or COM extension), DOS first searches the current default directory for the command file. If the file exists, DOS executes the command. Otherwise, DOS checks to see if you have defined a path of other subdirectories or disk drives to search for the command. Figure 6-17 is a flowchart that shows this process.

The format of the PATH command is

PATH [drive:][pathname][;[drive][pathname]...]

Enter the following command:

```
A> PATH B:;
```

If DOS fails to locate the external command in the current subdirectory, it will search the default directory on drive B for the command file. The flowchart in Figure 6-18 shows this process. Establish the path by entering

```
A> PATH \IBM;\DEC;\INTEL;\APPLE;
```

DOS will first examine the default directory for the external file and then sequentially search the pathnames provided through the PATH command for the command file. Figure 6-19 is a flowchart describing this process.

If DOS does not locate the file in the current directory, it will begin its search for the file in the subdirectory \IBM. DOS will continue its search sequentially through the pathnames specified until the file is found or the path is exhausted. If DOS does not

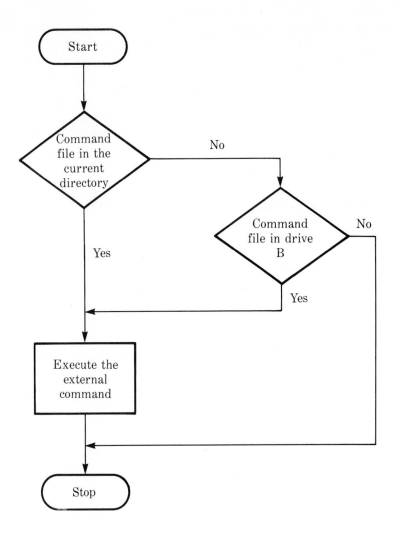

Figure 6-18. Flowchart showing failure of DOS to locate an external command

DOS: The Complete Reference

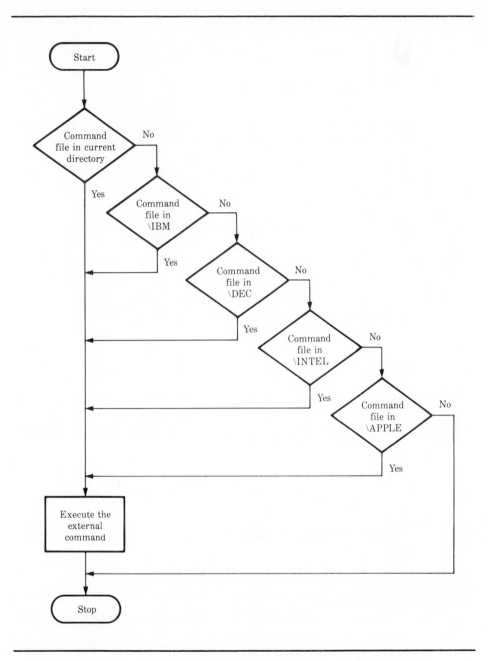

Figure 6-19. Flowchart showing sequential execution of PATH

find the command file, it will display the following error message:

```
Bad command or file name
```

If the pathname specified in the PATH command contains an invalid entry, DOS will skip the entry and continue with the next path. For example, assume you are using the directory structure shown in Figure 6-20. The entry \MYDIR in the following pathname does not exist:

PATH \IBM;\DEC;\MYDIR;\INTEL;\APPLE;

DOS will simply continue its search with the next entry in the path. It is important to note that the PATH command does not validate the path entries at the time you issue it. Instead, DOS will display the error message each time it attempts to access the invalid path. Enter the command

```
A> PATH ;
```

This deletes the previous path and directs DOS to examine only the current default directory for commands. If you issue the PATH command without any parameters, DOS will display the current path as follows:

```
A> PATH
PATH=\IBM;\DEC;\INTEL;\APPLE;
```

DOS Path Commands

As previously stated, a path is simply the route DOS will take through the directory structure to find files. Place a blank disk in drive A and your DOS disk in drive B. Issue the commands required to create the directory structure shown in Figure 6-20

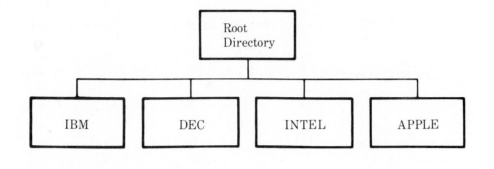

Figure 6-20.   Directory structure that does not contain MYDIR

on drive A. After entering the commands, DOS will display

```
A> MKDIR \IBM
A> MKDIR \DEC
A> MKDIR \INTEL
A> MKDIR \APPLE
A> DIR

 Volume in drive A has no label
 Directory of  A:\

IBM          <DIR>      10-28-86    9:52a
DEC          <DIR>      10-28-86    9:56a
INTEL        <DIR>      10-28-86    9:56a
APPLE        <DIR>      10-28-86    9:56a
         4 File(s)    357376 bytes free
```

Next, copy the *.SYS files from your DOS disk in drive B into the IBM subdirectory by entering one of the following:

```
A> COPY B:*.SYS \IBM\*.*
```

or

```
A> CD \IBM
A> COPY B:*.SYS *.*
```

List the contents of the IBM subdirectory by entering one of these:

```
A> DIR \IBM
```

or

```
A> CD \IBM
A> DIR
```

Next, copy the following file from the keyboard into the \DEC subdirectory with the name NOTES.DAT by entering

```
A> COPY CON \DEC\NOTES.DAT
THE VAXMATE IS DIGITAL'S
NEW 80826 MICROCOMPUTER.
```

DOS will display

```
A> COPY CON \DEC\NOTES.DAT
THE VAXMATE IS DIGITAL'S
NEW 80826 MICROCOMPUTER.
```

When you have entered the data, press the F6 key and press ENTER. The screen should now contain

```
A> COPY CON \DEC\NOTES.DAT
THE VAXMATE IS DIGITAL'S
NEW 80826 MICROCOMPUTER.
^Z

        1 File(s) copied
```

DOS uses the symbol ^Z to mark the end of a file. Set your current default subdirectory to \DEC and type the contents of the file NOTES.DAT. DOS will display

```
A> CD \DEC
A> TYPE NOTES.DAT
THE VAXMATE IS DIGITAL'S
NEW 80826 MICROCOMPUTER.
```

Now list all of the subdirectories on drive A by entering

```
A> TREE
```

List all of the files contained in each subdirectory by entering

```
A> TREE /F
```

Set your default directory to \APPLE and type the contents of the file NOTES.DAT in the subdirectory \DEC by entering

```
A> CD \APPLE
A> TYPE \DEC\NOTES.DAT
```

Issue the PATH command required to request DOS to search drive C for external commands if it fails to locate the command file in the current subdirectory.

```
A> PATH C:;
```

Modify the PATH command also to search the subdirectories on drive A in the order \APPLE, \DEC, \IBM, \INTEL.

```
A> PATH C:;\APPLE;\DEC;\IBM;\INTEL;
```

Executing External Commands
Contained in Subdirectories

As you increase the use of subdirectories in your day-to-day applications, eventually you must execute programs that are contained in a subdirectory. An external command is simply a program that DOS executes as a COM or EXE file. Create the subdirectory DOS on the disk in drive A with the following command:

```
A> MKDIR DOS
```

Next, copy the file TREE.COM from your DOS disk in drive B into the subdirectory DOS.

```
A> COPY B:TREE.COM \DOS
```

You have two choices for executing the DOS TREE command from drive A. You can set the current working directory to DOS and simply invoke the command

```
A> CD \DOS
A> TREE
```

or you can specify the complete pathname of the command at the DOS prompt.

```
A> \DOS\TREE
```

DOS will start at the root and examine the subdirectory DOS for the file TREE.COM. If DOS finds the file, it will execute the command. Otherwise, DOS will display the message

```
Bad command or file name
```

Assume your directory structure is that shown in Figure 6-21. The following are valid pathnames for external commands:

```
\DOS\DISKCOMP
\WORDSTAR\WS
\MISC\PASCAL\DATE
\MISC\MODULA\BUDGET
```

Copying a Disk Containing Subdirectories

Assume that you have the directory structure shown in Figure 6-12 in drive A and that each subdirectory contains the files illustrated. To make a complete copy of your disk, you must use the DISKCOPY command. The DOS COPY command copies files only in the current directory or subdirectory specified. Suppose

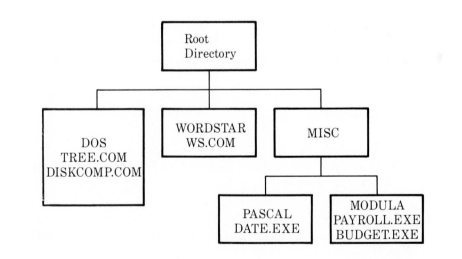

Figure 6-21.   Directory structure with DOS, WORDSTAR, and MISC directories

your current directory contains the following:

```
A> DIR

 Volume in drive A has no label
 Directory of   A:\

 IBM            <DIR>        10-28-86    9:52a
 DEC            <DIR>        10-28-86    9:56a
 APPLE          <DIR>        10-28-86    9:56a
 INTEL          <DIR>        10-28-86    9:56a
         4 File(s)      357376 bytes free
```

The COPY command will not copy the files contained in each subdirectory. You must use the DISKCOPY command in this case.

```
A> DISKCOPY A: B:
```

Renaming a Subdirectory

DOS does not provide an easy method for renaming a subdirectory. If you try to rename the subdirectory \IBM with the REN command, DOS will display

```
A> REN IBM IBMNOTES
Invalid path or file name
```

To rename a directory, you must perform the following steps:

• Create a new directory with the name desired.

• Copy the files contained in the old directory to the new directory.

• Verify that the copy procedure was successful.

• Delete the files from the old directory.

- Remove the old directory with RMDIR.

For example, suppose the subdirectory \IBM contains the following files:

```
A> DIR
 Volume in drive A has no label
 Directory of  A:\IBM

SEPT       DAT       4  10-28-86  11:13a
OCT        DAT      19  10-28-86  11:13a
           4 File(s)     355328 bytes free
```

If you want to rename the subdirectory to \IBMNOTES, you must perform the following steps:

- Create the new directory.

```
A> MKDIR \IBMNOTES
```

- Copy the files from the old directory to the new directory.

```
A> COPY \IBM\*.* \IBMNOTES\*.*
```

- Verify that the copy was successful.

```
A> DIR \IBMNOTES
```

- Delete the files from the old directory.

```
A> DEL \IBM\*.*
```

- Remove the old directory with RMDIR.

```
A> RMDIR IBM
```

Working Directories

As previously stated, the *working directory* is the directory DOS commands will affect by default if the command does not specify a different directory. The DOS command CHDIR sets the current working directory. Each disk drive has its own working directory. DOS keeps track of the working directory for each drive. The following commands set the working directory in drive A to DOS, the default in drive B to PAYROLL, and the current directory in drive C to WORDSTAR:

```
A> CD \DOS
A> CD B:\PAYROLL
A> CD C:\WORDSTAR
```

As you can see, you can use the terms *current directory, working directory,* and *default directory* interchangeably.

Other Applications

The use of subdirectories is almost unlimited. For example, you might use the directory structure shown in Figure 6-22 on a fixed disk. Most users have word processing, spreadsheet, and database

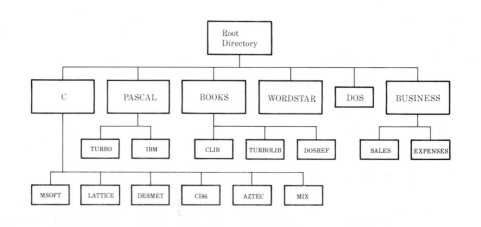

Figure 6-22. Sample directory structure of a fixed disk

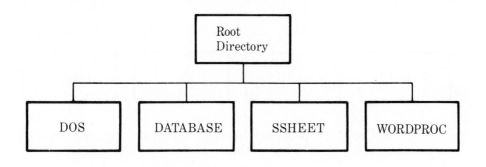

Figure 6-23.   Sample directory structure of disk containing database, spreadsheet, and word processing programs

applications. As a minimum, their directory structure should resemble Figure 6-23.

If you take time initially to create a sound directory structure, your disk organization will be enhanced, which will in turn increase your productivity.

Review

1. What is the purpose of subdirectories?

2. What is the root directory?

3. List the directory manipulation commands.

4. Issue the commands required to create the following directory structure on a blank disk:

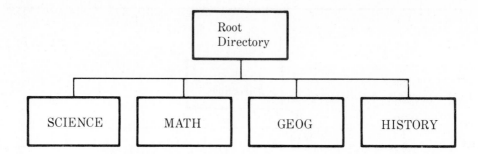

5. Using the previous directory structure, remove the MATH subdirectory.

6. Does DOS allow you to remove subdirectories containing files?

7. What are the steps required to rename a DOS directory?

8. You are given the directory listing

```
A> DIR

Volume in drive A has no label
Directory of  A:\EXAMPLE

.               <DIR>       10-28-86   11:18a
..              <DIR>       10-28-86   11:18a
        2 File(s)     355328 bytes free
```

What are the directories . and ..?

9. What is the command used to set the current default directory to the root directory?

10. How do you list all of the directories on a disk? How do you list the files that they contain?

11. What is the function of the PATH command?

12. What is the function of the following commands:

MKDIR \IBM\QTR1\REPORTS
PATH ;
COPY B:VDISK.SYS \NEWVDISK.SYS
DEL \DEC\NOTES.DAT
TREE /F

PATH
DEL \IBM*.*
\DOS\DISKCOPY

13. You are given the following directory structure:

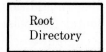

Draw the directory structure produced by the following commands:

MKDIR \CLASS1
MKDIR CLASS2
MKDIR CLASS1\NOTES
MKDIR \CLASS2\TEST
CD CLASS1
MKDIR ..\MISC
CD \CLASS2
MKDIR HOMEWORK
CD ..
RMDIR CLASS1\NOTES

Answers

1. *What is the purpose of subdirectories?*

Subdirectories enhance your disk organization by allowing you to group logically related files. In addition, subdirectories reduce the possibility of accidental file deletion, since most DOS commands affect only the current working directory or subdirectory specified.

2. *What is the root directory?*

By default, each DOS disk has a root or upper-level directory. The root directory provides the base (or root) for all other directories to grow from. DOS uses the backslash (\) to represent the root directory.

3. *List the directory manipulation commands.*

MKDIR or MD
CHDIR or CD
RMDIR or RD
PATH
TREE

4. *Issue the commands required to create the following directory structure on a blank disk:*

A> MKDIR \SCIENCE
A> MKDIR \MATH
A> MKDIR \GEOG
A> MKDIR \HISTORY

5. *Using the previous directory structure, remove the MATH subdirectory.*

A> RMDIR \MATH

6. *Does DOS allow you to remove subdirectories containing files?*

No. Before you may remove a subdirectory with RMDIR, you must delete all of the files it contains.

DOS: The Complete Reference

7. *What are the steps required to rename a DOS directory?*

Create a new directory with the name desired. Copy the files contained in the old directory to the new directory. Verify that the copy was successful. Delete the files from the old directory. Remove the old directory with RMDIR.

8. *You are given the directory listing*

```
A> DIR

 Volume in drive A has no label
 Directory of   A:\IBM

 .            <DIR>      10-28-86   11:18a
 ..           <DIR>      10-28-86   11:18a
         2 File(s)     355328 bytes free
```

What are the directories . and ..?

DOS uses the period (.) to represent the current default directory. In this case, the current default is \IBM. Suppose you issue the command

`A> DIR .`

DOS will display the same result as if you had issued the command

`A> DIR`

Likewise, DOS uses the double periods .. to represent the parent directory. The parent directory is the directory one level above the current directory. Assume your directory structure is

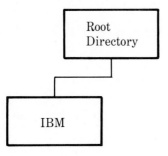

Also assume that the current directory is \IBM. In this setting, . will point to \IBM and .. will reference the parent (in this case, the root) directory.

9. *What is the command used to set the current default directory to the root directory?*

A> CD \

10. *How do you list all of the directories on a disk?*

The TREE command displays all of the subdirectories on a disk:

A> TREE

How do you list the files that they contain?

The /F qualifier to the TREE command requests TREE to display the files contained in each subdirectory:

A> TREE /F

11. *What is the function of the PATH command?*

The DOS PATH command provides you with a convenient method of telling DOS where to look for external commands. Each time you execute an external command (a file with extension EXE or COM), DOS first searches the current working directory for the command file. If the file exists, DOS executes the command. Otherwise, DOS checks to see if you have defined a path of other subdirectories or disk drives to search for the command via the PATH command.

12. *What is the function of the following commands:*

MKDIR \IBM\QTR1\REPORTS

Create the subdirectory REPORTS in the directory \IBM\QTR1.

PATH ;

Eliminate previous DOS paths and request DOS to search only the current default directory for external commands.

COPY B:VDISK.SYS \NEWVDISK.SYS

Copy the file VDISK.SYS from drive B and place it in the root directory with the name NEWVDISK.SYS.

DEL \DEC\NOTES.DAT

Delete the file NOTES.DAT from the subdirectory \DEC.

TREE /F

Display each subdirectory and the files each contains on the current default disk.

PATH

Display the current path DOS is using to find external commands.

DEL \IBM*.*

Delete all of the files in the subdirectory \IBM.

\DOS\DISKCOPY

Execute the external command DISKCOPY from the subdirectory \DOS.

13. *You are given the following directory structure:*

Draw the directory structure produced by the following commands:

MKDIR \CLASS1

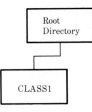

MKDIR CLASS2

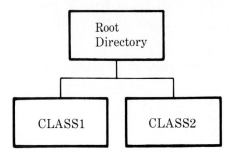

MKDIR CLASS1\NOTES

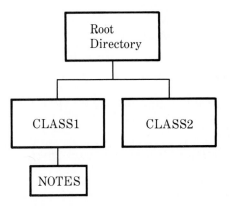

MKDIR \CLASS2\TEST

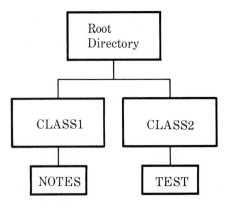

CD CLASS1
MKDIR ..\MISC

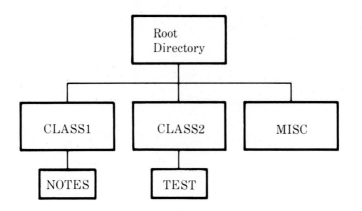

CD \CLASS2
MKDIR HOMEWORK

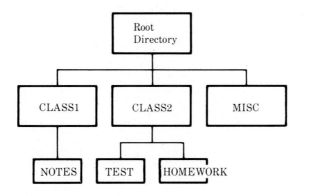

CD ..
RMDIR CLASS1\NOTES

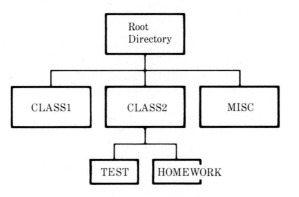

Redirection of Input and Output

MORE
FIND
SORT
DOS Pipe

Each of the preceding chapters introduced DOS commands. All of these commands displayed their results on the screen. For example, consider the following command:

```
A> DIR
```

DOS displays the output of the directory command on the screen. Most of the DOS commands send their output to a destination defined by DOS as standard output (stdout). By default, stdout points to the screen.

This chapter introduces the DOS I/O (input/output) redirection operators. As you will see, the function of these operators is simply to redirect I/O from the DOS default standard output (the screen) and standard input (the keyboard).

Issue the following command:

```
A> DIR > DIR.LIS
```

The output of the command DIR was not displayed on the screen. Instead, the redirection operator > directed DOS to place the output of the command into the file DIR.LIS, as illustrated in Figures 7-1 and 7-2.

A> DIR

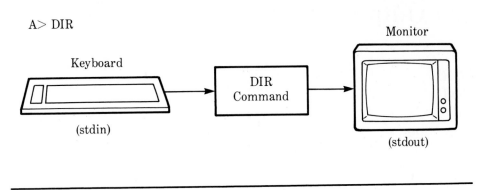

Figure 7-1. Communication path of DIR command

You can direct the output of DOS commands to files, the printer (PRN:), and even to other programs. Issue the following command:

```
A> DIR *.BAT > PRN:
```

A> DIR > DIR.LIS

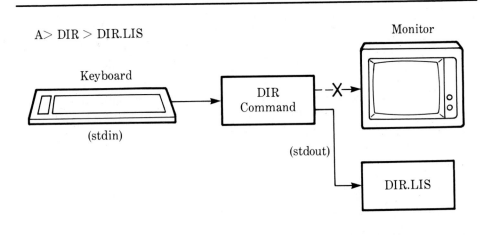

Figure 7-2. Communication redirection using DIR > DIR.LIS

If your system printer is turned on, the output of the directory listing is printed.

Issue the following command:

```
A> CHKDSK > DISK.STA
```

DOS will place the output of the command CHKDSK into the file DISK.STA.

The second DOS redirection operator, >>, appends the output of a command to the file specified. Consider the following command:

```
A> DIR *.SYS >> SYS.DIR
```

When DOS executes the command, it searches for the SYS.DIR file. If the file exists, DOS appends the result of the command to the end of the file. If the file does not exist, DOS creates it and places the output of the command into it.

```
A> DIR *.SYS >> SYS.DIR
```

If the files ANSI.SYS and VDISK.SYS are on the disk, the file SYS.DIR now contains

```
Volume in drive A has no label
Directory of   A:\

ANSI      SYS      1641   14/08/84     8:00
VDISK     SYS      3080   14/08/84     8:00
         2 File(s)    9024 bytes free
```

Type the file to verify this by entering the following command:

```
A> TYPE SYS.DIR
```

Now issue this command:

```
A> DIR K*.* >> SYS.DIR
```

The SYS.DIR file now contains the following:

```
Volume in drive A has no label
Directory of  A:\

ANSI     SYS     1641  14/08/84    8:00
VDISK    SYS     3080  14/08/84    8:00
       2 File(s)    9024 bytes free

Volume in drive A has no label
Directory of  A:\

KEYBSP   COM     2073  14/08/84    8:00
KEYBIT   COM     1854  14/08/84    8:00
KEYBGR   COM     2111  14/08/84    8:00
KEYBUK   COM     1760  14/08/84    8:00
KEYBFR   COM     2235  14/08/84    8:00
       5 File(s)    9024 bytes free
```

Both of the redirection operators examined thus far have dealt strictly with the redirection of output. DOS also allows you to redirect input from the standard input (stdin). The three DOS commands used here to demonstrate redirection of input are MORE, FIND, and SORT.

MORE

The MORE command gets its input from standard input and displays it, a screen at a time, to standard output. Each time a screen of information is displayed, MORE pauses and displays the following message:

```
-- More --
```

MORE waits for you to press any key to continue. If you want to see more output, simply press a key. If not, press CTRL-BREAK.

Enter the following command for redirection of output to create the file DIR.LIS:

```
A> DIR > DIR.LIS
```

You can now display the contents of the file a screen at a time as follows:

```
A> MORE < DIR.LIS
```

MORE will display the first page of data and prompt the user to press a key to continue, as shown here:

```
 Volume in drive A has no label
 Directory of  A:\

 COMMAND   COM    22042   14/08/84    8:00
 ANSI      SYS     1641   14/08/84    8:00
 SORT      EXE     1632   14/08/84    8:00
 SHARE     EXE     8544   14/08/84    8:00
 FIND      EXE     6363   14/08/84    8:00
 ATTRIB    EXE    15123   14/08/84    8:00
 MORE      COM      320   14/08/84    8:00
 ASSIGN    COM      988   14/08/84    8:00
 PRINT     COM     7811   14/08/84    8:00
 SYS       COM     3629   14/08/84    8:00
 CHKDSK    COM     9275   14/08/84    8:00
 FORMAT    COM     9015   14/08/84    8:00
 VDISK     SYS     3080   14/08/84    8:00
 BASIC     COM    17024   14/08/84    8:00
 BASICA    COM    26880   14/08/84    8:00
 FDISK     COM     8076   14/08/84    8:00
 COMP      COM     3471   14/08/84    8:00
 TREE      COM     2473   14/08/84    8:00
 BACKUP    COM     5440   14/08/84    8:00
 RESTORE   COM     5413   14/08/84    8:00
 -- More --
```

When you press a key, MORE displays the next page (if a full page exists) or to the end of the file, as shown here:

```
LABEL     COM     1260    14/08/84    8:00
DISKCOPY  COM     4165    14/08/84    8:00
DISKCOMP  COM     3752    14/08/84    8:00
KEYBSP    COM     2073    14/08/84    8:00
KEYBIT    COM     1854    14/08/84    8:00
KEYBGR    COM     2111    14/08/84    8:00
KEYBUK    COM     1760    14/08/84    8:00
KEYBFR    COM     2235    14/08/84    8:00
MODE      COM     5194    14/08/84    8:00
SELECT    COM     2079    14/08/84    8:00
GRAPHICS  COM     3111    14/08/84    8:00
RECOVER   COM     4066    14/08/84    8:00
EDLIN     COM     7183    14/08/84    8:00
GRAFTABL  COM     1169    14/08/84    8:00
           34 File(s)     100352 bytes free
```

The third redirection operator, <, directs DOS to obtain the input for the command from an alternate input source as shown in Figure 7-3.

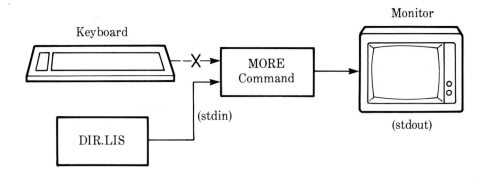

Figure 7-3.   Effect of redirection operator < on obtaining input from alternate source

The FIND command locates and displays each occurrence of a string within a file. The format of FIND is

[drive:][path]FIND [/C][/N][/V] "string" [file—specification [...]]

where the following is true:

drive: and *path* contain the disk drive and directory path of FIND.EXE.

/C directs FIND to display a count of the number of occurrences of the string in the file.

/N directs FIND to display the line number of each line containing the string specified.

/V directs FIND to display all lines that do not contain the string specified.

Assume the file STATES.LIS contains the following:

```
ALASKA, JUNEAU
ALABAMA, MONTGOMERY
ARIZONA, PHOENIX
ARKANSAS, LITTLE ROCK
CALIFORNIA, SACRAMENTO
NEVADA, LAS VEGAS
WASHINGTON, OLYMPIA
```

Enter the command

```
A> FIND "ARIZ" STATES.LIS
```

The command will display

```
---------- STATES.LIS
ARIZONA, PHOENIX
```

Now, enter the command

```
A> FIND/N "ALA" STATES.LIS
```

The command will display

```
---------- STATES.LIS
[1]ALASKA, JUNEAU
[2]ALABAMA, MONTGOMERY
```

Assume the current directory contains the files shown here:

```
Volume in drive A has no label
Directory of  A:\

.              <DIR>        9-16-86     7:43p
..             <DIR>        9-16-86     7:43p
STATES  LIS       256       9-20-86     8:48p
ART7    18        256       9-20-86     8:48p
ART7    3         128       9-16-86     7:53p
CHAP7          <DIR>        9-16-86     7:43p
ART7    4         128       9-16-86     7:54p
CHAP12         <DIR>        9-16-86     7:25p
ART7    6         128       9-16-86     7:55p
ART7    8         256       9-16-86     8:03p
SYS     DIR       512       9-16-86     8:02p
ART7    10        128       9-16-86     8:03p
       10 File(s)    9054208 bytes free
```

You can create a file containing each file name by entering the command

```
A> DIR > DIR.LIS
```

FIND will now display all of the subdirectories, as shown here:

```
A> FIND "<DIR>" < DIR.LIS

---------- DIR.LIS
CHAP7          <DIR>        9-16-86     7:43p
CHAP12         <DIR>        9-16-86     7:25p
```

Later in this chapter, you will see how to use FIND even more efficiently via the DOS pipe.

SORT

The SORT command sorts the data it obtains from standard input and writes the sorted information to standard output. The format of SORT is

[drive:][path]SORT [/+n][/R]

where the following is true:

drive: and *path* contain the disk drive and directory path of SORT.EXE.

/+n directs SORT to perform the sort based upon the data beginning in column *n*.

/R directs SORT to perform the sort in reverse (descending) order.

Suppose, for example, the NAMES.LIS file contains the following:

```
BARNES
VOHS
BRYANT
RICH
EUBANK
GUEBARD
ANDERSON
HUTCHINSON
SCHMAUDER
BOY
```

Enter the command

```
A> SORT < NAMES.LIS
```

The command will display

```
ANDERSON
BARNES
BOY
BRYANT
EUBANK
GUEBARD
HUTCHINSON
RICH
SCHMAUDER
VOHS
```

Now suppose the MAIL.LIS file contains

```
1234567890123456789

WA SEATTLE    93244
AZ PHOENIX    85023
NV LAS VEGAS  89126
NY NEW YORK   22021
OR PORTLAND   91122
CA OAKLAND    83233
MA BOSTON     01123
```

You can sort by city as shown here:

```
A> SORT/+4 < MAIL.LIS

MA BOSTON     01123
NV LAS VEGAS  89126
NY NEW YORK   22021
CA OAKLAND    83233
AZ PHOENIX    85023
OR PORTLAND   91122
WA SEATTLE    93244
```

Likewise, you can sort by ZIP code and place the result into the ZIP.SRT file, as shown here:

```
A> SORT /+15 < MAIL.LIS > ZIP.SRT

MA BOSTON      01123
NY NEW YORK    22021
CA OAKLAND     83233
AZ PHOENIX     85023
NV LAS VEGAS   89126
OR PORTLAND    91122
WA SEATTLE     93244
```

DOS Pipe

The final redirection operator is the DOS pipe, ¦. The pipe redirects the output of one program to become the input of a second program. If you enter

```
A> DIR ¦ MORE
```

the output of the DIR command is not written to the screen, but rather to the standard input of the MORE command, as shown in Figure 7-4.

You can use each of the commands MORE, FIND, and SORT with the DOS pipe, as illustrated in the following examples.

Enter the command

```
A> DIR ¦ FIND "<DIR>"
```

The command displays each of the subdirectories in the current directory.

Enter the command

```
A> DIR ¦ SORT > SORT.DIR
```

The command line writes a sorted directory listing to the file SORT.DIR.

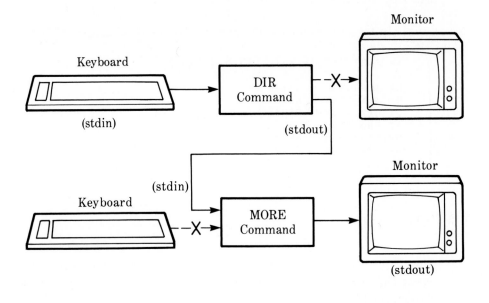

Figure 7-4. Output of DIR written to standard input of MORE

Enter the command

```
A> TYPE MAIL.LIS ¦ SORT ¦ MORE
```

The SORT command obtains its input from the MAIL.LIS file and displays it a screen at a time.

Now enter

```
A> TYPE MAIL.LIS ¦ FIND "ALA" > ALA.LIS
```

Each line in the MAIL.LIS file that contains the string "ALA" is written to the ALA.LIS file.

Applications that support the DOS pipe are easy to implement. Chapter 16 illustrates C and Turbo Pascal programs that utilize the pipe.

1. What are standard input and standard output? Where does DOS default each to?

2. Illustrate the four DOS redirection operators and explain the function of each.

3. For the following commands, label the standard input and output.

> A> SORT < MAIL.LIS
> A> FIND "<DIR>" < DIR.LIS > SUB.DIR
> A> DIR ¦ MORE

Example:

> A> DIR > DIR.LIS
>
> Command DIR
> Standard Input = keyboard
> Standard Output = DIR.LIS

4. What is the function of each of the following commands?

> A> DIR ¦ FIND "<DIR>"
> A> DIR ¦ SORT/R > DIR.SRT
> A> TYPE MAIL.LIS ¦ MORE

Answers

1. *What are standard input and standard output? Where does DOS default each to?*

Standard input and output are the DOS defaults for the source of input and destination of output for each command. By default, DOS assigns standard input to the keyboard and standard output to the screen display.

2. *Illustrate the four DOS redirection operators and explain the function of each.*

>   redirection of output. DOS uses > to place the output of a command into a file, or to a device (PRN:).

>> redirection of output. DOS uses >> to append the output of a command to a file.

<   redirection of input. DOS uses < to redirect the source of input for a command from a file or device.

¦   DOS pipe. DOS uses ¦ to redirect the output of one command to become the input of a second command.

3. *For the following commands, label the standard input and output.*

    A> SORT < MAIL.LIS

Command SORT
Standard Input = MAIL.LIS
Standard Output = screen display

    A> FIND "<DIR>" < DIR.LIS > SUB.DIR

Command FIND
Standard Input = DIR.LIS
Standard Output = SUB.DIR

    A> DIR ¦ MORE

Command DIR
Standard Input = keyboard
Standard Output = MORE command

Command MORE
Standard Input = DIR command
Standard Output = screen display

4. *What is the function of each of the following commands?*

   A> DIR ¦ FIND "<DIR>"

FIND searches each line of output from the DIR command for the string "<DIR>". In this case, the name of each subdirectory in the current directory is displayed to the screen.

   A> DIR ¦ SORT/R > DIR.SRT

SORT sorts the output of the DIR command in reverse order and places the result into the file DIR.SRT.

   A> TYPE MAIL.LIS ¦ MORE

DOS displays the contents of the MAIL.LIS file one page at a time until the entire file is displayed or the user enters CTRL-BREAK.

Batch Processing

Creating Batch Files
REM
PAUSE
ECHO
GOTO
IF
FOR
SHIFT
AUTOEXEC.BAT

Thus far, each time you have issued a command, you have waited for the command to finish before you entered a second command. You are in constant interaction with the computer. Processing of this type is *interactive processing*. The user types in a command at the system prompt and then waits for the command to complete before proceeding. Interactive processing constitutes the majority of the processing performed on computers today. There are, however, many instances in which processing does not require constant user interaction. Consider an application that calculates employee salaries, sorts the salaries, and prints the paychecks. If you assumed that the commands PAYROLL.EXE, SORTPAY.EXE, and PRINTPAY.EXE perform each step of the processing, you could issue each command interactively. In this case, you first issue the command PAYROLL.EXE as follows:

```
A> PAYROLL
```

When the processing is finished, you sort the salaries with the SORTPAY.EXE command, as follows:

```
A> PAYROLL

A> SORTDATA
```

Once the data is sorted, you can print the paychecks with the PRINTPAY.EXE command, as shown here:

```
A> PAYROLL

A> SORTDATA

A> PRINTPAY
```

At this point, the printing of payroll checks begins, and you can work on another task away from the computer. Because you performed all of the payroll commands interactively, you had to remain at the computer to issue subsequent commands as each process ended. Depending on the size of the company, the amount of time spent waiting to issue the next command could be considerable.

In this instance, none of the commands require user interaction once the program begins. In such cases, DOS allows you to group all of the commands into a file that DOS reads and executes in a sequential manner. Consider the previous payroll example. DOS allows you to group all three commands into a file with the extension BAT, as illustrated here:

```
PAYROLL
SORTDATA
PRINTPAY
```

If you place all three commands into the file DOPAY.BAT, you simply issue the command DOPAY at the DOS prompt. DOS will read and execute each command in the file sequentially. You are now free to perform other tasks away from the computer while DOS executes the batch file. Processing in which the system obtains the commands from a file, rather than from the user at a keyboard, is termed *batch processing*. Note that the extension BAT represents batch processing. This type of processing is shown in Figure 8-1.

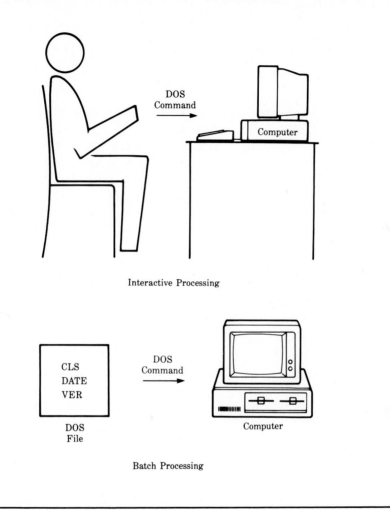

Interactive Processing

CLS
DATE
VER

DOS
File

DOS
Command

Computer

Batch Processing

Figure 8-1.　Comparison of interactive and batch processing

By default, DOS displays the name of each program on the screen as it executes. Executing the file DOPAY.BAT results in the following display:

```
A> PAYROLL

A> SORTDATA

A> PRINTPAY
```

Grouping the payroll commands into a single BAT file saves a significant amount of time that would otherwise be spent waiting for each program to finish so that the next command could be issued. In addition, some applications are composed of several small programs that execute sequentially. In these cases, batch processing not only saves time, but also saves much typing.

Create the file SETDATE.BAT to perform the following:

Clear the screen
Prompt the user for the date
Prompt the user for the time
Display the current DOS version

Your file should look like this:

```
CLS
DATE
TIME
VER
```

Executing SETDATE.BAT results in the following:

```
A> DATE
Current date is Thu 10-02-1986
Enter new date (mm-dd-yy):

A> TIME
Current time is 11:31:23.03
Enter new time:

A> VER

IBM Personal Computer DOS Version 3.00
```

The following rules provide guidelines for creating batch procedures:

• Do not name batch files to internal DOS commands such as CLS.BAT. DOS will not be able to find the BAT file.

• DOS will execute COM and EXE files before BAT files with the same name, subject to the search strategy named in the PATH command.

• Batch files must have the extension BAT.

• If you invoke a batch process that resides on a floppy disk and later remove that disk during processing, DOS will prompt you to reinsert the disk upon completion of the current program.

• Changing the default drive or directory during the execution of a BAT file will not affect batch processing.

• You can invoke other batch files from within a batch process. If the second batch procedure is the last command in the batch file, you simply reference its name as follows:

```
CLS
DATE
TIME
DOPAY
```

If the second batch procedure occurs in the middle of the batch file, you must invoke a secondary command processor:

```
CLS
DATE
TIME
COMMAND/C DOPAY
CLS
```

The statement COMMAND/C loads a secondary command processor to execute the batch procedure.

- Any command that can be issued from the DOS prompt can be issued from within a batch file.

Creating Batch Files

One of the easiest and fastest ways to create a batch file is simply to copy the series of commands from the keyboard as follows:

```
A> COPY CON FILENAME.BAT
```

Once you have entered the last line of the batch file, press the F6 key and then press ENTER. For example, the previous example created a batch file containing

```
CLS
DATE
TIME
VER
```

To enter the file from the keyboard, simply type

```
A> COPY CON SETDATE.BAT
```

Upon completion of the process, the screen will contain

```
A> COPY CON SETDATE.BAT
CLS
DATE
TIME
VER
^Z
        1 File(s) copied
```

Many DOS users will invoke word processors or the line editor EDLIN (see Chapter 13) to create their batch files.

DOS provides several commands that enhance batch processing. The commands, which are all internal DOS commands, are

REM [message]
PAUSE [message]
ECHO [on/off/message]
GOTO label
IF [NOT] condition DOS—command
FOR %%variable IN (set) DO DOS—command
SHIFT

REM

The batch command REM allows you to display messages to the screen during batch processing. The format of the command is

REM [message]

where

message is an optional character string containing up to 123 characters.

Note that when you enter the following REM commands within DOPAY.BAT, the messages displayed on the screen can be enhanced:

```
REM Beginning PAYROLL
PAYROLL
REM Sorting PAYROLL data
SORTDATA
REM Printing PAYROLL checks
PRINTPAY
```

Execution of DOPAY.BAT now results in

```
A> REM Beginning PAYROLL

A> PAYROLL

A> REM Sorting PAYROLL data

A> SORTDATA

A> REM Printing PAYROLL checks

A> PRINTPAY
```

As you will see, the DOS command ECHO OFF, presented later in this chapter, suppresses the display of messages via REM.

PAUSE

The batch command PAUSE is similar to REM in that it allows you to display messages from within a batch file. In addition to displaying messages, PAUSE temporarily suspends processing until you acknowledge the message by pressing any key to continue. If you do not want to continue, you enter CTRL-BREAK or CTRL-C, causing DOS to display

```
Terminate batch job (Y/N)?
```

Simply press Y to terminate batch processing or N to continue.

If you assume that the procedure DOPAY.BAT requires a blank disk in drive B prior to the sort, enter the PAUSE command as follows:

```
PAYROLL
PAUSE Enter blank diskette in drive B:
SORTDATA
PRINTPAY
```

Execution of DOPAY.BAT now results in

```
A> PAYROLL

A> PAUSE Enter blank diskette in drive B:
Strike a key when ready . . .

A> SORTDATA

A> PRINTPAY
```

ECHO

The batch command ECHO allows or prevents the display of the names of DOS commands as they are executed within a BAT file. When OFF, ECHO inhibits the display of command names and messages from REM. ECHO does not inhibit output produced by the commands.

The format of ECHO is

ECHO [ON/OFF/message]

where

   message is a message for ECHO to display

This message length should not exceed 117 characters.

When ECHO is ON, DOS displays all of the command names on the screen as it executes them. If you do not specify any parameters to ECHO, the current state (ON or OFF) is displayed on the screen as shown here:

```
A> ECHO
ECHO is on
```

GOTO

The batch command GOTO provides a mechanism for branching within a BAT file. The format of GOTO is

GOTO label

where

> *label* is the name of a label within the BAT file at which DOS may continue execution.

Labels can be virtually any length. Only the first eight characters of a label are significant, though. DOS, therefore, considers the labels :labelname1 and :labelname2 to be equivalent. Entering the following BAT procedure will repeatedly display a directory listing until the user presses CTRL-BREAK to terminate processing.

```
:loop
DIR
GOTO loop
```

IF

To support conditional processing within batch files, DOS provides the IF command. The format of IF is

> IF [NOT] condition DOS—command

where

> *condition* is the Boolean condition DOS evaluates.

It must be ERRORLEVEL number, EXIST file—specification, or string1==string2. ERRORLEVEL number evaluates as TRUE when the previous program exits to DOS with an error status greater than, or equal to, the decimal value contained in number.

One of the features that DOS provides to programmers is the ability to return a status value to DOS when the program terminates.

```
PAYROLL
SORTDATA
IF ERRORLEVEL 1 GOTO PRINT
REM ERROR IN SORT
GOTO DONE
:PRINT
PRINTPAY
:DONE
```

In the example BAT file, the following message appears:

```
REM ERROR IN SORT
```

The message is displayed on the screen if the program SORT-DATA exits to DOS with an error status less than 1. Otherwise, the procedure simply runs to conclusion.

EXIST file—specification evaluates as TRUE when the file name exists as specified. Consider the contents of the following BAT file:

```
PAYROLL
IF EXIST PAYROLL.SRT GOTO PRINT
SORTDATA
:PRINT
PRINTPAY
```

If the payroll data has already been sorted (PAYROLL.SRT), this BAT file prints the paychecks. Otherwise, the procedure invokes the SORTDATA program and then prints the checks.

The condition string1==string2 evaluates as TRUE when

the character string contained in string1 is identical to the one in string2. The comparison is case-dependent, so the strings must match exactly. If you enter the following, DOS will evaluate the condition as FALSE:

```
IF FIRSTSTRING==firststring GOTO DONE
```

The ability to perform string comparisons will become more vital when batch parameters are discussed later in this chapter.

The NOT operator simply reverses the result of the condition performed. Consider issuing the following command:

```
IF NOT EXIST PAYROLL.SRT SORTDATA
```

FOR

The FOR command provides a mechanism for repetitive processing within a BAT procedure. The format of FOR is

FOR %%variable IN [set] DO DOS—command

where the following is true:

%%variable is a variable DOS sequentially sets to members of the given set.

set is a collection of file names for DOS to use sequentially.

DOS—command is the command DOS performs with each iteration.

Consider the following BAT file:

```
FOR %%F IN (AUTOEXEC.BAT CONFIG.SYS TEST.BAT) DO TYPE %%F
```

The double percent signs in %%F tell DOS that F is a variable whose value DOS can change throughout the execution of the batch procedure. DOS first assigns the variable F the value AUTOEXEC.BAT and types its contents. Next, DOS assigns F the value of CONFIG.SYS and displays it. Finally, DOS assigns F the value TEST.BAT and types it, and the batch procedure concludes. As you will see, wildcard characters are valid as set members.

Entering the following example will type all of the BAT files in the current directory:

```
FOR %%F IN (*.BAT) DO TYPE %%F
```

If a member of the set is invalid for the DOS command, DOS simply continues the FOR loop with the next member.

One of the most powerful features DOS provides for batch processing is the ability to pass parameters (values) to a BAT procedure. Consider the following command line:

```
A> BATFILE PARAM1 PARAM2 PARAM3
```

In this case, BATFILE is the BAT file DOS will execute. PARAM1, PARAM2, and PARAM3 are the parameters, or values, you are passing to the batch procedure. DOS sequentially accesses parameters within a batch procedure. In the previous example, DOS assigns the parameters as follows:

%1 contains the first parameter, PARAM1
%2 contains the second parameter, PARAM2
%3 contains the third parameter, PARAM3

DOS supports ten batch parameters (%0 through %9). Previously, you saw the double percent sign used to denote a variable within a batch procedure. In this case, the single percent sign, %, followed by a single digit denotes a parameter or value that the user is passing to the batch procedure. Entering the following batch procedure will display parameters 1-9. If a parameter is not present, ECHO simply ignores its reference:

```
ECHO %1 %2 %3 %4 %5 %6 %7 %8 %9
```

Parameter 0 (%0) is unique in that it contains the name of the batch procedure. Consider a batch file called TIMESET.BAT that contains the following:

```
ECHO %0
DATE
TIME
```

Invoking TIMESET thus results in

```
A> TIMESET

A> ECHO TIMESET
TIMESET

A> DATE
Current date is Thu 10-02-1986
Enter new data (mm-dd-yy):

A> TIME
Current time is 12:02:22.22
Enter new time:

A>
```

Many applications require you to test whether the user has provided a specific parameter. DOS assigns the value NULL to any parameters not referenced by the user. To test for a NULL string, place the parameter within single quotes as follows:

```
IF '%1'=='' GOTO NOPARAM
```

If the parameter %1 does not exist, the DOS substitution results in

```
IF ''=='' GOTO NOPARAM
```

The DOS REN(ame) command does not allow you to rename a file across different drives. If you attempt such an action, the following message will be displayed:

```
A> REN CONFIG.SYS B:CONFIG.SYS
Invalid parameter
```

The following BAT file, DREN (drive rename), renames files across drives by first ensuring that the user has provided the source and destination file names. If both names are present, the procedure checks to see whether a file with the same name as the destination file name already exists. If so, the procedure prompts

```
PAUSE TARGET FILE ALREADY EXISTS
Strike a key to continue ...
```

To continue the rename procedure, simply press a key. If you do not wish to continue, press CTRL-BREAK. If processing continues, DREN copies the source file to the destination specified. DREN then prompts the user to press a key before it deletes the source file, as shown by the following display:

```
IF '%1'=='' GOTO NOPARAM
IF '%2'=='' GOTO NOPARAM
IF EXIST %2 PAUSE TARGET FILE ALREADY EXISTS
COPY %1 %2
PAUSE ABOUT TO DELETE SOURCE FILE
DEL %1
GOTO DONE
:NOPARAM
REM MUST SPECIFY SOURCE AND TARGET FILES
:DONE
```

Entering the following BAT procedure will type all of the files in the set specified by %1:

```
FOR %%F IN (%1) DO TYPE %%F
```

If you name the file T.BAT, you can enter

```
A> T *.*
```

The command displays the contents of all of the files in the current directory.

Enter the command

```
A> T *.BAT
```

You will display the contents of all of the BAT files in the current directory. Enter

```
A> T
```

No files are displayed.

SHIFT

If your application requires more than ten batch parameters, you can use the SHIFT command. The format of SHIFT is

SHIFT

SHIFT simply rotates each parameter to the left one location. In other words, %0 is assigned the value of %1, %1 the value of %2, and so on. This concept is illustrated in Figure 8-2.

If more than ten parameters exist, DOS assigns %9 the value of the next parameter in the list. If you enter the following procedure, DISPLAY.BAT, it displays each of the parameters it receives:

```
:LOOP
SHIFT
IF '%0'=='' GOTO DONE
ECHO %0
GOTO LOOP
:DONE
```

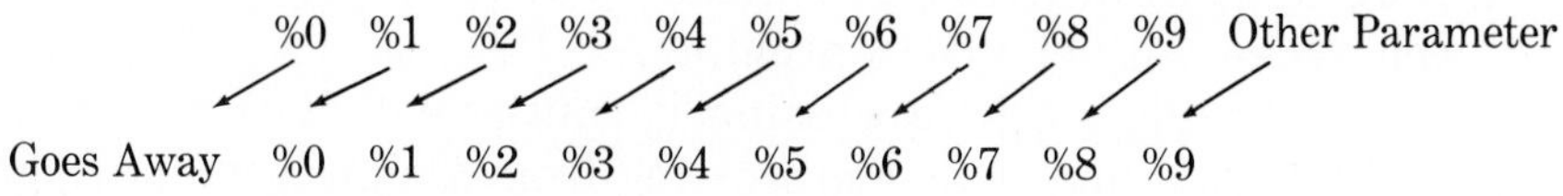

```
%0   %1   %2   %3   %4   %5   %6   %7   %8   %9   Other Parameter
   /   /   /   /   /   /   /   /   /   /
Goes Away   %0   %1   %2   %3   %4   %5   %6   %7   %8   %9
```

Figure 8-2.   Example of SHIFT rotating each parameter one location to the left

You invoke the procedure as

```
A> DISPLAY 1 2 3 4 5 6 7 8 9 10 11
```

AUTOEXEC.BAT

Each time the system boots, DOS examines the root directory for a file named AUTOEXEC.BAT. If the file is found, DOS executes all of the commands it contains. If it does not find the file, DOS issues the DATE and TIME commands.

AUTOEXEC.BAT is no different from other BAT procedures. All of the rules for creating batch procedures must be followed, and all of the batch commands are valid.

Consider the following AUTOEXEC.BAT procedure, which prompts the user for the date and time, clears the screen, and then displays the current DOS version.

```
DATE
TIME
CLS
```

If you are developing an application for users who want to run only your particular system, simply place the reference to your program within AUTOEXEC.BAT. The user will never have to be concerned with the DOS prompt.

Although batch processing is convenient, it is important to perform as much of your processing from a high-level language as possible. DOS BAT files execute slowly because DOS must interpret each command before it executes that command. Thus, BAT files are not meant to be used in programming language.

Review

1. How does batch processing differ from interactive processing?

2. What is the file extension for DOS batch files?

3. Create a batch procedure to clear the screen, display the current DOS version, and prompt the user to set the system time.

4. How does DOS treat batch files that have the same name as DOS commands?

5. List the DOS batch commands.

6. How must you reference a second batch procedure from within a batch procedure if the reference is not the last statement in the file?

7. Create the AUTOEXEC.BAT file that sets the date and time, invokes CHKDSK to examine the disk, and finally displays the current DOS version number.

8. Create a batch procedure that displays all of the .BAT files in the current directory. How can %1 be used to enhance the procedure's usefulness?

9. Write a batch procedure that compares the file name passed by the user in %1 to CONFIG.SYS. If the file name is equal to CONFIG.SYS, display its contents.

10. Write a batch procedure that simply displays the name of the batch procedure.

DOS: The Complete Reference

Answers

1. *How does batch processing differ from interactive processing?*

Interactive processing is processing in which the user is in constant interaction with the computer. At the system prompt, the user enters a command the computer is to perform, waits for the command to finish, and then issues a subsequent command.

Batch processing is processing in which the computer obtains commands from a file on disk, as opposed to receiving those commands from a user at a keyboard. The file contains a list of one or more commands that DOS executes sequentially.

2. *What is the file extension for DOS batch files?*

The DOS extension for batch procedures is BAT.

3. *Create a batch procedure to clear the screen, display the current DOS version, and prompt the user to set the system time.*

```
CLS
VER
TIME
```

4. *How does DOS treat batch files that have the same name as DOS commands?*

DOS will not find BAT files whose names are the same as DOS commands. In other words, the BAT file will never execute.

5. *List the DOS batch commands.*

```
REM
PAUSE
ECHO
GOTO
IF
FOR
SHIFT
```

6. *How must you reference a second batch procedure from within a batch procedure if the reference is not the last statement in the file?*

If the reference to the second batch procedure is not the last statement in the batch file, you must invoke a second command processor with the statement COMMAND/C, as in

    COMMAND/C SECOND.BAT

7. *Create the AUTOEXEC.BAT file that sets the date and time, invokes CHKDSK to examine the disk, and finally displays the current DOS version number.*

    DATE
    TIME
    CHKDSK
    VER

8. *Create a batch procedure that displays all of the BAT files in the current directory. How can %1 be used to enhance the procedure's usefulness?*

    FOR %%F IN (*.BAT) DO TYPE %%F

    You can use %1 as the member of the set

    FOR %%F IN (%1) DO TYPE %%F

You can now pass the files to display as a parameter.

9. *Write a batch procedure that compares the file name passed by the user in %1 to CONFIG.SYS. If the file name is equal to CONFIG.SYS, display its contents.*

    IF '%1'==CONFIG.SYS TYPE %1

10. *Write a batch procedure that simply displays the name of the batch procedure.*

    ECHO %0

Managing Your Disks

N
I
N
E

Disk Structure
File Allocation Table (FAT)
How Hard Disks Differ from Floppies
FDISK Command
Exploiting DOS Subdirectories Fully
Improving System Performance
VERIFY Command

To get the best performance from your disks, you must have a good understanding of disk structure and DOS disk-access methods. This chapter examines the structure of DOS disks, the impact of various FORMAT qualifiers, disk fragmentation, the DOS FDISK command (which prepares a hard disk for use by DOS), the use of DOS subdirectories to improve your file organization (and system performance), and finally, the DOS VERIFY command.

Disk Structure

The following types of disks have been discussed throughout this reference:

Standard 5 1/4-inch floppy disks

Microfloppy disks

Quad-density disks

Hard disks

In terms of disk structure and access methods, DOS treats all of these disks in the same manner. This simplifies the disk I/O routines that are built into DOS. Although most users will never be required to access disks at the lowest levels supported by DOS, it is important that you have a general understanding of DOS disk structure.

Most of the examples presented in this chapter will center around floppy disks, because they are in common use. It is important to remember, however, that all of the concepts that will be discussed also apply to hard disks.

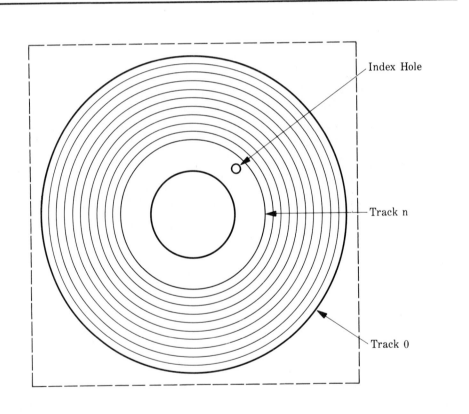

Figure 9-1.   Tracks that make up a disk

Visualize the floppy disk as a record album that you would play on your stereo. The disk is composed of tracks that begin at the center and work their way outward, as illustrated in Figure 9-1. The number of tracks present on the disk depends on the disk type. Standard 5 1/4-inch floppy disks contain 40 tracks, quad-density disks contain 80 tracks, and hard disks can contain several hundred tracks.

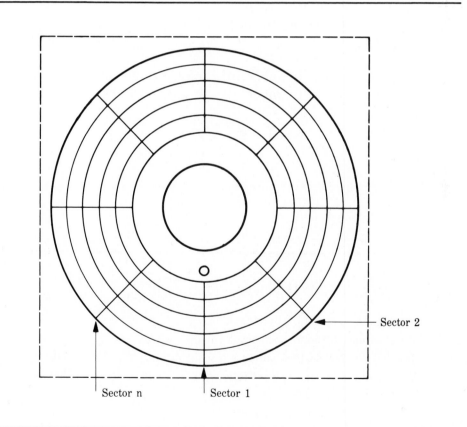

Figure 9-2.   Sectors that make up tracks

Each track on the disk is broken down further into units called sectors, as shown in Figure 9-2. The number of sectors again depends on the disk type. Common configurations include those shown in Table 9-1.

The amount of information that a disk can store depends upon the sector size, which is specified in bytes. Common sector sizes include 128, 256, 512, and 1024 bytes. As previously stated, disks are capable of storing information on both sides. To determine the amount of data a disk can store, use the following equation:

STORAGE = (number__of__sides) * (number__of__tracks) *
(number__of__sectors) * (sector__size)

An example in Chapter 2 showed that a double-sided, double-density disk formats to 368,640 bytes of storage. Consider the following:

STORAGE = (number__of__sides) * (number__of__tracks) *
(number__of__sectors) * (sector__size)

Disk Type	Tracks Per Side	Total Sectors
Single-sided, 8 sectors per track	40	320
Single-sided, 9 sectors per track	40	360
Double-sided, 8 sectors per track	40	640
Double-sided, 9 sectors per track	40	720
Quad-density, 9 sectors per track	80	1440
Quad-density, 15 sectors per track	80	2400

Table 9-1.   Configurations of Disk Types and Sectors

$$STORAGE = (2) * (40) * (9) * (512)$$

$$STORAGE = 368,640 \text{ bytes}$$

Reconsider the qualifiers supported by the DOS FORMAT command:

/1   Single-sided disk format (DOS will only format one side of the disk)

/8   Eight sectors per track format (DOS will only divide the disk into eight sectors per track)

/4   Format a double-sided, double-density disk in a quad-density disk drive

/B   Allocate space for the system files required to boot DOS, but do not place the files on the disk

/S   Allocate space for the system files required to boot DOS, and place the files on the disk

/V   Prompt the user for a volume label

The DOS FORMAT command defines the structure of each DOS disk. During formatting, DOS allocates sectors for the following:

Boot record

File allocation table (FAT)

Root directory entries

Data sectors

As you can see in Figure 9-3 (and will see in Chapter 14), each DOS disk contains a boot record in sector 1, side 0, track 0. The purposes of the boot record are to start the DOS boot process and to define the disk media characteristics. Examine the boot record shown in Figure 9-4.

The file allocation table (FAT) is simply a table that DOS uses to record disk sectors that are currently being used to store files, sectors that are available for file allocation, and, lastly, sectors

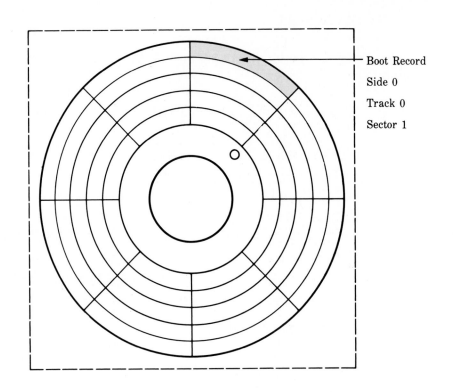

Boot Record
Side 0
Track 0
Sector 1

Figure 9-3.   Boot record in DOS

that are unusable because of media corruption. Each DOS disk contains two FATs. This prevents a single disk corruption from rendering the disk unusable. If one of the tables goes bad, a backup FAT always is available, although it is usually transparent to the user. Before seeing how the FAT tracks used and unused sectors, you will examine the basic unit of disk space allocation — the disk cluster.

Each time a DOS file grows, DOS must allocate space on the disk for the file. A simple method of space allocation would be for

8086 JMP instruction
IBM or Microsoft name and version number
Bytes per disk sector
Sectors per cluster
Number of reserved sectors
Max root directory entries
Total sectors
Media description
Number of sectors per file allocation table
Sectors per track
Number of disk heads
Number of hidden sectors
Bootstrap program

Figure 9-4.   Example boot record

DOS to allocate disk space a sector at a time as space is needed. Although this has some advantages that will be discussed later, it quickly leads to disk fragmentation.

Disk Fragmentation

Disk fragmentation occurs when several files on the disk are contained in sectors that are disbursed all around the disk (see Figure 9-5). Consider the file shown in Figure 9-6. The disk read/

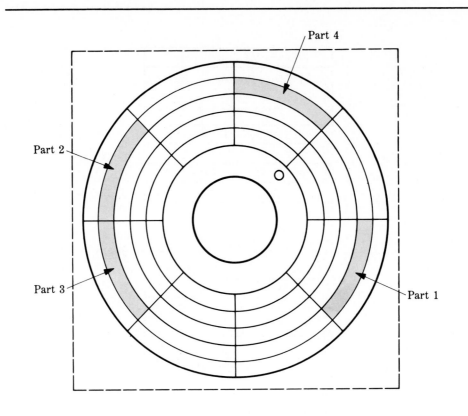

Figure 9-5.   Example of disk fragmentation

write head reads the sector that contains the first part of the file. Since the sectors are contiguous, the drive can read parts 2, 3, and 4 of the file in half a revolution of the disk. In the case of the fragmented disk shown in Figure 9-7, the disk drive will first read part 1 of the file and must rotate the disk half a revolution before reading part 2 (see Figure 9-8). To read part 3, the drive must rotate the disk almost a full revolution (see Figure 9-9).

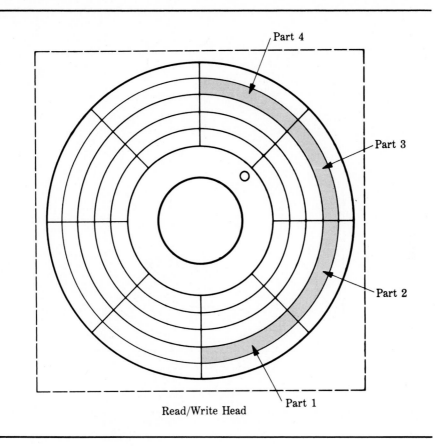

Figure 9-6. Sample file

Finally, a quarter-revolution of the disk allows the drive to read part 4. In this case, a small file required four times as many disk rotations when fragmented as the contiguous file.

Compared to the electronic speed of the computer, mechanical disk drives are slow. Excess disk rotations caused by disk fragmentation can be costly in terms of system performance. To minimize the possibility of disk fragmentation, DOS allocates disk

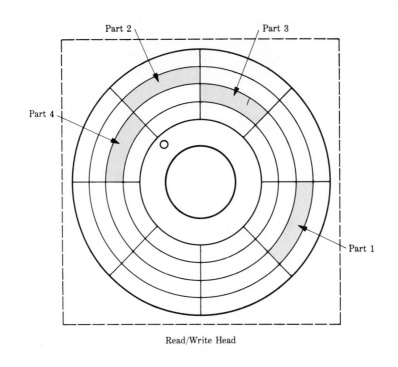

Part 2

Part 3

Part 4

Part 1

Read/Write Head

Figure 9-7.   Fragmented disk

space via clusters. A *cluster* is a set of contiguous disk sectors. The number of sectors per cluster is dependent on disk type (see Table 9-2).

The only drawback to allocating disk space via clusters occurs when each of your files requires only one sector and your cluster size is 2. In this case, each file would have one sector of wasted space, as shown in Figure 9-10.

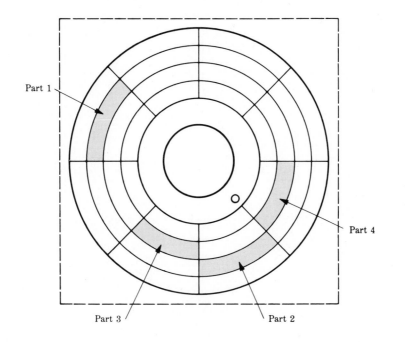

Figure 9-8.   Half of a revolution necessary to read part 2

If you are concerned about disk fragmentation (and you should be), the DOS CHKDSK command will report on specific files or on the entire disk. Once your disk becomes fragmented, you must back up the disk to a floppy disk via the DOS BACKUP command and then restore the files using the DOS RESTORE command. Chapter 11 provides a batch file to aid in this process.

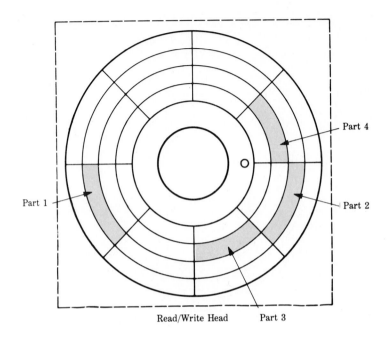

Figure 9-9.   Full revolution necessary to read part 3

Disk Type	Sectors Per Cluster
Single-sided, 8 sectors per track	1
Single-sided, 9 sectors per track	2
Double-sided, 8 sectors per track	1
Double-sided, 9 sectors per track	2
Quad-density, 8 sectors per track	2
Quad-density, 9 sectors per track	1
Fixed-disk, 9 sectors per track	4

Table 9-2.   Number of Sectors Per Cluster

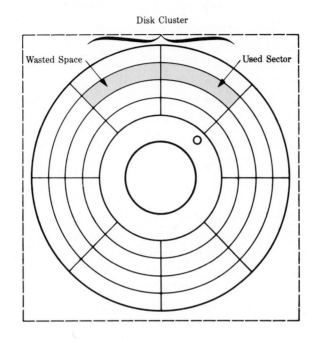

Disk Cluster

Wasted Space

Used Sector

Figure 9-10.   One sector of wasted space

File Allocation Table (FAT)

The FAT provides DOS with a list of used, available, and corrupted disk sectors. The table contains one entry for each cluster on the disk. As previously discussed, DOS allocates disk space in clusters. Table 9-3 provides the number of clusters of data space available on each DOS disk. The file allocation table for a double-sided, double-density disk with two sectors per cluster will have the status classifications shown in Table 9-4.

DOS uses cluster entries 0 and 1 for disk media identification. As you will see, DOS maintains a directory entry for each

Disk Type	Number of Data Clusters
Single-sided, 8 sectors per track	323
Single-sided, 9 sectors per track	630
Double-sided, 8 sectors per track	351
Double-sided, 9 sectors per track	708
Quad-density, 9 sectors per track	1422
Quad-density, 15 sectors per track	2371

Table 9-3.   Number of Clusters of Data Space Available

file on the disk. One of the fields in the directory entry is a pointer to the first cluster of the file. Given the disk shown in Figure 9-11, the file allocation table entry for the file would be that shown in Table 9-5.

DOS uses the hex value FFF to mark the end of a file. If the DOS FORMAT command finds corruptions on the disk, it places the hex value FF7 in the file FAT entry for the cluster containing the corruption. This prevents DOS from trying to use the bad area on the disk (see Figure 9-12).

Cluster Number	Status
2	3
3	FFF
4	FF7
.	.
.	.
.	.
354	0
355	0

Table 9-4.   Status Classifications on Double-Sided, Double-Density Disks

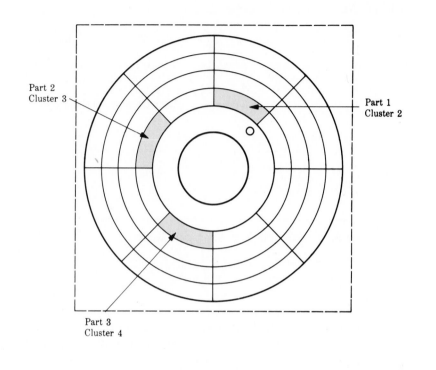

Figure 9-11. Clusters in sample disk

Each time DOS needs to allocate space for a file, it searches the FAT for unused disk clusters. DOS attempts to minimize disk fragmentation through its choice of clusters for each file. As previously stated, each DOS disk contains root directory sectors. Table 9-6 specifies the number of disk sectors DOS allocates disk space for in root directory entries for each disk drive type. Each file on the disk has an entry in a directory structure. The entry is a 32-bit record that contains the information shown in Table 9-7.

Chapter 6 discussed how the root directories on different types of disks are restricted to a specific number of files. If you consider the amount of disk space that DOS allocates for directory

Cluster Number	Status	
0		⎱ ← Disk Format Information
1		⎰
2	3	⎱ ← Next Cluster
3	4	⎰
4	FFF	← Last Cluster in the File
.	.	
.	.	
.	.	
355	0	

Table 9-5.   Example File Allocation Table

entries and the length of each directory entry (32 bytes), the following equation will determine the maximum number of files that DOS can store in the root:

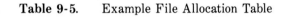

MAX_FILES = (sector_size) * (number_directory_sectors) / 32

Disk Type	Directory Entries
Single-sided	64
Double-sided	112
Quad-density	224
Hard disk	512

Table 9-6.   Disk Sectors in Root Directory

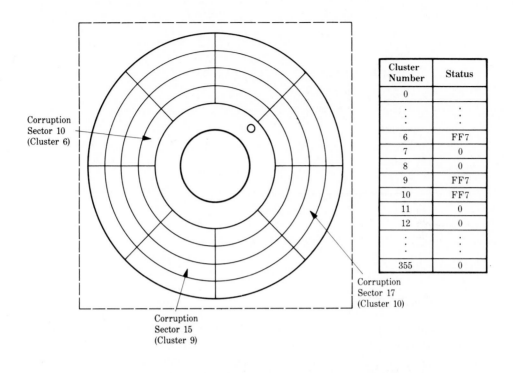

Cluster Number	Status
0	
⋮	⋮
6	FF7
7	0
8	0
9	FF7
10	FF7
11	0
12	0
⋮	⋮
355	0

Corruption
Sector 10
(Cluster 6)

Corruption
Sector 17
(Cluster 10)

Corruption
Sector 15
(Cluster 9)

Figure 9-12.   FAT preventing DOS from using a bad area on disk

For a double-sided, double-density disk, the maximum number of files in the root is

MAX__FILES = (512) * (4) / 32
MAX__FILES = 64

It is important to note that DOS only allocates disk space for directory entries in the root directory. To DOS, a subdirectory is simply a standard DOS file whose contents contain directory entries. DOS stores each subdirectory file in the disk data space described in the next section. Since DOS does not specifically allocate space for subdirectories, those subdirectories can contain an unlimited number of files.

Field	Offset
File name	0
Extension	8
Attribute byte	11
Reserved for DOS	12
Time	22
Date	24
Starting cluster number	26
File size	28

Table 9-7. Entry in Directory Structure

Data Space

The majority of a DOS disk is taken up by clusters that contain data. The data stored in this section of the disk can be programs, text, or data (database files, subdirectories, and so forth). Each time DOS creates or extends a file, it allocates clusters contained in the data space. The number of sectors that DOS allocates depends on the number of sectors per cluster for the disk type. Remember, the basic unit of file allocation is a disk cluster.

How Hard Disks Differ from Floppies

Thus far, all of the information presented in this chapter applies to fixed and floppy disks. This section examines the characteristics that make hard disks unique. First, most floppy disks store data on two sides only, as illustrated in Figure 9-13. Hard disks, however, can be composed of multiple disks called *platters*. Most

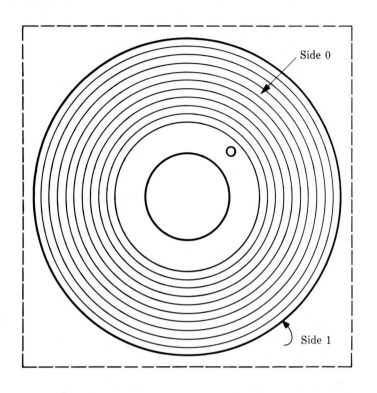

Figure 9-13.   Storage by floppy on two sides of disk

microcomputer hard disks use two platters that give each hard disk four sides on which to record information (see Figure 9-14). Floppy disks use tracks as a method of organizing information, as shown in Figure 9-15. Hard disks, on the other hand, combine tracks on multiple platters to form cylinders, as shown in Figure 9-16.

    One of the best features of hard disks is that one disk can hold multiple operating systems. For example, some computer users

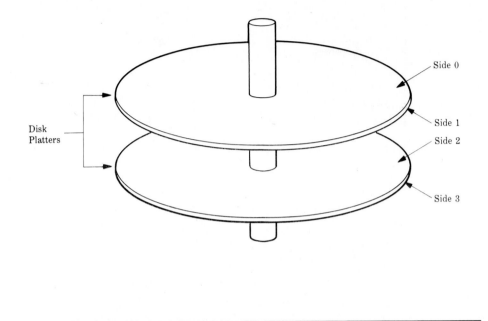

Figure 9-14. Two platters of hard disk

have DOS and possibly XENIX and CP/M. The DOS FDISK command allows you to partition the disk into separate areas for each operating system. In this case, you can have a disk with a single partition containing DOS (see Figure 9-17). You can also have a hard disk with any combination of the operating systems, as shown in Figure 9-18. Last, you can have a disk that contains all three, as shown in Figure 9-19.

As you will see, you can partition a fixed disk into a maximum of four partitions. The DOS FDISK command provides you with access to each of the disk sections.

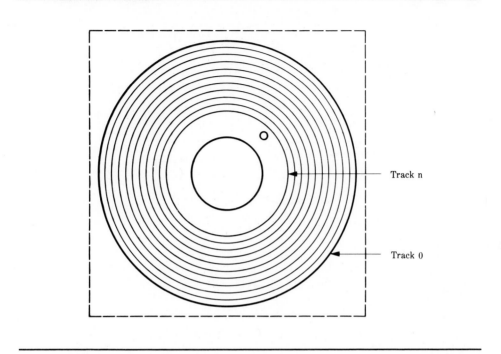

Track n

Track 0

Figure 9-15.   Tracks used by floppy disks

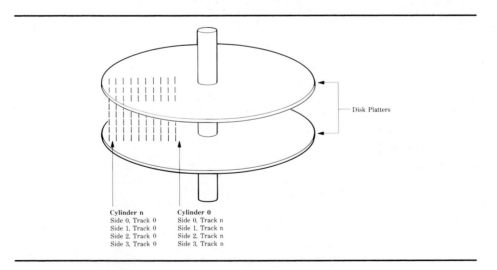

Disk Platters

Cylinder n
Side 0, Track 0
Side 1, Track 0
Side 2, Track 0
Side 3, Track 0

Cylinder 0
Side 0, Track n
Side 1, Track n
Side 2, Track n
Side 3, Track n

Figure 9-16.   Cylinders on hard disk

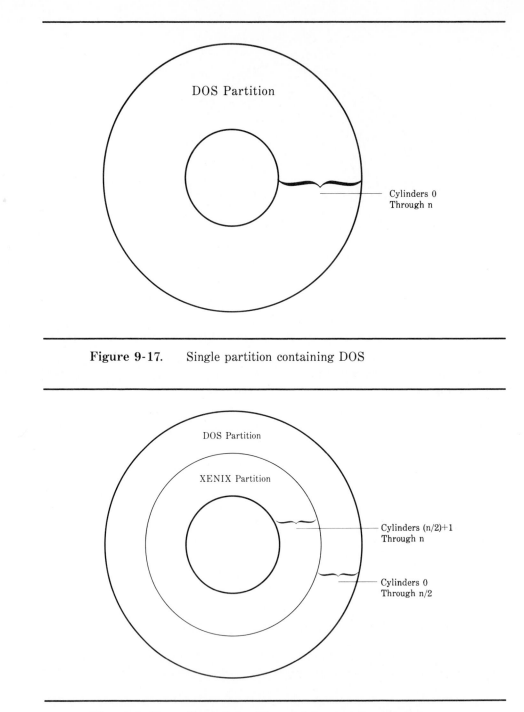

Figure 9-17. Single partition containing DOS

Figure 9-18. Hard disk with multiple operating systems

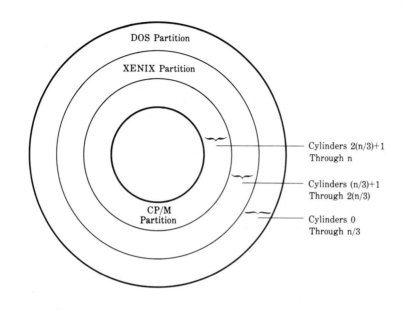

Figure 9-19. Hard disk containing all three sample operating systems

FDISK Command

Most computers are shipped from the manufacturer with the disk formatted with a single DOS partition. If your disk is not so formatted, or if you want to partition your disk, you must use the DOS FDISK command. Once you partition the disk, you must format each disk partition with the operating system you desire. (Note that users should exercise caution when using FDISK.) The format of the DOS FDISK command is

FDISK

FDISK will respond with the following menu:

```
IBM Personal Computer
Fixed Disk Setup Program Version 3.00
(C)Copyright IBM Corp. 1983,1984

FDISK Options


Choose one of the following:

     1. Create DOS partition
     2. Change Active partition
     3. Delete DOS partition
     4. Display Partition data
     5. Select Next Fixed Disk Drive

Enter choice: [1]


Press Esc to return to DOS
```

Creating a DOS Partition

As previously stated, you can divide your fixed disk into one to four disk sections called partitions. Before your hard disk can be used by DOS, you must create a DOS partition. To do so, select option 1 from the FDISK main menu. FDISK will respond with

```
Create DOS Partition

Current Fixed Disk Drive: 1


Do you wish to use the entire fixed disk
for DOS (Y/N).....................? [Y]
```

If DOS is the only operating system that you will ever use, you will probably want to allocate the entire disk as a single partition.

If so, simply press ENTER at the prompt, and FDISK will respond with

```
System will now restart
Insert DOS diskette in drive A:
Press any key when ready . . .
```

Place your DOS system disk in drive A and press any key to continue. If you want to cancel the operation, press CTRL-BREAK. DOS will reboot and prompt you for the system date and time. Once DOS reboots, the disk partition exists. You must now use the DOS FORMAT command to format the hard disk.

```
A> FORMAT C:/S
```

If you intend to use more than DOS on the disk, and you desire multiple disk partitions, press N to the prompt, as shown here:

```
Create DOS Partition

Current Fixed Disk Drive: 1


Do you wish to use the entire fixed disk
for DOS (Y/N).....................? [N]
```

FDISK will respond with

```
Total fixed disk space is nnnn cylinders
Maximum available space is nnnn
cylinders at nnnn.

Enter partition size.............: [nnnn]
```

FDISK tells you the total space on the disk and the maximum space available on the disk, both in cylinders. If you want to use all of the available space, simply press the ENTER key. Otherwise, type in the number of cylinders that you want to allocate for the disk partition. FDISK will respond with

```
Enter starting cylinder number..: [nnnn]
```

Normally, you will simply press ENTER and start the new partition at the cylinder specified. Again, this partition must be formatted before it is usable.

Changing the Active Disk Partition

Remember, your hard disk can have up to four disk partitions. Only one partition can be active at any given time. The active partition is the partition that receives control or is accessible each time the computer boots. To change the active partition, select option 2 from the FDISK main menu. FDISK will respond with

```
Change Active Partition

Current Fixed Disk Drive: 1

Partition  Status     Type    Start  End  Size
    1         A        DOS      000   299  300
    2         N      non-DOS    300   614  315

Total disk space is 615 cylinders

Enter the number of the partition you
want to make active...................: [ ]
```

In this case, FDISK is telling you that the first partition is the active partition. In addition, FDISK provides you with the information shown in Table 9-8. FDISK prompts you for the number of the partition that you want to make active. Simply type in the partition number and press ENTER.

DOS: The Complete Reference

On Screen	Information
Partition	A number assigned to each disk partition (1-4)
Status	A active partition N inactive partition
Type	(DOS) partition bootable only if the system files are present (non-DOS) partition containing an operating system other than DOS
Start	Starting cylinder number for the partition
End	Ending cylinder number for the partition
Size	Number of cylinders in the partition (End − Start + 1)
Total disk space	In cylinders

Table 9-8.   Information Provided by FDISK Command

Deleting a Disk Partition

If you want to delete a partition that you have created previously via FDISK, select the FDISK main menu option 3. For example, suppose your hard disk is partitioned as

```
Display Partition Information

Current Fixed Disk Drive: 1

Partition Status    Type    Start End Size
    1        A      DOS      000  299 300
    2        N      non-DOS  300  614 315

Total disk space is 615 cylinders
```

Also suppose that you want to delete partition 2. First, select option 2 from the FDISK main menu and set partition 2 as the active partition. (Note that you may have to refer to the documentation that accompanied the operating system used to create the non-DOS partition.) Next, select FDISK option 3 and delete the partition.

```
Delete DOS Partition

Current Fixed Disk Drive: 1

Partition Status    Type    Start End Size
    1         N       DOS     000   299   300
    2         A     non-DOS   300   614   315

Total disk space is 615 cylinders
```

FDISK will display

```
Warning! Data in the DOS partition
will be lost.  Do you wish to
continue........................? [N]


Press Esc to return to FDISK Options
```

If you press Y and then press ENTER, the space allocated to the partition will be released for use by another partition. Remember, all of the data contained in the partition will be destroyed. If you do not want to delete the partition, simply press ENTER, and FDISK will leave the partition intact.

Displaying Partition Information

If you simply want to display information about your disk partitions, select option 4 from the FDISK main menu. FDISK will display

```
Display Partition Information

Current Fixed Disk Drive: 1

Partition Status    Type    Start End Size
     1        A      DOS     000  299 300
     2        N    non-DOS   300  614 315

Total disk space is 615 cylinders
```

Again, FDISK will display the information shown in Table 9-8.

Selecting the Next Hard Disk

If you have multiple hard disks, FDISK main menu option 5 allows you to configure each disk. When the disks are configured, you must format each disk partition.

Exiting to DOS

If you do not want to perform any FDISK operations, or if you have finished your disk configuration, simply press the ESC key (Figure 9-20 shows the location of this key). FDISK will return control to DOS.

Exploiting DOS Subdirectories Fully

As stated in Chapter 6, the main function of DOS subdirectories is to enhance your disk organization. If you have just partitioned and formatted your disk, your root directory should contain the DOS hidden system files only, along with the COMMAND.COM file. With the exception of the files AUTOEXEC.BAT (discussed in Chapter 8) and CONFIG.SYS (discussed in Chapter 15), you should not add any other files to the root directory. Place all of your files into DOS subdirectories; this will improve your disk

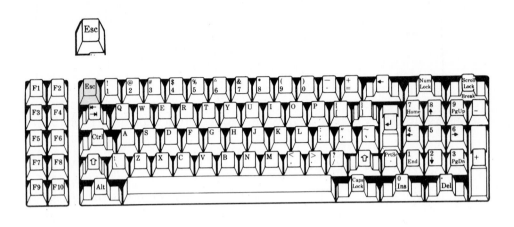

Figure 9-20. Location of ESC key

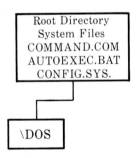

Figure 9-21. \DOS subdirectory

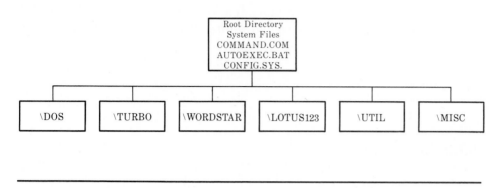

Figure 9-22.   Adding subdirectories for other programs

organization tremendously. First, create a subdirectory for your DOS system files on your hard disk. Many UNIX users call this subdirectory \BIN, for binary system files. You may also use the name \DOS, as shown in Figure 9-21. If you want to add other programs to your disk, create the appropriate subdirectories, as illustrated in Figure 9-22.

Improving System Performance

Many DOS commands require directory searches for a specific DOS file. The DOS PATH command specifies the series of drives and subdirectory paths that DOS examines in search of a command each time the command is not found in the current working directory. Consider the following PATH command:

```
A> PATH \UTIL;\MISC;\BUDGET
```

If the subdirectories \MISC and \UTIL contain a large number of files, DOS must examine each directory entry for the command until it finds it. Therefore, you should always position the directories most likely to contain the executable files early in the specified path. If two directories are equally likely to contain the command, place the directory that contains fewer files first in the path command. Likewise, minimizing the number of files in a directory by creating additional subdirectories will decrease the number of subdirectory entries DOS must examine in search of files.

VERIFY Command

Each time DOS reads or writes data to or from disk, it uses disk sectors. For example, issue the command

`A> COPY SOURCE.DAT TARGET.DAT`

DOS will read a disk sector from the file SOURCE.DAT and then write the sector to the file TARGET.DAT. DOS continues this process until it has read and written all of the sectors contained in the file SOURCE.DAT. This process is shown in Figure 9-23.

Although unlikely, a serious problem can occur during the writing of the disk sector that will leave the contents of the files SOURCE.DAT and TARGET.DAT different. DOS will not recognize the error unless you have turned on disk verification by entering

`A> VERIFY ON`

Each time DOS reads a disk sector from the file SOURCE.DAT, it places the sector into a disk buffer in memory (see Figure 9-24). DOS then writes the contents of the disk buffer to a sector on the disk containing the file TARGET.DAT, as illustrated in Figure 9-25. It is possible, however, for DOS to encounter errors when it writes the sector to disk. Normally this is the result of a hardware malfunction. If this occurs, the file TARGET.DAT will not have the same contents as the file SOURCE.DAT. By default, DOS will not check for this error. Suppose, however, you issue the command

`A> VERIFY ON`

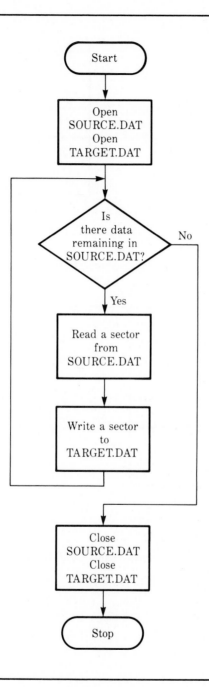

Figure 9-23. Process of DOS reading and writing sectors

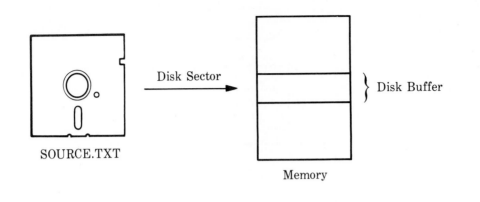

Figure 9-24. Dos placing sector into disk buffer in memory

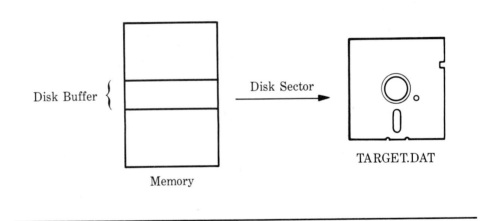

Figure 9-25. DOS writing contents of buffer to target sector

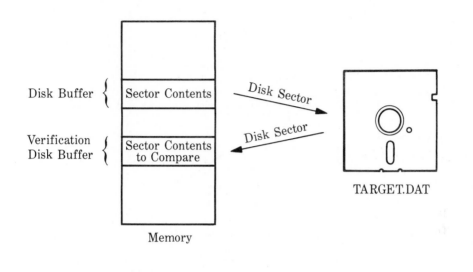

Figure 9-26. DOS verifying that target and source sectors are the same

DOS will reread each disk sector it writes to verify that the disk sector written is identical to the contents of the disk buffer in memory, as seen in Figure 9-26. If the contents differ, DOS is now capable of recognizing the error. This process is shown in Figure 9-27.

The DOS VERIFY command will be discussed further in Chapter 10 and disk buffers in Chapter 15. For now, it is only important that you understand that both deal with disk sectors.

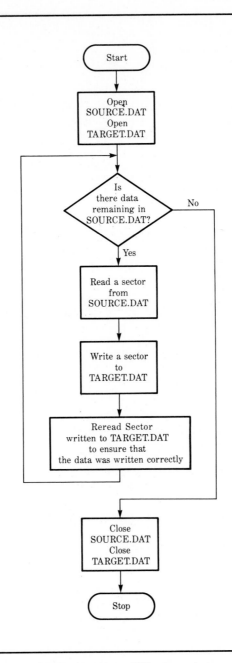

Figure 9-27. DOS recognizes differences between source and target sectors

1. Label the following:

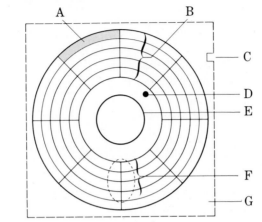

2. List the four items for which DOS allocates space on the disk.

3. Determine the storage space available (in bytes) for a double-sided disk with eight sectors per track and 512-byte sectors.

4. What is the boot record?

5. What is the DOS unit of disk space allocation?

6. What is disk fragmentation?

7. What is the FAT?

8. How does DOS track corrupted sectors on the disk?

9. Why can a double-sided disk store only 112 files in the root directory?

10. What is a disk partition?

11. What files should reside in your root directory?

12. What is the function of the DOS VERIFY command?

13. What is the maximum number of directory entries in a DOS subdirectory?

Answers

1. *Label the following*:

    A. Disk sector
    B. Disk tracks
    C. Write-protect notch
    D. Index timing hole
    E. Disk rotation hub
    F. Read/write opening
    G. Diskette envelope

2. *List the four items for which DOS allocates space on the disk.*

    boot record
    file allocation table
    root directory
    data space

3. *Determine the storage space available (in bytes) for a double-sided disk with eight sectors per track and 512-byte sectors.*

STORAGE = (number_of_sides) * (number_of_tracks) * (number_of_sectors) * (sector_size)

STORAGE = (2) * (40) * (8) * (512)

STORAGE = 368,640 bytes

4. *What is the boot record?*

Every DOS disk has a boot record in the first sector of the disk. The purpose of the boot record is to start the DOS boot process and, in addition, define the disk media characteristics for that specific disk. Nonbootable disks have boot records that contain the program required to display an error message that states that the disk is not bootable. For more specifics on the DOS boot record, refer to Chapter 14.

5. *What is the DOS unit of disk space allocation?*

DOS uses the cluster as its unit of disk space allocation. A cluster can contain one or more disk sectors.

6. *What is disk fragmentation?*

Disk fragmentation occurs when several files on the disk are contained in sectors that are disbursed all around the disk. The more disbursed the sectors are, the longer the period of time required to read the disk, since the disk must be rotated continuously to find the next sector.

7. *What is the FAT?*

The FAT is the file allocation table, which tracks which disk sectors are used currently to store files, available to store files, and unusable media corruptions.

8. *How does DOS track corrupted sectors on the disk?*

DOS marks each corrupted sector (that is, it marks the cluster containing the sector) as unusable in the file allocation table. Each time DOS needs to allocate disk space for a file, it searches the FAT for available clusters. Since the corrupted sectors have been marked unusable in the FAT by the DOS FORMAT command, DOS leaves the sectors unused.

9. *Why can a double-sided disk store only 112 files in the root directory?*

For double-sides disks, DOS allocates seven sectors for root directory entries. Each sector is 512 bytes long, and each directory entry requires 32 bytes.

MAX_FILES = (sector_size) * (directory_sectors) / 32

MAX_FILES = 512 * 7 / 32

MAX_FILES = 112

10. *What is a disk partition?*

Fixed disks can be organized into one to four distinct sections. This partitioning allows you to place more than one operating system on a disk. The DOS FDISK command performs disk partitioning.

11. *What files should reside in your root directory?*

The files in your root directory should be the DOS hidden system files, the file COMMAND.COM, and the optional files AUTOEXEC.BAT and CONFIG.SYS. The remainder of your files should be in subdirectories.

12. *What is the function of the DOS VERIFY command?*

The DOS VERIFY command ensures that each sector DOS writes to disk is written correctly. By default, DOS does not reread each sector it writes to disk to ensure the data was recorded correctly. Use of the VERIFY command is a trade-off between the overhead of the additional disk read versus the insurance of a correct disk write operation. The only time to use this command is usually during system backups because of the unlikeliness of disk write errors.

13. *What is the maximum number of directory entries in a DOS subdirectory?*

DOS does not restrict the number of entries in a subdirectory. DOS treats each subdirectory as a file and does not allocate a fixed amount of disk space for it. The fixed space allocation is the factor that restricts the number of entries in the root directory. Since subdirectories are simply DOS files, they can continue to grow as long as adequate disk space remains.

Advanced DOS Commands

APPEND (Specify a Search Path for Data Files)
ASSIGN (Assign a Drive Letter to Another Drive)
ATTRIB (Set a File's Read-only or Backup Attributes)
COMMAND (Invoke a Command Processor)
CTTY (Modify the Command Device)
EXE2BIN (Convert an EXE File to a COM File)
EXIT (Exit from a Secondary Command Processor)
JOIN (Join a Disk Drive to a DOS Path)
RECOVER (Recover a File or Disk Containing Bad Sectors)
REPLACE (Update Previous Versions of Files)
SET (Set an Environment String)
SHARE (Support File Sharing)
SUBST (Substitute a DOS Path with a Drive Letter)
SYS (Place Operating System on Disk)
VERIFY (Verify That Disk Output is Written Correctly)
XCOPY (Copy Files and Directories to a New Disk)
DOS Editing Keys

Chapters 1 through 9 examined several of the DOS commands. Most of these commands have been grouped by function (printer commands, directory commands, and so forth). This chapter presents the majority of the remaining DOS commands. Because the functions of these commands are diverse, they are grouped under the classification of "Advanced DOS commands." The commands presented in this chapter are

APPEND
ASSIGN
ATTRIB
COMMAND
CTTY
EXE2BIN
EXIT
JOIN
RECOVER
REPLACE
SET
SHARE
SUBST
SYS
VERIFY
XCOPY

In addition, the DOS command editing keys will be discussed.

APPEND (Specify a Search Path for Data Files)

The MS-DOS version 3.2 APPEND command is similar to the PATH command, which was presented in Chapter 6. APPEND defines the series of subdirectory paths that DOS should search each time it opens a data file. The format of the APPEND command is

[drive:][path]APPEND [d:][p][;[d:][p]...]

or

[drive:][path]APPEND ;

where the following is true:

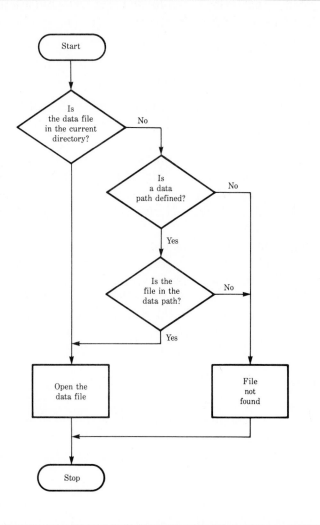

Figure 10-1.   Process of DOS searching a data path for a file

drive: is the disk drive containing the file APPEND.COM.

APPEND is an external DOS command; therefore, DOS must read the command from disk into memory each time the command is invoked. If you do not specify a disk drive, DOS will use the default drive.

path is the series of subdirectories DOS must traverse to find the file APPEND.COM. If you do not specify a path, DOS uses the current working directory.

d: is the name of a disk drive to include in the path DOS is to traverse to find data files.

p is a subdirectory path to include in the path DOS is to traverse to find data files.

Each time DOS attempts to open a file, it first checks to see if it can open the file as specified. If the file is found, DOS will open it. If DOS does not find the file, it will check to see if you have defined a data file path. If you have, DOS will start at the first entry in the data file path and begin searching for the file. DOS will continue to search for the file with each entry in the data file search path until either the file is found or the data path is exhausted. This process is shown in Figure 10-1. To determine if a file is in the data path, use the flowchart shown in Figure 10-2. Note that if two entries in the data file path contain a file with the specified name, DOS will find only the first reference.

Consider the following examples. Enter

```
A> APPEND A:;B:;C:
```

If DOS does not find the data file as specified, it will search drives A, B, and C (in order) for the specified data file. This process is shown in Figure 10-3. Enter

```
A> APPEND C:\DOS;C:\REPORTS
```

If DOS does not find the data file as specified, it will examine the subdirectories \DOS and \REPORTS on drive C. Enter

```
A> APPEND ;
```

The command removes the current data file path. DOS will not search any other locations for the data file if it does not find it as specified. Enter

```
A> APPEND
```

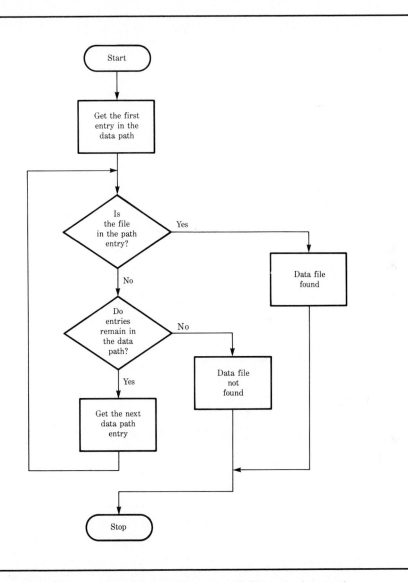

Figure 10-2. Flowchart to determine if file is in data path

If you invoke APPEND without any parameters, DOS will display the current data file path. It is important to note that the DOS APPEND command adds overhead each time DOS opens a file. If you intend to use the APPEND command, you will

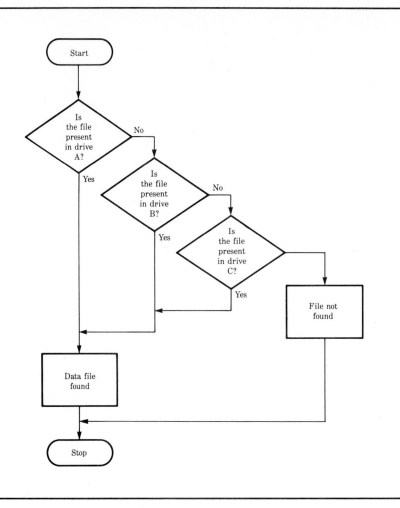

Figure 10-3. Process of searching drives for data file

improve your system performance by placing the directories most likely to contain the file early in the specified data file path. In addition, if the directories in the data file path contain many files, DOS will have to examine each one to see if it matches the file requested.

If you are using the DOS ASSIGN command presented in the next section, you must issue the APPEND command first. Some

DOS users choose to place the APPEND command in their AUTOEXEC.BAT file. This specifies the data file path to DOS each time the system boots.

ASSIGN (Assign a Drive Letter to Another Drive)

The DOS ASSIGN command allows you to assign a disk drive letter to another drive. If you have an application program that uses only drives A and B, the DOS ASSIGN command allows you to place the data on your hard disk (drive C) and then reassign drive A or B to point to drive C. The format of the DOS ASSIGN command is

[drive:][path]ASSIGN [d1=d2...]

where the following is true:

drive: is the disk drive containing the file ASSIGN.COM. ASSIGN is an external DOS command; therefore, DOS must read the command from disk into memory each time the command is invoked. If you do not specify a disk drive, DOS will use the default drive.

path is the series of subdirectories DOS must traverse to find the file ASSIGN.COM. If you do not specify a path, DOS will use the working directory.

d1 is the drive away from which disk references are directed.

d2 is the drive to which all references to drive d1 will be directed.

Consider the following examples. Enter

```
A> ASSIGN A=C
```

DOS will route all references to drive A to drive C. References to drive C will remain unchanged. Enter

```
A> ASSIGN A=C B=C
```

DOS will route references to either disk A or B to drive C. Invoke ASSIGN without any parameters, as follows:

```
A> ASSIGN
```

DOS will delete all disk reassignments. Do not use the ASSIGN command with the DOS BACKUP and PRINT commands. Doing so may produce unexpected results. The DOS FORMAT and DISKCOPY commands ignore drive assignments made via ASSIGN.

ATTRIB (Set a File's Read-only or Backup Attributes)

The DOS ATTRIB command allows you to prevent DOS from modifying or deleting a file. The format of the DOS ATTRIB command is

[drive:][path]ATTRIB [± r] [± a] file —spec

where the following is true:

drive: is the disk drive containing the file ATTRIB.COM. ATTRIB is an external DOS command; therefore, DOS must read the command from disk into memory each time the command is invoked. If you do not specify a disk drive, DOS will use the default drive.

path is the series of subdirectories DOS must traverse to find the file ATTRIB.COM. If you do not specify a path, DOS will use the current working directory.

+r sets a file to read-only

−r sets a file to read and write access

$+a$ sets a file as needing to be backed up

$-a$ sets a file as backed up

(Note: The qualifiers +a and −a are only available with DOS version 3.2.)

file—spec is the name of the file whose attributes are to be modifed. ATTRIB supports the DOS wildcard characters. Chapter 16 contains a complete discussion of file attributes.

Consider the following examples. Enter

```
A> ATTRIB +R *.COM
```

ATTRIB will set all of the files with the extension COM to read-only. This prevents the files from being deleted, renamed, or copied over. If you attempt to modify a file that has been marked read-only, DOS will display

```
Access denied
```

Consider the command

```
A> ATTRIB +R B:\BUDGET\JULY.RPT
```

In this example, ATTRIB will set the file JULY.RPT in the subdirectory B:\BUDGET to read-only. Suppose you enter

```
A> ATTRIB -R C:\OLDDATA\JULY.RPT
```

ATTRIB will set the file JULY.RPT in the subdirectory C:\OLDDATA to read/write attributes. This allows DOS to modify, rename, or delete the file.

Suppose you enter

```
A> ATTRIB +A *.*
```

ATTRIB will mark all of the files in the current directory as requiring backups. This qualifier requires DOS version 3.2.

The following command modifies the archive bit. Suppose you issue the ATTRIB command without any parameters, as in

```
A> ATTRIB FILENAME.EXT
```

ATTRIB will display the current attributes of a file. Issue the command

```
A> ATTRIB *.*
```

The attributes of all files are listed.

If you want a list of the files that are marked read-only, use the following command line and note the display:

```
A> ATTRIB *.* ¦ FIND "R        "
R        A:\ATTRIB.EXE
R        A:\FIND.EXE
R        A:\JOIN.EXE
R        A:\REPLACE.EXE
R        A:\SHARE.EXE
R        A:\SORT.EXE
R        A:\SUBST.EXE
R        A:\XCOPY.EXE

A>
```

This is one example of a "pipe" (see Chapter 7).

If ATTRIB cannot find the specified file, it will display

```
A> ATTRIB FILENAME.EXT
Invalid path or file not found
```

If the qualifier you specify is invalid, ATTRIB will display

```
A> ATTRIB +C FILENAME.EXT
Syntax error
```

It is a good idea to make files used in your application programs read-only. This prevents the end user from deleting or modifying the files accidentally. Chapter 16 will examine a Turbo Pascal procedure that sets a file's attributes. This allows your application program to set the file to read or write access when the program begins, use the file, and then set the file back to read-only when the program has been executed.

In addition to the ATTRIB command, the DOS commands BACKUP, RESTORE (see Chapter 11), and XCOPY (version 3.2) all use the file archive bit. As you will see, this bit explains how BACKUP knows that it should perform a backup on only those files that have been modified since the last backup.

COMMAND (Invoke a Command Processor)

COMMAND invokes a new command processor. A DOS command processor is the program that actually executes DOS internal and external commands, as illustrated in Figure 10-4.

The format of COMMAND is

[drive:][path]COMMAND [d:][p][/E:nnnnn][/C string][/P]

where the following is true:

drive: is the disk drive containing the file COMMAND.COM. COMMAND is an external DOS command; therefore, DOS must read the command from disk into memory each time the command is invoked. If you do not specify a disk drive, DOS will use the default drive.

path is the series of subdirectories DOS must traverse to find the file COMMAND.COM. If you do not specify a path, DOS will use the working directory.

d: is the disk drive containing the program to be used as the command processor. By default, DOS uses the file COMMAND.COM as the command processor. If you do not specify a disk drive, DOS will use the current default drive.

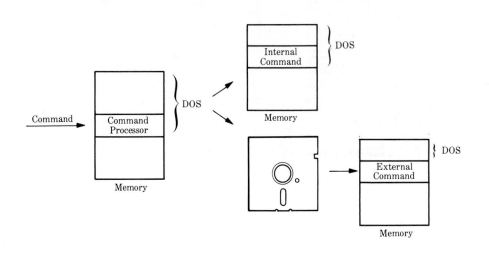

Figure 10-4. DOS command processor

p is the subdirectory path DOS must traverse to find the new command processor. By default, DOS will search the current working directory for the command processor.

/E specifies the size of the environment (see SET) in bytes. The value must be in the range 160-32,768.

/C string specifies a command that the command processor is to execute. If you do not specify a command, DOS will load the command processor and it will prompt you for commands. Otherwise, the command processor will remain in memory only for the execution of the command.

/P requests COMMAND to make the new command processor permanent in memory. The only way to remove the command processor is to reboot. If you do not specify the /P option, the DOS EXIT command will remove the command processor from memory. If you specify the /C qualifier, DOS ignores /P.

As illustrated in the chapter on batch processing (see Chapter 8), DOS must load a secondary command processor when you invoke a second batch procedure from the middle of a batch file, as shown here:

```
DATE
TIME
COMMAND /C BATFILE
CLS
VER
```

This is because DOS loads the command processor into memory in two parts: a resident part and a transient part (see Figure 10-5). Some user applications overwrite the transient portion of the command processor. If this happens, the resident part must reload the transient part from disk into memory. Conceptually, this can be viewed as in Figure 10-6.

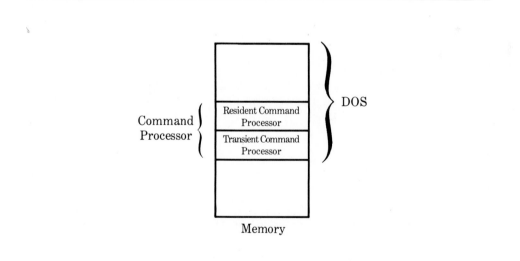

Figure 10-5.   Resident and transient parts of command processor

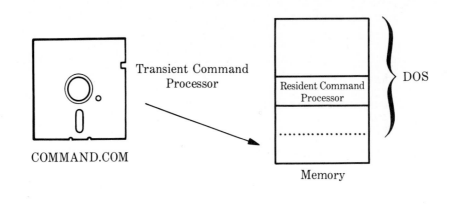

Figure 10-6. Reloading the transient part of command processor

Chapter 16 will examine a Turbo Pascal procedure that allows you to invoke DOS commands from within a Pascal program. This is one of the most useful features of the DOS COMMAND in that it allows you to exit from your application temporarily to access DOS. Consider the following examples. Enter

A> COMMAND

DOS will load a secondary command processor. Since no command is specified, the command processor will prompt you for input, as shown here:

```
A> COMMAND

The IBM Personal Computer DOS
Version 3.00 (C)Copyright IBM Corp 1981, 1982, 1983, 1984

A>
```

By default, DOS will load the file COMMAND.COM as the command processor. If DOS cannot find the file, it will display

```
A> COMMAND

Specified COMMAND search directory bad

Invalid COMMAND.COM

Cannot start COMMAND, exiting
```

To remove the command processor from memory, issue the DOS EXIT command (discussed later in this chapter).

```
A> EXIT
```

If you enter

```
A> COMMAND /E:32000
```

DOS will load a secondary command processor with an environment of 32,000 bytes. (A more detailed explanation of the DOS environment appears in Chapter 16.) If the size of the specified environment is too large, DOS will prompt

```
A> COMMAND /E:64000
Invalid environment size specified
```

If you enter the command

```
A> COMMAND /C CHKDSK
```

DOS will invoke a secondary command processor to issue the

DOS CHKDSK command. The processor will reside in memory only until the CHKDSK command has been executed (see Figure 10-7).

If you enter

```
A> COMMAND /P
```

DOS will load a command processor and make it permanent in memory.

Note the following file:

```
DATE
TIME
COMMAND /C SOMEFILE.BAT
VOL
CLS
```

You must use COMMAND to invoke a second batch procedure from the middle of a batch file. For more information on COMMAND, see the DOS EXIT command presented later in this chapter, along with the programming example presented in Chapter 16.

CTTY (Modify the Command Device)

The DOS CTTY command modifies the device from which DOS receives commands. By default, DOS looks to the CON: device for commands. The format of the DOS CTTY command is

CTTY device—name:

where the following is true:

device—name: is the name of the device from which DOS is to receive its commands. See Chapter 4 for DOS device names.

Consider the following examples. Enter

```
A> CTTY AUX:
```

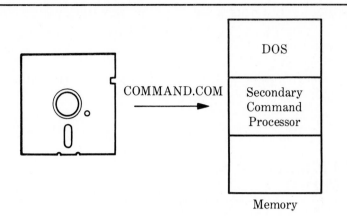

a. Secondary Command Processor Loaded

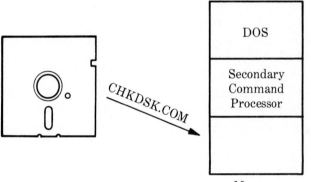

b. CHKDSK Loaded and Executed

c. Secondary Command Processor Terminates

Figure 10-7. Command processor residing in memory until CHKDSK is executed

DOS will obtain its input from the auxiliary device. If you enter

```
A> CTTY CON:
```

the DOS command device is set back to CON. Most users will never use the CTTY command.

EXE2BIN (Convert an EXE File to a COM File)

DOS executes programs with either the extension EXE or COM. Although both file types are executable, there are several subtle differences between them. These differences occur because EXE files are relocatable in memory. COM files, on the other hand, contain an exact image of how the file will appear in memory.

If you were to compare the contents of a COM file with the contents of the program in memory, as seen in Figure 10-8, they would be identical. EXE files are relocatable. This means that each time DOS loads an EXE file into memory, DOS must perform additional processing, as shown in Figure 10-9.

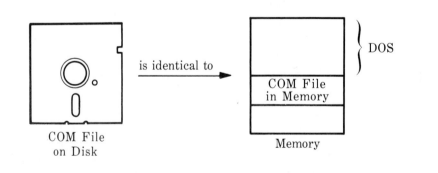

Figure 10-8.   Contents of COM file compared to program in memory

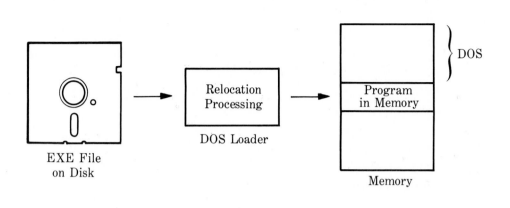

Figure 10-9. Additional processing required by EXE file loading

Since COM files do not require additional processing at load time, they load and execute faster than EXE files. In addition, because COM files do not contain relocation tables, they are more compact than EXE files. These qualities also restrict the size of COM programs to 64K, however. Relocatable images require DOS to change values in the program depending on where the program is loaded in memory. Relocation does, however, allow DOS to be more flexible in where it places the image in memory. A recent trend has been to keep files in EXE format to ensure that the programs remain portable as DOS migrates toward virtual memory. The format of the DOS EXE2BIN command is

[drive:][path]EXE2BIN file—spec1 file—spec2

where the following is true:

drive: is the disk drive containing the file EXE2BIN.COM. EXE2BIN is an external DOS command; therefore, DOS must read the command from disk into memory each time the command is invoked. If you do not specify a disk drive, DOS will use the default drive.

path is the series of subdirectories DOS must traverse to find the file EXE2BIN.COM. If you do not specify a path, DOS will use the working directory.

file—spec1 is the name of the file to convert from EXE format to COM format.

file—spec2 is the name of the converted COM file.

A program must meet several criteria before you can convert it to a COM file. These requirements are beyond the scope of this text, so refer to your DOS documentation. If EXE2BIN is unable to convert your program, it will display

```
A> EXE2BIN SOMEFILE.EXE SOMEFILE.COM
File cannot be converted
```

Some other messages may also appear.
Consider the following example. If you enter

```
A> EXE2BIN SOMEFILE.EXE SOMEFILE.COM
```

EXE2BIN will convert SOMEPROG.EXE, the relocatable program, into a COM file with the name SOMEPROG.COM.

EXIT (Exit from a Secondary Command Processor)

As previously illustrated, DOS allows you to invoke a second command processor via COMMAND. The most common use of COMMAND is in batch processing to invoke a second BAT file from the middle of a batch procedure. In batch processing, the secondary command processor remains in effect until the batch file has been completely invoked (see Figure 10-10).

It is also possible to invoke a second command processor from the DOS prompt or from within an application program. In these

START.BAT

DATE
TIME

DT.BAT

Step 1. Execute the CLS command
Step 2. Load secondary command processor from disk into memory to execute DT.BAT

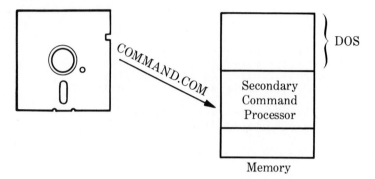

Step 3. Secondary command processor executes the commands in DT.BAT
Step 4. Release the memory allocated by the secondary command processor and return to the batch file START.BAT

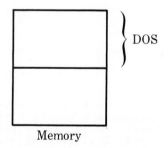

Step 5. Execute the VER command and terminate

Figure 10-10.   Batch processing and secondary command processor

Advanced DOS Commands

instances, the secondary command processor remains in effect until the system reboots or until EXIT is invoked. The purpose of the EXIT command simply is to terminate a secondary command processor and to return control to the original command processor. The format of the EXIT command is

EXIT

Issue the CHKDSK command and you will see the following:

```
A> CHKDSK

    362496 bytes total disk space
     45056 bytes in 3 hidden files
    294912 bytes in 39 user files
     22528 bytes available on disk

    524288 bytes total memory
    274080 bytes free

A>
```

Write down the amount of available memory.
Invoke a second command processor as follows:

```
A> COMMAND
```

Again, invoke the CHKDSK command and note the display:

```
A> CHKDSK

    362496 bytes total disk space
     45056 bytes in 3 hidden files
    294912 bytes in 39 user files
     22528 bytes available on disk

    524288 bytes total memory
    270992 bytes free

A>
```

Notice that the secondary processor allocates some memory. Terminate the secondary command processor and determine the amount of available memory as follows:

```
A> EXIT
A> CHKDSK

    362496 bytes total disk space
     45056 bytes in 3 hidden files
    294912 bytes in 39 user files
     22528 bytes available on disk

    524288 bytes total memory
    274080 bytes free

A>
```

As you can see, EXIT terminates the second command processor and frees memory the secondary command processor had allocated.

JOIN (Join a Disk Drive to a DOS Path)

The DOS JOIN command (version 3.1 or greater) allows you to make two drives appear as one. The format of the JOIN command is

[drive:][path]JOIN [d: [path]][/D]

where the following is true:

drive: is the disk drive containing the file JOIN.EXE. JOIN is an external DOS command; therefore, DOS must read the command from disk into memory each time the command is invoked. If you do not specify a disk drive, DOS will use the default drive.

path is the series of subdirectories DOS must traverse to find the file JOIN.EXE. If you do not specify a path, DOS will use the working directory.

d: is the disk drive to join to the specified directory path.

path is the subdirectory path to associate the disk drive to.

/D (when present) requests JOIN to disassociate the drive with a directory path.

Assume that you have the directory structure shown in Figure 10-11. Create a new directory called JOINDIR.

```
A> MKDIR \JOINDIR
```

Your directory structure should now resemble Figure 10-12. Issue the following command and note the display:

```
A> DIR \JOINDIR

Volume in drive A has no label
Directory of   A:\JOINDIR

       2 File(s)     21504 bytes free
```

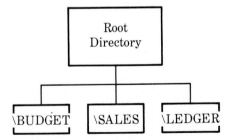

Figure 10-11.   Example directory structure

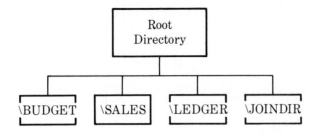

Figure 10-12. Directory structure with JOINDIR

Place your DOS disk in drive B and issue the command

```
A> JOIN B: \JOINDIR
```

The command associates the disk in drive B to the pathname
\JOINDIR. Perform the following directory command and note
the display:

```
A> DIR \JOINDIR

  Volume in drive A has no label
  Directory of  A:\JOINDIR

  COMMAND  COM     23210   3-11-86   10:00a
  ASSIGN   COM      1509   3-11-86   10:00a
  ATTRIB   EXE     15091   3-11-86   10:00a
  FORMAT   COM      6831   5-09-86    3:52p
  FDISK    COM     14448   5-13-86    9:47a
  DISKCOMP COM      3774   5-20-86    8:52a
  DISKCOPY COM      4099   5-20-86    8:52a
  TREE     COM      6306   5-03-86   11:19a
  EXE2BIN  EXE      2816   3-11-86   10:00a
  FC       EXE     14576   3-11-86   10:00a
  FIND     EXE      6403   3-11-86   10:00a
  JOIN     EXE     15971   3-11-86   10:00a
  LABEL    EXE      2750   3-11-86   10:00a
  SHARE    EXE      8304   3-11-86   10:00a
  SUBST    EXE     16611   3-11-86   10:00a
  SYS      EXE      2671   3-11-86   10:00a
```

```
MORE       COM        282    3-11-86   10:00a
SORT       EXE       1664    3-11-86   10:00a
CHKDSK     COM       9435    3-11-86   10:00a
DEBUG      COM      15552    3-11-86   10:00a
EDLIN      COM       7261    3-11-86   10:00a
PRINT      COM       8291    3-11-86   10:00a
RECOVER    COM       4050    3-11-86   10:00a
MODE       COM       2868    5-21-86   11:59a
ANSI       SYS       2563    5-12-86    1:42p
SELECT     COM       6052    5-08-86    8:54a
KEYBSP     COM       2317    5-08-86    6:10p
KEYBFR     COM       2395    5-08-86    6:13p
KEYBGR     COM       2310    5-08-86    6:15p
KEYBNR     COM       2335    5-08-86    6:10p
KEYBSF     COM       2331    5-08-86    6:23p
KEYBSG     COM       2360    5-08-86    6:20p
KEYBDK     COM       2335    5-08-86    6:25p
KEYBUK     COM       1972    5-08-86    6:08p
KEYBIT     COM       2011    5-08-86    6:06p
KEYBSV     COM       2259    5-08-86    6:18p
GFTPRN     COM        292    3-18-86   10:30a
GRAFTABL   COM       2145    3-11-86   10:00a
GRAPHICS   COM       5363    4-10-86   11:37a
COMP       COM       7194    5-03-86   11:19a
SHIPZONE   EXE        779    5-12-86    9:45a
SPEED      EXE       1196    5-09-86   11:34a
       42 File(s)        21504 bytes free
```

Issue the JOIN command without any parameters.

```
A> JOIN
```

JOIN will display the current joins, as shown here:

```
A> JOIN
B: => A:\JOINDIR

A>
```

If you try to reference a device that has been joined to a path, DOS will display

```
A> DIR B:
Invalid drive specification
```

To remove the join, issue the command

```
A> JOIN B:/D
```

The JOIN command may make disk organization somewhat confusing. Most applications will never require that you use the DOS JOIN command. A possible application for the DOS JOIN command, however, is one for users who may have multiple disk configurations. If you need to write data to a floppy disk drive, you have no way of knowing what the eventual disk configuration will be. To solve this problem, create a directory on the hard disk called \DATA.

```
A> MKDIR C:\DATA
```

The user's AUTOEXEC.BAT file issues this JOIN command to the appropriate drive:

```
JOIN A: C:\DATA
```

This application then simply opens files in the subdirectory C:\DATA. If, instead, the application references disk drive A and the drive breaks, the application would be unusable. In this case, the user would simply modify the JOIN command to join drive B to the directory C:\DATA, and the application could continue.

```
JOIN B: C:\DATA
```

RECOVER (Recover a File or Disk Containing Bad Sectors)

As illustrated in Chapter 9, DOS stores files on disk via chains of disk clusters. Periodically, intermediate sectors in the chain will go bad. In such a case, the DOS RECOVER command allows you to recover the contents of the file minus the bad sectors. If you discover that a part of a file is better than no file, the DOS RE-COVER command can be useful. RECOVER does not recover erased files. (Note: Several third-party packages exist that "un-erase" deleted files. DOS does not provide this function.) The format of the RECOVER command is

[drive:][path]RECOVER file_spec

or

[drive:][path]RECOVER d:

where the following is true:

drive: is the disk drive containing the file RECOVER.COM. RECOVER is an external DOS command; therefore, DOS must read the command from disk into memory each time the command is invoked. If you do not specify a disk drive, DOS will use the default drive.

path is the series of subdirectories DOS must traverse to find the file RECOVER.COM. If you do not specify a path, DOS will use the working directory.

file_spec is the name of the file to recover. RECOVER supports the DOS wildcard characters.

d: is the disk drive to recover.

The first format of RECOVER recovers a file that contains bad sectors. If you use DOS wildcard characters, RECOVER will only recover the first matching file. RECOVER only recovers one file at a time.

Consider the following examples. Enter

```
A> RECOVER BUDGET.DAT
```

RECOVER will recover the contents of the file BUDGET.DAT. You may have to edit the file to restore its original contents. This is because the file is missing disk sectors. Use the line editor EDLIN (see Chapter 13) to restore the file as required.

Enter

```
A> RECOVER *.DAT
```

RECOVER will recover the first file with the extension DAT. As previously stated, RECOVER recovers only one file at a time. If the file you specify does not exist, RECOVER will display

```
A> RECOVER FILENAME.EXT

Press any key to begin recovery of the
file(s) on drive A:

File not found

A>
```

If the directory on a disk has been damaged, you can use the second format of the RECOVER command to recover the files. In this case, DOS will recover all of the sector chains (see Chapter 9) on the disk into files with the file name FILEnnnn.REC (nnnn is a four-digit number, beginning with 0001). RECOVER will place the first file it finds into the file FILE0001.REC, the second into FILE0002.REC, and so on.4

Consider the following examples. If you enter the commands

```
A> RECOVER B:

Press any key to begin recovery of the
file(s) on drive B:

3 file(s) recovered

A> DIR B:

 Volume in drive B has no label
 Directory of  B:\

FILE0001 REC     45056  12-11-86    5:53p
FILE0002 REC     29184  12-11-86    5:53p
FILE0003 REC     41472  12-11-86    5:53p
        3 File(s)      78848 bytes free

A>
```

RECOVER will recover all of the files on drive B and place them in files with the name FILEnnnn.REC. If the disk drive that you specify is invalid, RECOVER will display

```
A> RECOVER E:
Invalid drive or file name
```

Once you have recovered the files, TYPE them and see if you can rename them with more meaningful names. If you have recovered executable files (EXE or COM), they will probably be unusable because of missing sectors. Be leery of invoking them. Again, you may need to edit text (readable) files to restore their original contents.

Note that bad sectors on your disk are an early warning of serious problems. If your disk has bad sectors, back it up immediately (see Chapter 11) and recover any files that you can. If your system continues to develop bad sectors, have it serviced immediately. It is a good practice to turn off a network before attempting to recover files (if your system is part of a local area network).

REPLACE (Update Previous Versions of Files)

DOS version 3.2 provides the REPLACE command, which simplifies the process of updating files. REPLACE works in one of two modes. By default, REPLACE replaces all of the files on the target disk with the files found on the source disk. As you will see, you can override this mode and only add files not already contained on the target disk. The format of the DOS REPLACE command is

[drive:][path]REPLACE file—spec [d:][p] [/A][/D][/P][/Q] [/S][/W]

where the following is true:

drive: is the disk drive containing the file REPLACE.COM. REPLACE is an external DOS command, which means DOS must read the command from disk into memory each time the command is invoked. If you do not specify a disk drive, DOS will use the default drive.

path is the series of subdirectories DOS must traverse to find the file REPLACE.COM. If you do not specify a path, DOS will use the working directory.

file—spec is the name of the target file name. REPLACE supports the DOS wildcard characters.

d: is the target drive for the file replacement.

p is the target path for the file replacement.

/A requests REPLACE only to copy files not contained in the target location. This prevents files from being overwritten by files in the source location.

/P requests REPLACE to prompt you as follows before it replaces a file:

```
Add FILENAME.EXT? (Y/N)
```

or

```
Replace FILENAME.EXT? (Y/N)
```

/R requests REPLACE to replace files that are marked read-only on the target drive.

/S requests REPLACE to search all subdirectories on the target for files whose names match the source. This qualifier is incompatible with the /A qualifier.

/W requests REPLACE to wait for you to press a key before it begins replacing files. If you are performing a complete replace, REPLACE will prompt

```
Press any key to begin replacing file(s)
```

If you have used the /A qualifier instead, REPLACE will prompt

```
Press any key to begin adding file(s)
```

Consider the following examples. Enter

```
A> REPLACE *.* B:*.*/S
```

REPLACE will update all of the files on drive B with files on drive A. Enter

```
A> REPLACE *.* B:/A
```

REPLACE will add all of the files found on drive A, but not on drive B, to drive B. Enter

```
A> REPLACE *.* B:/P
```

REPLACE will update all of the files on drive B with the files contained on drive A and prompt you before each replacement with

Replace FILENAME.EXT? (Y/N)

Enter

A> REPLACE *.* B:/S/R

REPLACE will update all of the files on drive B with the files contained on drive A, including files on drive B that are marked read-only.

Note that you cannot use REPLACE to upgrade from one version of DOS to another. REPLACE does not copy hidden or system

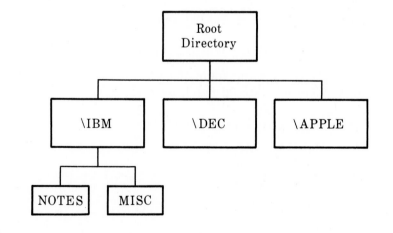

Figure 10-13.   Example directory structure

files. In addition, REPLACE will not search subdirectories in the source disk for files. For example, suppose your disk has the structure shown in Figure 10-13. You issue the command

```
A> REPLACE \IBM\*.* B:
```

The command will not examine the subdirectories \IBM \NOTES or \IBM \MISC for files to replace on drive B. If REPLACE does not find the file to replace, it will display

```
A> REPLACE FILENAME.EXT B:

REPLACE Version 3.20 (C) Copyright IBM Corp. 1985, 1986

No files found 'A:\FILENAME.EXT'
```

If the target directory is invalid, REPLACE will display

```
A> REPLACE FILENAME.EXT B:\TARGET

REPLACE Version 3.20 (C) Copyright IBM Corp. 1985, 1986
Path not Found 'B:\TARGET\'

No files replaced
```

REPLACE uses the following exit-status values that allow you to perform conditional batch processing:

    0   Successful replacement

    1   Command line error

    2   File not found

    3   Path not found

    5   Access denied

    8   Insufficient memory

    15   Invalid drive

It is a good practice to shut down a network during file replacements (if your system is part of a local area network).

SET (Set an Environment String)

Each time DOS boots, it creates an environment in which your programs can run. By default, the environment contains the following:

```
PATH=
COMSPEC=A:\COMMAND.COM
```

The *environment* is simply a location in memory where you can store information for use by DOS or other programs, as illustrated in Figure 10-14.

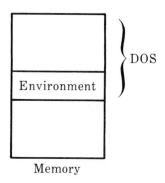

Memory

Figure 10-14.   Illustration of DOS environment

Issue the following commands and note the resulting displays:

```
A> SET
PATH=
COMMSPEC=A:\COMMAND.COM

A> PROMPT A:
A: SET
PATH=
COMMSPEC=A:\COMMAND.COM
PROMPT=A:

A:
```

```
A> SET
PATH=
COMMSPEC=A:\COMMAND.COM

A> PATH C:;B:;A:
A> SET
COMMSPEC=A:\COMMAND.COM
PATH=C:;B:;A:
```

Each time DOS executes a command, it uses the search strategy defined by the PATH string in the environment. The format of the SET command is

SET [string1=[string2]]

where the following is true:

string1 is the character string SET is to assign a value.

string2 is the character string value SET is to assign to *string1*.

Consider the following examples. Enter

```
A> SET
PATH=
COMMSPEC=A:\COMMAND.COM
```

If you invoke SET without any parameters, it will display the current environment.

```
A> SET PATH=C:;B:;A:
A> SET
COMMSPEC=A:\COMMAND.COM
PATH=C:;B:;A:
```

In this case, you are using the SET command to define the DOS command path. This command has the same effect as the command

```
A> PATH C:;B:;A:
```

The following command undefines an item in the environment:

```
A> SET PATH=
A> SET
COMMSPEC=C:;B:;A:
PATH=

A>
```

Last, use the SET command to set the system prompt, as shown here:

```
A> SET PROMPT=A:
A: SET
COMMSPEC=A:\COMMAND.COM
PATH=
PROMPT=A:

A:
```

Chapter 16 will examine a Turbo Pascal procedure that displays all of the items in the environment.

SHARE (Support File Sharing)

Many network applications require that two or more programs be able to access a data file simultaneously. Although it is possible to open the same file several times from within one program, the most common use of file sharing is in a local area network. A

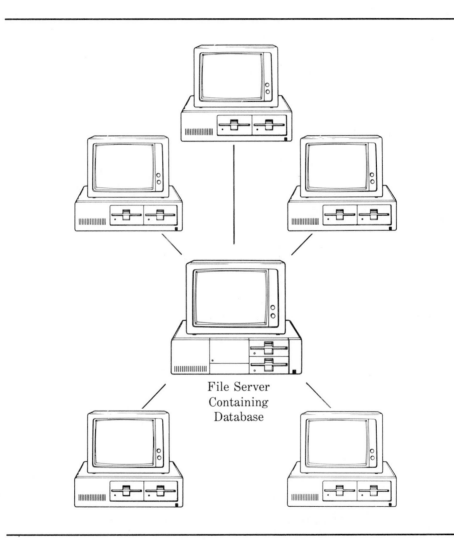

File Server
Containing
Database

Figure 10-15.   File sharing and local area networks

computer *network* is simply a collection of connected computers that share resources (files, disks, printers, and so on).

Most file-sharing applications occur in local area networks when multiple users are trying to access and update a database at the same time, as shown in Figure 10-15.

If your application requires file sharing, you first must install the DOS file-sharing code into memory via the DOS SHARE command.

```
A> SHARE
A>
```

Once the file-sharing code is installed (see Figure 10-16), all DOS read and write operations are validated against the code, as illustrated in Figure 10-17.

If you are sharing files in a network, you must first invoke the DOS SHARE command. The format for the SHARE command is

[drive:][path]SHARE [/F:filespace][/L:locks]

where the following is true:

    drive: is the disk drive containing the file SHARE.COM. SHARE is an external DOS command; therefore, DOS must

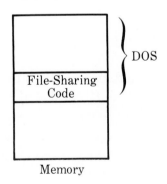

Figure 10-16.   Installation of file-sharing code

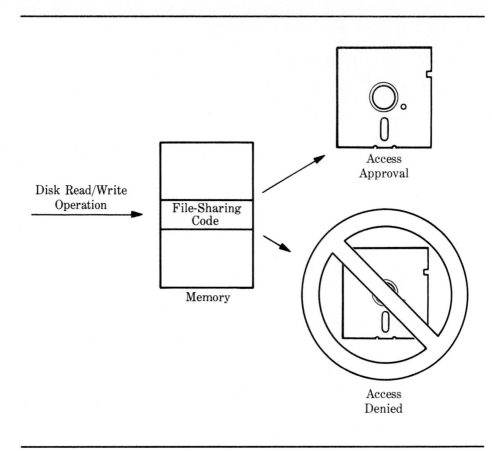

Figure 10-17. Validation of DOS read and write operations

read the command from disk into memory each time the command is invoked. If you do not specify a disk drive, DOS will use the default drive.

path is the series of subdirectories DOS must traverse to find the file SHARE.COM. If you do not specify a path, DOS will use the working directory.

/F:filespace specifies the amount of memory set aside for file sharing. By default, DOS sets aside 2048 bytes for file shar-

ing. This value supports a minimum of 27 files. Each shared file uses 11 bytes plus up to 63 bytes for its file name.

/L:locks specifies the number of simultaneous locks DOS can apply. The default value is 20. (See the DOS reference section at the end of this book.)

Consider the following examples. Enter

```
A> SHARE
A>
```

DOS will install file sharing with space for 27 shared files and 20 simultaneous locks. Enter

```
A> SHARE /F:4096
A>
```

DOS will install file sharing with minimum space for 55 (4096/(63+11)) shared files and 20 simultaneous locks. Enter

```
A> SHARE /L:30
A>
```

DOS will install file sharing with space for 27 shared files and 30 simultaneous locks. Note that the number of locks and the amount of space allocated for shared files increases the amount of memory allocated by DOS. The DOS SHARE command can only be invoked once. If you try to load file sharing a second time, DOS will respond with

```
A> SHARE
SHARE already installed

A>
```

The only way to remove file sharing is to reboot. If you don't need to share files, do not invoke the SHARE command, because it produces additional overhead on disk read/write operations.

SUBST (Substitute a DOS Path with a Drive Letter)

The DOS SUBST command associates a DOS path with a disk drive identification. This action allows you to abbreviate your path. The format of the DOS SUBST command is

[drive:][path]SUBST [d:] [p][/D]

where the following is true:

drive: is the disk drive containing the file SUBST.COM. SUBST is an external DOS command; therefore, DOS must read the command from disk into memory each time the command is invoked. If you do not specify a disk drive, DOS will use the default drive.

path is the series of subdirectories DOS must traverse to find the file SUBST.COM. If you do not specify a path, DOS will use the working directory.

d: is the drive identification of the disk drive you want to associate to the path. The drive cannot be the current disk drive. The letter specified for drive must be in the range A-Z. If you use a letter greater than E, you must modify the LASTDRIVE parameter in the file CONFIG.SYS (Chapter 15).

p is the DOS path that you want associated with the disk drive.

/D requests SUBST to delete a previously defined substitution.

Consider the following examples. If you enter

```
A> SUBST D: \IBM
```

DOS will now associate all references to drive D with the subdirectory \IBM on drive A. If you enter

```
A> DIR D:
```

DOS displays all of the files contained in the path associated with drive D, as shown here:

```
A> DIR D:

 Volume in drive D has no label
 Directory of   D:\

NOTES     TXT      30   12-13-86    9:53a
SEPT      RPT      78   12-13-86    9:54a
BUDGET    DAT      76   12-13-86    9:54a
          5 File(s)     358400 bytes free
```

If you invoke SUBST without any parameters, it will display the current path substitutions.

```
A> SUBST
D: => A:\IBM

A>
```

If you try to associate a path to the current drive, SUBST will display

```
A> SUBST A: B:\IBM
Invalid parameter
```

If the drive specified is invalid, SUBST will display

```
A> SUBST Z: \IBM
Invalid parameter
```

Also, if the path that you specify is invalid, SUBST will display

```
A> SUBST D: \PATHNAME
Path not found
```

If you attempt to substitute a drive that DOS is already associating with a path, SUBST will display

```
A> SUBST D: \DOS
Invalid parameter
```

Last, enter the command

```
A> SUBST D:/D
A>
```

This will remove the current association between drive D and the path A:\IBM.

SYS (Place Operating System on Disk)

The DOS SYS command places the hidden files on a disk that DOS requires in order for the disk to be bootable. The format of the DOS SYS command is

[drive:][path]SYS d:

where the following is true:

drive: is the disk drive containing the file SYS.COM. SYS is an external DOS command; therefore, DOS must read the command from disk into memory each time the command is invoked. If you do not specify a disk drive, DOS will use the default drive.

path is the series of subdirectories DOS must traverse to find the file SYS.COM. If you do not specify a path, DOS will use the working directory.

d: is the disk drive identification of the disk drive containing the disk onto which the operating system files are to be placed.

The disk you are upgrading via the DOS SYS command must have been originally formatted with the /B or /S qualifier and it may not contain any files. The DOS SYS command places the files IBMBIO.COM and IBMDOS.COM (for PC-DOS) or IO.SYS and MSDOS.SYS (MS-DOS), along with the file COMMAND.COM, onto the disk you specify, as shown in Figure 10-18.

Consider the following example. Enter

```
A> SYS B:
```

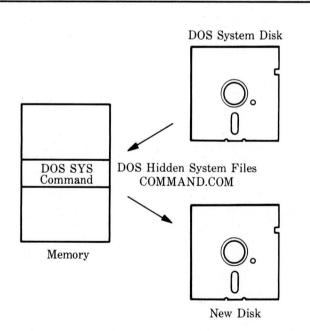

Figure 10-18.   System files placed on disk

The SYS command will place the files onto the disk in drive B. If you try to boot a disk that does not contain the hidden system files, DOS will display

```
Non-System disk or disk error
Replace and strike any key when ready
```

If the disk does not contain the file COMMAND.COM, DOS will display

```
Bad or missing Command Interpreter
```

In either case, simply place a bootable disk in the drive, and the boot process will continue.

If the disk in the drive specified was not formatted with the /B or /S option, and it contains files, SYS will display

```
No room for system on destination disk
```

See the DOS reference section at the end of the book for additional messages from SYS.

VERIFY (Verify That Disk Output Is Written Correctly)

The DOS VERIFY command toggles disk verification on and off. The format of the command is

VERIFY [ON | OFF]

The parameter [ON | OFF] is optional. The ON | OFF states that the value you specify must be either the word ON or the word OFF. When VERIFY is ON, DOS reads each disk sector it writes to ensure that the data was written correctly. This additional processing has a significant impact on processing time and system performance. Because of this overhead, normally you should set VERIFY=ON only during system backups (see Chapter 11).

Consider the following examples. If you invoke VERIFY without any parameters, DOS will display the current VERIFY status, ON or OFF.

```
A> VERIFY
VERIFY is off
```

Enter

```
A> VERIFY ON
A>
```

DOS will read each disk sector it writes to ensure that the data has been written to disk correctly. Enter

```
A> VERIFY OFF
```

DOS does not have the additional overhead of verifying the success of each disk output operation because OFF is the DOS default.

XCOPY (Copy Files and Directories to a New Disk)

The DOS XCOPY command is new with DOS version 3.2. The command allows you to copy files contained in a directory, or subdirectories, without having to invoke the DOS DISKCOPY command.

The format of the DOS XCOPY command is

[drive:][path]XCOPY file_spec1 file_spec2 [/A][/D][/E] [/M][/P][/S][/V][/W]

where the following is true:

drive: is the disk drive containing the file XCOPY.COM. XCOPY is an external DOS command; therefore, DOS must read the command from disk into memory each time the command is invoked. If you do not specify a disk drive, DOS will use the default drive.

path is the series of subdirectories DOS must traverse to find the file XCOPY.COM. If you do not specify a path, DOS will use the working directory.

file_spec1 is the source file(s) to copy.

file_spec2 is the destination file name(s) for the file copy.

/A copies only those files marked for backup. The archive attribute of the file is not changed.

/D:mm-dd-yy copies only those files whose date is the same or later than the specified date.

/E creates subdirectories on the target disk with the same contents as subdirectories on the source disk.

/M copies only those files marked for backup. The archive attribute of the file is changed when copying is completed. This allows XCOPY to be used in backup procedures.

/P requests XCOPY to prompt you before copying each file.

```
FILENAME.EXT (Y/N)?
```

If you press Y and then press ENTER, XCOPY will copy the file. Otherwise, XCOPY will ignore the file.

/S copies files in the source directory and all subdirectories below the source. Without the /S qualifier, XCOPY will ignore subdirectories.

/V requests XCOPY to verify that each disk sector is written correctly. Although this qualifier adds overhead, it ensures that the data XCOPY writes to the source disk is correct.

/W requests XCOPY to prompt as follows before beginning the file copy:

```
Press any key to begin copying file(s)
```

Consider the following examples. You ask for a directory and then invoke XCOPY.

```
A> DIR

 Volume in drive A has no label
 Directory of   A:\

IBM             <DIR>      12-13-86    9:53a
DEC             <DIR>      12-13-86   10:29a
ASSIGN    COM      1536    12-30-85   12:00p
ATTRIB    EXE      8247    12-30-85   12:00p
CHKDSK    COM      9832    12-30-85   12:00p
COMP      COM      4184    12-30-85   12:00p
XCOPY     EXE     11200    12-30-85   12:00p
        7 File(s)     316416 bytes free

A> XCOPY A:\*.* B: /S

Reading source file(s)...
ASSIGN.COM
ATTRIB.EXE
CHKDSK.COM
COMP.COM
XCOPY.EXE
IBM\NOTES.TXT
IBM\SEPT.RPT
IBM\BUDGET.DAT
```

```
DEC\BUDGET.DAT
DEC\PROFIT.DAT
DEC\REPORTS.TXT
        11 File(s) copied
```

XCOPY will copy all of the files on drive A to drive B. This command is similar to the DOS DISKCOPY command in that it also copies subdirectories. If you want to copy the current directory only, use XCOPY as follows:

```
A> DIR

 Volume in drive A has no label
 Directory of  A:\

IBM            <DIR>      12-13-86    9:53a
DEC            <DIR>      12-13-86   10:29a
ASSIGN    COM    1536     12-30-85   12:00p
ATTRIB    EXE    8247     12-30-85   12:00p
CHKDSK    COM    9832     12-30-85   12:00p
COMP      COM    4184     12-30-85   12:00p
XCOPY     EXE   11200     12-30-85   12:00p
         7 File(s)     316416 bytes free

A> XCOPY *.* B:

Reading source file(s)...
ASSIGN.COM
ATTRIB.EXE
CHKDSK.COM
COMP.COM
XCOPY.EXE
        5 File(s) copied
```

Issue the command

```
A> XCOPY A:\*.* B: /S/P
```

This directs XCOPY to copy all of the files on drive A to drive B and puts the following prompt before each file copy:

```
FILENAME.EXT (Y/N)?
```

Enter

```
A> XCOPY A:\*.* B: /S/W
```

XCOPY will copy all of the files on drive A to drive B and prompt you with

```
Press any key to begin copying file(s)
```

Enter

```
A> XCOPY A:\*.* B: /S/V
```

XCOPY will copy all of the files on drive A to drive B, verifying that each disk sector is written correctly. Enter

```
A> XCOPY A:\*.* B: /S/A
```

XCOPY will copy all of the files on drive A that require backing up to drive B. XCOPY will not modify the archive bit on the files. Enter

```
A> XCOPY A:\*.* B: /S/M
```

XCOPY will copy all of the files on drive A that require backing up to drive B. XCOPY will modify the archive bit on the files so that they no longer require a backup.

Assume that you have the directory structures shown in Figure 10-19. Enter

```
A> XCOPY A:\*.* B: /S
```

XCOPY will create on drive B the directories present on drive A and copy the contents of the directories to them, resulting in the directory structures shown in Figure 10-20.

Given the directory structures shown in Figure 10-21, enter

```
A> XCOPY \ORDERS\*.* B: /S
```

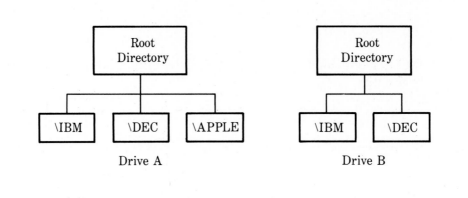

Figure 10-19. Example directory structures

XCOPY will create the subdirectory \ORDERS on drive B with its subdirectories intact, as shown in Figure 10-22.

Given the directory structure in Figure 10-20, enter the command

```
A> XCOPY \IBM\*.* B:\NEWIBM\*.* /S
```

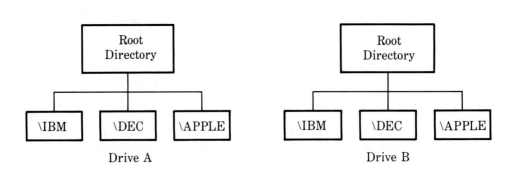

Figure 10-20. Result of copying directories

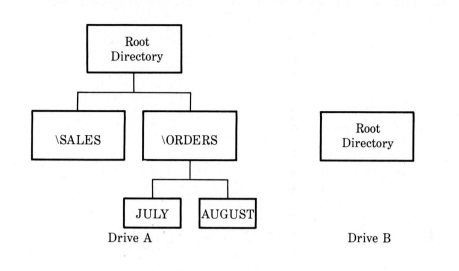

Figure 10-21. Example directory structures

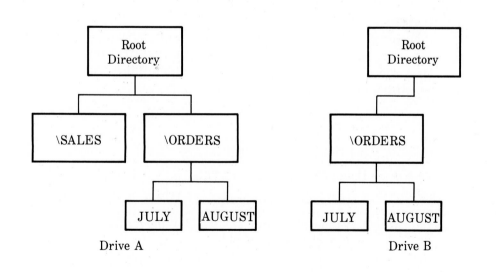

Figure 10-22. Directory structures with \ORDERS

XCOPY will copy the contents of the subdirectory \IBM on drive A to the directory \NEWIBM on drive B.

XCOPY is convenient for copying the contents of your hard disk or a large subdirectory to floppy disk. First modify the attributes of the files so that their attribute bit is set as follows:

```
A> ATTRIB +A C:*.*
```

Next, issue the command

```
A> XCOPY C:*.* B: /M
```

XCOPY will begin copying files to drive B. When the floppy disk fills, XCOPY will display

```
Insufficient disk space
        nn File(s) copied

A>
```

The program will exit. Simply place a new disk in drive B and issue the same command until all of the files are copied. XCOPY uses the following exit-status codes, which allow you to perform conditional batch processing:

0   Successful copy

1   No files found to copy

2   User termination via CTRL-C

4   Fatal processing error

5   DOS critical error (INT 24H), normally associated with a drive not ready

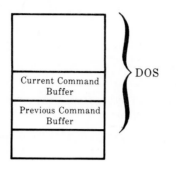

Figure 10-23. DOS storing commands in hidden buffer

DOS Editing Keys

Each time you type in a DOS command, DOS stores the command in a hidden buffer, as illustrated in Figure 10-23. In so doing, DOS allows you to repeat or modify the previous command in a simple fashion. Figure 10-24 shows the keys that DOS uses to edit the command in the command buffer.

Consider the following examples. Enter

`A> DIR B:`

If you press the F1 key, DOS will place the first character into the current command buffer from the previous command.

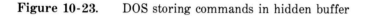

`A> D`

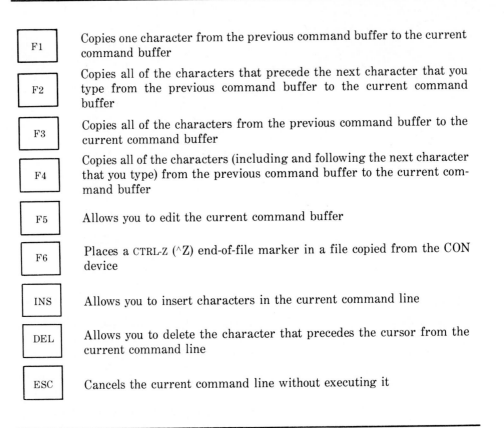

F1	Copies one character from the previous command buffer to the current command buffer
F2	Copies all of the characters that precede the next character that you type from the previous command buffer to the current command buffer
F3	Copies all of the characters from the previous command buffer to the current command buffer
F4	Copies all of the characters (including and following the next character that you type) from the previous command buffer to the current command buffer
F5	Allows you to edit the current command buffer
F6	Places a CTRL-Z (^Z) end-of-file marker in a file copied from the CON device
INS	Allows you to insert characters in the current command line
DEL	Allows you to delete the character that precedes the cursor from the current command line
ESC	Cancels the current command line without executing it

Figure 10-24. DOS editing keys

Press F1 five more times.

`A> DIR B:`

Invoke the command by pressing the ENTER key. At the DOS prompt, press the F3 key, and the following is displayed:

```
A> DIR B:

 Volume in drive B has no label
 Directory of   B:\

 ATTRIB    EXE      8247   12-30-85   12:00p
 FIND      EXE      6416   12-30-85   12:00p
 JOIN      EXE      8955   12-30-85   12:00p
 REPLACE   EXE     11650   12-30-85   12:00p
 SHARE     EXE      8580   12-30-85   12:00p
 SORT      EXE      1911   12-30-85   12:00p
 SUBST     EXE      9911   12-30-85   12:00p
 XCOPY     EXE     11200   12-30-85   12:00p
          8 File(s)        21504 bytes free

 A> DIR B:
```

DOS will place the entire previous command into the current command buffer, as shown in Figure 10-25.

Suppose you want to issue the command

```
A> DIR A:
```

Simply press the F3 function key and then use the DEL key to delete the characters B:. Type the characters A: and press ENTER. The previous command buffer now contains

```
A> DIR A:
```

The F2 function key copies all of the characters that precede the character that you type after pressing F2 in the previous command buffer to the current command buffer. For example, if you press F2 and then type the letter A, DOS will copy all of the

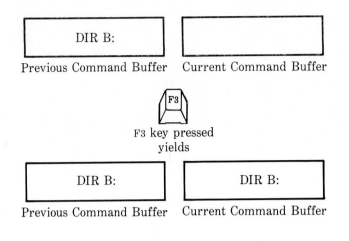

Figure 10-25. DOS placing previous command into buffer

letters in the previous command buffer to the current command buffer that preceded the letter A.

```
A> DIR A:

 Volume in drive A has no label
 Directory of  A:\

 ATTRIB    EXE     8247   12-30-85   12:00p
 FIND      EXE     6416   12-30-85   12:00p
 JOIN      EXE     8955   12-30-85   12:00p
 REPLACE   EXE    11650   12-30-85   12:00p
 SHARE     EXE     8580   12-30-85   12:00p
         5 File(s)       42504 bytes free

 A> DIR
```

DOS: The Complete Reference

The F4 function key deletes all of the characters up to, but not including, the characters that you type immediately after pressing F4. Suppose, for example, the previous command buffer contained

```
A> DISKCOPY
```

Pressing the F4 key and following that immediately with the letter C will result in the command buffer containing

```
A>      COPY
```

The F5 function key makes the current line that you are typing the previous command buffer. For example, suppose you type

```
A> DIKKCOPY A: B:
```

Press F5, and DOS will display

```
A> DIKKCOPY A: B:ə
   ▨
```

You can now use the other DOS function keys as described in Figure 10-24. For example, pressing the F1 key twice results in

```
A> DIKKCOPY A: B:ə
   DI▨
```

Simply type the letter S and press the F3 key and then ENTER.

As previously stated, the F6 function key places an end-of-file marker in a file that you are copying from the CON: device.

1. What is the function of the DOS APPEND command?

2. What is the result of the following DOS command?

    A> ASSIGN A=C

3. What are the two file attributes that the DOS ATTRIB command allows you to modify?

4. What is the result of the following command?

    A> ATTRIB +R CONFIG.SYS

5. What is a command processor? What is the function of COMMAND?

6. What is an environment?

7. What is the function of the DOS CTTY command?

8. What is the function of the DOS EXIT command?

9. How does an EXE file differ from a COM file?

10. What is the function of the DOS EXE2BIN command?

11. What is the function of the following DOS command?

    A> JOIN B: \JOINDIR

12. Does the DOS RECOVER command recover deleted files?

13. Why do text files recovered by the DOS RECOVER command require additional editing?

14. What is file sharing?

15. What is the result of the following command?

    A> SHARE /L:30/F:4096

16. What is the function of the following DOS command?

    A> SUBST F: \IBM\NOTES\1987

17. What is the function of the DOS SYS command?

18. What does the following DOS command do?

    A> VERIFY ON

19. What is the function of the DOS REPLACE command?

20. How does the DOS XCOPY command differ from the DOS COPY command?

21. What are the DOS command editing keys, and what is the function of each?

1. *What is the function of the DOS APPEND command?*

The MS-DOS version 3.2 APPEND command allows you to define a data path that DOS will search each time it opens a data file. If the file you specify does not exist in the current working directory, MS-DOS will check to see if you have defined a data path via the APPEND command. If you have, DOS will examine successive entries in the path until the file is found or the data path is exhausted.

2. *What is the result of the following DOS command?*

    A> ASSIGN A=C

The DOS ASSIGN command allows you to direct all references to a disk drive to a different disk drive. In this example, DOS will reroute all references to disk A to drive C. If, for example, you have a program that always searches drive A for a file, but you would rather have that file reside on a different disk, the DOS ASSIGN command allows you to do this.

3. *What are the two file attributes that the DOS ATTRIB command allows you to modify?*

The DOS ATTRIB command allows you to modify a file's read-only and archive attributes. If you set a file's read-only attribute bit to +r, DOS will not allow the file to be modified, deleted, renamed, or copied over. If you set a file's archive attribute to +a, the DOS BACKUP and XCOPY commands can perform selective file copies based on the need to archive the file.

4. *What is the result of the following command?*

    A> ATTRIB +R CONFIG.SYS

The command sets file CONFIG.SYS to read-only access.

5. *What is a command processor? What is the function of COMMAND?*

A command processor is a program that obtains and executes commands from the user or BAT files. The DOS command processor resides in the COMMAND.COM file. The function of COMMAND is to invoke a secondary command processor. If you attempt to invoke a second BAT file from the middle of a BAT file, you must use COMMAND as follows:

```
DATE
TIME
CLS
COMMAND /C SOMEFILE.BAT
CLS
VOL
```

As you will see in Chapter 16, COMMAND also allows you to exit from an application temporarily to access DOS commands and then return to the current state of the application.

6. *What is an environment?*

An environment is an area DOS sets aside in memory, in which you can place information, that is accessible by other programs. By default, the DOS environment contains

```
A> SET
PATH=
COMSPEC=C:\COMMAND.COM
```

The DOS SET command allows you to place entries into the environment.

7. *What is the function of the DOS CTTY command?*

By default, DOS receives its commands from the CON device. The DOS CTTY command allows you to change the source of DOS command input.

8. *What is the function of the DOS EXIT command?*

The DOS EXIT command terminates a secondary command processor. If, for example, an application spawns a DOS secondary command processor, the DOS EXIT command terminates the processor and returns control to the application.

9. *How does an EXE file differ from a COM file?*

Although both EXE and COM files are executable, there are several subtle differences. These differences occur because EXE files are relocatable in memory. COM files, on the other hand, contain an exact image of how the file will appear in memory. Because EXE files are relocatable, each time DOS loads an EXE file into memory, DOS must perform additional processing. Since COM files do not require additional processing at load time, they load and execute faster than EXE files. In addition, because COM files do not contain relocation tables, they are more compact than EXE files. COM files, however, are restricted to a size of 64K. Relocatable images require DOS to change values in the program, depending on where the program is loaded in memory. Relocation does, however, allow DOS to be flexible in where it places the image in memory.

10. *What is the function of the DOS EXE2BIN command?*

The DOS EXE2BIN command converts a relocatable EXE file to a memory-image COM file. Once desirable because of their compactness and quick execution, COM files will become less desirable as DOS migrates to virtual memory.

11. *What is the function of the following DOS command?*

    A> JOIN B: \JOINDIR

The DOS JOIN command (in DOS version 3.1 or greater) allows you to make two drives appear as one. The command associates the disk in drive B with the pathname \JOINDIR.

12. *Does the DOS RECOVER command recover deleted files?*

No, the DOS RECOVER command recovers files that have lost or damaged disk sectors. There are several third-party products that recover deleted files. DOS, however, does not provide this capability.

13. *Why do text files recovered by the DOS RECOVER command require additional editing?*

The DOS RECOVER command recovers files that have lost or damaged disk sectors. Because the recovered file is missing disk sectors, it no longer contains all of its previous information. Use the DOS line editor EDLIN (see Chapter 13) to restore the file to its previous contents.

14. *What is file sharing?*

Many network applications require that two or more programs be able to access a data file simultaneously. Although it is possible to open the same file several times from within one program, the most common use of file sharing is in a local area network. The DOS SHARE command must be invoked before your system can support file sharing. Once SHARE is installed, all disk read/write operations are validated against the file-sharing software.

15. *What is the result of the following command?*

    A> SHARE /L:30 /F:4096

The command installs the file-sharing software with support for 55 files and 30 simultaneous locks.

16. *What is the function of the following DOS command?*

    A> SUBST F: \IBM\NOTES\1987

The DOS SUBST command allows you to abbreviate a long DOS pathname. For instance, you don't have to refer to the pathname \IBM\NOTES\1987:

A> DIR \IBM\NOTES\1987

You can refer instead simply to drive F:

A> DIR F:

17. *What is the function of the DOS SYS command?*

The DOS SYS command places the hidden files on a disk that DOS requires for the disk to be bootable. The disk you are upgrading via the DOS SYS command must be originally formatted with the /B or /S qualifier and may not contain any files. The DOS SYS command places the files IBMBIO.COM and IBMDOS.COM (for PC-DOS) or IO.SYS and MSDOS. SYS (MS-DOS) along with the COMMAND.COM file on the disk you specify.

18. *What does the following DOS command do?*

A> VERIFY ON

With VERIFY=ON, DOS will read each disk sector it writes to ensure that the data has been written correctly to disk. The command does introduce additional overhead to all DOS disk read/ write operations.

19. *What is the function of the DOS REPLACE command?*

DOS version 3.2 provides the REPLACE command, which simplifies the process of updating files. REPLACE works in one of two modes. By default, REPLACE replaces all of the files on the target disk with the files found on the source disk. You can override this mode and add only those files not already contained on the target disk.

20. *How does the DOS XCOPY command differ from the DOS COPY command?*

The DOS COPY command copies files contained in the current directory or the specified directory. COPY does not copy files contained in subdirectories that reside in the source directory for the copy. In addition, COPY does not consider file attributes that allow selective copies. The DOS XCOPY command, however, does copy files that are contained in sub-directories and also considers file attributes.

21. *What are the DOS command editing keys, and what is the function of each?*

Each time you type in a DOS command, DOS stores the command in a hidden buffer. In so doing, DOS allows you to repeat or modify the previous command in a simple fashion. DOS uses the following keys to edit the command in the command buffer:

F1   Copies one character from the previous command buffer to the current command buffer

F2   Copies all of the characters that precede the next character that you type from the previous command buffer to the current command buffer

F3   Copies all of the characters from the previous command buffer to the current command buffer

F4   Copies all of the characters including and following the next character that you type from the previous command buffer to the current command buffer

F5   Allows you to edit the current command buffer

F6   Places a CTRL-Z (^Z) end-of-file marker in a file copied from the CON device

INS   Allows you to insert characters in the current command line

DEL   Allows you to delete the character that precedes the cursor from the current command line

ESC   Cancels the current command line without executing it

Backing Up
Your Disks

BACKUP
Backup Policies and Procedures
Problems with BACKUP
RESTORE (Retrieving Files from Backup Disks)

One of the most important functions you must perform on a regular basis is backing up your disks. The sole purpose of performing backups is to prevent, or minimize the effect of, accidental loss of data. Data stored on disk can be destroyed by power failure, fire, theft, accidental spills of food and drink, accidental file deletion, and programming errors. If you perform backups on a regular basis, however, and follow the guidelines set forth in this chapter, you will greatly reduce the possibility of losing data and minimize the effects of any actual data loss.

Several factors are involved in ensuring that you back up your disks properly. First, you must perform backups on a regular basis. Many users fail to perform backups, claiming that "backups take just too much time." Unless these users can tolerate a total loss of programs or data, failing to perform disk backups on a regular basis is inexcusable. This chapter examines a backup policy and schedule that ensures your backups are up-to-date.

Second, you need to establish a safe location for your backup disks. Some of the sources of data destruction (fire and theft) are as capable of destroying your backup disks as they are your working disks. It is essential, therefore, that you find a safe place in which to store your backups. Many users make one or more copies of all their software and data disks and place the originals in a safe deposit box. As a minimum precaution to protect against

Figure 11-1.   Media box for disk storage

dust and other damage, you should store your backup disks in a protected media box as illustrated in Figure 11-1.

Third, always document your backups. Before you get started with backups, purchase a three-ring binder to serve as your backup log. Write down the date the backup was performed, the name of the device backed up, the location of the backup disks, and the initials of the individual who performed the backup in the log, as shown in Figure 11-2.

Chapter 2 introduced the first form of disk backup, the DISK-COPY command. Place your DOS disk in drive A and issue the command

`A> DISKCOPY A: B:`

If the disk you are trying to back up is copy-protected, you will need to purchase a third-party software package that breaks the software protection and allows you to copy the disk. Note that distributing licensed software is against the law. Use software packages that break copy protection to create your own backup copies only. BACKUP and RESTORE are the DOS commands you will use to perform your disk backups.

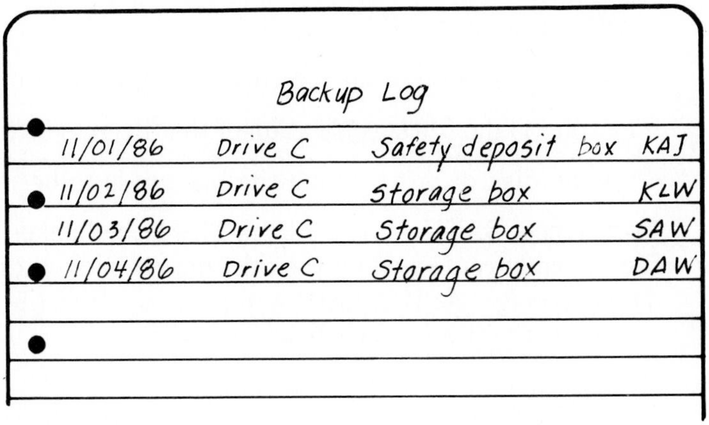

Figure 11-2. Backup log

BACKUP

Although the DOS BACKUP command supports floppy disk backup, it is most commonly used for hard disk backups. The format of the command is

[drive:][path]BACKUP d1:[file—spec] d2:[/A][/D:mm-dd-yy] [/M][/S]

where the following is true:

drive: is the disk drive containing the file BACKUP.COM. BACKUP is an external DOS command; therefore, DOS must read the file from disk into memory each time the command is invoked. If no disk is specified, DOS uses the current default drive.

Backing Up Your Disks

path is the series of subdirectories DOS must traverse to find the file BACKUP.COM. If no path is specified, DOS uses the current working directory or uses the search specified by the PATH command.

d1 is the disk containing the file(s) to be backed up.

file—spec is the file specification of the file(s) to be backed up.

d2 is the disk drive to which the backup is to be written.

/A requests BACKUP to add the files to be backed up to the files already contained on the destination backup disk. If you do not specify /A, BACKUP will destroy all of the files contained on the destination disk.

/D requests BACKUP to back up all files that have been created or modified since the date specified. Unless modified by a COUNTRY specification (see Chapter 15), the format of the date is mm-dd-yy where the following is true:

> *mm* is a two-digit number representing the desired month. The value must be in the range 1 (January) to 12 (December).

> *dd* is a two-digit number representing the desired day. The value must be in the range 1-31.

> *yy* is a two-digit number representing the desired year. The value must be in the range 80-99.

/M requests BACKUP to back up all files that have been created or modified since the last backup.

/S requests BACKUP to back up subdirectories contained in the current working directory.

Before you back up your hard disk, you need to know how many floppy disks will be required to store the data contained on your hard disk. Set your default drive to drive C and issue the DOS CHKDSK command. The following is displayed:

```
C> CHKDSK

Volume DOSDISK       created Nov 2, 1986 8:38p

21309440 bytes total disk space
  116736 bytes in 7 hidden files
  167936 bytes in 61 directories
13660160 bytes in 1729 user files
   20480 bytes in bad sectors
 7344128 bytes available on disk

  524288 bytes total memory
  274080 bytes free
```

Subtract the number of free bytes from the total number of bytes available as follows:

bytes used = total disk space − free bytes

Use the following equation to determine the number of floppy disks BACKUP will require to back up your hard disk:

number of disks = bytes used/floppy storage

Disk Type	Storage Capacity
Single-sided Double-density	184,320 bytes
Double-sided Double-density	368,640 bytes
Quad-density	1,228,800 bytes

Table 11-1.   Number of Bytes Available on Types of Disks

Table 11-1 gives you the number of bytes available on each type of floppy disk. For example, suppose you are given the disk

```
C> CHKDSK

Volume DOSDISK      created Nov 2, 1986 8:38p

21309440 bytes total disk space
  116736 bytes in 7 hidden files
  167936 bytes in 61 directories
13660160 bytes in 1729 user files
   20480 bytes in bad sectors
 7344128 bytes available on disk

  524288 bytes total memory
  274080 bytes free
```

You can determine the number of floppy disks required for the backup as follows:

number of disks = bytes used/floppy storage

$37.88 = (21309440 - 7344128)/368640$

38 disks needed

BACKUP requires all of the destination floppy disks to be formatted prior to use. Do not use the /S switch during disk formatting since doing so allocates a large portion of the disk for system files (such as IBMBIO.COM, IBMDOS.COM, and COMMAND.COM). Format your backup disks as follows:

```
A> FORMAT B:
```

Consider the following examples. Enter

```
C> BACKUP BUDGET.DAT B:
```

BACKUP will back up the file BUDGET.DAT in the current working directory to the backup disk in drive B. The contents of the disk in drive B will be destroyed. BACKUP will warn you as follows:

```
Insert backup diskette 01 in drive B:

Warning! Files in the target drive
B:\ root directory will be erased
Strike any key when ready
```

If you do not want to destroy the contents of the disk, simply terminate the command by pressing CTRL-C. Enter

```
C> BACKUP BUDGET.DAT B:/A
```

BACKUP will back up the file BUDGET.DAT in the current working directory, appending it to the contents of the disk in drive B. Enter

```
C> BACKUP *.DAT B:/M
```

BACKUP will back up all of the files in the current working directory with the extension DAT that have been created or modified since the last backup. The contents of the disk in drive B will be destroyed. Enter

```
C> BACKUP C:\ B:/S
```

BACKUP will back up all of the files on drive C to the disk(s) in drive B. If the backup requires more than one disk, it will prompt

```
Insert backup diskette 02 in drive B:

Warning! Files in the target drive
B:\ root directory will be erased
Strike any key when ready
```

The contents of the disk in drive B will be destroyed. Enter

```
C> BACKUP C:\ B:/S/M
```

BACKUP will back up all of the files on drive C that have been created or modified since the last backup. The contents of the disk in drive B will be destroyed. Enter

```
C> BACKUP C:\ B:/S/D:12-23-86
```

BACKUP will back up all of the files on drive C that have been created or modified since 12-23-86. The contents of the file in drive B will be destroyed. Enter

```
C> BACKUP C:\*.DAT B:/S
```

BACKUP will back up all of the files on drive C that have the extension DAT. The contents of the disk in drive B will be destroyed. Enter

```
C> BACKUP B:\ C:/S
```

BACKUP will back up the contents of the floppy disk contained in drive B to the fixed disk in drive C. BACKUP will create the directory BACKUP in the root directory and place the files in it. Most users will use either the DOS COPY command or the XCOPY command to copy the contents of a floppy disk to a hard disk.

Backup Policies and Procedures

Backups should be performed on a regular basis. The importance of your data will always affect your backup policies and procedures. The following procedure will minimize the possibility of data loss for most DOS users:

• Buy and format enough disks to perform three full backups of your hard disk. The number of disks required is shown in Table 11-2.

Hard Disk Size	Floppy Disk	Disks Required
10 megabytes	Double-sided Double-density	29
10 megabytes	Quad-density	9
20 megabytes	Double-sided Double-density	58
20 megabytes	Quad-density	18

Table 11-2.   Disks Required for Hard Disk Backup

• On the first day of the month, perform a complete disk backup as follows:

```
C> BACKUP C:\ B:/S
```

If your system is part of a local area network, turn off the network during the monthly backup. This ensures that the monthly backup is complete.

• Label your monthly disk backups as shown in Figure 11-3.

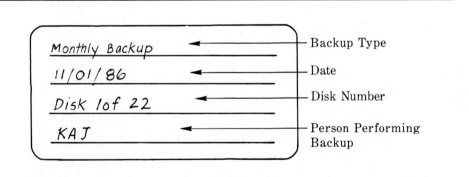

Figure 11-3.   Example of labels for monthly disk backups

- Each day, back up all of the changes for that day as follows:

```
C> BACKUP C:\ B:/S/M/A
```

- Label your daily (incremental) backup disk as shown in Figure 11-4.

- Log your backups in your backup log, as shown in Figure 11-5.

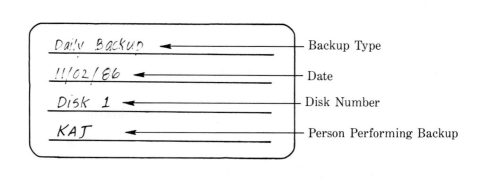

Figure 11-4.   Example of labels for daily disk backups

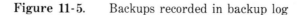

Figure 11-5.   Backups recorded in backup log

You can use batch procedures to simplify the backup process. The DOS BACKUP command uses the following error-status values; its use of them allows the batch procedures to perform conditional processing.

0   BACKUP completed successfully

1   BACKUP did not find any files to back up

2   BACKUP did not back up some files because of sharing conflicts

3   BACKUP was terminated by the user (CTRL-BREAK)

4   BACKUP was terminated because of an error

Create the batch procedures that follow for your monthly and daily backups.

In the file MONTHLY.BAT, include the following:

```
REM MONTHLY BACKUP PROCEDURES
BACKUP C:\ B:/S
IF ERRORLEVEL 4 GOTO FATAL_ERROR
IF ERRORLEVEL 3 GOTO USER_TERMINATED
IF ERRORLEVEL 2 GOTO SHARING_CONFLICT
IF ERRORLEVEL 1 GOTO NO_FILES
:SUCCESSFUL
PAUSE SUCCESSFUL BACKUP -- BACKUP COMPLETE
GOTO DONE
:NO_FILES
PAUSE NO FILES FOUND TO BACKUP
GOTO DONE
:SHARING_CONFLICT
PAUSE FILE SHARING CONFLICTS -- BACKUP INCOMPLETE
GOTO DONE
:USER_TERMINATED
PAUSE USER TERMINATION OF BACKUP -- BACKUP INCOMPLETE
GOTO DONE
:FATAL_ERROR
PAUSE FATAL BACKUP ERROR -- BACKUP INCOMPLETE
:DONE
```

MONTHLY.BAT

In the file DAILY.BAT, include the following:

```
REM INCREMENTAL BACKUP PROCEDURE
BACKUP C:\ B:/S/M/A
IF ERRORLEVEL 4 GOTO FATAL_ERROR
IF ERRORLEVEL 3 GOTO USER_TERMINATED
IF ERRORLEVEL 2 GOTO SHARING_CONFLICT
IF ERRORLEVEL 1 GOTO NO_FILES
:SUCCESSFUL
PAUSE SUCCESSFUL BACKUP -- BACKUP COMPLETE
GOTO DONE
:NO_FILES
PAUSE NO FILES FOUND TO BACKUP
GOTO DONE
:SHARING_CONFLICT
PAUSE FILE SHARING CONFLICTS -- BACKUP INCOMPLETE
GOTO DONE
:USER_TERMINATED
PAUSE USER TERMINATION OF BACKUP -- BACKUP INCOMPLETE
GOTO DONE
:FATAL_ERROR
PAUSE FATAL BACKUP ERROR -- BACKUP INCOMPLETE
:DONE
```

DAILY.BAT

At the end of the month, you should have the following disks:

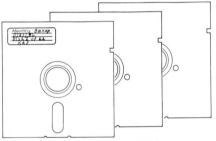

Monthly Backup Disks

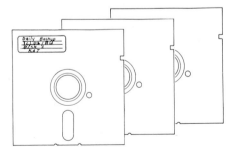

Daily Backup Disks

A convenient practice not provided directly by the DOS BACKUP command is to journalize the files that were backed up throughout the month. You can then search the journal file (BACKUP.BJL) to locate backed up files to determine which backup volume(s) contain the file(s) you need to restore. Chapter 16 provides a Turbo Pascal program that reads the file BACK-UP.BJL and provides a listing of the disk volumes containing the files desired. This program is available in the disk package offered by the author. In addition, you can use the DOS text editor EDLIN (see Chapter 13) to examine the journal file.

To produce the backup journal BACKUP.BJL, modify the monthly and daily batch procedures as follows:

```
REM MONTHLY BACKUP PROCEDURE
BACKUP C:\ B:/S > C:\BACKUP.BJL
IF ERRORLEVEL 4 GOTO FATAL_ERROR
IF ERRORLEVEL 3 GOTO USER_TERMINATED
IF ERRORLEVEL 2 GOTO SHARING_CONFLICT
IF ERRORLEVEL 1 GOTO NO_FILES
:SUCCESSFUL
PAUSE SUCCESSFUL BACKUP -- BACKUP COMPLETE
GOTO DONE
:NO_FILES
PAUSE NO FILES FOUND TO BACKUP
GOTO DONE
:SHARING_CONFLICT
PAUSE FILE SHARING CONFLICTS -- BACKUP INCOMPLETE
GOTO DONE
:USER_TERMINATED
PAUSE USER TERMINATION OF BACKUP -- BACKUP INCOMPLETE
GOTO DONE
:FATAL_ERROR
PAUSE FATAL BACKUP ERROR -- BACKUP INCOMPLETE
:DONE
```

MONTHLY.BAT

```
REM INCREMENTAL BACKUP PROCEDURE
BACKUP C:\ B:/S/M/A >> C:\BACKUP.BJL
IF ERRORLEVEL 4 GOTO FATAL_ERROR
IF ERRORLEVEL 3 GOTO USER_TERMINATED
IF ERRORLEVEL 2 GOTO SHARING_CONFLICT
IF ERRORLEVEL 1 GOTO NO_FILES
:SUCCESSFUL
PAUSE SUCCESSFUL BACKUP -- BACKUP COMPLETE
GOTO DONE
:NO_FILES
PAUSE NO FILES FOUND TO BACKUP
GOTO DONE
:SHARING_CONFLICT
PAUSE FILE SHARING CONFLICTS -- BACKUP INCOMPLETE
GOTO DONE
:USER_TERMINATED
PAUSE USER TERMINATION OF BACKUP -- BACKUP INCOMPLETE
GOTO DONE
:FATAL_ERROR
PAUSE FATAL BACKUP ERROR -- BACKUP INCOMPLETE
:DONE
```

DAILY.BAT

In this case you will use the DOS redirection operators > and >>
to create the file BACKUP.BJL. DOS redirects the name of each
file BACKUP backs up from the screen to the backup journal. All
of the messages requesting a new disk, or informative BACKUP
messages, are written to the screen.

Problems with BACKUP

There are a few problems that may arise during your backup processing. If you take the following steps, you will prevent these
problems from affecting your backups. First, some memory-
resident programs conflict with BACKUP. When you perform
your monthly backup, it is a good practice not to install memory-
resident programs. Second, always perform a directory listing on
the file BACKUPID.@@@ when you finish your backups. The
DOS BACKUP command sometimes causes the size of this file to
be 0. If the size of the file is 0, consider performing an intermediate complete backup of your disk and starting the monthly

backup cycle from the current date. In other words, invoke the procedure MONTHLY.BAT to obtain a complete disk backup, and then you can begin your incremental backups (DAILY.BAT) the following day.

RESTORE (Retrieving Files from Backup Disks)

The DOS RESTORE command restores one or more files from your backup disks. The format of the command is

[drive:][path]RESTORE d1: file—spec [/P][/S]

where the following is true:

drive: is the disk drive containing the file RESTORE.COM. RESTORE is an external DOS command; therefore, DOS must read the file from disk into memory each time the command is invoked. If no disk is specified, DOS uses the current default drive.

path is the series of subdirectories DOS must traverse to find the file RESTORE.COM. If no path is specified, DOS uses the current working directory.

d1 is the disk drive containing the backup disk.

file—spec is the name of the file(s) to back up from the backup disk (d1). This file specification also tells RESTORE where you want the files to be stored.

/P requests RESTORE to prompt you before restoring files that have been modified, or marked as read-only since the last backup:

```
Warning! File\FILENAME.EXT
was changed after it was backed up
Replace the file (Y/N)?
```

/S requests RESTORE to restore files in all of the subdirectories present.

Consider the following examples. Enter

```
C> RESTORE B: C:/S
```

RESTORE will restore all of the files on the backup disk in drive B to the disk in drive C, including files contained in subdirectories. Enter

```
C> RESTORE B: C:*.DAT
```

RESTORE will restore all of the files on the backup disk that came from the current directory in drive B that have the extension DAT. Files contained in subdirectories will not be restored. Enter

```
C> RESTORE B: C:*.DAT/P
```

RESTORE will restore all of the files on the backup disk in drive B that have the extension DAT. For all files with the extension DAT that have been modified or marked read-only since the backup occurred, RESTORE will prompt

```
Warning! File\FILENAME.EXT
was changed after it was backed up
Replace the file (Y/N)?
```

Enter

```
C> RESTORE B: C:/S/P
```

RESTORE will restore all of the files on the backup disk in drive B to the disk in drive C, including the files contained in subdirectories. For all files that have been modified or marked read-only since the backup occurred, RESTORE will prompt

```
Warning! File\FILENAME.EXT
was changed after it was backed up
Replace the file (Y/N)?
```

Use the following steps when you perform file restorations:

- Locate the file(s) to restore via your backup journal.

- If your computer is part of a local area network, turn off the network during the file restoration.

- Record the restoration in your backup log, as follows:

Backup Log			page 2
11/03/86	Drive C:	Storage box	KAJ
11/04/86	Drive C:	Restore	KAJ

The DOS RESTORE command also uses exit-status values, which allow you to perform conditional processing within batch procedures as follows:

0 RESTORE completed successfully

1 RESTORE did not find any files to restore

2 RESTORE did not back up some files because of sharing conflicts

3 RESTORE was terminated by the user (CTRL-BREAK)

4 RESTORE was terminated because of an error

As stated in Chapter 9, the only way that DOS can address disk fragmentation is to perform a complete backup and restoration of the disk. If you want to perform this process, you should first perform at least two complete backups of your hard disk. This decreases the possibility that a floppy disk error will prevent the restoration of your hard disk. In addition, there are several third-party products that address this problem. The following batch procedure addresses disk fragmentation. Include the following in the file FRAG.BAT:

```
REM DISK FRAGMENTATION PROCEDURE
BACKUP C:\ B:/S
IF ERRORLEVEL 4 GOTO FATAL_ERROR
IF ERRORLEVEL 3 GOTO USER_TERMINATED
IF ERRORLEVEL 2 GOTO SHARING_CONFLICT
IF ERRORLEVEL 1 GOTO NO_FILES
PAUSE FIRST BACKUP SUCCESSFUL -- BEGINNING SECOND BACKUP --
      USE NEW DISKETTES
BACKUP C:\ B:/S
IF ERRORLEVEL 4 GOTO FATAL_ERROR
IF ERRORLEVEL 3 GOTO USER_TERMINATED
IF ERRORLEVEL 2 GOTO SHARING_CONFLICT
IF ERRORLEVEL 1 GOTO NO_FILES
PAUSE SECOND BACKUP SUCCESSFUL -- BACKUP COMPLETE -- BEGINNING RESTORE
RESTORE B: C:/S
IF ERRORLEVEL 4 GOTO REST_FATAL_ERROR
IF ERRORLEVEL 3 GOTO REST_USER_TERMINATED
IF ERRORLEVEL 2 GOTO REST_SHARING_CONFLICT
IF ERRORLEVEL 1 GOTO REST_NO_FILES
PAUSE SUCCESSFUL DISK RESTORATION -- PROCESSING COMPLETE
GOTO DONE
:NO_FILES
PAUSE NO FILES FOUND TO BACKUP
GOTO DONE
:SHARING_CONFLICT
PAUSE FILE SHARING CONFLICTS -- BACKUP INCOMPLETE
GOTO DONE
:USER_TERMINATED
PAUSE USER TERMINATION OF BACKUP -- BACKUP INCOMPLETE
GOTO DONE
:FATAL_ERROR
PAUSE FATAL BACKUP ERROR -- BACKUP INCOMPLETE
GOTO DONE
:REST_NO_FILES
PAUSE NO FILES FOUND TO RESTORE
GOTO DONE
:REST_SHARING_CONFLICT
PAUSE FILE SHARING CONFLICTS -- RESTORE INCOMPLETE
GOTO DONE
:REST_USER_TERMINATED
PAUSE USER TERMINATION OF RESTORE -- RESTORE INCOMPLETE
GOTO DONE
:REST_FATAL_ERROR
PAUSE FATAL RESTORE ERROR -- RESTORE INCOMPLETE
:DONE
```

FRAG.BAT

The importance of performing backups of your disk cannot be overemphasized. You may never need to perform a file restoration. If you must, however, the few minutes you have spent backing up your disks on a daily basis will make you a true believer in the DOS BACKUP command. If you do not feel comfortable using the DOS BACKUP command, several third-party software packages provide menu-driven backups.

If you are developing applications for users, it is essential that you provide a mechanism to back up disks. This may just require providing user documentation on how and when to invoke the DOS BACKUP command. You may want to integrate the BACKUP and RESTORE commands into the application, however. Chapter 16 will examine a Turbo Pascal procedure that allows you to spawn a DOS command from within your application. If your data is very important, you may want to produce hard-copy backups of that data.

Review

1. What is the function of backups?

2. Will any backup procedure guarantee that no data will be lost?

3. What is the best method of backing up a floppy disk?

4. What are the functions of the following BACKUP qualifiers?

/D
/M
/S

5. What are the functions of the following BACKUP commands?

C> BACKUP MAIL.LST B:
C> BACKUP MAIL.LST B:/A
C> BACKUP C:\ B:/S
C> BACKUP C:\ B:/M/S

```
C> BACKUP C:\ B:/M/S/A
C> BACKUP *.DAT B:/A/D:12:23:86
```

6. What is the purpose of a backup journal?

7. What are the BACKUP exit-status codes?

8. What are the functions of the following RESTORE commands?

```
C> RESTORE B: C:/S
C> RESTORE B: C:*.COM
C> RESTORE B: C:BUDGET.DAT
C> RESTORE B: C:/S/P
```

9. What are the RESTORE exit-status values?

10. What are the steps in identifying and correcting fragmented disks?

11. Why should you perform two complete backups before restoring a fragmented hard disk?

12. How do you determine the number of floppy disks required to complete a hard disk backup?

Answers

1. *What is the function of backups?*

The purpose of backups is to prevent or minimize the accidental loss of programs or data.

2. *Will any backup procedure guarantee that no data will be lost?*

No procedure can guarantee that data loss will not occur. You must come to a happy medium between the amount of time and effort you want to spend completing your backups versus the amount of time you would be willing to spend re-creating lost programs or data.

3. *What is the best method of backing up a floppy disk?*

The DOS DISKCOPY command offers the easiest method of backing up a floppy disk. You should make backup copies of all of your floppy disks as soon as you buy them and place the originals in a safe location.

4. *What are the functions of the following BACKUP qualifiers?*

/D:mm-dd-yy requests BACKUP to back up only those files created or modified since the date specified. */M* requests BACKUP to back up all files modified since the last backup. */S* requests BACKUP to back up all of the files contained in subdirectories.

5. *What are the functions of the following BACKUP commands?*

> *C> BACKUP MAIL.LST B:*

BACKUP will place a backup copy of the file MAIL.LST on the disk in drive B. The contents of the disk in drive B will be destroyed.

> *C> BACKUP MAIL.LST B:/A*

BACKUP will place a backup copy of the file MAIL.LST on the disk in drive B. The file will be appended to the other backup files on that disk.

C> BACKUP C:\ B:/S

BACKUP will perform a complete disk backup of drive C, writing it to the disk(s) in drive B. All of the files on drive C will be backed up.

C> BACKUP C:\ B:/M/S

BACKUP will back up all of the files on drive C that have been modified since the last backup to the disk in drive B. The contents of the disk in drive B will be destroyed.

C> BACKUP C:\ B:/M/S/A

BACKUP will back up all of the files on drive C that have been modified since the last backup to the disk in drive B. The files will be appended to the contents of drive B.

*C> BACKUP *.DAT B:/A/D:12:23:86*

BACKUP will back up all of the files in the current working directory with the extension DAT that have been modified since 12-23-86.

6. What is the purpose of a backup journal?

A backup journal tells you which disk volumes contain backup copies of a file. See the procedures for creating a backup journal, presented in this chapter.

7. What are the BACKUP exit-status codes?

   0 BACKUP completed successfully
   1 BACKUP did not find any files to back up
   2 BACKUP did not back up some files because of sharing conflicts
   3 BACKUP was terminated by the user (CTRL-BREAK)
   4 BACKUP was terminated because of an error

8. *What are the functions of the following RESTORE commands?*

   C> RESTORE B: C:/S

RESTORE will restore all of the files on the backup disk in drive B to the disk in drive C, including files contained in subdirectories prompting you prior to restoring files that have been modified or marked read-only since the last backup.

   C> RESTORE B: C:*.COM

RESTORE will restore all of the files on the backup disk in drive B that have the extension COM. Files contained in subdirectories will not be restored.

   C> RESTORE B: C:BUDGET.DAT

RESTORE will restore the file BUDGET.DAT from the backup disk in drive B to the current directory in drive C, but only if it originally came from that directory.

   C> RESTORE B: C:/S/P

RESTORE will restore all of the files on the backup disk in drive B to the disk in drive C, including the files contained in subdirectories. For all files that have been modified or marked read-only since the backup occurred, RESTORE will prompt

```
Warning! File\FILENAME.EXT
was changed after it was backed up
Replace the file (Y/N)?
```

9. *What are the RESTORE exit-status values?*

   0   RESTORE completed successfully
   1   RESTORE did not find any files to restore
   2   RESTORE did not back up some files because of sharing conflicts

3   RESTORE was terminated by the user (CTRL-BREAK)

4   RESTORE was terminated because of an error

10. *What are the steps in identifying and correcting fragmented disks?*

To determine if your disk is badly fragmented, issue the CHKDSK command:

C> CHKDSK *.*

Next, perform two complete disk backups. Then use the DOS RESTORE command to replace the contents of the disk. The batch procedure FRAG.BAT, presented earlier in this chapter, illustrates these procedures.

11. *Why should you perform two complete backups before restoring a fragmented hard disk?*

You should always obtain two complete backups to provide added assurance that a floppy disk error in the first backup will not prevent hard disk restoration.

12. *How do you determine the number of floppy disks required to complete a hard disk backup?*

Issue the CHKDSK command, and the following will be displayed:

```
C> CHKDSK

Volume DOSDISK      created Nov 2, 1986 8:38p

 21309440 bytes total disk space
   116736 bytes in 7 hidden files
   167936 bytes in 61 directories
 13660160 bytes in 1729 user files
    20480 bytes in bad sectors
  7344128 bytes available on disk

   524288 bytes total memory
   274080 bytes free
```

Calculate the number of bytes used as follows:

bytes used = total disk space − free bytes
13965312 = 21309440 − 7344128

Next, use the equation

number of disks = bytes used/floppy storage
37.883 = 13965312/368640

This allows you to determine the number of disks required:

38

International DOS Concerns

Building an International Disk

With the international success of the IBM PC and DOS, the support of DOS for the keyboards, currency, and numeric standards of foreign countries became a must. With version 3.0 of DOS came many enhanced international capabilities. For example, many countries use different symbols for the following:

Date and time separators (/ − :)
Currency symbols and digits ($ F Lit.)
Thousands and decimal separators (, ; .)
List separators (, ;)

Thousands and decimal separators are simply the symbols that separate the digits in a number (for example, 4,356.07). List separators are simply delimiters used to separate items in a list.

DOS currently provides support for the countries shown in Table 12-1. Table 12-2 provides the symbols used by each country. All of the information provided in this table is available to application programs. Rather than having a version of a program for every country, you can have one program that looks up the country-specific symbols and responds accordingly.

In addition to specifying each country's symbols, DOS allows users to select one of six keyboard formats. If you list the directory of your DOS disk, you will note the files that follow.

```
A> DIR KEYB*.COM

Volume in drive A has no label
Directory of  A:\

KEYBSP   COM    2073   14/08/84    8:00
KEYBIT   COM    1854   14/08/84    8:00
KEYBGR   COM    2111   14/08/84    8:00
KEYBUK   COM    1760   14/08/84    8:00
KEYBFR   COM    2235   14/08/84    8:00
         5 File(s)    21792 bytes free
```

Each KEYBxx.COM program places code into memory to support one of the keyboard layouts shown in Figure 12-1. Later versions of DOS provide additional keyboard layouts. See the KEYBXX command in the DOS Reference section.

Each keyboard program allocates approximately 2K of memory. When you invoke a keyboard program, the foreign keyboard template remains resident in memory until you reboot the system. Once you have loaded a secondary keyboard, you can alternate between the foreign keyboard and the U.S. keyboard by pressing CTRL-ALT-F1 and CTRL-ALT-F2. The first combination, CTRL-ALT-F1, selects the U.S. keyboard layout. The sequence CTRL-ALT-F2 selects the foreign keyboard.

If you intend to use a foreign keyboard set permanently, you should place the desired KEYBxx.COM reference in the file AUTOEXEC.BAT. This ensures that DOS loads the keyboard template each time the system boots.

Most of the foreign character sets utilize the extended ASCII character set (ASCII values 128-255). The color graphics adapter, however, has problems displaying characters in this range when it is medium-resolution four-color mode. To compensate for this, DOS provides the command GRAFTABL. You use GRAFTABL to load an alternate character set into memory. To load this character set, simply issue the command

```
A> GRAFTABL
```

DOS will respond with

```
GRAPHICS CHARACTERS LOADED

A>
```

Country	Country Code
Australia	61
Belgium	32
Denmark	45
Finland	358
France	33
Germany	49
Israel	972
Italy	39
Netherlands	31
Norway	47
Spain	34
Sweden	46
Switzerland	41
United Kingdom	44
United States	1

Table 12-1.   Countries Supported by DOS and Corresponding Codes

Country Code	Country	Date Format	Currency Symbol	Thousands Separator	Decimal Separator	Date Separator	Time Separator	Decimal Significant Digits	Currency Format	Hour Format*	Data List Separator
1	United States	mm dd yy	$	,	.	—	:	2	0	1-12	,
31	Netherlands	dd mm yy	—	.	,	—	:	2	0	0-23	;
32	Belgium	dd mm yy	F	.	,	/	:	2	0	0-23	;
33	France	dd mm yy	F	.	,	/	:	2	0	0-23	;
34	Spain	dd mm yy	π	.	,	/	:	2	0	0-23	;
39	Italy	dd mm yy	Lit.	.	,	/	:	0	0	0-23	;
41	Switzerland	dd mm yy	Fr	,	.	.	:	2	0	0-23	,
44	United Kingdom	dd mm yy	£	,	.	—	:	2	0	0-23	,
45	Denmark	dd mm yy	DKR	.	,	/	.	2	0	0-23	;
46	Sweden	yy mm dd	SEK	.	,	—	.	2	0	0-23	;
47	Norway	dd mm yy	KR	.	,	/	.	2	0	0-23	;
49	Germany	dd mm yy	DM	.	,	.	.	2	0	0-23	;
61	Australia	dd mm yy	$	,	.	—	:	2	0	0-23	,
358	Finland	dd mm yy	MK		,	—	:	2	0	0-23	;
972	Israel	dd mm yy	—	,	.	/	:	2	0	0-23	,

* 1-12 is 12-hour format; 0-23 is 24-hour format.

Table 12-2.   Symbols Used by Each Country

French KEYBFR.COM

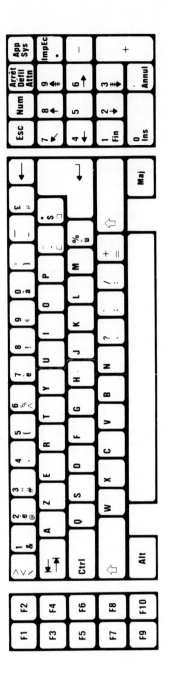

From *Disk Operating System Technical Reference*, 1986. Reprinted by permission of International Business Machines Corporation.

Figure 12-1. Keyboard layouts supported by DOS

German KEYBGR.COM

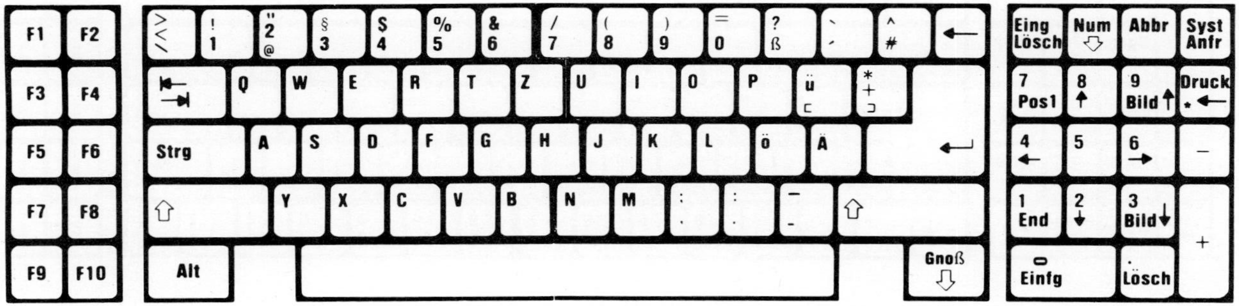

From *Disk Operating System Technical Reference*, 1986. Reprinted by permission of International Business Machines Corporation.

Figure 12-1. Keyboard layouts supported by DOS (*continued*)

Italian KEYBIT.COM

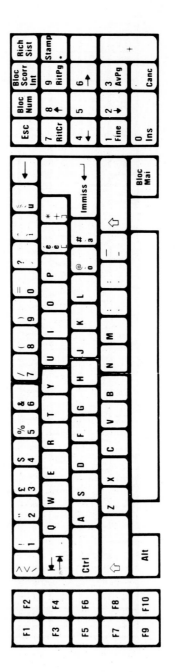

From *Disk Operating System Technical Reference*, 1986. Reprinted by permission of International Business Machines Corporation.

Figure 12-1. Keyboard layouts supported by DOS (*continued*)

U.K. English KEYBUK.COM

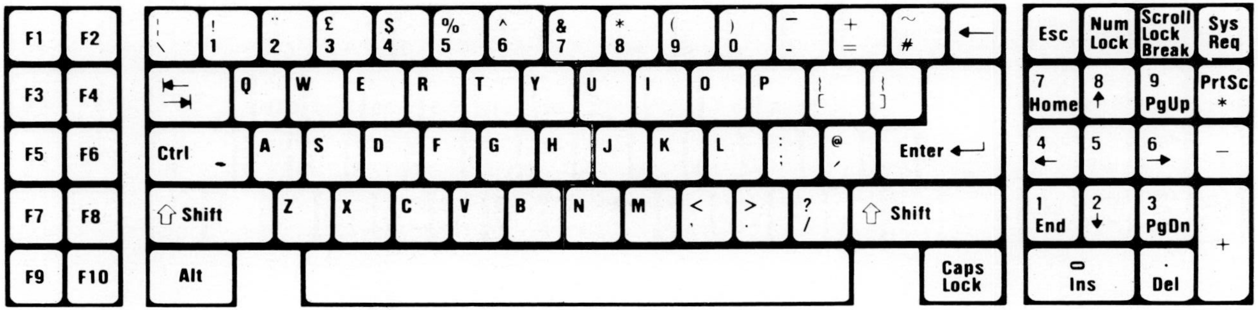

From *Disk Operating System Technical Reference*, 1986. Reprinted by permission of International Business Machines Corporation.

Figure 12-1. Keyboard layouts supported by DOS *(continued)*

Spanish KEYBSP.COM

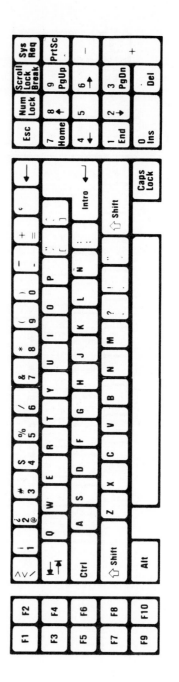

From *Disk Operating System Technical Reference, 1986. Reprinted by permission of International Business Machines Corporation.*

Figure 12-1. Keyboard layouts supported by DOS (*continued*)

DOS: The Complete Reference

U.S. English

From *Disk Operating System Technical Reference, 1986. Reprinted by permission of International Business Machines Corporation.*

Figure 12-1. Keyboard layouts supported by DOS (*continued*)

Tables 12-3 through 12-8 illustrate the extended ASCII characters used for each KEYBxx.COM.

Many users in foreign countries find it convenient to place the command GRAFTABL into the file AUTOEXEC.BAT. If you do not intend to use the extended character set often, you should not invoke GRAFTABL, since it allocates approximately 1.5K of memory.

Building an International Disk

To simplify the process of creating a system disk that utilizes the character set of a foreign country, DOS provides the command SELECT. The format of the command is

[drive:][path]SELECT country—code keyboard—layout

where the following is true:

drive: and *path* are the drive and path of the file SELECT.COM

country—code is the three-character value used to reference each country

keyboard—layout is the two-character mnemonic of the KEYBxx.COM of the country desired (IT, UK, FR, GR, SP)

SELECT creates a DOS system disk and builds the files CONFIG.SYS and AUTOEXEC.BAT containing the following entries:

CONFIG.SYS
    COUNTRY=country—code

AUTOEXEC.BAT
    KEYBxx

To invoke SELECT, place your DOS disk in drive A and a new disk in drive B. If you only have one floppy disk drive, SELECT will prompt you to enter the source and target disks at

Code	Char	Code	Char	Code	Char	Code	Char	Code	Char	Code	Char	Code	Char	Code	Char	Code	Char
96	`	135	ç	144	É	153	Ö	163	ú	172	¼	229	σ	238	ε	247	≈
127	⌂	136	ê	145	æ	154	Ü	164	ñ	173	¡	230	µ	239	∩	248	°
128	Ç	137	ë	146	Æ	155	¢	165	Ñ	174	«	231	τ	240	≡	249	·
129	ü	138	è	147	ô	157	¥	166	ª	175	»	232	Φ	241	±	250	·
130	é	139	ï	148	ö	158	Pts	167	º	224	α	233	Θ	242	≥	251	√
131	â	140	î	149	ò	159	ƒ	168	¿	225	ß	234	Ω	243	≤	252	ⁿ
132	ä	141	ì	150	û	160	á	169	⌐	226	Γ	235	δ	244	⌠	253	²
133	à	142	Ä	151	ù	161	í	170	¬	227	π	236	∞	245	⌡	254	■
134	å	143	Å	152	ÿ	162	ó	171	½	228	Σ	237	∅	246	÷		

From *Disk Operating System Technical Reference*, 1986. Reprinted by permission of International Business Machines Corporation.

Table 12-3. U.K. English Extended ASCII Set

96 `	148 ö	160 á	169 ⌐	226 Γ	235 δ	244 ⌠	253 ²
127 ⌂	150 ù	161 í	170 ¬	227 π	236 ∞	245 ⌡	254 ■
128 Ç	152 ÿ	162 ó	171 ½	228 Σ	237 ø	246 ÷	255
129 ü	153 Ö	163 ú	172 ¼	229 σ	238 ε	247 ≈	
131 â	154 Ü	164 ñ	173 ¡	230 µ	239 ∩	248 °	
132 ä	155 ¢	165 Ñ	174 «	231 τ	240 ≡	249 •	
134 å	157 ¥	166 ª	175 »	232 Φ	241 ±	250 ·	
135 ç	158 Pts	167 º	224 α	233 Θ	242 ≥	251 √	
136 ê	159 ƒ	168 ¿	225 β	234 Ω	243 ≤	252 ⁿ	
137 ë							
139 ï							
140 î							
142 Ä							
143 Å							
144 É							
145 æ							
146 Æ							
147 ò							

From *Disk Operating System Technical Reference*, 1986. Reprinted by permission of International Business Machiness Corporation.

Table 12-4. Italian Extended ASCII Set

127 ⌂	136 ê	145 æ	154 Ü	163 ú	172 ¼	229 σ	239 ∩	248 °
128 Ç	137 ë	146 Æ	155 ¢	164 ñ	173 ¡	230 µ	240 ≡	249 ∙
129 ü	138 è	147 ô	156 £	165 Ñ	174 «	231 τ	241 ±	250 ·
130 é	139 ï	148 ö	157 ¥	166 ª	175 »	232 Φ	242 ≥	251 √
131 â	140 î	149 ò	158 Pts	167 º	224 α	234 Ω	243 ≤	252 ⁿ
132 ä	141 ì	150 û	159 ƒ	168 ¿	225 β	235 δ	244 ⌠	253 ²
133 à	142 Ä	151 ù	160 á	169 ⌐	226 Γ	236 ∞	245 ⌡	254 ■
134 å	143 Å	152 ÿ	161 í	170 ¬	227 π	237 ∅	246 ÷	255
135 ç	144 É	153 Ö	162 ó	171 ½	228 Σ	238 ε	247 ≈	

From *Disk Operating System Technical Reference*, 1986. Reprinted by permission of International Business Machiness Corporation.

Table 12-5.   U.S. English Extended ASCII Set

123 {	156 £	172 ¼	230 µ	239 ∩	248 °
124 |	157 ¥	174 «	231 τ	240 ≡	249 •
125 }	158 Pts	175 »	232 Φ	241 ±	250 ·
126 ~	159 ƒ	224 α	233 Θ	242 ≥	251 √
127 ⌂	166 ª	225 β	234 Ω	243 ≤	252 ⁿ
134 å	167 º	226 Γ	235 δ	244 ⌠	253 ²
145 æ	169 ⌐	227 π	236 ∞	245 ⌡	254 ■
146 Æ	170 ¬	228 Σ	237 ∅	246 ÷	
155 ¢	171 ½	229 σ	238 ε	247 ≈	

From *Disk Operating System Technical Reference*, 1986. Reprinted by permission of International Business Machiness Corporation.

Table 12-6. Spanish Extended ASCII Set

Code	Char	Code	Char	Code	Char	Code	Char	Code	Char	Code	Char	Code	Char	Code	Char
123	{	136	ê	152	ÿ	167	º	224	α	234	Ω	243	≤	252	η
124	¦	139	ï	155	¢	168	¿	226	Γ	235	δ	244	⌠	253	²
125	}	140	î	156	£	169	⌐	227	π	236	∞	245	⌡	254	■
126	~	141	ì	157	¥	170	¬	228	Σ	237	∅	246	÷		
127	⌂	143	Å	158	Pts	171	½	229	σ	238	∈	247	≈		
128	Ç	145	æ	159	ƒ	172	¼	230	µ	239	∩	248	°		
131	â	146	Æ	164	ñ	173	¡	231	τ	240	≡	249	∙		
134	å	147	ô	165	Ñ	174	«	232	Φ	241	±	250	·		
135	ç	150	û	166	ª	175	»	233	Θ	242	≥	251	√		

From *Disk Operating System Technical Reference*, 1986. Reprinted by permission of International Business Machiness Corporation.

Table 12-7. German Extended ASCII Set

Code	Char	Code	Char	Code	Char	Code	Char	Code	Char
96	`	160	á	169	⌐	226	Γ	235	δ	244	⌠	254	■
123	{	161	í	170	¬	227	π	236	∞	245	⌡		
124	|	162	ó	171	½	228	Σ	237	Ø	246	÷		
125	}	163	ú	172	¼	229	σ	238	ε	247	≈		
126	~	164	ñ	173	¡	230	µ	239	∩	249	·		
127	⌂	165	Ñ	174	«	231	τ	240	≡	250	·		
128	Ç	166	ª	175	»	232	Φ	241	±	251	√		
134	å	167	º	224	α	233	Θ	242	≥	252	ⁿ		
141	ì	168	¿	225	β	234	Ω	243	≤	253	²		
143	Å
144	É
145	æ
146	Æ
149	ò
155	¢
157	¥
158	Pts
159	ƒ

From *Disk Operating System Technical Reference*, 1986. Reprinted by permission of International Business Machines Corporation.

Table 12-8. French Extended ASCII Set

the correct times. The following command creates a disk for the United Kingdom:

```
A> SELECT 044 UK
```

If you have two floppy disk drives, SELECT will display the following:

```
Insert SOURCE Diskette in Drive A:

Insert TARGET Diskette in Drive B:

Press any key when ready ...
```

SELECT will then invoke the DISKCOPY program to copy the contents of the DOS disk to the target drive. When finished, DISKCOPY will prompt you as follows:

```
Copy another diskette (Y/N)?
```

Press N, and SELECT will build the files CONFIG.SYS and AUTOEXEC.BAT on the target disk. If you are running DOS version 3.0, SELECT will invoke the DISKCOMP routine to verify a successful DISKCOPY. The target disk will now utilize the standards of the United Kingdom. Type the files CONFIG.SYS and AUTOEXEC.BAT on the target disk by entering the following commands:

```
A> TYPE B:CONFIG.SYS

COUNTRY=044

A> TYPE B:AUTOEXEC.BAT

KEYBUK
ECHO OFF
CLS
DATE
TIME
VER

A>
```

1. What countries are represented by the following keyboard programs?

    KEYBSP.COM
    KEYBIT.COM
    KEYBGR.COM
    KEYBUK.COM
    KEYBFR.COM

2. If a secondary keyboard program is loaded, how do you alternate between the U.S. and foreign keyboards?

3. What is the function of GRAFTABL?

4. Issue the SELECT command required to create a disk for Italy with the Italian keyboard layout.

5. Illustrate the entry in CONFIG.SYS to specify the country of France.

Answers

1. What countries are represented by the following keyboard programs?

KEYBSP.COM	Spain
KEYBIT.COM	Italy
KEYBGR.COM	Germany
KEYBUK.COM	United Kingdom
KEYBFR.COM	France

2. If a secondary keyboard program is loaded, how do you alternate between the U.S. and foreign keyboards?

CTRL-ALT-F1 selects U.S. keyboard

CTRL-ALT-F2 selects foreign keyboard

3. What is the function of GRAFTABL?

GRAFTABL loads an alternate character set into memory to be used in conjunction with the extended ASCII character set. The IBM color monitor blurs characters in this range when it is in medium-resolution four-color mode. Many of the foreign character sets utilize characters in this range.

4. Issue the SELECT command required to create a disk for Italy with the Italian keyboard layout.

SELECT 39 IT

5. Illustrate the entry in CONFIG.SYS to specify the country of France.

COUNTRY=33

EDLIN—The DOS
Line Editor

Getting Started with EDLIN
Advanced Text Editing
Searching for Words and Phrases
Replace
Creating Disk Labels with EDLIN

One of the most common uses of computers is to generate reports, memos, and letters. Although the cost of dedicated word processors has decreased greatly over the past few years, they are still expensive. Some users find that the DOS line editor, EDLIN, suits many of their word processing needs.

EDLIN is a text editor that allows you to create or modify text (readable) files. With EDLIN you can

- create text files

- examine the contents of a text file

- update the contents of a text file by inserting, deleting, or changing lines

- perform file-wide searches and replacements of keywords within a text file

EDLIN is a line editor, which means that you edit files one line at a time. A line in an EDLIN file can contain up to 253 characters. As stated, each time you use EDLIN you create, examine, or modify a file. If you use EDLIN to modify a file, EDLIN saves the previous version of the file and gives it the extension BAK, as illustrated in Figure 13-1.

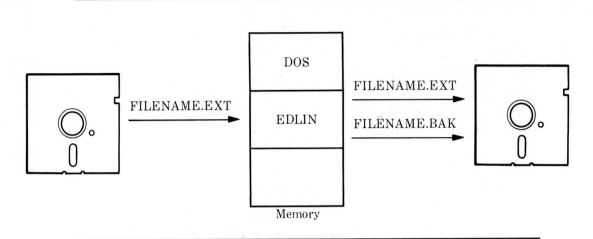

Figure 13-1. EDLIN saving previous version of a file

EDLIN is a DOS command that you can treat in the same manner as other DOS commands. Before you can use EDLIN, it must reside in memory, as shown in Figure 13-2. The format to invoke EDLIN is

[drive:][path]EDLIN file—spec [/B]

where the following is true:

drive: is the disk drive that contains the file EDLIN.COM. EDLIN is an external DOS command; therefore, DOS must read the command from disk into memory each time you invoke EDLIN. If you do not specify a disk drive, DOS will use the current drive.

path is the series of subdirectories DOS must traverse to find the file EDLIN.COM. If you do not specify a path, DOS will use the current working directory.

file—spec is the name of the text file that you want to edit.

/B is an advanced EDLIN qualifier that tells EDLIN that the text file may contain an embedded Control Z (^Z), the DOS

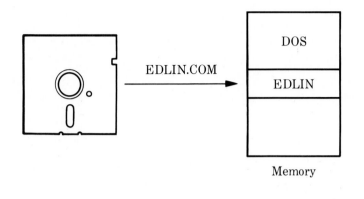

Figure 13-2.   EDLIN residing in DOS memory

end of file marker. If the /B qualifier is included in the command line, EDLIN will load the entire file regardless of embedded ^Z characters. Otherwise, EDLIN will use the first ^Z to mark the end of the file.

When you invoke EDLIN, you must specify a file to edit by entering

```
A> EDLIN FILENAME.EXT
```

If no file name is present, EDLIN will display

```
A> EDLIN
File name must be specified
```

EDLIN begins by loading into memory as much of the file you are editing as possible. EDLIN loads the file into memory until the file is completely loaded or memory is 75% full, as shown in Figure 13-3. EDLIN leaves 25% of memory free so that it has enough space to perform the editing it requires.

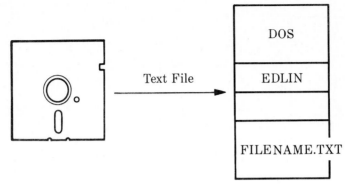

a. File completely loaded in memory

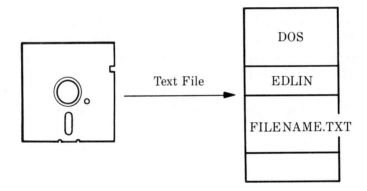

b. Memory 75% full

Figure 13-3.   EDLIN loading a file into memory

Once EDLIN has loaded the file, EDLIN displays one of two messages and then an asterisk, *, which is the EDLIN prompt. If the file you are editing is a new file, EDLIN will display

```
A> EDLIN NEWFILE.EXT
New file
*
```

If you are editing an existing file, EDLIN will display

```
A> EDLIN OLDFILE.EXT
End of input file
*
```

The EDLIN prompt, *, is similar to the DOS prompt in that it tells you that EDLIN is ready for you to issue a command. Before you examine EDLIN, however, it is important to examine the characteristics of EDLIN commands.

All EDLIN commands manipulate a single line of text, or multiple lines one line at a time. With the exception of the EDIT command, all EDLIN commands are called with a single letter.

A   Append lines from disk into memory

C   Copy lines

D   Delete lines

E   End edit and save changes

I   Insert lines

M   Move lines

P   Page display

Q   Quit edit and disregard changes

R   Replace a word or phrase

S   Search for a word or phrase

T   Transfer lines from another file

W   Write lines from memory back to disk

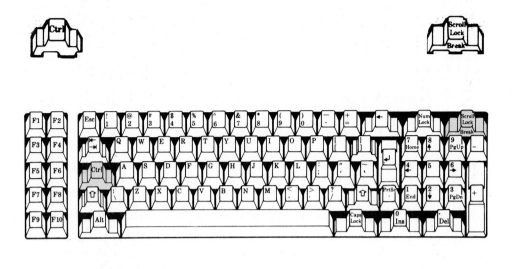

Figure 13-4. Position of CTRL and BREAK keys

All EDLIN commands are executed only after you press the ENTER key. EDLIN commands are terminated when you press CTRL-BREAK, as shown in Figure 13-4. The DOS editing keys from Chapter 10 are valid in EDLIN, as illustrated in Figure 13-5. To suspend the scrolling of output in EDLIN, press the CTRL and NUMLOCK keys at the same time, as shown in Figure 13-6. To resume scrolling, simply press any key.

EDLIN supports multiple commands on one line. To use multiple commands you must separate each command with a semicolon (;). To enter a control sequence in EDLIN, hold down the CTRL key while you press V (see Figure 13-7) and then the key desired. For example, for an ^I (the tab character), simply press CTRL and V at the same time, release the keys, and press I. Commands and string parameters can be entered in both uppercase and lowercase letters.

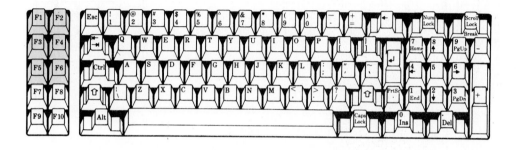

Figure 13-5.   Position of DOS editing keys

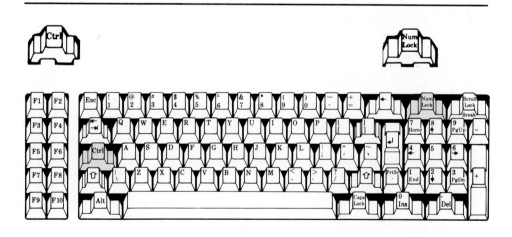

Figure 13-6.   Position of CTRL and NUMLOCK keys

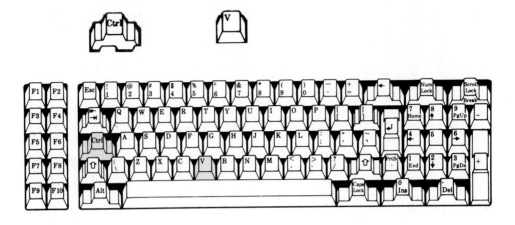

Figure 13-7. Position of CTRL and V keys

Getting Started with EDLIN

To get started, create the following batch file via EDLIN:

```
CLS
DATE
TIME
VER
```

The name of the file is TEST.BAT. Simply issue the EDLIN command as follows:

```
A> EDLIN TEST.BAT
```

Because TEST.BAT is a new file, EDLIN will respond with

```
A> EDLIN TEST.BAT
New file
*
```

Since there are no lines in the current file, you must issue the Insert command. Type the letter I and press the ENTER key; the following is displayed:

```
A> EDLIN TEST.BAT
*I
        1:*
```

As previously stated, EDLIN works with one line of text at a time. In this case, the 1:* tells you that EDLIN is ready for you to type in line 1. Type CLS and press the ENTER key.

```
A> EDLIN TEST.BAT
*I
        1:* CLS
        2:*
```

EDLIN is now ready for line 2. Type the word DATE and press ENTER.

```
A> EDLIN TEST.BAT
*I
        1:* CLS
        2:* DATE
        3:*
```

Continue this process for the words TIME and VER.

```
A> EDLIN TEST.BAT
*I
        1:* CLS
        2:* DATE
        3:* TIME
        4:* VER
        5:*
```

Since you have typed in all of the desired lines, you can now exit Insert mode. Press CTRL-BREAK to exit from the Insert mode, and the following is displayed:

```
A> EDLIN TEST.BAT
*I
        1:* CLS
        2:* DATE
        3:* TIME
        4:* VER
        5:*^C
*
```

To terminate this editing session and save the changes to the file, use the EDLIN Exit command.

```
A> EDLIN TEST.BAT
*I
        1:* CLS
        2:* DATE
        3:* TIME
        4:* VER
        5:*^C
*E

A>
```

At the DOS prompt, type the contents of TEST.BAT, and the following is displayed:

```
A> TYPE TEST.BAT
CLS
DATE
TIME
VER
```

Now that you have seen how to create a file with EDLIN, create the file CONFIG.NEW with the following data:

```
FILES=20
DEVICE=VDISK
```

```
A> EDLIN CONFIG.NEW
New file
*I
        1:* FILES=20
        2:* DEVICE=VDISK
        3:* ^C
*E

A>
```

Now use EDLIN to examine a file that already exists.

```
A> EDLIN TEST.BAT
End of input file
*
```

Type the number 1 and press the ENTER key.

```
A> EDLIN TEST.BAT
End of input file
*1
        1:* CLS
        1:*
```

EDLIN is displaying the current contents of line 1. If you want to change line 1, simply type the new line that you desire at the 1:* prompt. Otherwise, press the ENTER key, and EDLIN will not modify the line's contents. In this case, simply press the ENTER key.

```
A> EDLIN TEST.BAT
End of input file
*1
        1:* CLS
        1:*
*
```

Press the ENTER key six times.

```
A> EDLIN TEST.BAT
End of input file
*1
        1:* CLS
        1:*
*
        2:* DATE
        2:*
*
        3:* TIME
        3:*
*
        4:* VER
        4:*
*
```

EDLIN just allowed you to edit all four lines of the file. Type 1 and press the ENTER key.

```
*1
            1:* CLS
            1:*
```

Type the word VOL and press ENTER.

```
*1
            1:* CLS
            1:* VOL
  *
```

You have just modified the contents of line 1. EDLIN is now ready to edit line 2. Press the ENTER key.

```
*1
            1:* CLS
            1:* VOL
  *
            2:* DATE
            2:*
```

Press the ENTER key, and EDLIN will leave the line unchanged.

```
*1
            1:* CLS
            1:* VOL
  *
            2:* DATE
            2:*
  *
```

EDLIN commands assume that you want to use the current
line if you do not provide an alternate line number. The current
line in this case is line 2. Type the letter D (for Delete) and press
ENTER.

```
*1
          1:* CLS
          1:* VOL
*
          2:* DATE
          2:*
*D
*
```

EDLIN just deleted line 2 from the file. Starting at line 1, display
the current contents of the file.

```
*1
          1:* VOL
          1:*
*
          2:* TIME
          2:*
*
          3:* VER
          3:*
*
```

End the current editing session and return to DOS.

```
*1
          1:* VOL
          1:*
*
          2:* TIME
          2:*
*
          3:* VER
          3:*
*E

A>
```

Perform a directory listing of TEST and the following is displayed:

```
A> DIR TEST

  Volume in drive A is EDLIN
  Directory of  A:\

TEST      BAK      23   11-30-86   11:08a
TEST      BAT      27   11-30-86   11:27a
          2 File(s)      68608 bytes free
```

As you can see, EDLIN saves the previous version of the file and gives it the extension BAK. This action by EDLIN protects you from making permanent changes to a file that you may later decide you don't wish to make. By saving the previous version of a file, EDLIN allows you to restore a file to its original contents if necessary.

Assume that you have made several changes to a file and that you realize you didn't really want to make those changes. At the DOS prompt, copy the contents of filename.BAK to filename.EXT to restore the file to its original contents by issuing the following commands:

A> COPY FILENAME.BAK FILENAME.EXT

If you are still in the editing session and you realize that you don't really want to make the changes you have entered, you can use the EDLIN Quit command.

*Q

This allows you to terminate an editing session and disregard any of the changes you have made. In this case, EDLIN will prompt you with

```
  *Q
  Abort edit (Y/N)?
```

If you really want to terminate the editing session without saving your changes, press the letter Y.

```
*Q
Abort edit (Y/N)? Y

A>
```

Otherwise, press N and you will remain in the editing session.

```
*Q
Abort edit (Y/N)? N
*
```

Advanced Text Editing

The file TEST.BAT should now contain the following:

```
VOL
TIME
VER
```

If it doesn't, issue the EDLIN command with the file TEST.BAT and then issue the commands required to change the contents of TEST.BAT as desired.

```
A> EDLIN TEST.BAT
```

The EDLIN List command lists the contents of one or more lines in a file. The format of the List command is [first __line][,last __line]L

where the following is true:

first __line is the line number of the first line EDLIN is to display. If you don't specify a line number, EDLIN begins the display 11 lines prior to the current line.

last __line is the line number of the last line EDLIN is to list. If you don't specify a line number, EDLIN displays a total of 23 lines.

L is the abbreviation for the EDLIN LIST command.

By default, the List command displays 23 lines (11 lines before and after the current line). Use the List command to display the contents of TEST.BAT.

```
A> EDLIN TEST.BAT
End of input file
*L
        1:* VOL
        2:  TIME
        3:  VER
    *
```

Next, use line 2 as the first line, to display the following:

```
A> EDLIN TEST.BAT
End of input file
*L
        1:* VOL
        2:  TIME
        3:  VER
*2,L
        2:  TIME
        3:  VER
    *
```

Now, display the contents of line 2 only.

```
A> EDLIN TEST.BAT
End of input file
*L
        1:* VOL
        2:  TIME
        3:  VER
*2,L
        2:  TIME
        3:  VER
*2,2L
        2:  TIME
*
```

EDLIN uses the period (.) as the abbreviation for the current line. As you will see, this abbreviation proves convenient in the use of many of the EDLIN commands. Consider the following:

```
*.,L
        1:* VOL
        2:  TIME
        3:  VER
*
```

Since EDLIN uses the period to represent the current line (line 1), the command displays the contents of the file. The following command displays the current line and the line immediately following it.

```
A> EDLIN TEST.BAT
End of input file
*L
        1:* VOL
        2:  TIME
        3:  VER
*2,L
        2:  TIME
        3:  VER
*2,2L
        2:  TIME
*.,+1
        1:* VOL
        2:  TIME
*
```

In addition to recognizing line numbers, EDLIN commands understand offsets from the current line number in the + or − direction. For example, if you assume that the current line number is 10, then the following is true:

.   is line 10
−5 is line 5
+5 is line 15
−7 is line 3
+8 is line 18

Quit the current editing session without saving any changes to the file.

```
A> EDLIN TEST.BAT
End of input file
*L
        1:* VOL
        2:  TIME
        3:  VER
*2,L
        2:  TIME
        3:  VER
*2,2L
        2:  TIME
*.,+1
        1:* VOL
        2:  TIME
*Q
Abort edit (Y/N)?

A>
```

Invoke EDLIN to create the file NUMBERS.DAT that contains the following:

```
ONE
TWO
THREE
FOUR
FIVE
SIX
SEVEN
EIGHT
NINE
TEN
ELEVEN
TWELVE
THIRTEEN
FOURTEEN
FIFTEEN
```

```
A> EDLIN NUMBERS.DAT
New file
*I
        1:* ONE
        2:* TWO
        3:* THREE
        4:* FOUR
        5:* FIVE
        6:* SIX
        7:* SEVEN
        8:* EIGHT
        9:* NINE
       10:* TEN
       11:* ELEVEN
       12:* TWELVE
       13:* THIRTEEN
       14:* FOURTEEN
       15:* FIFTEEN
       16:* ^C
   *
```

Use the EDLIN List command to display the entire contents of
the file.

```
*1,L
        1: ONE
        2: TWO
        3: THREE
        4: FOUR
        5: FIVE
        6: SIX
        7: SEVEN
        8: EIGHT
        9: NINE
       10: TEN
       11: ELEVEN
       12: TWELVE
       13: THIRTEEN
       14: FOURTEEN
       15:*FIFTEEN
   *
```

Select line 10 as the current line number.

```
*10
        10:* TEN
        10:*
   *
```

List lines 5 through 15 by invoking either

```
*5,15L
        5:  FIVE
        6:  SIX
        7:  SEVEN
        8:  EIGHT
        9:  NINE
       10:*TEN
       11:  ELEVEN
       12:  TWELVE
       13:  THIRTEEN
       14:  FOURTEEN
       15:  FIFTEEN
   *
```

or

```
*-5,+5L
        5:  FIVE
        6:  SIX
        7:  SEVEN
        8:  EIGHT
        9:  NINE
       10:*TEN
       11:  ELEVEN
       12:  TWELVE
       13:  THIRTEEN
       14:  FOURTEEN
       15:  FIFTEEN
   *
```

In addition to the List command, EDLIN provides the Page command. The format of the command is

[first _line][,last _line]P

where the following is true:

> *first _line* is the line number of the first line the Page command is to display. If you do not specify a line number, Page begins at the current line plus one.

> *last _line* is the line number of the last line the Page command is to display. If you do not specify a line number, Page will display 23 lines at a time.

> *P* is the abbreviation for the EDLIN Page command.

Set the current line number to 1.

```
*1
        1:* ONE
        1:*
  *
```

Invoke the EDLIN Page command.

```
*1
        1:* ONE
        1:*
*P
        1: ONE
        2: TWO
        3: THREE
        4: FOUR
        5: FIVE
        6: SIX
        7: SEVEN
        8: EIGHT
        9: NINE
       10: TEN
       11: ELEVEN
       12: TWELVE
       13: THIRTEEN
       14: FOURTEEN
       15:*FIFTEEN
  *
```

If you do not specify a starting line number, the EDLIN Page command begins at the current line number plus one. By default, Page displays 23 lines at a time. After it has finished the display, Page increments the current line number to the last line it displayed, or, in this case, line 15.

Consider the following Page commands. Specify

```
*1,10P
         1:  ONE
         2:  TWO
         3:  THREE
         4:  FOUR
         5:  FIVE
         6:  SIX
         7:  SEVEN
         8:  EIGHT
         9:  NINE
        10:*TEN
  *
```

Page will display lines 1-10. Specify

```
*-5,P
         5:  FIVE
         6:  SIX
         7:  SEVEN
         8:  EIGHT
         9:  NINE
        10:  TEN
        11:  ELEVEN
        12:  TWELVE
        13:  THIRTEEN
        14:  FOURTEEN
        15:*FIFTEEN
  *
```

Page will display the lines of the file from line 5 (.−5 or 10 − 5) to the end of the file.

You have already used one form of the EDLIN Delete command to delete the current line. The complete format of the Delete command is

[first__line][,last__line]D

where the following is true:

first—line is the line number of the first line EDLIN is to delete. If you do not specify a line number, Delete uses the current line number.

last—line is the line number of the last line EDLIN is to delete. If you do not specify a line number, Delete only deletes the one line specified.

D is the abbreviation for the EDLIN Delete command.

Use Delete to delete lines 5-10 of the current file by invoking either of the following:

```
*5,10D
*1,L
        1: ONE
        2: TWO
        3: THREE
        4: FOUR
        5:*ELEVEN
        6: TWELVE
        7: THIRTEEN
        8: FOURTEEN
        9: FIFTEEN
*
```

or

```
*5
        5:* FIVE
        5:
*.,+5D
*1,L
        1: ONE
        2: TWO
        3: THREE
        4: FOUR
        5:*ELEVEN
        6: TWELVE
        7: THIRTEEN
        8: FOURTEEN
        9: FIFTEEN
*
```

Note that EDLIN updates line numbers of the text remaining in the file after the deletion of the other lines. The following EDLIN command deletes line 3 of the text file.

```
*5
             5:* FIVE
             5:
*.,+5D
*1,L
             1:  ONE
             2:  TWO
             3:  THREE
             4:  FOUR
             5:*ELEVEN
             6:  TWELVE
             7:  THIRTEEN
             8:  FOURTEEN
             9:  FIFTEEN
*3,3D
*1,L
             1:  ONE
             2:  TWO
             3:*FOUR
             4:  ELEVEN
             5:  TWELVE
             6:  THIRTEEN
             7:  FOURTEEN
             8:  FIFTEEN
*
```

Enter the command

```
*1,4D
*1,L
             1:*TWELVE
             2:  THIRTEEN
             3:  FOURTEEN
             4:  FIFTEEN
*
```

The command deletes lines 1-4 of the file. Finally, enter the command

```
*1,4D
*1,L
             1:*TWELVE
             2:  THIRTEEN
             3:  FOURTEEN
             4:  FIFTEEN
*.,4D
*L
*
```

This command deletes text from the current line through line 5. Exit from the current editing session. Issue the EDLIN command with the file TEST.BAT.

```
A> EDLIN TEST.BAT
```

The file should now contain

```
VOL
TIME
VER
```

Use the EDLIN Insert command as follows to modify the contents of TEST.BAT to

```
CLS
DATE
VOL
TIME
VER
```

```
A> EDLIN TEST.BAT
End of input file
*1I
        1:* CLS
        2:* DATE
        3:* ^C
*1,L
        1: CLS
        2: DATE
        3:*VOL
        4: TIME
        5: VER
*
```

The complete format of the EDLIN Insert command is

[insert __ before __ line]I

where the following is true:

> *insert__before__line* is the line number of the line in front of which you want EDLIN to insert the text. If you do not specify a line number, EDLIN will insert the text before the current line.

> *I* is the abbreviation of the EDLIN Insert command.

Use the EDLIN Insert command to modify the current file from

```
CLS
DATE
VOL
TIME
VER
```

to

```
CLS
DATE
CLS
DISKCOPY A: B:
VOL
TIME
VER
```

```
*1,L
        1: CLS
        2: DATE
        3:*VOL
        4: TIME
        5: VER
*3I
        3:*CLS
        4:*DISKCOPY A: B:
        5:*^C
*
```

List the new contents of the file TEST.BAT.

```
*1,L
        1: CLS
        2: DATE
        3: CLS
        4: DISKCOPY A: B:
        5:*VOL
        6: TIME
        7: VER
   *
```

Exit from the current editing session.

```
*1,L
        1: CLS
        2: DATE
        3: CLS
        4: DISKCOPY A: B:
        5:*VOL
        6: TIME
        7: VER
   *E

A>
```

At the DOS prompt, TYPE the contents of TEST.BAT. The following is displayed:

```
A> TYPE TEST.BAT
CLS
DATE
CLS
DISKCOPY A: B:
VOL
TIME
VER

A>
```

The Append command appends the specified number of text lines from disk to the file in memory. The format of the Append command is

[number_of_lines]A

where the following is true:

number_of_lines is the number of lines that the Append command is to append to the file in memory. If you do not specify a line number, EDLIN will load lines from disk until the entire file is loaded or memory is 75% full.

A is the abbreviation of the EDLIN Append command.

Consider the following example:

```
*A
End of input file
```

In this case, EDLIN tells you that it has loaded the entire file into memory.

Searching for Words and Phrases

One of EDLIN's best features is that it allows you to locate and replace words or phrases quickly within a file. The EDLIN Search command displays lines containing the word or phrase that you specify. The format of the EDLIN Search command is

[first_line][,last_line][?]S[string<F6>]

where the following is true:

first_line is the line number for which the EDLIN Search

command should begin the search. If you don't specify a line number, Search uses the current line number.

last___line is the line number of the line at which the EDLIN Search command should quit searching for the word or phrase. If you do not specify a line number, Search uses the last line in memory.

If *?* is specified, the Search command will prompt you with the following each time it finds the word or phrase specified in the command:

```
O.K.?
```

If you want to quit the search, press Y and press ENTER. Otherwise, press N and press ENTER, and the search will continue. If Search does not find the word or phrase, it will display the message

```
Not found
```

S is the abbreviation for the EDLIN Search command.

string is the word or phrase for which EDLIN is to search. If you do not specify a string, EDLIN uses the last string used in a search operation.

<F6> represents the F6 function key. EDLIN uses the F6 key to signify the end of the word or phrase.

Exit the current editing session and create the following file:

```
PC-DOS and MS-DOS are
almost identical. PC-DOS
is the IBM implementation
of DOS.  MS stands for
Microsoft.  This book
provides commands standard
to DOS.
```

```
A> EDLIN DOS.TXT
New file
*I
        1:* PC-DOS and MS-DOS are
        2:* almost identical. PC-DOS
        3:* is the IBM implementation
        4:* of DOS.  MS stands for
        5:* Microsoft.  This book
        6:* provides commands standard
        7:* to DOS.
        8:* ^C
    *
```

Consider the following search commands. Invoke

```
*1,SDOS<F6>
        1:* PC-DOS and MS-DOS are
        2:* almost identical. PC-DOS
        2:*
```

EDLIN will display the first line containing the string along with
the current line. Invoke

```
*1,?SDOS<F6>
        1:* PC-DOS and MS-DOS are
O.K.?
```

EDLIN finds the string on line 1 and asks you if you want to terminate the search. Press Y in response to the prompt

```
O.K.?
```

EDLIN will terminate the search. Invoke

```
*1,?SDOS<F6>
        1:* PC-DOS and MS-DOS are
O.K.? Y
        2:* almost identical. PC-DOS
        2:*
```

If you do not provide a string for which the Search command can look, it will use the string used in the previous Search operation. Invoke

```
*1,?S<F6>
        1:*PC-DOS and MS-DOS are
O.K.?n
        2: almost identical. PC-DOS
O.K.?n
        4: of DOS.  MS stands for
O.K.?n
        7: to DOS.
O.K.?n
Not found
        2:*almost identical. PC-DOS
        2:*
*
```

You told Search to continue looking for the string until the string is no longer found. Invoke

```
*1,5?S<F6>
        1:*PC-DOS and MS-DOS are
O.K.?n
        2: almost identical. PC-DOS
O.K.?n
        4: of DOS.  MS stands for
O.K.?n
Not found
        2:*almost identical. PC-DOS
        2:*
*
```

Search will display the first occurrence of the string in the range of lines between 1 and 5. Suppose you receive the message

```
*1,5?Sdos<F6>
Not found
        2: almost identical. PC-DOS
        2:*
```

This means Search did not find the string you entered. Remember that, to EDLIN, the string "DOS" is not equivalent to "dos".

Replace

The EDLIN Replace command is similar to the Search command. The format of the Replace command is

[first—line][,last—line][?]R[string1<F6>][string2]

where the following is true:

first—line is the line number at which the EDLIN Replace command should begin. If you don't specify a line number, Replace uses the current line number.

last—line is the line number of the line at which the EDLIN Replace command should quit searching for the word or phrase. If you do not specify a line number, Replace uses the last line in memory.

? if specified, the Replace command will prompt you with the following each time it finds the word or phrase specified in the command:

```
O.K.?
```

If you want to make the replacement, press Y and ENTER. Otherwise, press N. Either way, the replacement will continue. If Replace does not find the word or phrase, it will display the message

```
Not found
```

R is the abbreviation for the EDLIN Replace command.

string1 is the word or phrase to be replaced. If you do not specify a string, EDLIN uses the last string used in a search or replace operation.

<F6> represents the F6 function key. EDLIN uses the F6 key to signify the end of the word or phrase.

string2 is the word or phrase with which to replace *string1*. If you do not specify a string, EDLIN uses the last string used in a replace operation.

Now use the following file.

```
PC-DOS and MS-DOS are
almost identical. PC-DOS
is the IBM implementation
of DOS.  MS stands for
Microsoft.  This book
provides commands standard
to DOS.
```

Consider the EDLIN Replace commands. If you invoke

```
*1,Ralmost<F6>functionally
        2: functionally identical. PC-DOS
*
```

Replace replaces each occurrence of the word "almost" with the word "functionally". Invoke

```
*1,L
        1: PC-DOS and MS-DOS are
        2:*functionally identical. PC-DOS
        3: is the IBM implementation
        4: of DOS.  MS stands for
        5: Microsoft.  This book
        6: provides commands standard
        7: to DOS.
    *
```

Replace will continue to change each occurrence of the word "PC-DOS" with the string "PC DOS".

```
*1,RPC-DOS<F6>PC DOS
        1:*PC DOS and MS-DOS are
        2: functionally identical.  PC DOS
    *1,L
        1:*PC DOS and MS-DOS are
        2: functionally identical.  PC DOS
        3: is the IBM implementation
        4: of DOS.  MS stands for
        5: Microsoft.  This book
        6: provides commands standard
        7: to DOS.
    *
```

If Replace cannot find the string to replace, EDLIN will display

```
    Not found
```

```
*1,L
        1:*PC DOS and MS·DOS are
        2: functionally identical.  PC DOS
        3: is the IBM implementation
        4: of DOS.  MS stands for
        5: Microsoft.  This book
        6: provides commands standard
        7: to DOS.
*1,Rdos<F6>DOS
Not found
*
```

Invoke

```
*1,L
        1:*PC DOS and MS·DOS are
        2: functionally identical.  PC DOS
        3: is the IBM implementation
        4: of DOS.  MS stands for
        5: Microsoft.  This book
        6: provides commands standard
        7: to DOS.
*1,SPC DOS^Z
        1: PC DOS AND MS·DOS ARE
        2:*functionally identical.  PC DOS
        2:*
*1,R^ZPC·DOS
        1: PC·DOS and MS·DOS are
        2:*functionally identical.  PC·DOS
*
```

Replace uses the string from the Search command as the string to replace.

Creating Disk Labels with EDLIN

Many software packages use standard labels to identify disks. These labels feed easily through a printer, as illustrated in Figure 13-8. In the example used in this section, the disk label will contain the information shown in Figure 13-9.

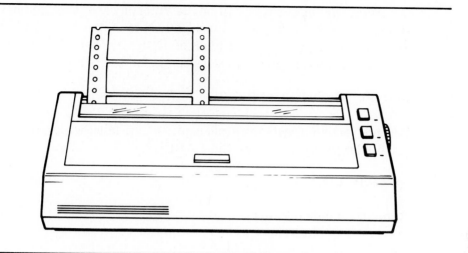

Figure 13-8. Labels being fed through printer

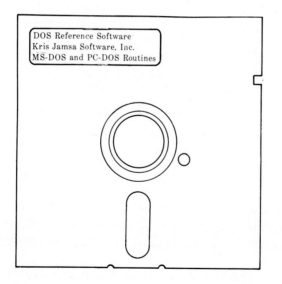

DOS Reference Software
Kris Jamsa Software, Inc.
MS-DOS and PC-DOS Routines

Figure 13-9. Sample disk label printed on printer

Since the lines of text will be the same on each label, you have several choices. First, you can use EDLIN to make one copy of the label and then issue the number of DOS COPY commands required to print the labels you desire, as follows:

```
A> COPY LABELS.TXT PRN:
```

Second, you can create multiple copies of the label within the file. Issue EDLIN to create the file LABELS.TXT as follows:

```
A> EDLIN LABELS.TXT
```

Enter the following text:

```
DOS Reference Software
Kris Jamsa Software, Inc.
MS and PC DOS Routines
```

```
A> EDLIN LABELS.TXT
New file
*I
        1:* DOS Reference Software
        2:* Kris Jamsa Software, Inc.
        3:* MS and PC DOS Routines
        4:* ^C
*E

A>
```

In this case, you will make multiple copies of the label within the file. EDLIN provides the Copy command, which simplifies this duplication. The format of the Copy command is

[first_line],[last_line],[destination_line][,count]C

where the following is true:

first_line is the line number of the first line to copy. If you do not specify a line number, Copy uses the current line.

last—line is the line number of the last line in the range of lines to be copied. If you do not specify a line number, Copy uses the current line.

destination—line is the line number before which the lines are to be copied. You must specify a line number.

count is the number of copies of the text to write to the destination. If you do not specify a number, Copy uses the value 1.

C is the abbreviation of the EDLIN Copy command.

TYPE the contents of the file LABELS.TXT.

```
A> TYPE LABELS.TXT

DOS Reference Software
Kris Jamsa Software, Inc.
MS and PC DOS Routines
```

To make a second copy of the text, invoke the command

```
A> EDLIN LABELS.TXT
End of input file
*L
        1:*DOS Reference Software
        2: Kris Jamsa Software, Inc.
        3: MS and PC DOS Routines
*1,3,4C
*L
        1: DOS Reference Software
        2: Kris Jamsa Software, Inc.
        3: MS and PC DOS Routines
        4:*DOS Reference Software
        5: Kris Jamsa Software, Inc.
        6: MS and PC DOS Routines
*
```

This command is equivalent to

```
*1,3,4,1C
*
```

If you need to make 100 more copies of the label, invoke the command

```
A> EDLIN LABELS.TXT
End of input file
*L
        1:*DOS Reference Software
        2: Kris Jamsa Software, Inc.
        3: MS and PC DOS Routines
*1,3,4C
*L
        1: DOS Reference Software
        2: Kris Jamsa Software, Inc.
        3: MS and PC DOS Routines
        4:*DOS Reference Software
        5: Kris Jamsa Software, Inc.
        6: MS and PC DOS Routines
*1,3,7,100C
*
```

Exit the current editing session.

In addition to the Copy command, EDLIN provides the Move command, which allows you to move a section of text to a new location within the file. The format of the Move command is

[first—line],[last—line],[destination—line]M

where the following is true:

first—line is the line number of the first line to move. If you do not specify a line number, Move uses the current line.

last—line is the line number of the last line in the range of lines to be moved. If you do not specify a line number, Move uses the current line number.

destination—line is the line number before which the lines are to be moved. You must specify a line number.

M is the abbreviation of the EDLIN Move command.

Invoke EDLIN to edit the file TEST.BAT.

```
A> EDLIN TEST.BAT
End of input file
*L
        1:*CLS
        2: DATE
        3: CLS
        4: DISKCOPY A: B:
        5: VOL
        6: TIME
        7: VER
*1,3,5M
*L
        1: DISKCOPY A: B:
        2:*CLS
        3: DATE
        4: CLS
        5: VOL
        6: TIME
        7: VER
*
```

Consider the following commands. Invoke

```
*1,1,8M
*L
        1: CLS
        2: DATE
        3: CLS
        4: VOL
        5: TIME
        6: VER
        7:*DISKCOPY A: B:
*
```

EDLIN will move line 1 to line 8. Invoke

```
*2,5,1M
*L
        1:*DATE
        2: CLS
        3: VOL
        4: TIME
        5: CLS
        6: VER
        7: DISKCOPY A: B:
*
```

EDLIN will move lines 2-5 to line 1. Invoke

```
*5,6,.M
*L
        1:*CLS
        2: VER
        3: DATE
        4: CLS
        5: VOL
        6: TIME
        7: DISKCOPY A: B:
   *
```

EDLIN will move lines 5 and 6 to the current line. Exit from the current editing session.

```
 *E

 A>
```

It is often convenient to combine several files into one file while you are editing. The EDLIN Transfer command allows you to transfer the contents of a file into your current file at the line number you specify. The format of the Transfer command is

[insert_before_line]Tfile_spec

where the following is true:

insert_before_line is the line number of the line before which you want to insert the contents of the specified file. If you do not specify a line number, Transfer uses the current line number.

T is the abbreviation of the EDLIN Transfer command.

file_spec is the name of the file to include in the current file.

Use EDLIN to create the following files:

DOS: The Complete Reference

```
PART1.TXT contains the first
two lines of the file.
```

PART1.TXT

```
PART2.TXT contains lines
three, four, and five of
the file.
```

PART2.TXT

```
PART3.TXT contains the last
two lines of the file.
```

PART3.TXT

Issue EDLIN to create the file WHOLE.TXT as follows:

```
A> EDLIN WHOLE.TXT
```

Consider the following commands. Invoke

```
A> EDLIN WHOLE.TXT
New file
*1TPART1.TXT
*L
        1:*PART1.TXT contains the first
        2: two lines of the file.
    *
```

Transfer will place the contents of PART1.TXT in the file. Invoke

```
    *L
        1:*PART1.TXT contains the first
        2: two lines of the file.
*3TPART3.TXT
*L
        1: PART1.TXT contains the first
        2: two lines of the file.
        3:*PART3.TXT contains the last
        4: two lines of the file.
    *
```

Transfer will append the contents of PART3.TXT to PART1.TXT. Invoke

```
*L
        1:*PART1.TXT contains the first
        2: two lines of the file.
        3: PART3.TXT contains the last
        4: two lines of the file.
*3TPART2.TXT
*L
        1: PART1.TXT contains the first
        2: two lines of the file.
        3:*PART2.TXT contains lines
        4: three, four, and five of
        5: the file.
        6: PART3.TXT contains the last
        7: two lines of the file.
*
```

Transfer will place the contents of PART2.TXT after PART1.TXT but before PART3.TXT. Exit from the current editing session. At the DOS prompt, TYPE the contents of WHOLE.TXT.

```
*L
        1: PART1.TXT contains the first
        2: two lines of the file.
        3:*PART2.TXT contains lines
        4: three, four, and five of
        5: the file.
        6: PART3.TXT contains the last
        7: two lines of the file.
*E

A> TYPE WHOLE.TXT
PART1.TXT contains the first
two lines of the file.
PART2.TXT contains lines
three, four, and five of
the file.
PART3.TXT contains the last
two lines of the file.

A>
```

The final EDLIN command is the Write command. The format of the Write command is

[lines]W

where the following is true:

lines is the number of lines to write from memory back to disk.

W is the abbreviation of the EDLIN Write command.

When the file you are editing becomes so large that it no longer fits into memory, EDLIN will read the contents of the file into memory only until memory is 75% full. To bring more of the file back into memory, you must write some of the contents of the file back out to disk. The Write command performs this function. Table 13-1 summarizes all of the EDLIN commands.

Command	Format
Append	[number_of_lines]A
Copy	[first_line],[last_line],destination_line[,count]C
Delete	[first_line][,last_line]D
Edit	[line_number]
End	E
Insert	[insert_before_line]I
Move	[first_line],[last_line],destination_lineM
Page	[first_line],[last_line]P
Quit	Q
Replace	[first_line],[last_line][?]R[string]<F6>[string2]
Search	[first_line],[last_line][?]S[string]<F6>
Transfer	[insert_before_line]Tfile name.ext
Write	W

Table 13-1.   EDLIN Commands

1. What is a text editor?

2. What is the function of the /B qualifier on the EDLIN command line?

3. What is the purpose of the asterisk (*) in EDLIN?

4. List the EDLIN commands.

5. How do you place control characters within a file in EDLIN?

6. Assuming the current line is line 5, what is the value of the following?

```
.
−4
+5
```

7. What is the command that allows you to search the entire file for the keyword DOS?

8. What is the command to replace each occurrence of the word "IBM" with the word "DEC"?

9. What lines will the following command display?

```
*1,L
```

10. What key combination is used to exit from the EDLIN Insert mode?

11. What is the function of the EDLIN Transfer command?

12. Use EDLIN to create the following file:

```
CLS
VOL
VER
DIR
```

Name the file TEST.BAT.

13. What are the functions of the following EDLIN commands?

    P
    Q
    W
    E

14. How does a line editor differ from a screen editor?

Answers

1. *What is a text editor?*

A text editor is a software program that allows you to manipulate text files. EDLIN is a text editor that allows you to

- Create text files
- Examine the contents of a text file
- Update the contents of a text file by inserting, deleting, or changing lines
- Perform file-wide searches and replacements of keywords within a text file

2. *What is the function of the /B qualifier on the EDLIN command line?*

The /B is an advanced EDLIN qualifier that tells EDLIN that the text file may contain an embedded control Z (^Z), the DOS end of file marker. If the /B qualifier is included in the command line, EDLIN will load the entire file regardless of embedded ^Z characters. Otherwise EDLIN will use the first ^Z to mark the end of the file.

3. *What is the purpose of the asterisk (*) in EDLIN?*

The asterisk is the EDLIN prompt that tells you that EDLIN is ready for you to enter a command or data.

4. *List the EDLIN commands.*

A	Append lines from disk into memory
C	Copy lines
D	Delete lines
E	End edit and save changes
I	Insert lines
M	Move lines
P	Page display
Q	Quit edit and disregard changes
R	Replace a word or phrase

S   Search for a word or phrase
T   Transfer lines from another file
W   Write lines from memory back to disk

5. *How do you place control characters within a file in EDLIN?*

To enter a control sequence in EDLIN, hold down the CTRL key while you type V and then the key desired. For example, for a ^I, the tab character, simply press CTRL and type V at the same time, release the keys, and type I.

6. *Assuming the current line is line 5, what is the value of the following?*

    .   is line 5
    −4   is line 1
    +5   is line 10

7. *What is the command that allows you to search the entire file for the keyword DOS?*

    * 1,SDOS<F6>

8. *What is the command to replace each occurrence of the word "IBM" with the word "DEC"?*

    *1,RIBM<F6>DEC

9. *What lines will the following command display?*

    *1,L

Lines 1-23.

10. *What key combination is used to exit from the EDLIN Insert mode?*

EDLIN uses the CTRL-BREAK keyboard combination to exit from the Insert mode.

11. *What is the function of the EDLIN Transfer command?*

The EDLIN Transfer command allows you to transfer the

EDLIN — The DOS Line Editor   **451** contents of a file into your current file at the line number you specify. For example, to insert the file AUTOEXEC.BAT into the file TEST.BAT at line 3, the EDLIN command is

  * 3TAUTOEXEC.BAT

12. *Use EDLIN to create the following file:*

  CLS
  VOL
  VER
  DIR

Name the file TEST.BAT.

```
A> EDLIN TEST.BAT
New file
*I
          1:* CLS
          2:* VOL
          3:* VER
          4:* DIR
          5:* ^C
*E

A>
```

13. *What are the functions of the following EDLIN commands?*

P is the EDLIN Page command, which displays one full page of information at a time.

Q is the EDLIN command to quit the current editing session without saving any changes to the file.

W is the EDLIN command to write specified lines from memory to the disk file.

E is the EDLIN command to exit from the current editing session, saving the changes made.

14. *How does a line editor differ from a screen editor?*

A line editor manipulates the information contained in a file one line at a time. A screen editor, on the other hand, displays a page of the file on the screen, allowing you to use the arrow keys and the function keys to move around in the file. With a screen editor, the contents of the file will be exactly as it appears on the screen. Whereas a screen editor allows you to manipulate a screenful of information at one time, line editors manipulate only a line at a time.

How DOS Really Works

The Anatomy of DOS
Command Processor
DOS Kernel
BIOS (Basic Input/Output System)
Hidden Files
Boot Record
System Generation
DOS Interrupts

All of the chapters presented thus far have dealt with DOS commands and their functions. This chapter presents a more technical description of DOS and its inner workings. If you are just starting with DOS, don't spend a great deal of time trying to understand fully the information presented in this chapter. It is only important that you have a basic understanding of the DOS command processor, the DOS system startup procedures, and DOS interrupts.

The Anatomy of DOS

Probably the best way to understand DOS is to examine it in terms of its functions. Consider the diagram shown in Figure 14-1. DOS is divided into three functional sections. The *command processor* is the portion of DOS that invokes each of the commands you issue. The DOS *kernel* provides the program interface

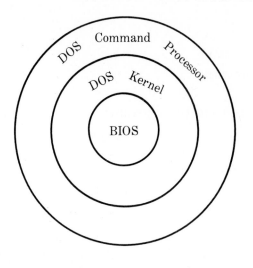

Figure 14-1. Three functional portions of DOS

to DOS. The DOS *BIOS* provides the input/output services used by DOS. Most users never have to be concerned with the DOS kernel or BIOS. Many users, however, do profit from an understanding of the DOS command processor.

Command Processor

The DOS command processor is the program responsible for performing the commands you issue (see Figure 14-2). By default, DOS uses the file COMMAND.COM as the command processor. It is possible, however, to specify a different program as the command processor via the COMMSPEC= entry in the file CONFIG.SYS.

```
COMMSPEC=SOMEFILE.COM
```

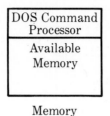

Memory

Figure 14-2.   DOS command processor

Most DOS users will never need to specify an alternate command processor.

The DOS command processor consists of three parts: a start-up portion, the resident section, and the transient area, as shown in Figure 14-3.

The *startup portion* of the DOS command processor exists solely to execute the procedure AUTOEXEC.BAT if that proce-

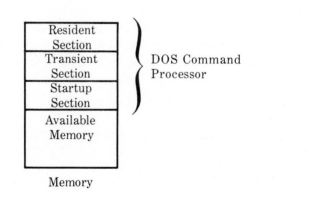

Memory

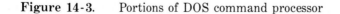

Figure 14-3.   Portions of DOS command processor

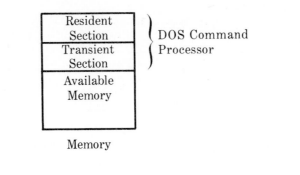

```
┌─────────────┐
│  Resident   │ ⎫
│  Section    │ ⎬ DOS Command
├─────────────┤ ⎬ Processor
│  Transient  │ ⎬
│  Section    │ ⎭
├─────────────┤
│  Available  │
│  Memory     │
│             │
└─────────────┘
```

Memory

Figure 14-4.   Termination and release of startup portion of command processor

dure is present in your root directory. When the AUTOEXEC. BAT procedure is finished, the startup portion of the command processor terminates, and the space it consumed in memory is released, as illustrated in Figure 14-4.

DOS keeps the *resident portion* of the command processor in memory at all times. This portion performs all of the essential functions to which DOS must be able to provide immediate response, such as the loading of the transient section of the command processor, finishing the execution of the programs, or user termination of programs via CTRL-BREAK processing. In addition, the resident portion of the command processor performs DOS critical error handling. This processing is responsible for the message

```
Not ready error reading device
Abort, Retry, Ignore?
```

The message appears when DOS can no longer continue without user intervention.

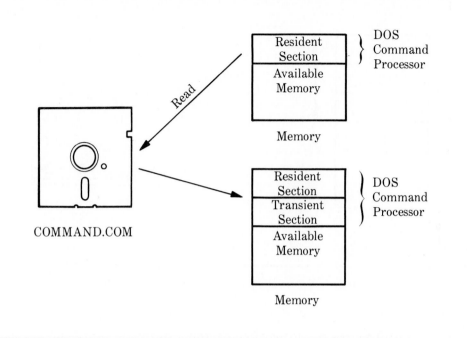

Figure 14-5. Resident portion of command processor reloading transient portion

The third portion of the DOS command processor is the *transient section*. As you will see, many DOS applications overwrite this section of the DOS command processor in memory. When this occurs, the resident section of the command processor reloads the transient portion from disk, as shown in Figure 14-5. If the resident portion of DOS cannot find the command processor (normally, COMMAND.COM), it will display the message

```
Insert disk with  COMMAND.COM in drive A
and strike any key when ready
```

Simply place a disk containing the command processor in the specified drive and strike any key.

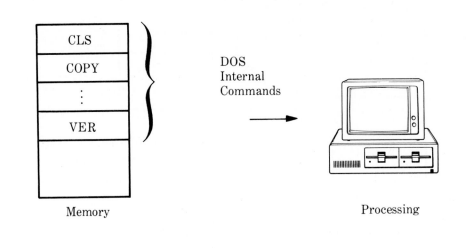

Figure 14-6. Internal DOS commands

The *transient portion* of the command processor receives commands from the interactive user or from DOS batch files. It is the responsibility of this section of DOS to execute each DOS command.

As you have learned in previous chapters, all DOS commands are classified as either internal or external. Internal DOS commands reside in memory within the DOS command processor. When you invoke one of these commands, DOS simply locates the command in memory and executes it, as shown in Figure 14-6. External commands, on the other hand, reside on disk. Each time you invoke an external command, DOS must load the command from disk into memory, as illustrated in Figure 14-7.

The transient portion of the DOS command processor contains all of the DOS internal commands. These are

BREAK	PATH
CHDIR	PROMPT
CLS	REN
COPY	RMDIR
CTTY	SET

DATE	TIME
DEL	TYPE
DIR	VER
ERASE	VERIFY
MKDIR	VOL

DOS maintains a list of these commands. Using this list, it can determine quickly whether the command entered by the user is an internal DOS command.

If a user command is not an internal DOS commmand, DOS must load the external command into memory. Each time the command processor loads an external command into memory, it places the contents of the file with an EXE or COM extension into the transient portion of the command processor and available memory, if required. When the command is finished, the space it consumed in memory is released.

All DOS commands, therefore, follow certain processing steps. Each time you invoke a command, DOS first examines its list of internal commands. If the command is found in memory, DOS executes it. Otherwise, DOS assumes it is an external command. For external commands, DOS first searches the current working directory for an EXE, COM, or BAT file whose name matches the command entered. If DOS finds the matching file, it loads the file from disk into the transient portion of the command processor and available memory, if required, and then executes it.

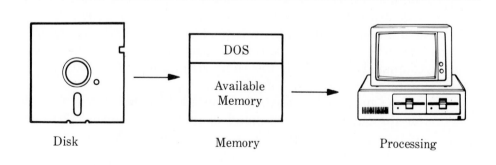

Figure 14-7.   External DOS commands

Otherwise, DOS examines each of the entries in the path you have defined via the PATH command. If DOS fails to locate a matching file, it displays the message

```
Bad command or file name
```

When the external command is finished, DOS releases the memory allocated for the command. These steps are shown in Figure 14-8.

If you are invoking a batch procedure (BAT file), the command processor simply reads each line of the file and performs the same processing listed previously. When the command processor is performing batch processing, many DOS users refer to it as the command interpreter. For example, consider the following BAT file:

```
CLS
DATE
DISKCOPY A: B:
```

The command interpreter takes control and opens the BAT file. In this case, it will first read the line containing the DOS command CLS. Since CLS is an internal DOS command, the command processor simply locates the command in memory and executes it to clear the screen. When CLS is finished, the command interpreter reads the second line of the BAT file and issues the DOS DATE command in the same manner. When the DATE command is finished, the command interpreter reads the line containing DISKCOPY A: B:.

As previously stated, the command processor will first look for the DISKCOPY command in the list of internal DOS commands. Since DISKCOPY is an external DOS command, the search will fail, so the command processor must search the current working directory for an EXE, COM, or BAT file with the file name DISKCOPY. If the command processor finds the file, it will load the file contents into memory and execute the file. Oth-

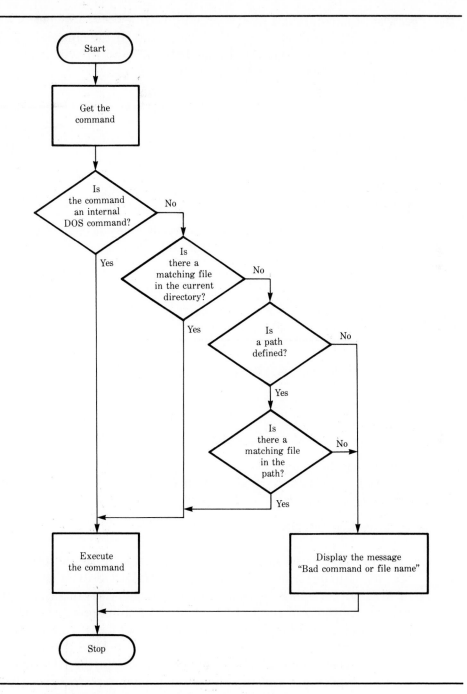

Figure 14-8.   Processing Steps for DOS commands

erwise, the command processor will search the list of paths you have defined via the DOS PATH command. If the command processor (COMMAND.COM) finds the command, it will load and execute it. Otherwise, it will display the message

```
Bad command or file name
```

When the DISKCOPY command is finished, the command interpreter will attempt to read the BAT file. In this case, no other lines reside in the file, so batch processing is completed. The processing performed by the command interpreter is illustrated in Figure 14-9.

DOS Kernel

The DOS kernel is the portion of DOS responsible for the following:

- file management
(creation, deletion, or modification of the DOS files)

- directory management
(creation, deletion, or modification of directories and directory entries)

- application interface to the DOS services

Many DOS users refer to this section of DOS as the "program section." During system startup, the file IBMDOS.COM (PC-DOS) or MSDOS.SYS (MS-DOS) is read into memory to create the DOS kernel. As you will see in Chapter 16, the functions provided by this section of DOS make it easy for programmers to develop powerful routines simply by accessing the built-in DOS services.

The most important fact to remember about the DOS kernel is that it provides the link between your programs and DOS.

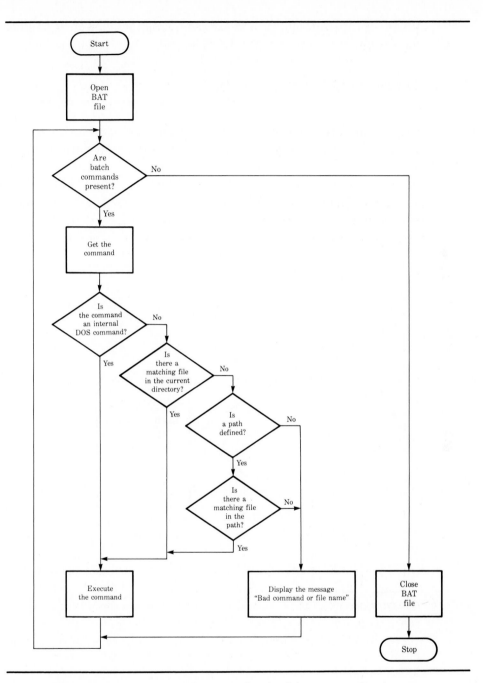

Figure 14-9. Processing steps involved in command processor

When a program writes to the screen, disk, or printer, it utilizes the services provided by the DOS kernel.

BIOS (Basic Input/Output System)

Every computer comes with a set of routines developed by the manufacturer that allow it to perform input and output at the lowest levels. These routines reside in an area of the computer called *read-only memory*, or ROM. Unlike the contents of the computer's RAM (*random-access memory*), which are lost each time the computer loses power, the contents of ROM exist indefinitely.

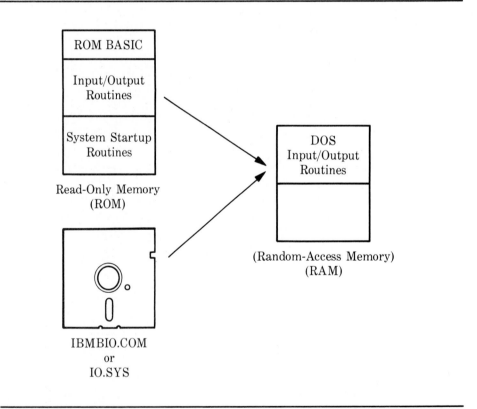

Figure 14-10.   DOS buiding a memory area for input and output

Each time the computer is turned on, DOS uses the routines found in ROM along with the file IBMBIO.COM (PC-DOS) or IO.SYS (MS-DOS) to build an area in memory responsible for input and output (see Figure 14-10).

DOS communicates with these routines by exchanging packets of information. In many cases, a program called a *device driver* is required to translate the packet of information from a format that DOS understands to a format understood by the hardware device.

Device drivers make it easy for you to add new hardware to the computer. Since each hardware device uses a known packet format, and DOS packets are well defined, the device driver software simply needs to ensure that DOS can communicate with the device and that all the messages between the hardware device and DOS are exchanged successfully. This is why it is necessary to specify the name of any device drivers you require to DOS (a mouse or plotter, for example) via the DEVICE= entry in the CONFIG.SYS file.

```
DEVICE=VDISK
DEVICE=MOUSE
```

Hidden Files

Issue the DOS CHKDSK command on your DOS system disk and the following is displayed:

```
A> CHKDSK B:

    362496 bytes total disk space
     37888 bytes in 2 hidden files
    324608 bytes available on disk

    524288 bytes total memory
    270992 bytes free
```

The two hidden files are IBMDOS.COM and IBMBIOS.COM (PC-DOS) or MSDOS.SYS and IO.SYS (MS-DOS). If these files are not present on your boot disk, DOS cannot create its first and second layers, and the boot will fail, resulting in the message

```
Non-System disk or disk error
Replace and strike any key when ready
```

In addition, if DOS cannot find the command processor (COMMAND.COM, by default), it will display the message

```
Bad or missing Command Interpreter
```

Simply place a disk containing the command processor in the specified drive and press a key. DOS will read the contents of the file into memory, completing its third layer.

Boot Record

As illustrated in Chapter 9, the first sector of the disk (track 0, sector 1, side 0) contains the DOS *boot record*. The boot record resides on every DOS disk. This ensures that DOS system disks are bootable and that nonbootable disks can produce the error message

```
Non-System disk or disk error
Replace and strike any key when ready
```

Each time DOS boots, it first looks for the boot record in the disk in drive A. If the disk in drive A is bootable, DOS will boot it.

If no disk is present in drive A, DOS will examine the active partition of the hard disk for a boot record. Many DOS users with a hard disk are confused as to why DOS will try to boot from drive A before using the hard disk. The reason for this is a safety factor built into DOS. If your hard disk becomes corrupted, or if you accidentally delete the file COMMAND.COM from the hard disk, you'll need a way to access the computer. Since DOS will always look to drive A first, it provides you with a method of booting your computer so you can repair your hard disk as required or boot another operating system.

In addition to getting the DOS boot process started, the boot record is responsible for defining the structure of the disk media

| 8086 JMP Instruction |
| IBM or Microsoft name
and
version number |
| Bytes per disk sector |
| Sectors per cluster |
| Number of reserved sectors |
| Max root directory entries |
| Total sectors |
| Media descriptor |
| Number of sectors per
file allocation table |
| Sectors per track |
| Number of disk heads |
| Number of hidden sectors |
| Bootstrap program |

Figure 14-11.   DOS boot record

DOS will be using for a system disk. Consider the boot record shown in Figure 14-11. Programs residing in the computer's ROM read the bootstrap program from disk into memory each time the computer is started up. The major function of the bootstrap program is to load the files IBMBIO.COM and IBMDOS.COM (PC-DOS) or IO.SYS and MSDOS.COM (MS-DOS) into memory and then to pass control to this section of memory to continue system startup (see Figure 14-12). When this portion of DOS receives control of the computer, it begins system generation (SYSGEN).

System Generation

As DOS boots, it takes into account the device drivers and system parameters you specify in the CONFIG.SYS file.

```
FILES=20
DEVICE=VDISK
```

If DOS finds CONFIG.SYS in the root directory of the boot device, it reads the contents of the file and uses that information to generate the operating system in memory. For the preceding file, for example, DOS will allocate space in memory for an additional 12 file handles (8 file handles is the default) and install the device driver for a RAM disk drive. Once DOS has examined the contents of CONFIG.SYS, it closes the file and loads the command processor from disk. As previously stated, DOS uses the COMMAND.COM file by default.

Once present in memory, the startup portion of the command processor searches the root directory for the AUTOEXEC.BAT file and executes the commands it contains if the file is present. Otherwise, it performs the DATE and TIME commands as described in Chapter 2. This process is shown in Figure 14-13.

Step 1: ROM program reads the bootstrap program from the boot record into RAM.

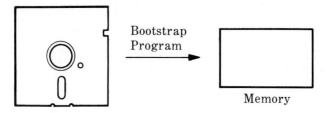

Step 2: Bootstrap program loads IBMBIO.COM and IBMDOS.COM (PC-DOS) or IO.SYS and MSDOS.SYS (MS-DOS) from disk.

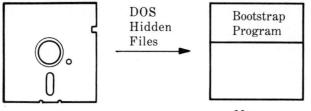

Step 3: The bootstrap program passes control to DOS.

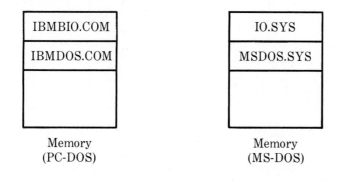

Figure 14-12. Function of bootstrap program

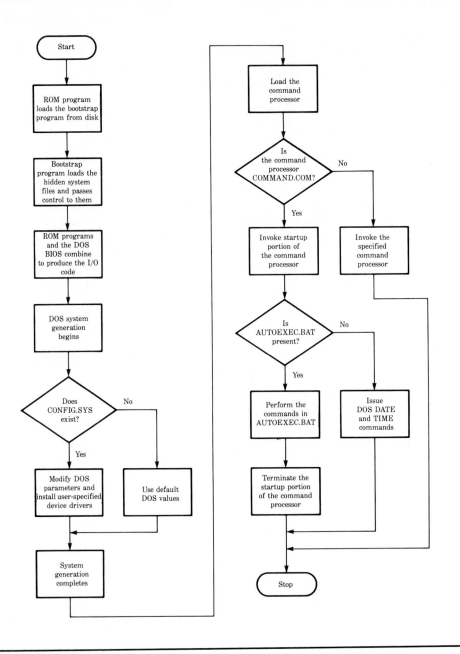

Figure 14-13. Processing steps involved in DOS startup operation

DOS: The Complete Reference

DOS Interrupts

An *interrupt* is a signal to the processor from a program or hardware device. Interrupts temporarily suspend the function that the CPU is performing so that it can perform another task. Each interrupt has a section of code, resident in memory, that the processor performs each time the interrupt occurs. This code is called an *interrupt handler* or an *interrupt service routine* (see Figure 14-14).

When an interrupt occurs, the processor locates the associated interrupt handler and executes that section of code. For example, when a user holds down the SHIFT and PRTSC keys on the keyboard, an interrupt temporarily suspends the currently running program and prints the contents of the screen. When the processor completes the interrupt handler, it returns processing to the function it was performing prior to the interrupt, as illustrated in Figure 14-15.

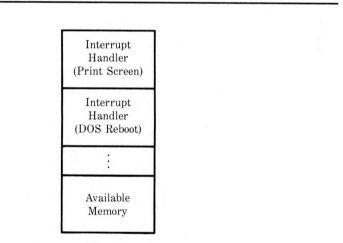

Memory

Figure 14-14.   Interrupt handler in DOS memory

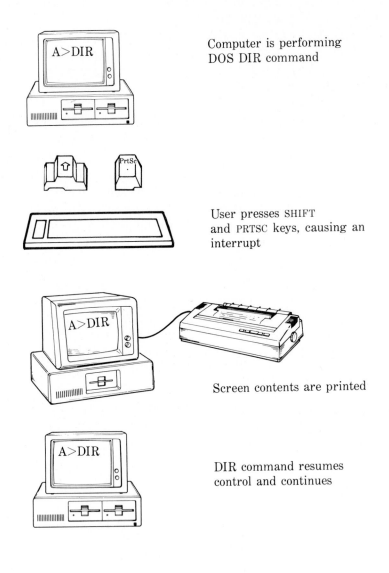

Computer is performing
DOS DIR command

User presses SHIFT
and PRTSC keys, causing an
interrupt

Screen contents are printed

DIR command resumes
control and continues

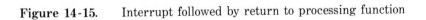

Figure 14-15.   Interrupt followed by return to processing function

Interrupt Number	Address
1	0070 01ED
2	3D28 09D2
3	0070 01ED
4	3D28 0998
5	F000 FF54
.	. .
.	. .
.	. .

Table 14-1.   DOS Interrupt Vectors

The processor finds interrupt handlers by using interrupt vectors. Visualize the interrupt vectors as a table containing the interrupt number and the address in memory of the interrupt handler, as shown in Table 14-1.

When an interrupt occurs, the processor uses the interrupt number as an index into the table to find the location in memory of the code to perform. As previously stated, the DOS kernel provides the interface between user programs and DOS. Chapter 16 will examine how to use this interface via DOS interrupts. As you will see, it is possible to generate powerful programs in minutes by utilizing the DOS services.

Review

1. What are the functional sections of DOS?

2. What are the three portions of the DOS command processor?

3. What is the default command processor?

4. How do DOS internal commands differ from DOS external commands?

5. What is a device driver?

6. What are the DOS hidden files? Why are they hidden?

7. What is the function of the boot record?

8. What is system generation?

9. What is an interrupt?

1. *What are the functional sections of DOS?*

DOS is functionally divided into three sections. The command processor is the portion of DOS that invokes each of the commands you issue. The DOS kernel provides the program interface to DOS. The DOS BIOS provides the input/output services used by DOS.

2. *What are the three portions of the DOS command processor?*

The DOS command processor consists of: a startup portion, the resident section, and the transient area. The startup portion executes the AUTOEXEC.BAT file, if the latter exists. The resident portion performs all of the essential functions to which DOS must always be able to provide immediate response, such as the loading of the transient section of the command processor or executing programs or terminating programs via CTRL-BREAK processing. In addition, the resident portion of the command processor performs DOS critical error handling. The third portion of the DOS command processor is the transient section. It contains the internal DOS commands and is responsible for the execution of both internal and external commands.

3. *What is the default command processor?*

By default, DOS uses the file COMMAND.COM as the command processor. It is possible, however, to specify a different command processor via the COMMSPEC= entry in the file CONFIG.SYS.

4. *How do DOS internal commands differ from DOS external commands?*

All DOS commands are classified as either internal or external. Internal DOS commands reside in memory within the DOS command processor. When you invoke one of these commands, DOS simply locates the command in memory and executes it. External commands, on the other hand, reside on disk. Each time you invoke an external command, DOS must load the command disk into memory.

5. *What is a device driver?*

DOS communicates with hardware devices by exchanging packets of information. In many cases, a program called a device driver is required to translate the packet of information from a format that DOS understands into a format understood by the hardware device.

6. *What are the DOS hidden files? Why are they hidden?*

The two hidden files are IBMDOS.COM and IBMBIOS.COM (PC-DOS) or MSDOS.SYS and IO.SYS (MS-DOS). If these files are not present on your boot disk, DOS cannot create its first and second layers, and the boot will fail. DOS hides the files; this prevents them from being deleted by DOS commands. If you accidentally deleted these files from your system disk, the disk would not be bootable. Since they are hidden, you may never see their names on any directory listing.

7. *What is the function of the boot record?*

The first function of the boot record is to get the DOS boot process started. In addition, the boot record is responsible for defining the structure of the disk media DOS will be using for a system disk.

8. *What is system generation?*

System generation describes the steps DOS uses to build the operating system to be used on your computer. Each time DOS boots, it takes into account device drivers or parameter values that you specify in the file CONFIG.SYS. Based on the information you supply, and several default DOS values, an operating system is created in memory. The process of creating this operating system is termed *system generation.*

9. *What is an interrupt?*

An interrupt is a signal to the processor from a program or hardware device. Interrupts temporarily suspend the function that the CPU is performing so that it can perform another task. Each interrupt has a section of code called an interrupt service routine that is resident in memory. Each time the interrupt occurs, the processor performs the interrupt service routine.

Customizing DOS

BREAK (Default: BREAK=OFF)
BUFFERS (Default: IBM PC BUFFERS=2;
                    IBM PC AT BUFFERS=3)
COUNTRY
DEVICE
DRIVEPARM
FCBS (Default: FCBS=4,0)
FILES (Default: FILES=8)
LASTDRIVE (Default: LASTDRIVE=E)
SHELL

This chapter examines ways that you can modify DOS to customize it for your specific needs. Many DOS users find that they can improve the performance and function of DOS by modifying one or more configuration values that DOS uses each time the system boots. If, however, you are not performing a great deal of programming or utilizing large database applications, the default values provided by DOS to configure the operating system should be adequate.

Each time DOS boots, it is loaded into memory with space allocated for internal commands, DOS data structures, and device drivers and other memory-resident programs (see Figure 15-1). The DOS internal commands have already been examined. DOS *data structures* are storage locations DOS uses to keep track of such things as open files, disk transfer buffers, and country-specific information for international DOS commands. As you will

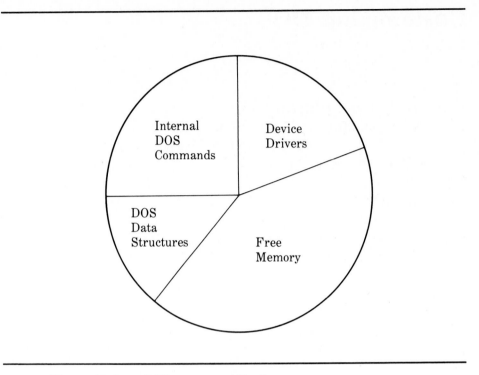

Figure 15-1. DOS memory utilization

see, *device drivers* are the software programs that allow DOS to communicate with hardware devices such as the printer, keyboard, and screen.

DOS allows you to modify several of its characteristics each time the system boots. To do so, you modify one or more of the configuration parameters in the file CONFIG.SYS, which must reside in the root directory. The parameters DOS allows you to modify are

BREAK
BUFFERS
COUNTRY
DEVICE
DRIVPARM

```
FCBS
FILES
LASTDRIVE
SHELL
```

Each time the system boots, DOS searches the root directory for the file CONFIG.SYS. If the file exists, DOS reads it sequentially and configures itself in memory with the values contained in the file. If the file does not exist, DOS uses default values for each of the parameters listed. Most DOS users use the text editor EDLIN or copy the file CONFIG.SYS from the keyboard as follows:

```
A> COPY CON CONFIG.SYS
```

BREAK (Default: BREAK=OFF)

Many times it is convenient to stop an application program by pressing CTRL-C. By default, DOS checks each time it writes to the screen or printer, or reads from the keyboard, to see whether or not the user has pressed a CTRL-C combination. It is possible for you to increase the number of functions that DOS will examine for CTRL-C upon completion. If you enter

```
BREAK=ON
```

in the file CONFIG.SYS, DOS will check for the CTRL-C upon completing disk reads and writes. This increases the likelihood of DOS intercepting the CTRL-C promptly and terminating the program as desired.

Setting BREAK=ON adds additional overhead. Because DOS must now test for CTRL-C following many functions, overall processing will be slower. To eliminate CTRL-C checking by DOS, simply issue the following command in CONFIG.SYS:

```
BREAK=OFF
```

Then reboot. DOS will still test for CTRL-C when it writes to the screen and printer or when it reads from the keyboard.

BUFFERS (Default: IBM PC BUFFERS=2; IBM PC AT BUFFERS=3)

The BUFFERS entry in CONFIG.SYS allows you to define the number of disk buffers DOS uses to hold data when it reads and writes to disk. A buffer is a 528-byte storage location in memory.

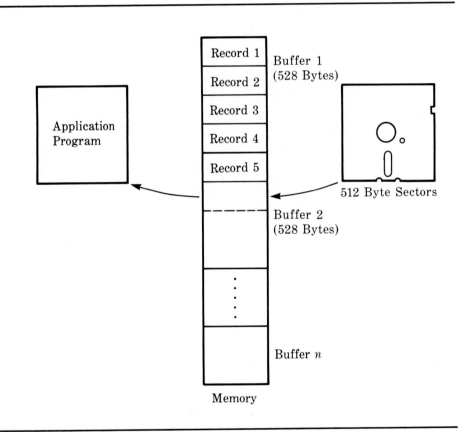

Figure 15-2. DOS record in disk buffer

DOS: The Complete Reference

Each time an application requests DOS to read and write a record from disk that is not an exact multiple of the disk sector size (an 80-byte record, for example), DOS places the record into a disk buffer. This is illustrated in Figure 15-2. Once the buffer fills during disk write operations, DOS writes (or flushes) the buffer contents to disk.

When DOS performs disk read operations, it first checks the list of buffers to see if the sector desired is already in memory. If it is, no disk I/O is required. Otherwise, DOS reads the sector from disk into a buffer (see Figure 15-3 and Figure 15-4).

If you increase the number of disk buffers DOS can access, a program that performs random-access disk I/O (a database program) is more likely to find the desired record already in memory. This eliminates many disk I/O operations that are slow processes, which in turn enhances the performance of your application.

Applications that read files sequentially will not see a performance increase by utilizing many buffers, since each record is used only once. Keeping records in disk buffers, therefore, provides no advantage when you use sequential file access programs.

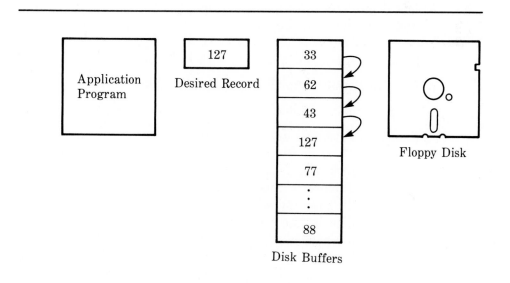

Figure 15-3.   Record found in disk buffer

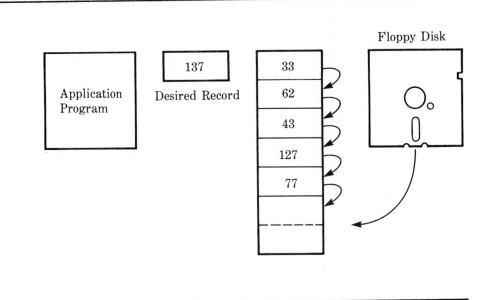

Figure 15-4. Record read from disk into buffer

General guidelines for determining the correct number of disk buffers are the following:

- Database applications use 10 to 25 buffers.
- Word processing applications use 5 to 20 buffers.
- Large numbers of subdirectories use 10 to 25 buffers.
- Fixed disk systems use three buffers minimum.

Many users often fall into the trap of thinking that "if more is better, much more is much better." Having too many buffers, however, will have an adverse effect on overall performance. First, each disk buffer requires 528 bytes of memory. If you use 60 buffers, you have allocated 30K of memory, which may be better utilized by the specific application. In addition, each time DOS performs disk I/O, it first searches the entire list of disk buffers to see if the record is already in memory. Increasing the number of buffers, therefore, also increases the amount of time

DOS must spend searching the list. If you make the number of buffers too large, you will actually see system performance decrease.

COUNTRY

Chapter 12 provides detailed information on creating and using international DOS disks. To create a disk for a foreign country, you issue the SELECT command. SELECT places the correct country entry into the file CONFIG.SYS. The country entry allows you to modify the following characteristics for foreign commands:

```
Country Code 1 United States

Date format mm dd yy
Currency symbol $
Thousands separator ,
Decimal separator .
Date separator -
Time separator :
Decimal significant digits 2
Currency format 0
12 hour time format (1-12)
Data list separator ,
```

Countries are specified as shown in Table 12-1. To select a country, specify the country code in CONFIG.SYS as follows:

```
COUNTRY=country_code
```

To select Italy, for example, place the following entry in CONFIG.SYS:

```
COUNTRY=039
```

If the country code value is invalid, DOS defaults to the U.S. format.

Each hardware device on the system requires a *device driver*, which is a program that DOS uses to communicate with the device. By default, DOS provides device drivers for standard input (the keyboard), standard output (the screen), the printer, the system clock, and fixed and floppy disk drives. DOS installs these drivers into memory each time the system boots. Devices that are not standard on PCs, such as a mouse, may require a unique device driver. Normally, the manufacturer provides the device driver with the hardware on floppy disk.

In order to inform DOS about the new device, you must install the device driver each time the system boots. To do so, place the following entry in CONFIG.SYS:

```
DEVICE=file_specification
```

Assume that the device driver is contained in the PLOTTER.SYS file; the entry in CONFIG.SYS is

```
DEVICE=PLOTTER.SYS
```

DOS provides two device drivers that you can install, ANSI.SYS and VDISK.SYS. You choose one or the other based on your requirements. The first driver, ANSI.SYS, provides enhanced keyboard and video support. Many applications utilize the screen-manipulation capabilities provided by ANSI.SYS in order to keep the application generic for different computers. The ANSI screen-manipulation capabilities allow programmers to clear the screen, clear lines on the screen, and set foreground and background colors, as well as position the cursor. The ANSI driver is an industry-wide standard for these functions. That means that a program that utilizes the ANSI capabilities on an IBM PC will run successfully on a DEC Rainbow, which uses entirely different video hardware. To install the ANSI driver, place the following entry in the file CONFIG.SYS, and reboot:

```
DEVICE=ANSI.SYS
```

(Chapter 18 provides several examples that utilize the ANSI driver from C, Pascal, and FORTRAN.)

The device driver VDISK.SYS allows you to imitate a disk drive in memory. A disk drive that resides in random-access memory (RAM) is known as a RAM drive or virtual disk. Virtual disks provide several useful capabilities. You can access files contained in a RAM disk quickly, since there are no mechanical devices to slow the access. In fact, most users find that RAM disks function up to ten times faster than standard disks.

In essence, you can treat RAM drives exactly as you would treat fixed or floppy drives. The only difference is that the RAM drive loses its contents when the power is turned off. Therefore, any information you have not saved from the RAM drive back to the floppy or fixed disk is lost when you turn off the computer.

DOS RAM drives have the following characteristics:

• The size of the drive is specified by the user.

• Virtual disks have volume labels and drive IDs. If you have a two-floppy-drive system with drives A and B, installing a RAM drive results in drive C. DOS allows you to install multiple RAM drives.

• Each RAM drive allocates approximately 768 bytes plus the number of bytes specified for the drive.

• The minimum size for a RAM drive is 64K.

• A minimum of 64K of memory must remain unused following the RAM drive installation. If not, VDISK will display an error message and modify the size of the RAM drive to ensure that a minimum of 64K is available.

The format to install a RAM drive at system startup is

DEVICE=VDISK.SYS size sectorsize numfiles [/E]

where the following is true:

size is the number of bytes to allocate for the RAM drive.

sectorsize is the size of each disk sector in bytes. Valid sizes are 128, 256, and 512 (128 is the default).

numfiles is the number of files the virtual disk may store. The default value is 64. The value must be in the range 2-512. Each entry uses 32 bytes. VDISK uses one of the entries for the disk volume name.

/E can be used with an IBM PC AT using extended memory. Extended memory occurs above 1MB address space. The /E qualifier forces VDISK to use extended memory for the virtual disk.

The following are valid entries for VDISK.SYS:

DEVICE=VDISK.SYS

(DOS will install a virtual disk drive with the default value of 64K, with 128-byte sectors and 64 file entries.)

DEVICE=VDISK.SYS 192 512 12

(DOS will install a 192K virtual disk with 512-byte sectors that supports 12 file entries.)

When the system boots, VDISK will display

```
VDISK Version 1.0 virtual disk C:
      Directory entries adjusted
      Buffer size:      192 KB
      Sector size:      512
      Directory entries:  16
```

DRIVPARM

DOS version 3.2 allows you to modify the characteristics of block devices at system boot time. The format of the DRIVPARM entry is

DRIVPARM drive [/checkdoor] [/f:formfactor] [/h:head-number] [/nonremoveable] [/s:sectors] [t:tracks]

where the following is true:

drive is the logical drive number to modify the characteristics of (A=0, B=1, C=2). The value must be in the range 0-255.

/checkdoor states that door lock-checking is required.

formfactor specifies the form of the device as shown in Table 15-1.

headnumber specifies the maximum head number. The value must be in the range 1-99.

/nonremoveable specifies that the device is nonremoveable.

sectors specifies the number of sectors per track.

tracks specifies the number of tracks per side.

Form Factor	Characteristic
0	320/360K
1	1.2MB
2	720K
3	8-inch single density
4	8-inch double density
5	hard disk
6	tape drive
7	other device

Table 15-1. Form Factors and Characteristics

Most users will never need to use the DRIVPARM entry. If you must modify the characteristics of a block device, first carefully review the technical reference manual that accompanied the device.

FCBS (Default: FCBS=4,0)

Early versions of DOS used file-control blocks (FCBs) to track each open file. A file-control block contains the state and structure of a specific file. If you are not running older application programs, you should never need to worry about the FCBS entry in CONFIG.SYS. If, however, you begin to experience problems with older programs as you migrate to newer versions of DOS, you should modify FCBS in CONFIG.SYS as follows:

FCBS = maxfiles, protected

where the following is true:

maxfiles specifies the maximum number of files that DOS can open concurrently via file-control blocks. The range of values for maxfiles is 1-255.

protected specifies the number of files that DOS cannot close automatically as it needs to open new files via file-control blocks. This value must be less than or equal to the value specified by maxfiles. The range of values for protected is 0-255.

As previously stated, newer programs do not use FCBs. The following example allows DOS to open 12 files concurrently via FCBs and restricts DOS from closing all 12 automatically:

```
FCBS=12,12
```

FILES (Default: FILES=8)

DOS 3.0 introduced file handles for file access. Most applications now open files via file handles and then perform read, write, and close operations by referencing the file handle. The FILES entry in CONFIG.SYS specifies the maximum number of files that DOS can have open at one time. If your application must open more than eight files concurrently, you must modify the FILES entry in CONFIG.SYS as follows:

FILES = numfiles

where

numfiles is the maximum number of files DOS can have open concurrently at any given time. The value must be in the range 8-255.

It is important to note that the FILES entry specifies the maximum number of files that DOS can open concurrently. DOS still limits each program to 20 open files. If you do not program, and you are not running large database applications, the default value of eight files should be adequate. Otherwise, you may want to allow for 20 files open concurrently by entering

```
FILES=20
```

Each file handle above the default 8 allocates 48 bytes of memory. It is important to note that DOS provides five file handles for each

File Handle	Default Device	Name	Operations
0	con:	stdin	keyboard
1	con:	stdout	screen
2	con:	stderr	screen
3	aux:	stdaux	aux:device
4	prn:	stdprn	printer

Table 15-2.   DOS File Handles and Applications

application that point to the locations shown in Table 15-2. This means that the eight default DOS file handles actually allow you to open three files within your application.

LASTDRIVE (Default: LASTDRIVE=E)

The entry LASTDRIVE in CONFIG.SYS allows you to specify the drive I.D. of the last disk drive DOS can refer to. The format of the entry is

LASTDRIVE=letter

where

letter is the letter (A-Z) of the LASTDRIVE DOS can reference. It must be equal to or greater than the number of drives installed on the system.

The following example sets the LASTDRIVE to drive C:

```
LASTDRIVE=C
```

SHELL

The SHELL entry in CONFIG.SYS allows you to specify an alternate command processor for DOS to use instead of COM-MAND.COM. The format of the entry is

SHELL=[drive:]file＿specification

where

file＿specification is the file containing the program that is to serve as the new command processor:

The following entry defines the file MYSHELL.EXE as the command processor:

```
SHELL=MYSHELL.EXE
```

Most users will never need to specify an alternate command processor. System programmers should first carefully read the DOS technical reference manual before installing their own command processor. The following example contains a CONFIG. SYS file for an IBM PC-AT with 512K of memory:

```
FILES=20
BUFFERS=25
DEVICE=ANSI.SYS
DEVICE=VDISK 192 512 12
```

1. List the DOS configuration parameters.

2. What is the function of CONFIG.SYS?

3. By default, when does DOS test for the CTRL-C combination?

4. When do the entries in CONFIG.SYS take effect?

5. What is a disk buffer? When should the number of disk buffers supported by DOS be increased? Why is having an overabundance of buffers undesirable?

6. When do file-control blocks become a concern to DOS users?

7. What is the entry in CONFIG.SYS that allows DOS to support 30 files that are open concurrently?

8. What is a RAM drive? Provide the entry in CONFIG.SYS to install a 128K RAM drive.

9. What is the ANSI driver?

1. *List the DOS configuration parameters.*

   BREAK

   BUFFERS

   COUNTRY

   DEVICE

   DRIVPARM

   FCBS

   FILES

   LASTDRIVE

   SHELL

2. *What is the function of CONFIG.SYS?*

CONFIG.SYS is the DOS configuration file. Each time DOS boots, it searches the root directory for the file CONFIG.SYS. If the file exists, DOS reads its contents sequentially and configures itself according to the entries provided. DOS allows you to specify new values for each of the configuration parameters listed in the previous answer. If CONFIG.SYS does not exist in the root directory, DOS uses default values for the parameters.

3. *By default, when does DOS test for the* CTRL-C *combination?*

By default (BREAK=OFF), DOS checks for the CTRL-C combination each time it writes to the screen or printer or when it reads from the keyboard. When you specify BREAK=ON, DOS also checks for CTRL-C after disk I/O operations.

4. *When do the entries in CONFIG.SYS take effect?*

Each time you modify the contents of CONFIG.SYS, you must reboot DOS in order for the entries to take effect in the system configuration.

5. *What is a disk buffer? When should the number of disk buffers supported by DOS be increased? Why is having an overabundance of buffers undesirable?*

A disk buffer is a storage location in memory that DOS uses each time it must read or write records from disk that are not a multiple of the disk sector size. If you are running large database applications that perform many random disk I/O operations, you should increase the number of disk buffers. This increases the likelihood of DOS finding the disk sector desired in memory, as opposed to having to read the sector from disk, which is a slower process. Because DOS examines the list of disk buffers with each disk I/O operation, having an overabundance of disk buffers will result in DOS spending a large amount of time performing sequential reads of the disk buffer list.

6. *When do file-control blocks become a concern to DOS users?*

Most DOS users will never be concerned with file-control blocks (FCBs). Early versions of DOS used FCBs for file I/O operations. Later versions of DOS use file handles instead. If you are running older programs under newer versions of DOS, you may experience problems until you increase the number of FCBs DOS will support with the FCBS entry in CONFIG.SYS.

7. *What is the entry in CONFIG.SYS that allows DOS to support 30 files that are open concurrently?*

FILES=30

8. *What is a RAM drive? Provide the entry in CONFIG.SYS to install a 128K RAM drive.*

A RAM drive is a disk drive that resides in random-access memory (RAM). The disk has the same function as a fixed or floppy disk. However, the information contained in the RAM drive is lost each time the computer loses power. Users often exploit RAM drives because of their tremendous speed. Since no mechanical devices are used with RAM drives, they are much faster than conventional disk drives.

> DEVICE=VDISK.SYS 128

9. *What is the ANSI driver?*

The ANSI driver is a device driver that increases the screen manipulation and keyboard capabilities of the PC. The driver contains a series of "standardized" routines that allow programmers to perform the following operations:

Clear the screen

Clear lines on the screen

Set foreground and background colors

Define keys on the keyboard

Extensive cursor positioning

DOS installs the ANSI driver at system boot time if you place the following entry in CONFIG.SYS:

> DEVICE=ANSI.SYS

Programming DOS

LINK
DEBUG
Programming the DOS Pipe
ANSI Driver
DOS System Services
Spawn
Command Line Arguments
Backup Log

All of the chapters thus far have considered the user interface to DOS. This chapter, however, examines several concerns for DOS programmers. If you develop any type of applications with PC-DOS or MS-DOS, the information presented in this chapter will be beneficial. The chapter will examine the DOS linker (LINK), the Microsoft librarian (LIB), the DOS debugger (DEBUG), the development of programs that support the DOS pipe, the ANSI driver, and the DOS system services. Several programming examples that utilize the DOS system services are also provided.

LINK

A critical phase of the program-development cycle is the link process. As you will see, you can place several qualifiers in the LINK command line that will simplify program development. Consider the following steps required to create and execute a program:

1. Create the following source file with a text editor:

```
A> EDLIN SAMPLE.C
New file
*I
        1:* main()
        2:*   {
        3:*     printf ("Hello\n");
        4:*   }
        5:*^C
*E

A>
```

2. Compile the source code into an OBJ file that contains object code.

```
A> CC SAMPLE.C
```

3. Link the object code with the run-time libraries provided with the compiler to create an executable file (file with an EXE extension).

```
A> LINK SAMPLE
```

4. Execute the program.

```
A> SAMPLE
```

This section uses the following keywords:

• *Source code* is the readable version of your program. In the previous example, SAMPLE.C contained the C source code. Source code is the input to the compiler.

• A *compiler* is a software program that converts source code into object code. The compiler ensures that you have not violated any of the syntactic or semantic rules of the programming language. If so, the compiler displays error messages; otherwise, the compiler generates object code.

- *Object code* is the output of the compiler. It contains the binary machine code instructions that make up your executable program. Object code is not yet executable because it may contain references to functions and symbols contained in another object file or library. The linker resolves these external references to create an executable EXE file.

- An *executable file* is the file containing the version of the program that you can execute from the system prompt. The linker produces an EXE file that contains executable machine instructions.

- A *linker* is a software program that combines one or more object files and libraries to produce an executable file. The OBJ and LIB files are the input to the linker. An EXE file is the linker output.

- A *loader* is the portion of COMMAND.COM that is responsible for loading an executable program from disk into memory and then executing it.

- A *list file* is an optional file created by the linker that contains the starting and stopping location of each routine in the executable file, along with its class name. Most programmers will never require the contents of a list file. However, some programmers find the list file a convenient debugging tool.

- *The run-time library* is a collection of routines provided with your compiler that your programs can access to perform common functions. Most of the input and output routines for a language, for example, reside in the run-time library.

- *The relocatable load module* is the name of a program (or overlay) that can reside anywhere in the computer's memory. If a program is relocatable, the loader (COMMAND.COM) must perform additional processing to it as it places the code into memory. The EXE files are relocatable; COM files are not.

In general, the linker combines separately compiled object modules with files contained in libraries to produce a relocatable, executable file. The linker can also produce an optional link map for use as a debugging tool, as shown in Figure 16-1.

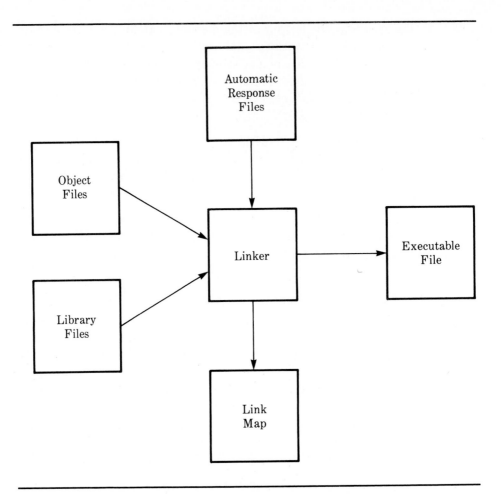

Figure 16-1.   Process of linker producing link map

The format of the DOS LINK command is

[drive:][path]LINK obj—files,exe—file,map—file,lib—files
[/DSALLOCATION][/HIGH][/LINE][/MAP][/PAUSE]
[/STACK:n][/X:n][/O]

where the following is true:

drive: is the disk drive identification that contains the file
LINK.EXE. LINK is an external DOS command, which

means that DOS must load the command from disk into memory each time the command is invoked. If you do not specify a disk drive, DOS will use the current default.

path is the list of subdirectories DOS must traverse to find the file LINK.EXE. If you do not specify a path, DOS uses the current working directory.

obj_files is the name of the OBJ file(s) that LINK is to combine.

exe_file is the name of the executable file that LINK is to create.

map_file is the name of the optional linker map.

lib_files is the name of optional library files that LINK is to search for external references.

/DSALLOCATION causes LINK to place all data contained in DGROUP at the high end of the group. All other groups are placed at the low end.

/HIGH directs the loader to place as much of the run image as possible in memory. Without this qualifier, the loader will place the image in low memory.

/LINE directs LINK to include the line numbers and addresses of the source statements in the modules in the list file. This qualifier only works for certain IBM compilers.

/MAP directs LINK to list in the list file all public symbols defined in the input modules. LINK will provide the segment and offset address in the file for each symbol.

/PAUSE directs LINK to pause and display the following message before writing the EXE file to disk:

/O sets the interrupt number of the overlay loading routine to number. The number can be any integer or value in the range 0-255.

```
About to generate .EXE file
Change diskette in drive n: and press <ENTER>
```

/STACK:n allows you to override the size of the stack specified by the assembler or compiler. The maximum stack size is 64K.

/X:n allows you to specify the number of segments an EXE file can contain. The default value is 256. You can specify a value from 0-1024.

Consider the following examples. Suppose you invoke the linker, without any parameters, as follows:

```
A> LINK
```

DOS will prompt you for the input file name, the executable file name, the optional list file, and the names of any additional libraries that you want to include, as shown here:

```
A> LINK
Object Modules [.OBJ]: SAMPLE
Run File [SAMPLE.EXE]:
List File [NUL.MAP]:
Libraries [.LIB]:
```

As you can see, LINK provides default values for responses within the brackets [ ]. LINK also allows you to specify one or more of the parameters in the command line as follows:

```
A> LINK SAMPLE, TEST
```

In this case, the input file SAMPLE was specified as the OBJ file for the linker to use. As you will see, TEST becomes the default file name for the executable program:

```
Microsoft (R) 8086 Object Linker   Version 3.05
Copyright (C) Microsoft Corp 1983, 1984, 1985. All rights reserved.

List File [NUL.MAP]:
Libraries [.LIB]:
```

Consider the following command:

```
A> LINK SAMPLE,TEST,SAMPLE
```

The linker will use the file name SAMPLE.OBJ for its input object file and the name TEST.EXE for the executable file. SAMPLE.MAP will contain the link map. If you want to specify a partial command line and have the linker use its default values, simply terminate the command line with a semicolon, as shown:

```
A> LINK SAMPLE;
```

In this case, LINK will not prompt you for any additional parameters. Instead, its default will be

```
Run File [SAMPLE.EXE]:
List File [NUL.MAP]:
Libraries [.LIB]:
```

There are many instances in which you may have multiple OBJ files or several LIB library files that you want to combine. Consider the example shown in Figure 16-2. In this case, you want to combine the contents of the files PART1.OBJ and PART2.OBJ to produce the file PROGRAM.EXE. Place the names of the two files on the command line as follows:

```
A> LINK PART1+PART2,PROGRAM
```

By default LINK will select the name of the first OBJ file as the name of the EXE file. If you want the linker to examine multiple libraries (in this case, the files MATH.LIB, TRIG.LIB, and CALC.LIB), simply group them as follows:

```
A> LINK SAMPLE,SAMPLE,,MATH+TRIG+CALC
```

LINK allows you to combine up to 16 libraries. LINK also allows you to place common responses into a file that LINK will read. Consider the following:

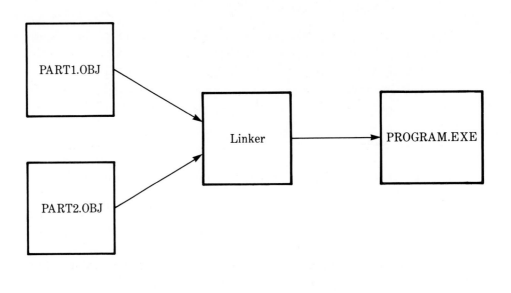

Figure 16-2. Combining OBJ or LIB files with linker

```
A> LINK @FILENAME
```

In this case, FILENAME contains the automatic responses to the LINK prompts. For example, examine the following command line:

```
A> LINK SAMPLE,TEST,SAMPLE,MATH
```

It can be placed into the file SAMPLE.LNK as follows:

```
SAMPLE
TEST
SAMPLE
MATH
```

Consider the following example:

```
A> LINK @OBJECT.LNK,SAMPLE,,@LIB.LNK
```

In this case, LINK will read the file OBJECT.LNK for the names of the object-code files. In addition, LINK will use the file LIB.LNK to determine which library files to search.

Rather than use automatic-response files, many users instead create BAT files for their more commonly linked files, such as

```
A> COPY CON L1.BAT
A> LINK SAMPLE,TEST,SAMPLE,MATH
^Z

        1 File(s) copied
A>
```

As previously stated, LINK supports multiple command-line qualifiers. Consider the following examples. Enter

```
A> LINK /MAP
```

LINK will produce a link map that contains the following:

```
Start  Stop   Length Name           Class
00000H 00012H 00013H AABASE         CODE
00020H 0164BH 0162CH CODE           CODE
01650H 01985H 00336H CODE           CODE
01986H 01986H 00000H APROG
01986H 01CDFH 0035AH _PROG
01CE0H 02CF2H 01013H _PROG
04E9DH 04F0DH 00071H _PROG
04F0EH 04F29H 0001CH _PROG
04F2AH 04F2AH 00000H _PROG
04F30H 053BFH 00490H DATA           DATA
055B0H 0563FH 00090H DOSVERSION     FLCODE
05640H 056A0H 00061H SETDRIVE       FLCODE
056B0H 05722H 00073H GETDRIVE       FLCODE

Origin    Group
04F3:0    DGROUP
09A6:0    SGROUP

Address         Publics by Name
```

```
055B:0006        DOSVERSION
0564:0006        SETDRIVE
056B:0006        GETDRIVE

Address          Publics by Value

055B:0006        DOSVERSION
0564:0006        SETDRIVE
056B:0006        GETDRIVE
```

Each public symbol is listed with its segment and offset address in the executable file.

Enter the LINK command

A> LINK /P

Before writing the executable file to disk, LINK will pause and display the message

```
About to generate .EXE file
Change diskette in drive n: and press <ENTER>
```

Place the disk on which you want the executable file to reside in the specified drive. Enter

A> LINK /S:32000

LINK will produce an EXE file with a 32,000-byte stack size. If you do not specify a stack size, the executable file will be created with a stack as specified by the assembler or compiler. Enter

A> LINK /X:512

LINK will produce an EXE file with 512 segments. The linker default is 256 segments. Linker segments will be defined later in this chapter. Enter

A>LINK /H

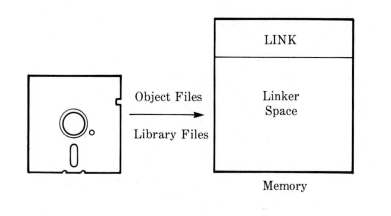

Figure 16-3. Linker reading OBJ and LIB files into memory

The linker will direct the loader (COMMAND.COM) to load the program into memory at as high a memory location as possible. The loader will place the program below the transient portion of COMMAND.COM. By default, the loader places the program in as low a memory location as possible.

How LINK Works

Each time you invoke the DOS linker, it reads into memory the object file(s) and libraries that you specify and begins creating the EXE file, as illustrated in Figure 16-3.

If the tables required by the linker become so large that they can no longer fit into memory, LINK creates a temporary file on the current drive in which to store the files, as shown in Figure 16-4.

When the link is finished, LINK deletes the file. When the linker creates the temporary file, it displays the message

```
VM.TMP has been created
Do not change the diskette in drive n:
```

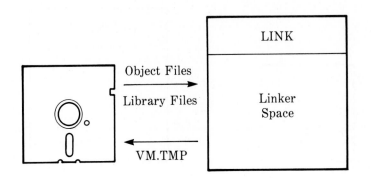

Figure 16-4.   Temporary file created by linker to store files

Once the LINK has created the executable image in memory, it writes it to disk, as specified in the LINK command line.

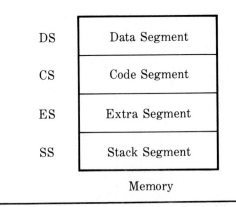

Figure 16-5.   Four segment registers of IBM PC and compatibles

Advanced LINK Concepts

The IBM PC and PC compatibles each use four segment registers as illustrated in Figure 16-5. It is also possible for segments to overlap, as shown in Figure 16-6.

Values are located in memory by first finding their segment address and then finding the offset of the storage location within the segment, as illustrated in Figure 16-7.

The various segment register configurations are referred to as memory models. Your compiler reference manual should provide an in-depth explanation of each model it supports. The following discussion is intended only as a brief overview of memory models. Each program requires separate segments for code and data; the minimum number of segments is two.

A small-memory model is the minimum executable configuration. In this model, the code and data each have a 64K segment. Because it is compact, the small-memory model produces fast code. Most of your applications should fall into this category.

A medium-memory model is used when you have a small amount of data and a large amount of code. Program code can reside in an unlimited number of segments, and data is restricted to 64K.

A large-memory model is used when you have a large amount of code and data. Both program code and data can reside in an

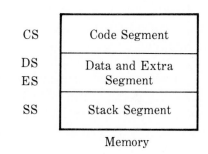

Figure 16-6.　Overlapping segment registers

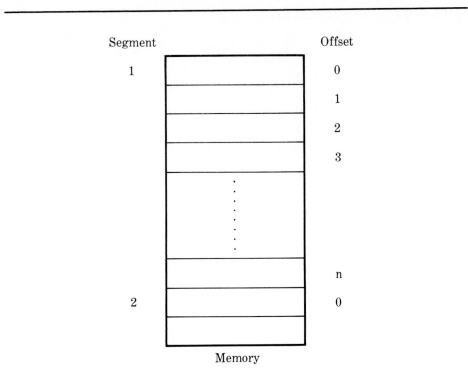

Segment   Offset

Memory

Figure 16-7.   Locating values in memory with segment address and offset address

unlimited number of segments. The only restriction is that the largest code module or variable must be 64K or smaller. Because of its tremendous flexibility as to size, this memory model produces the slowest code of all the models.

Because a segment can be located anywhere in memory, DOS breaks memory into 16-byte paragraph boundaries (see Figure 16-8). A segment address must begin at the start of a 16-byte paragraph boundary. By default, the DOS loader (COMMAND. COM) places executable programs as low as possible in memory. The /HIGH qualifier directs the loader to place the segments at as high a memory location as possible.

Many assembly language programmers are concerned with the actual placement of their code in memory. To assist them, the DOS linker supports segments, groups, and classes. A *segment* contains up to 64K of contiguous memory. When you develop assembly language programs, it is possible to divide the modules in your programs into distinct areas called segments. It is the job of the linker to combine all of these portions into one single segment.

A *group* is a collection of segments that fit together in a 64K-segment section of memory. Either your assembly language program or your language compiler puts segments in groups.

A *class* is a collection of segments that must be placed together in contiguous memory locations. These segments include your code and data segments.

Although most high-level language programmers will never need to be concerned with segments, groups, and classes, all pro-

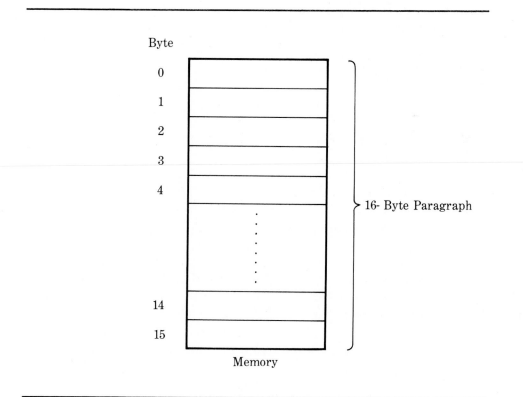

Figure 16-8. The 16-byte paragraph boundaries of DOS segments

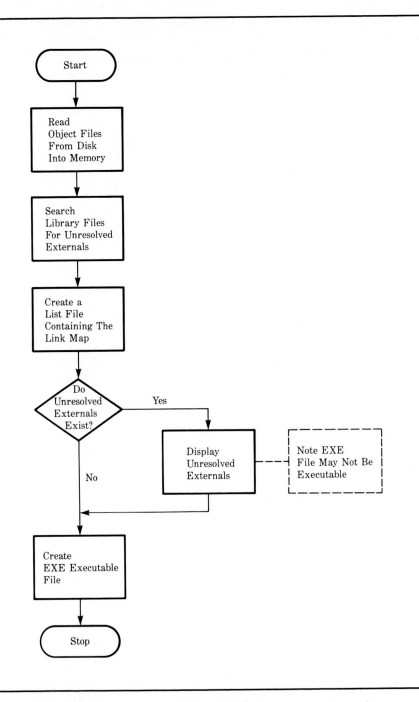

Figure 16-9. Inner workings of linker

grammers should have a basic understanding of the inner work-igs of the linker. Figure 16-9 is a flowchart of the linker process. Appendix C provides a complete overview of all of the LINK error messages.

Librarians

One of the most useful, and least used, capabilities provided with most compilers is a librarian. As previously stated, the linker combines OBJ object files and searches LIB library files to resolve external program references. It is often most convenient to compile your commonly used functions and procedures and place them in a library that can be linked to all of your applications. This prevents you from having to include additional source code in your programs that increases compile time.

In addition, if you link all of your applications to a standard library, you can ensure that they are all using the latest version of a routine. Likewise, maintaining libraries simplifies code sharing with other programmers and applications. Lastly, linking a library as opposed to OBJ files only includes the routines explicitly referred to in your program, which results in more compact code.

Although the syntax and commands may differ for the librarian provided with your compiler, this text will present the Microsoft librarian LIB, since its use is most common. You will find that the functioning of most librarians is identical.

The Microsoft librarian is a software program that allows you to create, update, and utilize run-time libraries. Specifically, the librarian allows you to

- Create LIB library files

- Add, delete, replace, or extract the contents of an object file to and from a library

- Produce a listing of all of the routines contained in a library

For example, if the file MATH.LIB contains the object modules TRIG.OBJ, CALC.OBJ, ALG.OBJ, and HEX.OBJ, the library can be visualized as shown in Figure 16-10. Within each object module are the related functions, procedures, and subrou-

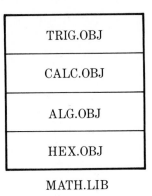

MATH.LIB

Figure 16-10. Object modules of MATH.LIB file

tines that you have compiled. If you append the file OCTAL.OBJ
to the library, its contents become those shown in Figure 16-11.
Likewise, if you delete the object module ALG.OBJ, visualize the
library as containing the modules shown in Figure 16-12.

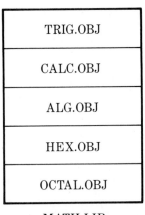

MATH.LIB

Figure 16-11. OCTAL.OBJ file appended to library

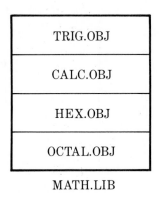

MATH.LIB

Figure 16-12.   MATH.LIB file with ALG.OBJ deleted

A library-replace operation deletes the current version of an object module within the library and replaces it with a new module (see Figure 16-13). Likewise, an extract operation places the contents of a library object module in a file on the disk, as shown in Figure 16-14.

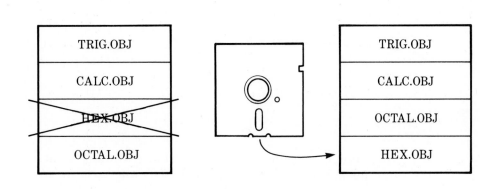

Figure 16-13.   Library-replace operation

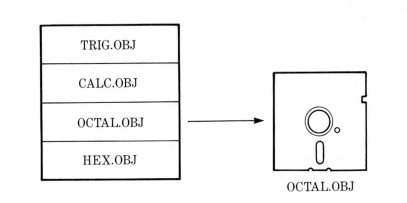

OCTAL.OBJ

Figure 16-14. Extract operation

The simplest way to invoke the Microsoft librarian is to type LIB at the DOS prompt.

`A> LIB`

The librarian will prompt you for the name of the file that you want to use, as follows:

```
A> LIB

Microsoft (R) Library Manager   Version 3.02
Copyright (C) Microsoft Corp 1983, 1984, 1985. All rights reserved.

Library name:
```

Type the name of the file and press ENTER. A library name has the same format as that of a standard DOS file, with an eight-character file name and a three-character extension. By default, the librarian uses the extension LIB. In this case, create the library file MATH.LIB.

```
A> LIB

Microsoft (R) Library Manager   Version 3.02
Copyright (C) Microsoft Corp 1983, 1984, 1985. All rights reserved.

Library name: MATH
```

Next, the librarian will prompt you for the operations that you want to perform. The following are valid LIB operations:

+ Append an object module to the library. Following the plus sign type the name of the object module to append.

```
Operations: + ALG.OBJ
```

− Delete an object module from the library. Following the minus sign, type the name of the object module to delete.

```
Operations: - CALC.OBJ
```

−+ Replace an object module in the library with a file found on disk. Following the plus sign, type the name of the module to replace.

```
Operations: -+ HEX.OBJ
```

* Extract an object module from the library to a file on disk. The file name on disk is given the same name. Following the asterisk, type the name of the object module.

```
Operations: * OCTAL.OBJ
```

−* Extract an object module from a library to disk and then delete the module from the library. Following the asterisk, type the module name.

```
Operations: -* ALG.OBJ
```

As you will see, it is possible to combine multiple operations on one line. After you enter the operation to be performed, the librarian prompts you for the list file name.

```
Microsoft (R) Library Manager   Version 3.02
Copyright (C) Microsoft Corp 1983, 1984, 1985. All rights reserved.

Library name: MATH
Operations: + ALG.OBJ
List file:
```

The list file provides two tables. The first list contains the names of all of the public symbols in the library. The second contains a listing of all of the object modules and the routines that they contain.

```
CHANGE_D..........MATH          CLOSE_FI..........MATH
CREATE_U..........MATH          CURSOR_S..........MATH
DELETE_F..........MATH          EXIT_TO_..........MATH
FIND_FIR..........MATH          FIND_NEX..........MATH
GET_ACTI..........MATH          GET_ATTR..........MATH
GET_CHAR..........MATH          GET_CURS..........MATH
GET_DATE..........MATH          GET_DIRE..........MATH

MATH            Offset: 00000340H   Code and data size: e81H
  CHANGE_D          CLOSE_FI          CREATE_U          CURSOR_S
  DELETE_F          EXIT_TO_          FIND_FIR          FIND_NEX
  GET_ACTI          GET_ATTR          GET_CHAR          GET_CURS
  GET_DATE          GET_DIRE
```

Lastly, the librarian prompts you for the name of the output library. If a library with the same name already exists, it is renamed to a BAK extension. This ensures that you have a backup version of the library that contains the contents of the library as they were prior to your operations. The complete format of the LIB command becomes

LIB library —name [/pagesize:n][;]operations...
[,listing, new —library —name]

where the following is true:

library —name is the name of the library that you want the operations performed on.

/pagesize: specifies the alignment of modules within the library. Modules in the library always start at a position that is a multiple of the page size from the start of the file. If you specify a small page size, less space is wasted within the library. However, decreasing the page size increases the number of disk I/O's required.

; causes a library consistency check. If LIB finds any errors, it will display the error messages. If a library module is inconsistent, simply replace it with a new OBJ file.

For programs that need to access routines contained in the library, simply reference MATH.LIB in the linker command line, as follows:

```
A> LINK file,file,,MATH
```

DEBUG

One of the most useful programming utilities provided with DOS is the program debugger DEBUG. Although DEBUG is most often used by assembly language programmers, it provides several convenient features that are quite easy to use. The DOS debugger allows you to

- Test programs in a controlled environment

- Load, display, or modify any file

- Execute DOS programs

- Perform physical disk sector read/write operations

- Create and assemble assembly language programs

As you will see, DEBUG (in the same fashion as EDLIN) uses single-letter commands:

Command	Format
Assemble	A [address]
Compare	C range or address
Dump	D [range] or [address]
Enter	E address [list]
Fill	F range list

Command	Format
Go	G [=address] [address [address...]]
Hexarithmetic	H value value
Input	I port_address
Load	L [address [drive sector sector]]
Move	M range address
Name	N [drive:] [path]file name[.ext]
Output	O port_address
Proceed	P [=address] [value]
Quit	Q
Register	R [register_name]
Search	S range list
Trace	T [=address] [value]
Unassemble	U [address] or [range]
Write	W [address [drive sector sector]]

The format of the DEBUG command is

[drive:][path]DEBUG [d:][p][file_name[.ext]] [param...]

where the following is true:

drive: is the disk drive identification of the disk that contains the file DEBUG.EXE. DEBUG is an external command; therefore, DOS must load the file from disk into memory. If you do not specify a drive, DOS will use the current default.

path is the list of subdirectories that DOS must traverse to find the file DEBUG.EXE. If you do not specify a path, DOS will use the current working directory.

d: is the disk drive containing the file that DEBUG is to examine.

p is the subdirectory path DOS must traverse to find the file that DEBUG is to examine. If you do not specify a path, DOS uses the current directory.

file_name[.ext] is the name of the file that DEBUG is to examine.

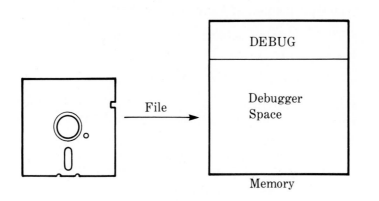

Figure 16-15. DEBUG copying file into memory

param is a command-line parameter for the program DEBUG to examine.

After it has been invoked, DEBUG copies the program or file from disk into memory so that you can display or modify its contents (see Figure 16-15).

The following discussion describes the initialization process DEBUG performs when it loads a file. It is intended for advanced users. Assume that you have invoked DEBUG without a file name, as shown here:

A> DEBUG

DEBUG then initializes the PC register contents as follows:

• The segment registers CS, DS, ES, and SS are set to the address of the first segment following the DEBUG program.

• The instruction pointer, IP, is set to 100H (the first statement following the program-segment prefix (PSP)).

- The stack pointer, SP, is set to the end of the segment or the transient portion of COMMAND.COM (whichever is lower).

- The remaining general-purpose registers are set to 0. The flags register is set to the following state:

    NV UP EI PL NZ NA PO NC

- If the DEBUG command line contains a file name, the segment registers DS and ES will point to the PSP, and the registers BX and CX will contain the size of the program.

To verify this information, invoke DEBUG with the file CHKDSK.COM. Issue the command

```
A> DEBUG CHKDSK.COM
```

The dash (-) is the DEBUG prompt. It is similar to the EDLIN prompt * in that it requests you to enter a command. At the DEBUG prompt, type R and press ENTER.

```
A> DEBUG CHKDSK.COM
-r
AX=0000  BX=0000  CX=243B  DX=0000  SP=FFFE  BP=0000  SI=0000  DI=0000
DS=40EB  ES=40EB  SS=40EB  CS=40EB  IP=0100     NV UP EI PL NZ NA PO NC
40EB:0100 E9C523          JMP      24C8
-
```

R is the DEBUG Register command that displays the contents of the register specified or all of the PC registers. The format of the command is

R [register __name]

In this case, you can invoke the command as follows:

```
-r
AX=0000  BX=0000  CX=243B  DX=0000  SP=FFFE  BP=0000  SI=0000  DI=0000
DS=40EB  ES=40EB  SS=40EB  CS=40EB  IP=0100     NV UP EI PL NZ NA PO NC
40EB:0100 E9C523          JMP      24C8
-r ip
IP 0100
:
```

DEBUG is prompting you to enter a new value for IP. Simply press ENTER to return to the DEBUG prompt with IP unchanged.

It is important to note that all of the DEBUG numbers are assumed to be in hexadecimal. To simplify your data entry, DEBUG provides the Hexarithmetic command. The format of the command is

H value value

The command displays the sum and difference (in hex) of the two values specified. Consider the following examples. Invoke

```
-H 12 10
0022   0002
-
-H FF FF
01FE   0000
-
-H A1 4F
00F0   0052
-
```

If you have not provided a file name in the DEBUG command line, the DEBUG command Name allows you to specify a file after invoking DEBUG. The following invokes the Name command:

```
-N CHKDSK.COM
-
```

The complete format of the DEBUG Name command is

N [drive:][path]file name[.ext]

The DEBUG Quit command allows you to exit from DEBUG and return to DOS.

```
-Q
A>
```

Invoke DEBUG with the file CHKDSK.COM.

```
A> DEBUG CHKDSK.COM
```

The DEBUG Go command executes the program that DEBUG has loaded into memory.

```
-g
Volume DOSDISK      created Nov 2, 1986 8:38p

 21309440 bytes total disk space
   116736 bytes in 7 hidden files
   221184 bytes in 74 directories
 18098176 bytes in 2905 user files
    20480 bytes in bad sectors
  2852864 bytes available on disk

   524288 bytes total memory
   258384 bytes free

Program terminated normally
-
```

The command starts execution at the address specified by CS:IP. Once DEBUG executes a command, the program must be reloaded by DEBUG before it can be executed again.

Using the Go command, DEBUG allows you to set up to ten checkpoints as follows:

G [=address] [address...]

The checkpoints can be specified in any order. In the case of CHKDSK.COM, you can issue the following Go command:

```
-G 24C8 FFFF 24Cf
```

DEBUG will execute until it finds the first checkpoint in the program. Once one checkpoint is found, DEBUG removes all of the remaining checkpoints.

Many of the hardware devices on the computer communicate via ports. The DEBUG Input and Output commands allow you to access the values contained in the ports. The formats of the commands are

I port—address

O port—address

For example, while you are in text mode, port 3D9 allows you to set the border color for color monitors. The following statement reads the current value of that port:

```
·I 3D9
FF
·
```

The next statement sets the border color to blue.

```
·O 3D9 F1
·
```

There are 16 possible border colors. Increment the current value by one to display each. In a similar fashion, port 3D8 allows you to enable and disable video display. The following statement displays the current value of this port:

```
·I 3D8
FF
·
```

The next statement disables the screen display.

```
·O 3D8 F7
·
```

Likewise, the statement enables screen display.

```
-O 3D8 FF
-
```

The DEBUG Dump command displays the contents of a portion of memory. The format of the command is

D [address] or [range]

A DEBUG range is specified as follows:

address [,] address

or

address [,] L [,] value

In the first example, DEBUG will display the contents of memory that falls within the two addresses specified. For example, examine the following:

```
-D 100,110
40D5:0100   5A 8A C7 0A C0 74 01 C3-8D 16 6C 47 9F 03 DA D1
            Z.G.at.C..lG..ZQ
            ^
40D5:0110   DE
-
```

```
-D CS:100, 110
40D5:0100   5A 8A C7 0A C0 74 01 C3-8D 16 6C 47 9F 03 DA D1
            Z.G.at.C..lG..ZQ
            ^
40D5:0110   DE
-
```

DEBUG only allows the first address to contain a segment address. If you try to place a segment address on the second value, DEBUG will display

```
•D CS:100, CS110
             ^ Error
•
```

The second format provides a starting address and the number of bytes to display.

```
•D 100,L,A
40D5:0100   5A 8A C7 0A C0 74 01 C3-8D 16                    Z.G.ət.C..
•
```

In this case, DEBUG will start at CS:100 and display ten bytes. The members of the IBM PC family contain their ROM dates at memory locations F000:FFF5 through F000:FFFC. The ROM dates are associated with PC family members as follows:

04/24/81: original IBM PC
10/19/81: updated PC ROM
08/16/82: original PC XT
10/27/82: updated PC XT ROM
11/08/82: PC portable
06/19/83: PC*jr*
01/10/84: PC AT

Consider the following examples:

```
•D F000:FFF5, FFFC
F000:FFF0               30 31 2F-31 30 2F 38 34        01/10/84
•
```

```
•D F000:FFF5,L,8
F000:FFF0                    30 31 2F-31 30 2F 38 34              01/10/84
•
```

The DEBUG Dump command will be used extensively throughout the remainder of this section.

The DEBUG Fill command places the contents of a list into a range of memory locations. The format of the command is

F range list

A *list* is simply a collection of one or more byte or string values. A *string value* is simply a collection of characters enclosed by double quotes (such as, "string"). For example, the IBM color monitor uses the memory locations starting at B800H for the video display. The following statement fills the screen with the letter K:

```
•F B800:0 L 4000 "K",7
•
```

In this case, "K" is the letter to display and 7 is its display attribute (in normal text mode).

The DEBUG Load command reads absolute disk sectors into memory. The format of the command is

L [address [drive sector sector]]

Suppose you don't specify any of the parameters, as in

```
•L
```

DEBUG will load the file whose name resides at CS:80 (the memory location where the Name command places it) into memory at location CS:100. As stated in Chapter 9, each DOS disk contains a boot record on the first sector on track 0. Load places this sector into memory at location CS:100 as follows:

```
-L 100 0 0 1
-
```

In this case, Load reads the boot record from drive A. As stated in Chapter 9, the boot record contains the 8-byte system identification at offset 3:

```
-D 103 L 8
40D5:0100          49 42 4D 20 20-33 2E 32          IBM   3.2
-
```

Likewise, the DEBUG Write command allows absolute disk sector writes. The format of the command is

W [address [drive sector sector]]

If you do not specify any of the following parameters, DEBUG will use the file name it finds at location CS:80.

```
-W
```

If you do not specify a starting address, DEBUG assumes CS:100. The Write command will be used in several examples later in this section.

The DEBUG Search command searches a range of memory locations for a list of bytes or string values. The format of the command is

S range list

For example, suppose you invoke

```
•S 100,L,100 "IBM"
40D5:0103

•
```

DEBUG will display the address of each location that contains the specified byte or string.

The DEBUG Move command allows you to move the contents from one range of memory to a new location. The format of the command is

M range address

For example, the following command fills the range of memory locations starting at CS:100 with the screen image of the letter K presented previously:

```
•F 100,L,4000 "K",7
•
```

The following command moves the image to the video display memory, resulting in the screen being filled with the letter K (note that for a monochrome monitor, you use B000):

```
-M 100,L,4000 B800:0
•
```

The source contents of the Move operation remain unchanged.

The DEBUG Enter command provides two functions. First, it allows you to replace the contents of one or more memory locations with the contents of a list. Second, the command allows modification of bytes in a sequential manner. The format of the command is

E address [list]

Consider the following example, which reads the system identification off the boot record and then updates it to SOFTWARE:

```
-L 100 0 0 1
-E 103 "SOFTWARE"
-W 100 0 0 1
-
```

The second option allows you to examine memory locations sequentially, as follows:

```
-E 100
40D5:0100  EB.
```

EB is the current contents of memory location CS:100. To change the contents, simply type the new value that you desire.

```
-E 100
40D5:0100  EB.25
```

To change the next memory location, press the SPACEBAR.

```
-E 100
40D5:0100  EB.25    34.
```

To leave the value 34 unchanged and examine the next value, press the SPACEBAR again.

```
•E 100
40D5:0100   EB.25      34.      90.
```

Press ENTER to return to the DEBUG prompt.

```
•E 100
40D5:0100   EB.25      34.      90.
•
```

The DEBUG Assemble command allows you to assemble 8088 assembly language statements with DEBUG. The format of the command is

A [address]

This is a useful method of developing an assembly language program when you do not have an assembler. For example, enter DEBUG as follows:

```
A> DEBUG TEST.COM
•
```

Create a simple program called TEST.COM that prints the contents of the screen. At the DEBUG prompt, issue the Assemble command.

```
File not found
•A 100
40D5:0100   INT 5
40D5:0102   MOV AH, 0
40D5:0104   INT 21
40D5:0106
```

Next, determine the number of bytes in the file by using the DEBUG Hexarithmetic command.

```
-H 106 100
0206   0006
```

Write the contents of the program to TEST.COM by first moving the size of the program into register CX.

```
-R CX
CX 0000
:6
```

Next, issue the Write command.

```
-W
Writing 0006 bytes
```

Exit from DEBUG and invoke the program as follows:

```
-Q

A> TEST
```

The contents of your screen should now be printing.

The DEBUG Unassemble command allows you to examine the object code that produced an EXE or COM file. The format of the command is

U [address] or [range]

Consider the following example:

```
A> DEBUG TEST.COM
-U 100,L, 6
40EB:0100 CD05          INT     05
40EB:0102 B400          MOV     AH,00
40EB:0104 CD21          INT     21
-
```

You want to change the program to

```
INT 18
MOV AH, 0
INT 21
```

You simply type

```
-U 100,L,6
40EB:0100 CD05          INT     05
40EB:0102 B400          MOV     AH,00
40EB:0104 CD21          INT     21
-A 100
40EB:0100    INT 18
40EB:0102
-U 100,L,6
40EB:0100 CD18          INT     18
40EB:0102 B400          MOV     AH,00
40EB:0104 CD21          INT     21
-W
Writing 0006 bytes
-Q
```

The program will now invoke the ROM BASIC provided with
your computer rather than printing the screen contents.

The DEBUG Compare command compares the contents of two memory ranges. The format of the command is

C range or address

Compare displays byte values that differ from each other in memory as follows:

address1 value1 value2 address2

Consider the following example:

```
]-C 100,L,10 200
40D5:0100   5A   8A   40D5:0200
40D5:0101   8A   D8   40D5:0201
40D5:0102   C7   A0   40D5:0202
40D5:0103   0A   9B   40D5:0203
40D5:0104   C0   46   40D5:0204
40D5:0105   74   0A   40D5:0205
40D5:0106   01   C0   40D5:0206
40D5:0107   C3   75   40D5:0207
40D5:0108   8D   05   40D5:0208
40D5:0109   16   A0   40D5:0209
40D5:010A   6C   39   40D5:020A
40D5:010B   47   46   40D5:020B
40D5:010C   9F   8A   40D5:020C
40D5:010D   03   D8   40D5:020D
40D5:010E   DA   A0   40D5:020E
40D5:010F   D1   6A   40D5:020F
-
```

The DEBUG Trace command allows you to step through a program, displaying the register contents after each command.

The format of the command is

T [=address] [value]

Given the program TEST.COM, you can step through it one instruction at a time, as follows:

```
A> DEBUG TEST.COM
-T

AX=0000  BX=0000  CX=0006  DX=0000  SP=FFF8  BP=0000  SI=0000  DI=0000
DS=40EB  ES=40EB  SS=40EB  CS=F600  IP=0000  NV UP DI PL NZ NA PO NC
F600:0000 E98F7E        JMP    7E92
-T

AX=0000  BX=0000  CX=0006  DX=0000  SP=FFF8  BP=0000  SI=0000  DI=0000
DS=40EB  ES=40EB  SS=40EB  CS=F600  IP=7E92  NV UP DI PL NZ NA PO NC
F600:7E92 FA            CLI
-T

AX=0000  BX=0000  CX=0006  DX=0000  SP=FFF8  BP=0000  SI=0000  DI=0000
DS=40EB  ES=40EB  SS=40EB  CS=F600  IP=7E93  NV UP DI PL NZ NA PO NC
F600:7E93 BA6000        MOV    DX,0060
-
```

Lastly, the DEBUG Proceed command is used to execute a subroutine call, an iterative instruction, or an interrupt to continue at the statement that immediately succeeds the instruction without the instruction executing. The format of the command is

P [=address] [value]

The command is similar to the Trace command.

Programming the DOS Pipe

Chapter 7 examined the DOS pipe and I/O redirection operators. As explained, DOS uses standard input (stdin) as the source of input for a program and standard output (stdout) as the output target. Since the pipe and I/O redirection operators are UNIX concepts, and since both UNIX and DOS are written in C, developing C programs that support the pipe and I/O redirection is easy.

If you are not familiar with C, Osborne/McGraw-Hill offers several C programming texts, including *The C Library* by Kris Jamsa (Berkeley, Calif.: Osborne/McGraw-Hill, 1985), which provides a complete chapter on programming the pipe.

The following C program obtains all of its input from the file descriptor stdin and writes all of its output to stdout with each line preceded by its line number:

```
#include <stdin.h>

#define MAX_LINE 255

main ()
  {
   int current_line = 0;

   char string[MAX_LINE];

   while (fgets (string, MAX_LINE, stdin))
     fprintf (stdout, "%d %s", ++current_line, string);
  }
```

Because the program gets its input from stdin and writes all of its output to stdout, it is possible to redirect both the program's input and output.

The compiler directive {$G256,P256} allows I/O redirection to occur within a Turbo Pascal program. Refer to the Turbo Pascal Reference Manual or *The Turbo Pascal Programmer's Library* by Kris Jamsa and Steven Nameroff (Berkeley, Calif.: Osborne/McGraw-Hill, 1986).

This C program implements the MORE command presented in Chapter 7 of this text:

```
#include <stdin.h>

#define MAX_LINE 255
#define PAGE 23

main ()
  {
   int current_line = 0;

   char string[MAX_LINE];
```

```
while (fgets (string, MAX_LINE, stdin))
  {
    fputs (string, stdout);
    if (!(++current_line % PAGE))
     {
      fputs ("--More--\n", stdout);
      fgets (string, MAX_LINE, stderr);
     }
  }
}
```

The following is a Turbo Pascal version of the same program:

```
{$G256,P256}

program More (input, output);

const
  SCREEN_SIZE = 24;              {number of lines to display on a screen}

type
  STRING79 = string[79];

var
  LINE : STRING79;              {line read from stdin}
  COUNT: integer;              {count of lines displayed}
begin
  COUNT := 0;

{read lines from stdin displaying them a page at a time.  prompt the
 user to hit return with each screenful of data}
  while (not EOF) do
    begin
      COUNT := COUNT + 1;
      Readln (LINE);
      Writeln (LINE);

{if a screenful has been displayed, prompt the user to hit return}
      if (COUNT mod SCREEN_SIZE = 0) then
        begin
          Write ('-- More --');

{read the carriage return from the keyboard as opposed to stdin which
 has been redirected by the operating system}
          Readln (KBD);
          Writeln;
        end;
    end;
end.
```

Last, the following program provides a tee for the DOS pipe.
Consider the following command:

A> DIR ¦ TEE DIR.LIS ¦ MORE

The DIR command pipes all of its output to the TEE program.

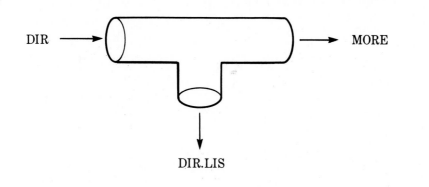

DIR → MORE

DIR.LIS

Figure 16-16. Creating intermediate files while piping DOS commands

TEE then performs two functions. First, TEE writes each line it receives to the file DIR.LIS. Second, TEE also writes each line to stdout, allowing the pipe to continue. This, in essence, allows you to create intermediate files as you pipe DOS commands (see Figure 16-16).

```c
#include <stdin.h>

#define MAX_LINE 255

main (argc, argv)
  int argc;
  char *argv[];
{
  char string[MAX_LINE];

  int tee_file;

  if (argc > 1)
   if ((tee_file = fopen (argv[1], "w")) != NULL)
     while (fgets (string, MAX_LINE, stdin))
       {
         fputs (string, stdout);
         fputs (string, tee_file);
       }
   else
     fprintf (stderr, "Error opening file %s\n", argv[1]);
   else
     fprintf (stderr, "No tee file specified command terminating\n");
  }
```

```
{$G256,P256}

program Tee (input, output);

type
  STRING79 = string[79];

var
  LINE    : STRING79;        {line read from stdin}
  TEE_FILE: text;            {the tee output file}

begin

{make sure the user provided an output file for the tee}
  if (ParamCount = 0) then
    Writeln ('tee: invalid usage: tee filename')

{an output file was provided so read each record from stdin and
 write it stdout and the output file}
  else
    begin
      Assign (TEE_FILE, ParamStr(1));
      {$I-} Rewrite (TEE_FILE) {$I+};
      if (IOresult <> 0) then
        Writeln ('tee: error opening the file ', ParamStr(1))
      else
        while (not EOF) do
          begin
            Readln (LINE);                      {read from stdin}
            Writeln (TEE_FILE, LINE);   {write to tee output file}
            Writeln (LINE);                     {write to stdout}
          end;
        Close (TEE_FILE);
    end;
end.
```

ANSI Driver

As previously stated, the ANSI driver (ANSI.SYS) is an install-able device driver that provides the following additional keyboard and screen display functions:

- Clear screen contents

- Save current cursor position

- Restore cursor to its saved position

- Move cursor up n rows

- Move cursor down n rows

- Move cursor left n columns

- Move cursor right n columns

FORTRAN		write (6,1) 27, 27
	1	format (1x, a1, '[H',a1,'[J'])
C		printf ("%c[H%c[J]", 27, 27);
Pascal		writeln (Chr (27), '[H', Chr (27), '[J');

Table 16-1.   Code Pieces to Clear the Screen

- Change character display attributes
- Set cursor position
- Set foreground and background colors
- Redefine keys

For example, Table 16-1 shows code pieces that clear the screen from FORTRAN, C, and Pascal.

The Escape character (ASCII 27) starts an ANSI character code sequence. Many programmers find that the ANSI driver provides a convenient method for performing I/O. Admittedly, using the ANSI driver is slower than making calls to the ROM-BIOS. Almost every operating system, however, supports the ANSI character codes. This means that if you write a C program that uses the ANSI codes on an IBM PC under DOS, that same program should run without modification on a larger computer running UNIX. Table 16-2 summarizes the character codes supported by the ANSI driver.

DOS System Services

If you have been writing applications under DOS and have not been using the DOS system services, you have been missing out on some of DOS's best features. The developers of DOS simplified their programming efforts by breaking each function required by DOS into a small piece of code called a *system service*. This means

ANSI Function	ANSI Code
Set cursor position	Esc[Row;COLH
Clear screen	Esc[HEsc[J
Cursor up n rows	Esc[nA
Cursor down n rows	Esc[nB
Cursor right n columns	Esc[nC
Cursor left n columns	Esc[nD
Save cursor position	Esc[s
Restore cursor position	Esc[u
Erase to end of line	Esc[K
Erase to bottom of screen	Esc[2J
Device status report	Esc[6n
Report cursor position	Esc[n;nR
Redefine a keyboard character (the ASCII character defined by ascii1 is redefined to the ASCII character defined by ascii2)	Esc[ascii1;ascii2p
Refine a function key key is defined as follows: F1 = 59 ... F10 = 68 F1 ... F10 = 59 ... 68	Esc[0;key;"string"; 13p

Table 16-2.   Character Codes Supported by ANSI

that they developed procedures and functions to create and manipulate files and directories, to perform I/O to the disk, screen, and printer, and to load and control the execution of programs.

Since all of these routines (services) are required for DOS to execute, the DOS developers have made them readily available to your programs. Before examining the actual services provided, an overview of the interrupts and 8088 registers is required.

Interrupts

An *interrupt* is a signal to the CPU from a program or hardware device. For each interrupt, a section of code known as an *interrupt service routine* is present in memory. The purpose of this code is to interrupt the processor temporarily to perform a specific task.

When an interrupt occurs, the processor locates the code associated with the interrupt and executes it. For example, when a user presses the CTRL-ALT-DEL keys, an interrupt handler reboots the operating system.

The CPU identifies interrupt handlers via interrupt vectors. An *interrupt vector* can best be viewed as a three-dimensional array that contains the interrupt number, along with the segment and offset address of the interrupt handler (as illustrated in Table 16-3).

When an interrupt occurs, the processor uses the *interrupt number* as an index into the table to locate the *interrupt handler*. Before the system invokes the interrupt handler, it stores information about the current program on the *system stack*. This allows the processor to resume its previous function when the interrupt handler completes.

Admittedly, this has been a brief and simplified overview of interrupt processing. Nevertheless, to exploit the ROM-BIOS and DOS services requires only a basic understanding of interrupt processing. As you will see, all the DOS services are invoked via the DOS interrupt 21H.

Interrupt	Segment Address	Offset Address
1	0070	01ED
2	3D28	09D2
3	0070	01ED
4	3D28	0998
5	F000	FF54
.	.	.
.	.	.
.	.	.
n	xxxx	xxxx

Table 16-3.   Interrupt Vectors

8088 Registers

The IBM PC and PC compatibles are based on a processor chip called the 8088. Within this chip are a set of storage locations known as *registers*. The CPU can manipulate values contained in registers quickly, since the storage locations are contained within the processor chip. The 8088 has 14 registers, each capable of storing 16 bits of data. The 8088 registers can be visualized as follows:

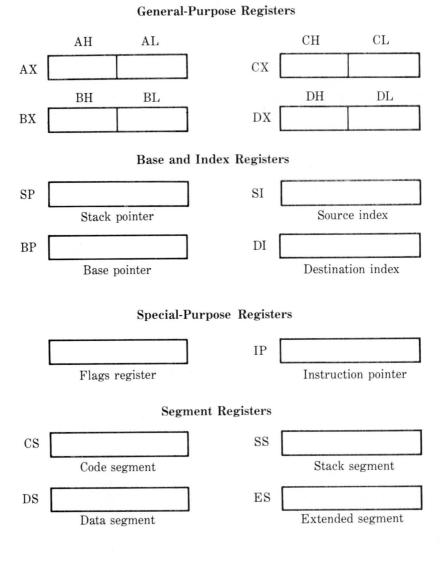

General-Purpose Registers

AH AL CH CL

AX CX

BH BL DH DL

BX DX

Base and Index Registers

SP SI

Stack pointer Source index

BP DI

Base pointer Destination index

Special-Purpose Registers

IP

Flags register Instruction pointer

Segment Registers

CS SS

Code segment Stack segment

DS ES

Data segment Extended segment

The way that your programs communicate with the services is through the 8088 registers. For example, if you want to determine the version of DOS that you are using, invoke the following DOS service:

Register	Entry Contents
AH	30H

Register	Exit Contents
AH	Minor DOS version number
AL	Major DOS version number

The value in register AH tells DOS what service you want to perform. Since you are simply requesting information from DOS in this case, you do not have to include information in any of the other registers. When DOS completes the service, it will return with the minor version number in register AH and the major version number in register AL, as illustrated in Figure 16-17.

Turbo Pascal provides a convenient method of requesting DOS services via the MSDOS function. To emulate the 8088 registers, you must define the following data type:

```
Type
  REGISTERS = record
                AX, BX, CX, DX, BP, SI, DI, DS, ES, FLAGS: INTEGER
              end;
```

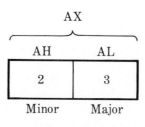

AX

AH	AL
2	3

Minor   Major

DOS Version 3.2

Figure 16-17.   DOS returning major and minor version numbers

Consider the following Turbo Pascal program, which displays the current DOS version:

```
program SYSTEM_TOOLS;

type
    REGISTERS = record
                    AX, BX, CX, DX, BP, SI, DI, DS, ES, FLAGS: INTEGER;
                end;

var
    REGS: REGISTERS;

begin
    with REGS do
      begin

        AX := $3000;                              {DOS function code}
        MSDos (REGS);
        writeln ('DOS Version ', Lo(AX), '.', Hi(AX));
      end;
end.
```

DOS Service Functions

The following section summarizes each DOS system service function.

00H: Terminate a Program

This service terminates the current program and performs the following:

• Restores the terminate CTRL-BREAK and critical-error handler addresses to the values they contained prior to the program's execution.

• Flushes all buffers for open file handles. If the file length has changed, the directory entry is updated.

Register	Entry Contents
AH CS	00H Program segment prefix address

Register	Exit Contents
	NONE

Notes This service performs the same function as service 20.

01H: Get Keyboard Input

This service checks whether characters are in the type-ahead buffer. If not, it waits for the user to enter a keyboard character. The service echos the character entered to the screen.

Register	Entry Contents
AH	01H

Register	Exit Contents
AL	The character entered from the keyboard.

Notes If the character entered is an extended ASCII code (such as a function key) you must invoke this interrupt twice. The first call will return the value 0 in the register AL. The second call will return the actual extended ASCII code:

Value	Character
3	Null character
15	Shift tab character
16-25	ALT Q W E R T Y U I O P
30-38	ALT Z X C V B N M
59-68	Function keys F1-F10
71	HOME key
72	Cursor UP ARROW key
73	PAGE UP key
75	Cursor LEFT ARROW key
77	Cursor RIGHT ARROW key
79	END key
80	Cursor DOWN ARROW key
81	PAGE DOWN key
82	INS key
83	DEL key
84-93	Function keys F11-F20 or SHIFT F1-F10
94-103	Function keys F21-30 or CTRL-F1-F10

02H: Display Character to
Standard Output Device

This service outputs the character contained in the register DL to the standard output device.

Register	Entry Contents
AH DL	02H Character to display

Register	Exit Contents
	NONE

Notes   DOS checks for a CTRL-BREAK upon completion of the output. If it is present, it executes interrupt 23H.

03H: Get Character From
Standard Auxiliary Device

This service waits for a character from the standard auxiliary device and then returns the character in register AL.

Register	Entry Contents
AH	03H

Register	Exit Contents
AL	Character input

Notes   The DOS I/O services to the standard auxiliary devices do not return error-status codes. Most users will access the ROM-BIOS services or use device drivers written for the standard auxiliary device.

04H: Output Character to
Standard Auxiliary Device

This service writes the character contained in register DL to the standard auxiliary device.

Register	Entry Contents
AH DL	04H Character to output

Register	Exit Contents
	NONE

Notes   The DOS I/O services to the standard auxiliary devices do not return error-status codes. Most users will access the ROM-BIOS services or use device drivers written for the standard auxiliary device.

05H: Output Character to
Standard Printer Device

This service writes the character contained in register DL to the standard printer device.

Register	Entry Contents
AH DL	05H Character to output

Register	Exit Contents
	NONE

06H: Direct Console
(Keyboard/Display) I/O

This service combines keyboard input and screen output into one DOS service. If the contents of DL is FFH, the service performs keyboard input; otherwise, the service writes the character contained in DL to the screen.

Register	Entry Contents
AH	06H
DL	FFH for input otherwise the character to output

Register	Exit Contents
AL	Character input if present and input service was performed
FLAGS	Zero flag is 1 if no character was present for input or 0 if a character is present

Notes　　If an input service is requested (DL = FFH), the service checks the input buffer to see if a character is present. If a character is present, the routine clears the zero flag and places the character in AL; otherwise, the service sets the zero flag and returns. The service does not echo character input to the screen.

　　If the character entered is an extended ASCII code (such as a function key), you must invoke this interrupt twice. The first call will return the value 0 in AL. The second call will return the actual extended ASCII code. The service does not check the character entered for CTRL-BREAK or other CTRL combinations.

07H: Direct Console Input Without Character Echo

This service gets a character from the standard input device without echoing the character input back to the screen. The character is returned in register AL.

Register	Entry Contents
AH	07H

Register	Exit Contents
AL	Character input

Notes   If the character entered is an extended ASCII code (such as a function key), you must invoke this interrupt twice. The first call will return the value 0 in AL. The second call will return the actual extended ASCII code. The service does not check the character entered for CTRL-BREAK or other CTRL combinations.

08H: Console Input Without Character Echo

This service gets a character from the standard input device without echoing the character input back to the screen. The character is returned in register AL.

Register	Entry Contents
AH	08H

Register	Exit Contents
AL	Character input

Notes   If the character entered is an extended ASCII code (such as a function key), you must invoke this interrupt twice. The first call will return the value 0 in register AL. The second call will return the actual extended ASCII code.

This service is similar to service 07H, except that it performs

CTRL-BREAK checking and executes interrupt service 23H if a CTRL-BREAK is present.

09H: Display a String

This service displays a string to the standard output device.

Register	Entry Contents
AH	09H
DS	Segment address of the string
DX	Offset address of the string

Register	Exit Contents
	NONE

Notes   The string must be terminated with the dollar sign ($) character, and this may limit the service's usefulness.

0AH: Buffered Keyboard Input

This service reads characters from the standard input device and places them in a user-defined buffer beginning at the third byte.

Register	Entry Contents
AH	0AH
DS	Segment address of the input buffer
DX	Offset address of the input buffer

Register	Exit Contents
	NONE

Notes   The maximum buffer size is 255 characters. The service fills the buffer as shown in Figure 16-18. The service continues to read characters until the ENTER key is pressed. If the

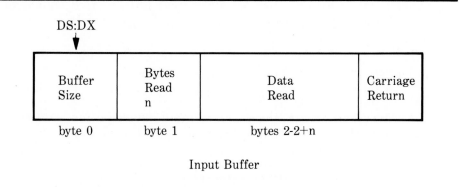

Figure 16-18. DOS function OAH filling buffer

buffer fills, the service ignores subsequent characters and rings the computer bell. The last character in the buffer is always the carriage-return character (ODH).

OBH: Check Standard Input Device Status

This service checks the status of the standard input device to determine whether input data is present. It returns FFH if input is present and 0H if no characters are available. The status returned is in register AL.

Register	Entry Contents
AH	OBH

Register	Exit Contents
AL	Standard input device status FFH for input available OH for no available characters

Notes   This service tests for CTRL-BREAK. If CTRL-BREAK is present, the service executes interrupt 23H.

0CH: Clear Keyboard Type-Ahead Buffer and Invoke Keyboard Function

This service clears the standard input device buffer and performs the keyboard function number contained in register AL.

Register	Entry Contents
AH	0CH
AL	Keyboard function number to perform

Register	Exit Contents
	NONE

Notes   This service forces the system to wait for keyboard input. The keyboard function specified in AL must be in the set (01H, 06H, 07H, or 0AH).

0DH: Flush All Disk Buffers

This service flushes all of the buffers for currently open files.

Register	Entry Contents
AH	0DH

Register	Exit Contents
	NONE

Notes   The service does not close the files, so directory entries for files whose sizes have changed will not be correct if you do not invoke the DOS close file service.

OEH: Select Default Disk Drive

This service selects the current default disk drive. The service also returns the total number of disk drives present in register AL.

Register	Entry Contents
AH	OEH
DL	Drive number desired

Register	Exit Contents
AL	Total number of disk drives present

Notes   Disk drive numbers are specified as 0 = A, 1 = B, 2 = C, and so forth.

OFH: Open File with File Control Block (FCB)

This service searches for the file specified in the file-control block and returns successful or unsuccessful open status in register AL.

Register	Entry Contents
AH	OFH
DS	Segment address of an unopened FCB
DX	Offset address of an unopened FCB

Register	Exit Contents
AL	File open status OOH is successful open FFH unsuccessful file open

Notes   The contents of a file-control block are shown in Figure 16-19. The file must exist before it can be opened. If the file does not exist, use the DOS create file service. Most newer applications

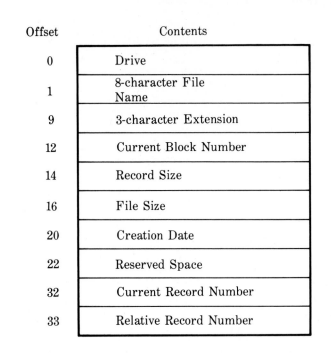

Offset	Contents
0	Drive
1	8-character File Name
9	3-character Extension
12	Current Block Number
14	Record Size
16	File Size
20	Creation Date
22	Reserved Space
32	Current Record Number
33	Relative Record Number

Figure 16-19. Contents of file-control block (FCB)

use file handles (DOS service 3DH) as opposed to file-control blocks. The use of file-control blocks is inadvisable. Use file handles instead, as they are easier to use. File-control blocks do not support paths.

10H: Close File Opened with File Control Block (FCB)

This service closes the file pointed to by the file-control block provided and flushes its buffers. If the file size has changed, the service updates the directory entry. The service returns the status in register AL.

Register	Entry Contents
AH	10H
DS	Segment address of the file's FCB
DX	Offset address of the file's FCB

Register	Exit Contents
AL	File close status
	00H successful close
	FFH file not found

Notes   The common cause for a return status of FFH is that the source disk for the file is no longer in the specified drive.

11H: Search for First Matching File Entry

This service searches the current disk directory for the first file name that matches the name specified in the file-control block (FCB) provided. If no matching files are found, the service returns the value FFH in register AL. Otherwise, the service sets AL to 00H, and the contents of the disk transfer address (DTA) are modified to match an unopened FCB. DOS wildcard characters are supported for file names (see also DOS function 4EH).

Register	Entry Contents
AH	11H
DS	Segment address of an FCB
DX	Offset address of an FCB

Register	Exit Contents
AL	File search status
	00H matching file found
	FFH matching file not found

Notes   This service is a powerful tool for directory-wide operations. It is used in conjunction with DOS service 12H, which finds subsequent matching file entries to allow operations to be performed on multiple files whose names meet the criteria specified in the file-control block.

12H: Search for Next Matching
File Entry

This service continues the search begun by the DOS service 11H. DOS examines the current disk directory for the next file name that matches the name specified in the file-control block (FCB) provided in the 11H service. If no matching files are found, the service returns the value FFH in register AL. Otherwise, the service sets AL to 00H, and the contents of the disk transfer address (DTA) are modified as specified in service 11H.

Register	Entry Contents
AH	12H
DS	Segment address of an FCB
DX	Offset address of an FCB

Register	Exit Contents
AL	File search status
	00H matching file found
	FFH matching file not found

Notes   This service is a powerful tool for directory-wide operations. It is used in conjunction with DOS service 11H, which finds the first matching file entry to begin operations to be performed on multiple files whose names meet the criteria specified in the file-control block.

13H: Delete File Specified by
File Control Block (FCB)

This service deletes the file specified in the file-control block from the current directory. The service returns the status in register AL.

Register	Entry Contents
AH	13H
DS	Segment address of an unopened FCB
DX	Offset address of an unopened FCB

Register	Exit Contents
AL	File deletion status 00H file deleted FFH file not found

Notes   The service will not delete files marked as read-only. Close all files before deleting them.

14H: Sequential Read from File Specified by File Control Block (FCB)

This service reads a record sequentially from a file opened with a file-control block. The record number for the service to read is specified in the file-control block. The data read from the disk is placed into the disk transfer area (see DOS service 1AH). The service returns the status in register AL.

Register	Entry Contents
AH	14H
DS	Segment address of an opened FCB
DX	Offset address of an opened FCB

Register	Exit Contents
AL	File read status 00H read successfully completed 01H end of file found (no data read) 02H disk transfer area too small for the record size specified 03H end of file found (partial data read)

Notes   The file-control block specifies the size of the record.

15H: Sequential Write to File
Specified by File Control Block (FCB)

This service writes records sequentially to a file opened with a file-control block. The record number for the service to write is specified in the file-control block. The data to write is obtained from the disk transfer area (see DOS service 1AH). The service returns the status in register AL.

Register	Entry Contents
AH	15H
DS	Segment address of an opened FCB
DX	Offset address of an opened FCB

Register	Exit Contents
AL	File write status
	00H write successfully completed
	01H diskette is full (no data written)
	02H disk transfer area too small for the record size specified

Notes   The file-control block specifies the size of the record. The service cannot write to read-only files.

16H: Find or Create Directory
Entry for File

This service searches the current directory for the file specified in a file-control block (FCB). If a directory entry is found, the service opens the file. Otherwise, the service creates a directory entry for the file. The service returns the status in register AL.

Register	Entry Contents
AH	16H
DS	Segment address of an unopened FCB
DX	Offset address of an unopened FCB

Register	Exit Contents
AL	File creation status 00H file successfully opened/created 01H diskette is full (no file created)

Notes　　Most users use this service to open files for output files; they use DOS service 0FH to open input files. It is desirable, however, to use file handlers.

17H: Rename File Specified by
File Control Block (FCB)

This service searches the current directory for the specified drive and renames the file specified to the name provided in the modified file-control block. The new name is specified (as illustrated) in the FCB. The service returns the status in register AL.

Register	Entry Contents
AH	17H
DS	Segment address of a modified FCB
DX	Offset address of a modified FCB

Register	Exit Contents
AL	File rename status 00H file successfully renamed 01H file not found

Offset	Contents
0	Drive
1	8-character File Name
9	3-character Extension
12	Current Block Number
14	Record Size
16	File Size
20	Creation Date
22	Second File Name

Figure 16-20.   Contents of modified file-control block (FCB)

Notes   The contents of a modified file-control block are shown in Figure 16-20. If the new file name contains question marks, the matching characters are taken from the previous file name. This service cannot rename read-only files.

19H: Return Current Disk Drive

This service returns the current default drive. The drive is returned in register AL.

Register	Entry Contents
AH	19H

Register	Exit Contents
AL	Current disk drive

Notes   Disk drives are specified as A = 0, B = 1, C = 2, and so forth.

1AH: Set Disk Transfer Address (DTA)

This service sets the disk transfer address to the specified address.

Register	Entry Contents
AH	1AH
DS	Segment address of the new DTA
DX	Offset address of the new DTA

Register	Exit Contents
	NONE

Notes   The default DTA is 128 bytes at offset 80H in the program segment prefix. DOS uses the disk transfer address for all file I/O.

1BH: Get Current Disk Drive File Allocation Table (FAT) Information

This service returns information for the file allocation table on the current drive.

Register	Entry Contents
AH	1BH

Register	Exit Contents
AL	Number of sectors/cluster
BX	Offset address of the media descriptor byte for the current drive
CX	Sector size in bytes
DS	Segment address of the media descriptor byte for the current drive
DX	Number of allocation units (clusters)

Notes   The contents of the media-descriptor byte are shown in Figure 16-21. Save the contents of the data segment register (DS) before invoking this DOS service.

1CH: Get Disk File Allocation Table (FAT) Information for Any Drive

This service returns information for the file allocation table on the specified drive.

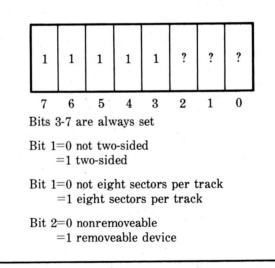

Bits 3-7 are always set

Bit 1=0 not two-sided
    =1 two-sided

Bit 1=0 not eight sectors per track
    =1 eight sectors per track

Bit 2=0 nonremoveable
    =1 removeable device

Figure 16-21.   Contents of media-descriptor byte

Register	Entry Contents
AH	1CH
DL	Drive number

Register	Exit Contents
AL	Number of sectors/cluster
BX	Offset address of the media descriptor byte for the drive specified in DL
CX	Sector size in bytes
DS	Segment address of the media descriptor byte for the drive specified in DL
DX	Number of allocation units (clusters)

Notes   Save the contents of the data segment register (DS) before invoking this DOS service. Disk drive numbers are specified as A = 0, B = 1, C = 2, and so forth.

21H: Random Read from File Specified by File Control Block (FCB)

This service reads one record specified in the file-control block from disk into the current disk transfer address. The service returns the status in register AL.

Register	Entry Contents
AH	21H
DS	Segment address of the file control block (FCB)
DX	Offset address of the file control block (FCB)

Register	Exit Contents
AL	Random read status
	00H successful read operation
	01H end of file (no data read)
	02H DTA too small for the record size specified
	03H end of file (partial data read)

Notes   DOS service 27H reads multiple records in a random fashion.

22H: Random Write to File Specified by File Control Block (FCB)

This service writes one record specified in the file-control block from disk into the current disk transfer address. The service returns the status in register AL.

Register	Entry Contents
AH	22H
DS	Segment address of the file control block (FCB)
DX	Offset address of the file control block (FCB)

Register	Exit Contents
AL	Random write status 00H successful write operation 01H disk full (no data written) 02H DTA too small for the record size specified

Notes   This service cannot write to read-only files.

23H: Return Number of Records in File Specified by File Control Block (FCB)

This service searches the current directory for the file specified by the file-control block and places the number of records in the file into the random record field of the FCB. The service returns the status in register AL.

Register	Entry Contents
AH	23H
DS	Segment address of the file control block (FCB)
DX	Offset address of the file control block (FCB)

Register	Exit Contents
AL	Record count status 00H file found FFH file not found

Notes   You must set the record size field of the FCB before invoking this function.

24H: Set Relative File Record Size Field

This service sets the random record field of the file specified by a file-control block (FCB). The random record field is set to the value contained in the current sequential and random record blocks of the FCB.

Register	Entry Contents
AH	24H
DS	Segment address of the file control block (FCB)
DX	Offset address of the file control block (FCB)

Register	Exit Contents
	NONE

Notes   You must invoke this function before performing random file access.

25H: Set Interrupt Vector

This service sets the segment and offset address of the code DOS is to perform each time the specified interrupt is invoked.

Register	Entry Contents
AH	25H
AL	Interrupt number to reassign the handler
DS	Segment address of the interrupt handler
DX	Offset address of the interrupt handler

Register	Exit Contents
	NONE

Notes   You normally will want to reset the interrupt handler to its previous vector before your application is finished. Use DOS service 35H to obtain the current vector address for an interrupt.

26H: Create New Program Segment Prefix (PSP)

This service copies the current program-segment prefix to a new memory location for the creation of a new program or overlay. Once the new PSP is in place, a DOS program can read a DOS COM or overlay file into the memory location immediately following the new PSP and pass control to it.

Register	Entry Contents
AH	26H
DX	Segment number for the new PSP

Register	Exit Contents
	NONE

Notes   The contents of the program-segment prefix are shown in Figure 16-22. DOS developers recommend that you use the newer DOS service 4BH instead of this older service.

27H: Random File Block Read From File Specified by File Control Block (FCB)

This service reads the number of records specified in register CX from the file address specified in the FCB to the disk transfer address. The service returns status in register AL and the actual number of records read in register CX.

Offset (Hex)	Contents
0	Int 20
2	Top of Memory
4	Reserved
5	OP Code
6	Number of Bytes in Segment
A	Terminate Address (Offset)
C	Terminate Address (Segment)
E	CTRL-BREAK Address (Offset)
10	CTRL-BREAK Address (Segment)
12	Critical Error Address (Offset)
14	Critical Error Address (Segment)
16	Reserved
2C	Environment Address (Segment)
2E	Reserved
50	DOS Call
52	Reserved
5C	File-Control Block One
6C	File-Control Block Two
80	Command-Line Length (Bytes)
81	Command-Line Parameters

Figure 16-22.   Contents of program-segment prefix (PSP)

Programming DOS   **571**

Register	Entry Contents
AH	27H
CX	Number of records to read
DS	Segment address of an opened FCB
DX	Offset address of an opened FCB

Register	Exit Contents
AL	Random block read status
	00H successful read
	01H end of file (no data read)
	02H DTA too small for record size specified
	03H end of file (partial data read)
CX	Number of records read

Notes   The record size is specified in the FCB. The service updates the current block/record fields to the first record not read.

28H: Random File Block Write to
File Specified by File Control Block (FCB)

This service writes the number of records specified in register CX from the file address specified in the FCB to the disk transfer address. The service returns status in register AL and the actual number of records written in register CX.

Register	Entry Contents
AH	28H
CX	Number of records to write
DS	Segment address of an opened FCB
DX	Offset address of an opened FCB

Register	Exit Contents
AL	Random block write status
	00H successful write
	01H disk full (no data written)
	02H DTA too small for record size specified
CX	Number of records written

Notes   The record size is specified in the FCB. The service allocates disk clusters as required.

29H: Parse the Command Line
for File Name

This service parses the command line for a file name in the form DRIVE:FILENAME.EXT. If a file name is found, DOS creates a file-control block for it. This service does not understand DOS pathnames. The service returns the status in register AL.

Register	Entry Contents
AH	29H
AL	Parse control bit mask
DI	Offset address of an unopened FCB
DS	Segment address of the command line to parse
ES	Segment address of an unopened FCB
SI	Offset address of the command line to parse

Register	Exit Contents
AL	Filename parse status
	00H no global filename characters found in command line
	01H global filename characters found in command line
	FFH invalid drive specifier
DI	Offset address of first byte of formatted FCB
DS	Segment address of first character after the filename
ES	Segment address of first byte of formatted FCB
SI	Offset address of first character after the filename

Notes The parse control bit mask works as follows:

Bit 0 set Causes the service to scan past leading separators such as blanks. Otherwise, the service assumes that the file name begins in the first byte.

Bit 1 set Causes the service to change the drive specifier in the FCB to the drive found in the command line. Otherwise, it is unchanged, which allows you to provide a default drive.

Bit 2 set Causes the service to change the file name specifier in the FCB to the name found in the command line. Otherwise, it is unchanged, which allows you to provide a default file name.

Bit 3 set Causes the service to change the extension specifier in the FCB to the extension found in the command line;

otherwise it is unchanged; this allows your to provide a default extension.

Bits 4-7   Must be zero.

If DOS wildcard characters are found in the command line, the service will replace all matching characters in the FCB with question marks (?). The service uses the characters : ; . , $+ < > | / $ " tab space and any control characters as file-name separators. If no valid file name was found in the command line, the value at ES:DI+1 is a blank.

2AH: Get the System Date

This service returns the day of the week, year, month, and day of the current system date.

Register	Entry Contents
AH	2AH

Register	Exit Contents
AL	Day of the week
CX	Year (1980-2099)
DH	Month (1-12)
DL	DAY (1-32)

Notes   The day of the week is specified as Sunday = 0 through Saturday = 6.

2BH: Set the System Date

This service sets the day, month, and year for the current system date.

Register	Entry Contents
AH	2BH
CX	Year (1980 - 2099)
DH	Month (1 - 12)
DL	DAY (1 - 31)

Register	Exit Contents
AL	00H if the date is valid FFH if the date is invalid

2CH: Get the System Time

This service gets the hours, minutes, seconds, and hundredths of seconds for the current system time.

Register	Entry Contents
AH	2CH

Register	Exit Contents
CH	Hours (0 - 23)
CL	Minutes (0 - 59)
DH	Seconds (0 - 59)
DL	Hundredths of seconds (0 - 99)

2DH: Set the System Time

This service sets the hours, minutes, seconds, and hundredths of seconds for the current system time.

Register	Entry Contents
AH	2DH
CH	Hours (0 - 23)
CL	Minutes (0 - 59)
DH	Seconds (0 - 59)
DL	Hundredths of seconds (0 - 99)

Register	Exit Contents
AL	00H if time is valid
	FFH if time is invalid

2EH: Set/Clear Disk Write VERIFY

This service sets VERIFY ON or clears VERIFY OFF for disk-write verification.

Register	Entry Contents
AH	2EH
AL	00H to set verify OFF
	01H to set verify ON
Register	Exit Contents
	NONE

Notes   Verification is not supported for network disks.

2FH: Get the Disk Transfer
Address (DTA)

This service returns the segment and offset address of the disk transfer area that DOS uses for all disk read/write operations.

Register	Entry Contents
AH	2FH

Register	Exit Contents
BX	Offset address of the disk transfer area
ES	Segment address of the disk transfer area

Notes   DOS service 1AH allows you to set the DTA.

30H: Get DOS Version Number

This service returns the DOS major and minor version numbers.

Register	Entry Contents
AH	30H
Register	Exit Contents
AH	Minor DOS version number
AL	Major DOS version number

Notes   For DOS version 3.2, 3 is the major version number and 2 is the minor version number.

31H: Terminate Current Program and
Remain Resident In Memory

This service terminates the current program, allowing it to remain resident in memory. Files opened by the program remain open.

Register	Entry Contents
AH	31H
AL	DOS return code
DX	Memory size to allocate in paragraphs

Register	Exit Contents
	NONE

Notes   Routines such as Borland International's *SideKick* are memory-resident programs. The memory size allocated is the amount of memory required for the program.

33H: Get or Set the State of
CTRL-BREAK Processing

This service gets or sets the current state of CTRL-BREAK processing (ON or OFF).

Register	Entry Contents
AH	33H
AL	00H to request current Ctrl-Break state
	01H to set the current Ctrl-Break state
DL	00H to set Ctrl-Break processing OFF
	01H to set Ctrl-Break processing ON

Register	Exit Contents
DL	Current Ctrl-Break state 00H = OFF, 01H = ON

35H: Get Segment and Offset Address
for an Interrupt

This service gets the current interrupt vector for an interrupt handler.

Register	Entry Contents
AH	35H
AL	Interrupt number desired

Register	Exit Contents
BX	Offset address of the interrupt handler
ES	Segment address of the interrupt handler

36H: Get Free Disk Space

This service gets the amount of free disk space for the specified disk drive.

Register	Entry Contents
AH	36H
DL	Disk drive for which free space is required

Register	Exit Contents
AX	FFFFH if the disk drive is invalid; otherwise, the number of sectors per cluster
BX	Available clusters
CX	Bytes per sector
DX	Clusters per drive

Notes   Free disk space is calculated as

$$Free\_Space = (AX * CX * BX)$$

38H: Return Country-Dependent Information

This service gets and sets country-dependent information (see Chapter 12). You get country information as follows:

Register	Entry Contents
AH	38H
AL	00H for current country
	Country code (Chapter 12) for countries with codes less than 255
	FFH for countries with codes greater than 255
BX	16 bit country code for countries with codes greater than 255
DS	Segment address of data buffer
DX	Offset address of data buffer

Register	Exit Contents
AX	Error code if carry flag is set
BX	Country code
DS	Segment address of data buffer
DX	Offset address of data buffer

You set country information in this way:

Register	Entry Contents
AH	38H
AL	Country code (Chapter 12) for countries with codes less than 255.
	FFH for countries with codes greater than 255.
BX	16 bit country code for countries with codes greater than 255.
DX	FFFFH

Register	Exit Contents
AX	Error code if carry flag is set

39H: Create Subdirectory (MKDIR)

This service creates the specified subdirectory. The service returns status codes in AX.

Register	Entry Contents
AH	39H
DS	Segment address of ASCIIZ subdirectory name
DX	Offset address of ASCIIZ subdirectory name

Register	Exit Contents
AX	Error status if carry flag is set

Notes   The ASCIIZ subdirectory name can contain a drive identification and DOS pathnames.

3AH: Remove Subdirectory (RMDIR)

This service removes the specified subdirectory. The service returns status codes in AX.

Register	Entry Contents
AH	3AH
DS	Segment address of ASCIIZ subdirectory name
DX	Offset address of ASCIIZ subdirectory name

Register	Exit Contents
AX	Error status if carry flag is set

Notes   The ASCIIZ subdirectory name can contain a drive identification and DOS pathnames.

3BH: Change Current Directory (CHDIR)

This service changes the default working directory to the specified subdirectory. The service returns status codes in AX.

Register	Entry Contents
AH	3BH
DS	Segment address of ASCIIZ subdirectory name
DX	Offset address of ASCIIZ subdirectory name

Register	Exit Contents
AX	Error status if carry flag is set

Notes   The ASCIIZ subdirectory name can contain a drive identification and DOS pathnames.

3CH: Create File and Return File Handle

This service creates a file or truncates an existing file and returns a file handle that DOS can use for I/O.

Register	Entry Contents
AH	3CH
CX	Attributes of the file
DS	Segment address of ASCIIZ filename
DX	Offset address of ASCIIZ filename

Register	Exit Contents
AX	Error status if carry flag is set, otherwise, the DOS file handle

Notes   The ASCIIZ file name can contain a drive identification and DOS pathnames.

3DH: Open File and Return File Handle

This service opens a file and returns a file handle that DOS can use for I/O.

Register	Entry Contents
AH	3DH
AL	Access code
DS	Segment address of ASCIIZ filename
DX	Offset address of ASCIIZ filename

Register	Exit Contents
AX	Error status if carry flag is set, otherwise, the DOS file handle

Notes   The ASCIIZ file name can contain a drive identification and DOS pathnames. Access codes contain the following:

> AL = 0 read-only access
> AL = 1 write access
> AL = 2 read/write access

If you are sharing files on a network, set the contents of AL as follows:

> Bit 4 = 1 Deny read/write access (exclusive mode)
> Bit 5 = 1 Deny write access
> Bits 4 and 5 = 1 Deny read mode
> Bit 6 = 1 Deny none

If you are creating subprocesses, use bit 7 of AL as follows:

> Bit 7 = 0 File is inherited by child
> Bit 7 = 1 File is restricted to current process

3EH: Close File Referenced by File Handle

This service closes a file referenced by a file handle. The service flushes the disk buffers and updates the directory entry for the file.

Register	Entry Contents
AH	3EH
BX	File handle

Register	Exit Contents
AX	Error status if carry flag is set

3FH: Read from File Referenced by File Handle

This service transfers the specified number of bytes from the file associated with the provided file handle into a buffer.

Register	Entry Contents
AH	3FH
BX	File handle
CX	Number of bytes to read
DS	Segment address of the data buffer
DX	Offset address of the data buffer

Register	Exit Contents
AX	Error status if carry flag is set, or the number of bytes read

40H: Write to File Referenced by File Handle

This service transfers the specified number of bytes from a buffer to the file associated with the provided file handle.

Register	Entry Contents
AH	40H
BX	File handle
CX	Number of bytes to write
DS	Segment address of the data buffer
DX	Offset address of the data buffer

Register	Exit Contents
AX	Error status if carry flag is set, or the number of bytes written

Notes   This service cannot write to a file marked read-only.

41H: Delete DOS File

This service deletes the file specified by an ASCIIZ string. The service returns the status register AX.

Register	Entry Contents
AH	41H
DS	Segment address of the ASCIIZ filename
DX	Offset address of the ASCIIZ filename

Register	Exit Contents
AX	Error status if carry flag is set

42H: Move File Pointer

This service moves the read/write pointer associated with a file handle as specified.

Register	Entry Contents
AH	42H
AL	Move technique
	AL = 0 pointer is moved from the start of the file
	AL = 1 pointer is moved from the current position
	AL = 2 pointer is moved from the end of file
BX	File handle
CX	CX and DX are combined to produce the number of
DX	bytes to move the pointer

Register	Exit Contents
AX	Error status if carry flag is set; otherwise,
DX	AX and DX combine to produce new pointer location

43H: Set/Return File's Attributes

This function sets or returns the value of a file's attribute byte.

Register.	Entry Contents
AH	43H
AL	Function code
	00 to return file attribute
	01 to set file attribute
CX	File attribute desired
DS	Segment address of the ASCIIZ filename
DX	Offset address of the ASCIIZ filename

Register	Exit Contents
AX	Error status if carry flag is set
CX	If no error and function 00 used CX
	contains file attribute

Notes   Attributes are specified as

01 Read-only   02 Hidden file
04 System file   08 Volume label
16 Subdirectory   32 Archive bit set

DOS Service 44H provides various I/O control services based on the contents of register AL (the function-code register).

44H: Device I/O Control (IOCTL)—
Get/Set Device Information

This service gets/sets device information.

Register	Entry Contents
AH	44H
AL	Function code
	00 Get device information
	01 Set device information
BX	File handle of device
DH	If AL=1, DH should be 0
DL	Device information for set

Register	Exit Contents
DX	Device information as shown

44H: Device I/O Control (IOCTL)—
Read/Write to Device

This service reads/writes to a device.

Register	Entry Contents
AH	44H
AL	Function code
	02 Read from device
	03 Write to device
BX	File handle of device
CX	Number of bytes to read/write
DS	Segment address of I/O buffer
DX	Offset address of I/O buffer

Register	Exit Contents
AX	Number of bytes read/written

44H: Device I/O Control (IOCTL)—
Read/Write to Block Device

This services reads/writes to a block device.

Register	Entry Contents
AH	44H
AL	Function code
	04 Read from device
	05 Write to device
BL	Drive number
CX	Number of bytes to read/write
DS	Segment address of I/O buffer
DX	Offset address of I/O buffer

Register	Exit Contents
AX	Number of bytes read/written

Notes   Drive numbers are specified as 0 = default, A=1, B=2, C=3, and so forth.

44H: Device I/O Control (IOCTL)—
Check Handle Status

This service returns status as to whether a handle is ready for input or output.

Register	Entry Contents
AH	44H
AL	Function code
	06 Get input status
	07 Get output status
BX	File handle to device

Register	Exit Contents
AL	If target is a file:
	FFH not end of file
	00H end of file
	If target is a device:
	00H device not ready
	0FH device ready

44H: Device I/O Control (IOCTL)—
Removeable or Nonremoveable Device

This service determines whether a device is removeable.

Register	Entry Contents
AH	44H
AL	Function code
	08 Removeable media?
BL	Drive number

Register	Exit Contents
AL	0H device is removeable
	1H device is fixed
	FH invalid drive specified

Notes   Drive numbers are specified as 0 = default, A=1, B=2, C=3, and so forth.

44H: Device I/O Control (IOCTL)—
Network or Local Device

This service determines whether or not a logical device is a member of a network.

Register	Entry Contents
AH	44H
AL	Function code
	09 Local or remote device?
BL	Drive number

Register	Exit Contents
DX	Remote devices return bit 12 set

Notes   Drive numbers are specified as 0 = default, A=1, B=2, C=3, and so forth.

44H: Device I/O Control (IOCTL)—
Network or Local Handle

This service determines whether or not a handle is associated with a network device.

Register	Entry Contents
AH	44H
AL	Function code
	AH Local or remote handle?
BX	File handle

Register	Exit Contents
DX	Remote handles return bit 15 set

44H: Device I/O Control (IOCTL)—
Retry on Locked Resources

This service specifies retry operations for locked resource conflicts.

Register	Entry Contents
AH	44H
AL	Function code
	BH Change retry count
CX	New delay loop count
DX	New retry count

Register	Exit Contents
AX	Error status if carry flag is set

44H: Device I/O Control (IOCTL)—
Get/Set Device Parameters

This service gets/sets the device parameters displayed here:

Register	Entry Contents
AH	44H
AL	Function code
	DH Generic device driver request
CL	Function code
	60H Get device parameters
	40H Set device parameters
CH	08H Function code
DS	Segment address of parameter block
DX	Offset address of parameter block

Register	Exit Contents
AX	Error status if carry flag is set

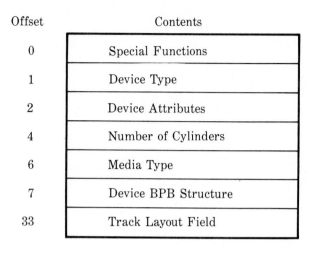

Offset	Contents
0	Special Functions
1	Device Type
2	Device Attributes
4	Number of Cylinders
6	Media Type
7	Device BPB Structure
33	Track Layout Field

Figure 16-23.   Definition of the parameter block

Notes   The definition of the parameter block is shown in Figure 16-23.

Special-Functions Field Values

Bit 0 set: Return the BPB that BUILD BPB would return
Bit 0 clear: Return the default BPB
Bit 1 set: Ignore all fields except TrackLayout
Bit 1 clear: Read all fields
Bit 2 set: All sectors are the same size
Bit 2 clear: Sector size may vary

Do not set Bits 0 and 1 at the same time.

Device-Type Field Values

0: 320/360K disk
1: 1.2Mb disk
2: 720K disk
3: 8-inch, single-density disk

4: 8-inch, double-density disk
5: fixed disk
6: tape drive
7: other device

Device Attributes Field Values

Bit 0 set: Nonremoveable device
Bit 0 clear: Device is removeable
Bit 1 set: Disk change line is supported
Bit 1 clear: Disk change line not supported

Media Type Values

0: quad-density
1: double-density

The device BPB field is shown in Figure 16-24.

44H: Device I/O Control (IOCTL)— Read/Write Logical Device Track

This service performs track read/write operations on a logical device.

Register	Entry Contents
AH	44H
AL	Function code
	DH Generic device driver request
CL	Function code
	61H Read track
	41H Write track
CH	08H Function code
DS	Segment address of parameter block
DX	Offset address of parameter block

Register	Exit Contents
AX	Error status if carry flag is set

Offset	Contents
0	Bytes Per Sector
2	Sectors Per Cluster
3	Reserved Sectors
5	Number of FATs
6	Number of Root Entries
8	Total Sectors
10	Media Descriptor Byte
11	Sectors Per FAT
13	Sectors Per Track
15	Heads
17	Hidden Sectors
21	Reserved

Figure 16-24.   Device BPB field

Notes   The contents of the parameter block are shown in Figure 16-25.

44H: Device I/O Control (IOCTL)—
FORMAT/VERIFY Logical Device Track

This service performs FORMAT or VERIFY track operations on a logical device.

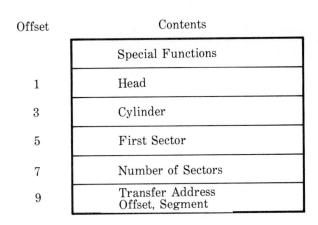

Offset	Contents
	Special Functions
1	Head
3	Cylinder
5	First Sector
7	Number of Sectors
9	Transfer Address Offset, Segment

Figure 16-25. Contents of parameter block

Register	Entry Contents
AH	44H
AL	Function code
	DH Generic device driver request
CL	Function code
	62H Verify track
	42H Format and verify track
CH	08H Function code
DS	Segment address of parameter block
DX	Offset address of parameter block

Register	Exit Contents
AX	Error status if carry flag is set

Notes The contents of the parameter block are shown in Figure 16-26.

Special-Functions Field Values

Bit 0 set: Determine if strange tracks are supported
Bit 0 clear: Format the track

44H: Device I/O Control (IOCTL)—
Determine Number of Logical Devices

This service determines the number of logical devices associated with a block device.

Register	Entry Contents
AH	44H
AL	Function code
	EH Return number of logical devices
BL	Drive number

Register	Exit Contents
AX	Error status if carry flag is set
AL	0 if only one logical drive assigned; otherwise, drive number of last drive to reference the device

Notes   Drive numbers are specified as 0 = default, A=1, B=2, C=3, and so forth.

44H: Device I/O Control (IOCTL)—
Set Logical Device

This service sets the next logical drive letter that will be used to reference a logical device.

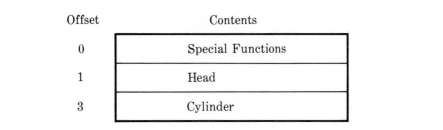

Offset	Contents
0	Special Functions
1	Head
3	Cylinder

Figure 16-26.   Contents of parameter block

Register	Entry Contents
AH	44H
AL	Function code
	FH Return number of logical devices
BL	Drive number

Register	Exit Contents
AX	Error status if carry flag is set
AL	0 if only one logical drive assigned; otherwise, drive number of last drive to reference the device

Notes   Drive numbers are specified as 0 = default, A=1, B=2, C=3, and so forth.

45H: Duplicate File Handle

This function creates a new file that points to the same file at the same position as the handle given.

Register	Entry Contents
AH	45H
BX	Current file handle

Register	Exit Contents
AX	Error status if carry flag is set; otherwise, new file handle

46H: Force a Duplicate File Handle

This function creates a new file that points to the same file at the same position as the given handle.

Register	Entry Contents
AH	46H
BX	Current file handle
CX	Second file handle

Register	Exit Contents
AX	Error status if carry flag is set

Notes   If the file handle currently contained in CX is open, this service first closes it.

47H: Get Current Directory

This function returns the current directory path.

Register	Entry Contents
AH	47H
DL	Drive number
DS	Segment address of 64 byte data buffer
SI	Offset address of 64 byte data buffer

Register	Exit Contents
AX	Error status if carry flag is set

Notes   If no errors occurred, the data buffer contains the directory name.

48H: Allocate Memory

This function allocates the number of 16-byte paragraphs requested.

Register	Entry Contents
AH	48H
BX	Number of paragraphs to allocate

Register	Exit Contents
AX	Error status if carry flag is set; otherwise, AX points to the memory allocated
BX	Size of largest available block if allocation failed

49H: Release Allocated Memory

This function releases allocated memory.

Register	Entry Contents
AH ES	49H Segment address of the block to return

Register	Exit Contents
AX	Error status if carry flag is set; otherwise, AX points to the memory allocated

4AH: Modify Allocated Memory

This function modifies allocated memory to contain the new specified block size.

Register	Entry Contents
AH BX ES	4AH New block size in paragraphs Segment address of the block

Register	Exit Contents
AX BX	Error status if carry flag is set Size of largest available block if request failed

Notes   DOS allows the block size to grow or shrink, but it can grow only if there is an empty space for it to grow into.

4BH: Load or Execute a Program (EXEC)

This function allows a program to load or execute a second program.

Offset	Contents
0	Environment Address (Segment)
2	Command Line Address (Offset)
4	Command Line Address (Segment)
6	File Control Block 1 Address (Offset)
8	File Control Block 1 Address (Segment)
10	File Control Block 2 Address (Offset)
12	File Control Block 2 Address (Segment)

Figure 16-27. Contents of parameter block for function code 0H

Register	Entry Contents
AH	4BH
AL	Function Code
	0H Load and execute the program
	3H Load but do not execute (overlay)
BX	Offset address of the parameter block
DS	Segment address of the ASCIIZ command name
DX	Offset address of the ASCIIZ command name
ES	Segment address of the parameter block

Register	Exit Contents
AX	Error status if carry flag is set

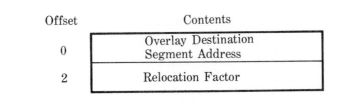

Offset	Contents
0	Overlay Destination Segment Address
2	Relocation Factor

Figure 16-28.   Contents of parameter block for function code 3H

Notes   For function code 0H, the contents of the parameter block are shown in Figure 16-27. For function code 3H, the contents of the parameter block are shown in Figure 16-28. The environment string is a series of ASCIIZ strings (up to 32K) that define the command environment. It is terminated by a byte of 0.

4CH: Terminate a Process (EXIT)

This function terminates the current program and returns an error-status level to DOS.

Register	Entry Contents
AH	4CH
AL	Return status code

Register	Exit Contents
	NONE

Notes   The DOS ERRORLEVEL batch-processing condition tests the exit status returned by this service.

4DH: Get Return Code of a Subprocess

This function obtains the return status code of a process created by the EXEC function.

Register	Entry Contents
AH	4DH

Register	Exit Contents
AX	Return code

Notes

Return Code Values

0H Normal termination
1H CTRL-BREAK termination
2H Critical device error forced termination
3H Termination by call 31H

4EH: Find First Matching File

This function finds the first file name that matches the provided file specification.

Register	Entry Contents
AH	4EH
CX	File attribute to use in search
DS	Segment address of ASCIIZ file specification
DX	Offset address of ASCIIZ file specification

Register	Exit Contents
AX	Error code if carry flag is set

Notes   The file information is offset from the DTA as shown in Figure 16-29. This function does not support network operations.

4FH: Find Next Matching File

This function finds the next file name that matches the file specification provided in service 4EH.

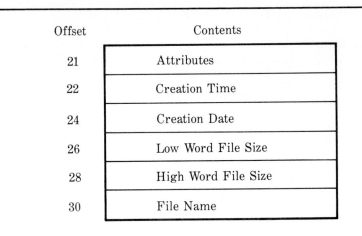

Offset	Contents
21	Attributes
22	Creation Time
24	Creation Date
26	Low Word File Size
28	High Word File Size
30	File Name

Figure 16-29.   File information offset from DTA

Register	Entry Contents
AH	4FH

Register	Exit Contents
AX	Error code if carry flag is set

Notes   This function does not support network operations.

54H: Get Disk Verification Status

This function returns the current status of VERIFY (ON or OFF).

Register	Entry Contents
AH	54H

Register	Exit Contents
AL	Verify status OH if VERIFY is OFF 1H if VERIFY is ON

Notes   Service 2EH sets disk verification.

56H: Rename a DOS File

This function renames a file as specified.

Register	Entry Contents
AH	56H
DI	Offset address of the ASCIIZ target filename
DS	Segment address of the ASCIIZ source filename
DX	Offset address of the ASCIIZ source filename
ES	Segment address of the ASCIIZ target filename

Register	Exit Contents
AX	Error status if carry flag is set

57H: Get/Set a File's Date and Time

This function gets/sets the creation date and time for the file associated with the file handle provided.

Register	Entry Contents
AH	57H
AL	Function Code
	0H Get time and date
	1H set time and date
BX	File handle
CX	New time if AL=1H
DX	New date if AL=1H

Register	Exit Contents
AX	Error status if carry flag is set
CX	System time if AL=0H
DX	System date if AL=0H

Notes   Specify the time as shown in Figure 16-30. Specify the date as shown in Figure 16-31.

59H: Get Extended Error Information

This function returns additional error status codes for DOS errors.

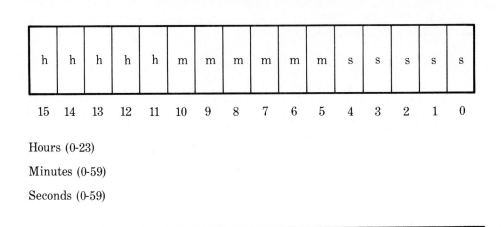

Bit	15	14	13	12	11	10	9	8	7	6	5	4	3	2	1	0
	h	h	h	h	h	m	m	m	m	m	m	s	s	s	s	s

Hours (0-23)

Minutes (0-59)

Seconds (0-59)

Figure 16-30.   Specifying the time

Register	Entry Contents
AH	59H
BX	OH for DOS Versions 3.0, 3.1, 3.2

Register	Exit Contents
AX	Extended error
BH	Error class
BL	Recommended action
CH	Locus

Notes

Errors

1 Invalid function number
2 File not found
3 Path not found
4 No file handles available
5 Access denied
6 Insufficient memory

y	y	y	y	y	y	y	m	m	m	m	d	d	d	d	d

Year (0-119) or (1980-2099)

Month (1-12)

Day (1-13)

Figure 16-31. Specifying the date

Classes
1 No resources available
2 Temporary error
3 Authorization error
4 Internal software error
5 Hardware error
6 System failure
7 Application software error
8 Item not found
9 Invalid format
10 Item locked
11 Media error
12 Item already exists
13 Unknown error

Actions
1 Retry operation
2 Delay and retry operation
3 User retry
4 Abort processing with clean-up
5 Immediate exit, no clean-up
6 Ignore error
7 Retry with user intervention

Locus

1 Unknown source
2 Block device error (disk)
3 Network error
4 Serial device error
5 Memory error

5AH: Create a Unique File Name

This function creates and returns a unique DOS file name.

Register	Entry Contents
AH	5AH
CX	Attribute byte of new file
DS	Segment address of ASCIIZ path
DX	Offset address of ASCIIZ path

Register	Exit Contents
AX	Error code if carry flag is set

Notes   If successful, the function will append the unique file name to the ASCIIZ path provided. The ASCIIZ path must be terminated with a backslash (\ ).

5BH: Create a DOS File

This function creates a DOS file.

Register	Entry Contents
AH	5BH
CX	Attribute byte of new file
DS	Segment address of ASCIIZ filename
DX	Offset address of ASCIIZ filename

Register	Exit Contents
AX	Error code if carry flag is set

5CH: Lock/Unlock File Contents

This function locks or unlocks a range of bytes in an open DOS file.

Register	Entry Contents
AH	5CH
AL	Function code
	OH Lock bytes
	1H Unlock bytes
BX	File handle
CX	High byte offset
DX	Low byte offset
SI	High byte length
DI	Low byte length

Register	Exit Contents
AX	Error code if carry flag is set

Notes Close all files before exiting or undefined results may occur.

5EH: Get Machine Name for Network Operations

This function returns the computer's network machine name.

Register	Entry Contents
AH	5EH
DS	Segment address of the 15 byte ASCIIZ name buffer
DX	Offset address of the 15 byte ASCIIZ name buffer

Register	Exit Contents
AX	Error code if carry flag is set
CL	NETBIOS name number

Notes This service requires the network software to be installed.

5E02H: Define Network Printer Setup

This function defines the computer's network printer.

Register	Entry Contents
AX	5E02H
BX	Redirection list index
CX	Length of setup string (MAX 64 bytes)
DS	Segment address of printer setup buffer
SI	Offset address of printer setup buffer

Register	Exit Contents
AX	Error code if carry flag is set

Notes   This service requires the network software to be installed.

5E03H: Get Network Printer Setup

This function returns the computer's printer setup.

Register	Entry Contents
AX	5E02H
BX	Redirection list index
DS	Segment address of printer setup buffer
SI	Offset address of printer setup buffer

Register	Exit Contents
AX	Error code if carry flag is set
CX	Length of the data returned
ES	Segment address of the printer setup string
DI	Offset address of the printer setup string

Notes   This service requires the network software to be installed.

5F02H: Get Redirection List Entry

This function returns network assignments.

Register	Entry Contents
AX	5F02H
BX	Redirection list index
DI	Offset address of 128 byte local device name buffer
DS	Segment address of 128 byte local device name buffer
EI	Offset address of 128 byte network device name buffer
ES	Segment address of 128 byte network device name buffer

Register	Exit Contents
AX	Error code if carry flag is set
BH	Device status flag
	Bit 0 set: device not valid
	Bit 0 clear: device is valid
BL	Device type
CX	Stored parameter value

Notes   This service requires the network software to be installed.

5F03H: Redirect a Network Device

This function creates a server connection.

Register	Entry Contents
AX	5F03H
BH	Device type
	3H Printer device
	4H File device
CX	Caller value
DI	Offset address of 128 byte local device name buffer
DS	Segment address of 128 byte local device name buffer
EI	Offset address of 128 byte network device name buffer
ES	Segment address of 128 byte network device name buffer

Register	Exit Contents
AX	Error code if carry flag is set

Notes   This service requires the network software to be installed. The network device name requires a password.

5F04H: Cancel Redirection of a Network Device

This function cancels a previous network connection.

Register	Entry Contents
AX	5F04H
DI	Offset address of 128 byte local device name buffer
DS	Segment address of 128 byte local device name buffer

Register	Exit Contents
AX	Error code if carry flag is set

Notes   This service requires the network software to be installed.

62H: Get Program Segment Prefix (PSP)

This function returns the address of the current program-segment prefix.

Register	Entry Contents
AH	62H

Register	Exit Contents
BX	Segment address of the program segment prefix

Notes   The contents of the program-segment prefix are displayed later in this chapter.

Using DOS Services

As previously stated, each DOS disk supports an optional 11-character volume label. The DOS VOL and LABEL commands allow you to display and set volume labels.

```
A> VOL

   Volume in drive A is DOSDISK

A>
```

If you have an application that uses the same file names year in and year out, but does so on a new disk each year, your program can examine the disk volume present on the disk to ensure that the correct floppy disk is in the desired drive. The following Turbo Pascal procedure returns the current volume label for the default disk:

```
Type
 VOLUMENAME = string[11];

procedure Get_Volume_Label (var VOLUME_LABEL: VOLUMENAME);
  type
    REGISTERS = record
                   AX, BX, CX, DX, BP, SI, DI, DS, ES, FLAGS: INTEGER;
               end;

  var
    REGS: REGISTERS;
    SEARCH_SPEC: VOLUMENAME;
    DTA_SEG,
    DTA_OFS : integer;   {address of disk transfer area}
    I       : integer;   {counter for loops}

  begin
    with REGS do
      begin
{convert the search specification to asciiz and set the registers
 to find the volume label}
        AX := $4E00;                        {DOS function code}
        SEARCH_SPEC := '*.*';
        DS := Seg(SEARCH_SPEC[1]);
        DX := Ofs(SEARCH_SPEC[1]);
        CX := 8;                            {attribute of label}

{invoke the DOS interrupt which finds the volume label}
        MSDos (REGS);

{set AX to request the disk transfer area}
        AX := $2F00;

{invoke the DOS interrupt which returns the disk transfer area}
        MSDos (REGS);

{return the segment and offset addresses}
        DTA_SEG := ES;
        DTA_OFS := BX;

        I := 0;
        while ((I < 11) and (Mem[DTA_SEG:DTA_OFS+30+I] <> 0)) do
          begin
            VOLUME_LABEL[I + 1] := Chr(Mem[DTA_SEG:DTA_OFS+30+I]);
            I := I + 1;
          end;

          VOLUME_LABEL[0] := Chr(I);
      end;            {with REGS}
  end;
```

As previously stated, each file has an attribute byte that defines whether the file needs to be backed up and whether the file is read-only. The DOS ATTRIB command allows you to modify file attributes from DOS. Likewise, the following Turbo Pascal procedure sets the attribute of the file you specify. Valid attribute values are

    0: read/write
    1: read-only
    2: hidden file
    4: system file
  16: subdirectory
  32: archive

```
procedure Set_File_Attributes (FILENAME: STRING79;
                               ATTRIBUTES: byte;
                               var STATUS: byte);
{
    This routine sets the attributes of the given file
    as specified.

    Common Return Status Values:
        2 - File not found          3 - Path not found
        5 - Access denied

}

  var
    REGS: REGISTERS;  {AX, BX, CX, DX, BP, SI, DI, DS, ES, FLAGS}

  begin
    with REGS do
      begin

{convert the file name to asciiz and set the registers to
 assign the file the attributes specified}
        FILENAME := FILENAME + Chr(0);     {convert to asciiz}
        AX := $4301;                       {DOS function code}
        DS := Seg(FILENAME[1]);
        DX := Ofs(FILENAME[1]);
        CX := ATTRIBUTES;

{invoke the DOS interrupt which assigns the file attributes}
        MSDos (REGS);

{return the status of the DOS operation}
        if Carry_Flag_Set (FLAGS) then     {error in operation}
          STATUS := Lo(AX)
        else
          STATUS := 0;                     {successful operation}
      end;
  end;
```

You should set all of the files used by your applications to read-only and allow the program to reset each file to read/write as required. This prevents you from accidentally modifying a file from DOS or a different application.

As previously stated, the DOS environment is an area in memory where DOS stores information that is available to all of your applications. The DOS SET command presented in Chapter

10 allows you to add or modify information contained in the environment. The Turbo Pascal program at the end of this section displays all of the information contained in the environment. You can modify it as required to meet your specific needs.

Each program that DOS executes contains a program-segment prefix (PSP), which is a 255-byte header that contains specific information about the program, as shown in Figure 16-22.

As you can see, offset 2CH contains the segment address of the environment used by the program. The environment is nothing more than a series of ASCIIZ strings (strings ending with a null character) that terminates with a zero byte. The following Turbo Pascal program first finds the location of the program-segment prefix by using DOS service 62H. Next, the program locates the segment address of the environment from offset 2CH in the PSP. Once this address is found, the program simply begins at the start of the environment and displays all of the information it contains until two successive bytes containing the value zero are found.

```
Program Display_Environment;

Type
  REGISTERS = record
                AX, BX, CX, DX, BP, SI, DI, DS, ES, FLAGS: INTEGER
              end;


Function Get_PSP: integer;
  var
    REGS: REGISTERS;  {AX, BX, CX, DX, BP, SI, DI, DS, ES, FLAGS}

  begin
    with REGS do
      begin

{set the registers to get the program segment prefix}
      AX := $6200;                        {DOS function code}

{invoke the DOS interrupt which returns the PSP}
      MSDos (REGS);

{return the address of the program segment prefix}
      Get_PSP := BX;
      end;
  end;


var
  I, J, PSP_SEG, ENVIRONMENT_SEG: integer;
  NULL: char;
  ENTRY: string[80];

begin
  NULL := Chr(0);

  PSP_SEG := Get_PSP;
```

```
     ENVIRONMENT_SEG := MemW[PSP_SEG: $2C];

     I := 0;

     repeat
      J := 0;

      repeat
        J := J + 1;
        ENTRY[J] := Chr(Mem[ENVIRONMENT_SEG: I]);
        I := I + 1;
      until (ENTRY[J] = NULL);

      ENTRY[0] := Chr(J-1);
      writeln (ENTRY);
      until (Mem[ENVIRONMENT_SEG: I+1] = 0);
     end.
```

Spawn

The following Turbo Pascal procedure allows you to issue DOS commands from within your Turbo Pascal program. For example, to issue the DOS DIR command, invoke the procedure as

```
Spawn ('DIR', STATUS);
```

Invoke the procedure without a command, as follows:

```
Spawn ('', STATUS);
```

The procedure will load a second command processor that allows you to issue DOS commands. Compile with the I and A options set to 400.

```
Type
  COMMAND_STRING = string[128];

procedure SPAWN (command_line: COMMAND_STRING;
                 var status: integer);
const
  STACK_SEGMENT: integer = 0;
  STACK_POINTER: integer = 0;

type
  REGISTERS = record
                AX, BX, CX, DX, BP, SI, DI, DS, ES, FLAGS: INTEGER
              end;

  PARAMETER_BLOCK = record
    ENVADDR,
    COMMOFS,
    COMMSEG,
    FCB1OFS,
```

```
      FCB1SEG,
      FCB20FS,
      FCB2SEG: integer;
      end;

   var
     REGS: REGISTERS;   {AX, BX, CX, DX, BP, SI, DI, DS, ES, FLAGS}
     PARAM: PARAMETER_BLOCK;
     COMMAND_FILE: COMMAND_STRING;

begin
  with PARAM do
    begin
      ENVADDR := 0;       {use PARENT process environment}

      if (ord(command_line[0]) <> 0) then
        command_line := '/C ' + command_line;

      command_line := command_line + chr(13);
      COMMSEG := Seg (command_line[0]);
      COMMOFS := Ofs (command_line[0]);
      FCB1SEG := -1;
      FCB10FS := 0;
      FCB2SEG := -1;
      FCB20FS := 0;
    end;

  with REGS do
    begin
      COMMAND_FILE := 'C:\COMMAND.COM' + chr(0) + chr(13);
      AX := $4B00;
      DS := Seg (command_file);
      DX := Ofs (command_file[1]);
      ES := Seg (PARAM);
      BX := Ofs (PARAM);

      STACK_SEGMENT := Sseg;                    { save the stack segment }
      inline ($2E/$89/$26/STACK_POINTER);   { save the stack pointer }

      MSDOS (REGS);

      inline ($2E/$8E/$16/STACK_SEGMENT);
      inline ($2E/$8B/$26/STACK_POINTER);

      if ((FLAGS and 1) = 1) then
        STATUS := AX
      else
        STATUS := 0;
    end;

end;
```

Lastly, as indicated in Chapter 5, the following Turbo Pascal procedure adds files to the DOS print queue:

```
type
 FILENAME = string[64];

procedure Print_File (FILE_NAME: FILENAME; var STATUS: integer);
  type
    REGISTERS = record
                  AX, BX, CX, DX, BP, SI, DI, DS, ES, FLAGS: INTEGER;
                end;

    SUBMIT_PACKET = record
```

```
                    LEVEL: Char;
                    OFFSET, SEGMENT: integer;
                  end;

  var
    REGS: REGISTERS;
    PACKET: SUBMIT_PACKET;

  begin
    FILE_NAME := FILE_NAME + Chr(0);

    with PACKET do
      begin
        LEVEL := Chr(0);
        OFFSET := Ofs (FILE_NAME[1]);
        SEGMENT := Seg (FILE_NAME);
      end;

    with REGS do
      begin
        AX := $0101;                              {DOS function code}
        DS := Seg(PACKET);
        DX := Ofs(PACKET);

        Intr ($2F, REGS);

        if ((FLAGS and 1) = 1) then
          STATUS := AX
        else
          STATUS := 0;
      end;

end;
```

The Turbo Pascal procedure MS DOS makes it simple to access
the DOS services from within Turbo Pascal programs. If, however, you are programming in FORTRAN or C, you need a similar interface. The disk packages The FORTRAN To DOS Interface, The C To DOS Interface, and The Turbo Pascal
Programmer's Library all implement the DOS services for the
specified languages. Each disk package is $59.95 plus $4 shipping. If you are developing applications that require the DOS services, these packages will simplify your programming efforts
greatly. Complete source code is provided with each package. For
more information, write to:

Kris Jamsa Software, Inc.
P.O. Box 26031
Las Vegas, NV 89126

Command Line Arguments

Each time you enter a command at the DOS prompt, the command that you enter becomes a command line. As you have seen, it is possible to specify parameters in the command line such as file names. Consider the following command:

```
A> COPY CONFIG.SYS CONFIG.SAV
```

In this case, the file names CONFIG.SYS and CONFIG.SAV constitute command-line parameters. They are simply values that you are passing to the program. As you will see, it is possible to access command-line parameters from within C and Turbo Pascal programs. In C, two variables, argv and argc, are used to support command-line processing. These variables are defined as follows:

```
main (argc, argv)
  int argc;
  char *argv[];
{
  /* program code here */
}
```

The variable argc contains a count of the number of command-line arguments. In the previous example, argc will contain the value 3 (C counts the command name as a parameter). The variable argv is an array of pointers to each command-line parameter. In the previous example, the elements of argv will point to the following:

argv[0] pointer to COPY
argv[1] pointer to CONFIG.SYS
argv[2] pointer to CONFIG.SAV
argv[3] pointer to NULL

Turbo Pascal differs slightly from C in that it provides two functions, ParamStr and ParamCount. The function ParamCount returns the number of command-line parameters. In the previous example, ParaCount will return the value 2. The function ParamStr returns the specified command-line parameter. In the previous example, ParamStr will return the following:

ParamStr(0) returns
ParamStr(1) returns ANSI.SYS
ParamStr(2) returns ANSI.OLD

Consider the following C and Turbo Pascal programs that display the contents of all of the command-line parameters:

```
main (argc, argv)
  int argc;
  char *argv[];
{
  int i;

  for (i = 1; i <= argc; i++)
    printf ("%s\n", argv[i]);
}



Program Echo ;

var
  I: integer;

begin
  for I := 1 to ParamCount do
    writeln (ParamStr(I));
end.
```

Probably the most useful purpose of command-line parameters is in specifying file names for the program to use. The following C and Turbo Pascal programs display the contents of the specified file by the first command-line argument:

```
#include "stdio.h"

#define LINE_SIZE 80

main (argc, argv)
  int argc;
  char *argv[];
{
  char line[LINE_SIZE];

  FILE *fopen(), *fp;
```

```
   if (argc < 2)
     printf ("SHOW: invalid usage: SHOW filename\n");
   else
    {
     if ((fp = fopen (argv[1], "r")) == NULL)
       printf ("SHOW: error opening the file %s\n", argv[1]);
     else
       {
       while (fgets (line, LINE_SIZE, fp))
         fputs (line, stdout);
       fclose (fp);
       }
    }
 }


program Show ;

type
  STRING79 = string[79];

var
  LINE    : STRING79;          {line read from the file}
  IN_FILE: text;              {the input file}

begin

{make sure the user provided an input file}
  if (ParamCount = 0) then
    Writeln ('SHOW: invalid usage: SHOW filename')

{an input file was provided so read each record and
 write it stdout}
    else
      begin
        Assign (IN_FILE, ParamStr(1));
        {$I-} Reset (IN_FILE) {$I+};
        if (IOresult <> 0) then
          Writeln ('SHOW: error opening the file ', ParamStr(1))
        else
          begin
            while (not EOF (IN_FILE)) do
              begin
                Readln (IN_FILE, LINE);
                Writeln (LINE);                {write to stdout}
              end;
            Close (IN_FILE);
          end;
      end;
end.
```

Backup Log

The following program allows you to determine on which backup
disk a file is contained. Simply compile the program to a COM
file. If you do not specify a file name, the program will display the
name of each file backed up, along with the backup disk number
it is contained on. If you specify a file name, the program will

display each occurrence of the file and its disk. The names that occur later in the list are the most current. The program requires the backup log created by the BAT procedures MONTHLY.BAT and DAILY.BAT in Chapter 11.

```
Program Read_Backup_Log;

type
  STRING79 = string[79];

var
  IN_TEXT: text[$FFF];
  FILE_SPEC, LINE, VOLUME_ID: STRING79;
  I, LENGTH, SUCCESS: integer;
  DISPLAY_LINE: boolean;

  begin

  if (ParamCount = 0) then
    FILE_SPEC := '*.*'
  else
    begin
      FILE_SPEC := ParamStr(1);
      Length := Ord (FILE_SPEC[0]);
      for I := 1 to Length do
        if ((FILE_SPEC[I] >= 'a') and (FILE_SPEC[I] <= 'z')) then
          FILE_SPEC[I] := Chr(Ord('A') + Ord(FILE_SPEC[I]) - Ord('a'));
    end;

  {$I-}
{open the input file}
    Assign (IN_TEXT, 'BACKUP.LOG');
    reset (IN_TEXT);
    SUCCESS := IOResult;

  if (SUCCESS <> 0) then
    writeln ('Error Opening BACKUP.LOG');

{go through the file looking for the first line to extract}
    while ((SUCCESS = 0) and (NOT EOF(IN_TEXT))) do
      begin
        readln (IN_TEXT, LINE);
        if (Ord(LINE[1]) = 10) then
          LINE := Copy (LINE, 2, 255);

        if (Pos ('Diskette Number:', LINE) <> 0) then
          VOLUME_ID := LINE
        else
          begin
            DISPLAY_LINE := FALSE;

            if (Ord(LINE[0]) > 0) then
              if (FILE_SPEC[1] = '*') then
                if (FILE_SPEC[3] = '*') then
                  if (Pos ('**', LINE) = 0) then
                    DISPLAY_LINE := TRUE;

            if (not DISPLAY_LINE) then
              if (Pos (FILE_SPEC, LINE) <> 0) then
                if (Pos ('**', LINE) = 0) then
                  DISPLAY_LINE := TRUE;

            if (DISPLAY_LINE) then
              writeln (VOLUME_ID,' ', LINE);
```

```
        SUCCESS := IOResult;
      end;
    end;
  close (IN_TEXT);
  {$I+}
end.
```

Review

1. What is the function of a linker?

2. What is an OBJ file?

3. What is a link map?

4. What is the function of the following command?

   A> LINK TEST1+TEST2,SAMPLE,,

5. What is a librarian?

6. What are the standard functions provided by a librarian?

7. What is a debugger?

8. List the DEBUG commands.

9. Is DEBUG an assembler substitute?

10. What are memory models?

11. Use DEBUG to determine the result of FFH + 2AH.

12. What statement is required in a Turbo Pascal program for it to support the DOS pipe?

13. List the functions provided by the ANSI driver.

14. What is an interrupt?

15. What are the DOS services?

16. How do you request DOS services from within a Turbo Pascal program?

17. What is an ASCIIZ string?

18. Write a Turbo Pascal program that displays the current disk drive.

Answers

1. *What is the function of a linker?*

The linker combines OBJ (object) files and searches LIB (library) files to resolve external references within a program to create an EXE (executable) file.

2. *What is an OBJ file?*

OBJ files contain object code. Object code is the output of the compiler. It contains the binary machine code instructions that make up your executable program. Object code is not yet executable because it may contain references to functions and symbols contained in another object file or library. The linker resolves these external references to create an EXE file.

3. *What is a link map?*

A link map is an optional file created by the linker that contains the starting and stopping location of each routine in the executable file, along with its class name. Most users will never require a link map. However, some programmers find it a convenient debugging tool.

4. *What is the function of the following command?*

   A> LINK TEST1+TEST2,SAMPLE,,

The command combines the object files TEST1.OBJ and TEST2.OBJ to create the executable file SAMPLE.EXE. The linker will use the default values for the list file and libraries.

5. *What is a librarian?*

It is often convenient to compile your more commonly used functions and procedures and place them in a library that can be linked to all of your applications. This prevents you from having to include additional source code in your programs that increases compile time and adds clutter to your code. In addition, if you link all of your applications to a standard library, you can ensure that they are all using the latest version of a routine. Likewise, maintaining libraries simplifies sharing code with other programmers and applications. A librarian allows you to add, delete, extract, or modify object files within a library.

6. *What are the standard functions provided by a librarian?*

• Create LIB library files

• Add, delete, replace, or extract the contents of an object file to/from a library

• Produce a listing of all of the routines contained in a library

7. *What is a debugger?*

A debugger is a software package that allows you to find errors in your program by testing it in a controlled environment. The DOS debugger is DEBUG. Specifically, DEBUG allows you to

• Test programs in a controlled environment

• Load, display, or modify any file

• Execute DOS programs

• Perform physical disk sector read/write operations

• Create and assemble assembly language programs

8. *List the DEBUG commands.*

```
Assemble [address]
Compare range or address
Dump [range] or [address]
Enter address [list]
Fill range list
Go [address] [address [address...]]
Hexarithmetic value value
Input port_address
Load [address [drive sector sector]]
Move range address
Name [drive:][path]file name[.ext]
Output port_address
Proceed [address] [value]
```

Quit
Register [register_name]
Search range list
Trace [address] [value]
Unassemble [address] or [range]
Write [address [drive sector sector]]

9. *Is DEBUG an assembler substitute?*

The DEBUG Assemble command allows you to create and modify small assembly language programs. Although this is convenient when working with small programs, the debugger is not a real assembler substitute.

10. *What are memory models?*

The various segment register configurations are referred to as memory models. Each program requires separate segments for code and data; the minimum number of segments is two. A small-memory model is the minimum executable configuration. In this model, the code and data each have a 64K segment. Because it is compact, the small memory produces fast code. Most of your applications should fall into this category. A medium-memory model is used when you have a relatively small amount of data and a large amount of code. Program code can reside in an unlimited number of segments, and data is restricted to 64K. A large-memory model is used when you have a large amount of code and data. Both program code and data can reside in an unlimited number of segments. The only restriction is that the largest code module or variable must be 64K or smaller. Because of its tremendous size flexibility, this memory model produces the slowest code.

11. *Use DEBUG to determine the result of FFH + 2AH.*

-H FF 2A
0129 00D5
-

12. *What statement is required in a Turbo Pascal program for it to support the DOS pipe?*

Examine the following statement:

{$G256,P256}

Turbo Pascal requires it to be the first statement in programs that are to support the DOS pipe.

13. *List the functions provided by the ANSI driver.*

The ANSI driver provides the following capabilities:

Clear the screen contents
Save the current cursor position
Restore the cursor to its saved position
Move the cursor up *n* rows
Move the cursor down *n* rows
Move the cursor left *n* columns
Move the cursor right *n* columns
Change character-display attributes
Set the cursor position
Set the foreground and background colors
Redefine keys

14. *What is an interrupt?*

An interrupt is a signal to the CPU from a program or hardware device. For each interrupt, a section of code known as an interrupt service routine is present in memory. The purpose of this code is to interrupt the processor temporarily to perform a specific task. When an interrupt occurs, the processor locates the code associated with the interrupt and executes it. For example, when a user presses the CTRL-ALT-DEL keys, an interrupt handler reboots the operating system.

15. *What are the DOS services?*

The developers of DOS simplified their programming efforts by breaking each function required by DOS into a small piece of code called a system service. This means that they developed procedures and functions to create and manipulate files and directories; to perform I/O to the disk, screen, and printer; and to load and control the execution of programs. Since all of these routines (services) are required for DOS to execute, the DOS developers have made them readily available to your programs.

16. *How do you request DOS services from within a Turbo Pascal program?*

Turbo Pascal provides an easy interface to DOS system services via the MSDOS procedure. To access the procedure, you must use the following structure:

```
Type
    REGISTERS = record
                    AX, BX, CX, DX, BP, SI, DI, DS,
                    ES, FLAGS: INTEGER;
                end;
```

17. *What is an ASCIIZ string?*

An ASCIIZ string is a character string that is terminated by a null (zero byte) character. Most of the DOS system services require ASCIIZ strings for all strings.

18. *Write a Turbo Pascal program that displays the current disk drive.*

```
    Program Show_Disk_Drive ;

Type
    REGISTERS = record
                    AX, BX, CX, DX, BP, SI, DI, DS,
                    ES, FLAGS: INTEGER;
                end;
var
    REGS: REGISTERS;
begin
    with REGS do
      begin
        AX := $1900;    {DOS function code}
        MSDos (REGS);
        writeln ('Current Drive: ', Chr(Lo(AX)+65));
      end;
end.
```

Microsoft Windows

What Is Windows?
Time-Sharing
Requirements
What Comes with Windows?
Installing Windows
Windows Products
MS Executive
System Menu
Selecting Programs from Icons
Windows Spooler

Many readers may wonder why two chapters on Microsoft Windows conclude this book on DOS. As you will see, Windows is an extension of DOS. By utilizing Windows, you expand all the features of DOS. In addition, Windows allows you to execute multiple programs simultaneously, quickly changing from one application to another. Lastly, Windows allows you to integrate multiple packages, exploiting the best features of each.

If you have used Microsoft Windows, you probably are already sold on its tremendous flexibility. If you have not used Windows, you will find that it is more than worth its cost, for several reasons. Most important, Microsoft Windows lays the foundation for future PC operating systems. If you understand the framework of Windows, you will find the transition to newer versions of DOS a smoother one. As you will see, the newer versions of DOS will offer features that closely resemble the functional features of Windows. Windows, like DOS, is written in the C language. Many programmers will benefit from having the ability to interface applications to Windows. In the future you will see many more programs integrated into Windows.

S
E
V
E
N
T
E
E
N

What Is Windows?

Before proceeding into the examination of Windows, it is important to establish a foundation for the thought processes used to develop Windows and the goals Windows attempts to meet. First, many PC users are not familiar with the DOS commands, nor do they desire to be. The first goal of Windows is to relieve users of the burden of having to memorize and understand DOS commands and their various options. As you will see, Windows has replaced the DOS prompt with pull-down menus and dialog boxes. DOS commands are represented by Windows' icons, and Windows supports a mouse interface. Windows makes the interface to the computer easy for novices to use and, therefore, nonthreatening. This has, in turn, reduced the time it takes to train users on systems new to them.

Second, Windows allows you to run multiple programs at one time. A computer with the ability to execute several programs simultaneously is called a *time-sharing system*. Later this chapter will examine how Windows performs time-sharing. For now, understand that Windows allows you to have several programs active simultaneously and also allows these programs to exchange information via Windows' built-in capabilities.

Third, Windows is called a *desktop system*. Windows provides many of the abilities normally associated with items on your desk, such as a notepad, calculator, and calendar.

In the future, you will see many of the concepts implemented in Windows (such as time-sharing and a convenient user interface) provided with newer versions of DOS.

Time-Sharing

As previously stated, Windows allows you to run multiple programs simultaneously, with each window appearing as an individual screen. For example, if you are running three programs on three individual computers, and you are not using Windows, the output would appear as in Figure 17-1. With Windows, each of the applications runs on the same computer, dividing the screen into

Figure 17-1.   Result of running three programs on three computers

three distinct regions, as in Figure 17-2. Windows works by time-sharing the central processing unit (CPU). Each time a program runs, the CPU finds the instructions for the program in memory and executes them, as illustrated in Figure 17-3.

Because of the tremendous speed of today's computers, the CPU spends the majority of its time idle, waiting to perform additional processing. For example, if you are using a word processing program, the CPU spends the majority of its time waiting for you to type in characters at the keyboard. During a 1-second time period, the CPU may be processing only 25% of the time, as illustrated in Figure 17-4.

Windows exploits the CPU's idle time and allows other programs to share the CPU. Given the example of three simultaneous programs, you can visualize CPU utilization as shown in Figure 17-5. Operating systems that share the CPU processing time in

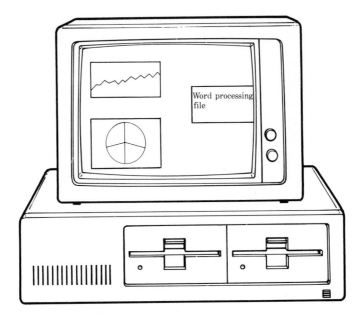

Figure 17-2. Result of running three programs on one computer

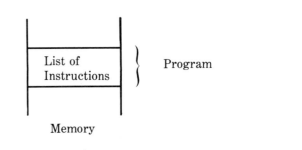

Figure 17-3. List of instructions in memory

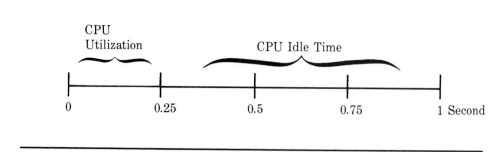

Figure 17-4. Processing time of CPU

this fashion are called time-sharing systems. Windows, therefore, can best be described as a time-sharing environment. As multiple programs are executed simultaneously, each program is allotted a segment of the CPU's processing time. Because transitions between segments are fast, it appears that several applications are executing simultaneously.

It is important to note that the processing ability of the PC is not unlimited. As the number of programs concurrently executing increases, the amount of CPU processing time available for each program eventually decreases. This, in turn, decreases the execution speed for each program, as illustrated in Figure 17-6.

A second major factor influencing the speed of execution of your applications is the amount of available memory. As previously illustrated, each time DOS executes a program, it first

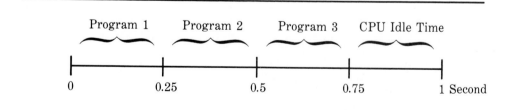

Figure 17-5. CPU utilization in time-sharing system

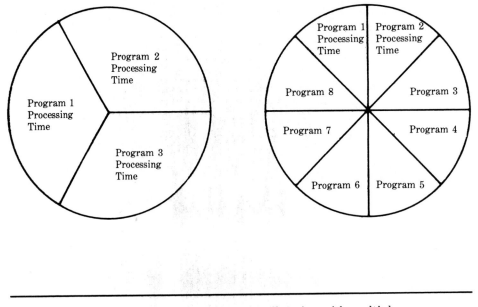

Figure 17-6. Effects on timeslice allocation with multiple programs

must load the program into memory. When you are executing multiple programs via Microsoft Windows, Windows will place as many of the programs into memory as possible (see Figure 17-7).

Unfortunately, the amount of memory in the system is limited. If you load several large programs under Windows, the majority of your system memory may be allocated. If you invoke additional programs, Windows must make space for the program in memory by swapping another program out of memory to disk temporarily (see Figure 17-8).

As the number of programs executing becomes very large, so does the amount of swapping that Windows must perform. Because of additional overhead, as swapping increases, the execution speed of your applications decreases. Chapter 18 will examine methods of minimizing the impact of swapping.

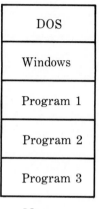

Memory

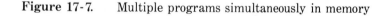

Figure 17-7.   Multiple programs simultaneously in memory

Requirements

Before you can invoke Windows, you must, as a minimum, have the following:

- Two double-sided disk drives or a hard disk
- A minimum of 256K of memory (512K recommended)
- DOS version 2.0 or greater
- A monochrome or color graphics adapter card

To exploit the functions of Windows fully, you should use at least 512K of memory and acquire a mouse. As you will see, Win-

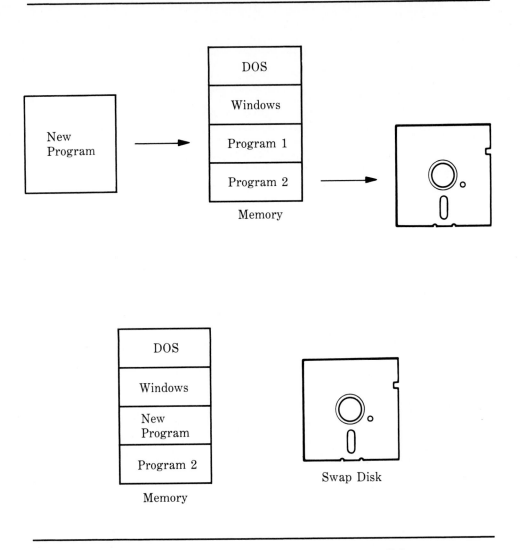

Figure 17-8.   Swapping program out of memory to disk

dows allows you to select options through use of the keyboard or use of a mouse. Using a mouse greatly enhances the speed of option selection. The Logitech Bus Mouse is illustrated in Figure 17-9. The Logitech mouse wins praise because of outstanding support software, product documentation, and support provided by Logitech personnel.

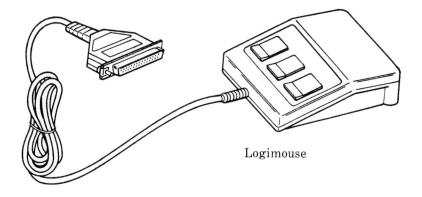

Logimouse

Figure 17-9.   Logitech's Bus Mouse

What Comes with Windows?

Included in your Windows package are the following:

• *Microsoft Windows Operating Environment User's Guide*, explaining use of Microsoft Windows

• *Microsoft Windows Paint User's Guide* explaining the use of the Windows Paint program that allows you to create diagrams to be integrated into reports and notes

• *Microsoft Windows Write User's Guide* explaining the use of Write, a simple word processing system provided with Microsoft Windows

• Microsoft Windows Operating Environment version 1.03 Update (depending on the version of Windows you purchased)

• The Windows Setup disk, to perform system installation

- The Windows Build disk, to create your Windows System disk

- The Windows Utilities disk, containing utility programs used by Microsoft Windows

- The Windows Fonts disk, containing the screen and printer fonts

- The Windows Desktop Applications disk, containing the Windows desktop applications, such as the calculator, clock, calendar, and notepad

- The Windows Program disk, containing the Write word processing program

This chapter clarifies Windows' system installation and familiarizes you with Windows applications.

Installing Windows

As previously stated, Windows requires either dual double-density disk drives or a hard disk. The Windows installation will vary, depending on your system configuration. Windows currently is in use on many dual floppy systems and hard-disk systems. This chapter will first examine the dual floppy disk installation.

Floppy Disk Installation

To create a Windows environment for a dual floppy system, perform the following steps:

1. To perform the installation correctly, you must create a backup copy of each Windows disk. Have six blank disks available.

2. The Windows system installation requires a DOS system disk that contains the command DISKCOPY.COM. Have a bootable DOS disk available.

3. Windows will create two disks. The first is the Windows Start-up disk that you will use to invoke Windows. The second is the Windows System disk. Have two blank disks available.

4. Boot DOS.

5. At the DOS prompt, place the Windows Setup disk in drive A and issue the command

A> SETUP

6. Perform the installation by following this text.

Windows will respond to the SETUP command with

```
Setup prepares Microsoft Windows to run on your computer.
It also helps you set up your disks in the most efficient way for:

        - starting Microsoft Windows
        - running Windows applications
        - printing from Microsoft Windows

When you're
ready:          TO                              PRESS

                Continue                          C
                Quit                              Q
```

If you are not ready to continue the Windows installation, press Q. Windows will return you to the DOS prompt. Otherwise, to continue the installation, press ENTER. Windows will display

```
You can set up Microsoft Windows to run from a floppy disk or
from a hard disk.  Please indicate the type of disk you want.

When you're
ready:          TO                              PRESS

                Setup on a floppy disk            F
                Setup on a hard disk              H
                Quit                              Q
```

At this point, Windows has no way of knowing whether you desire a hard disk or floppy disk system installation. In this case, type F. Windows will begin the floppy disk system installation by displaying

```
To setup Microsoft Windows on a floppy disk you need:

    - the Microsoft Windows Setup disk
    - the Microsoft Windows Build disk
    - the Microsoft Windows Utilities disk
    - the Microsoft Windows Font disk

You need to know the following:

    - what kind of pointer device (mouse) you have, if any
    - what kind of graphics adaptor you have
    - what kind of printer(s) you have, if any
    - how each printer is connected to your computer

When you're
ready:       ┌──────────────────────────────────────────────┐
             │ TO                               PRESS       │
             ├──────────────────────────────────────────────┤
             │ Continue                           C         │
             │ Quit                               Q         │
             └──────────────────────────────────────────────┘
```

If you do not know the information required, press Q and continue the installation at a later time. Otherwise, press ENTER, and Windows will respond with

```
                    Setup Menu
┌──────────────────────────────────────────────────────────────┐
│ TO                                                  PRESS     │
├──────────────────────────────────────────────────────────────┤
│ Backup master disks                                   B      │
│     Allows you to make copies of your master disks.          │
│                                                              │
│ Set up Windows System                                 S      │
│     Allows you to configure Windows to your system.          │
│                                                              │
│ Quit                                                  Q      │
└──────────────────────────────────────────────────────────────┘
 If this is the first time you have used Setup, do these in order.
```

Since this is the first time that you are performing a Windows system installation, select option B. Windows will prompt you to place your DOS System disk in drive A, as follows:

```
The backup procedure works by running your copy of the DOS utility
DISKCOPY.COM.  Please put your DOS disk in drive A:


                        ---|■|---


                     Put your DOS disk
                        into drive A:

When you're
ready:            ┌─────────────────────────────────────┐
                  │ TO                          PRESS    │
                  ├─────────────────────────────────────┤
                  │ Continue                      C      │
                  │ Return to Setup menu          M      │
                  └─────────────────────────────────────┘
```

With the DOS System disk in drive A, press ENTER to continue.
The Windows installation is ready to create your backup disk.
Place a blank disk into drive B and press ENTER. The following is
displayed:

```
This procedure copies or "backs up" your master disks so that
you may store them away for safekeeping.

    ---|■|---                              ---|■|---


  Put the master disk                   Put a blank disk
    into drive A:                         into drive B:

When you're
ready:            ┌─────────────────────────────────────┐
                  │ TO                          PRESS    │
                  ├─────────────────────────────────────┤
                  │ Continue                      C      │
                  │ Return to Setup menu          M      │
                  └─────────────────────────────────────┘
```

The familiar DISKCOPY prompt now will be displayed on
your screen.

```
Insert SOURCE Diskette in Drive A :

Insert TARGET Diskette in Drive B :

Press any key when ready . . .
```

Place your Windows Setup disk in drive A and a blank disk in drive B. Press ENTER to continue the backup process. When the process is finished, DISKCOPY will display

```
Insert SOURCE Diskette in Drive A :

Insert TARGET Diskette in Drive B :

Press any key when ready . . .

Copying 40 tracks
9 Sectors/Track, 2 Side(s)


Copy another diskette (Y/N)?
```

Press Y at the prompt and repeat this process for each of the Windows disks. When the process is finished, place your original Windows disks in a safe location. You will use the backup disks from now on. The Windows installation will now return to the following menu:

```
                            Setup Menu

 TO                                                      PRESS

 Backup master disks                                       B
     Allows you to make copies of your master disks.

 Set up Windows System                                     S
     Allows you to configure Windows to your system.

 Quit                                                      Q

If this is the first time you have used Setup, do these in order.
```

You are ready to create the Windows System disk. Type S. Windows will now prompt you to enter the type of keyboard your system is using.

```
In order to operate correctly, Microsoft Windows needs to know
what kind of keyboard you have.

Follow these            - Find your keyboard on this list.
steps:                  - Type the number for your keyboard.
                          (Or enter M to return to Setup menu)
                        - Press the ⏎ key.

 1: United States    11: France          21: Portugal
 2: Argentina        12: Ireland         22: Spain
 3: Australia        13: Italy           23: Sweden
 4: Austria          14: Japan           24: United Kingdom
 5: Belgium          15: Lebanon         25: Venezuela
 6: Brazil           16: Luxembourg      26: West Germany
 7: Canada           17: Mexico          27: AT&T 6300 or 6300 PLUS
 8: Chile            18: Netherlands
 9: Denmark          19: Norway
10: Finland          20: Peru

         keyboard: 1
```

In this case, Windows is adjusting itself for possible KEYBxx.COM files. Select the appropriate keyboard number and press ENTER.

Next, the Windows installation will prompt you for the type of mouse (pointing device) that you will be using.

```
In order to operate correctly, Microsoft Windows needs to know
what kind of pointing device you have.

Follow these            - Find your pointing device on this list.
steps:                  - Type the number for your pointing device.
                          (Or enter M to return to Setup menu)
                        - Press the ⏎ key.

 1: No pointing device
 2: Microsoft Mouse (Bus/Serial)
 3: Mouse Systems or VisiOn Mouse (COM1)
 4: Mouse Systems or VisiOn Mouse (COM2)
 5: Logitech Serial Mouse
 6: Kraft Joystick Mouse
 7: the Lite-Pen Company - Lightpen
 8: FTG Data Systems Lightpen and Single Pixel Board
 9: AT&T Mouse 6300 (plugs into keyboard)

         pointing device: 1
```

If you don't have a mouse, simply press ENTER, thus selecting the default value of 1. Lastly, the installation asks what type of graphics adapter your system is using.

```
In order to operate correctly, Microsoft Windows needs to know
what kind of graphics adapter you have.

Follow these          - Find your graphics adapter on this list.
steps:                - Type the number for your graphics adapter.
                        (Or enter M to return to Setup menu)
                      - Press the ⏎ key.

1: IBM (or compatible) Color/Graphics Adapter or COMPAQ Personal Computer
2: Hercules Graphics Card (or compatible) with Monochrome Display
3: Enhanced Graphics Adapter (EGA) with Monochrome Personal Computer Display
4: EGA with Enhanced Color Display (Black and White only)
5: EGA with Enhanced Color Display or Personal Computer Color Display
6: EGA (more than 64K) with Enhanced Color Display
7: AT&T PC 6300 or PC 6300 PLUS Display Adapter
8: AT&T Display Enhancement Board
9: Micro Display Systems GENIUS Graphics Adapter

          graphics adapter: 1
```

After you have responded to the three previous prompts, the Windows installation is ready to build the Windows System disk. Place the Windows Setup disk in drive A and a blank disk in drive B.

```
Setup is now ready to create the Windows System disk.
Please insert a blank disk in drive B:

                    +--+--█--+--+

                    Put a blank disk
                    into drive B:

When you're
ready:          +----------------------------------+
                | TO                        PRESS  |
                +----------------------------------+
                | Continue                  C      |
                +----------------------------------+
```

The Windows installation will copy files from the Setup disk to your Windows System disk, displaying

```
Setup is copying files from the Setup disk to the
Windows System disk.
```

When the process is finished, the procedure will prompt

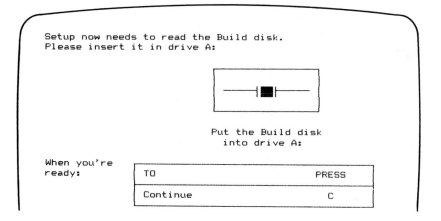

```
Setup now needs to read the Build disk.
Please insert it in drive A:
```

```
Put the Build disk
into drive A:
```

```
When you're
ready:
```

TO	PRESS
Continue	C

Place the backup copy of your Windows Build disk in drive A. Press ENTER to continue. The Windows installation procedures will begin copying files to your Windows System disk, displaying

```
Setup is copying files from the Build disk to the
Windows System disk.
```

When this process is finished, Windows will display

```
Your new System disk is ready.  Later you will add to it some
information about your hardware.  For now, please remove the
System disk from drive B: and label it "Microsoft Windows System disk"

When you're
ready:        ┌─────────────────────────────────────────┐
              │ TO                          PRESS        │
              ├─────────────────────────────────────────┤
              │ Continue                      C          │
              └─────────────────────────────────────────┘
```

Remove the disk from drive B and label it as shown in Figure 17-10.

The Windows installation procedure is now ready to build your Windows Startup disk. Place a blank disk in drive B and press ENTER to continue.

```
Setup is now ready to create the Windows Startup disk.
Please insert a blank disk in drive B:

                    ┌─────────────────────┐
                    │  ──────┤█├──────     │
                    │        ▄▄▄           │
                    └─────────────────────┘

                       Put a blank disk
                        into drive B:

When you're
ready:        ┌─────────────────────────────────────────┐
              │ TO                          PRESS        │
              ├─────────────────────────────────────────┤
              │ Continue                      C          │
              └─────────────────────────────────────────┘
```

The installation will now prompt you to specify whether or not the Windows installation disk should be a bootable disk. Normally, you will want this disk to be bootable. Type Y and press ENTER.

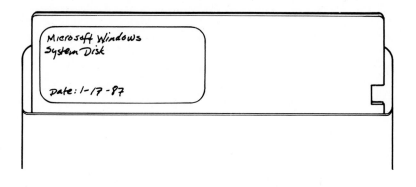

Figure 17-10. New Windows System disk

The installation procedures will prompt you to place your DOS system disk in drive A, as follows:

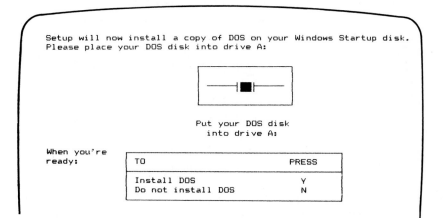

Windows now will complete the creation of your Startup disk by copying the required files to it.

```
Setup is writing the Windows startup files to the
Windows Startup disk.
```

After the files have been copied, the installation procedure will display

```
Your new Startup disk is ready.  Please remove it from drive
B: and label it "Microsoft Windows Startup disk"

When you're
ready:        TO                          PRESS
              Continue                      C
```

Remove the disk from drive B and label it as shown in Figure 17-11.

Next, the installation will complete the creation of your Windows System disk.

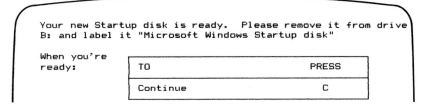

```
In this procedure, Setup goes to the Utilities disk for the
printer drivers and related fonts needed for the hardware you will
specify.  Setup then adds the information to your System disk.
```

Put the Utilities disk   Put the System disk
    into drive A: into drive B:

```
When you're
ready:        TO                          PRESS
              Continue                      C
```

Microsoft Windows
Startup Disk

Date: 1-17-87

Figure 17-11.   New Windows Startup disk

Place the backup copy of your Windows Utilities disk in drive A
and the Windows System disk that you have been creating in drive
B. Press ENTER when you have done so. The Windows installation
will prompt you, asking whether or not you want to configure a
printer or plotter to be used with Windows, as follows:

```
Would you like to set up a printer/plotter?

When you're
ready:        ┌──────────────────────────────────────────┐
              │ TO                            PRESS       │
              ├──────────────────────────────────────────┤
              │ Set up a printer/plotter        Y         │
              │ Continue                        N         │
              └──────────────────────────────────────────┘
```

If you have a printer, press Y; otherwise, press N. If you select
a printer configuration, the installation will display

```
In order to print correctly, Microsoft Windows needs to know what
kind of printer or plotter you have.

Follow these          - Find your printer in this list.
steps:                - Type the number for your printer.
                        (Or enter M to return to Setup menu)
                      - Press the ↵ key.

 1: Epson FX-80        11: NEC P2/P3           21: HP 7550A
 2: Epson MX-80 Graftrax  12: C-Itoh 8510      22: Generic / Text Only
 3: Epson LQ-1500      13: Toshiba P1351       23: PostScript/LaserWriter
 4: IBM Graphics       14: Star SG-10          24: HP ThinkJet (2225 C-D)
 5: IBM Proprinter     15: TI 850              25: Xerox 4020
 6: Okidata 92/93 (IBM)   16: TI 855
 7: Okidata 192/193 (IBM) 17: HP LaserJet
 8: Okidata 92/93 (Std)   18: HP LaserJet+
 9: Okidata 192/193 (Std) 19: HP 7470A
10: NEC 3550           20: HP 7475A

        Printer: 1
```

If your printer appears on the screen, enter its number. If your
printer does not appear on the screen, select the printer that most
closely behaves like your printer. Refer to your printer's reference
manual for more details.

Next, the procedure will prompt you to enter the port to
which your printer is connected.

```
Now Windows needs to know which port this printer or plotter is
connected to.  (If you're unsure which port you are using,
check the owner's guide for your device.)

Follow these          - Find the output port for this printer/plotter.
steps:                - Type the number for your printer/plotter.
                        (Or enter M to return to Setup menu)
                      - Press the ↵ key.

 1: LPT1:
 2: LPT2:
 3: LPT3:
 4: COM1:
 5: COM2:
 6: None
        Output port: 1
```

Normally, the printer is connected to LPT1. After you have specified the port, Windows will copy its utilities files to your Windows
System disk.

```
Setup is copying files from the Utilities disk to the
Windows System disk.
```

The installation provides you with the opportunity to configure multiple printers.

```
Would you like to set up another printer/plotter?

When you're
ready:          ┌─────────────────────────────────┐
                │ TO                        PRESS  │
                ├─────────────────────────────────┤
                │ Set up another printer      Y    │
                │ Continue                    N    │
                └─────────────────────────────────┘
```

If you have additional printers, type Y; otherwise, type N.

The installation procedure will now prompt you for the Font
disk.

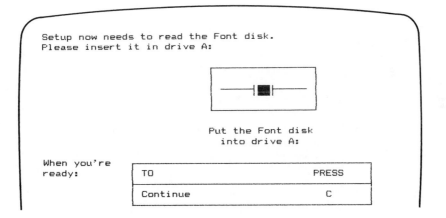

```
Setup now needs to read the Font disk.
Please insert it in drive A:

               ┌──────────────────────┐
               │   ──┤██├──            │
               └──────────────────────┘

                  Put the Font disk
                    into drive A:

When you're
ready:          ┌─────────────────────────────────┐
                │ TO                        PRESS  │
                ├─────────────────────────────────┤
                │ Continue                    C    │
                └─────────────────────────────────┘
```

Place the Windows Font disk in drive A and press ENTER to continue the file copy.

```
 Setup is copying files from the Font disk to the
 Windows System disk.
```

Windows will now redisplay the menu, as follows:

```
                            Setup Menu

     TO                                                    PRESS

     Backup master disks                                     B
          Allows you to make copies of your master disks.

     Set up Windows System                                   S
          Allows you to configure Windows to your system.

     Quit                                                    Q

 If this is the first time you have used Setup, do these in order.
```

Press Q. Your Windows installation is complete. The installation
will display

```
     Microsoft Windows is set up to operate on your computer.

     You can now start Windows.

     To start Microsoft Windows:

            - Put the Windows Startup disk in drive A:
            - Put the Windows System disk in drive B:
            - Type WIN
            - Press the ┘ key.

     A>
```

Hard Disk Installation

The Windows fixed disk installation is similar to the floppy disk
installation. Because of the significant number of Windows users
using hard disks, however, it is worth examining the complete
hard disk installation here. Using Windows from a hard disk
greatly simplifies your efforts, since all of the files reside on the

fixed disk. To install Windows on your fixed disk, perform the following:

1. Boot DOS and be sure that you have adequate disk space on the hard disk (approximately 1.5 M).

2. Place the Windows Setup disk in drive A and issue the command

A> SETUP

3. Perform the installation by following this text.

The Windows installation procedure will respond to the SETUP command with the following:

```
Setup prepares Microsoft Windows to run on your computer.
It also helps you set up your disks in the most efficient way for:

     - starting Microsoft Windows
     - running Windows applications
     - printing from Microsoft Windows

When you're
ready:        TO                          PRESS

              Continue                      C
              Quit                          Q
```

If you are not ready to perform the Windows system installation, type Q, and the installation procedures will return you to the DOS prompt. Otherwise, continue the installation by pressing ENTER. The setup procedure will respond with

```
You can set up Microsoft Windows to run from a floppy disk or
from a hard disk.  Please indicate the type of disk you want.

When you're
ready:        TO                          PRESS

              Setup on a floppy disk        F
              Setup on a hard disk          H
              Quit                          Q
```

In this case, you are performing a hard disk installation, so type H. The Windows installation will display

```
Now Setup will copy the Windows files to your hard disk.

Please type below the full pathname of the directory
where you would like SETUP to put the Windows files.

To accept \WINDOWS as the directory:
   - press the ⏎ key.

To specify a different directory:
   - Use the Backspace key to delete characters
   - Type the new directory name (for example: C:\PROGRAMS)
   - press the ⏎ key.

[C:\WINDOWS                                            ]
```

By default, the Windows system installation creates a directory called WINDOWS in the root directory of your fixed disk. To specify an alternate directory name, type in the name you desire. If the directory name WINDOWS is acceptable, press ENTER to continue the installation. The installation procedure will continue by displaying

```
To setup Microsoft Windows on a hard disk you need:

      - the Microsoft Windows Setup disk
      - the Microsoft Windows Build disk
      - the Microsoft Windows Utilities disk
      - the Microsoft Windows Font disk
      - the Microsoft Windows Desktop Applications disk
      - the Microsoft Write Program  disk

You need to know the following:

      - what kind of pointer device (mouse) you have, if any
      - what kind of graphics adaptor you have
      - what kind of printer(s) you have, if any
      - how each printer is connected to your computer

When you're
ready:          TO                         PRESS

                Continue                     C
                Quit                         Q
```

Press ENTER to continue the installation or Q to return to DOS. Next, the procedure will prompt you for the system keyboard.

```
In order to operate correctly, Microsoft Windows needs to know
what kind of keyboard you have.

Follow these              - Find your keyboard on this list.
steps:                    - Type the number for your keyboard.
                            (Or enter Q to quit Setup)
                          - Press the  ⏎  key.

 1: United States    11: France         21: Portugal
 2: Argentina        12: Ireland        22: Spain
 3: Australia        13: Italy          23: Sweden
 4: Austria          14: Japan          24: United Kingdom
 5: Belgium          15: Lebanon        25: Venezuela
 6: Brazil           16: Luxembourg     26: West Germany
 7: Canada           17: Mexico         27: AT&T 6300 or 6300 PLUS
 8: Chile            18: Netherlands
 9: Denmark          19: Norway
10: Finland          20: Peru

        keyboard: 1
```

Enter the number associated with the keyboard format that your system will be using. The procedure now prompts you for the pointing device that you will be using. (If you have not purchased a mouse yet, you should purchase either the Logitech Bus or C7 (Serial) mouse.)

```
In order to operate correctly, Microsoft Windows needs to know
what kind of pointing device you have.

Follow these              - Find your pointing device on this list.
steps:                    - Type the number for your pointing device.
                            (Or enter Q to quit Setup)
                          - Press the  ⏎  key.

1: No pointing device
2: Microsoft Mouse (Bus/Serial)
3: Mouse Systems or VisiOn Mouse (COM1)
4: Mouse Systems or VisiOn Mouse (COM2)
5: Logitech Serial Mouse
6: Kraft Joystick Mouse
7: the Lite-Pen Company - Lightpen
8: FTG Data Systems Lightpen and Single Pixel Board
9: AT&T Mouse 6300 (plugs into keyboard)

        pointing device: 1
```

Lastly, the Windows installation will prompt you to specify the graphics adapter present on your system.

```
In order to operate correctly, Microsoft Windows needs to know
what kind of graphics adapter you have.

Follow these          - Find your graphics adapter on this list.
steps:                - Type the number for your graphics adapter.
                        (Or enter Q to quit Setup)
                      - Press the ↵ key.

1: IBM (or compatible) Color/Graphics Adapter or COMPAQ Personal Computer
2: Hercules Graphics Card (or compatible) with Monochrome Display
3: Enhanced Graphics Adapter (EGA) with Monochrome Personal Computer Display
4: EGA with Enhanced Color Display (Black and White only)
5: EGA with Enhanced Color Display or Personal Computer Color Display
6: EGA (more than 64K) with Enhanced Color Display
7: AT&T PC 6300 or PC 6300 PLUS Display Adapter
8: AT&T Display Enhancement Board
9: Micro Display Systems GENIUS Graphics Adapter

        graphics adapter: 1
```

After you have responded to these three prompts, the installation procedure will begin copying files from the Setup disk to the WINDOWS directory on your hard disk.

```
Setup is copying files from the Setup disk to the
C:\WINDOWS\ directory.
```

Next, the procedure will load files from the Windows Build disk.

```
Setup now needs to read the Build disk.
Please insert it in drive A:




                        ┌─────────────┐
                        │  ─┤█■█├─     │
                        └─────────────┘



                    Put the Build disk
                      into drive A:

When you're      ┌──────────────────────────────────────┐
ready:           │ TO                          PRESS     │
                 ├──────────────────────────────────────┤
                 │ Continue                      C       │
                 └──────────────────────────────────────┘
```

Place the Windows Build disk into drive A and press ENTER. The procedure will copy files from the Build disk, displaying

```
Setup is copying files from the Build disk to the
C:\WINDOWS\ directory.
```

When this process is finished, the installation procedure will copy files from the Windows Utilities disk to your fixed disk.

```
Setup now needs to read the Utilities disk.
Please insert it in drive A:




                Put the Utilities disk
                    into drive A:

When you're
ready:      ┌──────────────────────────────────┐
            │ TO                        PRESS   │
            ├──────────────────────────────────┤
            │ Continue                   C      │
            └──────────────────────────────────┘
```

Place the Utilities disk in drive A and press ENTER.

The installation procedure now allows you to specify the printer that you will be using in conjunction with Windows. Type Y to configure your printer.

```
Would you like to set up a printer/plotter?

When you're
ready:      ┌──────────────────────────────────────┐
            │ TO                          PRESS     │
            ├──────────────────────────────────────┤
            │ Set up a printer/plotter      Y       │
            │ Continue                      N       │
            └──────────────────────────────────────┘
```

The procedure will display

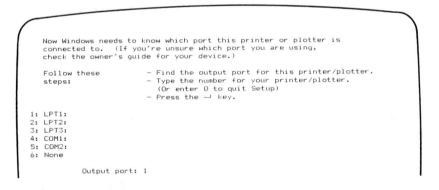

```
In order to print correctly, Microsoft Windows needs to know what
kind of printer or plotter you have.

Follow these          - Find your printer in this list.
steps:                - Type the number for your printer.
                        (Or enter 0 to quit Setup)
                      - Press the ↵ key.

 1: Epson FX-80       11: NEC P2/P3          21: HP 7550A
 2: Epson MX-80 Graftrax  12: C-Itoh 8510    22: Generic / Text Only
 3: Epson LQ-1500     13: Toshiba P1351      23: PostScript/LaserWriter
 4: IBM Graphics      14: Star SG-10         24: HP ThinkJet (2225 C-D)
 5: IBM Proprinter    15: TI 850             25: Xerox 4020
 6: Okidata 92/93 (IBM)   16: TI 855
 7: Okidata 192/193 (IBM) 17: HP LaserJet
 8: Okidata 92/93 (Std)   18: HP LaserJet+
 9: Okidata 192/193 (Std) 19: HP 7470A
10: NEC 3550          20: HP 7475A

          Printer: 1
```

If your printer is in the list of printers, enter its number and press ENTER. Otherwise, select the printer that behaves most like your printer. Refer to your printer reference manual.

Next, the installation will prompt you to specify the port to which your printer is attached.

```
Now Windows needs to know which port this printer or plotter is
connected to.  (If you're unsure which port you are using,
check the owner's guide for your device.)

Follow these          - Find the output port for this printer/plotter.
steps:                - Type the number for your printer/plotter.
                        (Or enter 0 to quit Setup)
                      - Press the ↵ key.

 1: LPT1:
 2: LPT2:
 3: LPT3:
 4: COM1:
 5: COM2:
 6: None

          Output port: 1
```

Normally, the port is LPT1. For more information on printer device names, refer to Chapter 4. The procedure continues by copying files from the disk to your fixed disk, displaying

```
Setup is copying files from the Utilities disk to the
C:\WINDOWS\ directory.
```

Next, the installation procedure allows you to configure multiple printers. If you have multiple printers, type Y and repeat the previous process. Otherwise, the installation continues by prompting you to place the Windows Fonts disk in drive A.

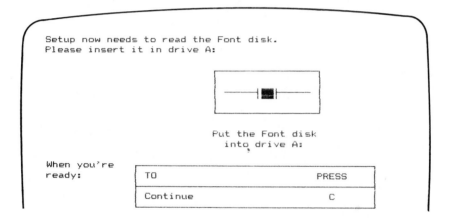

```
Setup now needs to read the Font disk.
Please insert it in drive A:




                              Put the Font disk
                               into drive A:

When you're
ready:        ┌─────────────────────────────────┐
              │  TO                      PRESS   │
              ├─────────────────────────────────┤
              │  Continue                  C     │
              └─────────────────────────────────┘
```

Place the disk in drive A and press ENTER to continue.

```
 Setup is copying files from the Font disk to the
 C:\WINDOWS\ directory.
```

After the Font copy is finished, the installation procedure will prompt for the Desktop Applications disk as follows:

```
Setup now needs to read the Desktop Applications disk.
Please insert it in drive A:


                    ──┤■├──


              Put the Desktop Applications disk
                     into drive A:

When you're
ready:           ┌────────────────────────────────────┐
                 │ TO                         PRESS    │
                 ├────────────────────────────────────┤
                 │ Continue                     C      │
                 │ Quit                         Q      │
                 └────────────────────────────────────┘
```

Place the disk in drive A and press ENTER.

```
Setup is copying files from the Desktop Applications disk to the
C:\WINDOWS\ directory.
```

Lastly, the Windows installation will prompt you for the Write Program disk, which contains the Write word processor.

```
Setup now needs to read the Microsoft Write Program  disk.
Please insert it in drive A:


                    ──┤■├──


            Put the Microsoft Write Program  disk
                     into drive A:

When you're
ready:           ┌────────────────────────────────────┐
                 │ TO                         PRESS    │
                 ├────────────────────────────────────┤
                 │ Continue                     C      │
                 │ Quit                         Q      │
                 └────────────────────────────────────┘
```

Place the disk in drive A and press ENTER.

```
Setup is copying files from the Microsoft Write Program  disk to the
C:\WINDOWS\ directory.
```

The Windows installation is complete, and the procedure will display

```
Microsoft Windows is set up to operate on your computer.
You are now in the Windows directory.

To start Microsoft Windows:

    - Type WIN
    - Press the ⅃ key.

C>
```

Windows Products

In addition to providing you with an environment that supports concurrent execution of programs, Windows provides you with several powerful desktop applications. Essentially, the developers of Windows tried to make the items that normally appear on your desktop available on your computer's screen.

The following programs are provided with Microsoft Windows:

- NOTEPAD allows you to create a "To Do" list with set priorities.

- CARDFILE allows you to organize facts on index cards.

- CALCULATOR provides a simple calculator.

- CALENDAR provides an on-line appointment system.

- CLOCK displays an analog clock with the current system time.

- TERMINAL provides terminal emulation for bulletin board access.

- REVERSI provides a challenging game.

Chapter 18 will examine each of these programs in detail, along with Microsoft Write (a simple word processor provided with Windows) and Paint (which allows you to create drawings for integration into reports and memos).

For now, however, you will learn about the Microsoft Executive, which is the Windows interface to DOS. After you've studied the following section, you should have a solid foundation for moving around Windows screens, applications, and menus.

Microsoft Executive

To invoke Windows, enter the following at the DOS prompt:

```
A> WIN
```

Windows will display the Windows logo on the screen and then the screen shown in Figure 17-12. The most obvious items displayed on the screen are the disk drive identifications across the top of the window, the names of the files contained in the current directory, the name of the current directory, and, lastly, the MS-DOS Executive name within the title bar.

As you will see, many of the commands that you will use can be invoked easily with a mouse or via the keyboard. This chapter will present both methods for each example presented. To get a feel for moving around in Windows, change the current default drives. If you are using a mouse, simply move the mouse pointer to the drive identification desired and press the mouse select button. If you are using the keyboard, press the CTRL key and the letter of the drive simultaneously. Toggle through all of the disk drives with either method.

Next, look at the list of files on the screen. Windows highlights one file by placing it in reverse video. As you will see, this file is the default for Windows file manipulation commands. If you

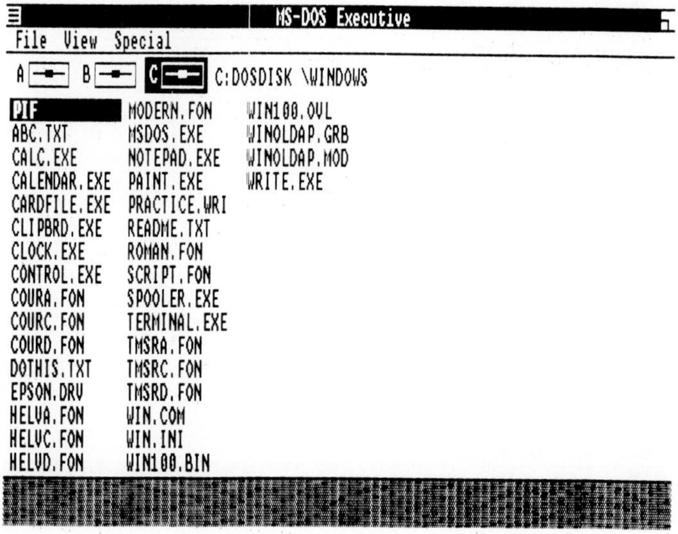

```
 ☰                        MS-DOS Executive                          ⌐
File  View  Special
 A ▭━▪  B ▭━▪  C ▭━▪  C:DOSDISK \WINDOWS

 PIF            MODERN.FON     WIN100.OVL
 ABC.TXT        MSDOS.EXE      WINOLDAP.GRB
 CALC.EXE       NOTEPAD.EXE    WINOLDAP.MOD
 CALENDAR.EXE   PAINT.EXE      WRITE.EXE
 CARDFILE.EXE   PRACTICE.WRI
 CLIPBRD.EXE    README.TXT
 CLOCK.EXE      ROMAN.FON
 CONTROL.EXE    SCRIPT.FON
 COURA.FON      SPOOLER.EXE
 COURC.FON      TERMINAL.EXE
 COURD.FON      TMSRA.FON
 DOTHIS.TXT     TMSRC.FON
 EPSON.DRV      TMSRD.FON
 HELVA.FON      WIN.COM
 HELVC.FON      WIN.INI
 HELVD.FON      WIN100.BIN
```

Figure 17-12. Opening Windows screen

are using the keyboard, select files via the cursor arrow keys. If
you are using a mouse, simply move the mouse pointer to the file
desired and press the mouse select button.

As you will see, Windows provides several drop-down menus
that allow you to perform additional processing. In general, a
drop-down menu is nothing more than a menu of options that is
displayed on top of the current window. Consider the screen display shown in Figure 17-13. The section labeled Menu Bar contains the list of available drop-down menus.

If you are using a mouse, point at the File menu. If you are
using the keyboard, press the ALT key while pressing the key
associated with the first letter of the menu desired—in this case,
ALT-F.

The File menu allows you to perform the functions shown in
Figure 17-14. If you are using the keyboard, you can select an
option from the drop-down menu via the cursor arrow keys or by
pressing the first letter of the option desired. If you are using a
mouse, point at the option desired. If you select the Run option,

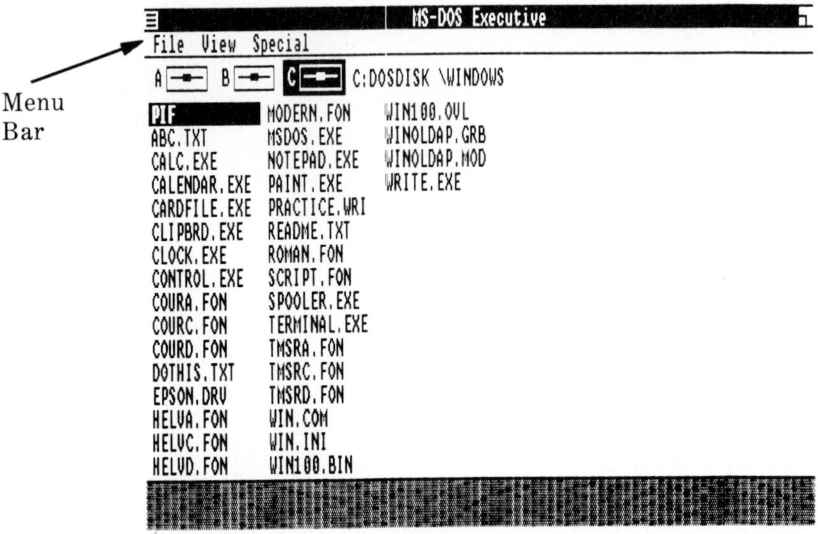

Figure 17-13. Sample menu

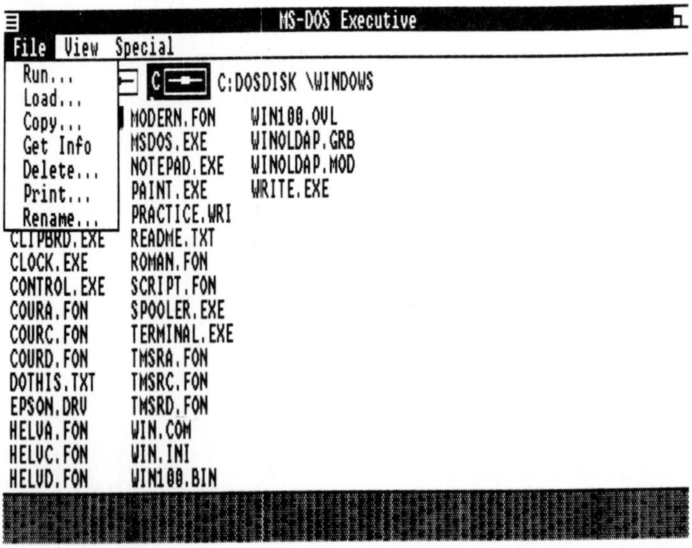

Figure 17-14. File menu

Windows will prompt you for the program to execute, as shown in Figure 17-15.

Type in the name of the program that you want Windows to execute and then press ENTER. In this case, press ENTER without specifying a file name. Windows defines boxes that prompt for information in this manner as *dialog boxes*. If you don't want to invoke a program, you can press the ESC key to exit from the dialog box.

The Windows Load command is unique in that it makes a program available as an icon. Later in this chapter will be a discussion on how to select an application from a list of icons. In this case, load the program CLOCK.EXE as an icon. Windows will display the screen shown in Figure 17-16.

There are two ways of selecting CLOCK.EXE as the program Windows is to load. First, you can select the file CLOCK.EXE as the Windows default file by using the cursor arrow keys or the mouse. Next, invoking the File menu and the Load option displays

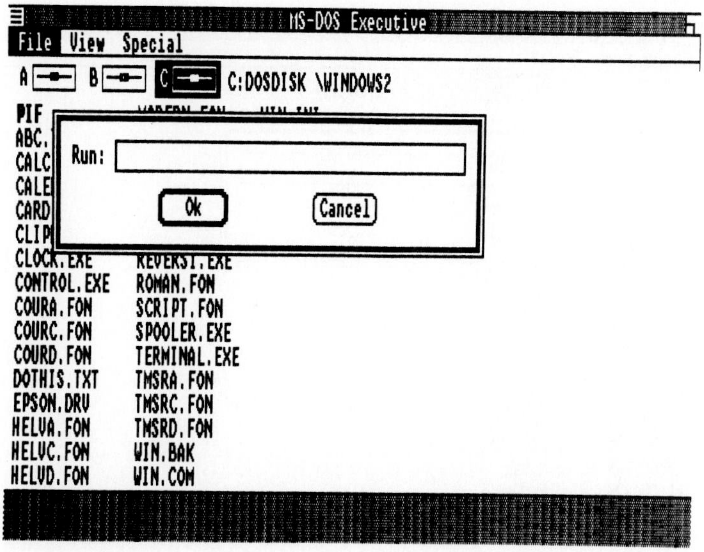

Figure 17-15. Run option

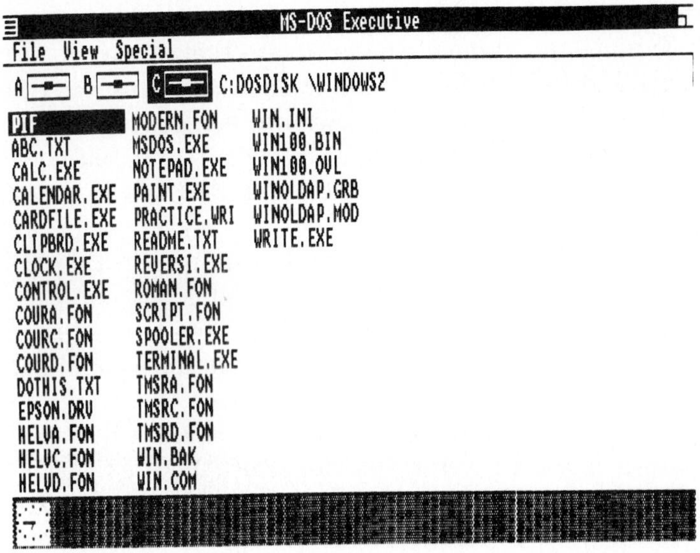

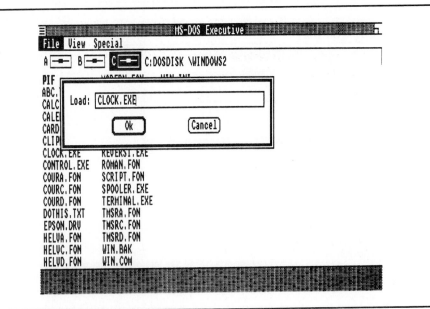

Figure 17-16.   CLOCK.EXE icon

Figure 17-17.   Load option

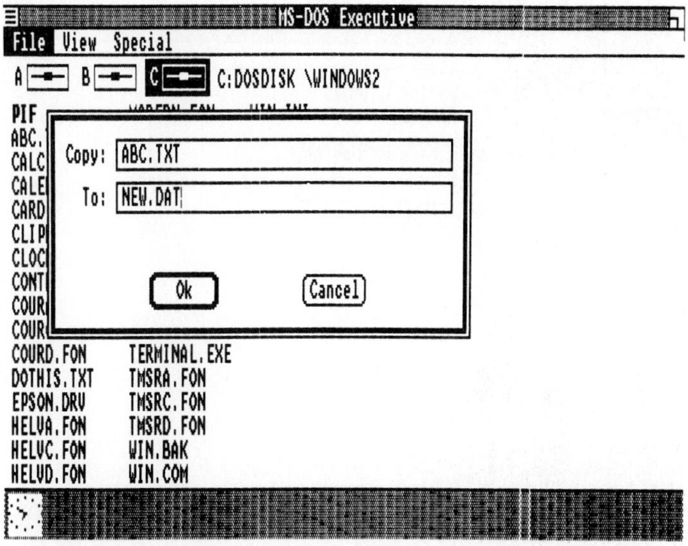

Figure 17-18. Copy command

CLOCK.EXE by default. The second method is to invoke the File menu and Load option, typing in the name CLOCK.EXE in the Windows dialog box (see Figure 17-17).

The Windows Copy command allows you to copy one or more files to a new location. By default, Copy will display the current default Windows file as the source file (see Figure 17-18). In this case, use the default source file and specify the target file as NEW.DAT.

The Get Info option simply displays the name, extension, size, and creation date and time for the Windows default file (see Figure 17-19).

The Windows Delete command is similar to the DOS DEL command. By default, Windows uses the default file as the file to delete. If you want to delete this file, simply press ENTER; otherwise, type in the name of the file to delete (see Figure 17-20). Windows will delete the specified file.

The Windows Print command is similar to the DOS PRINT command in that it places a file into a queue (the Windows spooler) for printing. By default, the command uses the Windows default file as shown in Figure 17-21. If you want to print a dif-

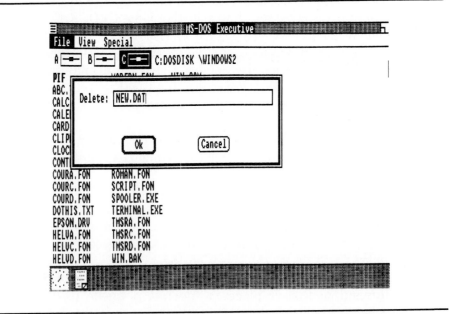

Figure 17-19. Get Info option

Figure 17-20. Delete command

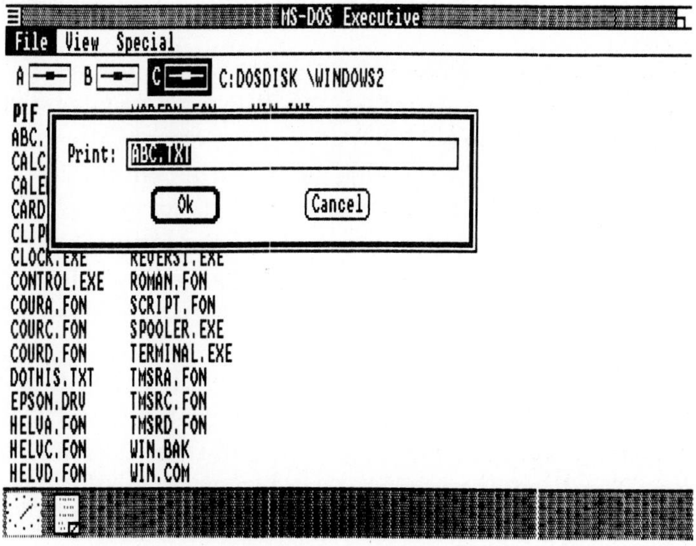

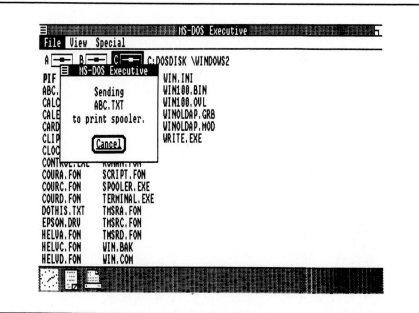

Figure 17-21. Print command

Figure 17-22. Default Print selection

ferent file, type in the name of the file that you desire. When you press ENTER, Windows will display the screen shown in Figure 17-22.

The Windows spooler is conceptually similar to the DOS PRINT queue. Once installed, the Windows spooler displays the icon shown in Figure 17-23. The complete abilities of the Windows spooler will be discussed later in this chapter.

The Windows Rename command allows you to rename the Windows default file. After you select the option, it will prompt you for the target file name via the dialog box shown in Figure 17-24. Simply type in the new file name that you desire and press ENTER.

The Windows View menu allows you to specify how Windows is to display files contained in the current directory. Select the View menu by pressing ALT-V or pointing at View with your mouse. The View menu allows you to specify the options shown in Figure 17-25. Again, you select options by using the cursor arrow keys, by typing the first letter of the option, or by pointing at the

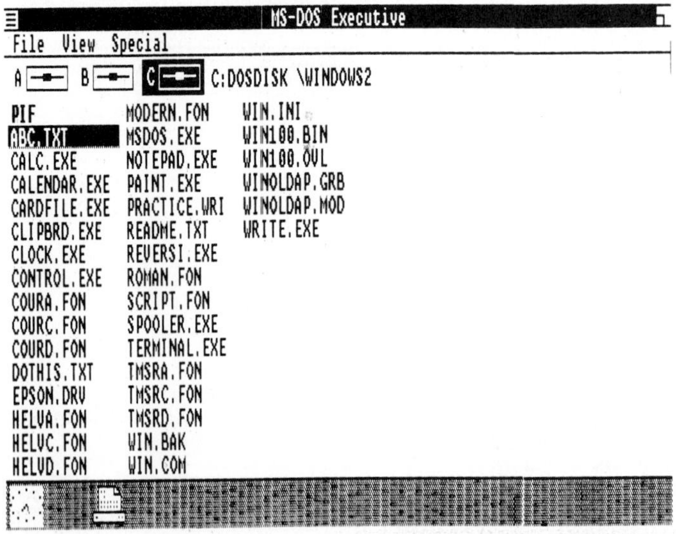

Figure 17-23.   Spooler icon

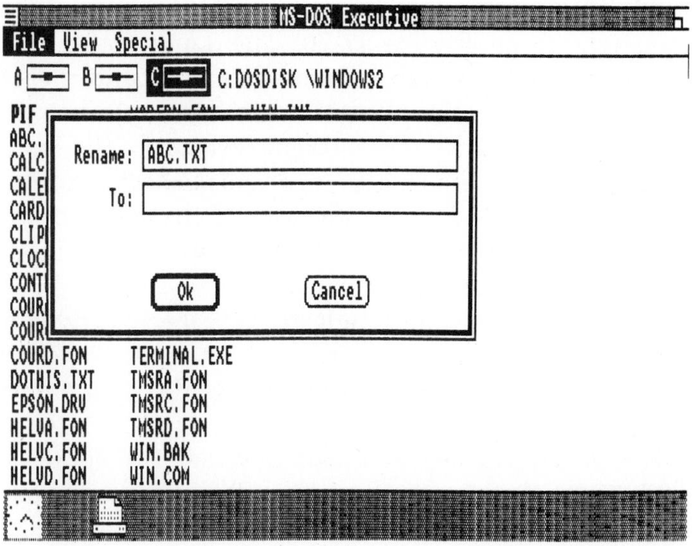

Figure 17-24. Rename command

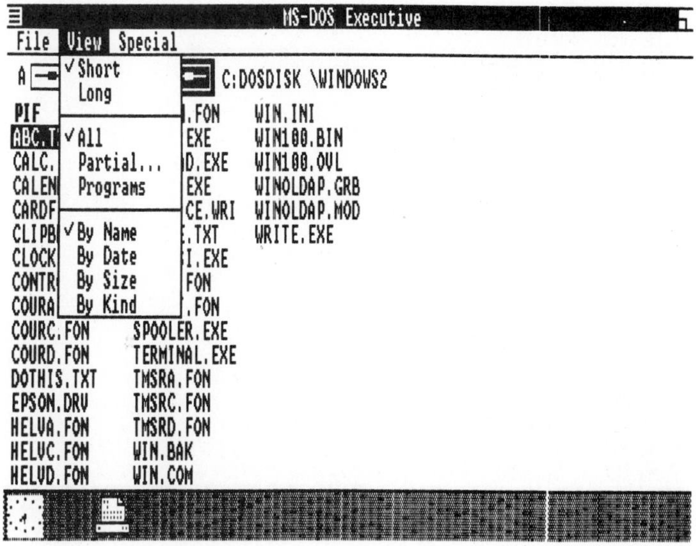

Figure 17-25. View menu

option with your mouse. The Short option directs Windows to display the file name and extension of each file in the current directory, as shown in Figure 17-26. The Long option displays the name, extension, size, and creation date and time of each of those files (see Figure 17-27). The All option directs Windows to list all of the files contained in the current directory. The Partial option causes Windows to display the dialog box shown in Figure 17-28. Simply type in the file specification of the file(s) that you want Windows to list. DOS wildcard characters are valid. To display only TXT files, enter *.TXT.

You use the By Name, By Date, By Size, and By Kind options to specify how you want the directory listing displayed and sorted by Windows. The checkmarks next to the View options display the current default values.

The Windows Special menu provides the options shown in Figure 17-29. The first option, End Session, allows you to terminate the current Windows session and return to DOS. After you invoke this option, Windows will display the dialog box shown in Figure 17-30. To terminate Windows, simply press ENTER. Other-

MS-DOS Executive		
File View Special		
A B C C:DOSDISK \WINDOWS2		
PIF	MODERN.FON	WIN.INI
ABC.TXT	MSDOS.EXE	WIN100.BIN
CALC.EXE	NOTEPAD.EXE	WIN100.OVL
CALENDAR.EXE	PAINT.EXE	WINOLDAP.GRB
CARDFILE.EXE	PRACTICE.WRI	WINOLDAP.MOD
CLIPBRD.EXE	README.TXT	WRITE.EXE
CLOCK.EXE	REVERSI.EXE	
CONTROL.EXE	ROMAN.FON	
COURA.FON	SCRIPT.FON	
COURC.FON	SPOOLER.EXE	
COURD.FON	TERMINAL.EXE	
DOTHIS.TXT	TMSRA.FON	
EPSON.DRV	TMSRC.FON	
HELVA.FON	TMSRD.FON	
HELVC.FON	WIN.BAK	
HELVD.FON	WIN.COM	

Figure 17-26.   Short option

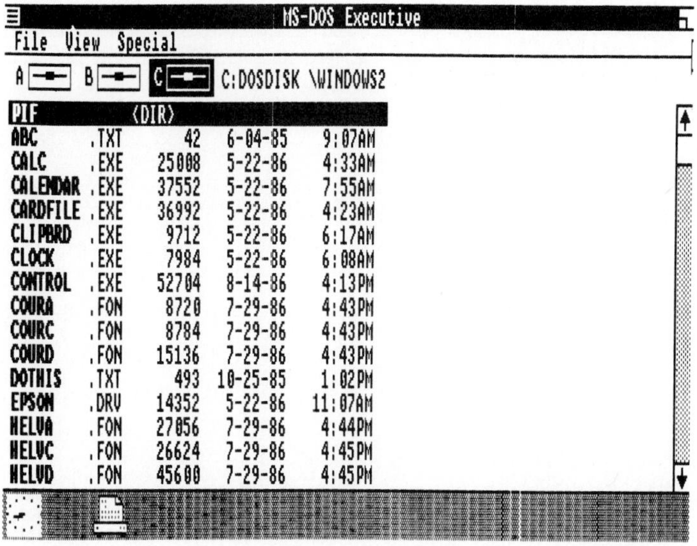

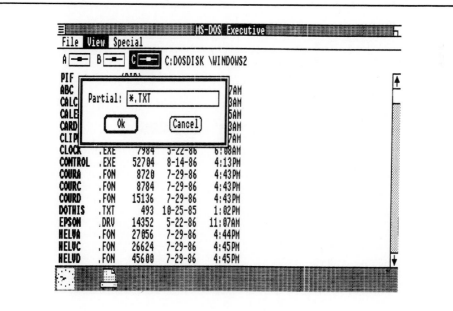

Figure 17-27. Long option

Figure 17-28. Partial option

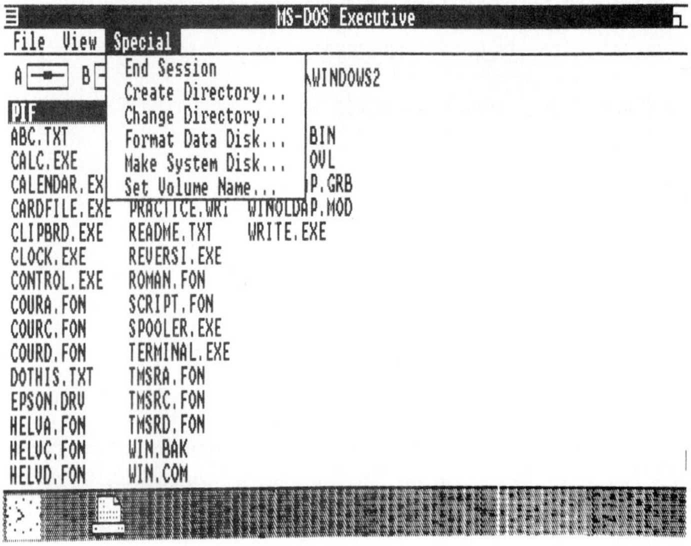

Figure 17-29. Special menu

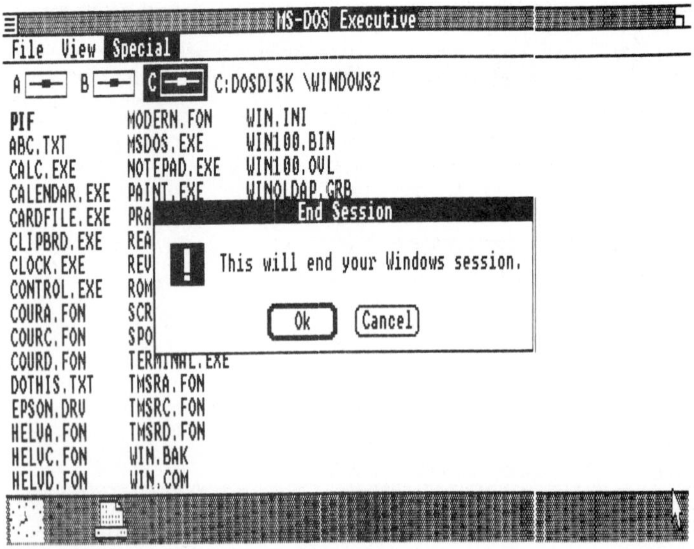

Figure 17-30. End Session dialog box

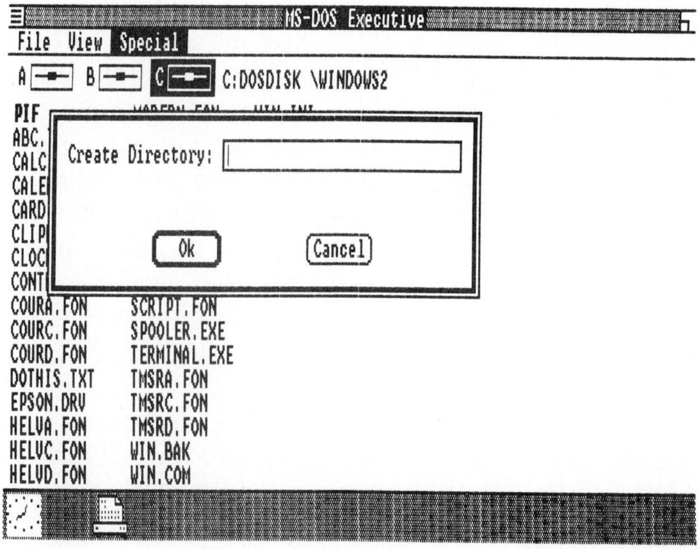

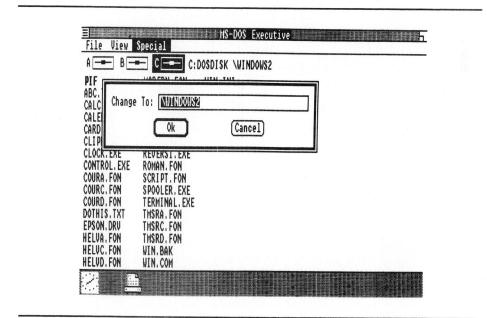

Figure 17-31.   Create Directory option

Figure 17-32.   Change Directory option

wise, press the TAB key to select Cancel, and then press the SPACEBAR.

The Create Directory option displays the dialog box shown in Figure 17-31, which allows you to create DOS subdirectories. Likewise, the Windows Change Directory option prompts you for the desired directory via the dialog box shown in Figure 17-32. Type in the name of the directory that you desire and press ENTER. In addition, you can set the default directory to a subdirectory that appears in the list of files displayed on the screen simply by selecting it as the default Windows file and pressing ENTER or the select button on your mouse. Likewise, by pressing the BACKSPACE key, you can move up one level in the directory structure.

The Format option allows you to format a disk contained in either drive A or drive B, as shown in Figure 17-33. Select the desired drive (via the TAB key) and press ENTER. If you don't want to format a disk, press the ESC key to exit from the dialog box.

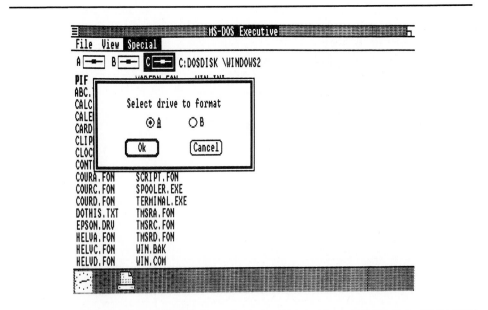

Figure 17-33.   Format option

The Make System option performs the DOS SYS command for the specified drive (see Figure 17-34). Select the desired drive (via the TAB key) and press ENTER. When you choose the drive the disk in that drive will be bootable.

Lastly, the Set Volume Name option allows you to specify the volume label for the current default disk, as shown in Figure 17-35. Type in the 11-character volume label that you desire and press ENTER. If you don't want to specify a volume label, press the ESC key. For more information on volume labels, refer to the VOL command in Appendix A, *DOS Reference Guide*.

System Menu

Every window has a System menu associated with it. You select this menu by pressing the ALT key and SPACEBAR simultaneously, or by pointing the mouse at the System menu box in the upper-

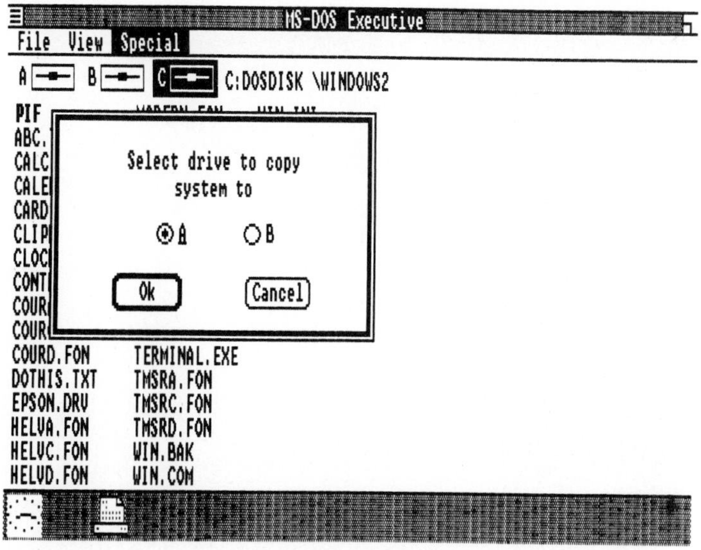

Figure 17-34.   Make System option

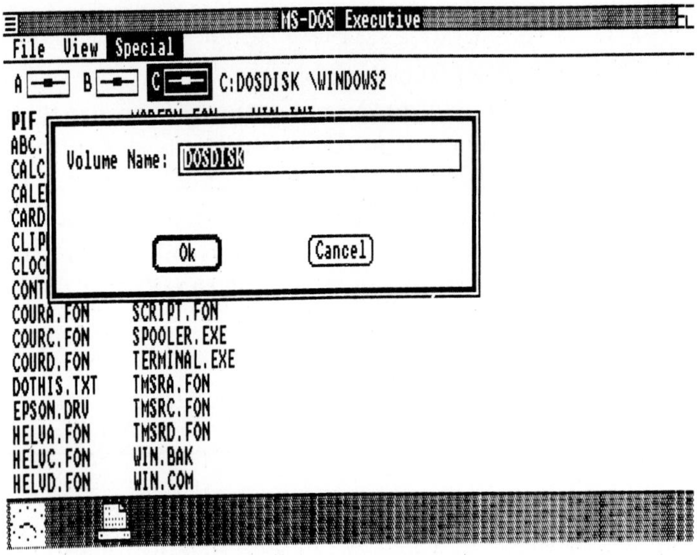

Figure 17-35. Set Volume Name option

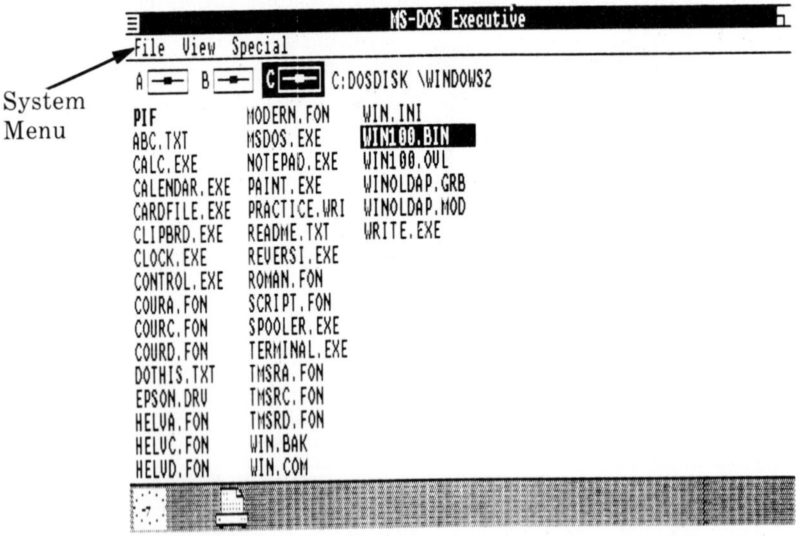

Figure 17-36. System menu

left-hand corner, as shown in Figure 17-36.

The menu provides the abilities shown in Figure 17-37. Note that one or more of the options may be dim. This means that the option currently is not available for the window. The Size option allows you to change the size of a window. If you have a mouse to use, some applications will support a size box. The use of Size is discussed in Chapter 18.

The Move option allows you to relocate a window on the screen or to move an icon to a window. The Icon option makes the current window an icon and places it in the lower-left-hand corner of the screen. The Zoom option expands a window to the full size of the screen, covering up any icons in the lower-left corner. The Zoom option works as a toggle (select it twice to shrink the size of the window). The Close option terminates the application running in the current window and removes it from memory. If you are closing the MS-DOS Executive, Windows will display the dialog box shown in Figure 17-38.

Figure 17-37.   System menu abilities

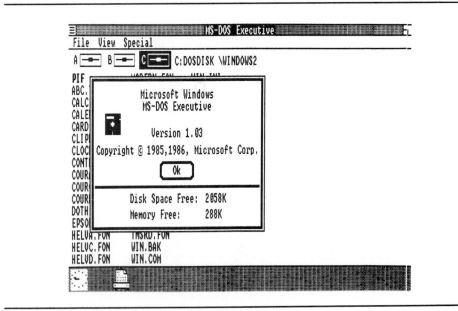

Figure 17-38. Dialog box for closing MS-DOS Executive

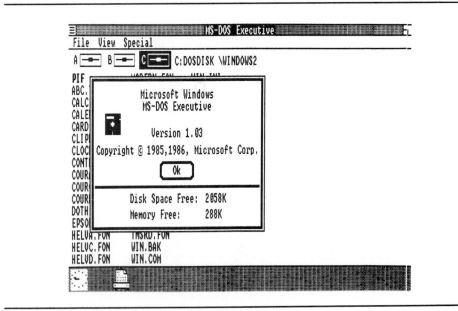

Figure 17-39. About option

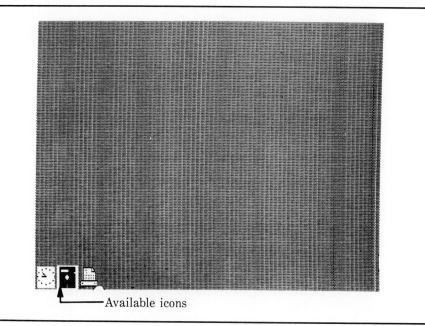

———Available icons

Figure 17-40.   Program icons

The About option displays information about the application in the current Window. For the MS-DOS Executive, About displays the dialog box in Figure 17-39.

Selecting Programs from Icons

To exploit the true power of Windows fully, you must invoke several programs simultaneously, switching from one program to the next as your needs require. As previously stated, Windows allows you to load programs into memory as icons and select them for execution at a later time. Windows will display the icon for the program in the lower-left-hand portion of the screen as shown in Figure 17-40.

If you load a program, the Windows spooler becomes available as an icon. Assume that you have no programs loaded and, therefore, no icons are displayed. Using the File menu, load the

```
 ≡                       MS-DOS Executive                        ⌐
  File  View  Special
  A ▬■▬ B ▬■▬ C ▬■▬ C:DOSDISK \WINDOWS2
  PIF           MODERN.FON    WIN.INI
  ABC.TXT       MSDOS.EXE     WIN100.BIN
  CALC.EXE      NOTEPAD.EXE   WIN100.OVL
  CALENDAR.EXE  PAINT.EXE     WINOLDAP.GRB
  CARDFILE.EXE  PRACTICE.WRI  WINOLDAP.MOD
  CLIPBRD.EXE   README.TXT    WRITE.EXE
  CLOCK.EXE     REVERSI.EXE
  CONTROL.EXE   ROMAN.FON
  COURA.FON     SCRIPT.FON
  COURC.FON     SPOOLER.EXE
  COURD.FON     TERMINAL.EXE
  DOTHIS.TXT    TMSRA.FON
  EPSON.DRV     TMSRC.FON
  HELVA.FON     TMSRD.FON
  HELVC.FON     WIN.BAK
  HELVD.FON     WIN.COM
```

Figure 17-41.   Loading CLOCK.EXE program

program CLOCK.EXE as an icon by executing the following
steps:

1. Press ALT-F.

2. Select Load.

3. Type in CLOCK.EXE and press ENTER.

Windows will display the screen shown in Figure 17-41.

Next, load the program CALC.EXE in the same fashion.
Your screen should now look like Figure 17-42.

To select an icon by using a mouse, simply point at the icon
and press the select button on your mouse. If you are using the
keyboard, use the ALT-TAB key combination to display the names
of the icons and the ALT-SPACEBAR key combination to toggle
through the icons.

Once the icon that you desire is highlighted, simply press
ENTER. In this case, select the clock icon. Windows will display an
analog clock on the screen, as shown in Figure 17-43.

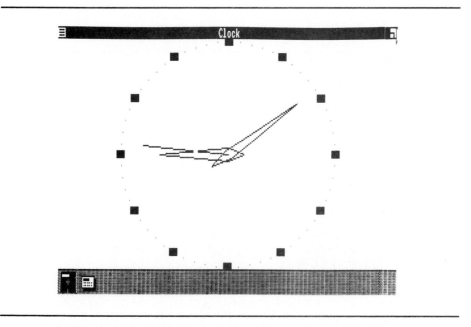

```
 ≣               • MS-DOS Executive                    ⌐
 File  View  Special
 A ▭▬  B ▭▬  C ▭▬  C:DOSDISK \WINDOWS2

 PIF          MODERN.FON    WIN.INI
 ABC.TXT      MSDOS.EXE     WIN100.BIN
 CALC.EXE     NOTEPAD.EXE   WIN100.OVL
 CALENDAR.EXE PAINT.EXE     WINOLDAP.GRB
 CARDFILE.EXE PRACTICE.WRI  WINOLDAP.MOD
 CLIPBRD.EXE  README.TXT    WRITE.EXE
 CLOCK.EXE    REVERSI.EXE
 CONTROL.EXE  ROMAN.FON
 COURA.FON    SCRIPT.FON
 COURC.FON    SPOOLER.EXE
 COURD.FON    TERMINAL.EXE
 DOTHIS.TXT   TMSRA.FON
 EPSON.DRV    TMSRC.FON
 HELVA.FON    TMSRD.FON
 HELVC.FON    WIN.BAK
 HELVD.FON    WIN.COM
```

Figure 17-42.   Load CALC.EXE program

Figure 17-43.   Analog clock from clock icon

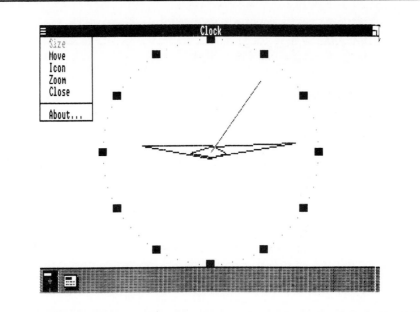

Figure 17-44. System menu box

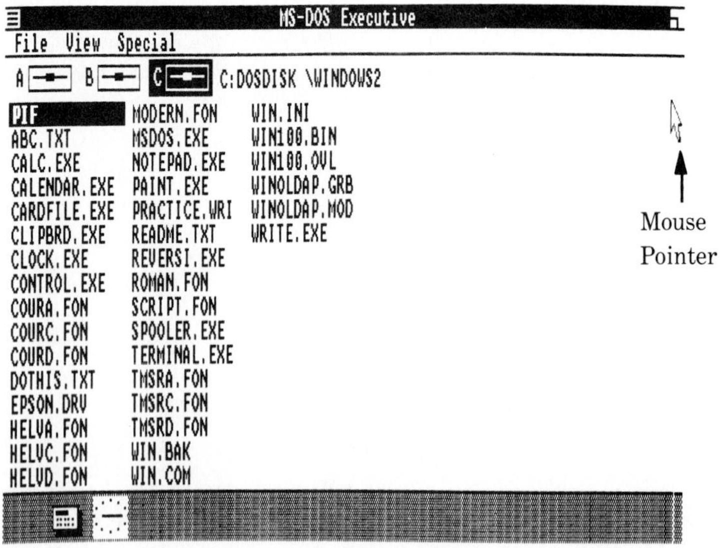

Figure 17-45. Executive main menu

When you grow tired of watching this clock, select the Windows System menu box by pressing the ALT-SPACEBAR key combination or by pointing your mouse at the System menu box in the upper-left corner. Windows will display the screen shown in Figure 17-44.

You have several choices. You want to return to the MS-DOS Executive, so you can either Close the clock program (removing it from memory) or select the icon option that places the clock icon back at the lower-left-hand corner of the screen. In this case, since there are multiple icons available, you must select the one that you desire. The floppy disk icon represents the Windows MS-DOS Executive. Select it and Windows will display the screen shown in Figure 17-45.

Windows Spooler

Each time you print a file from within Windows, the file is added to the Windows spooler. As you will see, you can gain additional control over the printer via the spooler icon. Select the spooler icon and Windows will display the screen shown in Figure 17-46.

If files reside in the Windows spooler, their names will be displayed on the screen. Select the Priority menu by pointing at the option with your mouse or by pressing ALT-P. The Priority menu allows you to perform the functions shown in Figure 17-47.

The High option allows you to speed up the printing of a job by distributing more of the CPU timeslices to the Windows print spooler. The Low command directs Windows to print jobs more slowly by distributing fewer CPU timeslices to the spooler.

The Controls menu provides you with direct control over files in the Windows print spooler (see Figure 17-48). First, the Pause option allows you to suspend printing temporarily, which allows the CPU timeslices normally allocated by the spooler to be distributed to other programs. The Resume option restarts printing by the Windows spooler. Lastly, the Terminate option allows you to remove files from the spooler. Windows will prompt, via a dialog box, for the file(s) to remove.

Periodically, the spooler will have messages that it must display. If the spooler is not the active window, the Spooler icon will

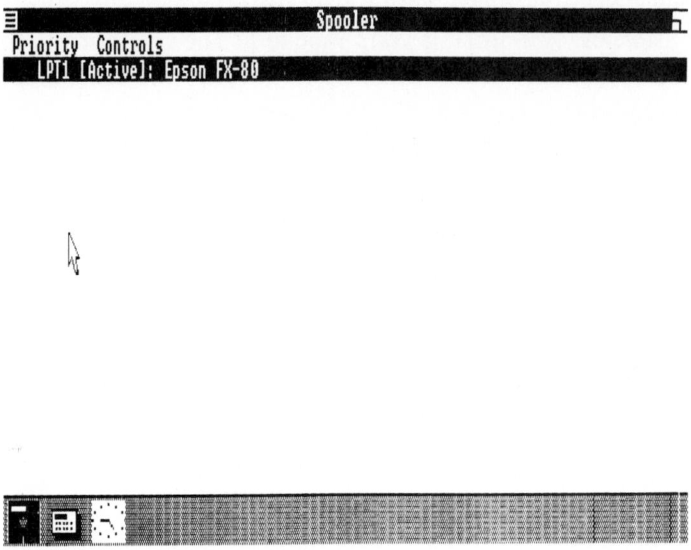

Figure 17-46. Result of selecting spooler icon

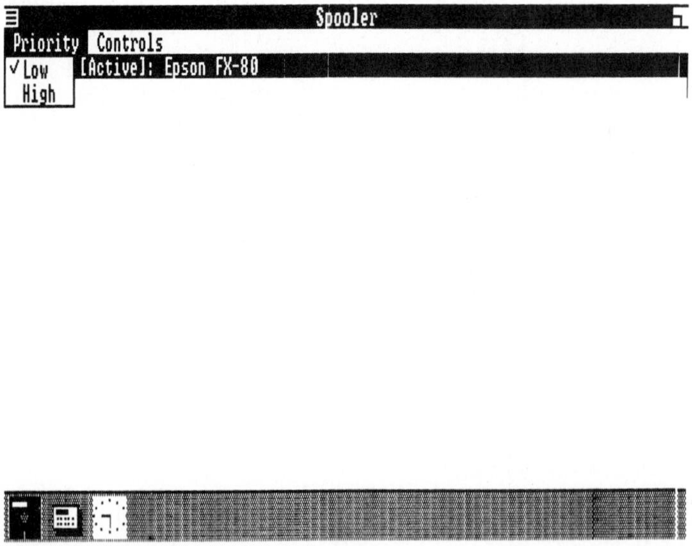

Figure 17-47. Priority menu

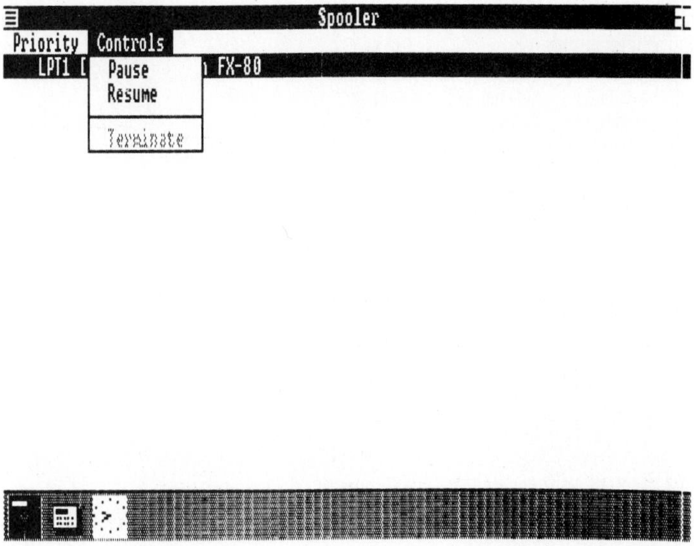

Figure 17-48. Controls menu

flash. Select the spooler icon as the active window to display the message.

Review

1. What is Windows?

2. What is time-sharing?

3. What are desktop applications?

4. List several of the design goals of Windows.

5. List and describe the applications provided with Windows.

6. Label each of the following.

```
 ┌─────────────────────────────────────────────────────────┐
 │ ≡            MS-DOS Executive                          ⬜ │
 ├─────────────────────────────────────────────────────────┤
 │ File  View  Special                                      │
 ├─────────────────────────────────────────────────────────┤
 │ A ⊶  B ⊶  │C ⊟│  C:DOSDISK \WINDOWS2                      │
 │ ┌────────┐  MODERN.FON      WIN.INI                       │
 │ ABC.TXT     MSDOS.EXE       WIN100.BIN                    │
 │ CALC.EXE    NOTEPAD.EXE     WIN100.OVL                    │
 │ CALENDAR.EXE PAINT.EXE      WINOLDAP.GRB                  │
 │ CARDFILE.EXE PRACTICE.WRI   WINOLDAP.MOD                  │
 │ CLIPBRD.EXE README.TXT      WRITE.EXE                     │
 │ CLOCK.EXE   REVERSI.EXE                                   │
 │ CONTROL.EXE ROMAN.FON                                     │
 │ COURA.FON   SCRIPT.FON                                    │
 │ COURC.FON   SPOOLER.EXE                                   │
 │ COURD.FON   TERMINAL.EXE                                  │
 │ DOTHIS.TXT  TMSRA.FON                                     │
 │ EPSON.DRV   TMSRC.FON                                     │
 │ HELVA.FON   TMSRD.FON                                     │
 │ HELVC.FON   WIN.BAK                                       │
 │ HELVD.FON   WIN.COM                                       │
 ├─────────────────────────────────────────────────────────┤
 │░░░░░░░░░░░░░░░░░░░░░░░░░░░░░░░░░░░░░░░░░░░░░░░░░░░░░░░░░░░░░│
 └─────────────────────────────────────────────────────────┘
```

7. How do you select menu options within the menu bar?

8. What is the System menu?

9. How does the Windows Load command differ from RUN?

10. What is the Windows spooler?

11. What is a dialog box?

12. How do you select an icon to execute?

13. How do you terminate a Windows session?

14. What are the functions provided by the Windows File menu?

15. What are the functions provided by the Windows View menu?

16. What are the functions provided by the Windows Special menu?

Answers

1. *What is Windows?*

Windows is an extension of DOS. By utilizing Windows, you can expand all the features of DOS. In addition, Windows allows you to execute multiple programs simultaneously, quickly changing from one application to another. Lastly, Windows allows you to integrate multiple packages, exploiting the best features of each.

2. *What is time-sharing?*

Because of the tremendous speed of today's computers, CPUs actually spend the majority of their time idle, waiting to perform additional processing. In a 1-second time period, for example, the CPU may be processing only 25% of the time. Windows exploits the CPU's idle time and allows other programs to share the CPU. Operating systems that share the CPU processing time in this fashion are called time-sharing systems. Windows, therefore, can best be described as a time-sharing environment. As multiple programs are executed simultaneously, each program gets a segment of the CPU's processing time. Because transitions between segments are fast, it appears as if several applications are executing simultaneously.

3. *What are desktop applications?*

A major goal of office automation software is to automate functions that you normally perform on a day-to-day basis. Windows' developers tried to make the items that normally appear on your desktop available on the computer screen. The items include an analog clock, an appointment calendar, a calculator, and a card file.

4. *List several of the design goals of Windows.*

The first goal of Windows is to relieve the user from the burden of having to memorize and understand DOS commands and their various options. Windows has replaced the

DOS prompt with pull-down menus and dialog boxes. DOS commands are represented by Windows icons, and Windows supports a convenient mouse interface. The interface to the computer is easy for novices to use, and, therefore, is non-threatening. This has, in turn, reduced the time required for users to learn how to use a system.

Second, Windows allows you to run multiple programs at one time. A computer with the ability to execute several programs simultaneously is termed a time-sharing system. Windows allows you to have several programs active simultaneously and also allows these programs to exchange information via Windows' built-in capabilities.

Third, Windows is called a desktop system. Windows provides many of the abilities normally associated with items on your desk, such as a notepad, calculator, and calendar.

5. *List and describe the applications provided with Windows.*

NOTEPAD allows you to create a "To Do" list.
CARDFILE allows you to organize facts on index cards.
CALCULATOR provides a simple calculator.
CALENDAR provides an on-line appointment system.
CLOCK displays an analog clock with the current system time.
TERMINAL provides terminal emulation for bulletin-board access.
REVERSI provides a challenging game.

6. *Label each of the following.*

7. *How do you select menu options within the menu bar?*

If you are using a mouse, point at the menu. If you are using the keyboard, press the ALT key while pressing the key associated with the first letter of the menu desired. ALT-F, for example, selects the File menu in the MS-DOS Executive.

8. *What is the System menu?*

Every window has a System menu associated with it. You select this menu by pressing the ALT key and SPACEBAR simultaneously or by pointing the mouse at the System menu box in the upper-left-hand corner of the window. The menu provides the following options: Size, Move, Icon, Zoom, Close, and About. Notice that one or more of the options may be dim. This means that the option currently is not available for the window.

9. *How does the Windows Load command differ from RUN?*

The Windows RUN command brings the specified program into memory and executes it immediately. The LOAD command brings the specified program into memory as an icon for later execution.

10. *What is the Windows spooler?*

The Windows spooler is similar conceptually to the DOS PRINT queue. Once installed, the Windows spooler displays a special icon. Each time you print a file from within Windows, the file is added to the Windows spooler. You can gain additional control over the printer via the spooler icon.

11. *What is a dialog box?*

Periodically, Windows requires you to type in information at a Windows prompt. In such cases, Windows displays a dialog box that contains the Windows prompt and a space for you to type in the required information.

12. *How do you select an icon to execute?*

To select an icon via a mouse, simply point at the icon and press the select button on your mouse. If you are using the keyboard, use the ALT-TAB key combination to display the names of the icons and the ALT-SPACEBAR combination to toggle through the icons. Once the icon that you desire is highlighted, simply press ENTER.

13. *How do you terminate a Windows session?*

In the MS-DOS Executive, select the End Session option from the Special menu. To return to DOS, simply press ENTER. To continue execution from Windows, press the TAB key to select Cancel and then press the SPACEBAR.

14. *What are the functions provided by the Windows File menu?*

The Windows File menu provides options for running, loading, copying, getting information about, deleting, printing, and renaming files.

15. *What are the functions provided by the Windows View menu?*

The Windows View menu view options include short and long; all, partial, and programs; and by name, by date, by size, and by kind.

16. *What are the functions provided by the Windows Special menu?*

The Windows Special menu provides options for ending a session, creating a directory, changing a directory, formatting a data disk, making a system disk, and setting a volume name.

Advanced Microsoft Windows

CLOCK
CALCULATOR
CALENDAR
CARDFILE
NOTEPAD
TERMINAL
REVERSI
The Clipboard
Running Multiple Applications Simultaneously
Microsoft WRITE and PAINT
The Windows Control Panel
What Is a PIF?
Providing Initialization Values to Windows
RAM Drives and Windows

Chapter 17 introduced Microsoft Windows, its development philosophy, time sharing, and moving between Windows menus and screens. This chapter builds upon your knowledge of Windows and examines each of its desktop applications; it also briefly discusses Microsoft WRITE, a simple word processor provided with Windows, and Microsoft PAINT, which allows you to incorporate diagrams and drawings into your reports and memos. In addition, this chapter discusses the simultaneous display of several applications on your screen and the traversal from one application to another. The configuration of Windows to maximize the capabilities of your system will also be discussed.

E
I
G
H
T
E
E
N

As you may recall from Chapter 17, Windows provides the following desktop applications:

- CLOCK displays an analog clock with the current system time.
- CALCULATOR provides a simple calculator.
- CALENDAR provides an appointment calendar.
- CARDFILE allows you to organize facts on index cards.
- NOTEPAD allows you to create a "To Do" list.
- TERMINAL provides terminal emulation for bulletin board systems.
- REVERSI provides a challenging game.

You can load each desktop application as an icon or load the application for immediate execution. In addition, each desktop application has its own system menu that provides the following type of information:

At the end of this chapter you will see each of the options on the system menu and note their effects upon the screen when multiple applications are displayed simultaneously, as shown here:

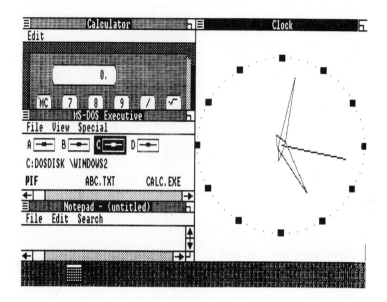

CLOCK

Items normally found on a desk are also available on your computer, in the form of programs called desktop applications. The first desktop application to be discussed is the analog clock. Invoke Microsoft Windows by issuing the following command:

A> WIN

Windows will display

```
≡▌                         MS-DOS Executive                    ▐EL
 File  View  Special
────────────────────────────────────────────────────────────────
 A ▭═▪  B ▭═▪  ▐C ▭═▪  D ▭═▪  C:DOSDISK \WINDOWS2              │
 ████   HELVD.FON   TMSRD.FON
 ABC.TXT        KAJ.CAL      VV.CAL
 CALC.EXE       LL.CAL       WIN.COM
 CALENDAR.EXE   MODERN.FON   WIN.INI
 CARDFILE.EXE   MSDOS.EXE    WIN100.BIN
 CLIPBRD.EXE    NOTEPAD.EXE  WIN100.OVL
 CLOCK.EXE      PAINT.EXE    WINOLDAP.GRB
 CONTROL.EXE    PRACTICE.WRI WINOLDAP.MOD
 COURA.FON      README.TXT   WRITE.EXE
 COURC.FON      REVERSI.EXE
 COURD.FON      ROMAN.FON
 DOS.CRD        SCRIPT.FON
 DOTHIS.TXT     SPOOLER.EXE
 EPSON.DRV      TERMINAL.EXE
 HELVA.FON      TMSRA.FON
 HELVC.FON      TMSRC.FON
```

Select CLOCK.EXE as the default Windows file either by using the cursor keys or by pointing at the file with your system mouse and pressing the select button. To invoke the program, simply press the ENTER key on your keyboard, or press the mouse select button twice, as illustrated here:

```
Keyboard Selection Of Executable Program

Select the file desired via the cursor arrow keys.
Press the Enter key to execute the program.




Mouse Selection Of Executable Program

Select the file desired via the select button on
the mouse.  Double clicking the select button
executes the program.
```

In this case, Windows will respond with

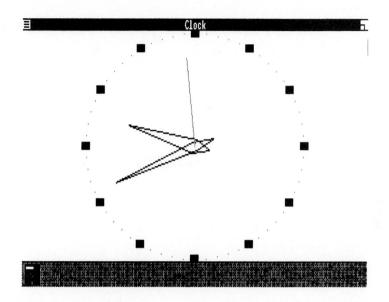

Note the MS-DOS Executive icon in the lower-left corner of the screen. It is possible to expand the clock display to the full size of the screen (covering up the icon section) by selecting the Zoom option from the system menu. Remember that the system menu is invoked by pressing ALT-S, or by selecting the menu with your mouse. If you expand the clock, Windows will display

In this case the Zoom option works as a toggle. Pressing it again will redisplay the icon area. Later in this chapter, you will gain greater control over the size of windows when you display several windows simultaneously. Save the CLOCK program as an icon and return to the MS-DOS Executive.

CALCULATOR

From the MS-DOS Executive, invoke the program CALC.EXE in the same manner as you invoked CLOCK.EXE. Windows will display

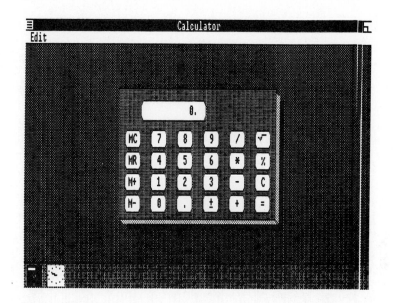

This is your desktop calculator. The calculator accepts the data entered from either the numbers along the top row of your

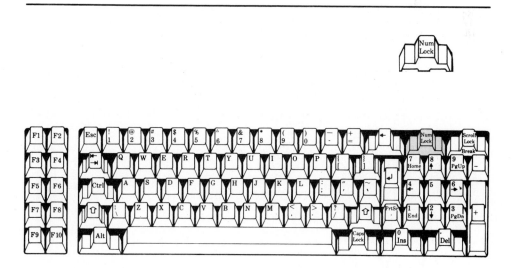

Figure 18-2. Location of NUMLOCK key on keyboard

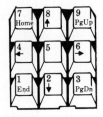

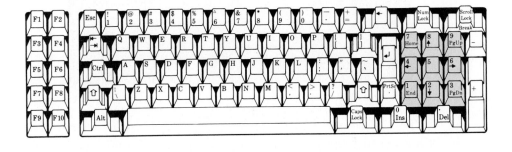

Figure 18-2.   Location of numeric keypad on keyboard

keyboard or from the numeric keypad. To use the numeric keypad, press the NUMLOCK key on your keyboard (see Figure 18-1). To add the numbers 45.66 and 3.77, for example, simply enter the number 45.66 and press the plus (+) key on the numeric keypad (see Figure 18-2). Next, enter the number 3.77 and press the equal (=) sign on the top row of your keyboard. The Windows calculator should now display

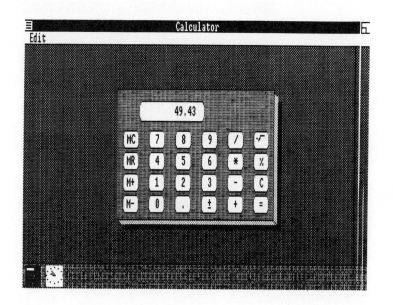

The calculator works the same way for subtraction, multiplication, and division. The calculator also provides a square root key. Before you can fully utilize the Windows calculator, however, you should know that Windows associates the following keyboard entries with the calculator:

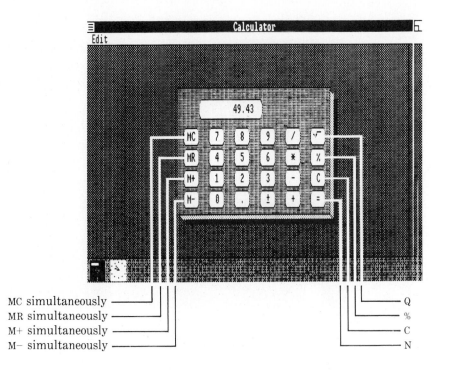

MC simultaneously ——————— Q
MR simultaneously ——————— %
M+ simultaneously ——————— C
M– simultaneously ——————— N

One of the most useful features of the calculator is to display the hexadecimal equivalent of a decimal value, as shown here:

```
Displaying Hexadecimal Equivalents

Enter the decimal value via the numeric keys.  Press
the H key and CALC will display the hexadecimal equivalent.
```

For example, enter the value 255 as follows:

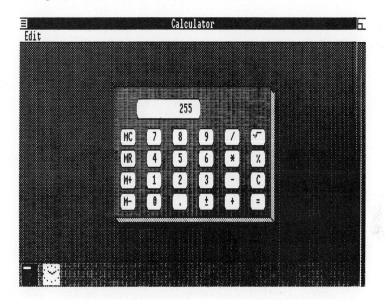

Next, press the H key. CALC will display the hexadecimal equivalent of the value 255, as follows:

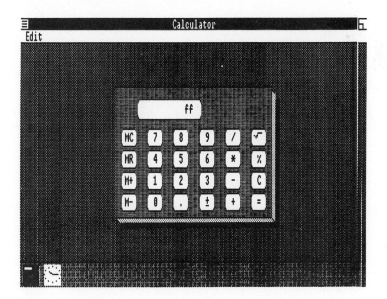

Later in this chapter you will see how to integrate calculations with other Windows applications via the Windows clipboard.

For now, save the calculator as an icon as shown here:

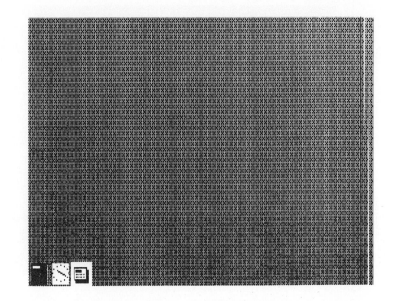

CALENDAR

The CALENDAR program provides you with a complete appointment calendar on your computer. With this program you can look up specific dates from January 1980 into the twenty-first century. In addition, CALENDAR allows you to select appointments or track your daily routine for each of these dates.

From the MS-DOS Executive, invoke CALENDAR.EXE.

Windows will display

CALENDAR would list today's appointments here. Examine the menu bar provided with CALENDAR. The first menu that you will select is File, which provides the following capabilities:

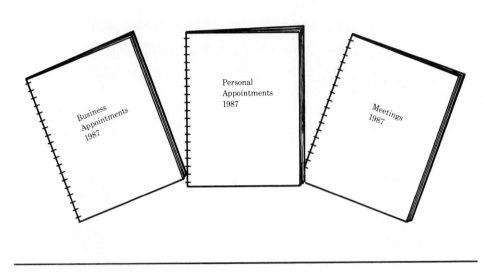

Figure 18-3.   Sample appointment books

The first File option, New, allows you to create a new calendar file. As you will see, the calendar allows you to specify several calendar files.

Visualize these files simply as different appointment books (see Figure 18-3). For example, if several people were sharing the same computer, each would want individual appointment calendars. Likewise, you might want separate appointment calendars for work and school. In such instances, each time you enter CALENDAR, you must specify which file to use.

The second File option, Open, allows you to specify which

DOS: The Complete Reference

appointment file that CALENDAR is to use. When you invoke Open, the screen displays the following:

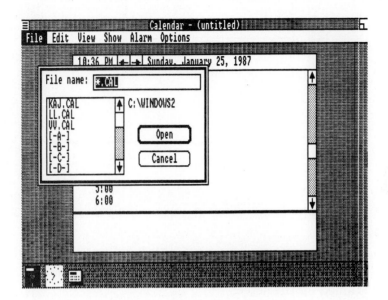

If calendar files exist, CALENDAR will display their names. To select a file, use your mouse or cursor keys, or simply type the name of the file desired. Each time you modify your appointment calendar, you must save the changes back to disk. You can change appointment calendars by adding, deleting, or modifying appointments.

The Save and Save As options of the File menu save to an appointment file the changes made to a calendar. When you invoke Save or Save As, the screen will display the following dialog box:

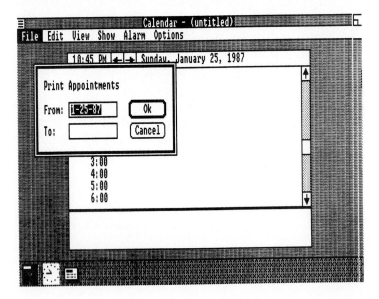

Simply enter the name of the file you want the calendar saved to and press ENTER. Or, you may simply press ENTER to save the file named on the screen.

The CALENDAR Print option is a powerful command. When you invoke Print, the following dialog box will be displayed:

This dialog box allows you to specify the range of dates for which you want to print appointments. The Print option creates a file containing the appointments in the specified range and sends the file to the Windows spooler. If you do not want to print any files, simply select the Cancel option or press the ESC key.

The Remove option works much like Print. When you invoke Remove, the command displays the following command box:

Enter the starting date from which to remove the appointments. Next, press the TAB key or point your mouse to the ending date box. Enter the date at which you want the appointment deletion to end and press ENTER. All of the appointments in the specified range will be deleted. If you don't want to delete any appointments, simply press the ESC key, or point to the Cancel option and press the select button on your mouse.

The second menu option, Edit, allows you to reschedule

appointments. When you invoke Edit, it displays the following menu:

```
┌─────────────────────────────────────────────────────────────┐
│ ☰              Calendar - (untitled)                      ┌─┐│
│ File Edit View Show Alarm Options                            │
│     ┌─────────┐                                              │
│     │ Cut  Del│                                              │
│     │ Copy  F2│  PM ←→  Sunday, January 25, 1987             │
│     │ Paste Ins│ 8:00 AM |                                 ▲ │
│     └─────────┘  9:00                                        │
│                 10:00                                        │
│                 11:00                                        │
│                 12:00 PM                                     │
│                  1:00                                        │
│                  2:00                                        │
│                  3:00                                        │
│                  4:00                                     ▒  │
│                  5:00                                        │
│                  6:00                                     ▼  │
│                                                             │
│                                                             │
│                                                             │
│  ┌─┐                                                        │
│  │▓│ ⊙ ▦                                                    │
└─────────────────────────────────────────────────────────────┘
```

Note that menu options that are not currently available are shown in light characters on the screen.

To demonstrate the use of each Edit option, enter the following appointment at 8:00 A.M.

```
┌─────────────────────────────────────────────────────────────┐
│ ☰              Calendar - (untitled)                      ┌─┐│
│ File Edit View Show Alarm Options                            │
│     ┌──────────────────────────────────────────────────┐    │
│     │ 10:59 PM ←→  Sunday, January 25, 1987             │    │
│     │  8:00 AM Call DOS User's Group |                ▲ │    │
│     │  9:00                                            │    │
│     │ 10:00                                            │    │
│     │ 11:00                                            │    │
│     │ 12:00 PM                                         │    │
│     │  1:00                                            │    │
│     │  2:00                                            │    │
│     │  3:00                                         ▒  │    │
│     │  4:00                                            │    │
│     │  5:00                                            │    │
│     │  6:00                                         ▼  │    │
│     └──────────────────────────────────────────────────┘    │
│                                                             │
│  ┌─┐                                                        │
│  │▓│ ⊙ ▦                                                    │
└─────────────────────────────────────────────────────────────┘
```

If you must reschedule the appointment for noon, simply move the cursor to the start of the 8:00 appointment and use either the mouse or keyboard as follows:

```
Keyboard Selection Of Paint Tools

Use the tab key to move right through the tools
or the shift and tab keys to move left.


Mouse Selection Of Paint Tools

Point at the paint tool desired and press the
mouse select button.
```

Next, select the Edit menu. Because you have selected an appointment to be moved, fewer options are shown in light characters. In this case, select the Cut option. The appointment should disappear from the appointment calendar. Next, move the appointment cursor to noon. Again select the Edit menu and choose the Paste option. The appointment is moved to the desired location, and the screen will contain the following:

```
≡        Calendar - (untitled)              ⌐|
File  Edit  View  Show  Alarm  Options

      11:04 PM ←|→ Sunday, January 25, 1987
          8:00 AM                              ▲
          9:00
         10:00
         11:00
         12:00 PM Call DOS User's Group
          1:00
          2:00
          3:00
          4:00
          5:00
          6:00                                 ▼
```

The same procedure can be used to move appointments from one day to the next, to delete appointments, and with the Copy option, to duplicate appointments. This process is called *cutting and pasting*. Windows applications can "cut" out a portion of the text from one location and either omit it or "paste" it in a new location.

The CALENDAR View menu allows you to examine either a day or a month calendar. When you invoke View, the screen will display the following:

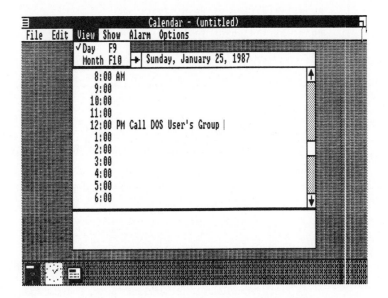

The F9 and F10 included in the menu tell you that CALENDAR predefines the function keys F9 and F10 to perform the options displayed. Press the F10 key; CALENDAR will display the following:

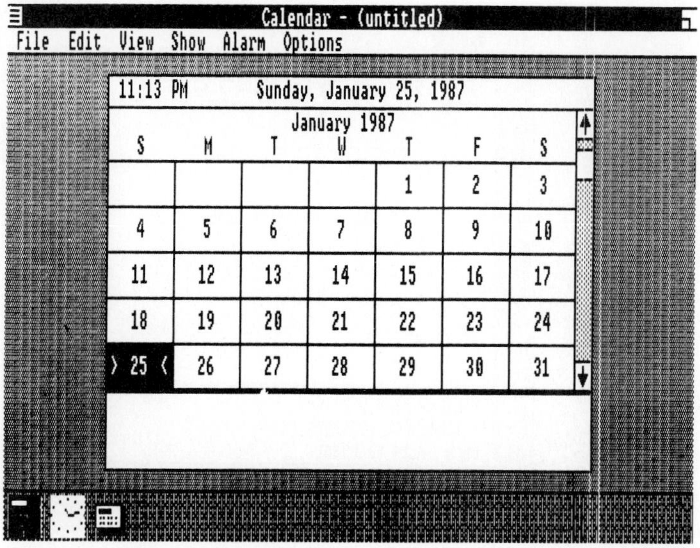

Experiment with the cursor keys (and the PG UP and PG DN keys) along with the mouse to toggle the dates displayed. Select the month to display. Note the box beneath the calendar. CALENDAR allows you to place a three-line note at the bottom of the calendar, as shown here:

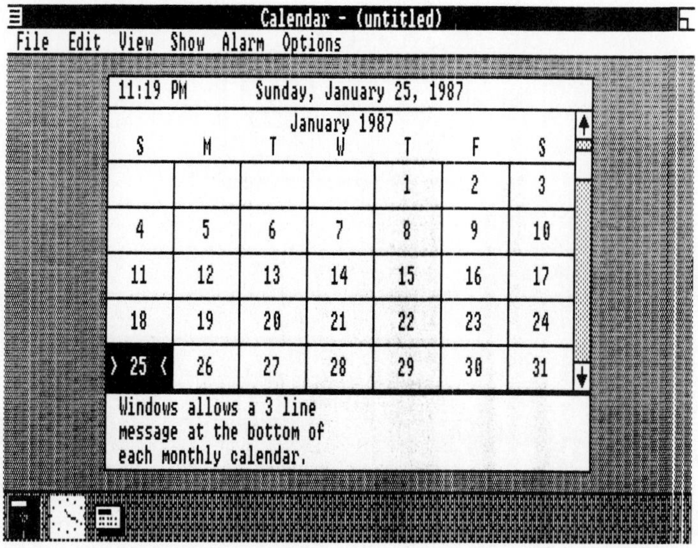

The CALENDAR Show menu provides the following capabilities:

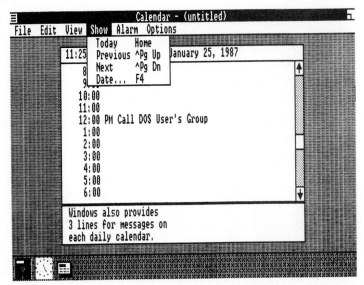

Note the predefined keys for each option. Again, experiment with each of the keys to note their effects on the date displayed. If you select the Date option, CALENDAR will display the following dialog box:

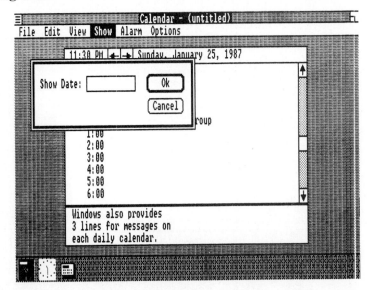

Enter the date you want to display appointments for and press ENTER.

DOS: The Complete Reference

One of the best features of the Windows appointment calendar is that it allows you to set alarms for important appointments. The Alarm menu provides the following capabilities:

```
 ≡           Calendar - (untitled)                    □
 File  Edit  View  Show  Alarm  Options
                         Set        F5
        11:35 PM  ←      Controls...    y 25, 1987
            8:00 AM                               ↑
            9:00
           10:00
           11:00
           12:00 PM Call DOS User's Group
            1:00
            2:00
            3:00
            4:00
            5:00
            6:00                                  ↓
        ┌─────────────────────────────────────┐
        │ Windows also provides               │
        │ 3 lines for messages on             │
        │ each daily calendar.                │
        └─────────────────────────────────────┘
 ■  ⟨⟩  ▤
```

The Set option sets an alarm for the appointment currently referenced by the appointment cursor. For example, place the cursor at the 12:00 P.M. appointment and select the Set option from the Alarm menu. CALENDAR will display a bell next to the time to notify you that an alarm has been set.

```
 ≡           Calendar - (untitled)                    □
 File  Edit  View  Show  Alarm  Options

        11:39 PM  ← →  Sunday, January 25, 1987
            8:00 AM                               ↑
            9:00
           10:00
           11:00
        ♫ 12:00 PM Call DOS User's Group
            1:00
            2:00
            3:00
            4:00
            5:00
            6:00                                  ↓
        ┌─────────────────────────────────────┐
        │ Windows also provides               │
        │ 3 lines for messages on             │
        │ each daily calendar.                │
        └─────────────────────────────────────┘
 ■  ⟨⟩  ▤
```

Later, when the time for the appointment arrives, the computer beeps and displays the following dialog box:

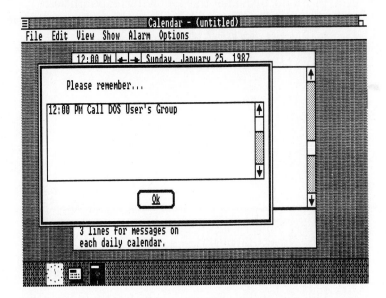

If at the designated time the CALENDAR package is active only as an icon, the computer will beep and the icon will flash. The calendar program must, however, reside in memory either as an icon or as an executable image.

The Controls option of the Alarm menu allows you to specify a number of minutes (0-10) before the appointment; the computer will then beep at that time, notifying you of the appointment. In addition, this option allows you to specify whether you want the computer to beep each time an alarm occurs. If you disable beeping, the dialog box is still displayed as long as CALENDAR is active, or the icon will flash. Selecting the Controls option results in the following dialog box:

```
≡                    Calendar - (untitled)                    ⌐
 File  Edit  View  Show  Alarm  Options
        12:04 PM ←|→ Sunday, January 25, 1987                ▲

    ┌──────────────────────────────────────┐
    │ Alarm Controls                       │
    │                                      │
    │ Early Ring (0 - 10): [0]  ┌─────────┐│
    │                           │   Ok    ││
    │ ⊠ Sound                   └─────────┘│
    │                           ┌─────────┐│  p
    │                           │ Cancel  ││
    └──────────────────────────────────────┘
            3:00
            4:00
            5:00
            6:00                                             ▼

        Windows also provides
        3 lines for messages on
        each daily calendar.
```

Simply enter the number of minutes before the appointment, or press the TAB key to enable or disable sound. Once the Sound option is selected, pressing the SPACEBAR will toggle sound on and off.

The last option, the Options menu, provides the following:

```
≡                    Calendar - (untitled)                    ⌐
 File  Edit  View  Show  Alarm  Options
                                   Mark          F6
        12:09 PM ←|→ Su   Special Time...  F7              ▲
                         Day Settings...
           8:00 AM
           9:00
          10:00
          11:00
        ♫ 12:00 PM Call DOS User's Group
           1:00
           2:00
           3:00
           4:00
           5:00
           6:00                                             ▼

        Windows also provides
        3 lines for messages on
        each daily calendar.
```

The Mark option places a box around an important date on the monthly appointment calendar. For example, if you select a mark for the current date, CALENDAR will display the monthly calendar as follows:

```
 ≡                    Calendar - (untitled)                      ⌐
  File  Edit  View  Show  Alarm  Options

      12:14 PM        Sunday, January 25, 1987
                          January 1987                    ▲
         S      M      T      W      T      F      S
                                     1      2      3
         4      5      6      7      8      9     10
        11     12     13     14     15     16     17
        18     19     20     21     22     23     24
      › 25 ‹   26     27     28     29     30     31      ▼
      Windows also provides
      3 lines for messages on
      each daily calendar.
```

The Mark option works as a toggle. The first time that you select the option, the box is displayed. Selecting the option a second time removes the box.

   The Special Time option allows you to enter a time that is not included on the daily appointment calendar. For example, if you are to call New York at 7:05, you can select the Special Time option and enter the following:

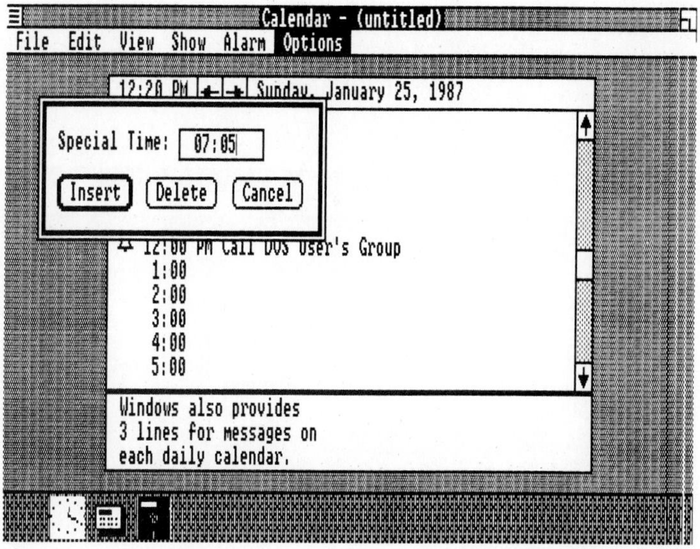

The daily appointment calendar will now display

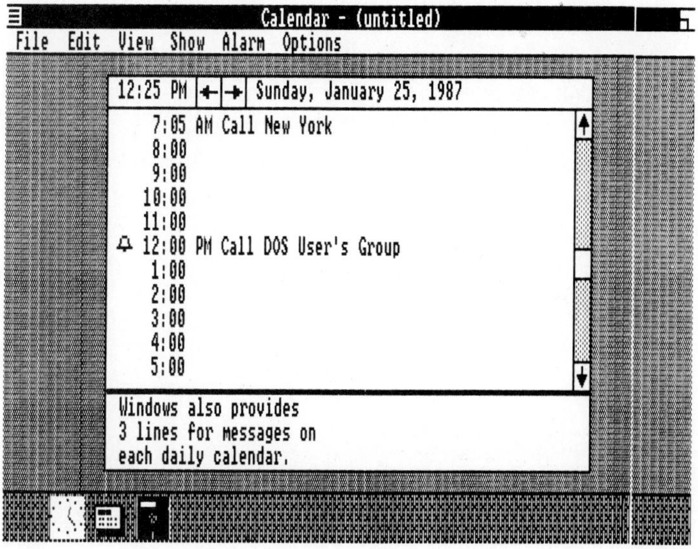

The Day Settings option allows you to configure the appointments calendar to meet your specific requirements. When you invoke Day Settings, it will display the following dialog box:

```
≡══════════════ Calendar - (untitled) ═══════════ ⬆
 File  Edit  View  Show  Alarm  Options

      ┌ 12:29 PM ┤◄│►├ Sunday, January 25, 1987      ▲
  ┌─────────────────────────────────────┐
  │ Day Settings                        │
  │                                     │
  │ Interval     ○ 15  ○ 30  ⦿ 60       │
  │                          ┌────────┐ │
  │ Hour Format ⦿ 12  ○ 24   │   Ok   │ │
  │                          └────────┘ │
  │ Starting Time: │ 8:00 AM │ ┌────────┐│
  │                          │ Cancel ││
  └─────────────────────────────────────┘
        3:00                              ▓
        4:00                              ▓
        5:00                              ▼
  ┌──────────────────────────────────────┐
  │ Windows also provides                │
  │ 3 lines for messages on              │
  │ each daily calendar.                 │
  └──────────────────────────────────────┘
```

Interval is the number of minutes that you want to appear between appointments on the calendar. By default, CALENDAR uses 60 minutes. If, however, you require an interval of 15 or 30 minutes, you can do so here. After you select 15-minute intervals, for example, your daily appointment calendar will appear as follows:

```
≣                    Calendar - (untitled)            ‖‖ 🬭
 File  Edit  View  Show  Alarm  Options
        ┌─────────┬───┬─────────────────────────┐
        │12:34 PM │← │→│ Sunday, January 25, 1987│
        ├─────────┴───┴─────────────────────────┬─┤
        │     8:00 AM                            │▲│
        │     8:15                               │ │
        │     8:30                               │ │
        │     8:45                               │ │
        │     9:00                               │ │
        │     9:15                               │ │
        │     9:30                               │ │
        │     9:45                               │ │
        │    10:00                               │ │
        │    10:15                               │ │
        │    10:30                               │▼│
        ├───────────────────────────────────────┴─┤
        │Windows also provides                     │
        │3 lines for messages on                   │
        │each daily calendar.                      │
        └──────────────────────────────────────────┘
```

If you select the 24-hour format, the calendar will use International time (0:00-23:00 hours). The Starting Time specifies the first time that you want to appear on your daily calendar. By default, CALENDAR uses 8:00 A.M.

CARDFILE

The Windows CARDFILE program allows you to create an on-line tracking system of 3×5 index cards. Simply record your information on the card, and Windows will automatically sort the cards for you.

From the MS-DOS Executive, run CARDFILE.EXE. Windows will display a 3 × 5 index card as follows:

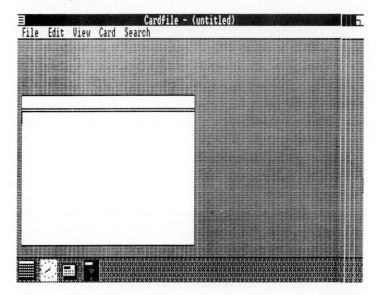

CARDFILE works much like the Windows CALENDAR program. For example, the File menu provides the following options:

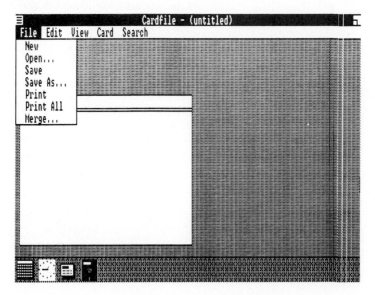

CARDFILE allows you to track 3 × 5 index cards for various subjects by means of an index card file. For example, you may have a series of index cards for DOS commands in the file DOS.CRD and a set of cards containing BASIC commands in the file BASIC.CRD.

The New option allows you to create a new deck of cards for recording information. Once a card file exists, you access it with the Open option. CARDFILE will display the following dialog box:

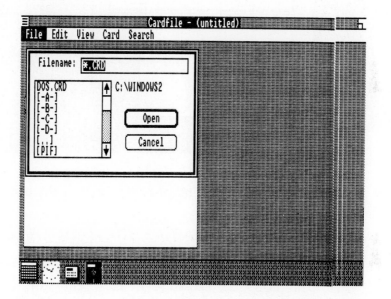

Simply enter the name of the card file you desire and press ENTER. After you modify entries in a card file, you must use the Save and Save As commands to record the updated information in a file. Each displays the following dialog box:

```
┌───────────────────────Cardfile - (untitled)────────────────────┐
│ File  Edit  View  Card  Search                                  │
│  ┌──────────────────────────────────────────┐                   │
│  │  Save file as:        C:\WINDOWS2         │                   │
│  │  ┌──────────────────────┐  ┌───────┐      │                   │
│  │  │                      │  │ Save  │      │                   │
│  │  └──────────────────────┘  └───────┘      │                   │
│  │                            ┌────────┐     │                   │
│  │                            │ Cancel │     │                   │
│  │                            └────────┘     │                   │
│  └──────────────────────────────────────────┘                   │
└─────────────────────────────────────────────────────────────────┘
```

The Print option prints the first card in the deck in the following format:

```
DOS CLS Command
─────────────────────────────────────────────────
The DOS CLS Command erases the contents
of the screen display and places the
cursor at the home position.

CLS does not effect video attributes.


A> CLS
```

The Print All option prints all of the cards in the deck.

The Merge option of the File menu allows you to include cards from another card file in your current deck. CARDFILE will automatically sort the new cards. When you invoke Merge, it will display the following dialog box:

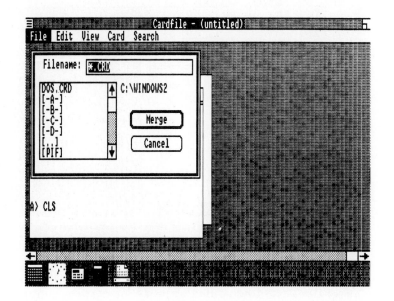

Simply enter the name of the file from which you want to include the cards.

The Edit menu allows you to easily delete, move, copy, or change text within the 3 × 5 card deck. When you invoke Edit, it will display the following:

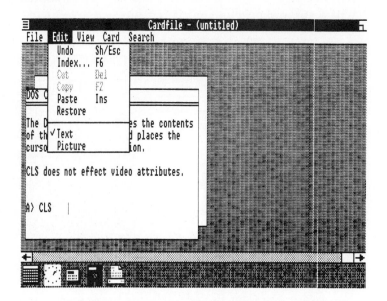

Note the predefined function keys for certain commands.

The first Edit command, Undo, allows you to reverse your latest change to a card. For example, if you use Cut to delete a section of text, Undo allows you to put it back.

The Index option is probably the most-used Edit option. Index allows you to enter the index label in the top line on the current card. CARDFILE does not allow you to place the cursor on the index line of a 3 × 5 card; you must select Index to place it there.

Once selected, Index will display the following dialog box:

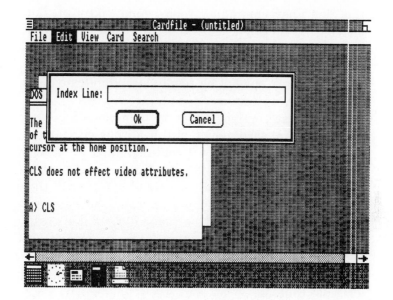

Simply enter the index label you desire and press ENTER.

The Cut option is similar to the Cut option used in CALEN-DAR. To move text, simply select the text as follows:

Keyboard Selection Of Text

Place the cursor at the first character to select.
Use the shift and cursor arrow key to select the
characters desired.

Mouse Selection Of Text

Place the cursor at the first character to select.
Use the mouse select button to select the characters
desired.

Next, invoke the Edit menu and select the Cut option. The selected text will disappear from the screen.

The Copy command works much like Cut, but rather than moving text, Copy creates a second copy of it. Again, select the text in the same manner as in the previous example. Place the cursor at the desired target location and invoke the Edit menu. Selecting the Copy option results in a duplicate of the text placed at the desired location.

The Paste option works with information contained in the Windows clipboard, which will be discussed in detail later in this chapter. For now, however, understand that Paste works in conjunction with Cut. After you use Cut to select the text to be moved from one location to another, place the cursor at the desired location. Invoke the Edit menu and select the Paste option; the text will be moved as desired. As you will find, it is possible to use Cut and Paste to move information from one card to another.

The Restore option works with the top card on the deck. If you have modified the top card, Restore allows you to restore its original contents.

The last Edit options, Text and Picture, specify the type of the contents on the clipboard. As you will see later in this chapter, it is possible to cut pictures from one application and place them in a second. Text specifies that the contents of the clipboard are text characters. If the clipboard instead contains art, use the Picture option before you issue a Paste command.

The View menu specifies how the cards are to be displayed on the screen. When you invoke View, the screen displays

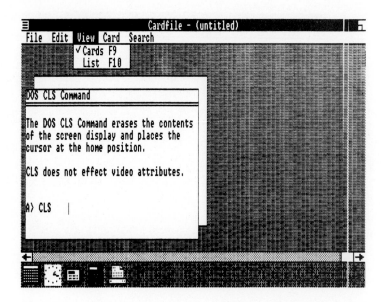

The Cards option will display the index cards in the following manner:

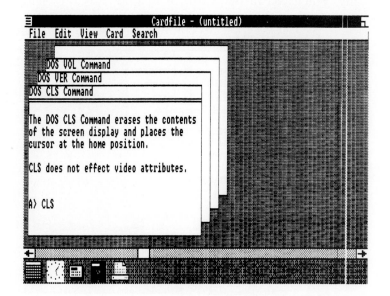

The List option displays the index section of each card as follows:

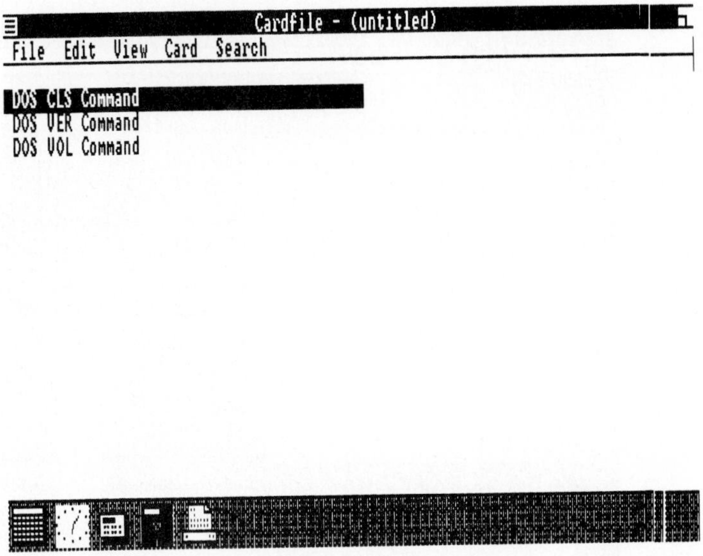

The CARDFILE Card menu allows you to add, delete, or duplicate cards, and it can use the first telephone number found on a card to dial a Hayes or Hayes-compatible modem automatically. When you invoke Card, it displays the following:

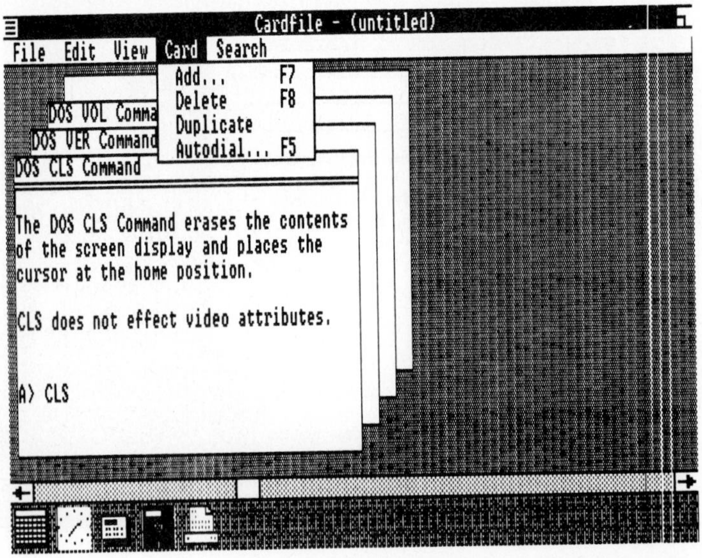

DOS: The Complete Reference

The Add option creates a new card and places it at the front of the deck, as follows:

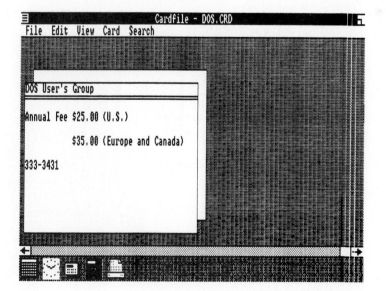

The Delete option deletes the card on the top of the deck. Duplicate creates an identical copy of the card at the top of the deck. The Autodial option searches the contents of the top card on the deck for a number greater than six characters and automatically dials it. For example, in the case of

Autodial will dial the number 333-3431.

The last menu, Search, allows you to perform quick lookups of cards in the deck. When you invoke it, the Search menu will display the following:

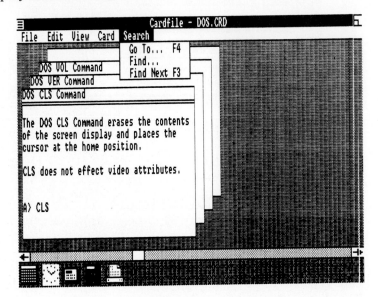

The Go To option will find the card containing the index you enter in the following dialog box:

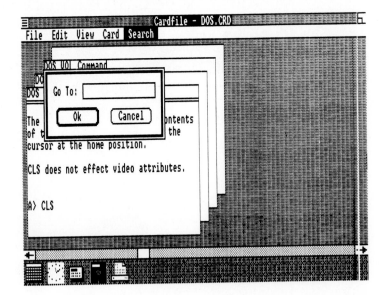

Simply enter as much of the index as you remember and press ENTER. CARDFILE will place the card with the index that matches your text on the top of the deck.

The Find option displays the following dialog box:

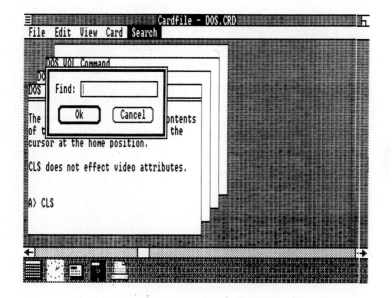

Enter the string for which you want CARDFILE to search the deck of cards and press ENTER. When CARDFILE encounters the first card having the string, it will place it at the top of the deck. The Find Next command continues the search for the previously defined string.

One of the best uses of CARDFILE is to create a list of DOS commands and their specific functions. Then, when you later need to access a command, simply bring up its card file for a quick reference, as shown here:

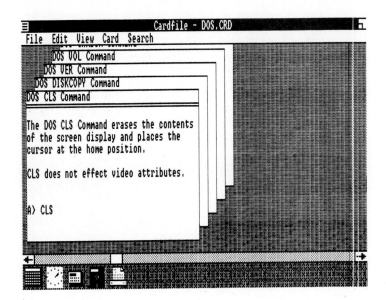

NOTEPAD

Windows allows you to create memos and small documents with NOTEPAD.EXE. From the MS-DOS Executive, run NOTEPAD.

EXE; Windows will respond with the following:

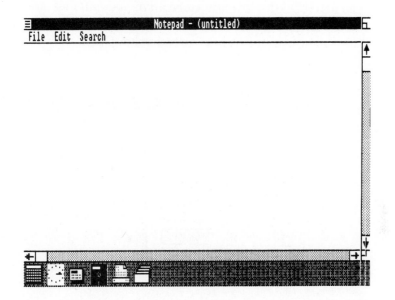

The screen represents a three-page notepad. The menu options provided with NOTEPAD are very similar to the menus examined thus far. Select the File menu, and NOTEPAD will display the following:

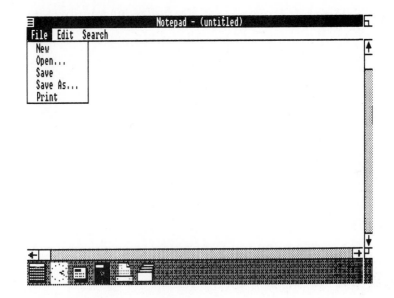

The New option gives you a new pad on which to write notes. NOTEPAD allows you to store all of your memos in separate files.

Once you have created a memo, you can later access it with the Open option. When you invoke Open, it will display the following:

Select the file name that you desire, or simply enter it and press ENTER.

The Save and Save As options allow you to save changes that you have made to memos. Each option displays the following dialog box:

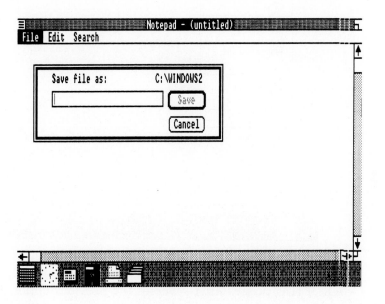

NOTEPAD uses the extension TXT by default. Once you have completed your memo, the Print option sends it to the Windows spooler.

Invoking the Edit menu will display the following:

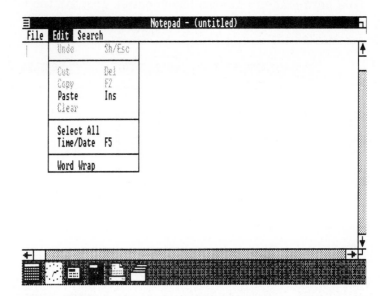

The Undo option is like the Undo option in the Windows CARDFILE program: it reverses the previous option. For example, if you enter a line of text while editing a memo, Undo will allow you to delete the line in one simple step.

The Cut, Copy, and Paste options all work as in the Windows CARDFILE program. Cut selects a section of text to be moved or deleted, erasing it from the screen. Copy selects a section of text for duplication. Paste restores a section of text that has been cut or copied to a new location.

The Clear option simply deletes a section of text. The Select All option is used when you want to copy the entire memo to the clipboard (discussed in detail later in this chapter).

The Time/Date option inserts the current system date and time at the current cursor position. It is good practice to time- and date-stamp all of your memos.

Last, the Word Wrap option directs NOTEPAD to automatically wrap text at the right column so that you do not need to press ENTER at the end of each line. Word Wrap works as a toggle. The first time that you select it, NOTEPAD will begin wrapping sentences; selecting the option a second time turns off Word Wrap.

Select the NOTEPAD Search menu. NOTEPAD will display the following:

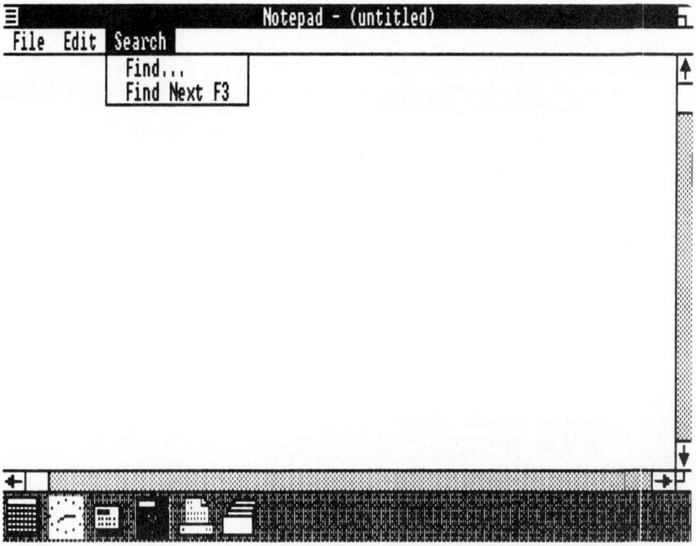

Selecting the first option, Find, results in the following dialog box, which prompts you for a text string to search for within the memo.

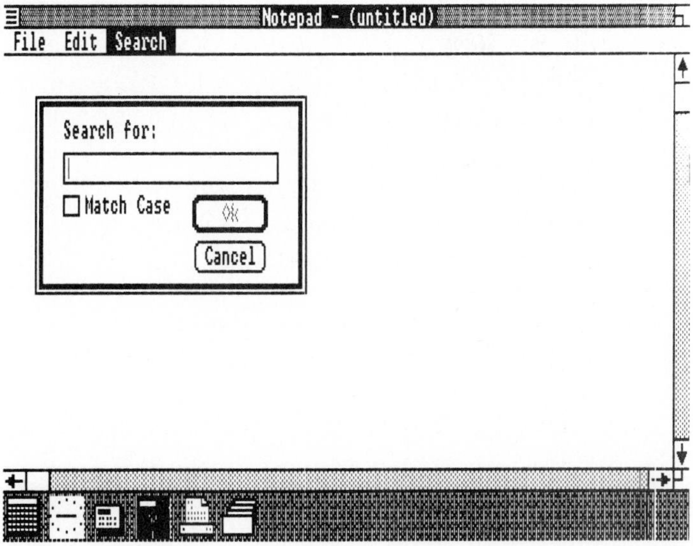

Simply enter the words that you are looking for and press ENTER. The Find Next option continues the search for keywords.

Here are two example memos entered on the Notepad. The first is a "To Do" list:

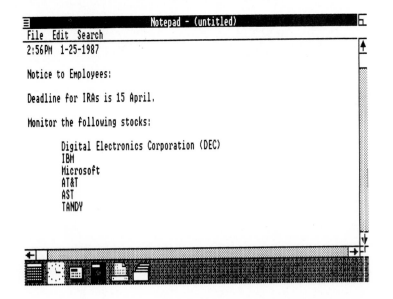

The second is an interoffice memo:

Windows offers more than its desktop features; its terminal-emulation program allows you to connect and share information with remote computers over telephone lines. If you don't have a modem connected to your system, you may want to skip this section. If you do, you should find the Windows communication package very simple to use. From the MS-DOS Executive invoke the program TERMINAL.EXE. Windows will display the following:

The screen format should look familiar by now. First select the File menu. TERMINAL will display the following:

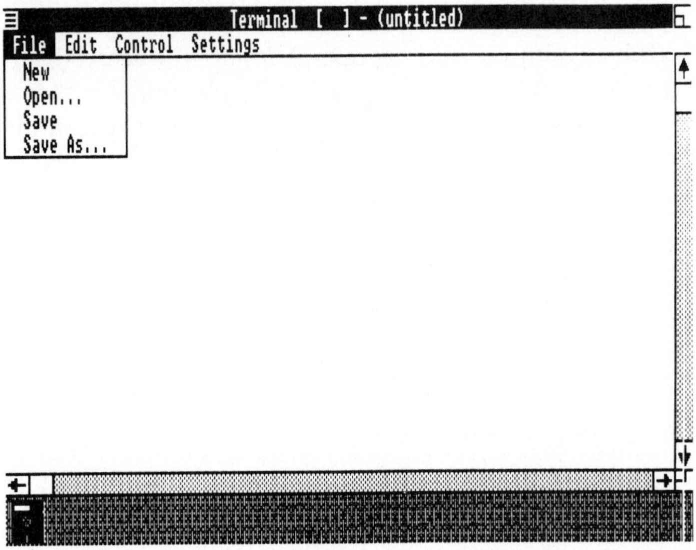

One of the most useful features of the Windows communication package is that once you configure your system for a particular bulletin board or on-line service, you can save the configuration in a file. The New option allows you to create a new configuration file. The Open option opens an existing configuration file and loads its communications options. When you invoke TERMINAL, it will display the following:

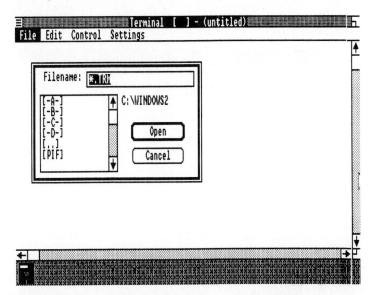

Select the file that you desire, or simply enter it and press ENTER. Once you have created or modified a configuration file, the TERMINAL Save and Save As options allow you to save the changes to a file. Both options will display the following dialog box:

Simply type in the name of the file to which you want the configuration saved.

Select the TERMINAL Edit menu. TERMINAL will display the following:

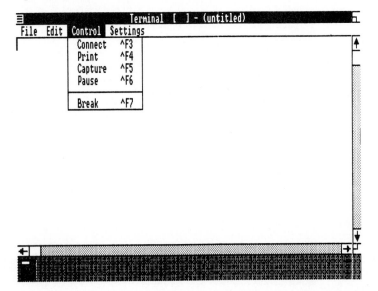

These options allow you to exchange information between Windows applications via the clipboard. The TERMINAL Control menu provides the following capabilities:

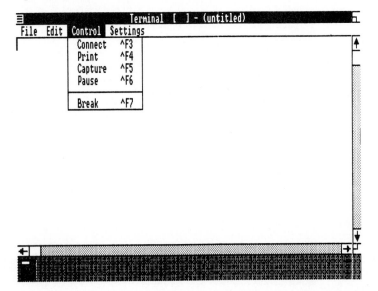

The Connect option uses all of the configuration options specified in the file and dials the number that you have specified for the desired service. To terminate the session at a later time, simply select Connect again. Connect works as a toggle. The first time you select Connect it establishes a connection; the second time terminates the connection.

The Print option causes all the information received (and displayed on the screen) to be echoed to the printer. The option uses the Windows spooler, so you are not constrained by a slow printer. This option also works as a toggle.

The TERMINAL Capture option allows you to capture into a file you can later edit all of the information received. When you invoke Capture, it displays the following dialog box:

Enter the name of the file in which you want to record the data, or press ENTER to use the default name.

The first time you select the Pause option, the screen stops scrolling; the second time, scrolling resumes.

The last option, Break, sends a break signal to the host computer, requesting that it terminate the current application. Again, note the predefined keys for each option.

Select the TERMINAL Settings menu. TERMINAL will display the following:

```
≡            Terminal [ ] - TEMP.TRM              ⌐
 File  Edit  Control  Settings
                      Terminal...              ▲
                      Communication...
                      Phone...
                                               ▼
 ←                                          → 
```

These options allow you to configure your system to meet the tele-communications requirements of the service to which you are connected. Select the Terminal option, and the TERMINAL program will display the following:

```
≡▓▓▓▓▓▓▓▓▓▓▓▓▓▓▓Terminal [  ] - TEMP.TRM▓▓▓▓▓▓▓▓▓▓▓▓▓⌐
 File  Edit  Control  Settings                        ▲

   ┌────────────────────────────────────────────┐
   │ Terminal Settings                          │
   │                                            │
   │ Terminal Type  ⊙ VT52      ○ ANSI          │
   │ □ New Line   □ Local Echo  ⊠ Auto Wraparound│
   │                                            │
   │ Text size      ⊙ Large     ○ Small         │
   │ Lines in Buffer:  [50]  Translation:┌─────┐▲│
   │                                     │None  ││
   │                                     │United Kingdom│
   │                                     │Denmark/Norway▼│
   │    ┌──────────┐      ┌──────────┐          │
   │    │    Ok    │      │  Cancel  │          │
   │    └──────────┘      └──────────┘          │
   └────────────────────────────────────────────┘
                                                  ▼
 ←▓░░░░░░░░░░░░░░░░░░░░░░░░░░░░░░░░░░░░░░░░░░░░░░░→
```

Most services will specify the terminal types that they support. VT52 and ANSI have been the standards for several years. Refer to the service documentation for more details.

The New Line option causes your computer to replace each linefeed sequence with a carriage return-linefeed. Some computers do not return the cursor to the beginning of the line when a new line begins, so select this option to compensate for this.

The Local Echo option is used when the service that you are communicating with does not echo the keys that you type as you type them. In this case, your terminal must do the echoing for you.

The Auto Wraparound option directs TERMINAL to automatically wrap each line at column 80.

Many advanced users will buffer in memory the information received and later scroll through it. The Lines in Buffer option allows you to specify the size of the buffer. Simply type in a value of up to 999 lines and press ENTER.

The Text size option allows you to reduce the size of the text on the screen to allow more information to be displayed.

The Communication option displays the following:

```
▤▤▤▤▤▤▤▤▤▤▤▤▤Terminal [ ] - TEMP.TRM▤▤▤▤▤▤▤▤▤▤▤▤🔲
 File  Edit  Control  Settings                       ▲
┌─────────────────────────────────────────────┐     ▐
│ Communications Settings                       │
│ Baud Rate:  ▐1200▌                            │
│ Word Length ○4  ○5  ○6  ◉7  ○8                │
│ Parity      ◉ Even    ○ Odd      ○ None       │
│ Stop Bits   ◉1        ○1.5       ○2           │
│ Handshake   ◉ XOn/XOff ○ Hardware ○ None      │
│ Connection  ◉ Modem   ○ Computer             │
│ Port        ◉ COM1:   ○ COM2:                │
│           ┌────────┐   ┌────────┐             │
│           │   Ok   │   │ Cancel │             │
│           └────────┘   └────────┘             │
└─────────────────────────────────────────────┘     ▼
```

Refer to the documentation of your specific service for this section. The only parameter that is independent of the service is Port, which specifies to what communications port your modem is attached, either COM1 or COM2.

The last option, Phone, displays the following:

```
▤▤▤▤▤▤▤▤▤▤▤▤▤Terminal [ ] - TEMP.TRM▤▤▤▤▤▤▤▤▤▤▤▤🔲
 File  Edit  Control  Settings                       ▲
┌────────────────────────────────┐                   ▐
│ Phone Settings                  │
│ Connect to: ┌────────────────┐  │
│             └────────────────┘  │
│ Dial Type    ◉ Tone  ○ Pulse   │
│ Speed        ○ Slow  ◉ Fast     │
│ Wait for Tone (2-15): ┌─┐2      │
│ Wait for Answer (1-256): ┌──┐60 │
│   ┌────────┐   ┌────────┐        │
│   │   Ok   │   │ Cancel │        │
│   └────────┘   └────────┘        │
└────────────────────────────────┘                   ▼
```

Enter the telephone number of the service in the Connect to box. Dial Type refers to your phone type. A pushbutton phone is a tone phone, and a rotary phone is a pulse phone. Speed refers to how fast the number should be dialed. Wait for Tone specifies the number of seconds that TERMINAL will wait for a dial tone. Likewise, Wait for Answer specifies the number of seconds that TERMINAL will let the phone ring.

If you have a modem connected to your system, you should find that the Windows TERMINAL program provides all of the functions you will need.

REVERSI

Windows also provides a board game called REVERSI. From the MS-DOS Executive, run the program REVERSI.EXE. Windows will display the following:

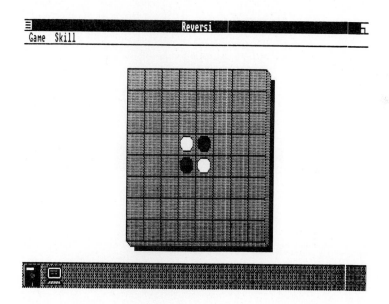

If you have played Othello, you should find REVERSI to be quite challenging.

Windows allows you to exchange information between applications via the Windows clipboard. The clipboard is simply a location where you can store text or graphics that other Windows applications can access. For example, the clipboard can store information from the calculator, the card file, the notepad, the PAINT application, the WRITE application, the terminal application, and the calendar.

Consider the following example. You have just written the following note with NOTEPAD:

```
≡          Notepad - (untitled)          ⌐
File  Edit  Search

CLS Command

The DOS CLS Command clears the
contents of the screen and places
the cursor at the home position.
```

Use the NOTEPAD Edit menu to choose the Select All option. All of the text should now be displayed in reverse video:

Again use the Edit menu to select the Copy option. All of the text in reverse video has now been copied to the Windows clipboard. Next, save NOTEPAD as an icon and invoke the program CLIPBRD.EXE from the MS-DOS Executive. Windows will display the following:

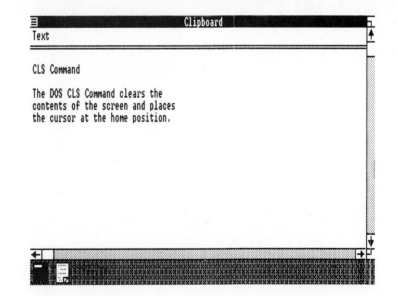

The CLIPBRD program allows you to view the information contained in the Windows clipboard. As you can see, the information that you just selected from NOTEPAD is displayed. When other applications perform Paste operations, the information that they paste is what is contained in the current clipboard. Save the CLIPBRD program as an icon.

From the MS-DOS Executive invoke CARDFILE.EXE. Windows will display the following:

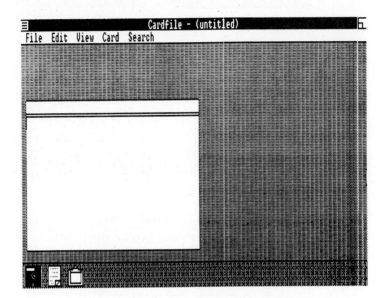

Next, use the Edit menu to select the Paste option. Your card should now contain the following:

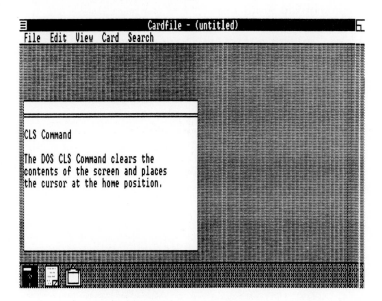

You have just exchanged information between two Windows applications. As you will see, it is possible to exchange information between all of the Windows applications in much the same way.

Running Multiple Applications Simultaneously

In this section you will see how to invoke several programs simultaneously, how to move the programs around the screen, and how the System menu becomes very powerful when multiple applications are running simultaneously.

From the MS-DOS Executive load the CLOCK, CALCULA-TOR, NOTEPAD, and CALENDAR as icons. Your screen should contain the following:

```
┌─────────────────────────────────────────────────────┐
≡              MS-DOS Executive                       ⌐┐
 File  View  Special
─────────────────────────────────────────────────────────
 A ═■ B ═■ C ═■ D ═■  C:DOSDISK \WINDOWS2

 PIF           HELVD.FON      TMSRD.FON
 ABC.TXT       KAJ.CAL        VV.CAL
 CALC.EXE      LL.CAL         WIN.COM
 CALENDAR.EXE  MODERN.FON     WIN.INI
 CARDFILE.EXE  MSDOS.EXE      WIN100.BIN
 CLIPBRD.EXE   NOTEPAD.EXE    WIN100.OVL
 CLOCK.EXE     PAINT.EXE      WINOLDAP.GRB
 CONTROL.EXE   PRACTICE.WRI   WINOLDAP.MOD
 COURA.FON     README.TXT     WRITE.EXE
 COURC.FON     REVERSI.EXE
 COURD.FON     ROMAN.FON
 DOS.CRD       SCRIPT.FON
 DOTHIS.TXT    SPOOLER.EXE
 EPSON.DRV     TERMINAL.EXE
 HELVA.FON     TMSRA.FON
 HELVC.FON     TMSRC.FON
```

Next, select the clock icon. Invoke the System menu for CLOCK and select the Move option. With the mouse or keyboard keys, move the clock icon to the title bar of the MS-DOS Executive, as shown here:

```
┌─────────────────────────────────────────────────────┐
≡              MS-DOS Executive        □             ⌐┐
 File  View  Special
─────────────────────────────────────────────────────────
 A ═■ B ═■ C ═■ D ═■  C:DOSDISK \WINDOWS2

 PIF           HELVD.FON      TMSRD.FON
 ABC.TXT       KAJ.CAL        VV.CAL
 CALC.EXE      LL.CAL         WIN.COM
 CALENDAR.EXE  MODERN.FON     WIN.INI
 CARDFILE.EXE  MSDOS.EXE      WIN100.BIN
 CLIPBRD.EXE   NOTEPAD.EXE    WIN100.OVL
 CLOCK.EXE     PAINT.EXE      WINOLDAP.GRB
 CONTROL.EXE   PRACTICE.WRI   WINOLDAP.MOD
 COURA.FON     README.TXT     WRITE.EXE
 COURC.FON     REVERSI.EXE
 COURD.FON     ROMAN.FON
 DOS.CRD       SCRIPT.FON
 DOTHIS.TXT    SPOOLER.EXE
 EPSON.DRV     TERMINAL.EXE
 HELVA.FON     TMSRA.FON
 HELVC.FON     TMSRC.FON
```

Press the ENTER key or your mouse select button. You should now have two applications on your screen. Select the calculator icon. Move it to the title bar of the analog clock and expand it in the same fashion. Your screen should now contain the following:

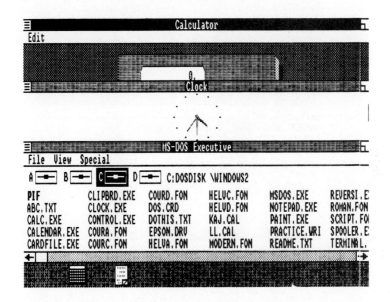

As you will see, by pressing ALT-TAB you move first through the applications windows on the screen and then through the available icons. Use ALT-TAB to select the clock window. When the title bar is displayed in reverse video, the window is the current default. Now select the System menu for CLOCK. Choose the Size option. With either the mouse or the cursor keys, move the small size box beyond the borders of the current clock window as shown here:

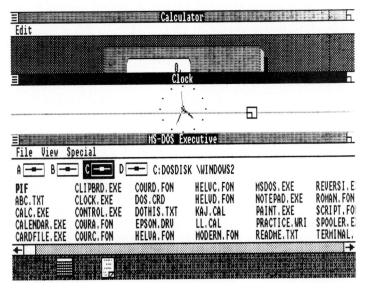

You should now have a moveable frame. Move the frame in both directions.

It is also possible to shrink and expand a window with the size option. In this case, make the clock window smaller, as shown here:

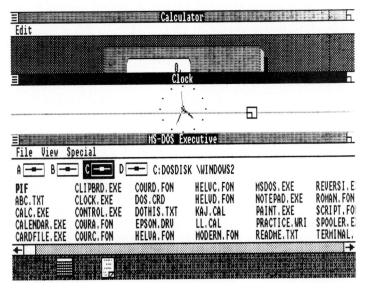

When you press the ENTER key or mouse select button, your screen will contain the following:

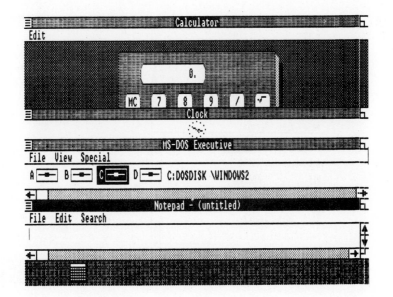

From the MS-DOS Executive load NOTEPAD.EXE as an icon. Move the program to the screen as shown here:

Now move the clock window from the top of the screen. Select the clock window and make it an icon. Next, move the icon to the right-hand border of the NOTEPAD window, as shown here:

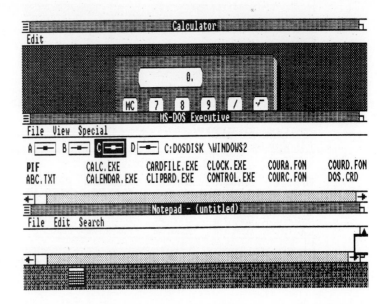

Press ENTER or the mouse select button, and your screen will contain the following:

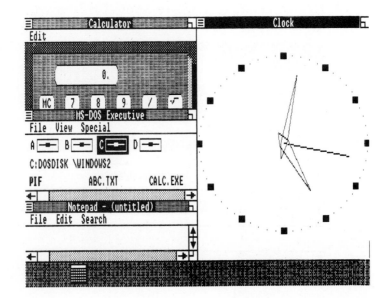

Next, load a second copy of the CLOCK program from the MS-DOS Executive and place it on the screen as follows:

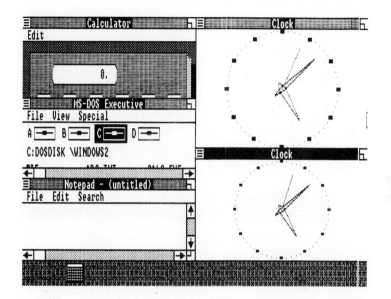

Now you can actually watch your system time-share. The two clocks appear to be running simultaneously. If you were to print a file to the Windows spooler, the file would print in the background, making the computer appear to be performing even more tasks at the same time. As you can see, Windows can utilize CPU time to its fullest capacity.

Microsoft WRITE and PAINT

Provided with Microsoft Windows are two additional applications packages for desktop publishing. The first, WRITE.EXE, is a simple word processor. Invoke WRITE.EXE from the MS-DOS Executive. Windows will display the following:

By this time, you should be able to traverse Windows menus and options on your own. Most of the options are the same as those already discussed, so simply experiment with WRITE. As you will find, WRITE is a convenient word processor that possesses significant capabilities, some of which are shown here:

WRITE HAS SEVERAL

DIFFERENT FONTS.

FONT SIZES CAN CHANGE.

BOLD CHARACTERS ARE SUPPORTED.

ITALICS ARE SUPPORTED.

<u>UNDERLINE IS SUPPORTED.</u>

PAINT allows you to create diagrams to include in other reports and memos. When you invoke PAINT, it will display the following:

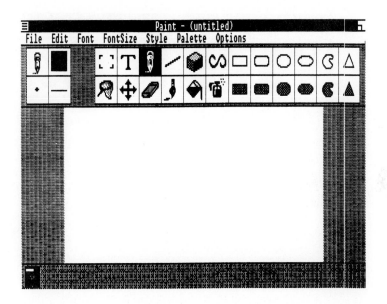

The options in the menu bar are selected as you would in all Windows applications. The 24 small boxes at the top of the screen are your drawing tools. If you are using a mouse, simply point at the desired tool and press the select button. If you are using the keyboard, simply press SHIFT-TAB.

The first printing tool is the pencil. To move the pencil with the mouse, simply move the mouse. If you are using the keyboard, use SHIFT-SPACEBAR. Using the pencil, draw the following box:

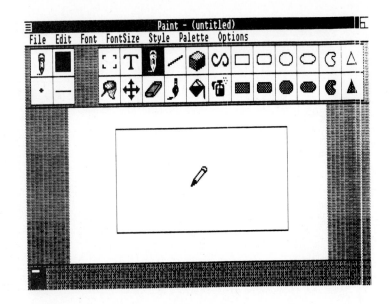

Next, divide the box into smaller boxes as follows:

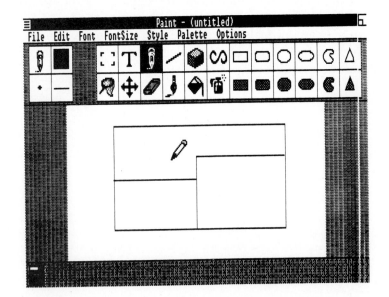

DOS: The Complete Reference

Select the large T from the tools shelf. Use this tool for text. Move the cursor below the box on the left and press the SPACE-BAR. Next, enter the label 1986 Sales as shown here:

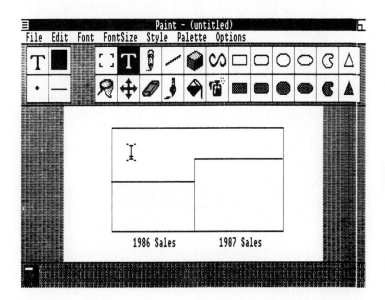

Space over to below the box on the right and enter the label 1987 Sales.

You can now place this picture on the clipboard for use by other applications. To do so, select the tool with the four corners. Frame the drawing as shown here:

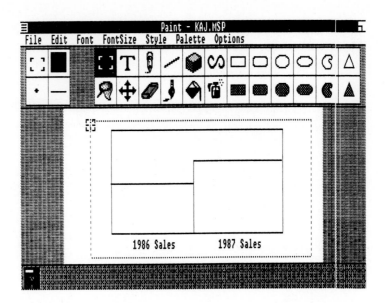

Select the Edit menu and the Cut option. The picture should disappear. It is available, however, on the clipboard for other Windows applications. CARDFILE, for example, can use it in a report.

The Windows Control Panel

One of the last programs provided with Microsoft Windows is CONTROL.EXE. CONTROL allows you to configure new printers, modify port communications parameters, set the color for systems using the Extended Graphics Adapter (EGA), set the system date and time, and modify the cursor blink rate and mouse double-click delay time. From the MS-DOS Executive, invoke CONTROL.EXE. Windows will display the following:

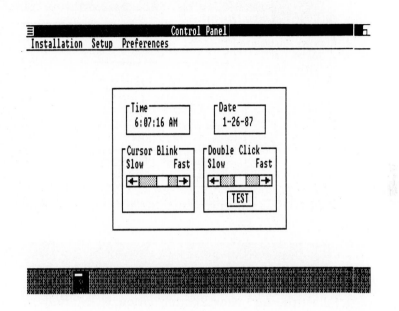

This is your control panel. To modify the system date or time, simply enter the desired time or date in the standard DOS time and date formats. To modify the cursor blink rate, use the TAB key or mouse to select the Cursor Blink box, and then use the cursor arrow keys or mouse to either speed up or slow down the blink rate. Each time you press the mouse select button, Windows delays a short period of time to see if you are double-clicking. The Double Click box allows you to increase or decrease this period of time. This allows you to configure your mouse to your own touch.

Select the Installation menu, and CONTROL will display the following:

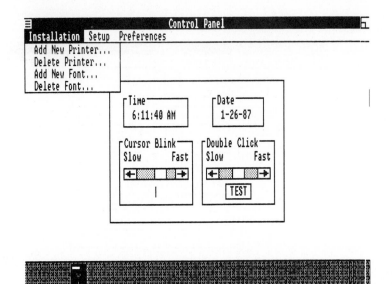

Select the Add New Printer option. CONTROL responds with the following dialog box to prompt you to enter the name of the printer device driver file:

DOS: The Complete Reference

You must still associate the new printer with a port. The Delete Printer option prompts you for the printer to remove, as follows:

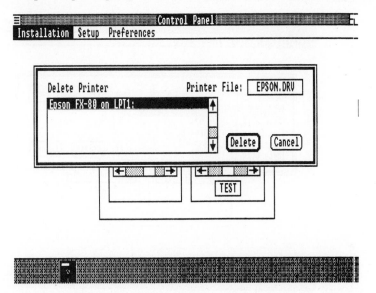

Simply select the desired printer. The printer will become unavailable to Windows.

Add New Font allows you to make additional fonts available to Windows applications programs. CONTROL will prompt you for the font as follows:

Likewise, the Delete Font option prompts you for the font to remove from Windows as follows:

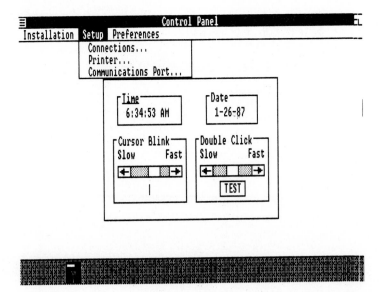

Simply use the keyboard cursor keys or your mouse to select the font to be removed.

Next, invoke the Setup menu. CONTROL will display the following:

Choose the Connections option. CONTROL allows you to specify the printer connected to each port, as follows:

```
≡                          Control Panel                     ᴸⵊ
 Installation  Setup  Preferences
─────────────────────────────────────────────────────────────

      ┌───────────────────────────────────────────────┐
      │  Printer                    Connection         │
      │ ┌─────────────────────────┐┌───────────────┐  │
      │ │ Epson FX-80 on LPT1:   ▲││None          ▲│  │
      │ │                        ▒││LPT1:          │  │
      │ │                        ▒││LPT2:         ▒│  │
      │ │                        ▒││LPT3:         ▒│  │
      │ │                        ▼││COM1:         ▼│  │
      │ └─────────────────────────┘└───────────────┘  │
      │        ┌────────┐      ┌──────────┐            │
      │        │   Ok   │      │  Cancel  │            │
      │        └────────┘      └──────────┘            │
      └───────────────────────────────────────────────┘
```

The Printer option defines the current Windows default printer, as follows:

```
≡                          Control Panel                     ᴸⵊ
 Installation  Setup  Preferences
─────────────────────────────────────────────────────────────

    ┌──────────────────────────────────────┐
    │  Default Printer                     │
    │ ┌─────────────────────────┐ ┌──────┐ │
    │ │ Epson FX-80 on LPT1:  ▲│ │  Ok  │ │
    │ │                       ▒│ └──────┘ │
    │ │                       ▒│ ┌────────┐│
    │ │                       ▼│ │ Cancel ││
    │ └─────────────────────────┘ └────────┘│st
    └──────────────────────────────────────┘
         ┌─────────────┐  ┌─────────────┐
         │◄─┌──┐──────►│  │◄─┌──┐──────►│
         └─────────────┘  └─────────────┘
                │          ┌──────┐
                            │ TEST │
                            └──────┘
```

The last option, Communications Port, allows you to specify the communications parameters for a specific port, as shown here:

```
▤░░░░░░░░░░░░░░░░░░░░░░Control Panel░░░░░░░░░░░░░░░░░░░░░░🔽
 Installation  Setup  Preferences
┌─────────────────────────────────────────────┐
│                                               │
│  Communications Settings                      │
│  Port          ⊙ COM1:      ○ COM2:           │
│                                          ⌐7   │
│  Baud Rate:   ┌──────┐                         │
│               │ 1200 │                         │
│               └──────┘                   ick   │
│  Word Length  ○4 ○5 ○6 ○7 ⊙8           Fast   │
│                                          ┌──►│ │
│  Parity       ○ Even  ○ Odd  ⊙ None           │
│                                               │
│  Stop Bits    ⊙1    ○1.5   ○2                 │
│                                               │
│  Handshake    ○ Hardware ⊙ None               │
│                                               │
│         ┌──────┐        ┌────────┐             │
│         │  Ok  │        │ Cancel │             │
│         └──────┘        └────────┘             │
└─────────────────────────────────────────────┘
```

The CONTROL Preferences menu will display the following:

```
▤░░░░░░░░░░░░░░░░░░░░░░Control Panel░░░░░░░░░░░░░░░░░░░░░░🔽
 Installation  Setup  Preferences
              Screen Colors...
              Mouse...                          │
              Country Settings...
         ┌────────────────────────────────────────┐
         │ ┌Time────────┐   ┌Date──────┐           │
         │ │ 12:52:27 PM │   │ 1-26-87  │           │
         │ └────────────┘   └──────────┘           │
         │                                          │
         │ ┌Cursor Blink┐   ┌Double Click┐          │
         │ │Slow    Fast│   │Slow    Fast│          │
         │ │┌─░░░──░░─►│   │┌─░░──░─►│          │
         │ │    │        │   │  ┌────┐     │          │
         │ │    │        │   │  │TEST│     │          │
         │ └────────────┘   └──────────────┘          │
         └────────────────────────────────────────┘
```

The Screen Colors option allows you to define the colors on the screen for the Extended Graphics Adapter, as follows:

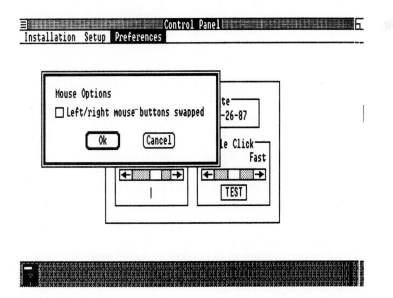

The Mouse option allows you to change the mouse select button from the left to the right button, as shown here:

Country Settings allows you to change the date, time, and currency formats as shown here:

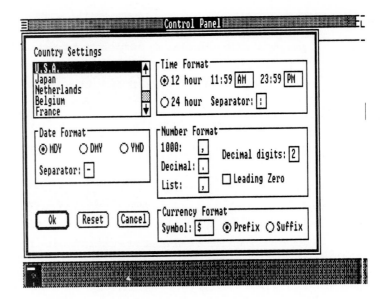

Most users will never invoke CONTROL. However, once you are confident using Windows, you may want to modify some of the default parameters.

What Is a PIF?

For many applications Windows requires additional information, such as the amount of memory the program will require, whether the program uses graphics, or a specific communications port. Windows places the information for these applications in a file with the extension PIF (Program Information File). Windows provides PIF files for most of the more widely used programs (see the PIF subdirectory). In addition, many applications will run with the default values used in Windows applications. If, however, your application performs memory-mapped graphics, you must create a PIF file for the program. To do so, set your current default to the

PIF subdirectory. Invoke the program PIFEDIT.EXE. Windows will display the following:

```
 ≣                    Program Information Editor                    ▙
 File
 Program Name:       [                                        ]
 Program Title:      [                                        ]
 Program Parameters: [                                        ]
 Initial Directory:  [                                        ]
 Memory Requirements: [52]  KB Required   [52]  KB Desired
 Directly Modifies    ⊠ Screen      □ COM1        □ Memory
                      □ Keyboard    □ COM2
 Program Switch       ○ Prevent    ⊙ Text    ○ Graphics/Multiple Text
 Screen Exchange      ○ None       ⊙ Text    ○ Graphics/Text
 Close Window on exit □
```

This dialog box allows you to specify the information required by Windows to run the application. First, enter the name of the application's executable file for which you are creating the PIF. Next, enter the title that you want displayed in the title bar for the application. Enter any required parameters for the program. Next, enter the amount of memory required for your application. In most instances, the default value of 52K is sufficient. Some programs execute more efficiently if additional memory is available. Enter the amount of memory that you would desire the application to have.

The Initial Directory prompt specifies to what DOS subdirectory Windows will set the current default upon invocation of the program. The next prompt inquires whether the program requires direct access to the video memory, the keyboard buffer, either communications port, or absolute memory addresses. Since each Windows application runs under the control of Windows, you must specify to what resources your program requires direct access.

The Program Switch option allows you to specify that your program requires sole control of the screen. Most applications use

Text. Next, the Screen Exchange option allows you to specify whether you want the ability to press CTRL-PRTSC to capture the current screen contents to the clipboard. This option requires additional memory allocation. Last, the Close Window on exit option specifies whether Windows removes the application's window upon completion of the program. By default, Windows uses the following values:

Program Title	None
Initial Directory	None
Memory Required	52K
Memory Desired	Available memory
Directly Modifies	Screen
Program Switch	Prevent
Screen Exchange	Text

Providing Initialization Values to Windows

Each time Windows starts, it searches the current directory for the file WIN.INI. This file is the Windows initialization file. It is similar to the CONFIG.SYS file, which DOS uses to configure itself in memory. Use the Windows NOTEPAD to edit the contents of WIN.INI. Before you begin, print a copy of the current WIN.INI.

Entries in WIN.INI are in the following format:

[section name]
keyword = setting [. . .]

The following are valid section names:

windows
extensions
colors
ports
devices
pif

The windows section allows you to specify the following:

DoubleClickRate=
CursorBlinkRate=
Device=   (for default printer)
Load= program__name

The Load keyword allows you to have programs automatically started as icons each time Windows starts. The following entry loads the CLOCK and CALENDAR programs:

Load=CLOCK CALENDAR

In addition to executable files, Windows allows you to load files for the various Windows applications. For example, the following entry loads the CALENDAR file KAJ.CAL at startup:

Load=KAJ.CAL

Within the extensions section you can specify the default file extensions for each application.

The colors option allows you to set the colors used by the Extended Graphics Adapter. See the file WIN.INI for the current default values. Most users choose to use CONTROL for specifying screen colors.

The ports section defines the communications parameters for each port. Entries are made as follows:

[port]
COM2:=baud,parity,databits,stopbits,retry

Again, most users choose to use CONTROL for configuring ports.

The devices section specifies printers and their port assignments. Refer to the current WIN.INI for examples. Use CONTROL to modify these assignments.

Last, the pif section allows you to modify the amount of memory dedicated to each application, as follows:

[pif]
test.com=64

Most of the parameters specified in WIN.INI are easily set via CONTROL.EXE. Many users only modify this file to load icons at startup.

RAM Drives and Windows

Windows provides its own driver for a virtual RAM disk. If you are currently using VDISK, modify CONFIG.SYS to instead reference the file RAMDRIVE.SYS provided with Windows. The functions of both drivers are the same. However, RAMDRIVE. SYS was designed especially for Windows. The installation for the driver is the same as VDISK with the exception that RAMDRIVE supports an /A option for the INTEL above-board expanded memory.

Review

1. List the applications provided with Microsoft Windows.

2. What is a PIF?

3. What is WIN.INI?

4. What is the clipboard?

5. Provide the entry in WIN.INI to load the Windows CALCULATOR and CALENDAR programs as icons upon Windows startup.

6. What is WRITE?

7. What is PAINT?

8. What are Cut and Paste operations?

Answers

1. *List the applications provided with Microsoft Windows.*

   SPOOLER
   MS-DOS
   CALC
   CALENDAR
   CARDFILE
   CLIPBRD
   CLOCK
   CONTROL
   NOTEPAD
   PAINT
   PIFEDIT
   REVERSI
   TERMINAL
   WRITE

2. *What is a PIF?*

   For many applications Windows requires additional information such as the amount of memory the program will require, whether or not the program uses graphics, or a specific communications port. Windows places the information for these applications in a file with the extension PIF (Program Information File). Windows provides PIF files for most of the more widely used programs (see the PIF subdirectory). In addition, many applications will run with the default values provided for Windows applications. However, if your application performs memory-mapped graphics, you must create a PIF file for the program. Set your current default to the PIF subdirectory. Invoke the program PIFEDIT.EXE to create a PIF file for a specific program.

3. *What is WIN.INI?*

   Each time Windows starts, it searches the current directory for the file WIN.INI. This file is the Windows initialization file. It is similar to the file CONFIG.SYS that DOS uses to configure itself in memory.

4. *What is the clipboard?*

Windows allows you to exchange information between applications via the Windows clipboard. In general, the clipboard is simply a location that you can store text or graphics on that other Windows applications can access.

5. *Provide the entry in WIN.INI to load the Windows CALCULATOR and CALENDAR programs as icons upon Windows startup.*

```
[windows]
Load=CALC CALENDAR
```

6. *What is WRITE?*

WRITE is a simple word processor provided with Microsoft Windows. WRITE is an integrated package that allows you to share information with other Windows programs.

7. *What is PAINT?*

PAINT is an applications program provided with Microsoft Windows. It allows you to create diagrams and pictures that can be integrated into reports and memos.

8. *What are Cut and Paste operations?*

Cut and Paste operations allow you to move text or graphics from one location to a new location. The second location may even be a different program. In such instances, Cut operations place the text or graphics to be moved on the Windows clipboard. Paste operations remove the contents of the clipboard and place them at the desired location.

DOS Reference Guide

This appendix provides a detailed explanation of the DOS commands. Each command is shown in the following format:

Command name (description)   Qualifiers

Command type (external or internal)   Options

Function   Notes

Syntax Chart   Examples

Format

Qualifiers are those components of the command format that contain slashes—anything that changes the way the command executes. Options are optional file names and drive identifications. If they are not provided, DOS will use default values or prompt the user for input.

The syntax charts for DOS are presented here for the first time. Before you examine the charts, it is important that you have a foundation for the concepts they represent. First, the purpose of syntax charts is to show you how to issue a correct command. As long as you follow the arrows within each chart, the format of your DOS commands will always be correct. The symbols used in the syntax charts throughout this reference are shown in Table A-1.

Consider one of the simplest charts, the syntax chart for the DOS CLS command:

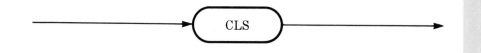

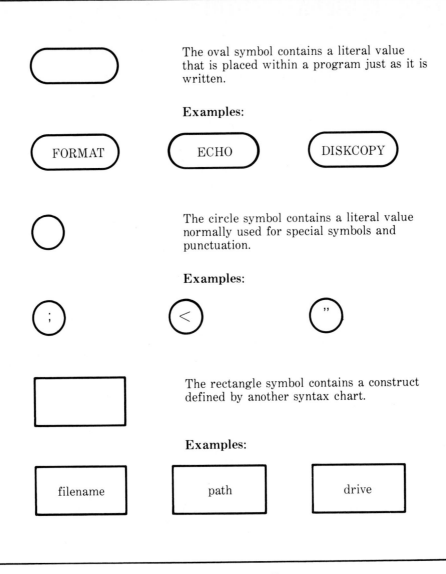

The oval symbol contains a literal value that is placed within a program just as it is written.

Examples:

The circle symbol contains a literal value normally used for special symbols and punctuation.

Examples:

The rectangle symbol contains a construct defined by another syntax chart.

Examples:

Table A-1.   Symbols Used in Syntax Charts

If you start at the left side of the syntax chart and work to the right, you will obtain the correct command. Likewise, the VOL syntax chart

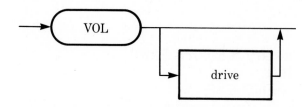

illustrates the optional disk drive. In this case, you must choose a direction to follow. Follow the chart in the direction of the arrows, and you will obtain a correct command.

Last, the syntax chart for the ECHO command shows three possible directions.

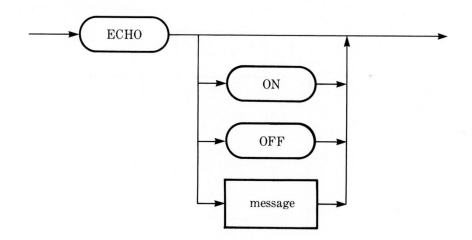

If you simply follow the direction of the arrows, you will always issue a correct command. Compare the syntax charts to the contents of the format entry for each of the following DOS commands. Once you are familiar with syntax charts, they will be very useful.

APPEND (Specify a Search Path for Data Files)
External APPEND.EXE

Function   Specify a search path for DOS data files in a similar manner to the DOS PATH command for executable files.

Syntax Chart

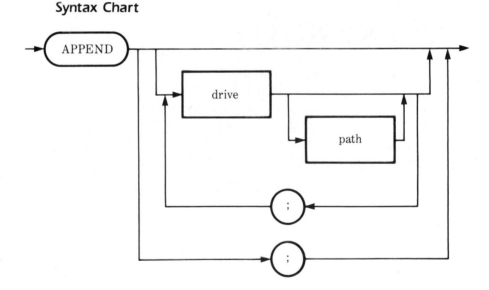

Format

        [drive:][path]APPEND [d:][p][;[d:][p]...]

or

        [drive:][path]APPEND ;

Qualifiers   None

Options

d: is a disk drive identification to include in the data file search path.

p is the DOS subdirectory path to include in the data file search path.

Notes   APPEND is provided by MS-DOS version 3.2.

Each time DOS opens a file, it first checks to see if it can open the file as specified. If the file is found, DOS will open it. If DOS does not find the file, it will check to see if you have defined a data file search path.

APPEND defines the series of subdirectory paths that DOS will search each time it fails to find a data file in the current directory or as specified.

If you invoke the command without any parameters, as in

A> APPEND

APPEND will display the current data search path.

APPEND does not validate the data paths that you specify. If DOS later finds an error (nonexistent or misspelled path), DOS will ignore the entry and continue processing the other entries in the list.

Examples

A> APPEND C:;A:;B:

If DOS cannot open a file as specified, it will search the current directories in drives C, A, and B, in that order.

A> APPEND C:\DOS\UTIL;A:\TOOLS

DOS will search the subdirectories \DOS\UTIL on drive C and then \TOOLS on drive A for files it cannot open as specified.

Function Route all disk I/O requests for a specific drive to a new disk drive.

Syntax Chart

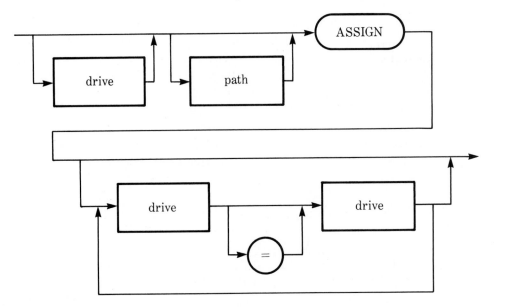

Format

[drive:][path]ASSIGN [old_drive [=] new_drive [...]]

Qualifiers None

Options

old—drive is the drive specification (A, B, or C) away from which you want to direct I/O requests.

new—drive is the drive specification (A, B, or C) to which you want I/O requests routed.

Notes   If no drive assignments are given, as in

```
A> ASSIGN
```

all normal drive assignments resume. The DOS commands FORMAT, DISKCOPY, and DISKCOMP ignore drive assignments.

Examples

```
A> ASSIGN A=B
```

All I/O requests to drive A will now be routed to drive B.

```
A> ASSIGN A=C B=C
```

DOS will route all I/O requests to drives A and B to drive C.

```
A> ASSIGN
```

All normal drive assignments will resume.

ATTRIB (Assign or Display File Attributes)
External ATTRIB.EXE

Function   Set or display a file's read-only/archive-bit status.

Syntax Chart

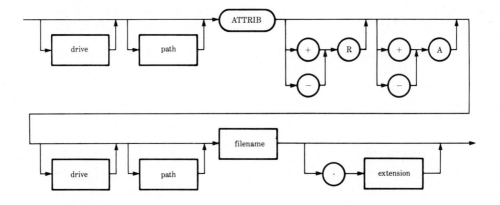

Format

[drive:][path]ATTRIB [+R ¦ −R] [+A ¦ −A] file—specification

Qualifiers

+*R* sets a file to read-only

−*R* sets a file to read/write access

+*A* sets a file's archive bit

−*A* clears a file's archive bit

Options

ATTRIB supports the DOS wildcard characters.

file—specification is the file(s) whose attributes are to be set or displayed.

Notes   By setting critical files to read-only, you can prevent inadvertent deletion or modification of the file from DOS.

Chapter 16 illustrates how to set a file's attribute byte from within an application.

The [+A | −A] option is available only with DOS version 3.2.

The ATTRIB command can be used conveniently with the XCOPY command presented in Chapter 10.

Examples

`A> ATTRIB *.SYS`

List the attribute byte of all files with the extension SYS.

```
A> ATTRIB + R CONFIG.SYS
A> DEL CONFIG.SYS
Access denied

A>
```

This command sets the file CONFIG.SYS to read-only to prevent deletion or modification of the file.

`A> ATTRIB ▸R CONFIG.SYS`

Set the file CONFIG.SYS back to read/write access.

BACKUP (Back Up One or More Files to a New Disk)
External BACKUP.COM

Function   Back up one or more files from a disk to a different disk.

Syntax Chart

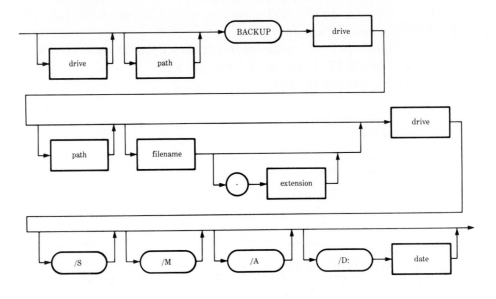

Format

> [drive:][path]BACKUP d1:[path][filename.[ext]] d2:
> [/A][/D:mm-dd-yy][/M][/S]

Qualifiers

> /A adds files being backed up to the files already present on the backup disk.
>
> /D:*mm-dd-yy* backs up only the files modified or created since the date specified.
>
> /M backs up only the files that have been modified or created since the last backup.
>
> /S backs up subdirectory files in addition to the files contained in the directory to be backed up.

Options

> *d1:* is the drive identification containing the file(s) to back up.
>
> *filename* is the file name of the file(s) to back up.
>
> *ext* is the optional three-character extension of the file(s) to back up.
>
> *d2:* is the drive identification of the drive containing the backup disk.

Notes   The backup disk must be formatted.

Unless the /A qualifier is used, all files on the backup disk are overwritten during the backup.

When the backup disk becomes full, BACKUP will prompt for a new formatted disk, as follows:

```
Insert backup diskette 02 in drive n:
```

Label your backup disks in sequential order, 1-n. When performing a RESTORE operation, you must enter the disks in the sequence that they were created.

BACKUP will modify each file's archive bit to specify that the file no longer requires a backup. This allows BACKUP to support the /M or /D qualifiers.

Every 10 megabytes of disk space requires approximately 25 double-sided, double-density disks or 6 quad-density disks.

BACKUP returns the following status values to support conditional batch processing:

0   successful backup

1   no files to backup

2   some shared files not backed up

3 user termination via CTRL-BREAK

4 error in processing

Examples

`A> BACKUP *.SYS B:`

  BACKUP will back up all of the *.SYS files in the current directory on drive A to the backup disk in drive B.

`A> BACKUP C:\ B:/S`

  BACKUP will back up the entire fixed disk (drive C) to the backup disks in drive B.

`A> BACKUP A:\ C:/S`

  BACKUP will back up the files on disk A to the fixed drive C. The files are placed in the subdirectory \BACKUP on the fixed disk.

`A> BACKUP C:\ B:/S/D:12-31-86`

  BACKUP will back up the files created or modified since 12-31-86.

BREAK (Enable/Disable CTRL-BREAK Processing)
Internal Command

Function Initiate or terminate CTRL-BREAK processing upon completion of DOS services. The default value is BREAK=OFF.

Syntax Chart

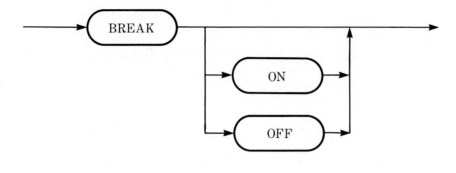

Format

BREAK [ON ¦ OFF]

Qualifiers   None

Options

If BREAK=ON, DOS will check for and process all CTRL-BREAK terminations upon completion of DOS services.

If BREAK=OFF, DOS will check for and process CTRL-BREAK terminations upon completion of standard input/output operations, standard print operations, or standard AUX operations.

Notes   If the command is issued without any parameters, as in

A> BREAK

DOS will display the current status of CTRL-BREAK processing —either ON or OFF.

```
BREAK is off
```

The default is BREAK=OFF.

By specifying BREAK=ON, you introduce additional overhead for CTRL-BREAK processing. This will, in turn, slow the speed of your applications. Many commercial programs do not allow CTRL-BREAK processing. Normally, you would only set BREAK=ON for program development.

Examples

```
A> BREAK ON
```

```
A> BREAK OFF
```

CHDIR (Change Default Directory)
Internal Command

Function Change or display the current directory for the specified drive.

Syntax Chart

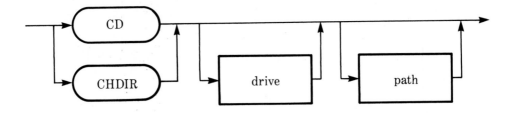

Format

    CHDIR [drive:][path]

or

    CD [drive:][path]

DOS: The Complete Reference

Qualifiers   None

Notes   If you do not specify a disk drive, CHDIR uses the current default.

If you do not specify a directory path, CD will display the current directory on the specified drive, as in

```
A> CD
A:\DOS
```

The root directory is specified by the backslash (\). The parent directory is specified by two periods (..). The current directory can also be represented by the period (.).

Examples

```
A> CHDIR
A:\DOS
```

Display the current directory on the default drive.

```
A> CD
A:\DOS
```

The commands CD and CHDIR are identical.

```
A> CD SUB1
```

Change the current directory to the subdirectory SUB1. Since no disk drive or path precedes SUB1, it must be a subdirectory in the current default drive.

```
A> CD B:\DOS\UTIL
```

Change the default directory on drive B to the directory \DOS\UTIL.

```
A> CD \
```

Change the directory on the current drive to the root directory.

CHKDSK (Check a Disk's Current Status)
External CHKDSK.COM

Function   Examine the files, directories, and file allocation table (FAT) for a specific drive and report findings. Display the amount of memory present in the computer along with the amount of memory unused by the operating system or other installed products. If the /F qualifier is present in the CHKDSK command line, correct errors in the FAT or directory entries.

Syntax Chart

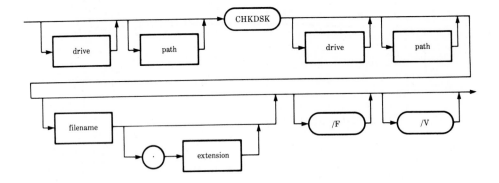

DOS: The Complete Reference

Format

[drive:][path]CHKDSK [file—specification][/F][/V]

Qualifiers

/F fixes errors found in the FAT or directories and writes corrections to the disk. Without the /F qualifier, CHKDSK will display only the inconsistencies and will not write the corrections to disk.

/V displays all of the files and their pathnames contained on the disk. If you are unsure where a file exists in your directory structure, the /V qualifier can be useful.

Options

file—specification causes CHKDSK to examine the files specified for disk contiguity. If you use the wildcard characters *.*, CHKDSK will examine the entire disk. See Chapter 9 for more information.

Notes   CHKDSK does not prompt you to enter a source disk. The program assumes that the desired disk is contained in the specified drive.

Badly fragmented files or disks degrade system performance because of the high number of disk seeks required. You should test for fragmentation of your disk periodically by using *.* as a CHKDSK file specification.

If CHKDSK finds lost clusters (see Chapter 9) on the disk, the program will prompt you to tell it whether or not it should convert the lost clusters into files. If you respond with Y and you have included the /F qualifier in the command line, CHKDSK will create files in the root directory with the name FILE0000.CHK. Examine these files to see if they contain useful information.

Examples

```
C> CHKDSK

Volume DOSDISK     created Nov 2, 1986 8:38p

 21309440 bytes total disk space
    16736 bytes in 3 hidden files
   227328 bytes in 76 directories
 18487296 bytes in 2981 user files
    20480 bytes in bad sectors
  2457600 bytes available on disk

   524288 bytes total memory
   273072 bytes free
```

In this example, the three hidden files are the DOS volume label and the system files (IBMBIOS.COM and IBMDOS.COM, or MSDOS.SYS and IO.SYS).

A> CHKDSK B:/F

CHKDSK will check the disk contained in drive B and correct any errors that it finds in the FAT or directory structure.

A> CHKDSK B:/V

CHKDSK will examine the disk in drive B and display the path and file name for each file on the disk.

A> CHKDSK B:*.*

CHKDSK will examine the disk in drive B for disk fragmentation.

CLS (Clear the Screen)
Internal Command

Function   Clear the screen display and place the cursor in the home position (upper left-hand corner).

Syntax Chart

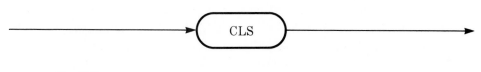

Format

CLS

Qualifiers   None

Notes   CLS does not affect video display attributes.

COMMAND (Invoke a Secondary Command Processor)
External COMMAND.COM

Function   Invoke a secondary command processor.

Syntax Chart

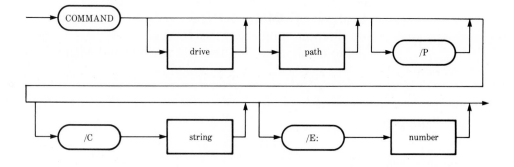

Format

[drive:][path]COMMAND [d:][p][/C string][/E:nnnnn][/P]

Qualifiers

/C string specifies the command that the secondary command processor is to perform. If this qualifier is omitted, COMMAND will prompt you for commands with the standard DOS prompt.

/E:nnnnn specifies the number of bytes to be allocated for the secondary command processor's environment. The value nnnnn must be in the range 160-32768.

/P directs DOS to install the secondary command processor permanently into memory. If the /C qualifier is also specified, DOS ignores /P.

Options

d: is the disk drive identification of the drive containing the command processor COMMAND.COM. If you do not specify a drive, DOS will use the COMMSPEC= value in the environment as the drive; this is normally the boot disk.

p is the path to the subdirectory containing the command processor COMMAND.COM. If you do not specify a path, DOS uses the COMMSPEC= value in the environment as the path.

Notes See Chapter 16 for a Turbo Pascal procedure that allows you to invoke COMMAND from within a Turbo Pascal program. See Chapter 8 on batch processing to see how a command is issued to invoke a second batch processor and with that a batch file.

Examples

```
A> COMMAND
```

Invoke a secondary command processor that will prompt for commands. The DOS EXIT command will terminate the secondary command processor.

`A> COMMAND /C CHKDSK`

Load a secondary command processor to execute the CHKDSK command.

COMP (Compare Two Files)
External COMP.COM

Function Compare the contents of two files and display the byte location of the first ten differences.

Syntax Chart

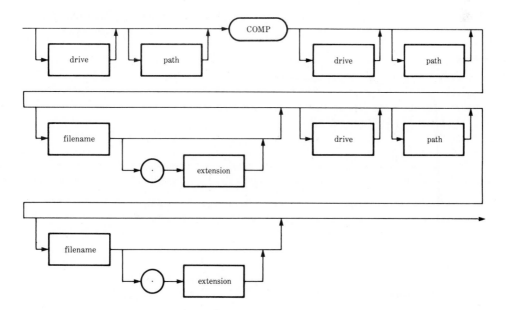

Format

[drive:][path]COMP [file—specification1] [file—specification2]

Qualifiers   None

Options

file—specification1 is the file name of the first file to compare.

file—specification2 is the file name of the second file to compare.

Notes   Files to be compared can reside in separate directories or disk drives.

COMP does not prompt you to enter a source disk. Be sure that the files that you want to compare are in the current drives before invoking the command.

COMP will not compare files of different sizes.

COMP supports wildcard characters as follows:

A> COMP *.DAT *.OLD

In this case, COMP will find DAT files whose file names match OLD file names. If you assume that the directory contains

```
Volume in drive A has no label
Directory of   A:\

SEPT      DAT        12     1-06-87     2:29p
SEPT      OLD        12     1-06-87     2:29p
JUL       DAT      7829     1-06-87     2:29p
JUL       OLD      7829     1-06-87     2:29p
JUN       OLD        16     1-06-87     2:29p
AUG       DAT        16     1-06-87     2:29p
          6 File(s)      342016 bytes free
```

then the command

A> COMP *.OLD *.DAT

will compare the specified file as follows:

```
A> COMP *.OLD *.DAT

B:SEPT.OLD and B:SEPT.DAT

Files compare ok


B:JUL.OLD and B:JUL.DAT

Files compare ok


B:JUN.OLD and B:JUN.DAT

B:JUN.DAT - File not found
```

If you do not specify a primary or secondary file name, COMP will prompt you for them as follows:

```
Enter primary file name
```

File differences are reported as follows:

```
A:FILE1 and A:FILE2

Compare error at OFFSET 6
File 1 = 35

File 2 = 34
```

The offset and byte values are in hexadecimal.

If you specify a drive only for the secondary file specification, COMP uses the name of the primary file for both.

If the files specified are identical, COMP will display

```
Files compare ok
```

If COMP finds more than ten differences, it will display

```
10 Mismatches - ending compare
```

When it is finished, COMP will prompt you to specify whether or not you want to perform additional comparisons, as shown here:

```
Compare more files (Y/N)?
```

Press Y to compare more files; otherwise, press N.

If COMP displays the message

```
Eof mark not found
```

it did not find an end-of-file marker in the last byte of the file. COMP failed to find the end-of-file marker in the byte that is the size of the file contained in the directory entry.

Examples

```
A> COMP ANSI.SYS B:ANSI.SYS
```

The command will compare the contents of the file ANSI. SYS on drive A to the contents of the same file on drive B.

The following commands are equivalent:

```
A> COMP *.C B:*.C

A> COMP *.C B:
```

The command will compare all C routines (files with a C extension) to their previous versions. If COMP cannot find one of the specified files, it will display

```
A:FILE1 - File not found
```

COPY (Copy One or More Files to a New Destination)
Internal Command

Function   Copy one or more files to a new target destination.

Syntax Chart

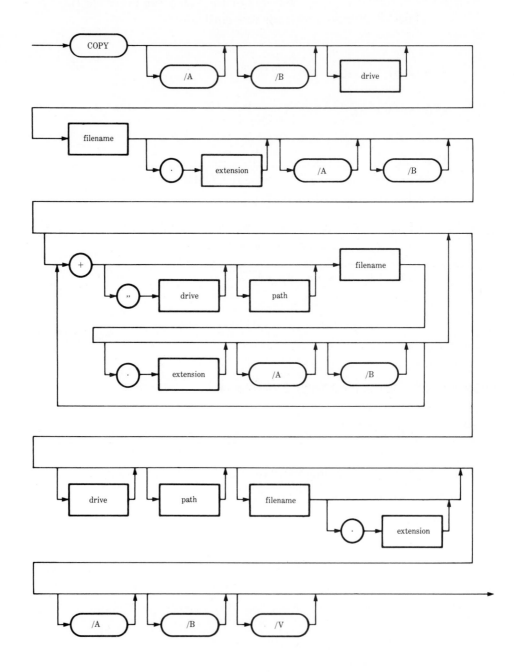

Format

COPY [/A][/B] file—specification1 [/A][/B]
[file—specification2][/A][/B][/V]

or

COPY [/A][/B] file—specification1
[/A][/B][+[[,,]file—specificationN
[/A][/B]...] [file—specification2][/A][/B][/V]

Qualifiers

/A directs COPY to treat the file as an ASCII file. The file's contents up to (not including) the Ctrl-Z end-of-file marker are copied.

/B directs COPY to copy the file based on the size entry in the file's directory entry.

/V directs COPY to read each sector it writes to disk to ensure that the data was recorded correctly.

Options

file—specification1 is the name of the source file(s) to copy. DOS wildcard characters are supported.

file—specification2 is the name of the target file(s). DOS wildcard characters are supported.

file—specificationN are the names of files to append to file— specification1 to create file—specification2.

Notes   COPY only copies files contained in the specified directory. It will not search lower-level directories.

COPY does not maintain file attributes. If you copy a read-only file, you will not create a second read-only file.

COPY does not support serial devices.

The source and target names must differ. If you attempt to use the same name, COPY will display

```
A> COPY CONFIG.SYS CONFIG.SYS
File cannot be copied onto itself
        0 File(s) copied
```

Examples

```
A> COPY B:CONFIG.SYS CONFIG.SYS
```

COPY the file CONFIG.SYS from drive B to drive A. The command is equivalent to

```
A> COPY B:CONFIG.SYS
```

The destination name defaults to the source name, default drive, and directory.

```
A> COPY PART1.TXT+PART2.TXT WHOLE.TXT
```

Append the file PART2.TXT to the file PART1.TXT to create the file WHOLE.TXT.

```
A> COPY CON D.BAT
DATE
TIME
CLS
^Z
        1 File(s) copied
```

COPY a batch file from the keyboard to the disk file D.BAT.

```
A> COPY D.BAT CON
DATE
TIME
CLS
        1 File(s) copied
```

Display a file to the console device.

CTTY (Change the Standard Input/Output Device)
Internal Command

Function   Change the standard input and output device to an auxiliary device.

Syntax Chart

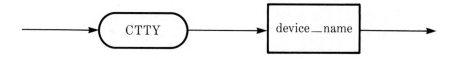

Format

    CTTY device_name

Qualifiers   None

Options

device—name is the name of the device to use for standard input and output.

Notes   The device-name specifier must be capable of performing both input and output.

Valid device names include AUX:, COM1:, and COM2:.

Examples

`A> CTTY COM1:`

The command requests DOS to use the COM1 port for standard input and output operations.

`A> CTTY CON`

The command causes DOS to resume using the CON device for standard input and output operations. If you entered the first example in this section, this command must come from the AUX device.

DATE (Set or Display the System Date)
Internal Command

Function   Set or display the system date known to DOS.

Syntax Chart

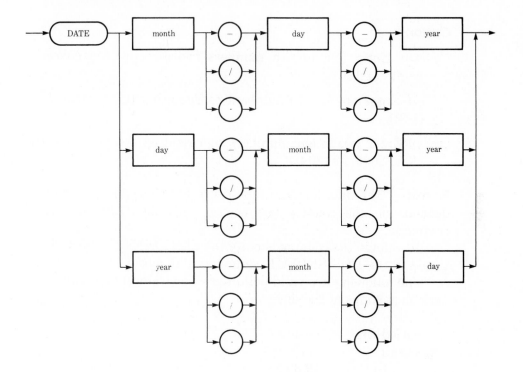

Format

DATE [mm-dd-yy]

DATE [dd-mm-yy]

DATE [yy-mm-dd]

Qualifiers   None

Options

mm Enter one to two numbers representing the current month (1-12).

dd Enter one to two numbers representing the current day (1-31).

yy Enter two to four numbers representing the current year (1980-2099) or (80-99).

Notes   The date format (mm-dd-yy, dd-mm-yy, or yy-mm-dd) depends on the country you choose with the DOS SELECT command.

To change the country, modify the file CONFIG.SYS as illustrated in the DOS SELECT command and reboot.

The following are valid delimiters (separators) to distinguish various portions of the date:

period (.)	9.30.87
slash (/)	9/30/87
dash (-)	9-30-87

If you enter an invalid date, DATE will display

```
Current date is Tue  1-06-1987
Enter new date (mm-dd-yy): 12-42-86


Invalid date
Enter new date (mm-dd-yy):
```

DOS computes and displays the day of the week (Sun-Sat) each time you issue the DATE command. Do not type it in yourself.

The DATE command does not set the system clock on the IBM PC AT. Use the Setup option of the diagnostic disk provided in the AT *Guide to Operations*.

If you do not want to modify the date displayed, simply press the ENTER key.

Examples

```
Current date is Tue  1-06-1987
Enter new date (mm-dd-yy): 9-30-87
```

Set the system date to September 30, 1987.

```
Current date is Mon  1-05-1987
Enter new date (mm-dd-yy):
```

Display the system date without modification.

```
Current date is Mon  1-05-1987
Enter new date (mm-dd-yy): 9.30.87
```

Periods, slashes, and dashes are all valid delimiters.

DEL (Delete File from Disk)
Internal Command

Function Delete the specified file(s) from disk.

Syntax Chart

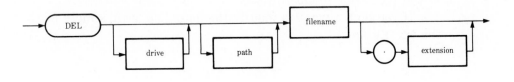

Format

DEL file_specification

or

DELETE file_specification

Qualifiers   None

Notes   Unless overridden with a drive or path specification, DEL will erase only those files in the current directory.

Files marked as read-only (via ATTRIB) cannot be deleted. If you attempt to delete such a file, DOS will display

```
Access denied
```

DEL will not delete subdirectories. To delete a subdirectory, you first must delete all of the files that it contains and then use RMDIR to remove the directory.

Warning: DEL works with the ASSIGNed disk. Be careful when you are deleting files if you are using the DOS ASSIGN command.

DEL supports the DOS wildcard characters. If you specify *.*

as the file specification, DEL will prompt

```
A> DEL *.*
Are you sure (Y/N)?
```

Then it will delete the files. If you want to delete the files, press Y and then press ENTER; otherwise, press N and then ENTER.

Examples

```
A> DEL CONFIG.OLD
```

Delete the file CONFIG.OLD from the current disk and directory.

```
A> DEL B:\OLDFILES\*.*
```

Delete all of the files contained in the directory OLDFILES on drive B.

If DEL cannot find the specified file, it will display

```
A> DEL FILENAME
File not found
```

DIR (Directory Listing of Files)
Internal Command

Function   List the specified file(s) for a given directory.

Syntax Chart

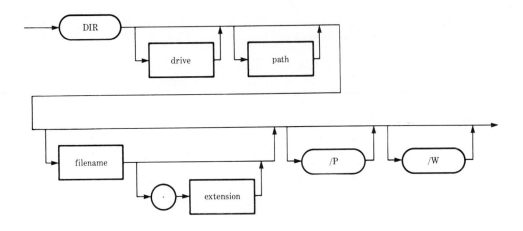

Format

DIR [file—specification] [/P] [/W]

Qualifiers

/P causes DIR to pause and display the prompt

```
Strike a key when ready . . .
```

This happens each time it displays a full screen of file names. To continue the directory listing, simply press any key.

/W directs DIR to display only file names, suppressing size, date, and time attributes for a file. DIR will display five file names across the screen.

Notes   The directory listing displays the file name and extension, file size in bytes, file creation date and time, volume identification, and free disk space.

DIR displays directory names without a size with the word <DIR>, as follows:

```
Volume in drive C is DOSDISK
Directory of  C:\DOSBOOK

.                <DIR>      9-14-86    8:44p
..               <DIR>      9-14-86    8:44p
CHAP6            <DIR>     10-25-86    4:06p
CHAP3            <DIR>     11-01-86    3:57p
CHAP7            <DIR>      9-16-86    7:43p
CHAP12           <DIR>      9-16-86    7:25p
CHAP2            <DIR>     11-08-86   11:14a
CHAP4            <DIR>     11-10-86   12:53p
NOTES            <DIR>     11-10-86    4:31p
CHAP8            <DIR>      9-28-86    4:52p
CHAP15           <DIR>     10-12-86    8:42a
CHAP5            <DIR>     11-16-86    4:52a
CHAP11           <DIR>     11-19-86    7:05a
CHAP1            <DIR>     11-20-86    9:25p
CHAP13           <DIR>     11-23-86    8:01a
CHAP10           <DIR>     11-23-86    1:26p
CHAP14           <DIR>     11-29-86    6:23a
CHAP9            <DIR>     12-07-86    1:07p
PREFACE          <DIR>     12-11-86    1:31p
CHAP16           <DIR>     12-13-86    4:48p
ERROR            <DIR>     12-15-86    2:21p
CARD             <DIR>     12-20-86    7:58p
DOSREF           <DIR>      1-01-87    2:05p
        23 File(s)    2367488 bytes free
```

If you do not provide a file specification, DIR defaults to *.*. If you do not provide an extension, DIR uses .*.

If the file you desire does not have an extension, you must use the period separator, as follows:

```
A> DIR FILENAME.

Volume in drive A is DOSDISK
Directory of  A:\

FILENAME            18    1-05-87    2:52p
        1 File(s)    2361344 bytes free
```

Examples

```
A> DIR
```

```
A> DIR *.*
```

These commands are equivalent.

```
A> DIR /P
```

DIR will pause and display the following message with each page of file names:

```
Strike a key when ready . . .
```

```
A> DIR /W

  Volume in drive A is IBM
  Directory of  A:\

ANSI     SYS    ASSIGN   COM    ATTRIB   EXE    BACKUP   COM    BASIC    COM
BASICA   COM    CHKDSK   COM    COMMAND  COM    COMP     COM    DISKCOMP COM
DISKCOPY COM    DRIVER   SYS    EDLIN    COM    FDISK    COM    FIND     EXE
FORMAT   COM    GRAFTABL COM    GRAPHICS COM    JOIN     EXE    KEYBFR   COM
KEYBGR   COM    KEYBIT   COM    KEYBSP   COM    KEYBUK   COM    LABEL    COM
MODE     COM    MORE     COM    PRINT    COM    RECOVER  COM    REPLACE  EXE
RESTORE  COM    SELECT   COM    SHARE    EXE    SORT     EXE    SUBST    EXE
SYS      COM    TREE     COM    VDISK    SYS    XCOPY    EXE    JOINDIR
       40 File(s)     21504 bytes free
```

DIR will display file names five across without specifying size, date, and time.

DISKCOMP (Compare Floppy Disks)
External DISKCOMP.COM

Function   Compare the contents of two floppy disks, and display the side and track numbers that differ between the two disks.

Syntax Chart

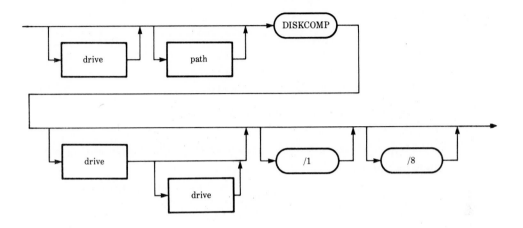

Format

[drive:][path]DISKCOMP [d1: [d2:]] [/1][/8]

Qualifiers

/1 directs DISKCOMP to compare only one side of the disk.

/8 directs DISKCOMP to make its comparison based on eight sectors per track as opposed to nine.

Options

d1: is the primary disk in the comparison.

d2: is the secondary disk in the comparison.

Notes   DISKCOMP allows you to use the same or different disk drives for comparisons. If you use the same drive, the program will prompt you to insert the proper disk at the correct time.

```
Insert SECOND diskette in drive A
```

If you invoke DISKCOMP without any drive specifications, DISKCOMP will perform a single-drive comparison.

```
A> DISKCOMP

Insert FIRST diskette in drive A

Press any key when ready . . .
```

If you omit the second disk drive, DISKCOMP will use the current default drive.

If the disks are identical, DISKCOMP will display the following message:

```
Compare OK
```

If a track difference is found, DISKCOMP will display the following:

```
Compare error on
side n track n
```

DISKCOMP does not support virtual drives (RAM drives), disk assignments via ASSIGN, fixed disk comparisons, or mixed-sided comparisons (double versus single).

If the disk types are incompatible, DISKCOMP will display

```
Drive types or diskette types
not compatible
```

After it finishes a comparison, DISKCOMP will display

```
Compare another diskette (Y/N)?
```

To compare additional disks, press Y; otherwise, press N.
DISKCOMP uses the following exit-status values to support conditional batch processing:

0   successful comparison (identical disks)

1   disks not identical

2   user termination via CTRL-BREAK

3   fatal disk error

4   invalid command

Examples

```
A> DISKCOMP
```

DISKCOMP will perform a single-drive comparison of the floppy disk that you insert, with another one that you will be prompted to insert.

```
A> DISKCOMP A: B:
```

DISKCOMP will compare the contents of the disk in drive A to those of the disk in drive B.

```
A> DISKCOMP B:
```

DISKCOMP will compare the contents of the disk in drive B to those of the disk in the current default drive.

If you specify a hard disk, DISKCOMP will display

```
A> DISKCOMP C:

Invalid drive specification
Specified drive does not exist,
or is non-removable
```

DISKCOPY (Copy Floppy Disks)
External DISKCOPY.COM

Function   Copy the contents of one floppy disk to another floppy disk.

Syntax Chart

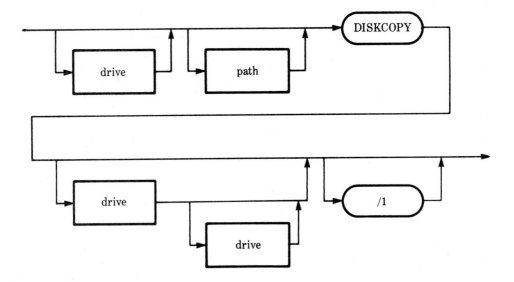

Format

[drive:][path]DISKCOPY [d1: [d2:]] [/1]

Qualifiers

/1 directs DISKCOPY to copy only one side of the disk.

Options

d1: is the disk to copy (source disk).

d2: is the disk d1 is copied to (target disk).

Notes   DISKCOPY allows you to use one or two disk drives during disk copies. If you use the same drive, DISKCOPY will prompt you to insert the correct disk at the proper time, as follows:

```
A> DISKCOPY A: A:

Insert SOURCE Diskette in Drive A :

Press any key when ready . . .
```

DISKCOPY performs single-drive disk copies under the following conditions:

• The user omits both drive specifications, as follows:

A> DISKCOPY

• The system is a single-floppy-disk system

If you omit the second drive specification, DISKCOPY will use the current default.

When you are performing a two-drive copy, DISKCOPY will

prompt you to enter the source and target disks prior to beginning the file copy:

```
A> DISKCOPY A: B:

Insert SOURCE Diskette in Drive A :

Insert TARGET Diskette in Drive B :

Press any key when ready . . .
```

Place the disks in the drives desired and press any key.

If the target disk is unformatted, DISKCOPY will format the disk and display the message

```
Formatting While Copying
```

DISKCOPY does not support virtual drives (RAM drives), disk assignments via ASSIGN, or fixed disk references.

DISKCOPY does not correct disk fragmentation (see Chapter 9). If CHKDSK reports that a disk is badly fragmented, FORMAT a new disk and use the XCOPY command.

When DISKCOPY is finished, it will ask whether or not you want to make additional copies.

```
Copy another diskette (Y/N)?
```

To copy an additional disk, press Y; otherwise, press N.

If DISKCOPY encounters errors on either the source or target disk, it will report the drive track and side containing the error. In such instances, the target disk may be unusable.

DISKCOPY provides the following exit-status codes to support conditional batch processing:

0   successful disk copy

1   unrecoverable error occurred

2   user termination via CTRL-BREAK

3   fatal disk error

4   invalid command

Examples

`A> DISKCOPY`

DISKCOPY will perform a single-drive disk copy of a disk.

`A> DISKCOPY A: B:`

DISKCOPY will copy the contents of the source disk in drive A to the target disk in drive B.

`A> DISKCOPY A:`

DISKCOPY will copy the contents of the disk contained in drive A to the disk contained in the current default drive. Since the specified drive is the same as the current default drive, DISKCOPY will prompt you to enter the target disk.

If the disk drive specified contains references to a fixed disk, DISKCOPY will display

```
A> DISKCOPY C: A:

Invalid drive specification.
Specified drive does not exist,
or is non-removable.
```

ECHO (Display Batch Command Names)
Internal Command

Function   Turn on/off the display of batch commands to standard output as they execute within BAT batch files.

Syntax Chart

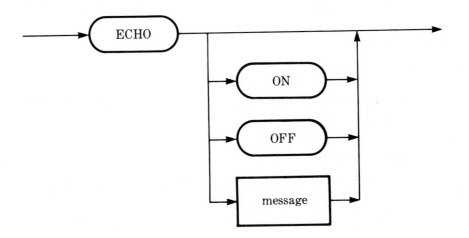

Format

ECHO [ON ¦ OFF ¦ message]

Qualifiers   None

Options

ON turns on the display of batch command names.

OFF turns off the display of batch command names.

message is an optional string of characters to display from within a batch file. The message can contain references to batch parameters.

Notes   None

Examples

Assume the following is contained in the file TEST.BAT:

```
ECHO GOING TO TURN ECHO OFF
ECHO OFF
VER
VOL
ECHO GOING TO TURN ECHO ON
ECHO ON
VER
VOL
```

The command

```
A> TEST
```

results in

```
A>ECHO GOING TO TURN ECHO OFF
GOING TO TURN ECHO OFF

A>ECHO OFF

IBM Personal Computer DOS Version  3.00

 Volume in drive A is DOSDISK
GOING TO TURN ECHO ON

A>VER

IBM Personal Computer DOS Version  3.00

A>VOL

 Volume in drive A is DOSDISK
```

Likewise, the batch file

```
ECHO ON
DATE
TIME
ECHO OFF
VER
```

results in

```
A>DATE
Current date is Mon  1-05-1987
Enter new date (mm-dd-yy):

A>TIME
Current time is 15:39:34.04
Enter new time:

A>ECHO OFF

IBM Personal Computer DOS Version  3.00
```

Last, to display batch parameters

```
ECHO %1 %2 %3 %4 %5 %6 %7 %8 %9
```

you issue the command

```
A> TEST A B C D E F G H
```

which will display

```
A> ECHO A B C D E F G H
A B C D E F G H
```

ERASE (Delete a File from Disk)
Internal Command

Function   Erase the contents of a file on disk and remove the file's directory entry.

Syntax Chart

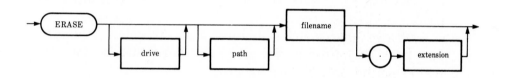

Format

ERASE file_specification

Qualifiers   None

Options

file_specification is the name of the file that you want to ERASE.

Notes   If a device or pathname is not specified, ERASE will use the current defaults.

ERASE cannot delete files marked as read-only. If you attempt to ERASE such a file, DOS will display

```
Access denied
```

ERASE supports the DOS wildcard characters. If you specify the characters *.*, ERASE will prompt

```
A> ERASE *.*
Are you sure (Y/N)?
```

To delete all of the files, press Y and press ENTER; otherwise, press N.

ERASE cannot delete subdirectories. To delete a subdirectory you first must ERASE all of the files that it contains and then issue the RMDIR command.

Examples

```
A> ERASE *.*
```

The command will ERASE all of the files in the current directory.

```
A> ERASE B:\OLDFILES\*.BAK
```

ERASE will delete all of the files contained in the subdirectory \OLDFILES on a disk contained in drive B.

EXE2BIN (Convert EXE File to COM)
External EXE2BIN.COM

Function   Convert files with an EXE extension to COM files.

Syntax Chart

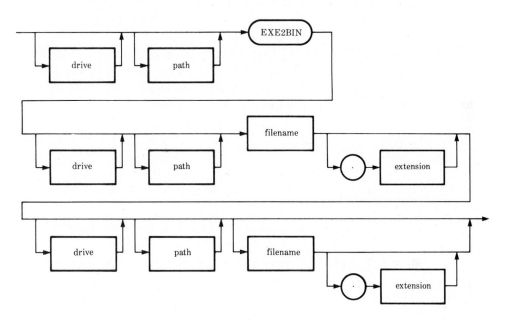

Format

[drive:][path]EXE2BIN file_specification1 [file_specification2]

Qualifiers   None

Options

file_specification1 contains the EXE file that you want to convert to a COM file.

file_specification2 is the name of the target COM file. If you do not specify a file, EXE2BIN creates a file with the same name as file_specification1 with the extension BIN.

Notes   If you do not specify an extension on file_specification1, EXE2BIN assumes EXE.

If you do not specify an extension on file_specification2, EXE2BIN assumes BIN.

If a drive or path is not provided for either file specification, EXE2BIN uses the current defaults.

COM files contain the memory image of a program. This format results in a more compact file and quicker loading by the DOS command processor at run time. For you to convert an EXE file to a COM file, the EXE file must have the following characteristics:

• The code and data portions of the program each contain less than 64K.

• There must be no stack segment.

• All program references must reside in the same segment.

If the file does not meet these qualifications, EXE2BIN will display

```
File cannot be converted
```

See the *Macro Assembler Manual* for more information on creating COM files.

In the past, because of their compactness and loading speed, COM files were highly desirable. EXE files, however, can reside anywhere in memory. The newer versions of DOS and MS Windows make it desirable for a program to reside anywhere in memory. You will see a shift away from the use of COM files.

Example

```
A> EXE2BIN TEST.EXE TEST.COM
```

Converts the file TEST.EXE to TEST.COM. This command is equivalent to

```
A> EXE2BIN TEST *.COM
```

EXIT (Terminate a Secondary Command Processor) Internal Command

Function   Terminate a secondary command processor and return control to DOS or the calling process.

Syntax Chart

Format

EXIT

Qualifiers   None

Notes   EXIT returns control to the calling process and releases the memory allocated by the secondary command processor.

FDISK (Fixed Disk Configuration) External FDISK.COM

Function   Configure and display information about fixed disk partitions. Specify the active partition.

Syntax Chart

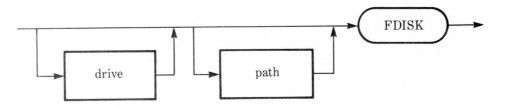

Format

[drive:][path]FDISK

Qualifiers   None

Notes   You can divide a fixed disk into one to four sections called partitions. A partition separates disk space into individual areas. Each area can contain a unique operating system. FDISK allows you to specify which partition the system is to boot from and, thus, which operating system is to be used.

Most DOS users create only one large DOS partition that uses the entire fixed disk.

FDISK is a menu-driven program. It provides you with default choices for each menu presented. If you want the default response, press ENTER. Otherwise, simply type the value desired and press ENTER.

A complete description of FDISK is provided in Chapter 9.

FIND (Search a File or Piped Input for a String) External FIND.EXE

Function   Search the file(s) specified for the character string and display lines containing the string.

Syntax Chart

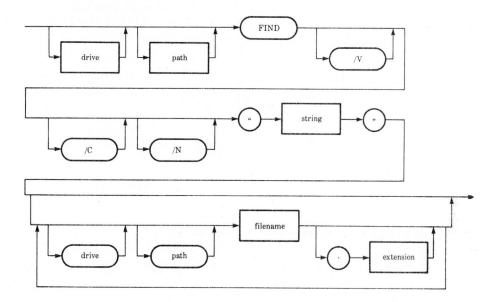

Format

[drive:][path]FIND [file—specification . . .] [/C][/N][/V]

Qualifiers

/C displays a count of the number of lines containing the string. If the /C qualifier is used with the /N qualifier, FIND ignores the /N.

/N displays the line numbers of each line within the file that contains the string.

/V displays each line that does not contain the string.

Options

file—specification is the file(s) you want to examine for the string. If you do not specify a file, FIND uses the standard input (stdin) to support redirection of I/O.

Notes FIND does not support DOS wildcard characters.

FIND will not match a lowercase string to an uppercase string.

The string desired must be contained in double quotation marks. If the string desired contains embedded double quotation marks, such as

"That's right", he said.

simply group the quotation marks as follows:

```
A> FIND """That's right"", he said." FILENAME.EXT
```

FIND treats two successive quotation marks as a single quotation mark.

Examples

```
A> FIND "NY" MAIL.LST
```

FIND will search the file MAIL.LST for the string NY.

```
A> FIND/C "NY" MAIL.LST
```

FIND will display a count of the number of occurrences of the string NY in the file MAIL.LST.

```
A> FIND /N "NY" MAIL.LST
```

FIND will display the line number and line for each line that contains the string NY in the file MAIL.LST.

```
A> FIND /V "NY" MAIL.LST
```

FIND will display each line in the file MAIL.LST that does not contain the string NY.

```
A> FIND "NY" MAIL.LST OLDLIST.DAT CITY.DAT
```

FIND will examine the files MAIL.LST, OLDLIST.DAT, and CITY.DAT for each occurrence of the string NY.

```
A> DIR ¦ FIND "<DIR>"
```

FIND supports I/O redirection. In this case, FIND will display the lines from the directory listing that contain the string <DIR>. This provides a quick method for listing all of the subdirectories in a directory.

FOR (DOS Iterative Processing Construct)
Internal Command

Function   Provide repetitive execution of DOS commands.

Syntax Chart

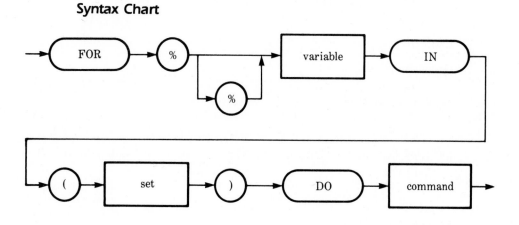

Format

FOR %%variable IN (set) DO dos—command

Qualifiers   None

Options

%%variable and *%variable* are simply variables that DOS sets to successive members of the set specified.

set is a list of valid DOS file names. The file names can appear in the list as

(file1, file2, file3)

or the set can contain DOS wildcard characters (*.*) or (*.DAT). If the set contains wildcard characters, the variable that you specify is set to the matching files in succession.

dos—command is the command that DOS is to execute iteratively.

Notes   The DOS FOR command is most common in DOS BAT files. It can, however, be invoked from the DOS prompt. If you are using the command from a BAT file, you must use the form %%variable. If, instead, you are using the command from the DOS prompt, you simply use %variable.

FOR loops cannot be nested.

Examples

(Iterative)

```
A> FOR %F IN (SEPT.DAT, OCT.DAT, NOV.DAT) DO SORT < %F
```

DOS will assign the variable F the file names SEPT.DAT, OCT.DAT, and NOV.DAT successively, displaying their contents in sorted order.

```
A> FOR %F IN (*.C) DO CC %F
```

DOS will successively compile all of your C files.

(Batch)

```
FOR %%F IN (*.FOR) DO ATTRIB +R %%F
```

DOS will set all of your FORTRAN (*.FOR) files to read-only.

FORMAT (Format Disk for Use by DOS) External FORMAT.COM

Function   Ready a disk for use by DOS. The disk can be a fixed or floppy disk.

Syntax Chart

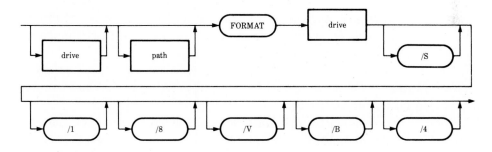

Format

[drive:][path]FORMAT [d:][/B][/S][/V][/1][/4][/8]

Qualifiers

/B requests FORMAT to allocate space on the disk for the DOS

system files but does not place them on the disk. This allows the DOS SYS command to be performed at a later time. Many software packages that require DOS FORMAT their disks in this fashion and then allow the end user to place DOS on the disk via SYS. In this case, DOS will FORMAT the disk with eight sectors per track.

/S requests FORMAT to place the operating system files on the disk, thus making the disk bootable. This qualifier cannot be used in conjunction with /B.

/V requests FORMAT to pause, prompting you to enter an 11-character volume label

```
Volume label (11 characters, ENTER for none)?
```

(See the DOS LABEL command for more information on volume labels.)

/1 directs FORMAT to format only a single side of the disk.

/4 requests FORMAT to format a double-sided disk in a quad-density drive. **Warning:** This format may not be readable in standard double-sided drives.

/8 directs FORMAT to format the disk with 8 sectors per track as opposed to the default 9 or 15. This qualifier cannot be used in conjunction with /V.

Notes   All new floppy disks and fixed disks must be formatted to be usable by DOS.

If you modify disk partitions via FDISK, the new partition must be formatted.

Formatting a disk always destroys the information previously contained on the disk.

FORMAT will prompt you to enter the disk to format in the specified drive, as follows:

```
Insert new diskette for drive B:
and strike ENTER when ready
```

If you format a disk with the /S option, DOS will place the system files on the target disk for you. Two of the files are hidden files and do not appear in the directory listing. You can verify their existence via CHKDSK.

`A> CHKDSK`

If the system files are not present on the current default disk, FORMAT will prompt you to place a disk containing the files into the default drive, as follows:

```
Insert DOS disk in drive A:
and strike ENTER when ready
```

Place your DOS system disk into the drive and press ENTER. If the default drive is a fixed disk, DOS will prompt you to place a DOS system disk into drive A.

Unless overridden by the /1 qualifier, FORMAT will examine the target drive and format the disk accordingly.

When the disk is formatted, FORMAT displays total disk space (bytes), disk space consumed by DOS (bytes), disk space unavailable because of damaged media (bytes), and available disk space (bytes).

```
A> FORMAT B:/S
Insert new diskette for drive B:
and strike ENTER when ready


Formatting...Format complete
System transferred

    362496 bytes total disk space
     60416 bytes used by system
    302080 bytes available on disk

Format another (Y/N)?
```

If you want to FORMAT an additional disk, press Y; otherwise, press N.

If you do not specify a target drive, FORMAT will use the default drive. If the default is a fixed disk, FORMAT will display

```
WARNING, ALL DATA ON NON-REMOVEABLE DISK
DRIVE C: WILL BE LOST!
Proceed with Format (Y/N)?
```

If you want to continue the FORMAT, press Y; otherwise, press N.

FORMAT uses the following exit-status values to support conditional batch processing:

0   successful format
1   unknown error
2   unknown error
3   user termination via CTRL-BREAK
4   termination because of fatal error
5   user termination to fixed disk prompt

Examples

`A> FORMAT B:`

FORMAT will format the disk in drive B with the default number of sectors per track.

`A> FORMAT B:/S`

FORMAT will format the disk in drive B, placing the DOS system files required to make the disk bootable on the disk.

`A> FORMAT B:/V`

FORMAT will format the disk in drive B and prompt you to enter a volume label as previously shown.

```
A> FORMAT
```

FORMAT will format the disk that you place in the current drive.

```
A> FORMAT B:/1
```

FORMAT will format the disk in drive B as a single-sided disk.

GOTO (DOS Branching Construct) Internal Command

Function   Branch to the label specified in a BAT file.

Syntax Chart

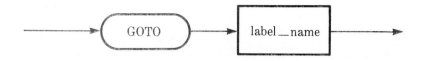

Format

GOTO label

Qualifiers   None

Options

label is a label that appears in the BAT file at which DOS is to continue executing the batch procedure. The label must be contained on its own line as follows:

    :label

Only the first eight characters of the label are significant. Therefore, DOS considers :doslabel1 and :doslabel2 as equivalent.

Notes If the label specified is not found in the BAT file, DOS terminates execution of the file and displays

```
Label not found
```

Examples

```
:LOOP
DIR
GOTO LOOP
```

The preceding BAT file displays directory listings until the user enters a CTRL-BREAK.

```
IF NOT EXIST NEWDATA.DAT GOTO DONE
SORT < NEWDATA.DAT > NEWDATA.SRT
PRINT NEWDATA.SRT
:DONE
```

The preceding BAT file checks for the existence of the file NEWDATA.DAT. If the file exists, it is sorted and printed. Otherwise, the procedure terminates.

GRAFTABL (Load Additional Character Set Data into Memory)
External GRAFTABL.COM

Function   Load an additional table of character set data into memory to support the color graphics adapter in medium-resolution graphics (320 x 200).

Syntax Chart

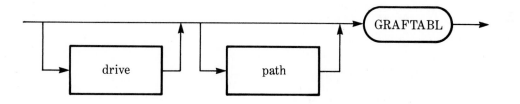

Format

[drive:][path]GRAFTABL

Qualifiers   None

Notes   In graphics mode, the color graphics adapter tends to blur ASCII characters in the range 120-255. Because most foreign character sets use this ASCII range, DOS provides GRAFTABL.

GRAFTABL loads memory-resident software that processes ASCII characters in the range 120-255. It can be installed only once. If you attempt to load GRAFTABL a second time, DOS will display

```
GRAPHIC CHARACTERS ALREADY LOADED
```

The memory-resident software allocates approximately 1K of memory. The only way to remove the software is to reboot.

Only use GRAFTABL with PCs that have a color graphics adapter. On other systems, the command will simply allocate memory; no performance value is added. GRAFTABL only affects characters in the range 120-255.

Example

```
A> GRAFTABL
GRAPHIC CHARACTERS LOADED
```

GRAPHICS (Print Graphics Display)
External GRAPHICS.COM

Function   Allow the screen contents with graphics to be printed.

Syntax Chart

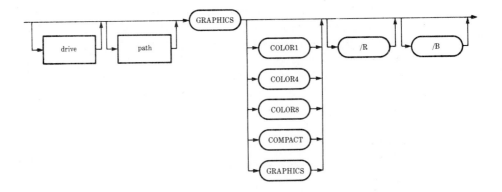

Format

[drive:][path]GRAPHICS [printer_type][/B][/R]

Qualifiers

/B requests GRAPHICS to print the background color. The default is not to print the background color.

/R directs GRAPHICS to reverse the screen image. Black images will be printed as white, and white images will be printed as black.

Options

printer_type specifies the type of printer to be used, as follows:

COLOR1	Color printer with black ribbon
COLOR4	Color printer with red, green, and blue ribbon
COLOR8	Color printer with cyan, magenta, yellow, and black ribbon
COMPACT	Compact printer
GRAPHICS	Graphics printer

If no printer type is specified, GRAPHICS assumes a graphics printer. Refer to your printer manual for additional information.

Notes   GRAPHICS loads memory-resident software that processes screen image prints of graphics displays. The memory-resident software allocates approximately 1-1.5K of memory. The only way to remove the software is to reboot.
    You can only load the GRAPHICS software into memory once.
    GRAPHICS supports the following:

• Print screen operations in text mode. This normally takes less than 30 seconds.

- Print screen operations in graphics mode. This may take up to three minutes. In 640 × 200 mode graphics, the screen image is rotated 90 degrees on the hard copy.

Example

```
A> GRAPHICS
```

GRAPHICS will load the memory-resident software and assume a graphics printer.

IF (DOS Conditional Processing Construct) Internal Command

Function   Provide conditional processing of DOS commands within batch files.

Syntax Chart

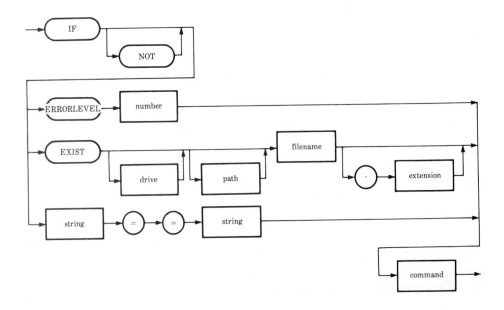

DOS: The Complete Reference

Format

IF [NOT] condition dos—command

Qualifiers   None

Options

NOT performs a Boolean NOT of the result of the condition. If the condition is true, NOT will result in a false and vice versa.

condition must be one of the following:

ERRORLEVEL value
EXIST file—specification
string1==string2

dos—command is the command to execute based upon a true condition.

Notes   ERRORLEVEL value is true if the previous DOS command exits with a status value greater than or equal to the specified value. The value must be specified as a decimal value, as illustrated here:

```
IF ERRORLEVEL 3 GOTO FATAL
```

EXIST file—specification is true if the specified file name is found by DOS, as shown here:

```
IF EXIST CONFIG.SYS PRINT CONFIG.SYS
```

string1==string2 evaluates as true if the contents of string1 are identical to the contents of string2.
When a condition evaluates as false, execution of the BAT file simply continues at the next statement.

Examples

```
IF EXIST %1 SORT < %1
IF NOT EXIST %1 ECHO FILE NOT FOUND
```

The preceding batch command checks for the existence of the file specified by %1 and, if it is present, sorts it. Otherwise, it displays the message "File not found."

```
REM MONTHLY BACKUP PROCEDURES
BACKUP C:\ B:/S
IF ERRORLEVEL 4 GOTO FATAL_ERROR
IF ERRORLEVEL 3 GOTO USER_TERMINATED
IF ERRORLEVEL 2 GOTO SHARING_CONFLICT
IF ERRORLEVEL 1 GOTO NO_FILES
:SUCCESSFUL
PAUSE SUCCESSFUL BACKUP -- BACKUP COMPLETE
GOTO DONE
:NO_FILES
PAUSE NO FILES FOUND TO BACKUP
GOTO DONE
:SHARING_CONFLICT
PAUSE FILE SHARING CONFLICTS -- BACKUP INCOMPLETE
GOTO DONE
:USER_TERMINATED
PAUSE USER TERMINATION OF BACKUP -- BACKUP INCOMPLETE
GOTO DONE
:FATAL_ERROR
PAUSE FATAL BACKUP ERROR -- BACKUP INCOMPLETE
:DONE
```

The preceding batch procedure tests the exit-status value returned by BACKUP and displays the appropriate message.

JOIN (Join a Disk Drive to a DOS Path) External JOIN.EXE

Function   Make two disk drives appear as one by joining a disk drive to a DOS path.

Syntax Chart

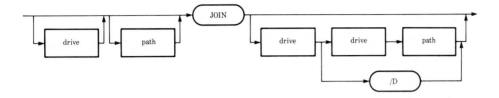

Format

[drive:][path]JOIN [d: [p]][/D]

Qualifiers

/D directs DOS to delete the JOIN specified.

Options

d: is the disk drive to JOIN to the DOS path.

p is the DOS path to JOIN the disk drive to.

Notes   JOIN will only JOIN a disk drive to an empty DOS directory.

If you issue the JOIN command without any parameters

```
C> JOIN
B: => C:\JOINDIR
```

JOIN will display the current joins.

Example

```
C> JOIN B: \JOINDIR
```

DOS will JOIN drive B to the path \JOINDIR on drive C. All references to C:\JOINDIR now will refer to drive B, as the following shows:

```
C> DIR \JOINDIR

 Volume in drive C is DOSDISK
 Directory of  C:\JOINDIR

ANSI     SYS     1651  12-30-85   12:00p
DRIVER   SYS     1115  12-30-85   12:00p
VDISK    SYS     3307  12-30-85   12:00p
        3 File(s)      21504 bytes free
```

KEYBxx (Load Foreign Keyboard Set) External KEYBxx.COM

Function   Load memory-resident software to support a foreign keyboard configuration to replace the keyboard program in the ROM-BIOS.

Syntax Chart

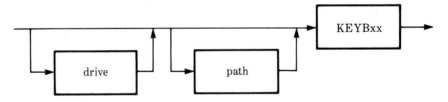

Format

[drive:][path]KEYBxx

Qualifiers None

Notes See Chapter 12.

Keyboard programs are specified as follows:

KEYBFR	FRANCE
KEYBGR	GERMANY
KEYBIT	ITALY
KEYBSP	SPAIN
KEYBUK	UNITED KINGDOM

Newer versions of DOS may support additional keyboard layouts. Refer to your documentation.

Load only one keyboard program into memory after booting DOS. If you load a second program into memory, it becomes the active keyboard. However, the space allocated by the first program remains allocated. Each keyboard program allocates approximately 2K of memory.

Once you have installed a keyboard program, you can change between that program and the U.S. keyboard by pressing CTRL-ALT-F1. To return to the foreign keyboard, press CTRL-ALT-F2.

See the SELECT command for more information on DOS international support.

Example

A> KEYBUK

Load the United Kingdom keyboard.

LABEL (Specify a Disk Volume Label) External LABEL.COM

Function Place an 11-character volume label on a disk.

Syntax Chart

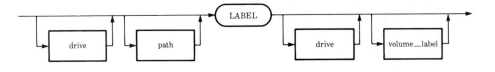

Format

[drive:][path]LABEL [d:][volume_label]

Qualifiers   None

Options

    d: is the disk drive identification containing the disk to place the volume label on. If you do not specify a drive, LABEL uses the current default drive.

    volume_label is the volume label to assign to the disk. If you do not specify a volume label, LABEL will prompt you for one as follows:

```
Volume Label (11 characters, ENTER for none)?
```

Any of the characters valid in DOS file names are valid volume-label characters.

Notes   If you want the disk unlabeled, simply press ENTER at the prompt

```
Volume Label (11 characters, ENTER for none)?
```

    Volume labels should be assigned to most disks. Chapter 16 presents the rationale for labeling your disk and a Turbo Pascal procedure that obtains the disk label from within a program so that you can verify that you are indeed processing the correct disk.

Examples

A> LABEL

The command allows you to assign or delete a disk volume label.

A> LABEL B:

This command allows you to assign or delete the disk volume label for the disk in drive B.

A> LABEL B:EXP1987

This command labels the disk in drive B as EXP1987.

MKDIR (Create a Subdirectory)
Internal Command

Function   Create a DOS subdirectory on the specified disk.

Syntax Chart

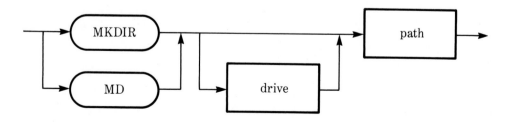

Format

   MKDIR [drive:]path

or

   MD [drive:]path

Qualifiers   None

Options

   drive: is the disk identification containing the disk on which
   to create the subdirectory.

   path is the name of the subdirectory. DOS directory names
   have the same format as DOS file names, except that the path
   may be longer than one file name.

Notes   The MKDIR command can be abbreviated to MD.

   If you do not specify a disk drive, MKDIR uses the current
default drive.

   You can create a large number of subdirectories. The maximum pathname that DOS can process, however, is 63 characters
long (including backslashes). Directory names can share the same
name as DOS files, since the attribute byte distinguishes them. It
is good practice, however, to keep the names unique.

   If you specify a directory path, the backslash (\ ) tells DOS to
begin at the root directory, as in the following:

A> MKDIR \IBM

   If no backslash is present, as in

A> MKDIR IBM

DOS will create the directory in the current directory.

Examples

```
A> MKDIR NEWDIR
```

MKDIR will create the subdirectory NEWDIR in the current directory.

```
A> MD B:NEWSUB
```

MKDIR will create a subdirectory called NEWSUB in the current directory on drive B.

```
A> MKDIR \DOS
```

MKDIR will create a subdirectory called DOS in the root directory of the current drive.

```
A> MKDIR \DOS\SUPP
```

MKDIR will create a subdirectory called SUPP within the directory DOS on the current drive.

MODE (Specify Device Characteristics)
External MODE.COM

Function   Set the device characteristics of the asynchronous communications adapter, the color graphics adapter, or the system printer.

Syntax Chart

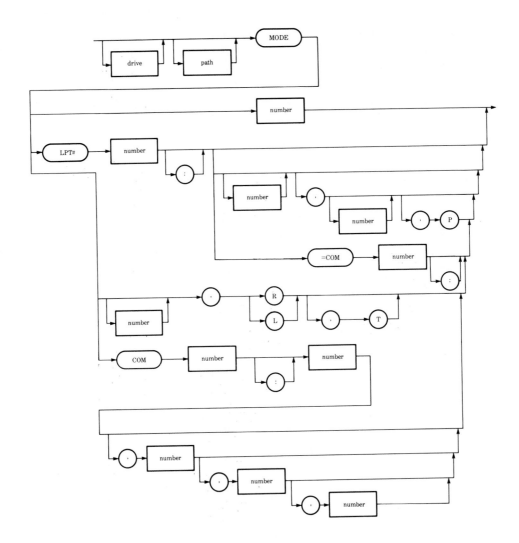

Format

    [drive:][path]MODE n

or

    [drive:][path]MODE [n],m[,t]

or

    [drive:][path]MODE COM#[:] baud [,parity[,databits[,stop-bits [,P]]]]

or

    [drive:][path]MODE LPT#[:] [n][,m[,P]]

or

    [drive:][path]MODE LPT#[:]=COM#[:]

Qualifiers   None

Options

    n sets the color graphics adapter as follows:

        40 creates a 40-column screen display.
        80 creates an 80-column screen display.
        BW40 sets the monitor to black and white with 40-column display.
        BW80 sets the monitor to black and white with 80-column display.
        CO40 sets the monitor to color with 40-column display.
        CO80 sets the monitor to color with 80-column display.
        MONO sets the display to the monochrome adapter with 80 columns.

    m is the letter R to shift the display right or L to shift the display left.

t requests a test pattern to aid in shifting the display.

n sets the printer as follows:

80 characters per line
132 characters per line

m sets the print vertical lines per inch as follows:

6 selects 6 lines per vertical inch.
8 selects 8 lines per vertical inch.

P requests continuous retries on time-out errors.

is the device number where 1, 2, or 3 is for printers and where 1 or 2 is for asynchronous communications adapters.

parity is specified as N for no parity, O for odd parity, and E for even parity.

databits specifies the number of data bits in a byte (7 or 8).

stopbits specifies the number of stop bits (1 or 2). If the baud rate is 110, the default is 2; otherwise, the default is 1.

Notes   The printer defaults are 80 characters per line and 6 lines per inch.

The P continuous retry option increases the amount of memory allocated by DOS for memory-resident code. You can break a continuous retry loop with a CTRL-BREAK. To disable retry operations, you must reinitialize the port with another MODE command.

The default protocol parameters are

Parity EVEN
Databits 7
Stopbits 1 (110 baud, stopbits = 2)

Baud rates are specified as

110 or 11
150 or 15
300 or 30
600 or 60
1200 or 12

```
        2400 or 24
        4800 or 48
        9600 or 96
```

The command MODE LPT#[:]=COM#[:] redirects parallel-printer output to a serial asynchronous communications adapter. Once printer output is redirected, you must issue a second MODE command to cancel redirection.

The colon is optional on LPT and COM device names.

MODE allows you to shift all of the characters on your display to the left or right. The command

```
A> MODE ,R,T
```

will display a test pattern to aid in the shift, as shown here:

```
012345678901234567890123456789012345678901234567890123456789012345678901234567890123456789
Do you see the leftmost 0? (Y/N)
```

If you press Y, the command completes and the screen is unaffected. If you press N, the screen will shift one character location in the specified direction. In 40-column mode, the screen shifts one character location. In 80-column mode, the screen shifts two characters. Chapter 4 provides a complete explanation of the MODE command.

Examples

```
A> MODE 80
```

Set the screen display to 80-column mode.

```
A> MODE BW40
```

Set the screen to black and white with 40 columns.

```
A> MODE LPT1: 80,8
```

Set the printer to 80 characters per line and 8 lines per inch.

```
A> MODE LPT1:=COM1:
```

Redirect parallel-printer output from LPT1 to the serial asynchronous communications port COM1.

```
A> MODE COM1: 96,N,8,1
```

Set COM1 to 9600 baud with no parity, 8 data bits, and 1 stop bit.

```
A> MODE COM1: 11,N,7,1
```

Configure COM1 for output with 110 baud, no parity, 7 data bits, and 1 stop bit.

MORE (Display Output a Screen at a Time)
External MORE.COM

Function   Read data from the standard input device, displaying it a page at a time. When a page is displayed, the prompt —MORE— appears; the user then presses any key to continue.

Syntax Chart

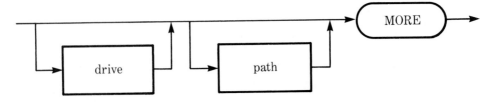

DOS: The Complete Reference

Format

[drive:][path]MORE

Qualifiers   None

Notes   At the —MORE— prompt, pressing any key causes the next page of data to be displayed.

MORE is primarily used with the DOS pipe. If you simply enter the command

```
A> MORE
```

the program will read and echo data from the keyboard until a CTRL-Z (end of file) is entered.

Examples

```
A> DIR | MORE
```

The output of the DIR command is displayed on the screen one page at a time.

```
A> MORE < PHONE.LST
```

MORE displays the contents of the file PHONE.LST one page at a time.

```
A> FIND "NY" PHONE.LST | MORE
```

Display each line in the file PHONE.LST that contains the string NY one page at a time.

PATH (Specify the Command Search Directories) Internal Command

Function　　Specify or display the list of drives and directory paths that DOS should traverse in search of a COM, EXE, or BAT file if the command is not found in the current working directory.

Syntax Chart

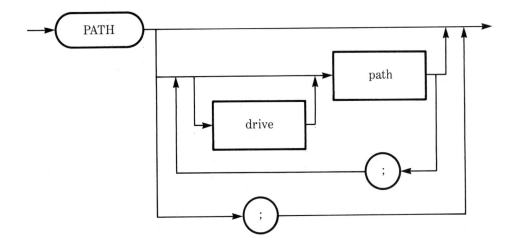

Format

　　　PATH [[drive:][path] [[;[drive:][path]]...]]

or

　　　PATH ;

Qualifiers　　None

Options

　　　drive: is a disk drive identification DOS is to search for command files. It can be used with a directory path.

　　　path is a series of subdirectories DOS is to examine.

Notes   When you enter a command that is not found by DOS in the current working directory, DOS uses the specified path to search for the command. DOS searches the path entries in the order that they are specified until the command is found, or the list is exhausted.

If you do not provide any command-line parameters, as in

```
A> PATH
PATH=C:\DOS;C:\UTIL;D:;A:
```

PATH will display the current command search path.

If you invoke PATH with a semicolon, as in

```
A> PATH ;
```

PATH will delete the command search path. In this case, DOS now will examine only the current working directory for the command.

The PATH command does not validate the paths that you enter. If DOS later experiences an error with a path (normally the path has been deleted or misspelled), it simply ignores the entry and continues searching the next path.

PATH only locates COM, EXE, and BAT files. MS-DOS version 3.2 provides the APPEND command, which works in a similar fashion for data files.

Most users define their command search path in their AUTOEXEC.BAT file.

Examples

```
A> PATH C:\DOS;C:\UTIL;A:
```

DOS will now search the directories \DOS and \UTIL on drive C, in that order, and if the file is still not found, examine the default directory in drive A.

```
A> PATH
PATH=C:\DOS;C:\UTIL;A:
```

PATH will display the current command search path.

```
A> PATH ;
```

PATH will delete the command search path.

PAUSE (Temporarily Suspend Batch Processing) Internal Command

Function   Temporarily suspend batch processing, display an optional message, and prompt the user to press any key to continue.

Syntax Chart

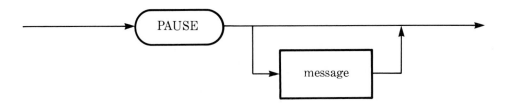

Format

PAUSE [message]

Qualifiers   None

Options

message is an optional character string of up to 123 characters that PAUSE displays prior to prompting, such as

```
Strike a key when ready . . .
```

Notes   To continue processing of the BAT procedure, simply press any key. To terminate processing, press CTRL-BREAK. If a CTRL-BREAK is entered, DOS will display

```
Terminate batch job (Y/N)?
```

To terminate processing, press Y; otherwise, press N.

PAUSE is a convenient method of pausing processing while the user inserts a new disk during batch processing, as in the following:

```
PAUSE INSERT DATA DISK IN DRIVE B:
```

Examples

```
PAUSE INSERT DATA DISK IN DRIVE B:
DATASORT
```

Execution of the preceding BAT file results in

```
A>PAUSE INSERT DATA DISK IN DRIVE B:
Strike a key when ready . . .
```

PRINT (Send File to the DOS Print Queue)
External PRINT.COM

Function   Print a file(s) on the system printer while you are performing other tasks on the computer.

Syntax Chart

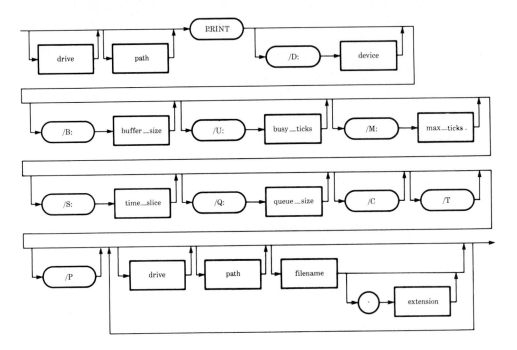

Format

[drive:][path]PRINT
[/B:buffer—size]
[/C]
[/D:device]
[/M:max—ticks]
[/P]
[/Q:queue—size]
[/S:time—slice]
[/T]
[/U:busy—ticks] [file—specification]

Qualifiers

/B:buffer—size sets the size of the memory buffer used by PRINT. The default size is 512 bytes. Increasing the size of

this buffer by multiples of 512 bytes (1024, 2048, 4096) will improve print performance by decreasing the number of disk I/Os required to print a file. Increasing this value does, however, allocate additional memory for DOS.

/C allows you to cancel specific files in the print queue. All file names found on the command line that precede the /C are removed from the queue, as in

A> PRINT FILE1.DAT /C

/D:*device_names* specifies the printer device. Valid device names include LPT1, LPT2, LPT3, and PRN. This qualifier is only valid the first time that you invoke the PRINT command.

/M:*max_ticks* specifies the maximum number of CPU clock ticks PRINT can have to print characters before it must return control of the CPU to DOS. The values for max_ticks range from 1-255. The default value is 2. This qualifier is only valid the first time that you invoke the PRINT command. Increasing this value will improve PRINT's performance by giving a higher priority to the print process and lower priority to the keyboard. If you make the value too large, the keyboard response may become slow.

/P adds all of the file names that precede the /P in the command line to the print queue. This allows you to add and delete files (via /C) in the same command.

/Q:*queue_size* specifies the number of file names the print queue can store. The range of values for queue_size is 1-32. The default value is 10. This qualifier is valid only the first time that you invoke the PRINT command.

/S:*time_slice* specifies the printer time-slice value. The range of values for time_slice is 1-255. The default value is 8. This qualifier is valid only the first time that you invoke the PRINT command.

/T removes all files from the print queue. If a file is being printed, it stops and a message notifying the operator of cancellation is printed. A form feed advances the paper in the printer to the next page.

/U:*busy_ticks* specifies the number of CPU clock ticks that

PRINT will wait until the printer becomes available. The range of values for busy—ticks is 1-255. The default value is 1. This qualifier is valid only the first time that you invoke the PRINT command.

Options

file—specification is the name of the optional file(s) to add or delete to or from the print queue.

Notes   A CPU clock tick occurs 18.2 times a second on an IBM PC.

PRINT installs the print queue the first time you invoke the PRINT command. PRINT allocates additional memory and places resident code into it. This, in turn, decreases the memory available for other applications.

If you do not specify a device name the first time that you invoke the PRINT command, the program will prompt you for the device you desire as follows:

```
Name of list device [PRN]:
```

Unless you have a printer connected to an asynchronous communications adapter, the default PRN: normally will be selected if you simply press ENTER.

Upon installation of the print queue, PRINT will display

```
Resident part of PRINT installed
```

PRINT supports the DOS wildcard characters, as in

```
A> PRINT *.DAT
```

PRINT always prints files in the order that they appear in the PRINT command.

Once the print queue has been installed, you can simply invoke PRINT with no file names to display the files currently queued, as shown here:

```
A> PRINT

    C:\DOSBOOK\DOSREF\DOSREF.2 is currently being printed
    C:\DOSBOOK\DOSREF\DOS.REA is in queue
    C:\DOSBOOK\DOSREF\DOSREF.3 is in queue
    C:\DOSBOOK\DOSREF\DOS.REF is in queue
    C:\DOSBOOK\DOSREF\ARTA.73 is in queue
```

If PRINT encounters a disk error while reading a file to print, the following will occur:

• The file currently being printed is cancelled.

• A disk error message is printed.

• A form feed advances the paper to the next page, and the printer alarm sounds.

• The files remaining in the queue are printed.

The qualifiers /T and /C cause PRINT to perform the following:

• The printer alarm sounds.

• If /T was issued, the message "ALL files cancelled by operator" is printed.

• If /C was issued, the message "filename: File cancelled by operator" is printed.

• A form feed advances the paper to the next page.

The disk containing the file to be printed must remain in the specified drive until printing is complete.

Files to be printed must not be modified or deleted until printing is complete.

An attempt to use the printer for other operations (such as print screen) while files are queued results in an out-of-paper condition.

Examples

`A> PRINT MAIL.LST`

PRINT the file MAIL.LST. If the PRINT command is being issued for the first time, PRINT will respond with

```
Name of list device [PRN]:
```

Press ENTER to send the output to the system printer.

`A> PRINT *.DAT`

PRINT supports DOS wildcard characters. All of the files with the extension DAT will be printed.

`A> PRINT /T`

PRINT will remove all files from the print queue.

`A> PRINT`

PRINT will list the files currently queued.

`A> PRINT MAIL.LST /C`

PRINT will remove the file MAIL.LST from the print queue.

`A> PRINT MAIL.LST /C MAIL.NEW /P`

PRINT will remove the file MAIL.LST from the print queue and add the file MAIL.NEW.

`A> PRINT /Q:32 /B:4098`

PRINT will install a print queue with support for 32 file names and a buffer size of 4098.

PROMPT (Set the System Prompt)
Internal Command

Function   Set the system prompt to the specified string.

Syntax Chart

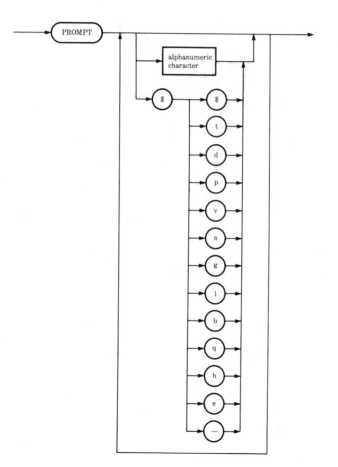

Format

PROMPT [prompt_string]

Qualifiers   None

Options

prompt_string is the text containing the desired system prompt. The prompt string can contain several metastrings that are in the format $c, where c is one of the following characters:

b the ¦ character
d the current system date
e the string Esc
h backspace character (deletes previous character)
g the > character
l the < character
n the current drive
p the current directory
q the = character
t the current system time
v the DOS version
_ carriage return line feed
$ the $ character

PROMPT ignores all other characters in metastrings.

Notes   If you issue the PROMPT command without a prompt string, the standard drive prompt (>) returns

```
A: PROMPT
A>
```

The prompt issued remains in effect until the system reboots or a new PROMPT command is issued.

Examples

```
A> PROMPT YES?
YES?
```

Change the system prompt to YES?.

```
A> PROMPT $P
A:\
A:\ CD DOS
A:\DOS
```

Use the current directory as the system prompt. Notice how the CD command modifies the prompt. Many users find this choice convenient for disk housekeeping chores.

```
A> PROMPT $T
17:19:15.22
```

Change the system prompt to the current system time. To remove the seconds and hundredths of seconds, use

```
17:20:21.12 PROMPT $T$H$H$H$H$H
17:20:
```

The following command displays the DOS version before each prompt:

```
A> PROMPT $V$_$N$G
IBM Personal Computer DOS Version  3.00
A>
```

RECOVER (Recover Corrupted File)
External RECOVER.COM

Function   Recover files from a disk that contains a corrupted sector or all of the files if a directory has been damaged. The files are truncated at the damaged sector, so data loss will occur. This service does not recover erased files.

Syntax Chart

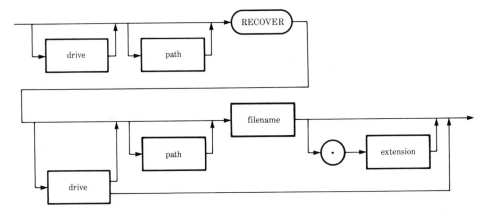

Format

[drive:][path]RECOVER file_specification

or

[drive:][path]RECOVER d:

Qualifiers None

Options

file_specification is the name of the file(s) to RECOVER. DOS wildcard characters are supported.

d: is a disk drive identification containing the disk to RE-COVER because of a corrupted directory.

Notes   RECOVER does not recover deleted files.

If a file or directory is not corrupted, *do not* issue this command.

To recover a single file containing a bad sector, enter

`A> RECOVER FILENAME.EXT`

If you use wildcard characters in the file name, RECOVER will recover the first matching file. RECOVER only works on one file at a time.

To recover an entire disk that has a damaged directory, use the command

`A> RECOVER drive:`

RECOVER will create files in the root directory of the default drive in the form

FILEnnnn.REC

In this case, *nnnn* is a sequential number starting at 0001.

RECOVER does not support networked drives.

Do not use RECOVER in conjunction with ASSIGN, JOIN, or SUBST.

Text files restored by RECOVER normally require editing. COM and EXE files are probably corrupted and should not be invoked unless absolutely necessary.

Do not rely on RECOVER. Do regular backups instead.

Examples

`A> RECOVER B:`

RECOVER the files contained on the disk in drive B.

`A> RECOVER CONFIG.SYS`

RECOVER the file CONFIG.SYS.

REM (Display Comments During Batch Processing) Internal Command

Function Display messages to standard output during the processing of a batch procedure.

Syntax Chart

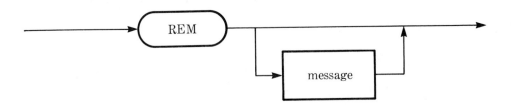

Format

REM [message]

Qualifiers None

Options

message is an optional character string of up to 123 characters to be displayed on the screen.

Notes If ECHO is OFF, messages from REM are suppressed.

Many programmers use REM within BAT files without a message, simply for spacing. Since the command processor must evaluate each statement within a BAT file, unnecessary REM statements will decrease the speed of your application.

Example

```
REM Starting batch procedure
VER
VOL
REM Ending batch procedure
```

Execution of the preceding BAT file results in

```
A> REM Starting batch procedure

A> VER

IBM Personal Computer DOS Version  3.00

A> VOL

  Volume in drive A is DOSDISK

A> REM Ending batch procedure
```

RENAME (Rename a DOS File)
Internal Command

Function   Change the name of the file specified by the first command-line parameter to the name specified by the second parameter.

Syntax Chart

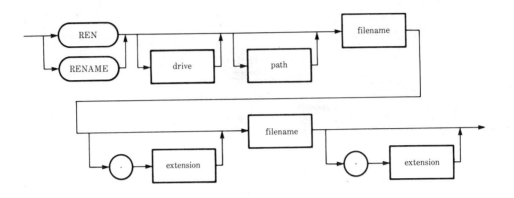

Format

RENAME file—specification filename[.ext]

or

REN file—specification filename[.ext]

Qualifiers   None

Options

file—specification is the name of the file to RENAME.

filename is the desired new eight-character filename.

ext is the optional three-character extension.

Notes   A complete path specification can be specified only on the first file. The new file will reside in the same directory and drive as the first file. This means that you cannot RENAME a file across different drives or directories.

RENAME supports DOS wildcard characters.

Examples

```
A> REN *.BAK *.SAV
```

RENAME all files with the extension BAK to files with the extension SAV.

```
A> REN B:MAIL.LST MAIL.OLD
```

RENAME the file MAIL.LST on the disk in drive B to MAIL.OLD.

```
A> REN \DOS\UTIL\CONFIG.SYS *.OLD
```

RENAME the file CONFIG.SYS in the subdirectory \DOS\UTIL to CONFIG.OLD.

REPLACE (Selective Replacement of Target Files) External REPLACE.EXE

Function   Create or replace files on the target disk with files with the same name from the source disk.

Syntax Chart

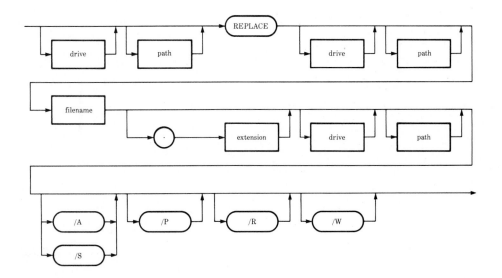

Format

[drive:][path]REPLACE file_specification [d:][p][/A][/P]
[/R][/S][/W]

Qualifiers

/A directs REPLACE to copy only those files from the source
disk that are not already contained on the target disk. This
qualifier cannot be used in conjunction with /S.

/P directs REPLACE to prompt you with the following before
replacing a file:

```
Replace FILENAME.EXT? (Y/N)
```

If /A is used, REPLACE will prompt

```
Add FILENAME.EXT? (Y/N)
```

/R directs REPLACE to replace files that have been marked
read-only on the target disk.

/S causes REPLACE to search all directories on the target
disk for a file matching the source file name. This qualifier
cannot be used in conjunction with /A.

/W directs REPLACE to prompt the following before it
begins:

```
Press any key to begin replacing file(s)
```

If /A is used, REPLACE will instead prompt

```
Press any key to begin adding file(s)
```

Options

file—specification is the name of the file(s) to add/replace from the source disk. REPLACE supports the DOS wildcard characters.

d: is the disk drive identification containing the target disk.

p is the pathname of the target path.

Notes   REPLACE does not find or update system or hidden files.

REPLACE returns the following exit-status codes to support conditional batch processing:

0	successful replacement of all files specified
2	source file not found
3	source or target path not found
5	access denied
8	insufficient memory
11	incorrect command format
15	invalid source or target drive
22	incorrect DOS version

Examples

`A> REPLACE A:\*.* B:/S/R`

This REPLACE command replaces all of the files from the source disk A to the target disk B, including files that have been marked read-only on drive B.

`A> REPLACE A:\*.* B:/A`

This REPLACE command adds all of the files from the source disk A that aren't contained on the target disk B.

RESTORE (Restore Files Saved by BACKUP) External RESTORE.COM

Function   Restore one or more files from a backup disk to another disk.

Syntax Chart

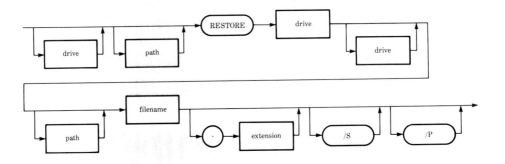

Format

[drive:][path]RESTORE d: file—specification [/P][/S]

Qualifiers

/P directs RESTORE to prompt the following before restoring files that have been modified or set to read-only since the last backup:

```
Warning! File FILENAME.EXT
is a read-only file
Replace the file (Y/N)?
```

/S directs RESTORE to restore all of the files contained in subdirectories.

Options

d: is the disk drive containing the backup disk.
file—specification is the name of the file(s) to RESTORE from the backup disk.

Notes   RESTORE only works with files placed on a disk via BACKUP.

When you are restoring all of the files on a disk, be sure to insert the disks in the correct order.

If you are only backing up a single file, but you don't know on which backup disk it is contained, start with the first disk and insert the disks sequentially.

Use the /P qualifier if you must RESTORE files that were created with a different version of DOS. This allows you to prevent the DOS system files from being restored.

When you are restoring multiple disks, RESTORE will prompt you for the next disk as follows:

```
Insert backup diskette n in drive n
```

RESTORE provides the following exit values to support conditional batch processing:

0   successful restoration
1   no files found to RESTORE
2   some files were not restored because of file-sharing conflicts
3   user termination via CTRL-BREAK
4   termination because of error

Examples

```
A> RESTORE A: B:ONEFILE.DAT
```

RESTORE the file ONEFILE.DAT from the backup disk in drive A to the current directory in drive B.

`A> RESTORE A: B:*.*`

RESTORE all of the files (excluding subdirectories) from drive A to drive B.

`A> RESTORE A: B:/S`

RESTORE all of the files (including subdirectories) from drive A to drive B.

`A> RESTORE A: B:/S/P`

RESTORE all of the files (including subdirectories) from drive A to drive B, resulting in the prompt

```
Insert backup diskette n in drive n
```

before restoring any files that have been modified or set to read-only since the last backup.

RMDIR (Remove a DOS Subdirectory)
Internal Command

Function   Remove a subdirectory from the specified disk.

Syntax Chart

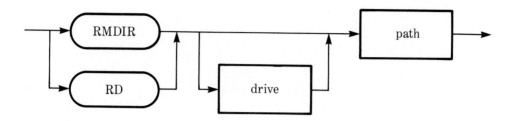

Format

> RMDIR [drive:]path

or

> RD [drive:]path

Qualifiers   None

Options

> *drive:* is the disk drive identification containing the disk from which to remove the subdirectory.
>
> *path* is the name of the subdirectory to delete.

Notes   RMDIR cannot delete the root or current directory. Attempts to do so will result in the following message:

```
A> RD .
Invalid path, not directory,
or directory not empty
```

> If a disk drive is not specified, RMDIR uses the current drive.

A subdirectory must be empty before it can be removed (excluding .. and .). If it is not empty, the following message is displayed:

```
A> RMDIR IBM
Invalid path, not directory,
or directory not empty
```

Examples

```
A> RMDIR OLD
```

```
A> RD OLD
```

Remove the subdirectory OLD from the current drive and directory. The two commands are identical.

```
A> RMDIR \DOS\OLD
```

Remove the subdirectory OLD from the directory DOS.

```
A> RD \DOS\OLD\SAV
```

Remove the subdirectory SAV from the subdirectory \DOS \OLD on drive B.

SELECT (Select International Format)
External SELECT.COM

Function   Specify the desired keyboard layout, as well as the date and time formats to be used by DOS.

Syntax Chart

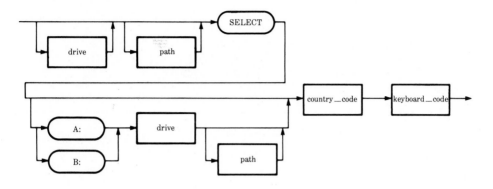

Format

[drive:][path]SELECT [[A: ¦ B:] d:[path]]
country—code keyboard—code

Qualifiers   None

Options

A: ¦ *B:* specifies the source drive for the keyboard commands.

d: is the target drive. If a drive is not specified, SELECT uses the current default.

path is the target path for the file copy.

country—code is the three-digit code that specifies the country format to use.

keyboard—code is the two-character identifier of the country keyboard layout to use.

country—code and keyboard—code are specified as shown in Table A-2.

Notes   SELECT uses the DISKCOPY command (DOS version 3.2 uses XCOPY) to make a copy of the DOS disk. SELECT creates the files CONFIG.SYS and AUTOEXEC.BAT on the target disk.

Country	Keyboard Code	Country Code
France	KEYBFR.COM	33
Germany	KEYBGR.COM	49
Italy	KEYBIT.COM	39
Spain	KEYBSP.COM	34
United Kingdom	KEYBUK.COM	44

Table A-2.   Country Codes and Keyboard Codes

The file CONFIG.SYS will contain the line

COUNTRY=country_code

AUTOEXEC.BAT will contain a keyboard command as follows:

KEYBxx

On a two-floppy disk system, SELECT will prompt you to enter your source disk in drive A and the target disk in drive B.

On a single-drive system, place your DOS disk in drive A and issue the SELECT command. SELECT will prompt you to place the target disk in the drive as required.

Example

```
A> SELECT 049 GR

Insert SOURCE Diskette in Drive A :

Insert TARGET Diskette in Drive B :

Press any key when ready . . .


Copying 40 tracks
9 Sectors/Track, 2 Side(s)
```

```
Copy another diskette (Y/N)?N

Insert FIRST diskette in drive A

Insert SECOND diskette in drive B

Press any key when ready . . .

Comparing 40 tracks
9 sectors per track, 2 side(s)

Compare OK

Compare another diskette (Y/N) ?
```

You select the German date and time formats, along with the German keyboard layout.

SET (Place or Display Entries in the Environment) Internal Command

Function   Insert the specified string into the command processor's environment.

Syntax Chart

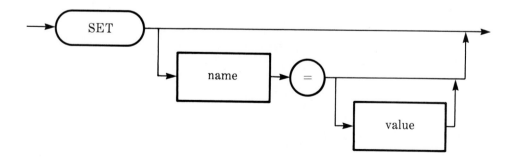

Format

SET [name=[value]]

Qualifiers   None

Options

name is the name of the entry in the environment to which you assign a value.

value is the string value to assign to name.

Notes   All lowercase strings are converted to uppercase before they are placed into the environment.

If the specified name already exists in the environment, it is replaced with the new value.

If you enter the SET command without parameters, SET will display the current environment contents as follows:

```
A> SET
COMSPEC=C:\COMMAND.COM
PATH=C:\DOS
```

If you specify a name with no value, as in

```
A> SET NAME=
```

SET will assign the value null.

At system startup, DOS places the COMSPEC= and PATH= entries in the environment.

The DOS PROMPT command also affects the environment, as follows:

```
A> PROMPT YYY
YYY SET
COMSPEC=C:\COMMAND.COM
PATH=C:\DOS
PROMPT=YYY
```

By default, DOS allocates 127 bytes for environment strings. If you have not installed any resident programs or code (GRAPH-ICS, GRAFTABL, PRINT, and so forth), DOS will allocate additional space for the environment as required. Otherwise, SET will display the message

```
Out of environment space
```

Examples

```
A> SET INPUT=SORTDATA.DAT
```

It is possible for applications to search the environment for entries. In this case, you have defined the input file for an application to use outside of the application. The application simply searches the environment for the string INPUT=SORTDATA. DAT and opens the specified file. Chapter 16 provides a Turbo Pascal program that displays the contents of the environment.

SHARE (Support DOS File Sharing) External SHARE.EXE

Function   Enable DOS file-sharing support.

Syntax Chart

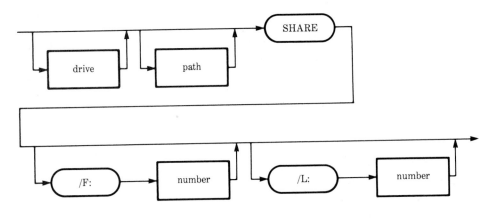

Format

[drive:][path]SHARE [/F:file__space][/L:locks]

Qualifiers

/F:file__space allocates memory (in bytes) for the area in which DOS records file-sharing information. Each open file requires 11 bytes plus the length of the file name (up to 63 characters). The default size is 2048 bytes.

/L:locks allocates memory for the number of locks desired. The default value is 20.

Notes   DOS versions 3.0 and greater support file and record locking. Each time a file open occurs, when file sharing is installed, DOS checks to see if the file is locked against the open operation. If so, the open fails. In addition, DOS checks for record locking during each read/write operation.

SHARE loads memory-resident software that performs the file and record locking. This software allocates memory. If you attempt to install SHARE more than once, SHARE will display

```
SHARE already installed
```

The only way to terminate file sharing is to reboot. Because of the overhead SHARE places on file I/O operations, only invoke SHARE when your applications require file or record sharing.

Examples

```
A> SHARE
```

Enable file sharing with the DOS defaults.

```
A> SHARE /L:30
```

Enable file sharing with space allocated for 30 locks.

SHIFT (Shift Batch Parameters Left) Internal Command

Function   Shift each batch parameter (%0-%9) left one position.

Syntax Chart

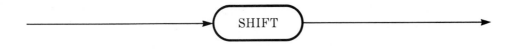

Format

SHIFT

Qualifiers   None

Notes   If more than ten parameters are passed to a batch file, you can use SHIFT to access each parameter past %9.

If no parameters exist to the right of a parameter, SHIFT replaces the parameter with a null string.

Examples

The following batch file displays all of the batch parameters that it receives.

```
ECHO OFF
:LOOP
IF '%1'=='' GOTO DONE
ECHO %1
SHIFT
GOTO LOOP
:DONE
```

If it is invoked with

A> TEST 1 2 3 4 5 6

the following is displayed:

```
A> ECHO OFF
1
2
3
4
5
6
```

DOS: The Complete Reference

The following batch file displays all of the files specified in the command until no files exist:

```
ECHO OFF
:LOOP
IF '%1'=='' GOTO DONE
TYPE%1
SHIFT
GOTO LOOP
:DONE
```

SORT (DOS Sort Filter)
External SORT.EXE

Function   Read data from standard input, sort the data, and write it to the standard output device.

Syntax Chart

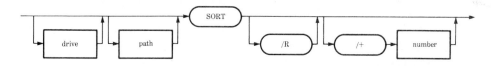

Format

[drive:][path]SORT [/R][/+n]

Qualifiers

/R directs SORT to sort the data in reverse order.

/+n directs SORT to sort the data based upon column n. By default, SORT uses column 1.

Notes   The maximum file size that SORT can sort is 63K.

If the I/O redirection operators > and < are used, the output file name must differ from the input file name.

SORT equates the lowercase letters (a-z) with uppercase (A-Z) characters for the duration of the SORT.

Examples

```
A> DIR ¦ SORT
```

In this example, SORT uses the piped output of the DIR command as its input and displays a sorted directory listing.

```
A> SORT < DATES
```

SORT will display the contents of the file DATES in sorted order to standard output.

```
A> SORT /+15 < SALARIES.LST > SALARIES.SRT
```

SORT will sort the file SALARIES.LST based on column 15 and write the result to the file SALARIES.SRT.

SUBST (Substitute a DOS Path with a Drive Letter) External SUBST.EXE

Function   Abbreviate DOS pathnames with a disk drive letter.

Syntax Chart

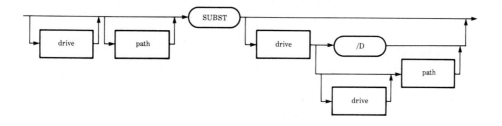

Format

[drive:][path]SUBST [d:] [p][/D]

Qualifiers

/D directs SUBST to delete the substitution specified.

Options

d: is the drive letter to use as the abbreviation.

p is the DOS pathname to abbreviate.

Notes   If you invoke the command without any parameters, as
in

```
A> SUBST
D: => A:\DOSBOOK\DOSREF
```

SUBST will display the current substitutions.

You may need to modify the LASTDRIVE= entry in the file CONFIG.SYS to support additional substitutions.

Examples

`A> SUBST F: \IBM\NOTES\1986\EXPENSES`

Abbreviate the DOS pathname \IBM\NOTES\1986\EX-PENSES as drive F.

`A> SUBST F:/D`

Delete the substitution referenced by drive F.

`A> SUBST`

Display all substitutions.

SYS (Transfer Operating System Files to a Disk)
External SYS.COM

Function   Transfer the operating system files required to make a disk bootable to the specified disk.

Syntax Chart

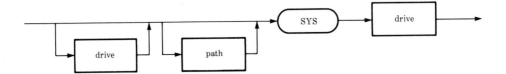

Format

[drive:][path]SYS d:

Qualifiers   None

Options

d: is the disk drive identification of the drive containing the disk to which the system files are to be transferred.

Notes   With some versions of DOS, you must COPY the file COMMAND.COM to the target disk to ensure that the disk is bootable.

The disk receiving the operating system files must meet one of the following characteristics:

• The disk must have an empty directory. DOS requires the hidden system files (IBMDOS.COM and IBMBIOS.COM for PC-DOS, and MSDOS.SYS and IO.SYS for MS-DOS) to be the first two files in the directory.

• Formatted with the /S qualifier, which places the system files on the disk, and the same version of DOS—in which case the files are already present.

• Formatted with the /B qualifier, which reserves space for the system files on the disk.

If SYS cannot transfer the files, it will display

```
No room for system on destination disk
```

Example

```
A> SYS B:
```

Transfer the system files to the disk contained in drive B.

TIME (Set the System Time)
Internal Command

Function   Change or display the system time. DOS uses this time to time-stamp all file creations/modifications.

Syntax Chart

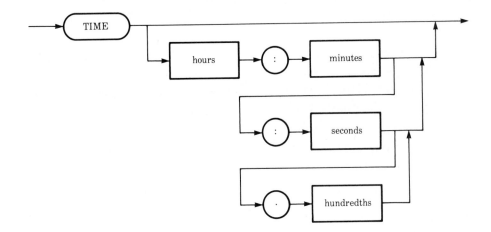

Format

TIME [HH:MM[:SS[.hh]]]

Qualifiers   None

Options

HH is the system hours. Type in 1 to 2 numbers in the range 0-23.

MM is the system minutes. Type in 1 to 2 numbers in the range 0-59.

SS is the system seconds. Type in 1 to 2 numbers in the range 0-59.

hh is the system hundredths of seconds. Type in 1 to 2 numbers in the range 0-99.

Notes   If you enter the TIME command with no parameters, the current system time is displayed, and you are prompted to enter a new system time, as follows:

```
 Current time is 18:20:48.78
 Enter new time:
```

If you do not want to modify the system clock, simply press ENTER. Otherwise, type in the time that you desire.

Colons or periods serve as delimiters (separators) for the time. The following are accepted by TIME:

12.59.59
12:59:59

If the time that you enter is invalid, TIME will display an error message and prompt you to enter a new system time as follows:

```
 Current time is 18:21:07.73
 Enter new time: 12:66:23

 Invalid time
 Enter new time·
```

If you enter only a portion of the time, TIME will set the remaining fields to 0.

The DOS TIME command does not affect the IBM PC AT system clock. (See the DOS DATE command.)

Examples

```
A> TIME 13:01
```

Set the system time to 13:01 (1:01 P.M.).

```
A> TIME 12:00
```

Set the system clock to noon.

```
A> TIME 00:00
```

Set the system clock to midnight.

TREE (Display Directory Structure)
External TREE.COM

Function   Display the directory paths on the specified drive. Optionally, display the files contained in each directory.

Syntax Chart

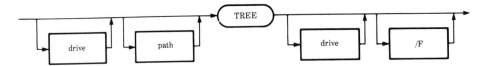

Format   [drive:][path]TREE [d:][/F]

Qualifiers

/F directs TREE to display each file contained in the subdirectories on the disk.

Options

d: is the disk drive that TREE is to examine. If you do not specify a disk drive, TREE uses the current default.

Notes   If requested by the /F qualifier, TREE will display the full pathnames of all files.

TREE writes all of its output to the standard output device so that it can be redirected.

Examples

Given the directory structure shown in Figure A-1, the command

```
A> TREE
```

will display

```
DIRECTORY PATH LISTING

Path: \IBM

Sub-directories: None


Path: \APPLE

Sub-directories: None


Path: \INTEL

Sub-directories: None
```

Likewise, the command

```
A> TREE /F
```

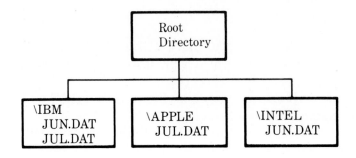

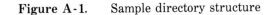

Figure A-1.   Sample directory structure

will display

```
DIRECTORY PATH LISTING

Path: \IBM

Sub-directories:   None

Files:             JUN     .DAT
                   JUL     .DAT

Path: \ APPLE

Sub-directories:   None

Files:             JUL     .DAT


Path: \INTEL

Sub-directories:   None

Files:             JUN     .DAT
```

TYPE (Display the Contents of a File)
Internal Command

Function   Display the contents of the specified file to the standard output device.

Syntax Chart

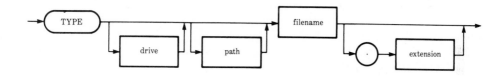

Format

TYPE file__specification

Qualifiers   None

Options

file__specification is the name of the file whose contents are to be displayed.

Notes   Only text files (ASCII files) can be displayed via TYPE. COM, EXE, and OBJ files contain nonprintable characters that prevent their display.

TYPE does not support DOS wildcard characters. If you attempt to use wildcard characters, TYPE will display

```
Invalid filename or file not found
```

TYPE expands tab characters to 8-column increments (columns 8, 16, 24, and so forth).

Examples

`A> TYPE CONFIG.SYS`

Display the contents of the file CONFIG.SYS.

`A> TYPE B:\DOS\UTIL\AUTOEXEC.BAT`

Display the contents of the file AUTOEXEC.BAT in the sub-directory \DOS\UTIL on the disk in drive B.

VER (Display DOS Version)
Internal Command

Function   Display the version of DOS that is currently executing to the standard output device.

Syntax Chart

Format

VER

Qualifiers   None

Notes   DOS version numbers consist of a minor and major number. Assuming DOS version 3.2, the major version number is 3 and the minor is 2.

Chapter 16 provides a Turbo Pascal program that uses the DOS services to obtain the DOS version number.

DOS: The Complete Reference

```
A> VER

IBM Personal Computer DOS Version  3.00
```

VERIFY (Verify Disk I/O)
Internal Command

Function   Enable or disable disk I/O verification.

Syntax Chart

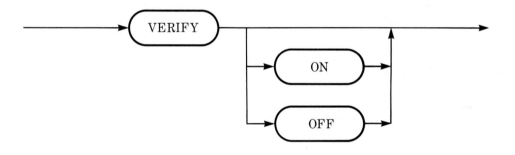

Format

VERIFY [ON ¦ OFF]

Qualifiers   None

Options

ON turns disk verification on. When disk output is finished, DOS will read the data written to disk to ensure that it was written correctly. This adds additional overhead to your processing, but ensures that the data is written correctly.

OFF turns disk verification off. DOS does not ensure that the data is recorded on disk correctly.

Notes   Disk I/O errors where the data written to disk is not correctly recorded are very rare. Normally, you turn on disk verification only during system backups.

If you invoke the VERIFY command without any parameters, VERIFY will display its current state, on or off, as follows:

```
A> VERIFY
VERIFY is off
```

Examples

```
A> VERIFY ON
```

Turn on disk verification.

```
A> VERIFY OFF
```

Turn off disk verification.

VOL (Display Volume Label)
Internal Command

Function   Display the volume label of the specified disk.

Syntax Chart

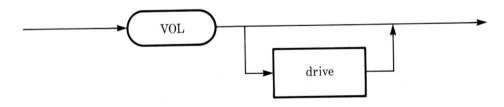

DOS: The Complete Reference

Format

VOL [drive:]

Qualifiers   None

Options

drive: is the disk drive identification containing the disk whose volume label is to be displayed.

Notes   If you do not specify a disk drive, VOL uses the current default.

Volume labels are created during formatting or via the LABEL command.

Examples

```
A> VOL

Volume in drive C is DOSDISK
```

Display the volume label of the default drive.

```
A> VOL B:
```

Display the volume label of the disk in drive B.

XCOPY (Copy Files to Include Subdirectories)
External XCOPY.EXE

Function   Copy a group of files to include files contained in lower-level subdirectories.

Syntax Chart

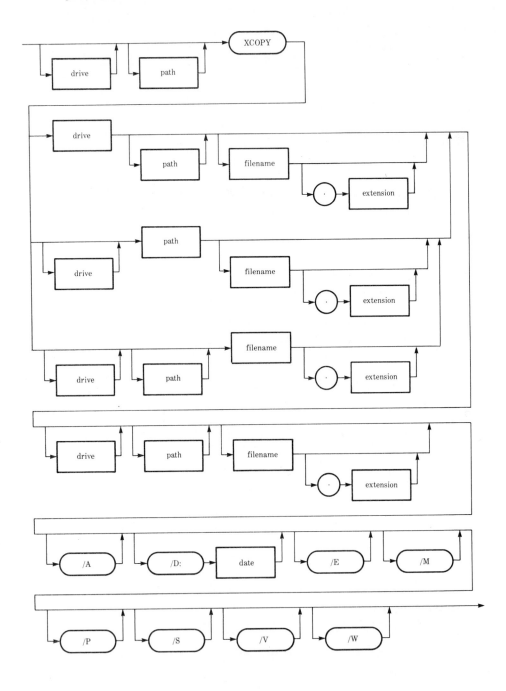

DOS: The Complete Reference

Format

[drive:][path]XCOPY file—specification1
file—specification2
[/A][/D:mm-dd-yy][/E][/M][/P][/S][/V][/W]

Qualifiers

/A directs XCOPY to copy all of the source files whose archive
bit is set. XCOPY will not modify the bit.

/D:mm-dd-yy directs XCOPY to copy all of the source files
that have been created or modified since the date specified.

/E requests XCOPY to create subdirectories on the target
even if they will end up empty.

/M directs XCOPY to copy all of the source files whose
archive bit is set. XCOPY will clear the file's archive bit when
it finishes.

/P XCOPY will prompt the following before copying each file:

```
FILENAME.EXT (Y/N)?
```

To copy the file, press Y; otherwise, press N.

/S directs XCOPY to copy files in all subdirectories below the
source directory.

/V directs XCOPY to use disk verification to ensure that the
data written to disk is recorded correctly.

/W requests XCOPY to prompt the following before beginning:

```
Press any key to begin copying file(s)
```

Options

file—specification1 is the source for the file copy. It can be a
file name, pathname, disk drive identification, or a combina-

tion of all three. DOS wildcard characters are supported. The default filename is *.*.

file_specification2 is the target for the file copy.

Notes   If you do not specify a source path, XCOPY uses the current directory.

XCOPY does not support file transfers to and from device names.

XCOPY does not copy hidden files from the source.

XCOPY does not overwrite read-only files.

XCOPY provides the following exit-status values to support conditional batch processing:

0	successful copy
1	no files found to copy
2	user termination via CTRL-BREAK
4	invalid command
5	critical error termination

Examples

```
A> XCOPY A:\ B:\ /S
```

Copy all of the files on drive A to drive B. XCOPY will create the subdirectories on the target drive.

```
A> XCOPY A:\ B:\ /S/A
```

Copy all of the files on drive A that require a backup to drive B. Do not clear the archive bit.

```
A> XCOPY A:\ B:\ /S/M
```

Copy all of the files on drive A that require a backup to drive B. Clear the archive bit.

`A> XCOPY A:\ B:\ /S/D:01-01-87`

Copy all of the files from the current directory in drive A to drive B that have been created or modified since 01-01-87.

ASCII Codes

Table B-1 lists the ASCII codes for characters.

DEC	OCTAL	HEX	ASCII		DEC	OCTAL	HEX	ASCII
0	000	00	NUL		10	012	0A	LF
1	001	01	SOH		11	013	0B	VT
2	002	02	STX		12	014	0C	FF
3	003	03	ETX		13	015	0D	CR
4	004	04	EOT		14	016	0E	SO
5	005	05	ENQ		15	017	0F	SI
6	006	06	ACK		16	020	10	DLE
7	007	07	BEL		17	021	11	DC1
8	010	08	BS		18	022	12	DC2
9	011	09	HT		19	023	13	DC3

Table B-1.   ASCII Character Codes

DEC	OCTAL	HEX	ASCII	DEC	OCTAL	HEX	ASCII
20	024	14	DC4	61	075	3D	=
21	025	15	NAK	62	076	3E	>
22	026	16	SYN	63	077	3F	?
23	027	17	ETB	64	100	40	@
24	030	18	CAN	65	101	41	A
25	031	19	EM	66	102	42	B
26	032	1A	SUB	67	103	43	C
27	033	1B	ESC	68	104	44	D
28	034	1C	FS	69	105	45	E
29	035	1D	GS	70	106	46	F
30	036	1E	RS	71	107	47	G
31	037	1F	US	72	110	48	H
32	040	20	SPACE	73	111	49	I
33	041	21	!	74	112	4A	J
34	042	22	"	75	113	4B	K
35	043	23	#	76	114	4C	L
36	044	24	$	77	115	4D	M
37	045	25	%	78	116	4E	N
38	046	26	&	79	117	4F	O
39	047	27	'	80	120	50	P
40	050	28	(	81	121	51	Q
41	051	29	)	82	122	52	R
42	052	2A	*	83	123	53	S
43	053	2B	+	84	124	54	T
44	054	2C	,	85	125	55	U
45	055	2D	—	86	126	56	V
46	056	2E	.	87	127	57	W
47	057	2F	/	88	130	58	X
48	060	30	0	89	131	59	Y
49	061	31	1	90	132	5A	Z
50	062	32	2	91	133	5B	[
51	063	33	3	92	134	5C	\
52	064	34	4	93	135	5D	]
53	065	35	5	94	136	5E	^
54	066	,36	6	95	137	5F	—
55	067	37	7	96	140	60	'
56	070	38	8	97	141	61	a
57	071	39	9	98	142	62	b
58	072	3A	:	99	143	63	c
59	073	3B	;	100	144	64	d
60	074	3C	<	101	145	65	e

Table B-1.   ASCII Character Codes (*continued*)

DEC	OCTAL	HEX	ASCII	DEC	OCTAL	HEX	ASCII
102	146	66	f	115	163	73	s
103	147	67	g	116	164	74	t
104	150	68	h	117	165	75	u
105	151	69	i	118	166	76	v
106	152	6A	j	119	167	77	w
107	153	6B	k	120	170	78	x
108	154	6C	l	121	171	79	y
109	155	6D	m	122	172	7A	z
110	156	6E	n	123	173	7B	{
111	157	6F	o	124	174	7C	|
112	160	70	p	125	175	7D	}
113	161	71	q	126	176	7E	~
114	162	72	r	127	177	7F	DEL

Table B-1. ASCII Character Codes (*continued*)

DOS Messages

Abort edit (Y/N)?

Source   EDLIN

Cause   EDLIN displays this message if you specify "Q" to quit an edit session.

User Action   To end the edit session press Y. No changes will be saved to disk. To continue the edit session press N.

Abort, Retry, Ignore

Source   DOS Commands

Cause   DOS cannot read/write to the device specified.

User Action   To terminate the command and return control to DOS, press A. To retry the command press R. To continue processing at the next step, press I. The section at the end of this appendix lists all the DOS errors that generate this message.

About to generate .EXE file
Change diskette in drive x: and press <ENTER>

Source   LINK

Cause   The /P qualifier was present in the LINK command line and LINK is ready to write the EXE file to disk.

User Action   Place the disk on which you want the EXE file to reside in the disk drive specified and press the ENTER key.

Access denied

Source   DOS Commands

Cause   The operation you attempted to perform violates the access mode for a file, directory, or device.

User Action   Modify the attributes of the file from read-only if you really want to perform the operation specified, or use a new file name.

Add drive: \ path \ filename?

Source   REPLACE

Cause   The /P qualifier was in the REPLACE command line and REPLACE is ready to add a file from the source to the target disk.

User Action   To replace the file, press Y and press ENTER. To ignore the file, press N and then press ENTER.

All files canceled by operator

Source   PRINT

Cause   An operator issued a PRINT/T command to cancel all of the files in the DOS print queue.

User Action   None

All specified file(s) are contiguous

Source   CHKDSK

Cause   All of the files matching the file specification in the CHKDSK command line are contiguous (Chapter 9).

User Action None

Allocation error for file, size adjusted

Source CHKDSK

Cause CHKDSK found an invalid cluster number in the file allocation table for the file name specified.

User Action If you did not specify the /F qualifier in the CHKDSK command line, do so now to correct the file size. If /F was present, CHKDSK will truncate the file to the last valid cluster number.

Amount read less than size in header

Source EXE2BIN

Cause The actual program section of an EXE file differed from the size specified in the file header.

User Action Recompile and relink the file before invoking EXE2BIN again.

APPEND/ASSIGN Conflict

Source APPEND

Cause APPEND cannot reference an ASSIGNed disk.

User Action Cancel the ASSIGN and issue the APPEND command. Reissue the ASSIGN command.

Are you sure (Y/N)?

Source DEL, ERASE

Cause A DEL or ERASE command was issued that will

delete all of the files in a directory. Because of its possible catastrophic effect, the command wants to ensure that you indeed
want to delete all of the files.

User Action   Press Y and then press ENTER to delete the files.
Press N and then press ENTER to cancel the command.

Array element size mismatch

Source   LINK

Cause   The same array is used in two different modules and
has been declared such that the sizes of the array's element
members differ. For example, one declaration is an array of type
integer, and the other is an array of type float.

User Action   Edit the source file and match the array types.
Compile and LINK the new source file.

Atempt to access data outside
of segment bounds

Source   LINK

Cause   An OBJ file is invalid.

User Action   Examine the source code for a segment violation
or illegal reference or instruction.

Attempt to put segment nnnnnn
in more than one group in file
nnnnnnnn.nnn

Source   LINK

Cause   The same segment name was declared in two different
groups.

User Action   Edit the source file and fix the conflict. Compile
and LINK the new source file.

Attempted write protect violation

Source   FORMAT

Cause   The disk to FORMAT is write-protected.

User Action   Insert a new disk, or remove the write-protect tab to continue the disk format.

** Backing up files to target drive n **
Target number: n

Source   BACKUP

Cause   BACKUP is specifying the sequence number of the disk it is using.

User Action   None

Backup file sequence error

Source   RESTORE

Cause   A file to be restored is contained on more than one disk. The RESTORE operation did not start with the first disk.

User Action   Invoke RESTORE with the correct disk sequence.

Bad command or file name

Source   DOS Command Line Interpreter

Cause   The command entered is not a valid DOS command.

User Action   Check the command spelling and then other possible locations (paths) for the command.

Bad internal reloc table

Source   LINK

Cause   Software error in the DOS linker.

User Action   Print the screen contents and notify IBM or Microsoft.

Bad or missing Command Interpreter

Source   DOS

Cause   The disk the system is booting from does not contain the file COMMAND.COM, or a disk error occurred when DOS was trying to access the file. Also, if the COMMSPEC= entry in an environment does not point to a path that contains COMMAND.COM, DOS will display this error.

User Action   If the boot disk is your hard disk, boot from a floppy disk in drive A and copy the contents of COMMAND.COM to the root directory of your hard disk. If the error is caused by an invalid environment parameter, correct the environment to point to a valid directory containing the file COMMAND.COM.

Bad or missing <filename>

Source   DOS

Cause   The DOS startup procedures could not find the device driver file specified in CONFIG.SYS, or an error occurred during the loading of the device driver into memory.

User Action   Check CONFIG.SYS to be sure that the device driver file name is correct. If so, the device driver contains a programming error. If you are developing the device, use DEBUG; otherwise, return the software to your dealer.

Bad Partition Table

Source   FORMAT

Cause   The disk partition table (Chapter 9) of a fixed disk does not contain a DOS partition, or the partition table contains errors.

User Action   Use the DOS FDISK command to create a new DOS partition.

Bad tracks found at start of partition
Partition size adjusted

Source   FDISK

Cause   The partition specified contained bad tracks/cylinders in the area allocated for DOS. The size of the disk partition was modified by FDISK.

User Action   None

Bad Unit

Source   DOS Commands

Cause   A device driver for a disk discovered an invalid device reference or experienced a critical error during I/O.

User Action   Perform a "print screen" of any additional messages displayed and contact IBM or Microsoft.

Batch file missing

Source   DOS

Cause   DOS cannot find the batch file it was processing. A previous step in the processing may have deleted or renamed the batch file.

User Action   Trace through the steps performed by the batch file and be sure that the BAT file is not deleted or renamed.

BF

Source   DEBUG

Cause   The flag code setting specified is invalid.

User Action　　Issue the DEBUG command with the correct flag code entry. Refer to Chapter 16.

BP

Source　　DEBUG

Cause　　More than ten breakpoints were specified for a DEBUG Go command.

User Action　　Issue the DEBUG Go command with ten or fewer breakpoints.

BR

Source　　DEBUG

Cause　　An invalid register name was specified.

User Action　　Reissue the command with the correct register name.

Break is ON ¦ OFF

Source　　BREAK

Cause　　If BREAK is OFF, DOS will not perform CTRL-BREAK checking after each disk I/O. If BREAK is ON, DOS will test for a CTRL-BREAK sequence upon completion of each disk I/O.

User Action　　None

Buffer size adjusted

Source　　VDISK

Cause　　The buffer size specified to VDISK was invalid for the current configuration. VDISK modified the size as required.

User Action　　None

Buffer size: n
Sector size: n
Directory entries: n
Transfer size: n

Source   VDISK

Cause   VDISK successfully installed a RAM drive with the buffer size, sector size, directory, and transfer size specified.

User Action   None

Cannot CHDIR to root

Source   CHKDSK

Cause   CHKDSK attempted to set the current working directory to the root and failed.

User Action   None. The disk is damaged.

Cannot CHKDSK a network drive

Source   CHKDSK

Cause   CHKDSK cannot be invoked using a disk that is part of a local area network.

User Action   Remove the disk from network access long enough to perform the CHKDSK command.

Cannot CHKDSK a SUBSTed or ASSIGNed drive

Source   CHKDSK

Cause   A path substitution hides information required by CHKDSK.

User Action   Remove the path substitution and invoke CHKDSK.

Cannot create Subdirectory BACKUP
on drive n:

Source   BACKUP

Cause   BACKUP cannot create the BACKUP subdirectory on the target disk specified.

User Action   Make sure that the disk is not write-protected. Use CHKDSK to determine that the root directory of the target disk is not full. Check to see if a directory with the same name already exists.

Cannot DISKCOMP to or from
a Network drive

Source   DISKCOMP

Cause   DISKCOMP cannot be performed on a disk that is currently part of a local area network.

User Action   Remove the disk from network access long enough to perform the DISKCOMP command.

Cannot DISKCOPY to or from
a Network drive

Source   DISKCOPY

Cause   DISKCOPY cannot be performed on a disk that is currently part of a local area network.

User Action   Remove the disk from network access long enough to perform the DISKCOPY command.

Cannot do binary reads from a device

Source   COPY

Cause   The /B qualifier was present in the COPY command

line and source of the COPY was a device name. With the /B qualifier COPY cannot recognize an end of file Ctrl-Z from the device.

User Action   Do not use the /B qualifier on the copy or place
the /A qualifier after the source device name.

Cannot edit .BAK file— rename file

Source   EDLIN

Cause   EDLIN will not edit BAK files because they are considered to be backup files to a more current version.

User Action   COPY or RENAME the BAK file to a meaningful name if you really need to edit its contents.

Cannot execute FORMAT

Source   SELECT

Cause   SELECT experienced an error invoking the DOS FOR-
MAT command.

User Action   Be sure that the DOS FORMAT command is
present on the source disk and invoke SELECT again.

Cannot execute XCOPY

Source   SELECT

Cause   SELECT experienced an error invoking the DOS
XCOPY command.

User Action   Be sure that the DOS XCOPY command is present on the source disk and invoke SELECT again.

Cannot FDISK a network drive

Source   FDISK

Cause   FDISK cannot be performed on a disk that is currently part of a local area network.

User Action   Remove the disk from network access long enough to perform the FDISK command.

Cannot find file filename
Change diskette and press <ENTER>

Source   LINK

Cause   LINK cannot find one of the OBJ files specified.

User Action   Insert the disk containing the OBJ file in the disk drive specified, or press CTRL-BREAK to terminate the LINK command.

Cannot find library filename
Enter new file spec:

Source   LINK

Cause   LINK cannot find one of the LIB files specified.

User Action   Insert the disk containing the LIB file in the disk drive specified, or press CTRL-BREAK to terminate the LINK command.

Cannot find system files

Source   FORMAT, SYS

Cause   The system files (IBMBIOS.COM, IBMDOS.COM for PC-DOS or IO.SYS, MSDOS.SYS for MS-DOS) cannot be found on the current disk.

User Action   Issue the command with a disk that contains the system files in the root directory.

Cannot FORMAT a network drive

Source   FORMAT

Cause   FORMAT cannot be performed on a disk that is currently part of a local area network.

User Action   Remove the disk from network access long enough to perform the FORMAT command.

Cannot FORMAT a SUBSTed or ASSIGNed drive

Source   FORMAT

Cause   FORMAT will not format a substituted or assigned disk drive.

User Action   Execute ASSIGN or SUBST to restore the disk to its original status. Invoke the FORMAT command.

Cannot JOIN to a network drive

Source   JOIN

Cause   JOIN cannot be performed on a disk that is currently part of a local area network.

User Action   Remove the disk from network access long enough to perform the JOIN command.

Cannot LABEL a network drive

Source   LABEL

Cause   LABEL cannot be performed on a disk that is currently part of a local area network.

User Action   Remove the disk from network access long enough to perform the LABEL command.

Cannot LABEL a SUBSTed or ASSIGNed drive

Source   LABEL

Cause   A path substitution hides information required by LABEL.

User Action   Remove the path substitution and invoke LABEL.

Cannot load COMMAND, system halted

Source   DOS

Cause   DOS could not find the command processor in the path specified by the COMMSPEC= entry, or the table that DOS uses to track available memory has been destroyed.

User Action   Reboot DOS.

Cannot nest response file

Source   LINK

Cause   An automatic response file for LINK contained a reference to a second automatic response file.

User Action   See Chapter 16. Fix the reference within the automatic file and reissue the LINK command.

Cannot open list file

Source   LINK

Cause   LINK cannot open the LIST file that contains the link map.

User Action   The source disk for the LIST file is probably full. Delete or move old files to make space for the file, or insert a new disk.

Cannot open overlay

Source   LINK

Cause   The target disk or directory is full.

User Action   Delete or move old files to make space for the overlay file, or insert a new disk. Invoke the LINK command.

Cannot open response file: filename

Source   LINK

Cause   LINK could not open the automatic response file specified.

User Action   Check the spelling of the file name. Be sure that the automatic response file exists and reissue the command.

Cannot open run file

Source   LINK

Cause   The target disk or directory is full.

User Action   Delete or move old files to make space for the EXE file, or insert a new disk. Invoke the LINK command.

Cannot open temporary file

Source   LINK

Cause   The target disk or directory is full.

User Action   Delete or move old files to make space for the temporary LINK file VM.TMP, or insert a new disk. Invoke the LINK command.

Cannot perform a cyclic copy

Source   XCOPY

Cause   The XCOPY command resulted in part of the destination being included in the source file. The /S qualifier was probably contained in the XCOPY command resulting in a destination subdirectory residing in a source directory above it in the directory tree.

User Action   A temporary file or disk may be required, dependent upon the directory tree structure.

Cannot RECOVER to a network drive

Source   CHKDSK

Cause   CHKDSK could not recover the entry specified.

User Action   None

Cannot RECOVER to a network drive

Source   RECOVER

Cause   RECOVER cannot be performed on a disk that is currently part of a local area network.

User Action   Remove the disk from network access long enough to perform the RECOVER command.

Cannot reopen list file

Source   LINK

Cause   The disk that contained the LIST file opened by LINK at the beginning of the link process was not replaced in the drive specified.

User Action   Reissue the LINK command.

Cannot start COMMAND, exiting

Source   DOS

Cause   DOS attempted to invoke a second copy of the command processor (COMMAND.COM) and insufficient memory existed.

User Action   Restart DOS. Remember that device drivers, shared files, and installed programs all allocate available memory.

Cannot SUBST to a network drive

Source   SUBST

Cause   SUBST cannot be performed on a disk that is currently part of a local area network.

User Action   Remove the disk from network access long enough to perform the SUBST command.

Cannot SYS to a network drive

Source   SYS

Cause   SYS cannot be performed on a disk that is currently part of a local area network.

User Action   Remove the disk from network access long enough to perform the SYS command.

Cannot use PRINT—use NET PRINT

Source   PRINT

Cause   PRINT does not support disk currently used in a local area network.

User Action   Use the NET PRINT command.

Cannot XCOPY from a reserved device

Source   XCOPY

Cause   The XCOPY source is a character device (printer) or asynchronous communication device, or NULL. XCOPY does not support this type of file copy.

User Action   Use a temporary file to perform the copy.

Cannot XCOPY to a reserved device

Source   XCOPY

Cause   The XCOPY destination is a character device (printer) or asynchronous communication device, or NULL. XCOPY does not support this type of file copy.

User Action   Use a temporary file to perform the copy.

CHDIR..Failed Trying alternate method

Source   CHKDSK

Cause   CHKDSK failed to change its current working directory.

User Action   Reboot DOS and reissue the DOS CHKDSK command.

Command format: DISKCOPY d: d: [/1]

Source   DISKCOPY

Cause   An invalid parameter was specified in the DISKCOPY command line.

User Action   See the DISKCOPY command format in Chapter 2 and reissue the command.

Common area longer than 65536 bytes

Source   LINK

Cause   The EXE program contains more than 64K of shared variables.

User Action   Modify the source program to utilize fewer than 64K of shared (communal) variables.

COMn: baud,parity,data bits, stop bits, device type initialized

Source   MODE

Cause   Device initialization was successful. See the DOS MODE in Chapter 4 command for further explanation of the message.

User Action   None

COMn: ,parity,data bits, stop bits

Source   MODE

Cause   MODE is displaying the data communications parameters for the COM device displayed.

User Action   None

COM port does not exist

Source   MODE

Cause   The COM port specified is invalid.

User Action   Review Chapter 4 and reissue the command.

Compare error at offset nnnnnnnn

Source   COMP

Cause   The files COMP was comparing differed at the offset specified. The offset is in hexadecimal.

User Action   None

Compare more diskettes (Y/N)?

Source   DISKCOMP

Cause   DISKCOMP has completed the disk comparison.

User Action   To compare additional disks press Y; otherwise, press N.

Compare more files (Y/N)?

Source   COMP

Cause   COMP has completed the file comparison.

User Action   To compare additional files press Y; otherwise, press N.

Compare process ended

Source   DISKCOMP

Cause   DISKCOMP has completed the disk comparison.

User Action   None

Comparing n sectors per track, n side(s)

Source   DISKCOMP

Cause   DISKCOMP is displaying the number of sectors per track and the number of disk sides it will compare between the two disks.

User Action   Be sure that the sectors per track and number of sides are correct. If not, reissue the DISKCOMP command with the qualifiers required.

Configuration too large for memory

Source   DOS

Cause   The combination of the FILES, BUFFERS, or environment specified does not leave sufficient memory available for COMMAND.COM to be loaded.

User Action   Reboot DOS and reduce the number of FILES, BUFFERS, or environment memory allocated.

Contains nnn non-contiguous blocks

Source   CHKDSK

Cause   The file name that precedes the message is noncontiguous (Chapter 9).

User Action   See Chapter 9 on disk fragmentation. Use the DOS COPY command to COPY the file to a new disk. Delete the current version of the file and restore the copy.

Content of destination lost before copy

Source   COPY

Cause   The source file for the COPY was overwritten before the command completed.

User Action   Examine the COPY command in Appendix A, "DOS Reference Guide." Restore the source file from your backup disk.

Convert directory to file (Y/N)?

Source   CHKDSK

Cause The subdirectory name that precedes this error message contains too much invalid information to be useful as a directory.

User Action Press Y to convert the directory to a file that you can examine with DEBUG or another software program. Press N to leave the directory intact.

Copy another (Y/N)?

Source DISKCOPY

Cause DISKCOPY wants to know if you desire additional disk copies.

User Action Press Y to copy another disk, or press N to return to DOS.

Copy complete

Source DISKCOPY

Cause DISKCOPY has completed the disk copy.

User Action None

Copying nnn tracks
n sectors per track, n side(s)

Source DISKCOPY

Cause DISKCOPY is displaying the number of tracks, number of sectors per track, and number of disk sides it will use for the disk copy.

User Action Be sure that the parameters displayed by DISKCOPY are correct. If not, reissue the DISKCOPY command with the command line qualifiers required.

Corrections will not be written to disk

Source   CHKDSK

Cause   CHKDSK discovered errors on the disk but will not write the corrections to the disk since the /F qualifier was not found in the command line.

User Action   Reissue the command with the /F qualifier.

Current date is mm-dd-yy

Source   DATE

Cause   DATE is displaying the current system date.

User Action   Enter the date that you desire, or press ENTER to use the date displayed.

Current drive is no longer valid

Source   DOS Command Interpreter

Cause   The DOS PROMPT command or SET PROMPT= command attempted to use the current drive via the $p meta-string and found the current drive to be invalid. This normally occurs with network drives that have been deleted.

User Action   Set the current default drive to a valid drive.

Current time is hh:mm:ss.hh

Source   TIME

Cause   Time is displaying the current system time.

User Action   Enter the time that you desire, or press ENTER to use the time specified.

Data record too large

Source   LINK

Cause   The object file created by the compiler or assembler produced an invalid object file record.

User Action   Notify the manufacturer of your compiler.

Delete current volume label (Y/N)?

Source   LABEL

Cause   The DOS LABEL command was issued for a disk drive that already contained a volume label.

User Action   Press N to keep the current disk volume label; otherwise, press Y.

DEVICE Support Not Present

Source   DISKCOMP, DISKCOPY

Cause   The disk drive specified is invalid for DISKCOPY or DISKCOMP commands.

User Action   Reissue the command with a different disk drive.

DF

Source   DEBUG

Cause   Conflicting codes were specified for a single flag.

User Action   Do not attempt to change a flag more than once per Register command.

Dir path listing for volume nnnnnnnnnnn

Source   TREE

Cause   The DOS TREE command is simply displaying the volume label for the disk.

User Action   None

Directory entries adjusted

Source   VDISK

Cause   The number of directory entries for the current RAM disk configuration was invalid. VDISK modified the number of entries as required.

User Action   None

Directory is joined,
tree past this point not processed

Source   CHKDSK

Cause   The current disk has been JOINed with another disk drive. CHKDSK is stopping its examination of the disk at this point.

User Action   None. CHKDSK only examines one device at a time.

Directory is totally empty, no . or ..,
tree past this point not processed

Source   TREE

Cause   The subdirectory found is not complete. This normally occurs only when DOS is unable to complete a directory update (power off or system reboot prior to completion).

User Action   Use the DOS RECOVER command to recover the directory and any files it contains, if possible.

Directory not empty

Source   JOIN

Cause   The target directory for a DOS JOIN command contains files. JOIN only uses empty directories.

User Action   Remove the files from the directory, or issue the JOIN command with a different directory name.

Disk boot failure

Source   DOS

Cause   The DOS startup procedures are unable to boot from the current system disk.

User Action   Try to reboot DOS. If unsuccessful, boot DOS from drive A.

Disk error reading drive n

Source   DOS

Cause   An application attempted to perform absolute sector reads on a disk contained in a local area network. DOS does not support this type of disk access.

User Action   Remove the disk from the network if the sector read is mandatory.

Disk error reading FAT n

Source   CHKDSK

Cause   The file allocation table (FAT) displayed is invalid.

User Action   DOS places two file allocation tables on each disk to ensure a backup is present. If both FATs are invalid, try rebooting the system to see if the problem disappears. If not, FORMAT the disk to make it usable again. If FORMAT fails, the disk is unusable.

Disk error writing drive n

Source   DOS

Cause   An application attempted to perform absolute sector writes on a disk contained in a local area network. DOS does not support this type of disk access.

User Action   Remove the disk from the network if the sector write is mandatory.

Disk error writing FAT n

Source   CHKDSK

Cause   The file allocation table (FAT) displayed is invalid.

User Action   DOS places two file allocation tables on each disk to ensure a backup is present. If both FATs are invalid, try rebooting the system to see if the problem disappears. If not, FORMAT the disk to make it usable again. If FORMAT fails, the disk is unusable.

Disk full. Edits lost

Source   EDLIN

Cause   The target disk for the file is full. The EDLIN E command exited the current editing session. All edited data is lost.

User Action   Delete or move old files, or obtain a new disk.

Disk not compatible

Source   FORMAT

Cause   The DOS FORMAT command cannot format the disk provided in the disk drive specified.

User Action   FORMAT the disk in an alternate disk drive.

Disk unsuitable for system disk

Source   FORMAT

Cause   The disk track that normally contains the DOS system files is defective. FORMAT cannot create a bootable system disk.

User Action   This disk will not be bootable. Use a new disk to create a bootable DOS system disk.

Diskette/Drive not compatible

Source   DISKCOPY, DISKCOMP

Cause   The source and destination disks are different types. DISKCOPY and DISKCOMP do not support operations on non-compatible disk types.

User Action   Use compatible disk and reissue the command.

Diskettes compare OK

Source   DISKCOMP

Cause   DISKCOMP found the disks compared identical.

User Action   None

Divide overflow

Source   DOS

Cause   An application program attempted to divide a number by 0, or an internal error caused DOS to invoke the divide by 0 interrupt. Control is returned to DOS.

User Action   Correct the programming error, if possible, or notify the manufacturer of the software package.

Do you see the leftmost 0 (Y/N)?

Source   MODE

Cause   The ,R, qualifier was found in the MODE command line. MODE is attempting to align the screen contents.

User Action   Press Y if you can see left-most 0; otherwise, press N. MODE will align the screen as required.

Do you see the rightmost 9 (Y/N)?

Source   MODE

Cause   The ,L, qualifier was found in the MODE command line. MODE is attempting to align the screen contents.

User Action   Press Y if you can see right-most 9; otherwise, press N. MODE will align the screen as required.

Do you wish to use the entire fixed disk for DOS (Y/N).............?

Source   FDISK

Cause   The Create DOS Partition option of FDISK is prompting whether or not you want to use the entire disk for a DOS partition.

User Action   If you press Y and then press ENTER, FDISK will allocate the complete hard disk for a DOS partition. If you press N, FDISK will prompt you for the partition size and starting cylinder location.

DOS partition already exists

Source   FDISK

Cause   A DOS partition already exists on the target disk.

User Action A new DOS partition cannot be created on that disk until the current DOS partition is deleted.

DOS partition created

Source FDISK

Cause FDISK has created the DOS disk partition as specified.

User Action FORMAT the DOS disk partition to make it usable.

DOS partition deleted

Source FDISK

Cause FDISK has deleted the DOS disk partition from the target disk.

User Action None

Drive letter must be specified

Source FORMAT

Cause The DOS FORMAT command requires a disk drive identification.

User Action Reissue the FORMAT command with the disk drive identification of the drive containing the disk to format.

Drive types or diskette types not compatible

Source DISKCOPY, DISKCOMP

Cause The source and target disks are not compatible. DISKCOPY and DISKCOMP do not support operations on noncompatible disk.

User Action Reissue the command with compatible disk.

Drive (x:) not ready
Make sure a diskette is inserted into
the drive and the door is closed

Source   DISKCOPY, DISKCOMP

Cause   The disk drive specified is empty or the door lock is not closed.

User Action   Be sure that the disk is properly placed in the drive and that the door is closed.

DUP record too complex

Source   LINK

Cause   A record in the object file contains an assembly language DUP record that is either nested too deeply or is too complicated for the linker to resolve.

User Action   Reduce the number of DUP statements or structures in the source code and reassemble. Reissue the LINK command.

Duplicate file name or file not found

Source   RENAME

Cause   RENAME could not find the source file to rename, or the target file name already exists on disk.

User Action   Perform a directory listing for the source or target file specified.

ECHO is ON ¦ OFF

Source   ECHO

Cause   ECHO is displaying its current state.

User Action   None

End of input file

Source   EDLIN

Cause   EDLIN has successfully read the entire file into memory.

User Action   None

Enter current Volume label for Drive n (Press ENTER for none):

Source   FORMAT

Cause   FORMAT is requiring you to enter a volume label that prevents you from inadvertently formatting your hard disk.

User Action   Press CTRL-BREAK to terminate the command or type in the volume label desired.

Enter new date:

Source   DATE

Cause   The previous date entered was invalid. DATE is prompting you for a new date.

User Action   Type in the DATE desired or press ENTER to use the default date displayed.

Enter new time:

Source   TIME

Cause   The previous time entered was invalid. TIME is prompting you for a new time.

User Action   Type in the TIME desired or press ENTER to use the default time displayed.

Enter partition size........:[nnnn]

Source   FDISK

Cause   The FDISK Create DOS Partition option is prompting you to enter the size of the DOS partition in cylinders.

User Action   If you press ENTER, DOS will use the number of cylinders contained between the left and right brackets [nnnn]. If you don't want the default value, enter the number of cylinders that you want to use for the partition and press ENTER.

Enter primary file name

Source   COMP

Cause   COMP is asking you to enter the primary file name for the file comparison.

User Action   Type in the file name of the first file that you want to compare and press ENTER.

Enter secondary file name

Source   COMP

Cause   COMP is asking you to enter the secondary file name for the file comparison.

User Action   Type in the file name of the second file that you want to compare and press ENTER.

Enter starting cylinder number..:[nnnn]

Source   FDISK

Cause   The FDISK Create DOS Partition option is prompting you to enter the cylinder number at which the partition is to begin.

User Action   If you press ENTER, FDISK will use the cylinder number contained between the left and right brackets [nnnn]. If you don't want to use the default cylinder, enter the cylinder number desired and press ENTER.

Enter the number of the partition you want to make active..........?

Source   FDISK

Cause   The FDISK Change Active Partition option is prompting you for the number of the partition that you want to make active.

User Action   Type in the partition number desired (1-4) for the active partition.

Entry error

Source   EDLIN

Cause   The EDLIN command you entered contained a syntax error.

User Action   See Chapter 13 and reissue the EDLIN command.

Entry has a bad attribute (or size or link)

Source   CHKDSK

Cause   CHKDSK has found a directory entry that contains invalid size or cluster links. If one or two periods precedes the error message, the current or parent directory contains the error.

User Action   Use the /F option of CHKDSK to repair the error.

EOF mark not found

Source   COMP

Cause   COMP examined two files and did not find an end of file CTRL-Z marker in the last block of a file. This normally occurs only in binary files.

User Action   See the COMP command in Appendix A, "DOS Reference Guide."

Error found, F parameter not specified
Corrections will not be written to disk

Source   CHKDSK

Cause   CHKDSK found errors on the disk specified. Since the /F qualifier was not present in the command line, no corrective measures were taken.

User Action   Invoke CHKDSK with the /F qualifier to repair the disk error.

Error in EXE file

Source   DOS Command Line Interpreter

Cause   The relocation information stored at the beginning of an EXE file is invalid. DOS cannot execute the command.

User Action   If you have the program's source or object code, recompile and relink the program. Otherwise, notify the manufacturer of the software package.

Error in EXE or HEX file

Source   DEBUG

Cause   The file to debug contains invalid records or data.

User Action   If possible, obtain a second copy of the file.

Error loading operating system

Source   DOS

Cause   The DOS startup procedures could not load the operating system from hard disk.

User Action   Reboot DOS. If the system cannot be restarted, boot DOS from drive A and issue the SYS command to the hard disk.

Error reading fixed disk

Source   FDISK

Cause   FDISK failed in five attempts to read the startup record from the current hard disk.

User Action   Reboot DOS and invoke FDISK again. If the problem persists, notify your dealer.

Error reading partition table

Source   FORMAT

Cause   FORMAT experienced an error reading the disk partition table.

User Action   Reboot and invoke FORMAT again. If the error persists, use the DOS FDISK command to repair the partition table.

Error writing fixed disk

Source   FDISK

Cause   FDISK failed in five attempts to write the startup record to the current hard disk.

User Action   Reboot DOS and invoke FDISK again. If the problem persists, notify your dealer.

Error writing to device

Source   DOS Commands

Cause   A DOS command experienced an error writing to a hardware device. The output has failed.

User Action   Examine the output request that failed. If the output is valid, reduce the number of bytes that it is attempting to write to the hardware device.

Errors on list device indicate that it may be off-line. Please check.

Source   PRINT

Cause   PRINT just received a new PRINT command and the device used for spooled printing is off-line.

User Action   Be sure that the printer is cabled correctly and the ON-LINE light is lit. DOS will print the file when the device becomes available.

EXE and HEX files cannot be written

Source   DEBUG

Cause   DEBUG does not allow you to write the contents of the program it is examining to an EXE file.

User Action   RENAME the file on disk to an extension other than EXE. Use DEBUG to read, rather than load, the file to make your changes. Later RENAME the file to an EXE file.

EXEC failure

Source   DOS Commands

Cause   DOS could not read a command from disk, or the FILES= entry in CONFIG.SYS contained a value too small for DOS.

User Action   Be sure that the FILES= entry in CONFIG.SYS uses a value greater than or equal to eight. If so, invoke the DOS CHKDSK command to examine the disk.

Extender card switches do not match the system memory size

Source   VDISK

Cause   The memory extender card DIP switches are incorrect, or you are accessing memory contained in an expansion unit. VDISK does not support memory contained in an expansion unit.

User Action   Examine the DIP switches on the memory extender card to be sure that they are correct.

FATAL: Internal Stack Failure, System Halted.

Source   DOS

Cause   DOS exceeded the available stack resources.

User Action   Place the entry STACKS=frames,size in the file CONFIG.SYS, where frames are in the range 8 to 64 (default 9) and size is in the range 32 to 512 (default 128). Each hardware interrupt temporarily allocates one frame from the stack pool.

File allocation table bad, drive n Abort, Retry, or Ignore?

Source   DOS

Cause   DOS cannot read the file allocation table (FAT, Chapter 9) for the disk specified.

User Action   Reboot DOS and invoke CHKDSK. If the problem persists, the disk is unusable and should be reformatted.

File cannot be converted

Source   EXE2BIN

Cause   The file to be converted from EXE format to COM format did not meet the requirements specified in Appendix A, "DOS Reference Guide" for EXE2BIN.

User Action   None. You cannot convert the file.

File cannot be copied onto itself

Source   COPY, XCOPY

Cause   The source and target names of a file to copy are identical. COPY and XCOPY will not allow you to copy a file's contents to itself.

User Action   Make sure that the target file name for the copy operation is complete (drive, path, file name, extension). If so, choose a new name or change the target disk drive.

File creation error

Source   DOS Commands

Cause   A file could not be created or replaced in the directory specified.

User Action   Check if a file already exists in the target directory with the name specified. If so, check the file's attributes to see if they are read-only. Also, use the DOS CHKDSK command to ensure that the directory is not full.

File filename.ext cancelled by operator

Source   PRINT

Cause   The user entered the /C qualifier in the PRINT command to remove the file specified from the print queue.

User Action   None

File is cross-linked:
on cluster nnn

Source   CHKDSK

Cause   CHKDSK found a cluster that is allocated by two files.

User Action   COPY both files to new file names. DELete the previous files. Examine the new files, if possible, to see which file contains the correct contents.

File is READ-ONLY

Source   EDLIN

Cause   The file you are attempting to edit has read-only attributes.

User Action   If you really want to edit the file, change its attributes with the DOS ATTRIB command.

File name must be specified

Source   EDLIN

Cause   EDLIN was invoked without a file name in the command line.

User Action   Reissue the EDLIN command and specify the file name EDLIN is to edit.

File not found

Source   DOS Commands

Cause   The file named in a command, or as a parameter to a command, does not exist as specified.

User Action   Reissue the command with the correct file name.

File not in print queue

Source   PRINT

Cause   A PRINT/C command was issued with a file name to cancel from the print queue and the file did not exist in the queue.

User Action   List the files in the print queue simply by invoking PRINT without any parameters and find the file name you desire.

File sharing conflict

Source   COMP

Cause   COMP could not open one of the files to compare because it is being accessed by another process.

User Action   Wait until the file is available and reissue the COMP command to perform the file comparison.

filename AND filename

Source   COMP

Cause   COMP is displaying the full path and file name for each file it is comparing.

User Action   None

filename.ext is currently being printed
filename.ext is in queue

Source   PRINT

Cause   The PRINT command has been issued with no other parameters in the command line.

User Action   None

filename is not a valid library

Source   LINK

Cause   The library name specified does not contain a valid library.

User Action   None

Files are different sizes

Source   COMP

Cause   COMP was invoked to compare two files of different sizes. COMP does not support this operation.

User Action   None

Files compare OK

Source   COMP

Cause   The files that COMP compared were identical.

User Action   None

Files were backed up mm/dd/yy

Source   RESTORE

Cause   RESTORE is telling you the date that the files were backed up.

User Action   Verify that the date displayed is the date that you anticipated based upon your backup log.

First cluster number is invalid, entry truncated

Source   CHKDSK

Cause   CHKDSK found an invalid cluster pointer for the file whose name precedes the error message.

User Action   Use the command CHKDSK /F and CHKDSK will truncate the data contained in the file at the bad cluster number.

DOS: The Complete Reference

Fixed Backup device is full

Source   BACKUP

Cause   The target destination device for the backup is full. No additional data can be written to it.

User Action   None

Fixup offset exceeds field width near nnnn in filename offset nnnnn

Source   LINK

Cause   The following errors cause this message to be displayed:

• A group (Chapter 16) exceeded 64K.

• The object code contains an intersegment short call or jump.

• A data name in the object code conflicts with a name in a library.

• An EXTRN statement appears in the body of a segment.

• A data item was declared outside of all segments.

• Segment register usage differs from the ASSUME qualifier used in the code.

User Action   Correct the error in the source code and reassemble and LINK.

Fixups needed — base segment (hex):

Source   EXE2BIN

Cause   The EXE file to convert requires an absolute segment address for the destination of the module load.

User Action   Enter the absolute segment address. Be leery of the COM file produced by EXE2BIN since it requires absolute memory addresses.

FOR cannot be nested

Source   DOS Batch Command Interpreter

Cause   The command that a FOR command was to execute was a second FOR command.

User Action   Edit the BAT file to ensure that only one FOR command is contained per line.

Format another (Y/N)?

Source   FORMAT

Cause   FORMAT completed successfully and is prompting you whether or not you want to FORMAT an additional disk.

User Action   Press Y to FORMAT another disk or N to return control to DOS.

Format complete

Source   FORMAT

Cause   FORMAT has successfully completed.

User Action   None

Format failure

Source   FORMAT

Cause   A disk error prevented FORMAT from completing.

User Action   The disk used is corrupted. Reissue the FORMAT command with a new disk.

FORMAT not supported on Drive n

Source   FORMAT

Cause FORMAT does not support operations to the disk drive type specified (normally a virtual disk drive).

User Action If the disk drive is not a virtual disk drive, reboot DOS and reissue the FORMAT command. If the error persists, be sure that an alternate disk device driver is not specified in CON-FIG.SYS. If so, remove it and reboot. If not, contact your manufacturer.

Formatting while copying

Source DISKCOPY

Cause The target disk for the DISKCOPY operation contained unformatted tracks. DISKCOPY is formatting the disk as it continues.

User Action None

Graphics characters already loaded

Source GRAFTABL

Cause The graphics characters have already been loaded into memory and the GRAFTABL command was reissued.

User Action None

Graphics characters loaded

Source GRAFTABL

Cause GRAFTABL has successfully loaded the graphics characters into memory.

User Action None

Has invalid cluster, file truncated

Source CHKDSK

Cause   CHKDSK found an invalid cluster in the file whose name precedes this message. If the /F qualifier is in the CHKDSK command line, CHKDSK will truncate the information contained in the file at the bad cluster number. Otherwise, the bad cluster pointer still remains.

User Action   Use CHKDSK /F to repair (truncate) the bad file.

Head: n Cylinder: n

Source   FORMAT

Cause   FORMAT is displaying the current disk head and cylinder number it is formatting.

User Action   None

Illegal device name

Source   MODE

Cause   An invalid device name was specified in the MODE command line. Use LPT1, LPT2, LPT3, or COM1, COM2.

User Action   Reissue the MODE command with the correct device name.

Incompatible system size

Source   SYS

Cause   The target disk contained DOS system files that are smaller than the new system files. SYS cannot place the new files into the smaller disk space.

User Action   FORMAT a new disk with the /S qualifier and then use the DOS XCOPY command to copy all files contained on the original disk to the new system disk.

Incorrect DOS version

Source   DOS Command Line Interpreter

Cause   The command that you entered will not run under the current DOS configuration.

User Action   Boot DOS under the later version number and reissue the command.

Incorrect DOS version, use DOS 2.00 or later

Source   LINK

Cause   The linker will not run on a system running a DOS version less than 2.0.

User Action   Boot DOS with a version number 2.0 or greater.

Incorrect number of parameters

Source   DOS Commands

Cause   The command line entered did not contain a sufficient number of parameters for the command that you invoked.

User Action   Examine the command in Appendix A, "DOS Reference Guide," and reissue the command with the correct number of parameters.

Incorrect parameter

Source   SHARE

Cause   A parameter in the SHARE command line is invalid.

User Action   Examine the DOS SHARE command in Appendix A, "DOS Reference Guide," and reissue the command.

Infinite retry not supported on network printer

Source   MODE

Cause   The P parameter was specified in MODE command line, which requests continuous retries on device time-out errors, and the device is connected to a local area network. DOS cannot sense device time-outs over the network.

User Action   Do not specify the P qualifier on network devices, or use a different device.

Infinite retry on parallel printer time-out

Source   MODE

Cause   The P parameter was specified in MODE command line, which requests continuous retries on device time-out errors.

User Action   None

Insert backup diskette nn in drive n:
Strike any key when ready

Source   RESTORE

Cause   RESTORE is prompting you to place the next disk in the restoration sequence in the drive specified and then to press any key to continue.

User Action   Place the disk required in the drive specified. Press any key to continue or CTRL-BREAK to terminate the command.

Insert backup source diskette in drive n
Strike any key when ready

Source   BACKUP

Cause   BACKUP has paused, prompting you to place the disk containing the source files in the disk drive specified.

User Action   Place the source disk in the drive specified and press any key to continue.

Insert backup target diskette n in drive n
Strike any key when ready

Source   BACKUP

Cause   BACKUP is prompting you to place the next disk in the backup sequence in the drive specified and then to press any key when you are ready to continue.

User Action   Place a formatted disk in the disk drive specified and then press any key to continue.

Insert disk with batch file
and strike any key when ready

Source   DOS

Cause   During the execution of a BAT file, the disk that contains the file has been removed. DOS is prompting you to replace the disk so that it can continue processing.

User Action   Place the disk containing the BAT file currently executing in the correct disk drive and press any key to continue.

Insert disk with \COMMAND.COM in drive A
and strike any key when ready

Source   DOS

Cause   DOS is attempting to reload the command processor (COMMAND.COM) and the file is not contained on the disk.

User Action   Insert a disk containing COMMAND.COM in drive A and press any key when ready.

Insert diskette for drive n and press any key when ready

Source   DOS

Cause   A DOS system with logical disk drives experienced a disk reference to a drive that is not the current drive. DOS is prompting you to enter the correct disk in that drive.

User Action   If the disk is already contained in the drive specified, simply press any key. Otherwise, place the disk that you desire in the drive and press any key when you are ready to continue.

Insert DOS disk in n and strike any key when ready

Source   FORMAT

Cause   A FORMAT /S command has been issued and the current disk does not contain the DOS system files.

User Action   Place a DOS system disk in the drive specified and press any key to continue.

Insert DOS diskette in drive A: Press any key when ready...

Source   FDISK

Cause   The DOS partition has been successfully created and FDISK is preparing to reboot your computer.

User Action   Place a DOS system disk in drive A and press any key to continue. Once the system is rebooted, use the DOS FORMAT command to format the hard disk.

Insert first diskette in drive n
Insert second diskette in drive n

Source   DISKCOMP

DOS: The Complete Reference

Cause   DISKCOMP is directing you to place the disks that you want to compare in the drive specified.

User Action   Place the disks to compare in the correct drives and press any key to continue.

Insert KEYBxx.com diskette in drive n: and strike any key when ready

Source   SELECT

Cause   The keyboard software requested resides on a disk other than the current default.

User Action   Place the disk containing the KEYBxx.COM file in the drive specified and press any key to continue.

Insert last backup target in drive n

Source   BACKUP

Cause   The /A qualifier appeared in the BACKUP command line. BACKUP is prompting you to place the last disk that you used for backups in the drive specified.

User Action   See Chapter 11. Place the last disk that you used for incremental backups in the drive specified and press any key to continue.

Insert new diskette for drive n and press ENTER when ready

Source   FORMAT

Cause   FORMAT wants to enter the disk that you want to format in the drive specified.

User Action   Place the disk to FORMAT in the drive specified and press the ENTER key when ready.

Insert restore target nn in drive nn
Strike any key when ready

Source   RESTORE

Cause   RESTORE is ready to restore files from a backup disk to a floppy disk. It is prompting you to enter the disk that you want the files restored to in the drive specified.

User Action   Place the disk that you want the restored files on in the disk drive specified and press any key when you are ready to continue.

Insert source diskette in drive n
Insert target diskette in drive n

Source   DISKCOPY

Cause   DISKCOPY is ready to copy the contents of one disk to another. It is prompting you to place the source and target disks in the drives specified.

User Action   Place the disk to copy in the source drive and the disk you want the new copy to go on in the target drive and press any key when you are ready.

Insert System disk in n
and strike any key when ready

Source   SYS

Cause   SYS is trying to load the system files to the target disk but the current default disk does not contain the hidden system files.

User Action   Place a DOS system disk in the drive specified and press any key to continue.

Insert target diskette in drive B:
Strike any key when ready

Source   SELECT

Cause   SELECT is ready to create the new disk.

User Action   Place the target disk in drive B and press any key to continue.

Insert target diskette in drive D:
Strike any key when ready

Source   SELECT

Cause   This command appears when you are using a single drive system. SELECT is prompting you to place the disk that you are creating into the drive specified.

User Action   Place the disk that you are creating via the SELECT command into the drive specified and press any key to continue.

Insufficient disk space

Source   DOS Commands

Cause   The disk that the command was writing the file to does not contain sufficient space.

User Action   Delete or move old files from the disk or use a new target disk for the operation.

Insufficient memory

Source   DOS Commands

Cause   The amount of available memory is insufficient for the command to execute.

User Action   Remove nonessential device drivers, file-sharing locks and file space, and disk buffers from memory. Many of these modifications require you to edit the CONFIG.SYS file. See Chapter 15.

Insufficient memory for system transfer

Source   FORMAT, SYS

Cause   Either FORMAT was invoked with the /S qualifier, or SYS command failed to move the DOS system files to the target disk because of insufficient memory.

User Action   None

Insufficient room in root directory
Erase files from root and repeat CHKDSK

Source   CHKDSK

Cause   CHKDSK was instructed to convert lost clusters into files and the root directory is full, prohibiting further recoveries.

User Action   Provide directory space in the root directory and reissue the CHKDSK command.

Insufficient space on disk

Source   DEBUG

Cause   DEBUG attempted to write to a disk that had insufficient space for the file.

User Action   Place a disk with sufficient space in a disk drive and write the data to it.

Insufficient stack space

Source   LINK

Cause   Insufficient system memory is available for the LINK command to execute.

User Action   Remove nonessential device drivers, file-sharing locks and shared file space, and disk buffers from memory. Many of these modifications require you to edit the CONFIG.SYS file.

See Chapter 15. Reissue the LINK command.

Intermediate file error during pipe

Source   DOS

Cause   DOS pipe operations create temporary files in the root directory of the current default drive. Insufficient disk space or insufficient directory entries prevented the temporary file creation.

User Action   Delete or move nonessential files from the current root directory and reissue the command.

Invalid baud rate specified

Source   MODE

Cause   The baud rate specified for a device is invalid.

User Action   Use a baud rate defined as follows:

    11 or   110
    15 or   150
    30 or   300
    60 or   600
    12 or   1200
    24 or   2400
    48 or   4800
    96 or   9600

and reissue the MODE command.

Invalid characters in volume label

Source   FORMAT

Cause   A character used in the volume name entered is invalid.

User Action   See the DOS VOL command in Chapter 3 and reissue the command with a valid name.

Invalid COMMAND.COM in drive n

Source   DOS

Cause   DOS attempted to reload the transient portion of the command processor from disk but found that file COMMAND. COM on the current drive contains an incorrect version of DOS.

User Action   Insert a DOS system disk with the correct version of the DOS command processor.

Invalid country code

Source   SELECT, COUNTRY=

Cause   The country code specified in either the SELECT command or COUNTRY= entry in CONFIG.SYS is invalid.

User Action   See Chapter 12 to determine the correct country code.

Invalid current directory

Source   CHKDSK

Cause   CHKDSK found an unrecoverable error while attempting to read the current directory.

User Action   Reboot DOS and reissue the CHKDSK command. If the error persists, the disk may require formatting.

Invalid date

Source   DOS Commands

Cause   The date specified was invalid or contained invalid delimiters.

User Action   See Chapter 2 and respecify the command.

Invalid device

Source   CTTY

Cause   The device name in the CTTY command is invalid.

User Action   See the CTTY command in Appendix A, "DOS Reference Guide," and reissue the command with a valid device name.

Invalid device parameters from device driver

Source   FORMAT

Cause   The DOS partition does not begin on a track boundary.

User Action   Use the DOS FDISK command to correct the hard disk partition. Reissue the FORMAT command.

Invalid directory

Source   DOS Commands

Cause   A directory in the path specified does not exist.

User Action   Examine the directory path specified. Reissue the command with the correct directory path.

Invalid disk change

Source   DOS

Cause   A disk in a high-capacity, 1.2MB floppy drive was removed while DOS had files open on the disk.

User Action   Place the correct disk back into the drive and complete the operation.

Invalid drive in search path

Source   DOS Commands

Cause   A path in the DOS PATH command contains an invalid disk drive specifier.

User Action   Correct the DOS search path with the DOS PATH or SET PATH= commands. Reissue the DOS command that previously failed.

Invalid drive or file name

Source   DOS Commands

Cause   Either the drive specifier or file name specified in the command line was invalid.

User Action   Correct the drive identification or file name and reissue the DOS command.

Invalid drive specification

Source   DOS Commands

Cause   An invalid or nonexistent disk drive was specified in the command or a command parameter.

User Action   Correct the drive identification and reissue the DOS command.

Invalid drive specification
Specified drive does not exist,
or is non-removable

Source   DOS Commands

Cause   An invalid or nonexistent disk drive was specified in the command or a command parameter.

User Action   Correct the drive identification and reissue the DOS command.

Invalid drive specification
Source and Target drives are the same

Source   BACKUP, RESTORE

Cause   BACKUP and RESTORE do not allow the source and target disk drives to be the same.

User Action   Reissue the DOS command with the correct source and target disk drive identification.

Invalid environment size specified

Source   DOS

Cause   The size of the environment is larger than 32K or contained non-numeric characters.

User Action   See Chapter 10 on the DOS environment and reissue the DOS command.

Invalid file name
or file not found

Source   RENAME, TYPE

Cause   The file name specified as a parameter to RENAME or TYPE is either not found or invalid.

User Action   Examine the RENAME and TYPE commands in Chapter 3 and reissue the command.

Invalid format file

Source   LINK

Cause   A library specified is invalid.

User Action   Restore the library from the original or a backup disk.

Invalid keyboard code

Source   SELECT

Cause   An invalid keyboard code was entered with the DOS SELECT command.

User Action   See Chapter 12. Reissue the SELECT command with a valid keyboard code.

Invalid media or track 0 bad — disk unusable

Source   FORMAT

Cause   Track 0 on the disk to be formatted is corrupted, which renders the disk unusable by DOS. Track 0 contains the mandatory DOS boot record.

User Action   Issue the command with a new disk.

Invalid number of parameters

Source   DOS Commands

Cause   The command line entered contained too few or too many parameters for the command entered.

User Action   Examine the command in Appendix A, "DOS Reference Guide," and reissue the command.

Invalid numeric parameter

Source   LINK

Cause   A link qualifier requiring a numeric value contained non-numeric characters.

User Action   Examine the LINK command in Chapter 16 and reissue the LINK command with a valid numeric value.

Invalid object module

Source   LINK

Cause   One of the OBJ files LINK is to combine is invalid.

User Action   Recompile the source code that created the OBJ file. If the problem persists, invoke CHKDSK to examine the disk.

Invalid parameter

Source   DOS Commands

Cause   The command line entered contained one or more invalid parameters. The parameters may simply be out of order.

User Action   Examine the command in Appendix A, "DOS Reference Guide," and reissue the command.

Invalid parameters

Source   MODE

Cause   A command line parameter is invalid.

User Action   Examine the mode command in Chapter 4 and reissue the MODE command.

Invalid partition table

Source   DOS

Cause   The DOS startup procedures could not read the hard disk because of a partition table error.

User Action   Reboot DOS. Invoke the FDISK command to repair the disk partition table.

Invalid path

Source   DOS Commands

Cause   The pathname specified is invalid or contained invalid characters.

User Action   Be sure that the pathname is valid (63 characters or fewer).

Invalid path, not directory or directory not empty

Source   RMDIR

Cause   RMDIR could not remove the directory specified for one or more of the following reasons:

- Cannot remove the current directory
- Directory still contains files
- Pathname is invalid

User Action   Delete any files from the directory and remove it. Be sure that the pathname specified is correct. Change the default directory to an alternate directory and then remove the directory desired.

Invalid path or file name

Source   ATTRIB, COPY

Cause   The file name or directory specified does not exist.

User Action   Correct the file name or pathname and reissue the DOS command.

Invalid subdirectory

Source   CHKDSK

Cause   The subdirectory name that precedes the error message contains invalid information.

User Action   Use the CHKDSK /F command to repair the directory.

Invalid switch

    Source   LINK

    Cause   The LINK command line contained an invalid qualifier.

    User Action   Examine the LINK command in Chapter 16 and reissue the command.

Invalid switch character

    Source   VDISK

    Cause   A qualifier to the VDISK entry in CONFIG.SYS is invalid. The virtual disk will still be installed in low memory.

    User Action   Examine VDISK in Chapter 15 and modify CONFIG.SYS as required.

Invalid time

    Source   TIME

    Cause   The time specified, or a delimiter used to separate the entries in the time, is invalid.

    User Action   Examine the TIME command in Chapter 2 and reissue the command.

Invalid volume label

    Source   FORMAT

    Cause   The volume label specified does not match the volume label on the disk to be formatted.

    User Action   Issue the DOS VOL command to determine the volume name and reissue the FORMAT command.

Is KEYBxx.COM on another diskette (Y/N)?

Source   SELECT

Cause   The KEYBxx.COM file specified was not found on the disk specified.

User Action   Examine the keyboard programs in Chapter 12 and press Y if the file is on another disk. If the keyboard file is not present, simply press N to terminate the command.

Keyboard routine not found

Source   DOS

Cause   The keyboard routine specified does not exist in the current directory of the disk specified.

User Action   Modify the disk as required and reissue the command.

Label not found

Source   Batch Command Interpreter

Cause   A GOTO command in a DOS BAT file referenced a label that does not exist.

User Action   Examine Chapter 8 on Batch Processing and edit the BAT file to correct the error.

Last backup target not inserted

Source   BACKUP

Cause   The /A qualifier is present in the BACKUP command line but the disk entered is not the last disk in the BACKUP sequence.

User Action   Place the correct disk in the drive and reissue the command.

** Last file not backed up **

Source   BACKUP

Cause   The target disk is full, resulting in the last file not being backed up.

User Action   None

Line too long

Source   EDLIN

Cause   An EDLIN line exceeded 253 characters. The EDLIN operation did not complete as desired.

User Action   Convert the line into two or more EDLIN lines.

List output is not assigned to a device

Source   PRINT

Cause   PRINT cannot print to the device specified.

User Action   Review Chapter 5 on the DOS PRINT command and reissue the command.

Lock violation

Source   XCOPY

Cause   The XCOPY source file is locked by the file-sharing code restricting access.

User Action   Retry the command at a later time.

LPT#: not rerouted

Source   MODE

Cause MODE is stating that the parallel device specified will receive all data written to it, despite previous redirections.

User Action None

LPT#: rerouted to COMn:

Source MODE

Cause MODE is stating that the parallel device specified will have all the data that is written to it rerouted to the serial device shown.

User Action None

LPT#: set for 80

Source MODE

Cause MODE is stating that it has set the number of characters per line on the printer at 80.

User Action None

LPT#: set for 132

Source MODE

Cause MODE is stating that it has set the number of characters per line on the printer at 132.

User Action None

Make sure a diskette is inserted into the drive and the door is closed

Source DISKCOMP, DISKCOPY

Cause One of the disk drives specified does not contain a disk, or the drive door is open.

User Action   Close the disk drive door, or place a disk in the drive specified.

Maximum available space nnnn
cylinders at cylinder nnnn

Source   FDISK

Cause   FDISK is telling you the maximum number of cylinders available on the disk and their starting addresses.

User Action   None

Memory allocation error
Cannot load COMMAND, system halted

Source   DOS

Cause   The DOS memory allocation table has become corrupted by an application.

User Action   Reboot DOS.

Mismatch DOS level number

Source   LINK

Cause   The linker has an internal fatal error.

User Action   Print the screen contents and notify IBM or Microsoft.

Missing operating system

Source   DOS

Cause   The DOS startup procedures cannot continue because a bootable DOS partition does not contain DOS.

User Action   Reformat the DOS partition with the FORMAT/S command.

—MORE—

Source   MORE

Cause   MORE has displayed a page of information and is pausing for you to press any key to continue.

User Action   Press any key to see the next screenful of information or CTRL-BREAK to terminate the command.

Must specify COM1 or COM2

Source   MODE

Cause   The MODE command line is invalid.

User Action   Review the MODE command in Chapter 4 and reissue the command.

Must specify destination line number

Source   EDLIN

Cause   An EDLIN Move or Copy command did not contain a mandatory destination line.

User Action   Examine Chapter 13 on EDLIN and reissue the command.

Must specify ON or OFF

Source   BREAK

Cause   The BREAK command line contained a value other than ON or OFF.

User Action   Reissue the BREAK command specifying either ON or OFF.

n is not a choice. Enter a choice.

Source   FDISK

Cause   An invalid FDISK menu option was entered.

User Action   Select an option number from the FDISK menu or press ESC to return to DOS.

n is not a choice. Enter Y or N.

Source   FDISK

Cause   Invalid user response. FDISK expects a Y or N answer.

User Action   Press Y or N.

nnn lost clusters found in nnn chains.
Convert lost chains to files (Y/N)?

Source   CHKDSK

Cause   CHKDSK was interrupted by a user CTRL-BREAK. It is prompting you to determine whether or not it should convert lost cluster chains in the FAT (Chapter 9) to files.

User Action   To convert the lost chains into files that you can edit, press Y; otherwise, press N. See Chapter 9 on disks and Chapter 3 on CHKDSK.

nnnn error on file filename

Source   PRINT

Cause   The PRINT command encountered a fatal error trying to read the file specified.

User Action   Be sure that the file is still available as specified.

nnnn files added

Source   REPLACE

Cause   REPLACE is telling you the number of files that it added to the target disk.

User Action   None

nnnn lost clusters found in nnnn chains. Convert lost chains to files (Y/N)?

Source   CHKDSK

Cause   CHKDSK found several lost disk clusters in its examination of the file allocation table.

User Action   If you want CHKDSK to convert the chains of clusters to files, press Y. Otherwise, press N and CHKDSK will free up the clusters so they can be allocated by DOS. If the /F qualifier is not present in the CHKDSK command line, the message is purely informational.

nnnnnn of nnnnnn bytes recovered

Source   RECOVER

Cause   RECOVER is specifying the number of bytes of the file specified it recovered. The directory entry for each file contains an entry for the actual file length.

User Action   None

nnnnnnnn bytes disk space freed

Source   CHKDSK

Cause   CHKDSK released all allocated disk space that was not associated with a file. If the /F qualifier was found in the command line, CHKDSK actually freed the disk space. Otherwise, it simply displayed the message.

User Action   To free the disk space, invoke CHKDSK with the /F option.

Name of list device [PRN]:

Source   PRINT

Cause   This message appears the first time you invoke PRINT so that PRINT can determine to what device it can send all of its output.

User Action   Type in the name of the device that you want PRINT to use, or simply press ENTER to use the device name PRN:.

NEAR/FAR conflict

Source   LINK

Cause   A shared variable has conflicting NEAR and FAR definitions.

User Action   Edit the source code to correct the definitions and recompile. Reissue the LINK command with the updated object file.

Network support loaded
Unable to FDISK

Source   FDISK

Cause   FDISK does not support operations on a disk that is part of a local area network.

User Action   Remove the device from the network and perform the FDISK operation. When FDISK is complete, add the disk back into the network.

New file

Source   EDLIN

Cause   EDLIN did not find a file with the name specified and will create a file with the name provided.

User Action   None

No COM: ports

Source   MODE

Cause   The computer does not contain any asynchronous communications ports.

User Action   None

No DOS partition to delete

Source   FDISK

Cause   The Delete DOS Partition option was selected from the FDISK main menu and no DOS partition exists on the disk.

User Action   Examine the partitions available via the Display Partition Data option on the FDISK main menu.

No files added

Source   REPLACE

Cause   The /A qualifier was present in the REPLACE command line and the file(s) specified already resided on the disk.

User Action   None

No files found

Source   REPLACE

Cause   None of the source files specified were found in the target location.

User Action   None

No files replaced

Source   REPLACE

Cause   The /P qualifier was present in the REPLACE command line and the user responded with N to all of the prompts.

User Action   None

No fixed disk present

Source   FDISK

Cause   FDISK was invoked on a system that does not have a fixed disk, or the fixed disk is incorrectly installed.

User Action   If you did not install your own fixed disk, have your dealer examine the cabling. If it is an external disk, be sure that it has power.

No free file handles
Cannot start COMMAND, exiting

Source   DOS

Cause   An attempt to load a secondary command processor failed because of insufficient file handles.

User Action   Increase the number of file handles available via the FILES= entry in the file CONFIG.SYS.

No object modules specified

Source   LINK

Cause   No object files were specified for the linker to link.

User Action   Object files are input source to the DOS linker. Specify the file(s) that you want linked.

No partitions to make active.

Source FDISK

Cause The Change Active Partition option of the FDISK main menu was selected and no partitions were available to become active.

User Action A partition must be created with the FDISK option Create DOS Partition before you can activate it.

No path

Source APPEND

Cause A path was not specified in the APPEND command line.

User Action Examine the APPEND command in Chapter 10 and reissue the command.

No path

Source PATH

Cause No alternate command path is defined.

User Action See the DOS PATH command in Chapter 6.

No retry on parallel printer time-out

Source MODE

Cause The MODE command line did not specify printer time-out retry operations.

User Action See Chapter 4 on the DOS MODE command.

No room for system on destination disk

Source SYS

Cause   SYS cannot transfer the DOS system files to the destination disk because the space used by the system files has already been allocated by files on that disk.

User Action   If you need to make the disk bootable, first FORMAT a blank disk with the /S qualifier and then use the DOS XCOPY command to copy the contents of the disk to a newly formatted bootable disk.

No room in directory for file

Source   EDLIN

Cause   EDLIN could not write the editing changes to disk because no free directory entries (Chapter 9) were present. The editing changes have been lost.

User Action   Use a different disk/directory to edit the file, or free up directory entries by deleting unwanted files.

No room in root directory

Source   LABEL

Cause   LABEL could not write the disk volume label to the disk because of insufficient space in the root directory.

User Action   Free up a directory entry in the root directory and reissue the LABEL command.

No space for a nnnn cylinder partition.

Source   FDISK

Cause   The partition size specified exceeds the number of available disk cylinders.

User Action   Specify a smaller cylinder number or use the default value provided by FDISK.

No space to create a DOS partition

Source   FDISK

Cause   FDISK is unable to create a DOS partition on the fixed disk because of insufficient space.

User Action   Make space available on the disk by modifying the size of the other partitions.

No subdirectories exist

Source   TREE

Cause   The drive examined did not contain any subdirectories.

User Action   None

No system on default drive

Source   SYS

Cause   SYS could not transfer the system files to the target disk because the files did not reside on the current disk.

User Action   Reissue the command with a disk that contains the system files.

Non-DOS diskette

Source   DOS Commands

Cause   The format of a disk is nonrecognizable.

User Action   Issue the DOS FORMAT command to make the disk usable under DOS. Any information it contains will be destroyed.

Non-System disk or disk error
Replace and strike any key when ready

Source   DOS

Cause   The DOS startup procedures could not find the files IBMBIOS.COM and IBMDOS.COM (PC-DOS) or IO.SYS and MSDOS.SYS (MS-DOS) in the root directory.

User Action   Boot DOS with a disk containing the system files.

** Not able to back up file **

Source   BACKUP

Cause   BACKUP cannot back up the file specified because of a file-sharing conflict.

User Action   Retry the BACKUP command at a later time.

** Not able to restore file **

Source   RESTORE

Cause   RESTORE cannot restore the file specified because of a file-sharing conflict.

User Action   Retry the RESTORE command at a later time if required.

Not a graphics printer file

Source   GRAPHICS

Cause   The file you are printing does not contain graphics.

User Action   None

Not enough memory

Source   SHARE

Cause   Insufficient memory is available to install the file-sharing code.

User Action   Remove any unnecessary installed images, file handles, file buffers, and so forth, from the file CONFIG.SYS and reboot DOS.

Not enough memory to merge the entire file

Source   EDLIN

Cause   An EDLIN Transfer command that was issued was unable to complete because of insufficient memory.

User Action   Break the file that you are merging into several files and manipulate them one at a time.

Not found

Source   EDLIN

Cause   EDLIN could not find the source string for a Replace or Search operation.

User Action   Be sure that the string you specified is correct. Remember that EDLIN differentiates between uppercase and lowercase letters.

O.K?

Source   EDLIN

Cause   An EDLIN Search or Replace operation is being performed and EDLIN wants to know whether to continue.

User Action   Press Y to terminate the search or replace. Any other key directs EDLIN to continue.

Out of environment space

Source   SET

Cause   The SET command could not complete because all of the DOS environment space has been allocated.

User Action   None

Out of space on list file

Source   LINK

Cause   LINK could not continue writing to the LIST file because the target disk ran out of disk space.

User Action   Write the LIST file to a different disk, or free up space for the file on the current disk.

Out of space on run file

Source   LINK

Cause   LINK could not continue writing to the EXE file because the target disk ran out of disk space.

User Action   Write the EXE file to a different disk, or free up space for the file on the current disk.

Out of space on VM.TMP

Source   LINK

Cause   LINK could not continue writing to the temporary file VM.TMP because the target disk ran out of disk space.

User Action   Free up space for the file on the current disk.

Parameters not compatible

Source   DOS Commands

Cause   The command line entered contained parameters that are incompatible.

User Action   Review the command syntax in Appendix A, "DOS Reference Guide," and reissue the command.

Parameter not compatible with fixed disk

Source   FORMAT

Cause   A /1 or /8 qualifier was specified in the FORMAT command line for a fixed disk. FORMAT does not support this operation.

User Action   Review Chapters 2 and 9. Reissue the FORMAT command.

Parity error or nonexistent memory error detected

Source   DEBUG

Cause   DEBUG detected a memory board problem.

User Action   Cycle the power on your system. If the problem persists, have your dealer perform diagnostics on your computer's memory.

Partition n is already active

Source   FDISK

Cause   FDISK is specifying the partition number of the currently active partition.

User Action   None

Partition nn made active

Source   FDISK

Cause   FDISK is specifying that the partition number displayed is now active the next time DOS boots.

User Action   None

Path not found

Source   DOS Commands

Cause   A parameter, command file, or path specified does not exist.

User Action   Reissue the command with the correct file name or pathname.

Path too long

Source   DOS Commands

Cause   A parameter or command path contained more than 63 characters.

User Action   Review Chapter 6 and reissue the command with a pathname that contains fewer than 63 characters.

Pathname too long

Source   PRINT

Cause   The pathname for a file to be printed contained more than 63 characters.

User Action   Reissue the command with a pathname that consists of fewer than 63 characters. You may need to change your current directory or move the file.

Please replace original diskette in drive A: and press <ENTER>

Source   LINK

Cause   The /P qualifier was present in the LINK command line and the EXE file has been written to the disk desired. LINK now requires the original disk to continue.

User Action   Place the disk that was in the drive when LINK was issued back in the drive and press any key to continue.

Press any key to begin adding files

Source   REPLACE

Cause   The /W qualifier was present in the REPLACE command line and REPLACE is prompting you to place the target and source disk in the correct drives before proceeding.

User Action   Place the source and target disk in the correct drives and press any key to continue.

Press any key to begin
copying file(s)

Source   XCOPY

Cause   The /W qualifier was present in the XCOPY command line and XCOPY is prompting you to place the target and source disk in the correct drives before proceeding.

User Action   Place the source and target disk in the correct drives and press any key to continue.

Press any key to begin recovery
of the file(s) on drive n

Source   RECOVER

Cause   RECOVER is pausing, allowing you to cancel the command with CTRL-BREAK.

User Action   To continue the file restoration, simply press any key. Otherwise, press CTRL-BREAK to cancel the command.

Press any key to begin replacing file(s)

Source   REPLACE

Cause   The /W qualifier was present in the REPLACE command line and REPLACE is prompting you to place the target and source disk in the correct drives before proceeding.

User Action   Place the source and target disk in the correct drives and press any key to continue.

Print queue is empty

Source   PRINT

Cause   No files are currently in the queue to be printed.

User Action   None

Print queue is full

Source   PRINT

Cause   The file(s) specified could not be added to the print queue because the queue ran out of queue entries.

User Action   Review Chapter 5 on the DOS PRINT command and reissue the command.

Printer error

Source   MODE

Cause   MODE could not complete its operation because of one of the following conditions:

- Printer is off.
- Printer is out of paper.
- Printer is off-line.

- Printer has timed-out.

- A printer I/O error occurred.

User Action   Determine the source of the MODE error and reissue the command.

Printer lines per inch set

Source   MODE

Cause   MODE is specifying the number of lines per vertical inch on printer output.

User Action   None

Probable non-DOS disk
Continue (Y/N)?

Source   CHKDSK

Cause   The disk that CHKDSK is examining does not have a recognizable format. CHKDSK wants to know if you want to continue.

User Action   To continue, press Y; otherwise, press N. If the disk is unusable, invoke the DOS FORMAT command with the disk.

Processing cannot continue

Source   CHKDSK

Cause   CHKDSK cannot continue processing because of the error that it will display following this error message.

User Action   Correct the problem if possible and reissue the command.

Program size exceeds capacity of
LINK, limit 704K

Source   LINK

Cause   The EXE file created by LINK exceeds the maximum 704K limit.

User Action   Break the program into several smaller programs.

Program terminated normally

Source   DEBUG

Cause   A DEBUG Go, Trace, or Proceed command successfully completed the program execution.

User Action   None

Program too big to fit in memory

Source   DOS

Cause   The DOS loader (COMMAND.COM) cannot load the executable file into memory because of insufficient free space.

User Action   Remove any unnecessary installed images, file handles, file buffers, and so forth, from the file CONFIG.SYS and reboot DOS.

Read error in:
drive: \path \filename

Source   EDLIN

Cause   EDLIN could not read the file specified from disk into memory.

User Action   Use COPY or XCOPY to create a new copy of the file on another disk and repeat the EDLIN operation.

Reinsert diskette for drive n and strike Enter when ready

Source   FORMAT

Cause   FORMAT is ready to write the system files from memory to the disk being formatted with the /S qualifier.

User Action   Place the disk being formatted back in the disk drive.

Relocation table overflow

Source   LINK

Cause   The object files contained more than 13,000 FAR operands.

User Action   Edit the source file and replace any FAR operands with short operands when possible.

REPLACE <drive: \path \filename> (Y/N)?

Source   REPLACE

Cause   The /P qualifier was found in the REPLACE command line, so REPLACE will prompt you before it replaces any files to the target location.

User Action   To replace the file, press Y; otherwise, press N.

REPLACE filename (Y/N)?

Source   REPLACE

Cause   Use of the /p switch before replacing a target file or adding a source file results in this prompt.

User Action   None

Replacing <drive: \path \filename>

Source   REPLACE

Cause   REPLACE is simply telling you that it is replacing the file specified.

User Action   None

Resident part of PRINT installed

Source   PRINT

Cause   This message appears the first time that you invoke the DOS PRINT command to tell you that the print queue software is now present in memory.

User Action   None

Resident portion of MODE loaded

Source   MODE

Cause   MODE required software to be installed in memory to perform a specific function.

User Action   None

Restore file sequence error

Source   RESTORE

Cause   The file specified was not restored because the disks were not inserted into the drive in the correct order.

User Action   Reissue the command placing the disk in the drive in the correct sequence.

** Restoring files from drive n **
Source: n

Source   RESTORE

Cause   RESTORE is specifying that it is in the process of restoring files with the drives displayed.

User Action   None

** Restoring files from drive n **

Source   RESTORE

Cause   RESTORE is simply specifying that it is in the process of restoring files from the disk specified.

User Action   None

Sector size adjusted

Source   VDISK

Cause   During the installation of a RAM drive, VDISK found it necessary to change the size of the sectors for the virtual disk.

User Action   None

Sector size too large in file filename

Source   DOS

Cause   A device driver that the DOS startup procedures were to install specified an invalid sector size.

User Action   If you have written the device driver yourself, correct the error. Otherwise, return the software package.

Segment limit set too high, exceeds 1024

Source   LINK

DOS: The Complete Reference

Cause   The /X qualifier was found in the LINK command line and it contained a value that was too large. The maximum number of link sectors is 1024.

User Action   Reissue the LINK command with a new sector value.

Segment limit too high

Source   LINK

Cause   The /X qualifier was found in the LINK command line and it contained a value that was too large for your current memory configuration.

User Action   Remove any unnecessary installed images, file handles, file buffers, and so forth, from the file CONFIG.SYS and reboot DOS. Reissue the LINK.

Segment size exceeds 64K

Source   LINK

Cause   The linker attempted to combine segments that exceeded the maximum 64K size restriction.

User Action   Change the names of the segments containing several of your modules. Recompile and LINK the files.

SHARE already installed

Source   SHARE

Cause   The SHARE command was invoked and the file-sharing code was already present in memory. SHARE can be invoked only once.

User Action   None

Sharing violation

Source   XCOPY

Cause   XCOPY could not complete a file copy because either a source or target file was opened, thus yielding sharing conflicts.

User Action   Wait for the file to be closed, thus resolving the conflict, and reissue the command.

Source and target drives are the same

Source   BACKUP, RESTORE

Cause   The source and target disk drive identifiers were the same. BACKUP and RESTORE do not support this type of operation.

User Action   Reissue the command with the appropriate drive identifications.

Source diskette bad or incompatible

Source   DISKCOPY

Cause   DISKCOPY experienced an error reading the source disk. The target disk may be unusable.

User Action   Use CHKDSK to examine the source disk.

Source does not contain backup files

Source   RESTORE

Cause   The source disk did not contain any backup files.

User Action   Perform a directory listing of the source disk to verify its contents.

Source path required

Source   REPLACE

Cause   The REPLACE command requires at least one pathname.

User Action   Review the REPLACE command in Chapter 10 and reissue the command.

Specified command search directory bad

Source   DOS Commands

Cause   A specified pathname is invalid.

User Action   Reissue the command with the correct pathname.

Specified drive does not exist, or is non-removable

Source   DISKCOPY, DISKCOMP

Cause   A drive specifier in the command line is for a hard disk. DISKCOPY and DISKCOMP do not support this operation.

User Action   Reissue the command referencing only floppy disk drives.

Stack size exceeds 65536 bytes

Source   LINK

Cause   The stack size for a program cannot exceed 64K.

User Action   Decrease the stack size and reissue the LINK command.

Symbol defined more than once

Source   LINK

Cause   The linker found two or more modules that define objects with the same name.

User Action   Be sure that each object module is included only once on the command line. If so, examine the source code for duplicate module names.

Symbol table overflow

Source   LINK

Cause   The object modules contain more than 256K of public, external segments, groups, classes, and files.

User Action   Review the LINK command in Chapter 16 and try to minimize the number of symbols defined.

Syntax error

Source   DOS Commands

Cause   The command line is invalid for the command specified.

User Action   Examine the command in Appendix A, "DOS Reference Guide," and reissue the command.

System files restored
The target disk may not be bootable

Source   RESTORE

Cause   RESTORE restored the DOS system files. If the files are for an earlier version of DOS, the system may not be bootable.

User Action   If the system is not bootable, boot a valid DOS system disk and use the SYS command to make the disk bootable.

System transferred

Source   FORMAT

Cause   The /S qualifier was present in the FORMAT command line and FORMAT has successfully transferred the DOS system files.

User Action   None

System will now restart
Insert DOS diskette in drive A:
Press any key when ready

Source   FDISK

Cause   FDISK requires DOS to reboot in order to update the disk partition table information.

User Action   Place a DOS system disk in drive A and press any key to continue.

Target cannot be used for backup

Source   BACKUP

Cause   BACKUP could not back up the files specified to the target disk.

User Action   If the target disk is a floppy disk, try a new formatted disk; otherwise, reboot DOS and reissue the command.

Target diskette may be unusable

Source   DISKCOPY

Cause   DISKCOPY encountered unrecoverable read, write, or verify errors while processing the disk. The copy of the target disk may be unusable because of the errors.

User Action   Issue the command with a new target disk.

Target diskette unusable

Source   DISKCOPY

Cause   DISKCOPY encountered too many fatal errors on the target drive to continue processing.

User Action   Issue the command with a new target disk.

Target diskette write protected
Correct, then strike any key

Source   DISKCOPY

Cause   The target disk for the disk copy operation is write-protected, thus preventing the operation.

User Action   Use a new target disk, or remove the write-protect tab from the disk and reissue the command.

Target is full

Source   RESTORE

Cause   The target disk for the file restoration is full.

User Action   Delete any unwanted files from the target disk and reissue the command.

10 Mismatches - ending compare

Source   COMP

Cause   COMP found 10 differences between two files and is terminating the comparison.

User Action   None

Terminate batch job (Y/N)?

Source   DOS

Cause   A CTRL-BREAK was issued during the execution of a

DOS batch file. DOS is prompting you to specify whether you want to continue or terminate processing of the BAT file.

User Action   Press Y to terminate the batch procedure; otherwise, press N and the processing will continue.

Terminated by user

Source   LINK

Cause   A CTRL-BREAK was issued in response to a LINK prompt.

User Action   None

The current active partition is n.

Source   FDISK

Cause   FDISK is displaying the number of the currently active disk partition.

User Action   None

The last file was not restored

Source   RESTORE

Cause   RESTORE was terminated by the user, or a disk ran out of space during the restoration.

User Action   If the disk is full, delete sufficient unwanted files and reissue the command.

There were n errors detected

Source   LINK

Cause　LINK is displaying the number of errors that occurred during the link process.

User Action　None

Too many block devices

Source　DOS

Cause　The DOS startup procedures found that you are trying to install more than the maximum of 26 block devices.

User Action　Modify CONFIG.SYS to ensure that only 26 block devices are being installed.

Too many external symbols, limit 510 per module

Source　LINK

Cause　LINK supports only 510 symbols per module. One of the modules being linked exceeds this limit.

User Action　Modify the module, or create a second module to reduce the number of symbols per module.

Too many files open

Source　EDLIN

Cause　EDLIN could not open the file specified because of insufficient file handles.

User Action　Increase the number of file handles supported by DOS via the FILES= entry in CONFIG.SYS and reboot.

Too many group-, segment-, class-names, limit 254 per module

Source　LINK

Cause   A source module exceeds the group, class, or segment limit of 254.

User Action   Reduce the number of groups, classes, or segments in the module; recompile and reissue the LINK command.

Too many groups

Source   LINK

Cause   The object module contains more than 9 groups.

User Action   Reduce the number of GRPDEFs in the module to 8.

Too many libraries, limit 16

Source   LINK

Cause   The LINK command specifies more than 16 libraries.

User Action   Use the librarian to combine libraries.

Too many libraries, limit 16

Source   XCOPY

Cause   XCOPY could not complete the copy operation because of too few file handles.

User Action   Modify the FILES= entry in CONFIG.SYS to increase the number of file handles present. Reboot DOS.

Too many overlays

Source   LINK

Cause   The program exceeds the maximum of 63 overlays.

User Action   Reduce the number of overlays in the program.

Too many public symbols

Source   LINK

Cause   The linker input exceeds the maximum of 2048 public symbols.

User Action   Reduce the number of public symbols in the source code and recompile and LINK.

Too many segments or classes

Source   LINK

Cause   The object module contains more than 255 segments.

User Action   Combine segments, or break the module into two or more modules.

Too many segments, use /X:N(256<N<1025)

Source   LINK

Cause   The default number of segments has been exceeded.

User Action   Use the /X LINK qualifier to specify a new segment value.

Too many TYPDEFs, limit 255 per module

Source   LINK

Cause   LINK supports a maximum of 255 TYPDEF statements and this limit has been exceeded.

User Action   Break the input module into multiple files and distribute the shared variables among them. Recompile and LINK the file.

Top level process aborted, cannot continue

Source   DOS

Cause   A critical error during system startup or a secondary command processor invocation was handled by the user selecting the Abort option.

User Action   Reboot with a different DOS disk.

Total disk space is nnnn cylinders

Source   FDISK

Cause   FDISK is displaying the total number of disk cylinders present.

User Action   None

Transfer size adjusted

Source   VDISK

Cause   An invalid transfer size was specified in the file CONFIG.SYS for VDISK.

User Action   Examine Chapter 15 and modify CONFIG.SYS to correct the error.

Tree past this point not processed

Source   CHKDSK

Cause   CHKDSK cannot proceed past the directory name that precedes the error message.

User Action   Reboot DOS and reissue the CHKDSK command.

Unable to copy keyboard routine

Source   KEYBxx

Cause   DOS could not open a KEYBxx.COM file.

User Action   Invoke CHKDSK to examine the disk.

Unable to create directory

Source   DOS Commands

Cause   The directory cannot be created because of one of the following:

- A directory with the same name already exists.
- One of the entries in the directory path cannot be found.
- The directory is to be added to the root directory, which is full.
- The directory name matches a file with the same name.
- The directory name is invalid.

User Action   Use a new disk or reboot and reissue the command.

Unable to shift screen left

Source   MODE

Cause   MODE cannot shift the screen any more columns to the left because of hardware limits.

User Action   None

Unable to shift screen right

Source   MODE

Cause   MODE cannot shift the screen any more columns to the right because of hardware limits.

User Action   None

Unable to write BOOT

Source   FORMAT

Cause   The /S qualifier was present in the DOS FORMAT command and the first track or cylinder in the partition could not be written to, thus rendering the disk unbootable.

User Action   Use a new disk or reboot and reissue the command.

Unexpected end-of-file on library

Source   LINK

Cause   A library file specified in the LINK command line contains invalid data. LINK will continue processing the number of bytes specified in the file's directory entries.

User Action   None

Unexpected end of file on VM.TMP

Source   LINK

Cause   The DOS linker required the temporary file VM.TMP during the link process and the disk containing it has been removed.

User Action   Reissue the LINK command.

Unrecognized command in CONFIG.SYS

Source   DOS

Cause   The DOS startup procedures detected an invalid directive in the file CONFIG.SYS.

User Action   Review Chapter 15 and edit CONFIG.SYS to correct the error. Reboot DOS.

Unrecognized printer

Source   GRAPHICS

Cause   The system printer is invalid for the GRAPHICS support.

User Action   Refer to the GRAPHICS command in Appendix A, "DOS Reference Guide."

Unrecognized printer port

Source   GRAPHICS

Cause   The printer device name specified is invalid.

User Action   Refer to the list of device names in Chapter 4 and reissue the command.

Unrecognized switch error: nnnnn

Source   LINK

Cause   The LINK command line contained an invalid qualifier.

User Action   Examine LINK in Chapter 16. Reissue the command.

Unrecoverable error on directory

Source   CHKDSK

Cause   CHKDSK experienced a fatal error processing the directory specified.

User Action   Reboot DOS and reissue the command. If the error persists, use RECOVER to attempt to recover the directory.

Unrecoverable file sharing error

Source   DOS Commands

Cause   The command cannot proceed because of file-sharing conflicts.

User Action   Wait for the file to become available and reissue the command.

Unrecoverable read error on drive n
Track nn, side n

Source   DISKCOMP

Cause   DISKCOMP failed to successfully read the track on the disk specified after four attempts.

User Action   COPY all of the undamaged files from the disk to a new disk. The disk is corrupted or copy-protected.

Unrecoverable write error on drive n
Track nn, side n

Source   DISKCOPY

Cause   DISKCOPY failed to successfully read the track on the disk specified after four attempts.

User Action   COPY all of the undamaged files from the disk to a new disk. The disk is corrupted or copy-protected.

Unrecoverable write error on drive n
Track nn, side n

Source   DISKCOPY

Cause   DISKCOPY failed to successfully write the track on the disk specified after several attempts.

User Action   Reissue the command with a new target disk. Use the DOS FORMAT command to format the disk that caused the errors during the DISKCOPY.

Unresolved externals:

Source   LINK

Cause   The external symbols listed were referenced in the object code input to the linker but were not defined.

User Action   Be sure that all of the object modules and libraries required are in the LINK command line. Update the source code and recompile and LINK if necessary.

VDISK not installed - insufficient memory

Source   VDISK

Cause   VDISK will not install a RAM drive if less than 64K of memory will result upon completion of the drive. Likewise, if the /E qualifier is present and the system does not have extended memory, VDISK will display this message.

User Action   None

VDISK Version 3.20 Virtual Disk x

Source   VDISK

Cause   VDISK is specifying the drive letter of the virtual drive it is installing.

User Action   None

VERIFY is ON | OFF

  Source VERIFY

  Cause VERIFY is specifying its current state.

  User Action None

VM.TMP is an illegal file name
and has been ignored

  Source LINK

  Cause LINK does not allow the file name VM.TMP to be used as an object file name.

  User Action Reissue the LINK command with a new object file name.

Volume label (11 characters,
ENTER for none)?

  Source FORMAT

  Cause The /V qualifier was found in the FORMAT command line and FORMAT is prompting you for the name of the volume label.

  User Action Type in the 11-character volume label name and press ENTER.

Warning! All data on non-removable disk drive n
will be lost
Proceed with FORMAT (Y/N)?

  Source FORMAT

  Cause FORMAT is warning you that the target disk is a fixed disk and the information that it contains will be destroyed.

User Action   If you want to FORMAT the hard disk, press Y and then press ENTER. Otherwise, press N and then press ENTER.

Warning! Data in the DOS partition could be DESTROYED. Do you wish to continue.............?[n]

Source   FDISK

Cause   FDISK is warning you that the Delete DOS Partition option will destroy all of the information contained in the DOS partition.

User Action   To delete the partition, press Y and then press ENTER. Otherwise, press N and then press ENTER.

Warning-directory full
nnn file(s) recovered

Source   RECOVER

Cause   RECOVER terminated without completing the file recover because of a full directory.

User Action   Free up space on the target directory by deleting files or moving files to a new disk.

Warning! Diskette is out of sequence
Replace the diskette or continue
Strike any key when ready

Source   RESTORE

Cause   RESTORE is warning you that you have not inserted the disks in the correct sequence.

User Action   If you want to intentionally skip disks, press any key to continue. Otherwise, place the proper disk in the drive and press any key.

Warning! File filename
is a read only file
Replace the file (Y/N)?

Source   RESTORE

Cause   The /P qualifier was found in the RESTORE command line and RESTORE is prompting you whether or not a file marked as read-only should be copied over on the target disk.

User Action   To restore a file over the contents of the read-only file, press Y. Otherwise, press N.

Warning! File filename
was changed after it was backed up
Replace the file (Y/N)?

Source   RESTORE

Cause   The /P qualifier was found in the RESTORE command line and RESTORE is prompting you whether or not a file that has been modified since the BACKUP should be copied over on the target disk.

User Action   To restore a file over the contents of the modified file, press Y. Otherwise, press N.

Warning! Files in the target drive
Drive: \BACKUP directory will be erased
Strike any key when ready

Source   BACKUP

Cause   BACKUP is warning you that all of the files on the target directory will be erased.

User Action   To continue the BACKUP, press any key. Otherwise, press CTRL-BREAK.

Warning! Files in the target drive
Drive: \root directory will be erased
Strike any key when ready

Source   BACKUP

Cause   BACKUP is warning you that all of the files on the target root directory will be erased.

User Action   To continue the BACKUP, press any key. Otherwise, press CTRL-BREAK.

Warning! No files were found
to back up

Source   BACKUP

Cause   BACKUP did not find any files to back up.

User Action   Be sure that the BACKUP command line is correct.

Warning! No files were found to restore

Source   RESTORE

Cause   RESTORE did not find any files matching the file specification.

User Action   Be sure that the RESTORE command line is correct.

Warning! No stack segment

Source   LINK

Cause   None of the input modules in the command line contain a module that allocated stack space.

User Action   Be sure that all of the object files have been specified correctly in the linker input.

Warning! Target is Full

Source   BACKUP, RESTORE

Cause   BACKUP or RESTORE cannot continue because the target device is full.

User Action   Make space available on the target device and reissue the command.

Writing nnn bytes

Source   DEBUG

Cause   DEBUG is displaying the number of bytes it is writing to disk.

User Action   None

The following DOS errors all generate the message **Abort, Retry, or Ignore.**

Bad call format

Source   DOS

Cause   A device driver received a request header of incorrect length.

User Action   If you are developing the device driver, use DEBUG. If you purchased the software, return it to the dealer.

Bad command

Source   DOS

Cause   A device driver issued an invalid command.

User Action   If you are developing the device driver, use DEBUG. If you purchased the software, return it to the dealer.

Bad unit

Source   DOS

Cause   A device driver received an invalid subunit number.

User Action   If you are developing the device driver, use DEBUG. If you purchased the software, return it to the dealer.

Data

Source   DOS

Cause   DOS was unable to read/write the data correctly.

User Action   Use CHKDSK to examine the source/target disk.

Drive not ready error

Source   DOS

Cause   DOS cannot read or write to the drive specified.

User Action   Be sure that the disk drive door is closed and that the drive contains a disk.

FCB unavailable

Source   DOS

Cause   File sharing has been installed and you attempted to open more files than FCBs were available to support.

User Action   Increase the number of FCBs present in the file CONFIG.SYS. Reboot DOS.

General failure

Source   DOS

Cause   DOS cannot access a disk because of one of the following:

- Disk is not properly inserted in the drive.
- Disk is not properly formatted.
- Disk type and drive are not compatible.

User Action   Correct the problem and reissue the command.

No paper

Source   DOS

Cause   The system printer is out of paper or not turned on.

User Action   Check the system printer.

Non-DOS disk

Source   DOS

Cause   The disk specified contains an invalid format.

User Action   Use CHKDSK to examine the disk. Invoke FOR-MAT to make the disk usable.

Not ready

Source   DOS

Cause   DOS cannot read/write to the device.

User Action   If the device is a disk, be sure that the drive door is closed and a disk is present. If the device is a printer, be sure that it has paper and is on-line.

Read fault

Source   DOS

Cause   DOS cannot read from the device.

User Action   Be sure that the disk is properly placed in the disk drive and reissue the command.

Sector not found

    Source   DOS

    Cause   DOS could not find the data sector on disk.

    User Action   Use CHKDSK to examine the disk.

Seek

    Source   DOS

    Cause   The disk could not find the track specified.

    User Action   Be sure that the disk is properly inserted in the drive. Use CHKDSK to examine the disk.

Sharing violation

    Source   DOS

    Cause   You attempted to access a file that someone has already opened in a mode that does not allow your access.

    User Action   Wait for the file to become available and then reissue the command.

Write fault

    Source   DOS

    Cause   DOS was unable to write to the device.

User Action   Be sure that the disk is properly inserted in the drive. Use CHKDSK to examine the disk.

Write protect

Source   DOS

Cause   DOS cannot write to a write-protected disk. If you are using a nine-sector disk with a version of DOS below 2.0, or a single-sided drive, DOS will display this error.

User Action   Remove the write-protect tab from the disk if you really desire to write to it.

Upgrading Your
DOS Version

Many users are confused about the steps required to upgrade their systems to a newer version of DOS. This appendix provides general guidelines for you to follow when upgrading your system.

1. Boot the new version of DOS and verify that all of your applications work. Test each program thoroughly.

2. If an application does not work under the new DOS version, contact your dealer or the software developer for additional information.

3. If all of your applications work correctly under the new DOS version, you are ready to complete the system upgrade. Be sure to have a disk ready that contains a complete DOS system for the version of DOS you are using currently. This is your backup disk. Boot the new version of DOS. Place the new DOS system disk in drive A and use the DOS SYS command to upgrade all of your disks (fixed and floppy). The system upgrade is complete.

The entire upgrade process is shown in Figure D-1.

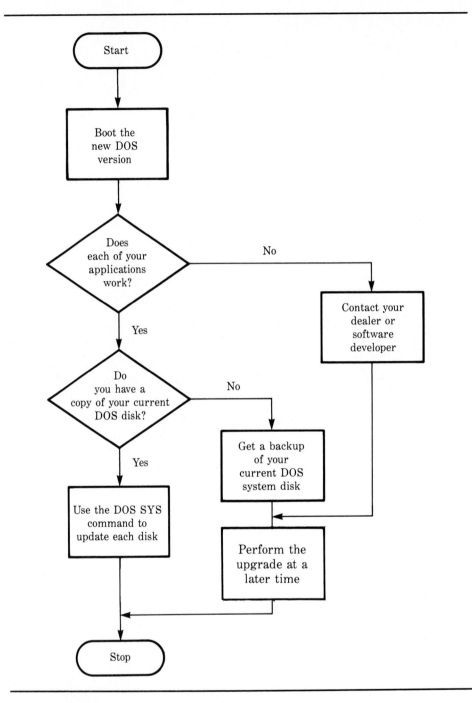

Table D-1. Upgrade Process

DOS: The Complete Reference

Apple®	Apple Computer, Inc.
CP/M®	Digital Research, Inc.
DEC™	Digital Equipment Corp.
DEC Rainbow™	Digital Equipment Corp.
IBM®	International Business Machines Corporation
IBM Extended Graphics Adapter™	International Business Machines Corporation
IBM PC AT®	International Business Machines Corporation
Intel®	Intel Corporation
Microsoft®	Microsoft Corporation
Microsoft Windows™	Microsoft Corporation
MS-DOS®	Microsoft Corporation
SideKick®	Borland International, Inc.
Turbo Pascal®	Borland International, Inc.
UNIX™	AT&T Bell Laboratories
WordStar®	MicroPro International Corporation
XENIX®	Microsoft Corporation

TRADEMARKS

The manuscript for this book was prepared and submitted to Osborne/McGraw-Hill in electronic form. The acquisitions editor for this project was Cynthia Hudson, the technical editor was Kevin Shafer, the technical reviewer was Seth Pratt, and the project editor was Fran Haselsteiner.

Cover art by Bay Graphics Design Associates. Cover supplier is Phoenix Color Corp. Book printed and bound by R.R. Donnelley & Sons Company, Crawfordsville, Indiana.

* (asterisk), use of, in EDLIN, 406, 450
8088 registers, 546
%%variables, 240

A

About option (Windows), 679
Advanced DOS commands, 289-356
Alarms, setting, with Windows Calendar, 713
Allocate memory, 597
Allocation error, 919
Anatomy of DOS, 453
ANSI
    codes, 544
    driver, 497, 542, 626
ANSI.SYS, 486, 542
APPEND, 290, 350, 780, 990
APPEND/ASSIGN conflict, 919
Append command, EDLIN, 431
Appending files, 72
Application software, 22, 33
Applications, Windows, 775
Appointment calendar, Windows, 702-719
ASCII character set
    extended, 384
    French extended, 397
    German extended, 397
    Italian extended, 394
    Spanish extended, 396
    U.K. extended, 393
    U.S.extended, 395
ASCII codes, 913-917
ASCIIZ string, 627
Assemble (DEBUG), 521, 534
ASSIGN, 295, 350, 782
Asynchronous ports, 130
ATTRIB, 296, 350, 611, 784
Attributes
    codes for file, 586
    file, 342
    setting file, 296
Autodialing with CARDFILE (Windows), 728
AUTOEXEC.BAT file, 245, 468
    specifying keyboard layout in, 392
AUX, 123, 304

Auxiliary device, service for output to, 550

B

Background commands, 138, 160
Backing up data, batch file for, 367
Backing up disks, 357-382
Backslash key, 170
BACKUP, 259, 359, 377, 785, 921, 926, 993, 1023
    error-status values for, 367
    problems with, 370
Backup
    attribute, 296
    files, batch file for restoring, 374
    log, 619
    policies and procedures, 364
BACKUP.BJL (backup journal file), 369
Bad sectors, 262, 316
BAK file extension, 417, 927
Basic Input/Output System, 464. *See also* BIOS
BAT files, 232
Batch file, missing, 923
Batch file for backing up data, 367
Batch files
    creating, 234
    creating, with EDLIN, 410
Batch processing, 229-248, 308
    definition of, 230
BAUD, 130
Baud rate error, 971
Binary
    digits, 3, 30, 124
    reads, 926
    system, 30
BIOS, 454, 464
Block devices, 488
Boot record, 253, 285, 466, 476
Bootable disk, 55, 79
Booting DOS, 35
Bootstrap program, 469
Border colors, 527
BREAK, 481, 788
BREAK key, 75
    using, with EDLIN, 408
Break message, 924

INDEX

Buffer, type-ahead, 556
Buffer size, 924
    print, 150
Buffered keyboard input, 554
BUFFERS, 482
Buffers
    determining number of, 484
    disk, 282
Byte, 3, 30
Bytes, recovered, 986
Bytes available on types of disks, 361

C

C, 539, 617
CALC.EXE (Windows), 680
CALCULATOR (Windows), 696-702
CALENDAR (Windows), 702-719
CARDFILE (Windows), 719-732
Central processing unit, 2. *See also* CPU
Character
    codes, ANSI, 544
    echo, controlling, 552
    sets, alternate, 384
Characters, shifting display of, 132
Chassis, 2, 30
CHDIR (CD), 176, 581, 790, 934
Chips, processor, 2
CHKDSK, 101, 259, 304, 310, 380, 465,
    792, 925, 937, 951, 985
    corrections, 939
Class, 512
Clearing screen, code pieces for, 543
Clipboard (Windows), 748
CLIPBRD program (Windows), 750
CLOCK (Windows), 693-696
CLOCK$, 123
CLOCK.EXE (Windows), 629
Close option (Windows), 677
CLS, 90, 460, 795
Clusters, 258, 260
    lost, 985
Color monitors, 4
COM and EXE files, 351
COM files, 198
    converting to, 306
COM port errors, 935
COM#, 123, 130
COMMAND, 299, 351, 795

Command
    buffer, 346
    device, modifying, 304
    interpreter, 922, 939
    line arguments, 617-619
COMMAND/C, 233
COMMAND.COM, 54, 299, 362
Command processor, 453-454
    exiting from, 308
    invoking, 299-300
    portions of, 475
    processing steps involved in, 463
    resident and transient parts of, 301
Commands
    advanced DOS, 289-356
    background, 138
    DEBUG, 521-542
    EDLIN, 407
    external, 56, 80, 90, 459, 475
    internal, 56, 80, 90, 458, 475
    processing steps for DOS, 461
    reference guide of DOS, 777-911
    summary of EDLIN, 447
    terminating, 72
Communications
    port, setting, in Windows, 768
    program, Windows, 739
COMP, 110, 119, 797
Compare (DEBUG), 521, 537
Compiler, 500
COMSPEC, 454
CON, 123, 304
Conditional processing, 238
CONFIG.SYS, 246, 468, 480, 486, 490,
    493
    specifying country codes in, 392
Configuration error, 937
Configuration parameters, list of, 495
Contiguous sectors, 256
CONTROL program (Windows), 762
Control Z (^Z) character, 404, 450
COPY, 68, 80, 126, 801, 937
Copy command, EDLIN, 440
Copying
    disks with subdirectories, 199
    files to subdirectories, 180
    using XCOPY, 335
COUNTRY, 485

Country codes, 384, 392
    invalid, 972
Country-dependent information, 579
CP/M, 23, 268
CPU, 2, 30, 631
    background commands and, 142
    time-sharing of, 631
    utilization of, 631
CTRL key, 74
    combinations, 80
    using, with EDLIN, 408
CTRL-ALT-DEL, 46, 547
CTRL-BREAK, 548
    processing, setting, 578
CTRL-C, 76, 481
CTRL-PRTSC, 155, 160
CTRL-S, 72
CTTY, 304, 351, 805
Customizing DOS, 479-498
Cut and paste (Windows), 710, 725
Cylinder number, 949
Cylinders, 269, 983, 1015

D

Data
    bits, 131
    files, searching for, 291
    sectors, 253
    structures, DOS, 479
Data, corrupted, 262
Database applications
    buffers required for, 484
    required file handles for, 491
DATE, 38, 43, 79, 806, 939
Date, 37
    errors, 973
    format, 38
    service function for specifying, 605
Date and time of files, get/set, 603
DEBUG, 521-542, 624
    messages with, 923-924
Debugger, 624
Default drive, 557, 564
    changing, 58
    program for displaying, 627
DEL, 97, 119, 809
DEL key, 344
Delete command (Windows), 665

Delete command, EDLIN, 425
Deleting files, 97
    service function for, 560, 585
Deleting lines with EDLIN, 416
Delimiters, date, 79
Density, disk storage, 12
Desktop applications, 687
Desktop system, 628
DEVICE, 486
Device
    BPB field, 593
    characteristics, specifying, 853
    customizations, 131
    drivers, 465-476, 480, 486
    errors, 952
    I/O control (IOCTL) service func-
        tions, 587-595
    name error, 962
    names, 61, 123-135
    names, referencing, 126
    parameters, get/set, 590
Device, modifying command, 304
Device-type field values, 591
Dialog boxes, Windows, 629
DIR, 61, 811
Direct console I/O, 552
Directories. *See also* Subdirectories
    copying, 335
    service function for changing cur-
        rent, 581
Directory
    errors, 973, 991-992, 1016, 1018
    finding or creating, 562
    get current, 597
    listing, sorted, 223
    names, 170
    options (Windows), 674
    parent, 182
    root, 167
    structure, displaying, 187
Disk
    errors, 942, 974, 990, 993, 1006, 1026
    fragmentation, 255, 374
    hub, 11
    index hole, 12
    jacket, 11
    labels, creating with EDLIN, 438
    media, 20

Disk, *continued*
    Operating System, 22
    organization, 167
    organization, affect of JOIN command on, 315
    output, verifying, 334
    sectors, recovering bad, 316
    spindle, microfloppy, 19
    structure, 249
    unusable error, 976
    verification status, 602
Disk boot failure, 942
Disk buffers, 482, 496. *See also* Buffers
    flushing, 556
Disk drive
    in-use light, 8, 37
    latch, 8
    selecting default, 557
    service for returning current, 564
Disk drives, 4, 36
    default, 58
    floppy, 6
    hard, 7
    joining, to DOS path, 311
Disk space
    getting free, 579
    how DOS allocates, 254
    insufficient, 969
Disk transfer address (DTA), 565
    getting, 576
Disk transfer area, 561
DISKCOMP, 114, 119, 814, 926, 936, 940
DISKCOPY, 47, 358, 377, 460, 818, 926, 934, 938, 940
Disks
    backing up, 357-382
    bootable, 55, 79
    comparing, 114
    copying, 47
    copying, with subdirectories, 199
    differences between hard and floppy, 266
    displaying status of, 101
    DOS system, 28, 36
    floppy, 6
    formatting, 52
    international, 392

Disks, *continued*
    managing, 249-288
    microfloppy, 18
    non-DOS, 1000
    number of bytes available on types of, 361
    rules for handling floppy, 9
    single-sided versus double-sided, 55
    storage capabilities of floppy, 12
    target and source, 48
    unbootable, 1017
    virtual, 487
    write-protecting, 31, 77
Display character, sending to output device, 550
Display I/O, 552
Displaying a string, 554
Divide overflow, 944
DOS
    definition of, 22
    disks, 28
    prompt, 42, 56, 79
    prompt, setting, 117
    version, displaying current, 91
    versions of, 24. *See also* Versions
Double periods, 178
Drive errors, 974
Drive letters
    assigning to another drive, 295
    substituting, for subdirectories, 330
DRIVPARM, 488
Drop-down menu, 661
Dump (DEBUG), 521, 530

E

ECHO, 237, 822, 947
Editing keys, 343, 355
    EDLIN, 408
EDLIN, 403-452
    /B option, 404, 450
    commands, 407, 447
EGA monitor, 4
English (U.K.) keyboard layout, 389
English (U.S.) keyboard layout, 391
Enter (DEBUG), 521, 532
ENTER key, 16

Environment, 323, 351, 612
    errors, 975, 995
    option, command processor, 303
    string, setting, 323
ERASE, 97, 119, 825
Error
    messages, DOS, 917-1029
    status codes, 603
ERRORLEVEL, 238, 367, 600, 845
ESC key, 344
Escape character, 543
EXE and COM files, 351
EXE file, 198, 501, 508
EXE files, converting, to COM files, 306
EXEC function, 599
Executable files, 501
EXE2BIN, 306, 352, 827, 919, 954
EXIT, 308, 829
Exiting from secondary command processor, 310
Expansion slots, 4
Extended error information, 603
Extended memory, 488
Extender card error, 954
Extension, file, 60
External commands, 56, 459
    executing, in subdirectories, 198
Extract operation, 518

F

F1 key, 343-344
F2 key, 344
F3 key, 344
F4 key, 344
F5 key, 344
F6 key, 126, 134, 344
    using, with EDLIN, 432
FAT, 285. *See also* File Allocation Table
FCBs, 1026. *See also* File-control blocks)
FDISK, 268, 271, 829, 987, 989
File
    creation error, 955
    entries, searching for matching, 559-560
    errors, 956-958, 975
    extension, 60, 80

File, *continued*
    handle status, checking, 588
    pointer, 585
    specifications, 68, 80
File allocation table (FAT), 253, 261
    bad, 954
    service for accessing, 565
File attributes
    codes for, 586
    setting and returning, 586
File contents, lock/unlock, 607
File control blocks (FCBs), 490, 557, 560, 564, 567
File handles, 548
    duplicating, 596
    network or local, 589
    returning, 582
    service functions for, 582-584
    specifying number of, 491
File names, 60, 79
    reserved, 61
    service function for finding, 573
    unique, 606
File-naming conventions, 66
File-sharing, 326
    error, 1019
FILES, 491
Files
    appending, using COPY, 72
    batch, 229-248
    categories of DOS, 67
    closing, 558
    comparing, 110
    contiguous, 918
    controlling access to, 296
    copying, 335
    copying, to subdirectories, 180
    cross-linked, 955
    deleting, 97
    displaying contents of, 92
    DOS, 60
    editing, with EDLIN, 403-452
    executable, 306, 501
    get/set date and time of (service function), 603
    hidden, 465, 469, 476
    intermediate, 541

Files, *continued*
    library, 515
    linking OBJ and LIB, 506
    listing, 79
    managing, 165-213
    opening, 557
    recovering, with bad sectors, 316
    renaming, 95, 875
    restoring, from backup disks, 371
    restoring fragmented, 374
    returning number of records in, 568
    searching for data, 291
    service function for creating, 582, 606
    service function for deleting, 585
    service function for finding, 601
    service function for renaming, 563, 603
    sharing, 326
    system, 362
    types of, 66
    updating previous versions of, 319
    Windows NOTEPAD, 735
Fill (DEBUG), 521, 530
FIND, 219, 830
Fixed disk errors, 952
Fixups, 959
Flags register, 524
Floppy disk drives, 5, 6
Floppy disks
    rules for handling, 9
    storage capabilities of, 13
Fonts, Windows, 765
FOR, 240, 833
Form factors (DRIVPARM), 489
FORMAT, 51-52, 79, 109, 835, 929, 960, 1021
    command options, 253
Format option (Windows), 674
FORMAT/VERIFY logical device track, 593
Fragmented files, restoring, 374
French extended ASCII character set, 398
French keyboard layout, 386
Function-code register, 586
Function keys, 15, 32, 344, 355

Functional sections of DOS, 475

G

German extended ASCII character set, 397
German keyboard layout, 387
Get Info option (Windows), 665
Go (DEBUG), 522, 526
GOTO, 238, 839
GRAFTABL, 384, 401, 841, 961
GRAPHICS, 156, 160, 842, 993
Graphics, printing, 157
Graphics characters, alternate, 384
Group, 512

H

Hard disk errors, 952
Hard disks, 7, 266
    backing up, 357-382
    copying contents of, 342
    floppy disks required for backing up, 365
    multiple, 277
Hardware, 2, 32
Hexadecimal
    byte offset, 112
    equivalents, displaying, with Windows, 700
Hexarithmetic (DEBUG), 522, 525
Hidden files, 465, 469, 476
Hub, disk, 11

I

I/O. *See also* Input and Output
    direct console, 552
    random-access, 483
    redirecting, 213-228, 548
    sequential access, 483
IBMBIO.COM, 54, 333, 362, 465, 469
IBMDOS.COM, 54, 333, 362, 462, 466, 469
Icons, 628
    selecting programs from (Windows), 679
IF, 238, 844
In-use light, 37
Index card system (Windows), 719-732
Index hole, 12, 250

Initialization values, Windows, 772
Input, 28
    redirecting, 213
    sources of, 31
Input (DEBUG), 522, 527
Input buffer, 555
Input-processing-output, 28, 31
INS key, 344
Insert
    command, EDLIN, 428
    disk messages, 964-969
    mode, EDLIN, 411
Instruction pointer (IP), 523
Insufficient
    disk space, 969
    memory, 969
Intel 8088, 80286, and 80386 chips, 2
Interactive processing, 229
Internal commands, 56, 458
International formats and standards,
    383-402
Interrupt, 477
Interrupt service routine, 471, 544
Interrupt vectors, 473, 545
    setting, 569
Interrupts, 471, 544, 626
IO.SYS, 54, 333, 465-466, 469
IOCTL service functions, 587-595
IPO, 28
Italian extended ASCII character set,
    394
Italian keyboard layout, 388

J

Jacket, disk, 11
JOIN, 311, 352, 846
JOIN.EXE, 311

K

Kernel, DOS, 453, 462
Keyboard, 14
    codes, 549
    formats, international, 383
    I/O, 552
    input, buffered, 554
    input, service for, 549
    layouts, foreign, 386
    type-ahead buffer, clearing, 556

KEYBXX, 384, 401, 848, 967, 980
Keys, special purpose, 14
Keywords, programming, 500

L

LABEL, 104, 610, 849, 929, 991
Label format, disk, 10
Labels, disk backup, 365
Large-memory model, 511
LASTDRIVE, 330, 492
LIB file, 501
Librarians, 515, 623
Libraries, limit of, 1013
Library files, 515
Library-replace operation, 517
Line editor, 403
LINK, 499, 987
    command options, 503
    map, 623
    messages with, 917, 920, 930, 1004,
        1011-1014
Linker, 499, 501, 623
    inner workings of, 514
List
    device, 987
    file, 501
List command, EDLIN, 418
Load (DEBUG), 522, 530
Load or execute program (EXEC), 598
Loader, 501
Local area networks, 318, 326. *See also*
    Network
Local device, 589
Locked resources, retry on, 590
Logical device, set, 595
Logical device track, 592
Logitech Bus Mouse, 635
Lost clusters, 104
LPT#, 123, 130, 981-982

M

Machine name, get, for network opera-
    tions, 607
Make System option (Windows), 675
Media-descriptor byte, 566
Medium-memory model, 511

Memory, 3, 30
    allocation error, 983
    errors, 994, 1001
    extended, 488
    how interrupts are used in, 471
    how used by DOS, 455
    insufficient, 969
    locations, replacing contents of, 533
    management within DOS, 57
    model configurations, 511
    modify allocated, 598
    release allocated, 597
    utilization, 480
Memory-resident programs, 578
Messages, DOS, 917-1029
Microfloppy disk, 18, 31
Microsoft PAINT, 757
Microsoft Windows, 627-689
    advanced, 691-776
Microsoft WRITE, 757
MKDIR (MD), 171, 580, 851
MODE, 128, 134, 853
Modify allocated memory, 598
Modules, library, 520
Monitors, 4
Monochrome monitor, 4
MORE, 216, 858, 984
Mouse, 634
    interface, 628
    option, Windows, 769
Move (DEBUG), 522, 532
Move command, EDLIN, 442
Move option (Windows), 677
MS-DOS, definition of, 22
MS-DOS Executive, Windows, 660-675
MSDOS.COM, 333
MSDOS.SYS, 54, 462, 466, 469
Multiple applications, running simul-
    taneous, 751

N

Name (DEBUG), 522, 525
NEAR and FAR, 987
Network. *See also* Local area networks
    device, 589
    printer, service function for, 608
    service function for machine names
        on, 607

Networks, service functions for, 607-609
Non-contiguous blocks, 937
Non-DOS disk, 1000
Nonremoveable device, 588
NOTEPAD (Windows), 733-738
NUL, 133

O

OBJ file, 501, 623
Object code, 501
Object modules, 515
Offset address, getting, 578
Operating system, 22, 32. *See also* DOS,
    COMMAND.COM
    copying, to disk, 332
    error loading, 951
Output, 28
    redirecting, to other devices, 214
    sources of, 31
Output (DEBUG), 522, 527

P

Page command, EDLIN, 424
PAINT, Microsoft, 757
Parallel data communication, 123, 134
Parallel redirection, 131
Parameter block, 591
Parameter errors, 963, 976, 995
Parameters, passing, to batch procedures,
    231
Parent directory, 182
PARITY, 130
Parity error, 996
Partition
    changing active, 274
    creating DOS, 272
    deleting disk, 274
    disk, 268
    errors, 945, 996
    size, 949
    table, bad, 922
    table, invalid, 977
Passing parameters to batch procedures,
    231
PATH, 191, 279, 290, 860
Path
    commands, 194
    errors, 977-978, 997
    name, 171

Paths, specifying, with APPEND, 291
PAUSE, 236, 862
PC-DOS, definition of, 22. *See also* DOS
PIF (Windows), 770
Pipe, DOS, 223, 538-542
Pipe error, 971
Platters, hard disk, 266
Pointers, damaged, 104
Ports, accessing values of, 527
Power-on diagnostics, 26
Power strip, 25
PRINT, 138, 863-864, 919, 933, 955
Print buffer, 160
    size, 144
Print command (Windows), 665
PRINT command options, 150
Print qualifiers, 160
Print queue, 139, 999
    procedure for adding files to, 615
Print queues, allocating size of, 152
Print screen command, 156
Printer
    defaults, 856
    device, service for output to, 551
    errors, 964, 1018
    modes, 130
    types, 158
Printers
    adding, in Windows, 764
    using, 137-164
Printing, stop, 153
Printing graphics, 157
PRN, 123, 139, 987
Proceed (DEBUG), 522, 538
Processing, 28
    steps for DOS commands, 461
    steps in DOS startup operation, 470
    steps involved in command proces-
      sor, 463
Program, 21
Program, load or execute (EXEC), 598
Program Information File (PIF), Win-
    dows, 770
Program interfaces to DOS, 615
Program segment prefix (PSP), 523, 570
    get, 610
Programming DOS, 499-627

Programs
    running, within DOS, 58
    terminate and stay resident, 577
PROMPT, 117, 869
Prompt, DOS, 42, 56, 79, 117

Q

Queue, print, 139, 160
Quit (DEBUG), 522

R

RAM, 464
RAM drive, 487, 497
    using, with Windows, 774
Random-access I/O, 483
Random file
    access, 569
    block read, 570
    block write, 572
Random read, 567
Random write, 568
Read and write errors, 1019
Read-only attribute, 296
Read/write
    opening, 11
    pointer, 585
Rebooting, 46, 78
Record size field, 569
Records, returning number of, 568
RECOVER, 316, 353, 872, 932, 986, 1022
Redirection list entry, 608
Redirection of input and output, 213
Register (DEBUG), 522, 524
Registers, 8088, 546
Relative file record size, 569
Release allocated memory, 597
Relocatable load module, 501
Relocation table overflow, 1002
REM, 235, 874
Removeable device, 588
RENAME, 95, 875
Rename command (Windows), 668
Rename icon (Windows), 668
Renaming
    files, service function for, 563
    subdirectories, 200

REPLACE, 319, 353, 877, 919, 985, 988, 1002
Replace command, EDLIN, 435
Reserved device names, 123
Resetting the computer, 46
Resident portion of the command processor, 456
RESTORE, 259, 371, 379, 880, 921, 993, 1003, 1011, 1022
    exit-status values for, 373
Restoring backup files, batch file for, 374
Retrieving files from backup disks, 371
Return code of subprocess, 600
REVERSI (Windows), 747
RMDIR (RD), 183, 581, 882
ROM, 464, 536
    determining date of IBM PC, 529
ROM-BIOS, 545
    services, 550
Root directory, 167
    entries, 253
Run-time library, 501

S

Screen
    clearing, 90, 119
    code to clear, 543
    colors, setting, in Windows, 769
    display, 72
    modes, 159
    output, echoing to the printer, 155
    printing contents of, 156
Screen-echo mode, 155
Scrolling, 73
Search (DEBUG), 522
Search command, EDLIN, 431
Searching for words and phrases, 431
Secondary command processor, 233, 301
    exiting from, 308
Sector notch, microfloppy, 19
Sector size, 1004
Sectors, 251
    bad, 55, 316
    reading and writing, 281
    source and target, 284
Segment, 512
    address, getting, 578

Segment, *continued*
    limit, 1004
    registers, 510, 523
Segments, 1014
SELECT, 392, 399, 884
Sequential
    file access, 483
    read, 561
    write, 562
Serial communication, 123, 134
Service functions, DOS, 548-610
SET, 323, 612, 887
Set Volume Name option (Windows), 675
Setting system date and time, services for, 575-576
Setup option, IBM PC AT, 38
SHARE, 326, 353, 890, 1005
SHELL, 493
SHIFT, 244, 891
SHIFT-PRTSC, 156, 160
Shutter, microfloppy, 18
Single-disk system, 50
Small-memory model, 511
Software, 32
    definition of, 21
SORT, 221, 893
Source code, 500
Source disk, 48, 1006
Spanish extended ASCII character set, 396
Spanish keyboard layout, 390
Spawn, 614
Special-functions field values, 591
Spooler (Windows), 683
Spooler icon (Windows), 665, 668
Stack
    failure error, 954
    pointer (SP), 524
    segment, 1024
    size, 508, 1007
    space, insufficient, 970
Standard auxiliary device, 550
Standard input device, checking status of, 555
Standard printer device, 551
Starting DOS, 35
Startup portion of DOS command processor, 455

Stop bits, 131
Storage, disk, 252
Subdirectories, 165-213. *See also* Directories
    copying, 335
    creating, 171
    definition of, 167
    maximum number of, 177
    service function for creating, 580
    service function for removing, 581
    substituting drive letters for, 330
    using, with hard disks, 277
SUBST, 330, 353, 894, 933
Switch, invalid, 979
Symbol table, 1008
Symbols, international, 385
SYS, 332, 353, 896, 992-993
System
    date, service function for, 574-575
    files, missing, 927
    generation, 468, 476
    memory utilization, checking, 119
    menu (Windows), 675
    services, 543
    size, incompatible, 962
    software, 22, 33
    stack, 545
    time, service function for, 575

T

Target disk, 48, 1009
TERMINAL (Windows), 739-747
Terminal output, echoing to printer, 155
Terminal types supported by Windows TERMINAL, 745
Terminate a process (EXIT), 600
Terminate and stay resident, 577
Terminating current program, service for, 548
Text editing, advanced, 418
Text editor
    definition of, 450
    EDLIN, 403-452
TIME, 40, 44, 79, 898, 939
Time format, 41
Time, service function for specifying, 604
Time-sharing, 687
    system, 628

Timeslice, 142
Trace (DEBUG), 522, 537
Track read/write operations, 592
Tracks, 250
    bad, 923
Transfer command, EDLIN, 444
Transient section of command processor, 457
TREE, 187, 900, 941
Turbo Pascal, 539
    procedure for returning volume label, 611
    program, Spawn, 614
    requesting DOS services from, 547, 627
Turning on system, 25
TYPE, 92, 119, 903
Type-ahead buffer, clearing, 556

U

U.K. keyboard layout, 388
U.K. English extended ASCII character set, 393
U.S. English extended ASCII character set, 395
U.S. keyboard layout, 391
Unassemble (DEBUG), 522, 535
Undo option (Windows), 724
UNIX, 23, 539

V

VDISK, 941, 1015, 1020
VER, 91, 119, 904
VERIFY, 280, 285, 334, 353, 905
    qualifier, 70
    setting, 576
Version
    errors, 963
    numbers, getting DOS, 577
    numbers, returning DOS, 547
Versions of DOS, 24
    displaying, 91
    upgrading, 1031
Video display modes, 129
    controlling, with DEBUG, 527
View menu (Windows), 668
Virtual disk, 487
VM.TMP, 1021. *See also* LINK

VOL, 109, 610, 906-907
Volume label, 119, 1021
    procedure for returning, 611
Volume labels, 971
    creating, 104
    displaying, 109

W

Wildcard characters, 64, 70, 559, 574
WIN.INI file, 772
Windows, 627-689
    advanced, 691-776
    applications of, 688
    CALCULATOR, 696-702
    CALENDAR, 702-719
    CARDFILE, 719-732
    Clipboard, 748
    CLOCK, 693-696
    control panel, 762
    definition of, 627, 687
    design goals of, 687
    installing, on hard disk, 650-659
    installing, on floppy disks, 636-650
    NOTEPAD, 733-738
    products and applications of, 659
    requirements of, 633

Windows, *continued*
    REVERSI, 747
    running simultaneous applications in,
        751
    spooler, 683
    TERMINAL, 739-747
    what comes with, 635
Word processing, buffers required for,
    484
Working directory, 201
Write (DEBUG), 522, 531
Write errors, 1028
WRITE, Microsoft, 757
Write-protect notch, 11, 19, 78
Write-protecting, 31
    disks, 77
    errors, 921, 1029

X

XCOPY, 335, 353, 907, 927, 933
XENIX, 23, 268

Z

Zoom option (Windows), 677, 695
^Z character, 404, 450

Order Today
Call Toll-Free 800-227-0900

Use Your American Express, Visa, or MasterCard

Here's More Help From the Experts

Now that you've developed even better computer skills with *DOS: The Complete Referemce*, let us suggest the following related titles that will help you use your computer to greater advantage.

DOS: The Pocket Reference
by Kris Jamsa

Picture yourself working away efficiently on the computer when all of a sudden . . . that DOS command you need just slips out of your mind and into space. Here, for the first time ever, is a *Pocket Reference* for PC and MS-DOS® through version 3.3. In this handy guide, you'll find complete examples of every DOS command with easy-to-follow tips and explanations. All the commands are listed alphabetically.

$5.95 p
0-07-881376-X, 128 pp., 4¼ x 7

The Osborne/McGraw-Hill MS-DOS® User's Guide
by Paul Hoffman and Tamara Nicoloff

A comprehensive guide to the MS DOS® operating system, this book is designed to familiarize you with all the versions of this powerful system from Microsoft. Ideal for beginners and experienced users alike, this guide covers each computer running MS DOS®, gives the version it runs and any improvements the manufacturer has made to the system. It also gives complete information on the PC DOS version designed for the IBM® PC. Additional programs and reference material make this guide a tool of lasting value.

$18.95 p
0-07-881131-7, 250 pp., 7½ x 9¼

DOS Made Easy
by Herbert Schildt

If you're at a loss when it comes to DOS, Herb Schildt has written just the book you need, *DOS Made Easy*. Previous computer experience is not necessary to understand this concise, well-organized introduction that's filled with short applications and exercises. Schildt walks you through all the basics, beginning with an overview of a computer system's components and a step-by-step account of how to run DOS for the first time. Once you've been through the initial setup, you'll edit text files, use the DOS directory structure, and create batch files. As you feel more comfortable with DOS, Schildt shows you how to configure a system, handle floppy disks and fixed disks, and make use of helpful troubleshooting methods. By the time you've gone this far, you'll be ready for total system management—using the printer, video modes, the serial and parallel ports, and more. *DOS Made Easy* takes the mystery out of the disk operating system and puts you in charge of your PC.

$18.95 p
0-07-881295-X, 385 pp., 7⅜ x 9¼

DOS: Power User's Guide
by Kris Jamsa

Professional DOS users and programmers with an interest in OS/2™, this book is a must for you! Jamsa, the author of the best-selling *DOS: The Complete Reference*, now shows experienced DOS users how to wield this operating system in powerful ways. If you're already familiar with C or Pascal, you'll gain even more insight from Jamsa's expertise. As a special highlight, the advanced features of DOS are compared with those of the new OS/2 operating system throughout the book. *DOS: Power User's Guide* shows you how to utilize fully the DOS pipe, memory map, system services, and subdirectories. Learn how to adapt the DOS environment to meet your specific needs. DOS pretender commands, disk layout, and system configuration are additional topics that Jamsa covers as he instructs you in the art of becoming a truly sophisticated user.

$22.95 p
0-07-881310-7, 700 pp., 7⅜ x 9¼

Order Today
Call Toll-Free 800-227-0900

Use Your American Express, Visa, or MasterCard

OS/2™: The Pocket Reference
by Kris Jamsa

Computer user's memory loss is a common ailment that plagues even the most competent OS/2™ aficionado. Now, Osborne/McGraw-Hill has a remedy that's guaranteed for immediate results—*OS/2™: The Pocket Reference*. In these pages, you'll find complete examples of every important OS/2 command and system configuration entry, each accompanied by easy-by-follow tips and explanations. All entries are listed alphabetically.

$5.95p
0-07-881377-8, 128 pp., 7³/₈ x 9¹/₄

OS/2™ Made Easy
by Herbert Schildt

This "Made Easy" guide contains simple, clear instructions for using OS/2™, the new operating system from IBM and Microsoft that runs on the 286, 386, and PS/2™ computer families. Schildt, the author of numerous bestsellers, including *DOS Made Easy*, teaches the fundamentals to first-time OS/2 users, as well as experienced DOS users. Start with OS/2 basics, such as formatting diskettes and backing up files. Schildt then pursues more advanced techniques. Learn to manipulate directories and files, use OS/2 commands, run DOS applications under OS/2, operate multiple tasks, and manage your hard disk. Like all the "Made Easy" books, each chapter presents a step-by- step lesson that includes plenty of examples and hands-on exercises.

$19.95p
0-07-881360-3, 350 pp., 7³/₈ x 9¹/₄

Using OS/2™
by Kris Jamsa

Microsoft's new operating system is now described for beginners and experienced computer users alike. *Using OS/2™* quickly moves from fundamental to advanced techniques and covers major OS/2 strengths in detail, including multi-tasking. Jamsa, a programmer for the United States Air Force and the highly regarded author of the acclaimed *DOS: The Complete Reference* and other Osborne books, draws on his extensive programming background to present OS/2 concepts in a clear, concise manner. You'll learn how to install OS/2 and learn the use of basic and advanced commands. Then you'll be ready for important techniques—redirection of I/O, system configuration and multi-tasking. A complete OS/2 command summary is provided.

$19.95p
0-07-881306-9, 600 pp., 7³/₈ x 9¹/₄

OS/2™ Programmer's Guide
by Ed Iacobucci
Foreword by Bill Gates

Learn OS/2™ from an expert! Ed Iacobucci, who lead the IBM® OS/2 design team, shows experienced programmers how to use version 1.0 of the new and powerful multi-tasking operating system built expressly for 80286 and 80386-based personal computers. Iacobucci gives you a complete overview of 80286 protected mode, including valuable tips and techniques which you can use to build your first protected mode programs. Iacobucci provides a complete overview of the OS/2 system, filled with insights which help you understand how and why the system works. Learn about dynamic linking and the system API; memory management in a protected environment; OS/2 multitasking; advanced inter-process communications facilities; the system I/O capabilities; session management, user interface, utilities, and more. You'll also learn how to use many of these concepts in practical programming examples that include using the I/O facilities, allocating and managing memory, using basic and advanced multitasking features, and building a "pop-up" application with keyboard monitors.

$24.95p
0-07-881300-x, 650 pp., 7³/₈ x 9¹/₄

Order Today
Call Toll-Free 800-227-0900

Use Your American Express, Visa, or MasterCard

C: The Complete Reference
by Herbert Schildt

For all C programmers, here's an encyclopedia of C terms, functions, codes, and applications. Arranged for quick fact-finding, *C: The Complete Reference* includes sections covering C basics, C library functions by category, various algorithms and C applications, and the C programming environment. You'll also find coverage of C++, C's newest direction, as well as full information on the UNIX® C de facto standard and the new proposed ANSI standard. Includes money-saving coupons for C products.

$27.95 p, Hardcover Edition
0-07-881313-1, 740 pp., 7³/₈ x 9¹/₄
$24.95 p, Paperback Edition
0-07-881263-1, 740 pp., 7³/₈ x 9¹/₄

C: The Pocket Reference
by Herbert Schildt

Speed up your C programming with *C: The Pocket Reference*, written by master programmer Schildt, the author of twelve Osborne/McGraw-Hill books. This quick reference is packed with vital C commands, functions, and libraries. Arranged alphabetically for easy use.

$5.95 p
0-07-881321-2, 120 pp., 4¹/₄ x 7

C Made Easy
by Herbert Schildt

With Osborne/McGraw-Hill's popular "Made Easy" format, you can learn C programming in no time. Start with the fundamentals and work through the text at your own speed. Schildt begins with general concepts, then introduces functions, libraries, and disk input/output, and finally advanced concepts affecting the C programming environment and UNIX™ operating system. Each chapter covers commands that you can learn to use immediately in the hands-on exercises that follow. If you already know BASIC, you'll find that Schildt's C equivalents will shorten your learning time. *C Made Easy* is a step-by-step tutorial for all beginning C programmers.

$18.95 p
0-07-881178-3, 350 pp., 7³/₈ x 9¹/₄

Advanced C, Second Edition
by Herbert Schildt

Experienced C programmers can become professional C programmers with Schildt's nuts-and-bolts guide to advanced programming techniques. Now thoroughly revised, *Advanced C, Second Edition* covers the new ANSI standard in addition to the Kernighan and Ritchie C used in the first edition. All the example code conforms to the ANSI standard. You'll find information you need on sorting and searching; queues, stacks, linked lists, and binary trees; dynamic allocation, interfacing to assembly language routines and the operating system; expression parsing; and more. When you finish reading *Advanced C*, you'll be ready for the slick programming tricks found in Schildt's twelfth book for Osborne, C: Power User's Guide.

$21.95 p
0-07-881348-4, 353 pp., 7³/₈ x 9¹/₄

C: Power User's Guide
by Herbert Schildt

Make your C programs sizzle! All the bells, whistles, and slick tricks used to get professional results in commercial software are unveiled to serious programmers in *C: Power User's Guide*. In his eleventh book for Osborne/McGraw-Hill, Schildt shows you how to build a Borland type interface, develop a core for a database, create memory resident programs, and more. Schildt combines theory, background, and code in an even mix as he excites experienced C programmers with new features and approaches. Learn master techniques for handling menus, windows, graphics, and video game programming. If hashing is what you're after, it's here too, along with techniques for using the serial port and sorting disk files. OS/2™ level programming with specific OS/2 functions is also covered. Before you send your programs out to market, consult Schildt for the final touches that set professional software apart from the rest.

$22.95 p
0-07-881307-7, 384 pp., 7³/₈ x 9¹/₄

Order Today
Call Toll-Free 800-227-0900

Use Your American Express, Visa, or MasterCard

Artificial Intelligence Using C
by Herb Schildt

With Herb Schildt's newest book, you can add a powerful dimension to your C programs—artificial intelligence. Schildt, a programming expert and author of seven Osborne books, shows C programmers how to use AI techniques that have traditionally been implemented with Prolog and LISP. You'll utilize AI for vision, pattern recognition, robotics, machine learning, logic, problem solving, and natural language processing, Each chapter develops practical examples that can be used in the construction of artificial intelligence applications. If you are building expert systems in C, this book contains a complete expert system that can easily be adapted to your needs. Schildt provides valuable insights that allow even greater command of the systems you create.

$21.95p
0-07-881255-0, 432 pp., 7³/₈ x 9¹/₄

Advanced Graphics in C: Programming and Techniques
by Nelson Johnson

Add graphics to your C programs and you'll add significant capabilities to your software. With *Advanced Graphics in C* you'll be able to write graphics programs for the IBM® EGA (Enhanced Graphics Adapter), the de facto standard for high-quality graphics programming on the IBM PC. *Advanced Graphics in C* features a special, complete graphics program called GRAPHIQ, that provides a whole toolkit of all the routines you'll need for graphics operations, and even gives you code for a rotatable and scalable character set. Johnson shows you how to use GRAPHIQ to implement or adapt graphics in your C programs. GRAPHIQ is full of tools not available elsewhere. *Advanced Graphics in C* also offers an entire stroke/front character set; code for the AT&T Image Capture Board; and information on serial and parallel interfacing to mice, light pens, and digitizers.

$22.95p
0-07-881257-7, 670 pp., 7³/₈ x 9¹/₄

These titles available at fine book stores and computer stores everywhere.

Or Call Toll-Free 800-227-0900
Use your American Express, Visa, or Master Card

For a FREE catalog of all our current publications, call 800-227-0900 or write to Osborne/McGraw-Hill, 2600 Tenth Street, Berkeley, CA 94710

Prices subject to change without notice.